Maria Grazia Guido

The Acting Translator

Embodying Cultures in the Dubbing Translation of American Sitcoms

New York Ottawa Toronto

Library and Archives Canada Cataloguing in Publication

Guido, Maria Grazia
The acting translator : embodying cultures in the dubbing translation of American sitcoms / Maria Grazia Guido.

(Language, media & education studies ; 54)
Includes bibliographical references.
ISBN 978-1-897493-38-0

1. Dubbing of television programs. 2. Situation comedies (Television programs)--United States--Translations into Italian. 3. Language and culture. I. Title. II. Series: Language, media & education studies ; 54

P306.93.G85 2012 418'.0379145617 C2012-907317-2

http://www.legaspublishing.com

LEGAS

P. O. Box 149	3 Wood Aster Bay	5201 Dufferin Street
Mineola, New York	Ottawa, Ontario	Toronto, Ontario
USA 11501	K2R 1B3	M3H 5T8

Printed and bound in Canada by Gauvin Press

Published under the aegis of

Center for Communication and Information Sciences

(Victoria University; University of Toronto;
University of Helsinki; Universidad Sao Paulo, Brasil; Indiana University;
University of Lugano; University of Ottawa)

Series: *Language, Media & Education Studies*

Edited by: Marcel Danesi & Leonard G. Sbrocchi

1. M. Danesi, *Interpreting Advertisements. A Semiotic Guide*
2. M. Angenot, *Critique of Semiotic Reason*
3. S. Feigenbaum, *The Intermediate Sign in the System of French and Hebrew Verbs*
4. A. Bailin, *Metaphor and the Logic of Language Use*
5. C. D. E. Tolton, ed., *The Cinema of Jean Cocteau*
6. C. Madott Kosnik, *Primary Education: Goals, Processes and Practices*
7. F. Nuessel, *The Esperanto Language*
8. M. G. Guido, *The Acting Reader: Schema/Text Interaction in the Dramatic Discourse of Poetry*
9. F. Ratto, *Hobbes tra scienza della politica e teoria delle passioni*
10. S. Battestini, *African Writing and Text*
11. T. A. Sebeok, *Essays in Semiotics I: Life Signs*
12. T. A. Sebeok, *Essays in Semiotics II: Culture Signs*
13. A. Ponzio and S. Petrilli, *Philosophy of Language, Art and Answerability in Mikhail Bakhtin*
14. R. Beasley, M. Danesi, P. Perron, *Signs for Sale. An Outline of Semiotic Analysis for Advertisers & Marketers*
15. F. Merrell, *Signs for Everybody, or, Chaos, Quandaries and Communication*
16. P. Perron, L.G. Sbrocchi, P. Colilli, M. Danesi (eds.) *Semiotics as a Bridge between the Humanities and the Sciences*
17. A. Makolkin, *Anatomy of Heroism*
18. P. Perron, M. Danesi, J. Umiker-Sebeok, A. Watanabe (eds.) *Semiotics and Information Sciences*
19. T. A. Sebeok, *The Swiss Pioneer in Nonverbal Communication Studies. Heine Hediger (1908-1992)*
20. M. Danesi (ed.), *The Invention of Global Semiotics*
21. T. A. Sebeok, *Semiotic Prologues*
22. R. Dalvesco, *Fuller Speak*
23. F. Merrell, *Learning Living, Living Learning: Signs Between East and West*
24. J. Kelly (ed.), *Looking Up; Science and Observation in the Early Modern Period*
25. A. Valdman, *Études sur les variétés du français*
26. A. Valdman, *Essays in Applied French Linguistics*
27. D. A. Koike, *La co-construcción del significado en el español de la Américas: acercamientos discursivos*

Cover: Roy Lichtenstein, *Interior with Shyline.*
Compugraphics by Pierre Bertrand

28. P. Perron and M. Danesi, *Classical Readings in Semiotics*
29. J. Deely, *Why Semiotics?*
30. S. Petrilli and A. Ponzio, *Views in Literary Semiotics*
31. F. Nuessel and A. Cedeño, *Selected Literary Commentary in the Literature of Spain*
32. A. Ponzio and S. Petrilli, J. Ponzio, *Reasoning with Emmanuel Levinas*
33. M. Solimini, *Anthropology, Otherness, and Existential Enterprise*
34. Maria Grazia Guido, *The Imaging Reader. Visualization and Embodiment of Metaphysical Discourse*
35. J.Deely, S. Petrilli, A. Ponzio, *The Semiotic Animal*
36. R. Iannacito-Provenzano, *Il dialetto molisano di Villa San Michele (Isernia)*
37. A. Ponzio, *The Dialogic Nature of Sign*
38. W. Weiss, *Towards a Mobile Voice*
39. R. Williamson, *La historia verdadera de la conquista de la Nueva España* de Bernal Díaz del Castillo. Apuntes para una historia de su lenguaje
40. P. G. Marteinson, *On the Problem of the Comic. A Philosophical Study on the Origin of Laughter*
41. F. Merrell, *Processing Cuiltural Meaning*
42. S. Petrilli and A. Ponzio, *Semiotics Today. From Global Semiotics to Semioethics, a Dialogic Response*
43. G. Marrone, *The Ludovico Cure. On Body and Music in* A Clockwork Orange
44. A. Ponzio, *Emmanuel Levinas, Globalization, and Preventive Peace*
45. R. Longo Lavorato, *De vulgari eloquentia: lingua e dialetti nella cultura italiana*
46. Wang Ning, *Translated Modernities: Literary and Cultural Perspectives on Globalization and China*
47. J. Deely, *Semiotics Seen Synchronically. The View as of 2010*44.
48. Carolina Travalia, *El concepto de colocación en español: propuesta de una nueva taxonomía y delimiutación de sus funciones*
49. M. Danesi, Lorraine Bryers, Ned Gudinskas, *Interpreting Advertisements: A Semiotic Guide* (second edition)
50. Sergej G. Proskurin, *Essays in Contemporary Semiotics*
51. M. Pasquarelli Clivio (ed.) *Lingue in contatto e plurilinguismo nella cultura italiana*
52. Stefania Ventura, *Teaching Languages Through Activities, Games, and Projects*
53. P. Arancibia, V. Fulginiti, K. Gaudet, J. Granata, W. Santini, L. A. Ouji (eds.) *Shaping an Identity. Adapting, Rewriting and Remaking Italian Identity*
54. Maria Grazia Guido. *The Acting Translator. Embodying Cultures in the Dubbing Translation of American Sitcoms*

To my beloved Grandparents

Contents

Introduction

1. Book Rationale

What kind of cognitive processes does the humorous language of a sitcom activate in our mind to make us laugh? Are humorous triggers to be specifically identified in the linguistic construction of sitcom scripts? Or are they rather to be recognized in our socio-cultural and personal experience that induces us to consider as humorous a particular use of the language which may instead leave other people unaffected? Furthermore, is it possible to reproduce the same humorous effects at both linguistic and experiential levels through the dubbing translation of sitcom scripts? And what kind of professional training should a dubbing translator receive to become capable of recreating in the target audiences' minds an experience of the sitcom humour equivalent to the experience of humour in the original version? Target audiences of television viewers in fact come from different socio-cultural and linguistic backgrounds but, together with the dubbed dialogues, they actually receive the same movie images of the sitcom referred to the source culture.

These are the research questions that justify the Acting Translator Model proposed in this book, which is grounded on the tenet that a dubbing translation is successful when it is appropriated into the identity of the translator, and, accordingly, needs to be 'embodied' and even 'dramatized' through personal experience. This theory of the 'embodied interpretation' has informed the previous two volumes issued in this series (Guido 1999, 2005) dealing respectively with the language of dramatic poetry and of metaphysics, which are both specialized discourses about fictitious 'possible worlds'. In the present book, this theory is applied to the humorous language of the North-American 'situation comedy', an audiovisual television genre (originally conceived for the radio) centred on a number of fixed characters interacting within the same environment, usually a home or a workplace, and dealing again with fictitious situations that reflect reality by filtering it through the perspective of humour – thus amplifying the paradoxes of contemporary social behaviours through the magnifying glass of irony.

In addition, the dubbing translation of sitcoms emphasizes the sense of displacement that humour induces in audiences, first by deroutinizing reality as it comes to be dislocated in the parallel 'possible world' of the sitcom and, then, by displacing such fictitious reality into the target language and culture—in the case in point, Italian language and culture. The 'experiential embodiment' of the original dialogue, situated in the source context, is therefore essential for the dubbing translator to understand it and its humour and, eventually, to render it into an equivalent dialogue in translation conveying the significance of the source context to a target audience.

The underlying assumptions are that: *(a)* translation is a process of meaning interpretation and intercultural negotiation, and *(b)* the translator in general, and the dubbing translator in particular, is an actual 'intercultural mediator'. This view would indeed challenge the traditional, and still widespread, notion of translation meant as a 'transmission of meanings', according to which the translator's interpretation is believed to be equivalent to the author's original intention insofar as meanings are regarded as inherent in the text and, in principle, entirely recoverable in translation. Contrary to this conventional view, the notion of translation as a 'process', advocated in this book, would instead entail two phases: 'interpreting' and 'rendering' (cf. Widdowson 1991), so that the translator, in moving from one phase to the other, shifts from the role of second-person reader (who makes continuous adjustments of his/her interpretation of culturally-marked meanings in the source text in order to accommodate them within the schematic structures of his/her own knowledge) to the role of first-person writer in the process of rendering a text into another language and culture. To this two-phase model of 'translation as a process' (cf. Bell 1991) another middle phase is here added, namely, the phase of the Acting Translator 'embodying' his/her own interpretation, thus 'inhabiting' the meanings that s/he achieves from the original text before rendering them into the target language. In rendering interpretations into equivalent texts, Widdowson remarks that three different perspectives on meaning are involved: "what the text means, what the writer means by the text, what the text means to the reader. These three perspectives are related to the three kinds of meaning in respect to indexical value: reference, force, and effect." (*ibidem*: 153). Reference, force and effect, in the case of the dubbing translation of humorous sitcoms, are referred to what the Acting Translator manages to achieve from the original text in terms of culture-bound referential meanings, to the force of the author's intentions, and to the effects of humour on the source audience, to be rendered into equivalent ways for the target audience of its dubbed version. Crucial in this respect is, therefore, the cultural background that informs pragmalinguistic uses and generic conventions in the source text of the sitcom and that, in the translator's processes of interpreting it and, then, rendering it into another language and culture, could make culture-bound meanings not only 'cognitively and linguistically inaccessible' to audiences from different linguacultural backgrounds, but also 'conceptually unavailable' to them. In fact, if a translation simply aims to convey the original referential meaning of the source text through the target language, then target audiences may find it difficult, if not impossible, to understand culture-bound concepts and discourse behaviours that are alien to their native socio-cultural and pragmalinguistic schemata (Rumelhart 1980; Carrell 1983). By 'schemata' it is here meant the background knowledge of culturally-determined linguistic and social behaviours and experiential conceptualizations, stored in people's minds, that are actualized into the forms and functions of their native language.

On the other hand, if the translator aims at recovering the force of the author's intentionality, often s/he will end up by interpreting it with reference not to the author's schemata but, indeed, to his/her own native schemata. In turn, the language of the translated text comes to be interpreted by the target receivers with reference to the effects that it produces on their own native schemata, which may not coincide with the author's intentionality, or with the translator's interpretation. Furthermore, in such 'top-down' processes accounting for the centrality of the translator's schemata in interpreting a text and rendering it into another language, also the typological divergences between source and target language structures may play their crucial role (cf. Guido 2008). For instance, when the two languages involved in the translation process are typologically similar in their cognitive-semantic and syntactic structures, then they are not expected to cause divergences in the translator's process of interpretation, so that they may have good probabilities of converging syntactically and semantically in the rendering phase, thus producing an almost literal translation whose language is received as 'natural' by the target audience. This is so because the grammatical and experiential features of the two languages involved are perceived by the translator as 'unmarked', and this sense of familiarity with the text, produced by such typological convergence, is expected to facilitate the translator's pragmatic negotiation of meanings in rendering a text into a target one.

Conversely, two typologically-different languages involved in the translation process (e.g., an SVO-accusative one and an OVS-ergative one) may make the translator perceive the syntactic and cognitive-semantic structures of the source text as unfamiliar and 'marked'. In such cases, if these typological, experiential structures are not recognized during the translator's interpretation process, the risk may be the activation of schema-biased presuppositions and, thus, the translated text may be rendered into a 'displaced' and 'transidiomatic' language (cf. Silverstein 1998), disconnected from the native contexts of its use and recontextualized within estranged communicative situations (cf. Guido 2008). The same may be said with the case of culture-bound humour structures that, when they come unrecognized or misinterpreted by the translator, represent another case of displaced, transidiomatic use of language. A translator, instead, should respect the 'situatedness' (Gumperz 1982) of the original text even though, in making it accessible to the target receivers, s/he has also to transpose it into the cognitive-experiential structures, the pragmalinguistic uses and the generic norms of the target language and culture.

This book, therefore, specifically presents a view of the discourse of humour in sitcom dubbing translation as the outcome of the ongoing process of interaction between the dubbing translator's schemata and the socio-culturally marked formal organization of the original script. In investigating such 'interactive' process of dubbing translation, a number of original concepts already explored in the above-mentioned books in this series (Guido 1999, 2005) will be examined: first, it will be claimed that schemata are not just to be conventionally considered as mere 'cognitive constructs' as in most literature on Schema Theory (cf. Schank *et al.* 1975; Chomsky 1980; Sanford and Garrod 1981; van Dijk and Kintsch 1983), but also experiential and 'embodied' images (Johnson 1987), as the body is the primary way to experience the world and, consequently, an essential way to semiotic conceptualization. However, differently from any other fictional genre where the receiver's schemata are totally involved in imaginatively shaping contexts, actors and actions, the very nature of an audiovisual script is essentially 'physical', 'dramatic', and already 'visualized' on the screen—thus apparently leaving no space to the receivers' diverse imaginative visualizations in their mind's eye. And yet, the discourse structure of humour 'in action'—as part of an audiovisual text like a sitcom—'diverges' from any normal pattern of language at the semantic, phonological, perceptual, and discursive levels insofar as any humorous reference can imply at least two interpretations: one overtly referred to the script actualized in the audiovisual context, and another covertly referred, instead, to a totally opposite script that is just evoked by the use of language and that, with its displacing sense of surprise, represents the humorous prompt. The assumption here is that the evoked, covert script in such 'script opposition' (Attardo 1994), peculiar to the humorous language of audiovisual texts, can indeed have the power of 'reviving' the translators' schemata by which they normally interpret reality according to shared conventional categories of meaning.

The covert script, indeed, prompts dubbing translators to explore its implications by 'acting puns out' physically and vocally, exploring the experiential effects the humorous language produces on them. This represents the novel methodological issue advanced in this book, which entails that the specific form of a particular pun, or a wordplay, is intrinsically connected with the translators' subjective schematic reactions to it. The contention, therefore, is that the humorous discourse in a sitcom context has to be made dynamic by being first of all 'activated' in the translators' diverse personal reactions to the peculiar form of its language. Furthermore, a sitcom script is also inherently 'dramatic' as it involves 'voices' within its very structural arrangement of language. This implies that, since their very first reading of the sitcom script, dubbing translators should feel the need to 'appropriate', 'embody' and 'enact' the dramatic potentialities of such 'humorous voices' according to their own different 'individual voices' precisely because humour, and especially sitcom humour, has always the implication of a direct speech act. This entails that a sitcom script is made up by 'humorous utterances' that—it is here claimed—should prompt translators to feel 'authorized' to appropriate them by imaginatively displacing their own individual schematic system of symbolization into the sitcom textual structure.

This book, therefore, intends to propose a methodological approach according to which the dramatic appropriation of the 'humorous voices' in a sitcom script performed by a team of dubbing translators should occur within an actual 'stage of enactment' where translators can co-create 'embodied' humorous situations equivalent to the verbal, 'scripted' ones and, likewise, explore by physical improvisation the 'unscripted' situations evoked by the humorous language. This represents the crucial creative basis upon which the team of sitcom dubbing translators would subsequently build their translation process, since also the translators' physical and vocal rendering of the humorous implications 'on stage' are expressions of their own interpretations, and lend themselves to further creative re-interpretations when translators set up to render the dialogues into the target language. Obviously, this method runs counter the discouraging reality of today's dubbing translation practice, carried out by underpaid and often unprofessional translators—as a norm working to strict deadlines—hired by productions and multinational companies that impose their own commercial and even ideological standards upon the translation product. However, despite the many marketing and political pressures conditioning the job of a dubbing translator, this book contends that an effective, principled and methodologically-sound approach to dubbing translation is much needed today, especially when humorous discourse is involved.

Hence, the central claim of this book is that to achieve a total experience of the sitcom, dubbing translators need to engage their own schemata in their body/thought entirety. For this purpose, dubbing translators have to free themselves from their customary silent approach to the sitcom script by giving it new, multidimensional semiotic contexts in space, to be 'inhabited' physically and vocally first in its source language, and then in the target language of its translation. This implies that dubbing translators should not limit themselves to the mentalist practice of 'sounding' the 'humorous voices' they achieve from the script just within their own 'inward ear', but they have to 'embody' them, 'inhabit' them within a 'physical space of representation', thus experiencing a first-person bodily and mental involvement with the humorous situations they inhabit, which has the potential of reviving the translators' own conventionalised schemata. In doing so, the dubbing translators become 'Acting Translators' who can generate 'in action' first an interpretation of the source script and, then, its rendering into a target script that is coherent with the effects that the original humorous forms and functions continually produce on their own socio-cultural and experiential schemata. In this way, acting translators activate a search for a pragmatic equivalence in the target language which is not just mental, but involves every level of experience—thus, this theory of the 'Acting Translator' locates the cognitive-linguistics enquiry within the context of the Experientialist approach to language (Johnson 1987; Lakoff 1987; Sweetser 1990; Langacker 1991). The book, then, also provides a practical demonstration of how 'drama techniques', consistent with the Experientialist approach, can be devised to induce in dubbing translators not only an understanding of the discourse of sitcom humour made up by spoken locutions, whose ambiguous language evokes two different and conflicting scripts, but also an apprehension of comic effects in both source and target cultures. Here the theoretical arguments will acquire a pedagogic dimension (cf. Barbe 1996) and become actualized in the experience of groups of students, majoring in English language and translation at two Italian universities, who were trained to become 'acting translators'. The pedagogical effectiveness of this Experientialist approach to humour embodiment and dubbing translation will therefore be systematically illustrated in this book by a series of case studies students/acting-translators were involved in. The choice of the protocol analysis (Ericsson and Simon 1984) to explore collected data is meant to support the argument that overt and collectively-shared 'embodiments of meanings', accomplished through the adoption of drama techniques, can enhance the translation students' awareness of the humorous sitcom language. This implies an interplay of the following three cognitive/affective translation strategies, each marking a phase of the theoretical enquiry:

Phase 1. A 'top-down', affective and deconstructive strategy involving the acting translators' drama improvisation on the plot of a series of sitcom episodes, first in the source language and, eventually, in the target one, and their subsequent creative-writing re-textualizations.Such 'schema-based' strategy presupposes the acknowledgement of only a low degree of textual constraint from the original scripts. This would allow acting translators to overcome their initial sense of estrangement felt towards the sitcom script and to 'familiarize' themselves with the peculiar structural and semantic arrangement of the humorous text, and with the situation that actualizes the scripted text as performed discourse. Such top-down process of 'familiarization' is expected to occur when acting translators impose their own 'voice' on the initial 'dramatic voices' they achieve from the sitcom script on their first approach to it. In this way, acting translators would appropriate not only the first-person, authorial perspective of the sender/author of the sitcom, but also the third-person perspective of the receiver by perceiving their own interpretation of the sitcom humour as if they were part of an audience.

Phase 2. A 'bottom-up', cognitive strategy of script analysis focused on the translators' reflection on the pragmatic actualization 'in space' of the move-&-act structure of the sitcom script. Such text-based strategy is expected to 'defamiliarize' the acting translators from the humorous language of the sitcom as they come to focus on the textual form and functions of the script and its constraints. This would allow them to identify—and then, eventually, to embody—the 'voices' of the sitcom characters as the addressers and the addressees in the scripted dialogue.

Phase 3. An 'interactive', 'top-down/bottom-up' strategy meant to gradually enable acting translators to appropriate the script and possibly to communicate their interpretative discourse to the other acting translators in the dubbing team. This is a context in which acting translators inter-act with each other as if they were a team of actors rehearsing the script in both the languages involved in the translation process. The interplay of familiarizing/defamiliarizing perspectives would allow the acting translators to position themselves variably in relation to their perception of—and response to—their own dramatic representation of the humorous sitcom discourse. One of the most suitable forums for realizing this interactive strategy is certainly the translation classroom which, under such circumstances, would indeed resemble the rehearsal room.

In focusing on a principled application of this Acting Translator Model in all its three phases, then, the book shall illustrate how this discourse principle of sitcom humour ultimately will lead to certain classroom activities that would enable dubbing translators to develop a sense of identity with the sitcom language and characters by creating their own interpretation, their own dramatic discourse out of them. This will set the principled grounds for the empirical investigation consisting in 'dialogic' classroom implementations of each of the three phases outlined above.

2. Methodological Approach

The research methodology that informs the three phases of the theoretical enquiry is specifically grounded on an Experientialist approach to Conversation Analysis (CA) focused on an 'embodied' investigation of the move-&-act patterns identified in a number of extracts from the episode-scripts of five North-American sitcoms aired at the turn of the century—namely, *The Nanny*, *Roseanne*, *Dharma & Greg*, *Friends*, and *Will & Grace*—all of them representing instances of novel developments of the traditional family unit. Initially, the analysis shall concern the selected script extracts first in their original English language and, then, in their respective dubbing translations for Italian television. The Experientialist approach to CA, adopted for the exploration of the humorous fictional contexts of the sitcoms, shall require an original revision of the traditional Structuralist and Ethnomethodological CA models which shall be eventually integrated with the Appraisal Framework of dialogic analysis (Martin and White 2005) in order to adapt them to the investigation of the new cultural dynamics that disrupt the conventional social roles and the related discourse strategies within contemporary family units in the western world, in particular the United States, as represented in the sitcoms under analysis. It will be argued that the scripts and frames upon which the traditional CA models are grounded are in fact unsuitable for describing such new discourse strategies taking place within atypical family units where the identities of their members are in a continuous evolution and, thus, characterized by a constant negotiation of roles, judgements, and attitudes through the use of humour, which allows a dialogic mediation between latent interpersonal and intercultural conflicts.

A revised CA model is therefore advanced here precisely to enquire into such unusual roles and strategies. Hence, further Acts and Moves shall be introduced to focus on negotiation processes in the sitcom dialogues, where the tension between different social groups find a solution through the application of a number of Humour constructs facilitating the strategies of mediation and conflict resolution. Furthermore, the selected sitcom extracts shall introduce instances of so-called 'Revelation plots' marking a new type of humour based on a dialogic pattern of Revelation/Negotiation Acts aimed at mediating conflicts. Then, a contrastive analysis will be carried out between the original sitcom dialogues in American-English and their versions for the Italian television, showing evidence of how the producers of the Italian versions did not consider as 'acceptable' for Italian audiences such new social roles and the original scripts that characterize these sitcoms, which explains why they were often completely reformulated in translation. More specifically, the choice of these sitcoms for the analysis is justified by the fact that whereas *Friends* and *Will & Grace* are examples of 'product globalization'—or 'foreignization' (Venuti 1995, 1998)—because their dubbing translation for the Italian television conveys semiotic aspects typical of the source culture (which makes it close to the lexical-semantic construction and to the spoken rhythm and intonation of the American speech), *The Nanny* and *Roseanne* are instead two examples of 'product localization'—or 'domestication' (*ibidem*). In *The Nanny*, in particular, the Italian dubbing translation conveys a regionalization of contexts and dialogues aiming at producing a sense of familiarity in Italian audiences which nullifies every sociolinguistic and cultural specificity of the original version. Also in *Roseanne* there is a pragmalinguistic transfer of a standardized diatopic (and diastratic) variation into the Italian translation to render in an equivalent way a US diatopic/diastratic accent. The selected episode from *Dharma & Greg*, instead, is an example of 'product neutralization' as, in it, a non-existent Italian variation was devised in order to reproduce a diatopically-marked American accent.

On such grounds, therefore, a contrastive 'critical discourse analysis' (Fairclough 1995) was carried out on the original American-English scripts and their dubbing translation for the Italian television in order to identify discourse similarities and differences in the move-&-act patterns of the original and the dubbed versions of the sitcom scripts. Starting from the assumption that translators as 'intercultural mediators' need to develop multicultural schematic representations underlying the pragmatic competence of the languages they deal with (Guido 2004), it is here argued that in the TV dubbing translation of these sitcom dialogues the respective dubbing translators frequently impose their own subjective, ethnocentric representations of contexts and pragmatic uses upon the original American-English conversation patterns. By adopting such purely 'top-down' interpretative procedures and disregarding the subsequent 'bottom-up' and 'interactive' phases of the analysis, these translators actually behaved as socio-cultural 'gatekeepers'—rather than mediators—for the Italian audiences, denying them access to socio-cultural, experiential and humorous peculiarities of the original dialogues. In other cases, on the other hand, such dubbing translators often seem to display a belief that the more they reproduce 'faithfully' the structure and the semantic sense of the source script, the better they render the translated sitcom in an equivalent way. Again, by adopting this strict bottom-up approach they miss the spontaneity of a spoken humorous discourse and its effects on the target audience from a different culture.

Subsequently, the results of this conversation analysis shall be compared with the outcome of a number of related longitudinal case-studies carried out with a convenience sample of research subjects represented by groups of Italian undergraduate students from two Italian Faculties of Foreign Languages majoring in Translation. The case studies implemented with reference to each episode extract under analysis has aimed to investigate the possibility of developing new dubbing translations of the same sitcom episodes which, differently from the 'official' ones for the Italian TV, could instead provide an appropriate sociopragmatic and pragmalinguistic equivalence to the original move-&-act patterns and, at the same time, still retain the spontaneity of natural Italian conversational styles (cf. Niemeier 1991; Bialystok 1996). Such novel dubbing-translation process is here defined as 'transmediation' aimed at the achievement of a 'product naturalization' on the assumption that a dubbing translator is actually an intercultural mediator working towards the achievement of a balance between 'globalization' and 'localization' trends culminating in a kind of 'glocalized' natural rendering of the original audiovisual product into another language and culture.

The convenience sample of Italian university students participating in the case studies was, in each case, subdivided into two groups: an experimental Group A, applying the Acting Translator Model, and a control Group B, applying a conventional approach to sitcom dubbing translation (cf. Cronin 2003; Robinson 2003; Hatim 2004; Olohan 2004). Group A, in the course of the 'top-down' phase of their analysis, was pilot-prompted to use role-play as an elicitation technique to improvise conversations (in English and Italian) on open-ended situations, each characterized by the Moves and Acts identified in the original script. Improvised conversations were audio/video-taped and transcribed. Group B (the control group) did not receive this initial pilot treatment and, thus, focused on the dubbing translation task straight away (cf. Bollettieri Bosinelli 1996; Dìaz-Cintas 2008). The research hypothesis was that such impro-drama sessions on move-&-act realizations carried out by Group A would help dubbing translators experience first-hand the proper diamesic level of sitcom communication which is not just written, but 'written to be spoken' at an interactional level. This was assumed to determine spontaneity and more appropriate pragmalinguistic equivalence in subsequent sitcom translations. Then, during the following bottom-up phase of their analysis, both groups of students were asked to examine units from the original scripts and videos by analyzing the interactional structures (Acts, Moves, Exchanges etc.) of the original conversations (Edmonson 1981) in all their degrees of indirectness, formality and patterns of humour, and correlating them to their possible sociolinguistic value and cultural meaning as illocutionary acts (cf. Pomerantz and Fehr 1997).

The think-aloud technique that was adopted (Faerch and Kasper 1987; Nisbett and Wilson 1977) allowed the monitoring of the analytical strategies that students developed in their minds as they focused on the phonological and textual aspects, and the socio-cultural dimensions of the sitcom humorous conversations. This means that while students analyzed the original scripts, they externalized their mental processes and associations on possible cross-cultural interpretations of dialogic patterns in order to render them appropriately and equivalently in translation. In doing so, they subsequently justified their translation choices at both pragmalinguistic and sociopragmatic levels of variability. A third, 'interactive' phase involved students as 'acting translators' enacting as a team, in a space of physical representation, their dubbing translations as if they were the characters of the sitcom. This phase allowed various adjustments in terms of spontaneity and socio-culturally plausible equivalent rendering of the original humorous cues into Italian. Such acting sessions were tape recorded, transcribed into protocols and finally analyzed in parallel with the original versions. Then, they were checked against the actual sitcom scenes to adjust lip-synchronization and timing. Such protocols of think-aloud and acting-session data showed evidence that the students in Group A, who underwent the 'top-down' pilot phase, produced translations with a spontaneous conversation style in the target language, as they felt they could easily identify themselves with the sitcom characters and 'embody' their voices. Students in Group B, instead, produced translations into Italian in almost artificial and often stilted dialogic tones, marked by pragmatically-biased transfer and reversetransfer patterns of language (Selinker and Lakshmanan 1992), and often reproducing typical literary written styles. Finally, results of a comparative analysis between Group-A translations and the dubbing translations for Italian TV evidenced a higher frequency of cross-cultural discourse equivalence in the patterns realized by Group-A students than in the 'official' dubbed patterns.

3. The Chapters

The theoretical and practical issues outlined so far inform the six chapters of this book, the first three ones focused on theory, whereas the last three ones on its principled applications.

Chapter 1 opens Part One by setting up the grounds for a theory of Humour that will contextualize the analysis of the US sitcoms later in the book. It introduces a cognitive-pragmatic model for the analysis of the effects produced by the type of discourse defined as 'humorous', which essentially characterizes sitcom scripts. The argument starts from a definition of the 'Humour construct' and then it proceeds by focusing on the theoretical and empirical aspects inherent in it. The theoretical aspects regard, at the beginning, the nature of the cognitive contrasts upon which the 'Humour construct' is grounded. The concepts of 'Incongruity' and 'Incongruity-Resolution' are thus discussed through an assessment of the relevant literature. Then, the linguistic dimension of the construct is analyzed by emphasizing the structural-semantic patterns which characterize humorous texts. It is argued that these two cognitive and linguistic dimensions necessarily interact in a model that assesses Humour neither from an exclusively psychological perspective (which generally defines Humour simply as a 'deviant' mental structure with reference to the receiver's schemata categorizing reality), nor from an exclusively formalist perspective (which characterizes it simply as a particular linguistic organization of the text). In fact, the model proposed in this book intends to assess Humour from a socio-cultural perspective which includes also the other two ones in an ongoing process of interaction between *(1)* the schematic categories of the receivers of a humorous text (i.e., the source audience, the translator, and the target audience) who interpret it from their respective socio-cultural stances (by applying a top-down approach to humour interpretation—and, eventually, its rendering into another language and culture), and *(2)* the formal-linguistic structures of the humorous text (to be explored by applying a bottom-up approach to the analysis of the humorous discourse). On such grounds, therefore, it will be demonstrated that the 'Humour construct' is not universal, and this is particularly evident when translation is involved insofar as humour, viewed from a cross-cultural perspective, immediately reveals its true nature—namely, of language which is interpreted differently according to the different pragmatic norms of the cultures that produce the humorous message, and the cultures that interpret it as humorous discourse. The Acting Translator Model presented in this book, therefore, is of an interpragmatic and cross-cultural kind and, as such, it is validated in the chapters that follow through its empirical applications to the analysis of the sitcom humour characterizing US culture at the turn of the century. At first, such humour will be explored in the context of the original, shared socio-cultural schemata. Then, it will be remarked how the effects produced by this type of humour may vary, also radically, with reference to both the motivational 'relevance' and the structural 'salience' (cf. Guido 2001) that the discourse of humour exerts on the different subjective schemata of its implied source and target receivers—which, in this specific cross-cultural case, also include the dubbing translators' schemata.

Chapter 2 introduces the North-American sitcom genre as an atypical multimodal type of text insofar as it engages language in an ambiguous 'written-to-be-spoken' comic register entertaining a two-way dialogic relation—one between the actors directly interacting on stage, and the other between the actors indirectly interacting with the audience as the actual receiver of the comic gags. The chapter provides an outline of the development of US sitcom structure over the second half of the twentieth century, focusing on the ways in which it has reflected changes in the American society and culture and has likewise influenced the western society as a whole. In fact, the sitcom genre, as an audiovisual type of text, also involves non-linguistic, semiotic elements whose related moving images and soundtracks are socio-culturally marked. Therefore, in switching from one culture to another in the translation process, the dubbing translators as intercultural mediators need further professional techniques since their concern is not simply a search for lip-synchronization (cf. Zabalbeascoa 1994, 1997), but to convey sociopragmatic aspects of the source culture to the target audience. On such basis, the chapter sets the grounds for the argument to come, focusing on the problems inherent in the dubbing translation of such complex audiovisual genre by advancing the tenet that dubbing translators have to overcome their consolidated habit of reading and translating sitcom scripts silently, sounding the characters' voices and experiencing fictional situations only in their minds. In fact it is here argued that translators should 'inhabit' such voices in a physical space of representation, and then once they have familiarized themselves with characters and situational contexts both physically and mentally, they can 'enact' the script—again, in both languages, by activating processes of intra-lingual and inter-lingual translation (cf. Gotti 1996). In this way, dubbing translators would experience a truly first-person bodily and mental involvement with the humorous situations they inhabit—an involvement that has the power of reviving their own conventional and predictable schemata, and would thus turn dubbing translators into actual 'acting translators'.

Chapter 3 introduces the Model of the Acting Translator who, as such, needs to undertake an experiential embodiment of the sitcom script, first by improvising on it and then acting it out, thus activating in his/her mind top-down (schema-based) processes of familiarization with its dialogic, experiential and socio-cultural patterns of 'comic language'. Then, the Acting Translator is expected to focus on such script patterns by activating bottom-up (text-based) processes of defamiliarization in order to render such patterns into appropriate equivalent and synchronized ways in the target language. Such bottom-up 'audiovisual awareness' is here assumed to modify the acting translators' initial sense of familiarity that they developed during the initial 'top-down' phase—when they 'improvised' on the original script by inventing parallel versions, which were meant to explore characters and situations in depth so as to allow them to 'appropriate' the script to their own schemata. In the second bottom-up' phase, instead, the dubbing translators' acquisition of the awareness that conversation is carefully constructed according to precise patterns of humour is expected to induce in their minds a sense of displacement which, in any case, humour itself would create by 'deroutinizing' reality. This sense of displacement becomes even more marked as the dubbing translators start displacing the original patterns of humour into the target culture and language in the translation process. Hence the importance given to the dubbing translators' experiential embodiment of the source situation as an essential prerequisite for them to understand its humour structure before rendering it into another language and culture. In order to explore the dialogic structure of humour that an Acting Translator is expected to embody and, then, to analyze before the actual dubbing translation phase, this chapter will introduce a conversation frame for the investigation of humorous dialogic exchanges organized into Moves and Acts that crucially diverge from the expected ones in everyday conversation to create the comic effect. As acting translators become aware of such conversation patterns of humour, then they can exploit them as if they were a *canovaccio*—an improvisation frame—typical of the Italian *Commedia dell'Arte*, which would allow them first to give vent to their imagination and creativity during the top-down phase of 'script familiarization' and, then, to reflect upon the humorous deviations from the expected conversation turns during the bottom-up and interactive phases of the sitcom-script analysis which introduce the actual dubbing translation process.

Chapter 4 opens Part Two of the book by focusing on a comparative conversation analysis of a script from *The Nanny* sitcom and of its dubbing translation for the Italian television (*La Tata*, in the Italian version), characterized by a top-down 'sociopragmatic transfer' of Italian stereotypes to the American cultural, inter-ethnic, contextual and linguistic patterns of the original version. This implies that several serious modifications were operated by the dubbing translator in the Italian scripts. Such modifications occur not only at the diatopic level of move-&-act realization, but also at the diastratic and even at the diaphasic levels (Trudgill 1983; Berruto 1987), insofar as neither social-status and family-relation parameters, nor the protagonist's typical New-York Jewish speech style (cf. Tannen 1981) and socio-cultural, ethnic, and situational references are respected in the Italian dubbing translation. Indeed, such references are all completely subverted to fit into Italian stereotypical values and taboos. The resulting schematic mismatches and dislocations—arising from the translator's socio-culturally biased assessments of speech-act realizations which affect his pragmatic choices in the target language—end up determining a 'sociopragmatic failure' (Thomas 1984) in the target audience's interpretative processes of the comedy situations. Contrary to the official translated version of this sitcom, the protocols—analyzed in this chapter—reporting the parallel scripts created by the students/acting-translators 'embodying' the original script, demonstrate that it is possible to produce more 'natural' and alternative equivalent versions of the same script in Italian.

Chapter 5 applies the Appraisal framework (Martin and White 2005) to the comparative conversation analysis of the original scripts and dubbing translations for the Italian television versions of two extracts, respectively from *Roseanne* (*Pappa e Ciccia*, in the Italian version) and *Dharma & Greg*. *Roseanne*, in its Italian version, is characterized by a top-down 'pragmalinguistic transfer' of a standardized Neapolitan variation to the rendering into Italian of the original white-American working-class Illinois pragmalect. As the data of a contrastive script analysis demonstrate, such diatopic and diastratic dislocations towards the target Italian culture affect and often modify the original socio-culturally marked humour of the sitcom. This means that the inappropriate transfer of typical Neapolitan conversation strategies to the American context of the sitcom—together with the transfer of expressions that are semantically or syntactically equivalent, but that differ in their pragmatic implications (cf. Anderman and Dìaz-Cintas 2009)—can actually produce a 'pragmalinguistic failure' (Thomas 1983) in the Italian audience's reception processes (i.e., a displacing sense of socio-cultural familiarity—and yet contextual confusion due to a mismatch between the pragmalinguistic dimension of the dubbed sitcom and its original visual dimension of the American context). This also implies that the original interplay of the characters' attitudes and judgements comes to be altered as it goes through the process of adaptation to the new socio-cultural context of the dubbed sitcom. In the dubbing translation of an episode from *Dharma & Greg*, instead, the top-down invention of an Italian accent which does not exist in reality to replace a real American diatopic accent actually modifies and neutralizes the original socio-culturally marked implications of this sitcom episode. Also in this case, the protocol analysis of the students/acting-translators embodying the original script before producing their dubbing translation demonstrates that it is possible to develop more natural and equivalent alternative versions in Italian by applying the 'Acting Translator' method.

Chapter 6 analyzes some extracts from *Friends* and *Will & Grace*, whose dubbing translation—differently from the sitcoms examined in the previous chapters—is instead characterized by a bottom-up 'sociopragmatic and pragmalinguistic reverse transfer' of the American conversational styles and idiomatic expressions (socio-culturally marking the original version of the sitcom) almost literally rendered into the Italian version. As the untranslated title of *Friends* anticipates, this means that to render the 'foreign flair' of the original sitcom episodes, the 'official' dubbing translators of this sitcom often reproduce literally the formal—even the idiomatic—aspects of the American-English speech-act realizations. In doing so, they operate unnatural stylistic distortions in the Italian dialogues which also affect the spoken rhythms and intonations of the dubbed version, but cannot be identified with any of the corresponding variations and jargons used by real groups of Italian young (twenty-something) people (cf. Titone 1995). The pragmatic effect of such stylistic displacement on the Italian audience may be an impression of watching the sitcom as if it were in its original American version (cf. Kilborn 1989). And yet, by viewing in parallel the actual original one, it becomes evident that the Italian language used in the dubbed dialogues is unnatural and, indeed, sounds 'recited'. The same bottom-up translation strategy is also adopted in *Will & Grace* where, however, the continuous in-jokes referred to the 'gayness' of the male protagonists make dubbing-translation equivalence particularly difficult to achieve. In both cases, a protocol analysis of the students/acting-translators' processes of 'script embodiment' is carried out by rigorously applying and assessing established models of humour translation, thus showing that there can be possibilities of translating in pragmatically equivalent ways the language spoken by specific socio-culturally marked groups of people.

In conclusion, the discussion on the results of the cross-linguistic analysis upon the parallel sitcom conversations highlights how, in all the examined cases, the process of translating the sitcom 'original voices' for the Italian TV, far from revealing creativity within textual constraints (Chaume-Varela 1998), actually turns into a series of strategies of re-authoring dialogues in the corresponding Italian versions with the dubbing translators taking rigid ethnocentric stances (cf. Yampolsky and Joseph 1993). The outcome of the case studies, instead, shows evidence that, by adopting the Acting Translator Model, dubbing translators can explore ways of embodying the sitcom 'original voices' through their own experience which would allow them to empathize and better understand the original patterns of humour. The book ends by re-defining the notion of intercultural communicative competence in the field of dubbing translation, meant as a cognitive process by which the Acting Translator develops 'embodied' sociopragmatic and pragmalinguistic representations of both source and target cultures. Such a competence underlies the acting translators' awareness of Moves and Acts in sitcom dialogues through a process of 'experiential appropriation' of the humorous script, which facilitates its rendering into a target language that would sound natural and spontaneous to the target audience, but also faithful to the source culture.

4. Acknowledgements

In writing this book, I have benefited from the help and encouragement of numerous people. First of all, I would like to thank Elena Sansonetti, Italian Story Editor at Mediaset Television Group, for sharing with me her expertise in the dubbing-translation process and for granting me access to original scripts, draft translations, and both working copies and final versions of videotapes of the dubbed sitcoms *The Nanny*, *Roseanne*, and *Dharma & Greg*, which I analyzed in my research and used in my classroom fieldwork. My thanks also go to Rosario Ponzio, Head Manager, and Silvana Ceci, Material Servicing Manager, at Warner Bros. International Television, Italy, for their precious information on the mechanisms of sitcom production and for letting me have working copies of translated scripts from *Friends*. I've also benefited from suggestions by Ornella Francioni at RAI, Italy's Public Broadcaster, and by Bruno Michelotto, Production Manager of the dubbed version of the sitcom *Will & Grace* at Multimedia Network. Physical-theatre director Freda O'Byrne, with her drama methods applied to the exploration of fictional characters, has represented a stimulus for me in the development of my cognitive-experiential approach to 'language embodiment' at the grounds of the Acting Translator Model introduced in this book. I'm also grateful to Prof. Henry Widdowson for his inspiring influence—over the years at the University of London, Institute of Education—on my ideas about translation as 'interpretation' and 'rendering' of discourse across cultures; to Prof. Larry Selinker, whose teachings on 'language transfer', at the University of London Birkbeck College, have let me gain insights into the analysis of 'non-natural' varieties of the target language in dubbing; and to Prof. Maurizio Gotti for his approach to intra- and inter-lingual translation that has had an effect on the top-down phase of my approach to dubbing translation advanced in this book. A special word of thanks is for my brother, Prof. Gianluigi Guido, for his thought-provoking Theory of Salience that I have applied to the discourse of humour. I also wish to express my appreciation to my many students at the Faculties of Foreign Languages for Translation, Interpreting and Intercultural Mediation first at the University of Rome "S. Pio V" and, then, at the University of Salento (Italy), who have been, over the years, enthusiastic subjects of my empirical application of the Acting Translator Model. Finally, a debt of gratitude is due to Prof. Leonard Sbrocchi at Legas, whose unfailing support, advice and encouragement have made the publication of this book possible.

PART ONE

Theoretical Aspects of the 'Humour Construct' Applied to the Sitcom Genre

Pictures: ensemble casts of *The Mary Tyler Moore Show*; *Three's Company*; *All in the Family*; *Happy Days*; *I Love Lucy; Bewitched; Family Ties; Married ... with Children.*

Chapter 1

The Discourse of Humour

1.1 The Grounds of Humorous Discourse: Setting the Scene

Dubbing translators who have to cope with the rendering of a sitcom into another language need first of all to develop a deep knowledge of the cognitive, socio-cultural, and linguistic mechanisms of Humour. Research has so far focused on approaches to the translation of humour in audiovisual texts aimed at the achievement of pragmatic equivalence in the target language (cf. Delabastita 1989; Luyken *et al.* 1991; Gaiba 1994; Zabalbeascoa 1996b, 2003; Vandaele 1999; Chiaro 2004, 2007; Schroter 2004; Martinez-Sierra 2005a; Bucaria 2007, 2008; Corrius 2008). The purpose of this chapter is to present a new Cognitive-Experiential model for the analysis of the effects produced by a type of discourse defined as 'humorous', which essentially characterizes sitcom scripts. The argument will start from a definition of the 'Humour construct' and, then, it will proceed by focusing on the theoretical and empirical aspects inherent in it. The theoretical aspects considered in the first part of this chapter will initially regard the nature of the schema-cognitive contrasts upon which the 'Humour construct' is grounded. The concepts of Incongruity and Incongruity-Resolution will be thus discussed through an assessment of the relevant literature. Then, the linguistic dimension of the construct shall be analyzed by emphasizing the structural-semantic patterns which characterize humorous texts. It will be argued that these two cognitive and linguistic dimensions necessarily influence each other in a model that assesses Humour neither from an exclusively psychological perspective (which generally defines Humour simply as a 'deviant' cognitive structure with reference to conventional schemata categorizing reality), nor from an exclusively formalist perspective (which characterizes it simply as a particular linguistic organization of the text). In fact, the model proposed in this volume intends to assess Humour from a socio-cultural perspective which includes also the other two ones in an ongoing process of interaction between *(1)* the schematic categories of those people who interpret the humorous text from their own socio-cultural stances, and *(2)* the formal-linguistic structures of the text itself. On such grounds, it will be demonstrated that the 'Humour construct' is not universal, but—particularly when translation is involved—it is 'differentiated' according to the different pragmatic norms of the cultures that, respectively, produce the humorous message and interpret it as humorous discourse. The model presented in this chapter, and theoretically substantiated in Part

One of this book, will be therefore of an inter-pragmatic and cross-cultural kind. As such, in Part Two it will be validated through empirical applications of its construct to the analysis of instances of sitcom humour. At first, the main characteristics of such humour shall be contextualized within the schemata of US culture. Then, it will be remarked how the effects produced by this type of humour may vary, also radically, with reference to both the motivational 'relevance' and the structural 'salience' (cf. Guido 2001) that the discourse of Humour exerts on the different schemata of its receivers. The book shall thus report a number of pedagogic lines of enquiry which critically emphasize the socio-cultural dimension of the discourse of Humour in the wider context of the sitcom dubbing-translation methodology.

In his essay on the nature of Humour, Munro (1951) points out the essential interpretative relativism of the humorous message by stating that it is impossible to reach an agreement on the identification of the characteristics of Humour and of specific behaviours or stimuli that humour may induce in people. Humour—Munro concludes—is simply what makes us have fun. Obviously, the issue is not so simplistic, although it is possible to agree with Munro on the impossibility of establishing an absolute definition of the humorous message and its interpretative effects (cf. Chapman *et al.* 1995; Ross 1998; Gruner and Gruner 1999; Attardo 2001; Billig 2005; Carr and Greeves 2006; Fleet 2010).

Humour, indeed, is a cognitive construct and, as such, it has a specific purpose—namely, to organize the data of both abstract knowledge and empirical experience and, thus, to describe or explain aspects of the world. Like any other construct, also the 'Humour construct' has therefore at least two types of meaning—i.e., a 'systemic' meaning and an 'observational' meaning (Kaplan 1964). 'Systemic meaning' assumes that the interpretation of what the construct stands for depends upon the theory informing the construct itself. 'Observational meaning', in its turn, assumes that if a construct has to be explicatory, it must be clearly put into practice, in direct or indirect ways (Togerson 1958). If a construct does not presuppose an observational meaning, then it is simply a metaphysical notion. By the same token, if a concept does not presuppose a systemic meaning, it is no longer a construct but merely an observational notion. In the case of the sitcoms to be analysed in this book, it is impossible to validate the 'Humour construct' if its underlying theoretical-systemic foundations cannot be verified through the application of an empirical-observational methodology.

This chapter, therefore, shall examine first the theoretical-systemic aspects of the construct, and then also a number of empirical-observational aspects of its application.

1.2 The Cognitive-linguistic Dimension of the 'Humour Construct'

The rationale justifying the present study considers Humour as a cognitive construct principally grounded upon socio-pragmatic parameters shared by a particular group of people. Accordingly, the 'Humour construct' is constituted by three interrelated dimensions which are, respectively, cognitive, linguistic, and socio-cultural.

1.2.1 *Schematic contrasts*

The cognitive dimension of the 'Humour construct' is justified by the involvement of the mental structures in the process of the interpretation of a humorous message. In the amused reaction to a joke, for instance, schematic, cognitive contrasts induced by specific linguistic-structural divergences between a predicted situation and its infringement come to be part of the interpretative process. This is due to the fact that the human mind categorizes reality into 'schemata' representing situational and functional-linguistic 'prototypes' (cf. Rosch and Mervis 1975) based upon a shared experience of particular socio-cultural contexts and of procedural and behavioural 'scripts' (Schank and Abelson 1977) which are inherently contingent and transient. The infringement of such prototypes —particularly by means of their contradictory or paradoxical re-interpretation—is believed to provoke the humorous reaction since it induces a reconsideration of the socially-accepted schemata under a different perspective, thus challenging them.

In the light of such Schema Theory, the approach to the discourse of Humour advanced in this book is therefore neither confined to a merely structural analysis of language, nor it is limited to a kind of cognitive-psychological approach that tends to overlook the linguistic dimension which, instead, characterizes the construct. On the contrary, in this book it is contended that in the 'Humour construct' the structural-linguistic and the psychological dimensions are inseparable insofar as one informs and affects the other in a mutual and ongoing conditioning throughout the process of interpretation of the humorous discourse.

Yet, some scholars still consider the two dimensions of the analysis as independent, if not quite irreconcilable. What follows is a brief outline of these alternative positions, starting from the theoretical stance that advocates the 'psychological' dimension of the interpretation of a humorous message.

1.2.2 *The concept of Incongruity/Resolution*

An important school of 'psychological' thought on Humour has laid emphasis on how crucial the cognitive structures and the interpretative processes are in determining the 'response' to a humorous message

(Herzog and Larwin 1988). At the centre of these theories there is the concept of 'Incongruity', or deviation from the normal schematic expectations (Shultz 1974a, 1974b, 1976), which occurs *(a)* every time it is impossible to integrate one or more elements of a stimulus-situation (e.g., a joke, or a funny story) into a unique procedural schema, or *(b)* when the whole stimulus-situation does not conform to the normal schematic expectations associated with that specific type of situation. Suls (1983), for instance, claims that incongruity represents the necessary and sufficient condition for producing humour. In line with this position, Nerhardt (1979) asserts that the more marked the deviation from the normal expectations is, the more salient the understanding and appreciation of the humorous message will be.

Yet, other theories hypothesize that incongruity alone is not always sufficient to produce a humorous effect and an adequate response to it. One of them, for instance, maintains that 'cognitive humour' has a bi-phasic structure of 'Incongruity/Resolution' (Jones 1970; McGhee 1972, 1976; Shultz 1972, 1977; Suls 1972, 1977, 1983). Shultz (1976) asserts that incongruity alone can only produce nonsense insofar as it is based on 'logical interruption', 'perceptive contrast' and 'joyful confusion'. Yet, incongruity, if it is not followed by its resolution, cannot produce a genuine humour insofar as humour, to be defined as such, needs a coherent solution of the incongruous schema contrast – namely, a schematic re-integration with the consequent discovery of the hidden logical meaning. Suls (1983: 42) explains that, according to this position, humour is the result of an incongruity resolution and the sense of a joke can be achieved only by considering the information already given in it. In this sense, the disrupted schemata are not so fundamental in the process of understanding a joke since only and exclusively the structural and contextual contents of the joke are important in its appreciation.

A basic principle of the Incongruity/Resolution construct is that humour is a form of problem-solving since incongruity without resolution leaves receivers puzzled or frustrated as they do not 'understand the joke'. In brief, the supporters of this construct suggest that a full appreciation of the humorous message depends upon: *(a)* the initial manipulation of a schema; *(b)* the reaction to such a manipulation (i.e., the awareness of a schematic incongruity); *(c)* the consequent cognitive uncertainty; *(d)* the rapid resolution of the incongruity. As a corollary to these conditions, there are two more elements to be explored with the purpose of producing a humorous effect: *(1)* a 'funny' context, with jokes that signal that the given information is 'divergent' from reality, so that it is not to be taken seriously; *(2)* a 'humorous' language, triggering a 'frame of mind' in receivers that allows them to perceive such a language as 'appropriate' to the context. There are several studies in support of this position on the nature of the humorous stimuli (e.g., Chapman and Foot 1977; Wicker *et al.* 1981; Herzog and Larwin 1988; Oppliger and

Sherblom 1988). Suls (1983), in his turn, emphasizes how the Incongruity/Resolution Theory of Humour prevails in the field of verbal humour over the simple Theory of Incongruity. The next section, therefore, shall focus on the purely verbal, linguistic dimension of Humour.

1.2.3 *Semantic Incongruity: The concept of Real/Unreal Script Opposition*

From a linguistic perspective, the Incongruity/Resolution structure of Humour can be analysed exclusively at the semantic level of language. At the basis of the linguistic theories of Humour there is the principle that language is codified—in its variety of uses—in a functional way and according to a number of incongruous situational 'scripts' which determine the contexts within which it is normally used. Prior to the introduction of the cognitive-semantic notion of 'script' in the discourse of humour, however, there is Greimas's (1983/1966) Structuralist notion of 'incongruous isotopies' at the basis of jokes—an isotopy being a coherent set of meaning options connected to a lexical item present in the humorous text. More precisely, Greimas's Isotopy/Disjunction Model of Humour postulates that a joke is made up of two opposite isotopies: when the intended isotopy is identified, then the meaning is disambiguated and the joke is solved. Another forerunner of the 'script-incongruity' theory of Humor is represented by Koestler's (1964) Bisociation Theory—i.e., a semiotic theory which introduces the cognitive notion of 'two colliding lines of thought' that determine the joke. Raskin's (1985: 81) definition of script as "a large chunk of semantic information surrounding the word or evoked by it" determines the actual cognitive turn in Humour studies. Attardo (1994), in his 'Script Opposition' Theory of Humour, enhances Raskin's notion of script by redefining it as "a cognitive structure internalized by the speaker which provides the speaker with information on how things are done, organized, etc." (*ibidem*: 199), and containing "information which is typical, such as well-established routines and common ways to do things and to go about activities" (*ibidem*: 200). Thus, for instance, the script that represents the 'restaurant' situation (i.e., the 'restaurant' script) includes not only every contextual aspect typical of a restaurant (e.g., tables, chairs, waiters, menu, etc.), but also every linguistic routine pertaining to the communicative functions of the restaurant context (reading the menu, calling the waiter, ordering the first course, etc.).

In the discourse of Humour, the linguistic structures codified in the scripts are constantly infringed by means of a Semantic-Situational Incongruity—which produces linguistic ambiguity—and then resolved through double meaning. This entails that incongruity in the humorous message has to generate 'salience' (cf. Guido 2001)—in other words, a humorous message, to be such, has as its purpose to attract attention (i.e., to be salient) with its semantic incongruity within a specific situational script it seems at first to refer to. The salience of the message, in its turn, has to motivate the humorous resolution of the incongruity through the awareness of the contrast between the 'normal' reference script and its explicit linguistic infringement (Kuhlman 1985). A typical example of semantic incongruity can be found in the discourse of 'nonsense humour' devised by Monty Python, the famous English team of comedians, in their celebrated "spam scene". This scene takes place within a modern 'cafe' whose conventional script suddenly becomes incongruous for the presence of ancient Vikings as well as for the linguistic infringement of the normal discourse routine due to the obsessive repetition of the nonsense word "spam" as the ingredient of every dish on the menu (another deviation is represented by the male comedians playing female roles). Here is an extract from this humorous script:

> *Scene: A cafe. One table is occupied by a group of Vikings wearing horned helmets. Whenever the word "spam" is repeated, they begin singing and/or chanting. A man and his wife enter. The man is played by Eric Idle, the wife is played by Graham Chapman (in drag), and the waitress is played by Terry Jones, also in drag.*
>
> *Man:* You sit here, dear.
> *Wife:* All right.
> *Man:* Morning!
> *Waitress:* Morning!
> *Man:* Well, what've you got?
> *Waitress:* Well, there's egg and bacon; egg sausage and bacon; egg and spam; egg bacon and spam; egg bacon sausage and spam; spam bacon sausage and spam; spam egg spam spam bacon and spam; spam sausage spam spam bacon spam tomato and spam;
> *Vikings:* Spam spam spam spam...
> *Waitress:* ...spam spam spam egg and spam; spam spam spam spam spam spam baked beans spam spam spam...
> *Vikings:* Spam! Lovely spam! Lovely spam!
> *Waitress:* ...or Lobster Thermidor a Crevette with a mornay sauce served in a Provencale manner with shallots and aubergines garnished with truffle pate, brandy and with a fried egg on top and spam.
> *Wife:* Have you got anything without spam?
> *Waitress:* Well, there's spam egg sausage and spam, that's not got much spam in it.
> *Wife:* I don't want ANY spam!
> *Man:* Why can't she have egg bacon spam and sausage?
> *Wife:* THAT'S got spam in it!
> *Man:* Hasn't got as much spam in it as spam egg sausage and spam, has it?
> *Vikings:* Spam spam spam spam... *(Crescendo through next few lines...)*
> [...]

Raskin (1985) suggests a semantic theory, he defines as Semantic Script Theory of Humour, according to which a written or spoken communicative act can be considered humorous when the text is perfectly compatible with two distinct scripts and these scripts are diametrically opposed, like 'good/bad', 'real/unreal'. The third element—namely, the quip—makes listeners immediately shift from a script to the other, which produces the 'joke effect'. In Raskin's view, the two scripts involved in the humorous message are opposed (or 'incongruent') in that one of them represents a real linguistic situation (i.e., the 'normal' reference script), whereas the other represents a completely unreal one—or at least ambiguous, or paradoxical—which is incompatible with the former real situation and which determines the infringement of the 'normal' script, thus causing the humorous effect (*ibidem*: 108). Raskin himself (*ibidem*: 100-107) acknowledges that Grice's (1975) Cooperative Principle of routine communication needs to be infringed in a humorous exchange because, in such a context, the Real/Unreal script opposition cannot fulfil the maxims of quality, quantity, relevance and manner principally based on the truth of what is being said. In fact, the sender and the receiver of a joke need to 'suspend their disbelief' and pretend to believe that what is represented in the joke is true. Hence, it can be said that the Real/Unreal opposition in the humorous message is grounded on an explicit semantic infringement of the situational scripts which conventionally encode the linguistic behaviour. The following two jokes (Widdowson 1991) can be considered examples of this semantic infringement:

> *A notice in a laundry:* Ladies, leave your clothes here and spend the afternoon having a good time.
>
> *A notice in a zoo:* Please do not feed the animals. If you have any suitable food, give it to the guard on duty.

In both cases the joke initially refers to a real situational script (the 'laundry' and the 'zoo' scripts, respectively) which, however, comes to be immediately infringed by ambiguous linguistic implications deriving from a different script that is suddenly evoked by the words of the joke and that is completely incongruent with the previous one. Humour is thus generated by the recognition of the incongruity between the two scripts. In the case of the former joke, therefore, the situational script explicitly referred to is the normal one of the 'laundry'—an ordinary, real place where a promotional notice encourages female clients to 'unburden themselves' of the cumbersome laundry task by leaving the clothes for the washing in that place, so they could feel free to spend more time elsewhere in pleasant occupations. The implicit, unreal script, instead, completely flouts the 'laundry' script by superimposing upon it the scene of an imaginary licentious place where women 'unburden themselves' of their clothes in the dressing room, signalled by the notice, and then move to other rooms of the place 'to have fun'. According to the Incongruity/Resolution model, it is reasonable to assume that the incongruity of the message in the notice is resolved by becoming aware that undoubtedly it can mean only one thing, but unintentionally implies another.

In the same way, also in the latter joke the real situational script is, once again, a normal notice in a zoo which forbids the public to give food directly to animals, asking people who intend to do so to give the food to the guard on duty who will decide whether it is suitable for animals or not. The implied unreal script, in this case, plays on the ambiguity of 'giving the food to the guard on duty' who is thus paradoxically regarded like an animal or, even worse, like a hungry human being reduced to an animal condition as he hopes—as it were—to receive food from the zoo visitors.

Furthermore, the Real/Unreal script opposition, in Raskin's (*ibidem*: 111) view, can be actualized into three different joke sub-types: *(1)* Actual/Non-Actual (or Existent/Non-Existent) opposition, in which the actual situation can be misinterpreted as an incompatible, non-actual one; *(2)* Normal/Abnormal (or Predicted/Unpredicted) opposition, in which an expected event is replaced by an unexpected one; *(3)* Possible/Impossible opposition, in which a plausible situation is misunderstood for an implausible one. The first sub-type can be represented by the two jokes examined above in which the humorous contrast is based on the opposition between an 'existent' situation (i.e., the normal notices in the laundry and the zoo) and a 'non-existent' one (i.e., the implied unreal ones). An example of the 'predicted/unpredicted' contrast can be identified in the following joke:

> A doctor says to a man: "your wife needs a complete rest. Here are some sleeping pills." "When shall I make her take them?", asks the man. "You shall not make her take them", replies the doctor, "it's you that must take them!"

In this case the contrast implies both the normal and predicted action of a doctor prescribing a medicine for an exhausted woman, and the unpredicted, unexpected action of the doctor prescribing the medicine for the woman's husband, a healthy, but unbearably wearing, causing his wife's exhaustion.

The third contrast identified by Raskin accounts for the 'possible/impossible' opposition. The following joke is an instance of this type:

> Samson was so strong that he succeeded in lifting himself from the ground for three meters by picking himself up by his own hair.

In this case, the first part of the joke points to the possible situation of Samson being a very strong man. The second part, however, shifts to the hyperbolic and impossible situation of a man capable of lifting himself from the ground with his own strengths by picking himself up by his own hair. This humorous strategy of 'hyperbolic exaggeration' is indeed typical of the comic 'tall tales'.

Raskin's linguistic theory, therefore, can be viewed in the light of the cognitive dimension of the Incongruity/Resolution theory of Humour since—as it is here contended—the cognitive and the linguistic dimensions are not to be regarded as alternative, but complementary, as they interact with each other according to the model introduced in the following sub-section.

1.2.4 *Incongruity/Resolution in the Interactive Model of Humour*

Attardo (1994, 2001, Attardo and Raskin 1991) revises Raskin's semantic model of humour by emphasizing its cognitive component in the receiver's 'schema/text' interactive process of interpretation, thus elaborating the so-called General Theory of Verbal Humour. In particular, he pointed out the need to elaborate a theory that could encompass not only single jokes, but whole humorous texts (such as comedy), and that, furthermore, could account for the distinction between 'verbal humour', based on language (such as puns, wordplay, etc.), and 'content humour' based on culturally-marked subjects—e.g., based on ethnic, gender disparagement). On such grounds, Attardo (1994: 143) claims that humour implies an intentional process of creation grounded on a mechanism of Incongruity/Resolution (cf. Vandeale 2002) which needs to be perceived and interpreted as such by its receivers in order to be appreciated as humorous discourse. In Attardo's view, the receiver has first to interpret the linguistic cues of the text so as to activate in his/her mind the relevant script, but, then, the punch line prompts him/her to perceive another—hidden—script which is incongruous with the previous one. The realization of the incongruity between the two opposite scripts involved in the joke forces the receiver to reinterpret its linguistic cues according to the new, unexpected script thus achieving the resolution of the ambiguity inherent in the joke and its consequent appreciation. This interactive process of humour interpretation involving the structure of the comic text and the receiver's schemata is further described in its cognitive details by Attardo (1994: 223-224), who identifies six parameters, or 'knowledge resources', that an interpreter of a humorous discourse needs to activate in his/her mind, and that are: *(1)* the recognition of a 'script opposition' in the textual structure of the joke; *(2)* the activation of a 'logical mechanism' which allows an understanding of how the two opposite scripts have been brought together and which crucially helps the interpreter to resolve their incongruity; *(3)* the identification of the 'situation' that contextualizes the joke; *(4)* the identification of the 'target' of the joke; *(5)* the familiarity with the 'narrative strategy' adopted to tell the joke; *(6)* the mastery of the 'language' used to construct the humorous text. In applying his theory to longer humorous texts, Attardo (1998, 2001, 2002; Ruch *et al.* 1993) points out that whereas jokes may contain only one script opposition, longer humorous texts are built on a complex interplay of opposite scripts that an interpreter has to unravel (Attardo 2001: 38). A preliminary distinction, therefore, is necessary between 'punch lines', or humorous triggers at the end of a text (usually an utterance), and 'jab lines', or humorous triggers within the text (*ibidem*: 82-85), although their identification is not so simple as it may at first appear (cf. Tsakona 2003).

In the light of Attardo's General Theory of Verbal Humour, therefore, it is possible to outline a cognitive model of humour according to which the semantic scripts that codify language use—and that collide with each other to generate a humorous joke—directly refer to the schemata people unwittingly use all the time to categorize reality. Hence, the abstract cognitive schemata and the semantic scripts people adopt—and adapt—to the various communicative situations, in which they are daily involved, interact with each other, thus determining linguistic (and non-linguistic) behaviours. The interaction between the cognitive level of schemata—i.e., the 'ideational' level in Halliday's (1973) terms - and the linguistic-semantic level of the scripts—i.e., the interpersonal level (*ibidem*) - in the specific case of humour can be analysed from two different perspectives defined as 'bottom-up' and 'top-down'. The 'bottom-up'—or 'text-based'—perspective implies a 'language-to-mind' approach which tries to explain humour by starting from an analysis of the linguistic dimension of the joke in order to access, on the one hand, the situational scripts that it entails and flouts, and, on the other, the cognitive categories (or schemata) that come to be challenged by such situational incongruity. The 'top-down'—or 'schema-based' —perspective, instead, implies a 'mind-to-language' approach which attempts to explain humour by starting from the analysis of the conflicting schematic categories involved at the cognitive level to proceed by examining the effects of their schematic incongruity at a situational level (i.e., the scripts) and, thus, at a linguistic level, focusing on the linguistic deviations from the expected scripts and on the resulting ambiguities.

These cognitive-linguistic approaches can definitely be considered as dimensions of the same interactive process underlying the production and reception of the discourse of Humour. Yet, in both the linguistic, 'bottom-up' and in the cognitive, 'top-down' approaches to Humour outlined so far, the prevailing perspective is a formal, universalist one, whereas the socio-cultural dimension of humour has almost been neglected. The next section, therefore, will try to shed some light on this dimension.

1.3 The Socio-cultural Dimension of the 'Humour Construct'

1.3.1 *The universalist fallacy*

Although Attardo's General Theory of Verbal Humour may implicitly suggest that Humour is definitely a universal construct of which Incongruity is one of the central cognitive-structural principles, Attardo himself (1994: 204) eventually points out that this theory needs to be adapted to different cultural parameters in its script actualization. Indeed, the theoretical trends that support the concept of the universality of Humour can be classified into three groups:

(1) Linguistic theories belonging to the 'Cognitive-Formal' trend in language studies, principally informed by the theory of Linguistic Universals meant as semantic categories present in the mind of all human beings independently of linguistic and cultural differences. This trend can be traced back to Greenberg's (1963) theory of Universals of Language and—from a different, purely mentalist perspective—to Chomsky's (1965, 1980) theory of Linguistic Competence.

(2) Linguistic theories belonging to the 'Behaviourist-Functional' trend in discourse analysis, according to which it is possible to reach a high degree of typological-linguistic and behavioural universality by starting from the analysis of the structures and functions of various languages directly derived from different situational and cultural contexts. This trend takes its origin from specific anthropological studies (Malinowski 1935; Firth 1957) and has influenced Behaviourist scholars, such as Bloomfield (1935), as well as Structuralist scholars, such as Fries (1952), Lado (1957), but also Halliday's (1973) Functional theory of language, and Hymes' (1972) theory of Communicative Competence.

(3) Linguistic theories belonging to the 'Structuralist' trend in textual analysis, according to which meaning is unique and invariable across languages and cultures since it is inherent in the text itself - not in the mind of its interpreters. This, for instance, is what Empson (1961) contends with reference to ambiguity as a textual—not mental—dimension, a view informed by the literary theory of the New Critics, with Wimsatt (1946) who warns against possible subjective interpretative fallacies.

On such theoretical grounds, a number of conclusions can be drawn:

(a) The linguistic theories encompassed by the 'Cognitive-Formal trend' include those cognitive approaches to Humour that acknowledge the existence of universal schematic categories whose application to the most diverse cultural realities allows the attribution of a meaning to the flow of information human beings are continually exposed to. This explains how all human beings develop expectations based on norms established by schematic categories. When such norms are flouted—by means of incongruity, and independently of the differences in culture or language—then they can produce humour (Rosch 1977; Pick 1980).

(b) The linguistic theories encompassed by the 'Behaviourist-Functional trend' include those anthropological views of humour according to which the humorous response based on incongruity is universal in that it is inherent in the cognitive structure of the human mind. Fry (1987) emphasizes that in the old Egyptian chronicles, as well as in the Old Testament, there are many examples of humour. Also Berger (1987: 6) asserts that every culture in every historical period, without exception, has its own 'sense of humour'. This is corroborated by the

work of those anthropologists who have discovered that humorous structures that imply jokes, tricks, pranks, mockery and hoax are present in the most ancient and traditional societies, as well as in the most industrialized contemporary ones (Apte 1983: 185; Fine 1983). Jocular behaviours have been observed even among the primates (Fry 1987). Moreover, incongruent, deviant, or abusive manifestations of personality and behaviour are also relevant in this kind of jocular activities (Apte 1983: 186). For instance, the evidence of the universal significance of incongruity in humour can be traced back to the 'wrong-way-round' behaviour (e.g., sitting back-to-front on a horse and riding it), which is one of the fundamental components of the ritual humour in the Indian-American culture, as well as in the African and Indian tribal cultures (Apte 1983: 190). Suls (1983), in supporting this position, even goes so far as to claim that, in every socio-cultural context, humour has a functional structure of an Incongruity/Resolution type. As evidence of this he produces Shulz's (1972: 47) experiments on Humour in the folk literature of non-Western societies, in which the conclusion is that the presence of the Incongruity/Resolution components can be found in most of the collected data.

(c) The linguistic theories encompassed by the 'Structuralist trend' include those views according to which the cognitive-structural characteristics of incongruity can be identified in most of the humorous verbal messages in the world. More specifically, incongruity is considered the fundamental component of humorous advertising, independently of the cultural and linguistic differences of each nation (Raskin 1985). In other words, Humour is regarded as a standardized textual structure applicable on global bases.

Contrary to the perspectives on Humour outlined so far, this book contends that the Universalist Theory of Humour is fallacious insofar as it cannot be applied to the different sociolinguistic and cultural realities of whole communities, as well as of small groups of people sharing the same interests. As a consequence, the principle of humorous Incongruity/Resolution needs to be reconsidered on cross-cultural grounds.

1.3.2 *Linguistic and cross-cultural differences*

In sub-section 1.2.4 two jokes have been examined (respectively contextualized in a laundry and in a zoo), presenting them as instances of the principle of incongruity between two different scripts (a 'real' one and an 'unreal' one). It has been contended that the humorous effect that such jokes provoke depends on the resolution of such an incongruity—that is, on the recognition of both scripts, one of which is real and explicit, whereas the other is unreal and implicit and in total contrast with the explicit one. The supporters of the universality of semantic and cognitive structures underlying the construction of a humorous message do not hesitate to assert that also the cognitive process of recognition of the incongruity between the two scripts is universally shared by human beings. But is it really so?

How could, for instance, an inhabitant of an underdeveloped and economically depressed African village recognize the incongruity of the joke on the zoo and its hungry guard on duty if, on the one hand, in his society the institution—and thus the very concept—of the zoo does not exist since wild animals live in freedom and, on the other, he cannot see anything humorous in the concept of hunger since it is a painful part of his daily experience?

And yet it is not necessary to make reference to cultures that are so far from the Western one to demonstrate the untenability of the universality principle in Humour. The following English joke can be regarded as a case in point:

> An English bishop received the following note from the vicar of a village in his diocese: "My lord, I regret to inform you of my wife's death. Can you possibly send me a substitute for the weekend?"

The humorous effect of this joke, for instance, not only is untranslatable into Italian, but it can also be obscure for those people who are not familiar with the British socio-cultural reality. This being so because, first of all, the humorous effect of this joke is grounded on the ambiguity of the word 'substitute' which, in the English language, does not reveal the feminine gender or the masculine one. In the Italian language, on the contrary, the gender of a word must be specified in translation—in the case in point, 'substitute' should be translated either as 'sostitut*o*' (masculine) or as 'sostitut*a*' (feminine), but this would disambiguate the joke and, thus, nullify its effect, as it would be translated in the following way:

> Un vescovo inglese ricevette un biglietto dal parroco di un paesino della sua diocesi: "Monsignore, mi duole informarla della morte di mia moglie. Potrebbe mandarmi un sostituto per questo fine settimana?"

Translated into Italian this joke would not be humorous at all. An Italian receiver can in fact understand only the real situational script—namely, the situation of an English vicar who asks his bishop to send him another priest to substitute him (hence a 'male substitute'—'sostitut*o*') for the weekend since he is in mourning for his wife who has just died. Even the normal script may be misunderstood if the Italian receiver has no knowledge of the fact that the joke is a British one and that in the Anglican Church priests are allowed to get married. The unreal script which generates the humorous incongruity—and which may not be grasped in Italian—is the one that implies the situation of a vicar who has just lost his wife and who asks his bishop to send him a 'substitute wife' for the weekend. The term 'substitute', in this case, cannot be translated with the masculine gender as it does not refer to the priest who has to substitute the vicar, but to a new 'substitute woman' who has to replace the late wife. The opposition between these two scripts implies, thus, a contrast between the spirituality expected from a religious person and the unexpected, implicit licentious relationship between the vicar and the 'substitute' for his wife.

The hypothesis of the universality of humour, therefore, is disproved by examples like this since only by recognizing these specific sociolinguistic details does it become possible to solve the incongruity between the two scripts.

1.3.3 *Types of sociolinguistic contrast*

The argument so far has considered how, although there may be cross-cultural similarities in cognitive principles and typological-linguistic structures of Humour, it is possible to find considerable socio-cultural and pragmatic differences in situations, contexts and subjects employed to create and communicate a humorous message. Such differences can be categorized. A useful model for categorization is the one proposed by Hofstede (1983) who demonstrates how national cultures can be classified on the basis of a number of dimensions. Two of the dimensions that he identifies regard the contrasts defined as 'Individualism/Collectivism' and 'Power Distance'.

In considering the dimension of 'Individualism/Collectivism', Triandis *et al.* (1988) notice how the subordination of the individual's objectives to the objectives of a large group of people is a crucial characteristic of the collectivist cultures (such as, for instance, the cultures of Thailand and Korea). The individualist cultures (e.g., those of the US and Germany), on the contrary, tend to be characterized by smaller, multiple and less rigid groups—till nearing individualism. To this it is possible to add that: *(a)* in collectivist cultures, both schemata categorizing reality, and situational and linguistic-semantic scripts organizing everyday experience are almost homogeneous and socially sanctioned. This implies that also the construction of a humorous message involves the entire community that interprets and resolves it in the same way; *(b)* in individualist cultures, both schemata and situational-linguistic scripts vary according to the various groups, whose components share the same cultural and social interests and express them through specific registers and language styles. In this case, the humorous message to be appreciated and correctly interpreted has to conform to such linguistic and socio-cultural specificities.

Hofstede's (1983) second dimension—i.e., 'Power Distance'—entails the ways in which power is unequally distributed within a national culture (Ronen 1986), as well as within specialized 'micro-cultures' shared by particular groups of people. This implies that the national cultures with a high level of power distance tend to be hierarchical in their interpersonal relations, whereas those with a low level of power distance tend to be more egalitarian. From such considerations it is possible to deduce that: *(a)* in cultures with a 'high level of power distance'—generally the 'collectivist' ones—the relationships between the characters of jokes are often marked by a great power distance; *(b)* in cultures with a 'low level of power distance'—generally the 'individualist' ones—the relationships between the characters of jokes are often egalitarian.

Furthermore, a sociolinguistic perspective of Humour can involve types of situational contrasts that add a multifaceted pragmatic depth to the typical Incongruity/Resolution cognitive structure examined above. What follows is an assessment of the two more relevant structures of sociolinguistic contrast—namely, the contrast of an 'Arousal/Safety' type and the contrast of a 'Humorous Disparagement' type—viewed in the light of Hofstede's (1983) dimensions.

1.3.4 *The Arousal/Safety contrast*

The Arousal/Safety contrast represents a kind of semantic mechanism of Humour based on the Relief construct explored from different disciplinary perspectives and in its diverse facets regarding the sense of safety and relief after having: *(a)* realized one's own expectations (Kant 1790), *(b)* used up all one's energy to achieve something (Spencer 1860), *(c)* made all the efforts to repress feelings and impulses and succeeded (Freud 1963), or *(d)* experienced high and excessive levels of tension (Berlyne 1960, 1969, 1972). Studies on the Theory of Safety have been carried out by Keith-Spiegel (1972), McGhee (1983), Morreall (1983) and Rothbart (1977). Other studies on the Safety construct explicitly maintain that Humour is directly associated with a sensation of arousal (Godkewitsch 1972, 1976; Goldstein and McGhee 1972; Chapman and Foot 1976).

Rothbart (1973, 1976) claims that the fundamental variable is neither arousal, nor the intensity changes of arousal, but rather—by applying Schachter and Singer's (1962) theory—the interpretative act which is associated to arousal. Hence, by making a distinction between physiological states (like arousal) and emotional states (like anxiety), Rothbart offers an explanation of the Arousal/Safety contrast in Humour - here reinterpreted under a fresh sociolinguistic light. According to Rothbart's (1973) theory, the humorous effect occurs when a person has experienced an excessive sensation of arousal, but at the same time (or immediately after the arousal), s/he manages to evaluate the stimulus that provoked arousal as harmless and devoid of dangerous consequences. When, on the contrary, a situation causing arousal is deemed harmful, then it induces a cautious attitude aimed at the resolution of the implicit problem, which nullifies every playful disposition necessary to produce a humorous effect. Therefore, the same event can give rise to either fear or fun. Neither fear nor fun, however, depend on the state of arousal which both feelings in any case would generate, but it is rather determined by the interpretative judgement (namely, the positive or negative evaluation) that a person associates with the stimulus that caused the sense of arousal.

In this book it is contended that the positive or negative evaluation by a person who interprets this stimulus is of a sociolinguistic nature, not simply of a cognitive one, insofar as this is an attempt to restore a social, semantic and schematic order which the sense of arousal puts in danger. The 'humorous safety', hence, is the sense of safety felt by the person who, though experiencing the thrill of trespassing the order that the group s/he belongs to has established, succeeds in projecting such transgressive impulse on to a playful and unreal dimension thus exorcizing it and making its actual realization impossible in reality.

In conclusion, the Arousal/Safety process entails a person's judgement (hence a relative judgement, not an absolute and universal one) in reference to a source of 'sociolinguistic arousal' and his/her consequent sense of safety and relief as soon as s/he realizes the innocuous—and thus 'humorous'—intention of that source. The effect of such a contrast is therefore of an 'affective' nature. Rothbart's Arousal/Safety hypothesis is in line with the theories on Humour Motivation by Shultz (1976), Apter and Smith (1977), and Apter (1982). More specifically, this hypothesis involves the dimension of Individualism/Collectivism insofar as it represents the unconscious and transgressing arousal associated with the individual's attempt to distance himself/herself from the group s/he belongs to, followed by a sense of safety at the realization that, eventually, the status quo is restored (cf. Franklyn 2008). It seems sensible therefore to state that the Arousal/Safety contrast is characteristic of the collectivist cultures with a high and established level of power distance.

1.3.5 *Humorous Disparagement*

Another contrast of a sociolinguistic nature is the one based on the mechanism of 'Humorous Disparagement'. The theories on humorous disparagement can be traced back to Aristotle (a review on this tradition can be found in Munro 1951; Keith-Spiegel 1972; La Fave *et al.* 1976; Zillmann and Cantor 1976; Morreall 1983; Zillmann 1983). These theories contend that humour is basically 'social' since, as Purpel (1981) claims, humour is so all-engaging to become one of the most insidious forms of hostility. Hence satire, ethnic humour, and disparaging humour are the most notorious components of this type of humorous discourse.

The disparaging humour always implies a triadic relationship following Jakobson's (1960) communicative model, which can be summed up in the formula "the Sender sends a Message to the Receiver". In the disparaging humour, thus, such a triadic relationship entails: *(1)* the teller of the joke (i.e., the Sender of the humorous message), *(2)* the listener (i.e., the

Receiver), and *(3)* the 'victim' or 'target' of the humorous joke (i.e., the subject of the humorous Message). This relationship is defined by Freud (1963) as the 'humorous paradigm'. If the Sender's intention is mainly didactic (i.e., to give a lesson to the Receiver, or to the 'victim'), then humour is of a satiric type. If instead the Sender intends to embarrass the 'victim' in the presence of other people and, in agreement with the Sender, most Receivers of the humorous joke are ready to condone the attack, then in this case it is possible to talk of disparaging humour. When, however the Sender produces disparaging humour without minding whether the others appreciate the attack, or not, then the result will be sarcasm. In the special case of self-disparaging humour, the Sender produces humour that is prejudicial to himself/herself. Furthermore, ethnic, racist, and sexist jokes can serve the same purposes. Disparagement in itself, however, is not funny (La Fave *et al.* 1976; Zillmann and Cantor 1976; Morreall 1983; Zillmann 1983). As Zillmann (1983) notes, the humorous disparagement actually is a theory of humorous facilitation: playfulness and jokes are only useful to make disparagement pass for humour. Following Freud (1963), Zillmann remarks how humorous disparagement needs the wrong attribution of a cause that could justify it. For instance, when listeners laugh for a racist joke, they need to think that they do so because they have attributed the stimulus to laugh not to the racist content of the joke, but to its formal construction, that is, to its play of words and wit. This confusion between the pleasure associated with the structure of the joke and the pleasure associated with its purpose (i.e., the racist attack) gives listeners the opportunity of rationalizing what otherwise would represent an ethically unacceptable behaviour.

There are, however, some circumstances in which it becomes easy for the listener to enjoy the humorous disparaging attack. This occurs when the victimization seems to be out of his/her control, when it seems to be well deserved, when the listener's approval of the attack does not run the risk of being subject to criticism and, finally, when also the other listeners join in the disparaging attack. In this last case, the listener's individual responsibility decreases in inverse relation to the size of the group. The Humorous Disparagement, thus, requires a particular attitude towards those people who are disparaged by humour. This implies: *(a)* a playful manipulation of the situational script; *(b)* the induction of a state of arousal associated with disparagement; *(c)* a sense of uncertainty towards one's own stance; *(d)* some elements of Incongruity/Resolution that can facilitate the necessary wrong attribution of a cause to the disparagement in order to justify the humorous joke. The effects of Humorous Disparagement, therefore, are principally of a conative type since they induce the expression of disparaging reactions and feelings.

In conclusion, generally speaking, if a joke has to be perceived as 'humorous', its Sender and Receivers must be well aware of the negative moral evaluation attributed to disparagement (or, at least, they must demonstrate that they agree on such an evaluation). This can allow the acceptance of racist, sexist, or ethically deplorable jokes and, paradoxically, if also the 'victims' of the joke agree on such negative evaluation, the result may even be the end of the arousal and tension between different groups. Indeed, Humorous Disparagement, by emphasizing social contrasts through jokes, could be capable of establishing a certain type of communication based on different sociolinguistic and cultural codes (cf. Billig 2005; Ryan 2007). In this sense, it mainly involves the dimension of Power Distance as it exorcises it only by emphasizing it through the lightness of a joke. Therefore, this type of disparaging humour principally characterizes individualist cultures with a low level of power distance and with more fluid and ongoing sociolinguistic scripts than those highly consolidated and hierarchical ones typical of the collectivist cultures.

1.3.6 *The argument so far*

So far the discussion has focused on more or less compact, wide and well-differentiated socio-cultural groups who *(a)* consciously share ethical judgements at the basis of humorous expressions (as in the case of the Humorous Disparagement), or *(b)* can however recognize behaviours and values of other groups so that they can decide whether acknowledging them (as it happens in the cultures characterized by a a low level of power distance and, thus, less social distance between the different groups), or rather rejecting them (as in the case of the humorous Arousal/Safety contrast, typical of the collectivist and hierarchical cultures with a high level of power distance and with consolidated sociolinguistic and behavioural scripts).

As mentioned before, schemata (usually considered as universal), as well as situational and linguistic-functional scripts organizing everyday experience, have often been regarded as 'unconsciously shared'. This assumption is quite controversial indeed, and it will be discussed in the next section with the introduction of a novel pragmatic model of humorous discourse which, in this book, shall inform the subsequent case-study analysis of the dubbing translation of American sitcoms.

1.4 The Pragmatic Model of Humorous Discourse

1.4.1 *Limits of the traditional pragmatic approach*

What happens, then, if the Receiver of a humorous message does not acknowledge it as such—or, at least, s/he does not succeed in grasping all the linguistic and socio-cultural implications of the joke?

From the perspective of classical Pragmatics, such a case would be defined as 'cooperation failure'. Grice (1975), in his seminal theory of the four Cooperative Maxims (i.e., Quality, Relevance, Quantity and Manner), aimed at granting successful linguistic communication, focuses almost exclusively upon the 'communicative intentionality' of the Sender of a message, who sets its qualitative—and hence 'ethical'—parameters as well as the criteria for establishing their relevance, the quantity of information necessary to its clarity, and finally the formal style—or manner—of the message. Grice, however, did not seem to recognize at all the process of 'interpretative cooperation' activated by the Receiver of the same message. In Grice's theory, in fact, the Receiver is simply expected to conform perfectly to the schematic and sociolinguistic parameters adopted by the Sender (Guido 1996: 59-61). Grice (1975: 50) states this explicitly:

> "The speaker thinks (and would expect the hearer to think that the speaker thinks) that it is within the competence of the hearer to work out, or grasp intuitively, that the supposition mentioned [...] IS required." (*Grice's emphasis*)

The concept of 'implicature'—a crucial aspect of Grice's (*ibidem*) 'cooperative principle'—is, indeed, grounded on such schematic conformity as it concerns exclusively the Sender's 'intentionality' in creating the message, whereas the Receiver's subjective interpretative 'inferences' are totally excluded, as well as any possible attempt at a 'meaning negotiation' between Sender and Receiver. All this, however, is contrary to the traditional theory of Speech Acts (Austin 1962; Searle 1969) which considers a verbal message in its full communicative dimension—namely, as constituted by *(a)* a 'locution' (i.e., the linguistic referent—or the 'text'—of the message), *(b)* an 'illocution' (i.e., the Sender's intentionality implied in the message—or the 'force' of the message), and *(c)* a 'perlocution' (i.e., the interpretation that the Receiver infers from the 'effects' that the 'illocutionary force' of the message has had on him/her). Conversely, according to Grice's paradigm, the 'illocutionary force' of the message (namely, the Sender's meaning implications) and the 'perlocutionary effects' that such a message has on the Receiver's interpretation, perfectly coincide in his concept of 'implicature'. The Receiver can only decide whether to flout the Sender's intentionality, or to disagree with it, but s/he is not supposed not to recognize it, or to misunderstand its implicatures. This indeed emphasizes Grice's univocal socio-cultural perspective, from which it is possible to deduce that in order to obtain an appropriate linguistic communication, all that senders and receivers need to do is to converge on a number of interpretative schemata sanctioned by a particular speech community with a homogeneous socio-cultural background both Sender and Receiver belong to—hence the 'authority of an interpretative community' as described by Fish (1980). Obviously, the implication is that this kind of 'expected communication' automatically excludes all those multicultural situations of language use where different speakers with different pragmatic schemata interact, often provoking unintentional obscurity and ambiguity (cf. Guido 2008). If Grice's (1975) theory is applied to humorous discourse, this clearly means that, on the one hand, the sharing of schemata and sociolinguistic codes within a specific group of people facilitates the understanding of the implications of the humorous message. Yet, on the other hand, this also means that other culturally different groups may not succeed in accessing the humorous implications of the message and, therefore, they may not interpret such a discourse as humorous. A case in point is produced by the English artist Robert Haydon (quoted in Wannan 1981: 12) when he describes, from his perspective, an accident occurred in Paris in 1814, when in the zoo of the town a five-franc note slipped from the hands of a man and ended up into the bears' cage. The day after, early in the morning, an elderly grenadier stealthily entered the cage to seize it. A bear was awake, so it rushed at the grenadier, killing him and devouring part of his body. In England—Haydon remarks—the bear would have been shot down and a public raising of funds would have been promoted in favour of the grenadier's widow. In France, instead, the accident was ridiculed: the bear was given the name of the grenadier and the public used to call its name out throwing food at it as a kind of reward for its deed.

This paradoxical episode of 'interpretative discordance' between two culturally different groups is emblematic as it represents the French group exorcising the violent 'arousal' provoked by a tragic situation through the sense of 'safety' induced by a humorous reaction that is totally incongruous to the situation. Conversely, the English group is here depicted in opposition to the French one as its members would have never shared with the French the incongruous humorous interpretation of such tragic situation, resolving instead the 'arousal' it provoked in a 'schematically logical' way—namely, in a way that was deemed congruous to the actual situation and, thus, non-humorous. Yet, in this report, a further 'English' stance is represented namely, Haydon's stance, as he embodies the narrator who deplores the French group's incongruous emotional reaction to tragedy by activating a humorous response of an Arousal/Safety type, and overtly attacks the French by using a 'humorous disparagement' strategy in targeting them—but, covertly, he probably appreciates them for their humorous resolution of the situation. This example, in sum, shows how a univocal interpretation of the humorous message cannot exist because there is always a multiplicity of interpretative perspectives. This pragmatic principle is indeed at the basis of the Cross-cultural Model of Humorous Discourse to be introduced at this point.

1.4.2 *The Cross-cultural Model of Humorous Discourse*

The cross-cultural model of humorous discourse to be discussed at this stage is assumed to be useful for its applications to the process of sitcom dubbing translation and, more specifically, for its affinity with the Acting Translator model advanced in this book. The model is pragmatic, yet it does not concern the analysis of a humorous 'message', but of humorous 'discourse'. The difference between 'message' and 'discourse' is crucial insofar as a 'message' entails a univocal 'Sender→Receiver' communication based on a total convergence of schemata (Jakobson 1960; Grice 1975), whereas a 'discourse' implies an ongoing negotiation of meanings developing from the interaction between the different socio-cultural schemata of people participating in a communicative exchange (and, thus, 'taking turns' and alternating in the roles of Sender and Receiver).

In the light of this theory of Discourse as a pragmatic negotiation of meaning (cf. Brown and Yule 1983; Widdowson 1984; Cook 1989; Guido 1996, 2008), the perspective on humour advanced in this book entails that the very socio-cultural nature of humorous communication cannot exclude other interpretative perspectives which are different from the perspective of the Sender of a humorous joke. In their interpretation of the joke, therefore, receivers may interact with each other, which would reveal how a joke may be interpreted by each of them as more or less humorous. So far the sociolinguistic approach to humour has not substantially diverged from the traditional pragmatic trend which sets at the centre of the interpretative process the intentionality of the Sender in devising a joke—who is also the only one capable of disambiguating the message. But reality is quite different. In fact, different interpretative perspectives can coexist as there are different types of humorous discourse achieved from the text of the same joke—this being due to the fact that the various empirical receivers can infer different interpretations from its linguistic arrangement. Hence the humorous discourse is here defined as the pragmatic achievement of meaning in reference to a linguistic text constructed on cognitive-schematic and cultural-semantic parameters of incongruity. This entails that there could be as many different interpretative 'discourses' derived from the same 'text' of a joke as are the receivers of a joke. Obviously, the text of the joke operates a strict control on its different interpretations, and yet, the socio-cultural backgrounds that inform the receivers' schemata determine the discourse interpretation that a receiver infers from a humorous text, which may differ from the discourse that another receiver, in his/her turn, may infer from the same text. Generally speaking, the Receiver of a humorous joke, in deriving from its textual construction his/her interpretative discourse, may adopt two types of perspectives that can be defined as *(1)* a 'motivational perspective' of 'familiarity', and *(2)* a 'structural perspective' 'estrangement'. Pointing out once again that the text of a humorous joke is formally characterized by various typologies of cognitive and situational incongruity aimed at stimulating the receivers' schematic memory and attention (cf. Goldsten *et al.* 1972; Alden and Hoyer 1993; Alden *et al.* 1993), it is possible to state that:

(1) A Receiver adopts the 'motivational perspective' when, in deriving his/her own interpretative discourse from the text of a joke, s/he feels

a sense of 'familiarity' with the cultural schemata and the sociolinguistic scripts that the Sender has flouted in order to create the incongruity of the joke. This means that the Receiver experiences a 'first-person' emotional, affective involvement with the socio-cultural group within which the humorous joke has been produced, thus succeeding in understanding all the topic and content implications intended by the Sender because s/he judges them as 'relevant', for instance, to the fulfilment of some of his/her impulses, like the 'transgressive' ones which otherwise would have been kept repressed (cf. Freud 1963; Dworkin and Efran 1967; Singer 1968; Landy and Metee 1969; Goldstein 1970; Baron 1978a, 1978b; Lamb 1978; Trice 1982; Mueller and Donnerstein 1983).

(2) A Receiver adopts the 'structural perspective' when, in deriving his/her own interpretative discourse from the text of a joke, s/he feels a sense of 'estrangement' towards the cultural schemata and the sociolinguistic scripts by which the Sender achieves incongruity in the joke. The Receiver, in this case, does not share the same schemata with the Sender, therefore, s/he does not feel any emotional involvement in the content of the joke since s/he neither judges it in its socio-cultural significance, nor knows its motivational value, thus considering the joke from a 'third-person' detached perspective of 'estrangement'. The Receiver's attention, rather than concentrating on the incongruity of the content, focuses instead on the procedural variables that determine the semantic-structural incongruity of the joke, and thus on the 'cognitive dissonance' to be solved. Such a dissonance is not, therefore, emotionally relevant and motivational to the Receiver, but only 'salient' (Guido 2001), in that it attracts his/her attention only upon the linguistic form that induces in the Receiver a merely physiological stimulus—like the sense of pleasure produced by the humour based on plays of words and wit, or on nonsense incongruity meant as schematic violation with no resolution. Focusing on the semantic-structural incongruity of a joke, however, means that a joke can be appreciated only in the language that produces it, with serious problems as regards the rendering of the joke into another language, as illustrated in the following case in Italian (from Guido 2005: 214):

> "Ho saputo che il suo ultimo libro ha avuto un ottimo successo [...] Per il prossimo anno ha qualcosa in serbo?" domandò la ragazza. "No, no..." rispose il Marchese, "tutto in italiano". *(Literal back-translation: "I've heard that your latest book has been a best-seller [...] For next year have you anything in store?" The young lady asked. "No, no..." the Marquis replied, "all in Italian").*

As evident, the literal back-translation of this exchange does not convey at all the humorous effect of the original pun, based on the homophonic/homographic coincidence of the phrase "in serbo", whose double meaning can be rendered either into 'in store' (as intended by the young lady in the exchange), or into 'in Serb' (as misunderstood by the Marquis—hence his pointing out that all his writings are "in Italian"). This pun, therefore, totally based on semantic-structural incongruity, cannot be rendered verbatim into English, unless the translator operates an analogue transformation by rendering it into another pun in English that is equivalent in meaning, but also in its wordplay form (Veisbergs 1997), as proposed in the following translation based on the "finish"/"Finnish" homophonic pun, in association with the 'domestication' strategy (Venuti 1995) of turning the original term "Italian" into "English" (but also for its assonance with "Finnish") as the language used for his writings by the Marquis (here rendered as "Marquess" in line with the British tradition):

> "For next year have you anything in store? I adore the exquisite finish of your works!" The young lady asked. "Well, no..." the Marquess replied, "all my works are in English".

Furthermore, it should be added that, from a 'motivational' perspective, the humorous contrast between the 'predictable' event and the unexpected, 'unpredictable' one is generally perceived as more comic than the contrast between the 'predictable' event and the 'impossible' one, which is instead more appreciated from a 'structural' perspective—as Alden and Hoyer (1993), for instance, demonstrate by applying a similar theory to the humour employed in the field of advertising. If Speck's (1991) theory of Incongruity is applied to the case of Humour, then it is possible to define as 'unexpected' the motivational effect obtained when the whole stimulus-event does not conform to the expectations that an individual has in reference to the same event. The definition of 'impossible' can, instead, be attributed to that structural effect of incongruity obtained every time two or more elements of a stimulus cannot be integrated within the same schema.

In sum, when the content of a humorous joke flouts established behavioural principles through sociolinguistic incongruity, then it is possible to define Humour from a 'motivational' perspective. Conversely, when the linguistic structures of the joke flout the logical principles at the level of semantic-formal and schematic reasoning, then it is possible to define Humour from a 'structural' perspective. Alford (1982) applies a similar theory to the description of 'taboo humour', analysed from a motivational perspective as it flouts 'idealized expectations', and of 'incongruent humour', explored from a structural perspective as it flouts 'phenomenological expectations'.

So far a model of Humour based on a type of multi-levelled pragmatic communication has been outlined. The main perspectives from which the Receiver of a joke can analyze it at the 'discourse' level are the following two ones:

(1) If the Receiver of a humorous joke is part of the same socio-cultural and linguistic group the Sender belongs to—sharing with him/her

the same mental and procedural schemata—then s/he will not have problems either in interpreting the text of the joke as 'humorous', or in achieving from that text a discourse interpretation which corresponds to the Sender's intentional discourse. In fact, the Receiver feels culturally motivated by the humorous incongruity of such a discourse.

(2) If, instead, the Receiver of the humorous joke is not part of the Sender's same group—and, therefore, s/he does not share the Sender's cultural background, then s/he can choose to: *(a)* adopt the perspective of 'estrangement' and appraise the joke only from the perspective of semantic-structural incongruity, focusing exclusively on its linguistic structure. In doing so, the Receiver actually flouts (consciously or not) the Sender's socio-cultural schemata by adopting a kind of 'Gulliver's perspective' of socio-cultural estrangement; *(b)* interpret the joke according to his/her own cultural schemata, thus flouting, once again, the Sender's socio-cultural schemata; *(c)* decide to 'acculturate' (Schumann 1986) and 'familiarize' with the Sender's socio-cultural schemata, thus adopting his/her perspective; *(d)* attempt to establish a cross-cultural pragmatic communication with the Sender, thus starting an 'interactive discourse' with him/her by trying to find similarities and divergences between his/her own socio-cultural schemata (by which s/he interprets the joke as a Receiver) and the Sender's ones—or the ones shared by the group the Sender belongs to. Most likely, the Receiver will interpret the joke in his/her own way, and yet, despite the possible interpretative discrepancies with the Sender's intentions, a reciprocal communication of their own intentions and interpretations can actually produce a new and stimulating humorous discourse, characterized by multiple dimensions of incongruity. Indeed, the reciprocal perception of diversity can indeed refresh and renew both Sender's and Receiver's mental and socio-cultural schemata which are usually atrophied by everyday uses.

The interactive and cross-cultural dimension outlined in point *(d)* is here believed to make the interactive model of humorous discourse, here introduced, valid for its applications to follow in the next chapters, focused on the analysis of humorous discourse in American sitcoms and in their dubbing translations for the Italian television. The discrepancies between the two cultures make this type of comparative discourse analysis quite complex, but also very challenging for the dubbing translator, meant as the receiver of the original humorous discourse as well as the sender of the new translated one.

Chapter 2

American Sitcom Humour: Source Structure and Target Versions

2.1 The Structure of the American Sitcom Genre

2.1.1 *Prototype sitcom frames*

In this chapter, some specific formal and dialogic aspects of the American sitcoms will be analysed as they inform both factual and procedural competences that a dubbing translator needs to acquire in order to develop specific professional skills as an 'Acting Translator'.

As an audiovisual genre, the North-American situation comedy, or sitcom, is a kind of play performed season after season on a three-stage TV theatre, with the aim to create an effect of history and realism by appealing to its viewers' long-term memory and personal experiences. The sitcom developed from television stand-up comedy, but managed to reach higher standards of dramaturgy thus becoming 'mass-culture' and accessible to everybody. Indeed, one of the most striking influences of this genre is can found in spoken English usage set within specific, and often domestic, contexts, as sitcoms contributed to the evolution of grammar structures and pragmatic conventions from its dialogic scripts. This is due to the fact that such scripts are contextualized within everyday situations that prompt television audiences to suspend their disbelief and perceive the pretence of fiction as reality. This feeling of witnessing true-to-life situations is even more emphasized by the comic dimension of 'comedy' which—especially in its tradition of stand-up comedy—has always been deeply rooted in real facts and social contexts that comedians typically criticize through their use of humour. Indeed, Marc (1998: 14) observes, "the stand-up's refusal to respect sharp distinctions between the 'play' world and the 'real' world results in the violation of a primary convention of Western theatre. The audience is explicitly asked *not* to suspend its disbelief". However, differently from the stand-up comedy genre which is only in part scripted (as most of the stand-up comedians' skill lies in their quip improvisation prompting audiences' laughter and interacting remarks with the comic on stage), sitcoms are carefully-constructed dialogic scripts whose humorous jokes are initially tested on audience samples, to be subsequently refined and finally even emphasized by canned laughter in their televised post-production. To make the artifice of such scripts look 'true-to-life' usually the domestic archetypes of 'men versus women', 'neighbour versus neighbour', 'young versus old' are all employed for humorous purposes, as in the early-

1950s examples of American 'domesticoms', such as *I Love Lucy* (*ibidem*: 17). However, in the early US sitcom productions, this sense of familiarity and identification of the audience with the inconsistencies of everyday domestic situations, represented through the magnifying glass of the sitcom humour, never included any infringement of social norms and taboos—which instead was very frequent in stand-up comedians' monologues. Threatened family ties were always restored at the end of the episodes by applying the Arousal/Safety mechanism of humour. In fact, family and a comfortable home setting have always provided the physical and psychological context for the development of sitcom stories up until the late eighties, an example of which being the famous series *Family Ties*. Furthermore, class-consciousness, racism, and male chauvinism were always underplayed by covertly applying techniques of Humorous Disparagement, since they were perceived as 'expected' and, after all, 'accepted' (cf. Himmelstein 1985). This is especially true with male chauvinism within the family, which is already present in the very first American sitcom—namely, *Mary Kay and Johnny* (1947-50)—with Johnny, the husband, as a well-organized banker characterized by an economic and even moral superiority, and Mary Kay, his wife, as a messy eccentric who provided 'Arousal' cues ending with 'Safety' resolutions often completed by Johnny's sexist 'Humorous-Disparagement' remarks at her. As for racism, throughout the sixties the question of ethnicity was instead totally overlooked. For instance, as for the Jewish component of the American society, although some sitcoms cast Jewish actors as their leading performers, yet productions chose not to mark their characters as 'Jewish'. An example of this is represented by *The Dick Van Dyke Show*, broadcast in the sixties, where emphasis was never put on the Jewish background and speech-style of the protagonist, but rather on the WASP environment of the sitcom, symbolized by a very fashionable living room and by the introduction, for the first time, of more fixed characters outside the protagonist's family circle—e.g., friends, co-workers and, as a new entry, a single 'career woman' who, however, worked for a living being very conscious that the real aspiration for a woman was marriage.

The conventional domestic structure of the sitcom focused on a married couple and essentially marked by male sexism is reaffirmed in the sixties with the magicom *Bewitched*, where the married couple is composed by a 'normal' husband, typically a breadwinner, and a 'paranormal' wife, Samantha, who is a witch with exceptional magical power, but who is also determined to behave as a simple suburban wifette and to keep her magic at bay only to please her husband's conservative expectations about her role in their marriage. However, at the end of the sixties, this representation of family relationships was already doomed, defeated by new dimensions of the domestic and social reality reflected in the generic structure of some hit sitcoms of the seventies, such as *The Mary Tyler Moore Show*, *All in the Family* and *The Jeffersons*.

2.1.2 *Deviations from generic norms*

In the sitcoms of the seventies, although the WASP social and domestic norms were kept, socio-cultural and ethnic differences began to be acknowledged, principally because they were at last recognized as crucial parts of a successful marketing strategy in mass-communication aimed at prompting the viewer to identify himself/herself with sitcom characters and contexts (cf. Castleman and Podrazik 1982; Eisner and Krinsky 1984). This explains the 'updating' of the social and domestic order that, since then, has marked this television genre for years so as to appeal commercially to a wider audience of 'sitcom consumers'. *The Mary Tyler Moore Show*, for instance, was a sitcom aimed at a share of educated audience that were experiencing new dimensions of domestic and social life in the seventies (Bryars 1977). Whereas in the same period sitcom representations of traditional American families still continued to exist, such as the famous *The Jeffersons* and *All in the Family* (with family members openly discussing for the first time crucial issues, such as race relationships), *The Mary Tyler Moore Show* was instead centred on the protagonist, Mary, a young, elegant, optimistic and single career woman living in a big city, Minneapolis, who does not care about getting married and does not need the support of a traditional family. The support she finds comes from her friends (thus anticipating the trend set by *Friends* in the nineties), in particular from her friend Rhoda, a single and self-disparaging Jewish woman, and Lou Grant, her boss (a married man who later got divorced but who was never sentimentally or sexually involved with Mary). Mary's neighbours, conversely, are represented as a dull married couple. This new picture of reality actually reflected the developments of the North-American society in the seventies, with a very low birth rate, fewer marriages and increasing divorces, marked by the eclipse of the traditional nuclear family.

However, a picture of what was actually meant by 'living in a nuclear family' was provided by another successful sitcom of the seventies, *All in the Family*. Set in a working-class context, this sitcom allowed racist, sexist, homophobic, and xenophobic prejudices to emerge through mechanisms of Humorous Disparagement that permeated the dialogues in which the protagonist of the series, the family head Archie Bunker, was involved. Archie, a white Protestant warehouse loading-dock worker, despises black people by defining them 'coloreds' and is intolerant towards Jews, calling them 'hebes'. On the other hand, Jews in this sitcom behave according to the expected Jewish stereotype, making audience laugh by uttering expressions like 'oy, oy, oy' or 'bar mitzvah'. In this way, then, the protagonist of this sitcom gave voice to the American prejudices of the time and audiences were expected laugh at the sense of 'Safety' triggered by the awareness that those politically unacceptable and controversial utterances were only aimed at achieving a comic—and, thus, harmless—effect. This working-class sitcom, however, lacks the elegance and sophistication of the previous middle-class series, and this is reflected in the furniture of Archie's home, "old, worn, and without style" (Newcomb 1974: 219), and in the structure of his house—with no separation between the dining and the living rooms and with only one bathroom. What is more, Archie shares his small house with his Polish son-in-law Mike, a Catholic-liberal immigrant that Archie himself maintains at university where he is preparing for an academic career. Mike and his wife—and Archie's daughter—Gloria, represent the hippie stereotypes of the seventies with their liberal ideologies that crash against Archie's 'conservative' sarcasm informing his 'disparaging humour'. Edith, Archie's wife, triggers audience's humorous response precisely because she does not recognize her husband's racist and sexist sarcasm. In fact, although Edith is portrayed as a slow-witted middle-aged woman, she is indeed morally superior to Archie as she manages to establish spontaneous sympathetic relations with everybody, including those categories of people that her husband despises (such as her black neighbours, the Jeffersons), and thus she represents the key to family unity and reconciliation. A spin-off of *All in the Family* was precisely represented by the hit sitcom *The Jeffersons*, bridging two decades by running from 1975 to 1986. The protagonist of this sitcom is an African-American family, with the father as the owner of a chain of dry-cleaning shops striving to adapt himself to middle-class manners by denying his socio-cultural background—a contrast that triggers audience's humorous response.

Despite the fact that both *All in the Family* and *The Jeffersons* bring to light many reprehensible prejudices of the American mind of that period, the two sitcoms after all reaffirm the centrality of family and the importance of its unity and values, a concept which in the seventies was restated in the structure of other hit American sitcoms (like *Happy Days* and *Mork and Mindy* which, however, were set in other historical periods—in the socially-idyllic fifties and in a science-fictional future, respectively), but only in part was reiterated in the eighties, as in the sitcom *Family Ties*, and also in *Diff'rent Strokes*, where a WASP millionaire adopts two Afro-American orphans. In fact, in the new decade, new affective alternatives to the conventional nuclear family began to emerge and to be portrayed in sitcoms, being rather in the tradition of the earlier series *The Mary Tyler Moore Show* where the group of friends provided the affective support to the protagonist.

2.1.3 *The merging of new and old sitcom frames*

A case in point in the eighties is represented by *Three's Company*, yet already *Happy Days* depicts the teenager protagonist, Richie Cunningham, who does not elect his father as his reference person, as expected—although his family offers him all the love and wisdom necessary for his proper raising—but an older friend outside the middle-class world he and his two close friends belong to—i.e., the egocentric biker the Fonz, famous for his tall-tales about himself. Furthermore, Richie, the son, and not his father, sets the perspective in the sitcom. Hence, in taking the Fonz's pathetic tall tales at face value, Richie represents the naïve stance from which humour—of a possible/impossible type (cf. Raskin 1985)—develops.

In *Three's Company*, the idea of a viable alternative to traditional family life is overtly put forward as the situation is wholly centred on a young man, Jack, sharing an apartment, simply as a roommate, with two young women, Janet and Chrissy. This idea was still perceived as naughty at the end of the seventies and in the early eighties—as evident from the fact that the entire sitcom contains recurrent gags, quips and sexual double-meanings all referred to such unusual situation. Even physically, the protagonist Jack Tripper (played by John Ritter) performs a series of slapstick numbers emphasizing all the awkwardness and temptation involved in such a life-style. The excuse found by the three friends that Jack is gay was meant to refrain their homophobic landlords (Mr. Roper first, and then Mr. Furley) from giving them notice to quit for immoral behaviour, thus introducing the homosexual issue in a jovial way. Jack tackles such an issue by embodying for fun the physical stereotype of the gay man in a manner which today would be considered as politically incorrect, if not offensive, but that at that time represented a covert type of liberating 'Humorous Disparagement' towards homosexuals, simultaneously providing a sense of Safety at knowing that Jack is just 'pretending' to be gay.

The non-traditional family unit composed of friends, introduced by *Three's Company*, was soon juxtaposed to other sitcoms, such as *Family Ties* and *The Cosby Show*, emblematically focused, once again, on the centrality of the traditional family in people's life despite divergences among its members emerging from different cultural, ideological, or even ethnic stances. Marc (1998: 182) defines in particular *Family Ties* as "the resurrection of the nuclear family sitcom"—in this specific case, an upper-middle-class family composed by two ex-hippie liberal parents (who look like Archie Bunker's daughter Gloria and her husband Mike after a decade), and their grown-up children, among whom one, the yuppie Alex (played by Michael J. Fox), fully embodies the Reaganian Republican ideology (looking like Archie in a sort of generational upside-down re-edition of *All in the Family*).

However, this improbable representation of harmonious nuclear family could not last simply because it was actually rare even in the eighties. Hence, to represent society in a more truthful way, though retaining the generic coherence of the conventional domesticom structure, the series *Married... With Children* was launched in 1987. Actually, this series turned out to be subversive as a deconstruction and a parody of the traditional sitcom structure focused on family as source of affection and of ethical and social education for children. In fact, no one of the components of the family portrayed in *Married ... With Children* can be defined as morally correct: from the selfish and pointless father, Al Bundy, to the materialistic mother, Peg, who cannot stand her husband and housework, up to their children: the spoiled, dull teenage son Bud, and the slut daughter Kelly. Humour, in this case, emerges from expected/unexpected mechanisms of Humorous Disparagement, as audience would never expect that a child or a wife insult or ridicule the father/husband, or that the deplorable behaviour of children is not only approved of, but even encouraged by their parents (who are instead expected to educate them according to shared social and moral values).

The collapse of the family myth reflected in the sitcom structure is thus already completed at the beginning of the nineties, when the need for devising new forms of sitcom entertainment was strongly felt so as to comply with new forms of social organization. It is at this point, therefore, that novel sitcom structures began to emerge in the US as a reflection of a new urban reality, and this renewal lasted until the 9/11 global tragedy of the terrorists' attack and destruction of the 'Twin Towers' in New York City at the turn of the 21st century, when traditional values started to re-emerge as people began to feel again the need and the reassurance of traditional life-styles and long-term relationships. This justifies the choice of turn-of-the-century North-American sitcoms for the analysis carried out in Part Two of this book, since they revived the 'group-of-friends' sitcom, successful in the seventies, such as *The Mary Tyler Moore Show* and *Three's Company*, and the ethically-reprehensible family sitcom, like *All in the Family*, thus contributing to the development of new hybrid forms of humour that reflect a different perception of what is to be considered as funny and entertaining and what cannot be regarded as such, mainly for cross-cultural political or ethical reasons.

However, before analyzing the structure of Humour in the selected sitcoms, it seems useful to introduce some of the main language patterns of humorous discourse to be identified in such sitcoms.

2.2 Language Patterns of Humour in American Sitcoms

2.2.1 *Culture-specific sitcom conventions*

The traditional socio-cultural structure of the US sitcom outlined so far (and, consequently, also the deviations from such a structure) are reflected in a series of humorous conversation patterns that have become conventionalised. Indeed, quips, puns and wordplay in sitcoms are carefully constructed in order to prompt a humorous effect on the audience, meant as a sample of television public sharing the same socio-cultural, national and language background, on the assumption that an audience's response to a humorous stimuli is conditioned by culture-specific and language-specific norms. Such specificity would thus make the reception of humour by other cultural and linguistic groups difficult—if not, very often, impossible. Chiaro (1992: 6-7) remarks:

> "In Italy, for example, where most television situation comedies are imported from either Britain or the United States, a series is only successful if the situation depicted is not too culture specific. For example, in the early 1980s the series *George and Mildred* and *Different Strokes* became extremely successful in Italy. Both programmes are basically farcical in structure with dramatic irony used as an indispensable feature in each episode. The main character is usually responsible for a misdeed which is worsened when he tries to remedy it. [...] On the other hand, the problems of a priest trying to outdo his Anglican counterpart in a parish somewhere in England (*Bless me, Father*) are far too culture-specific to hope to amuse Roman Catholic Italy. In fact, the latter series was quickly relegated to off-peak viewing time on one of the country's minor commercial channel. Situation comedy frequently plays on stereotypes. John Cleese's bowler-hatted business man (*Monty Python*) and hotelier (*Fawlty Towers*), members of the French resistance (*'Allo, 'Allo*) and typical civil servants (*Yes, Prime Minister*) are all figures belonging to the British culture which are instantly recognized in their inflated parodied forms by home audiences. Outside the British Isles, the stereotypes do not necessarily correspond as being comic in intent."

Indeed, even within the same speech community of native speakers of English—such as the broader one to which British and US sitcom viewers belong to—socio-cultural divergences may determine dissimilar perceptions of the comic structure of dialogues and, thus, prompt diverse responses to humour. That is why, paradoxically, British sitcoms in the US have often been 'remade' so as to comply with different native contexts of humorous language use. This is the case, for instance, of the British sitcom of the seventies *Man About the House*, whose US remake in the eighties—i.e., *Three's Company*—on the one hand faithfully kept to the original situation (namely, two young women who decide to allow a student chef, for whom they have no romantic interest whatsoever, to move permanently in the flat they share, telling their landlord that he is gay to get the permission for the young man to live with them). Even the two spin-offs of this British sitcom—namely, *Robin's Nest* and *George and Mildred* (i.e., their landlord and his wife)—were eventually remade in the US as spin-offs of *Three's Company*—namely, *Three's a Crowd* and *The Ropers*. In all these cases, the whole humorous construction of the US parallel series was reorganized upon the culture-specific norms of what was deemed as comic in the American society of the eighties and, more specifically, with reference to the Californian setting where the three young characters of the sitcom acted.

Having said so, it is however possible to identify a number of linguistic conventions which may be considered as 'shared' on a cross-cultural basis, to the point that they have been regarded as 'universal' and thus suitable to define the discourse of Humour as a specific genre, and the comic sitcom as one of its audiovisual sub-genres. As specified in Chapter 1, Humorous Disparagement is a common strategy aimed at producing a comic effect on audiences. This strategy comes under the 'Superiority' theories of humorous discourse (Zillmann 1983) according to which jokes and plays of wit are grounded upon the pleasure people covertly take in the other fellows' misfortunes—which is obviously unavowed under normal circumstances. Hence the joke becomes a safe discourse domain where it is possible to laugh at physical or mental handicaps, socially-disadvantaged categories of people, discredited professions, citizens of economically-depressed nations and, likewise, also at women, homosexuals, non-white ethnic groups (all categories of people that, in early US sitcoms, were often disparagingly referred to as 'dull'). Bier (1988), however, advances the hypothesis that derogatory humour may be an emotional strategy which, at least in the cases under his consideration, is activated by the American dominant WASP groups to exorcize the menace that communities of immigrants—such as Polish, Jews, Afro-American, or Latinos—can represent to their social, economic and even sexual supremacy. By belittling them, the dominant groups attempt to reassert their alleged superiority. On the other hand, socially or economically disadvantaged groups may activate Arousal/Safety strategies of humour (cf. Morreall 1983), belonging to the 'Relief' theories of humorous discourse which trigger laughter as a release of the tensions caused by social restrictions. Both Disparagement and Arousal/Safety strategies of humour cannot be rendered linguistically without the contribution of cognitive-semantic constructions principally based on Incongruity (cf. Bergson 1900; Schultz 1974a, 1974b, 1976). Chapter 1 provided some illustrations of the humorous mechanism of Incongruity which presupposes the Receiver's identification of two different schema dimensions of meaning in the same story, so that what is at first interpreted as belonging to a specific schema and a script by activating a cognitive 'commonsense default', is suddenly perceived from a different schematic perspective which contextualizes it within a new script. Such unexpected contextual associations—or 'bisociation' in Koestler's (1974) definition—triggered by the language of the joke, prompts the Receiver's amusement and laughter. Typically, amusement is triggered by the final punch line of the joke which produces ambiguity, due to the two overlapping schemata and their relative scripts normally considered as mismatched. Laughter, therefore, is prompted by the solution of ambiguity, consisting in the Receiver's recognition that the script s/he expected before the punch suddenly does not correspond to the script disclosed after the punch (cf. Raskin 1985).

In the longer text of a sitcom episode, however, humour is constructed within the conversation structure. Sacks (1974) focuses on conversational jokes which have the same structure as the narrative ones, with an introduction, the storytelling, and the final pun triggering the Receiver's amused reaction, only that jokes are distributed across the dialogic turns and often involve idiomatic and formulaic expressions conveying double meaning, usually at the end of an exchange (cf. Sherzer 1978). In Norrick's (1993: 5) view, natural-occurring conversational humour "helps to relieve the tension and foster friendly interaction" (cf. Tannen 1984), but also to defy and offend the interlocutor, thus asserting the speaker's superiority (*ibidem*: 63). Such interpersonal dynamics can be detected also in television comedy. Palmer (1994: 142) stresses the importance of "narrative flow and the joke theme" that give coherence to "the flow of gags" in a sitcom, thus ensuring the audience's understanding of the comic effect. Walte (2007), however, claims that television comedy does not attempt to reproduce reality and natural-occurring conversation, but only to represent an ideal community, although it tries to replicate the use of everyday language (cf. Tagliamonte and Roberts 2005). In this sense, Attardo's (1994: 319) notion of conversational humour that disrupts the expected sociocultural routines and appropriateness norms (encoded in the expected script) to create the humorous effect (by triggering a new, opposite script in the Receiver's mind) may well be applied to the fictional structure of sitcom conversation. Indeed, the parameters advanced by the General Theory of Verbal Humour (Attardo and Raskin 1991; Ruch *et al.* 1993; Attardo 1994), introduced in Chapter 1 (*1.2.4*), grounded on the Incongruity/Resolution pattern triggered by two 'mismatched scripts', can be likewise applied to the description of sitcom conversation, insofar as: *(a)* the 'Script Opposition' occurs in conversation by means of one or more wordplays, often split into two characters' respective turns, making the joke be congruent with two different situational scripts which are opposed to each other; *(b)* the 'Logical Mechanism' is thus determined by the audience's perception of an apparent truth and consistency of the story told in the joke followed by their sudden recognition that it is only a pseudo-logic due the simultaneous juxtaposition of the two possible scripts implied in the joke which determine ambiguity and emphasize the pun; *(c)* the 'Situation' should be easily recognizable as it is determined by the contextual details given in a joke which the Receiver initially attributes to a particular script but then, suddenly, s/he has to re-contextualize within a different script as soon as the punch line is uttered; *(d)* the 'Target' is an optional parameter in sitcom conversation and it may regard the person or event the joke is referred to, usually with derogatory aims; *(e)* the 'Narrative Strategy', shaping the double logic structure of the joke, as well as the precise collocation and timing of the punch line, is part of the fictional structure of the sitcom conversation, which is not natural, but artificially constructed; *(f)* the 'Language' is what shapes the 'surface structure' of the sitcom jokes classifying them into a specific genre.

Furthermore, Short (1989) and Clark and Schaefer (1992) identify a double structure of fictional conversation in which audiences play the role of receivers as 'overhearers' of the conversation between the characters alternatively playing the roles of addressers and addressees. This entails that the effect of humorous jokes in sitcoms can be different—often diametrically opposite—on the characters that interpret them within the dialogic context of the fictional situation, and on the audiences that 'overhear' them from the outside. Hence, whereas sitcom characters may react negatively to a joke, the audience may find it hilarious. The way characters react to other characters' jokes in sitcom conversation is crucial for the construction of their fictional personality, which is often rendered prototypical to allow predictable attitude, behaviours and consequent humorous reactions to interpersonal interactions (cf. Culpeper 2001). The audience's understanding of the comic situation and its characters, therefore, is crucial in their process of humour interpretation in a sitcom since, as Snell (2006) points out, audiences have to activate their relevant socio-cultural and experiential schemata to make sense of the implied script incongruity and resolve it, even when the characters within the situational context seem not to be able to understand it and to come to a solution. In this sense, Snell (*ibidem*) advocates the application of the General Theory of Verbal Humour to the analysis of television comedy. Hence, applied to the structure of humour in American sitcoms, the 'knowledge resources' identified by Attardo (1994) are crucial for the audience to understand the socio-cultural, logical, and pragmalinguistic background informing the scripts which construct the joke. The application of the 'Language' parameter, for instance, determines the sitcom 'template' characterizing the 'surface structure' of the situational contexts typical of this genre (thus allowing audiences to classify it as domesticoms, magicoms, etc.). The 'Narrative Strategy' parameter, instead, marks the humorous style of a sitcom and defines the socio-cultural and psychological personality of its characters who 'inhabit' the scripts and 'embody' the humorous language as addressers and addressees in conversation. The 'Target' parameter represents the temporary or permanent object of scorn in a sitcom exchange. This is usually a stereotypical character representing a category of people who, in specific contexts, are regarded as inferior, dull, or endowed with negative connotations that are perceived as a threat by those characters that, in the sitcom, establish the perspective meant to be shared (overtly or covertly) with the implied audience of receivers. Seen under this light, the parameter of 'Logical Mechanism' is adjusted to the main character's perspective to the point that it can justify as 'humorous' even the racist, homophobic, or sexist puns, which are conveyed by the unexpected script juxtaposed to the expected, logical, and socially-sanctioned one. The 'Situation' parameter, therefore, is crucial to the setting of all the other parameters in a sitcom insofar as it determines not only its 'Narrative Strategy', but also the 'Language' used by the characters. 'Language', in its turn, has to adapt itself to the 'Logical Mechanism' activated by characters in producing jokes and by audiences in interpreting them—a 'mechanism' that has to comply with the 'Script Opposition' parameter.

2.2.2 *Shared knowledge and its disruption*

Crucial to this General Theory of Verbal Humour, therefore, is the concept of knowledge shared between the Sender of the joke and its (implied) Receiver. Without such 'shared knowledge', in fact, Humour would not be perceived as such by its receivers. The implication is that the 'universal' generic conventions illustrated so far cannot in practice work unless they are applied to a culture-specific domain of humorous discourse within which shared socio-cultural information is crucial to the interpretation of a joke as such. Obviously, shared socio-cultural information is not just referred to the synchronic dimension of geographical, cultural and linguistic differences, but also to their diachronic dimension, insofar as if a joke is produced within the same homogeneous socio-cultural and pragmalinguistic community, but in a past historical period, then it may not be perceived as 'humorous' in the present. This is especially evident when contemporary audiences watch sitcoms produced in earlier decades, where references to former ways of life, values, beliefs, historical people and events, and—crucially—jargon, do not contribute any longer to the achievement of the same humorous effect they produced in the past. Also wordplay is culture-specific and requires a socio-cultural and pragmalinguistic knowledge shared by both Sender and Receivers to be understood as a humorous pun conveying two unrelated meanings. This lack of relation in meanings should instead occur at any of the linguistic levels of morphology, phonology, lexis, syntax and pragmatics, and the expected outcome is ambiguity, at the basis of the joke. Hence, when lexical and phonological levels are involved, ambiguity can be conveyed, for instance, by homophony (where the same sound of two words with different meanings represents the comic punch), homonymy (where the punch is instead represented by two words with the same form but different sounds), or by the polysemous coexistence of various meanings in a single word, as in Raskin's (1985: 26) example: "The first thing which strikes a stranger in New York is a big car"—with the word "strikes" evoking the stranger's 'astonishment' as well as his being "run down" by a big car. Hockett (1977) classifies wordplay into two categories: 'prosaic' and 'poetic'. Prosaic wordplays involve a shared socio-cultural knowledge informing the two juxtaposed schemata and related scripts, whereas poetic wordplays entail a shared knowledge of the language which helps understand ambiguity based on language patterns. One of the most common 'poetic wordplays' that in a sitcom dialogue function as a humorous punch is the 'slip of the tongue', or 'speech error', consisting in substituting, deleting, or adding sounds, words, or phrases, thus modifying the intended meaning and usually provoking a hilarious effect on receivers. Indeed, the comic effect produced by slips of the tongue may be considered as a universal pattern of humour since it has been observed in almost all languages and cultures, and across geographical spaces and historical times (cf. Sherzer 1978). Differently from the slips of the tongue unconsciously occurring in everyday conversation, and thoroughly described by Freud (1963), those ones occurring in sitcom dialogues are instead deliberately constructed for humorous effects. It can happen, for instance, that a character finding himself in an embarrassing situation, through an apparently accidental slip of the tongue may reveal to the audience, and/or to the other interacting characters, his actual hidden, inappropriate, and often naughty thoughts. In such cases, a slip of the tongue can take the form of 'malapropism' (i.e., the substitution of words similar in sound but different in meaning), or of 'spoonerism' (i.e., the swap of the corresponding sounds of two words occurring in the same utterance), or of 'methatesis' (i.e., the substitution of a single sound or a syllable in a word) (cf. Hockett 1967). All these cases involve a new syntagmatic form of the utterance organized upon unintended paradigmatic alternatives of sounds, words, or phrases which totally modify its sense to achieve a humorous effect. At the morphological level, for instance, wordplay in sitcoms often entails the creation of humorous neologisms by adding incorrect affixation to words by parallelism to similar ones. At the level of syntax, humorous effects are often obtained by the ambiguous use of pronouns referring to two different words in the same sentence, although this structure is less frequent in sitcom dialogues as they are based on conversation speed and require from audiences a quick grasp of the punch which provokes their prompt laughter, with no time for reflection on syntactic subtleties. The pragmatic level, instead, is crucial in the structure of sitcom conversation based on two juxtaposed scripts, so that the form of an utterance can actually fulfil the different functions of the explicit script and the implicit one. The possibility of a double interpretation of a sitcom character's utterance may prompt another interacting character to activate in his/her mind precisely the interpretative option that is inappropriate to the context in which the utterance occurs, thus misunderstanding its intended speech act and, consequently, triggering a comic effect on the audience of receivers as soon as they grasp his/her misinterpretation. In this comic mechanism, therefore, punch plays a central role in the construction of the humorous effect in a sitcom. A punch, indeed, prompts sitcom audiences' laughter as, in Chiaro's (1992: 48) terms, it is "the point at which the recipient either hears or sees something which is in some way incongruous with the linguistic or semantic environment in which it occurs but which at first sight had not been apparent". A punch, thus, introduces in the humorous discourse a Problem/Solution pattern (*ibidem*: 50), which is made complex by the fact that some of Grice's (1975) cooperative maxims are overlooked, especially those ones requesting speakers to 'be clear, avoid ambiguity, and avoid obscurity'. The violation of the pragmatic principles of successful communication prompts the receivers of a pun, who expect a specific script (usually the conventional one that their minds activate by default), to be suddenly, amusingly surprised as they realize that the intended script is another one.

2.2.3 *Equivalence in translating humorous patterns*

Obviously, solving ambiguity and obscurity implied in a joke becomes more difficult when translation is needed to render the humorous discourse into another language and culture—and it becomes almost impossible when the target audience is unable to understand the cultural references implied in the source text of the joke. Linguistically, the lack of correspondence between the source and the target semantic systems makes the translation of puns and wordplay particularly complicated (cf. Delabastita 1994). Furthermore, differences in the discourse organization of source and target languages may not even guarantee pragmatic equivalence in joke translation, particularly in terms of humorous effect on the target receivers who may totally misunderstand quips and punch lines. Some joke patterns can indeed be rendered into other languages and cultures by simply substituting few surface and culturally-marked elements —as in the case with the 'underdog jokes' where the 'losers' are, respectively, Poles in the United States (as Archie Bunker's son-in-law Mike in *All in a Family*); Irish in England; Belgian in France; but also workers' categories, such as the *carabinieri*, a police-force category in Italy. Joke patterns based on inter-racial and inter-gender relationships are instead not so automatically translatable. It is true that up to a certain extent they may be considered as universals of Humorous-Disparagement discourse, yet they work differently across cultures, and even across historical periods. For instance, the 'universal' sexual pattern of man's prowess as opposed to woman's degradation does not meet the same widespread and unreserved appreciation any longer as they are stigmatized as 'antisocial', if not 'improper'. There are cases in which religious heritage plays a role in sanctioning a joke as acceptable, or rather as intolerable and offensive. The case of the anti-Muslim humorous cartoons produced in Europe and fiercely disallowed by the Muslim communities is a case in point. The sexual degradation of the Mother figure in Italy represents another crucial instance, as in the Italian culture, 'Mother' (but also, to a lesser extent, the other female components of a family) is still associated to the Holy Mother-Virgin, hence every joke based on this topic—especially with reference to the receiver's own mother—has to adopt an Arousal/Safety strategy to work at a humorous level in order to defuse the affront. The same may be said of jokes based on the humorous disparagement of Jews, which in Europe are blameworthy since as memory of the Holocaust is still painfully vivid, whereas in the United States they are acceptable when referred to the stereotypical peculiarities of the Jewish-American community, though with no reference whatsoever to the past tragedy. These cultural discrepancies are evident, for instance, in the Italian dubbing translation of the American sitcom *The Nanny* (to be analysed in Chapter 4 of this book) where every reference to the Jewish origin of the protagonist, as well as to the sexual exuberance of her mother, are totally obliterated by a radical rewriting of its scripts into the target language to make them acceptable to the Italian audience. Sometimes, however, the practice of rewriting sitcom scripts into the target language is justified by the fact that this television genre is characterized by the presence of canned laughter from a virtual audience (but also genuine laughter from a real theatre audience present on the sitcom set) signalling the occurrence of a pun. Such a pun, in fact, may be either untranslatable, since it is based on lexical and phonological ambiguity in the source language, or inaccessible to the target television audience if the pun is translated literally, since its socio-cultural and pragmalinguistic references can be understood and appreciated as 'humorous' only by the speech community producing that sitcom. The rewriting practice which produces a dubbing translation of a script that is almost completely different from the original one is precisely a strategy aimed at making the sitcom structure accessible to the target audience who may otherwise be unable to grasp the sense of puns underscored by canned laughter. This rewriting strategy in translation is also supported by Nida (1964) who is in favour of restructuring a source text to render it into a pragmatically equivalent one in the target language and culture. In this way, he asserts, 'formal equivalence' becomes less relevant than 'dynamic equivalence', meant as the pragmatic correspondence of purpose and effect of a discourse in both its original and translated versions. A more recent translation theory in support of Nida's notion of dynamic equivalence is the Skopos Theory (Vermeer 1994), where 'skopos' is meant as the 'intended aim' of a translation, not its literal rendering of a text into another language. Applied to the humorous discourse of comedy, such 'intended aim' often entails acknowledging the impossibility of 'formally' preserving in the target script the original quips and puns, and even the original meaning, of the source script. The only solution, therefore, is the substitution of language-based or culture-based puns with totally different—yet 'dynamically' equivalent—ones in the dubbing translation. Equivalence, however, has to account for the source socio-cultural context of the sitcom in which the humorous pun occurs, and also this context may be unfamiliar, and even inaccessible, to the target audience's experience. This explains Basnett-McGuire's (1980) suggestion that equivalence in translation is not just to be achieved linguistically, but also contextually, that is, by reformulating the whole situational context in which the pun occurs so as to produce a parallel humorous situation in the target language and culture which does not necessarily correspond to the original one in a literal way, but only in a pragmatic way. Contrary to this view, it is here argued that, relevantly, in a sitcom, the visual context cannot be eliminated (as it happens instead with the US remade versions of foreign movies or television series) because, however hard a translator works to make the script linguistically and socio-culturally accessible and familiar to the target receivers, the visual setting will always be on the screen with all its physical, behavioural and situational references, reminding viewers that the sitcom belongs to a context that is different from their own. Indeed, the visual dimension of the sitcom represents the 'fixed frame' which constrains all the possible realizations of dynamic equivalence in dubbing translation, thus excluding those ones which are too inconsistent. The other crucial constraint is lip-synchronization, which discloses a whole range of difficulties related to the dubbing translation of the sitcom genre.

2.3 Issues in the Dubbing Translation of American Sitcoms

2.3.1 *Parameters of sitcom dubbing translation*

The way in which the dubbing translation of sitcoms has to be assessed differs from the ways in which other types of translations are conventionally judged. In fact, sitcom translations are evaluated in relation to whether they achieve or not their primary aim, that is, to make the dubbed sitcom successful with the target audience. In this sense the issue of the source and target contexts that respectively produce the source and the translated versions of the sitcom is of the utmost importance for the audience's reception of this television genre. Indeed, this is a genre that, to be successful, has to be recognized as an accessible and acceptable communicative act. The importance of the sitcom context, therefore, contributes to the classification of the translated version of this television genre as, in Nida's (1969) terms, an 'intersemiotic' one, which means that this is not simply an 'interlinguistic' translation, like most translated text types that do not rely on the visual dimension of the situational context. In fact, the crucial dimensions that a dubbing translator of sitcoms needs to account for are:

(1) the intersemiotic context of the source text (i.e., the sitcom original script), with its particular conditions of production and reception that are conditioned by pragmalinguistic, socio-cultural, temporal and situational dimensions of discourse which, in their turn, determine the register parameters of this audiovisual genre – namely, its tenor, field and mode (Halliday 1978);

(2) the intersemiotic context of the target text (i.e., the sitcom trans-

lated script) in all its production and reception dimensions of discourse mentioned above in relation to the source text;

(3) the professional context in which the dubbing translator operates, which includes not only his/her specialized skills and experience, but also the other participants in this communicative process, such as the sitcom producer who, in agreement with the national television distributor, sets both the marketing and the socio-political parameters for the dubbed sitcom version—parameters that constrain the sitcom translation into making it consistent with popularity expectations, as well as possible censorship requirements;

(4) lip-synchronization, which does affect the whole dubbing-translation process because of the presence of other participants—namely, the dubbing actors and their director who will be using and adjusting the translation to fit lip-movement within the time-limits set by turn-taking in sitcom dialogues.

Working within such constraints may often mean for the dubbing translator having to give up every attempt at achieving a sense of spontaneity in conversation, as s/he tries to render in equivalent ways language-based or culture-specific quips and puns into the target language (cf. Zabalbeascoa 1996) with no possibility of relying on longer sentence-structures or explicative paraphrases to make them accessible to the target audience.

Zabalbeascoa's (1994) classification expands the above outlined dimensions by stating that a dubbing translator of television comedy series, during his/her translation process, should account not only for the 'lip movement' parameter, but also for other crucial parameters such as: *(a)* the original 'utterance timing' to be reproduced in the target version; *(b)* the 'conversation pauses' to be kept or 'compensated for' (e.g., with the addition of off-screen characters' voices to disambiguate some otherwise obscure cues); *(c)* the 'conversation exchange' (meant as a series of utterances, usually included in a take) to be respected in its pragmatic turn-taking outcome so as to render it into an equivalent exchange in the target version; *(d)* a 'chapter' of the comedy series; *(e)* the 'whole series'. In applying these parameters to the dubbing translation of sitcom scripts, the translator should always keep in mind the divergent schemata and background knowledge of both source and target audiences, which often entail conflicting social, cultural and moral values, as well as different generic conventions which define what is 'humorous' in different cultures. This casts a new light on the notion of pragmatic—or 'dynamic' (Nida 1969)—equivalence to be achieved in translation by adapting socio-culturally marked references present in the source text to parallel socio-cultural situations familiar to the receivers of the target text, so as to give preference to the dynamic translation of a 'humorous effect' that may vary across cultures, rather than to the literal translation of the joke which may mean absolutely nothing to a foreign audience of receivers. A dynamic equivalence in dubbing translation can be achieved even by resorting to 'compensation', obtained by adding to the dubbing translation either 'explicative utterances', spoken by the voices of off-screen characters taking part in the exchange to compensate for meaning obscurity, or 'voice intonations' that do not correspond to the original ones. Such strategies are often adopted in dubbing to make up for the loss of an untranslatable joke, or of a quick pun that prompts the original audience's laughter. Sitcom original or canned laughter, in fact, is normally retained in the target-version soundtrack, so that, if a joke is not appropriately rendered into the target language, then laughter will not be understood by the target audience.

2.3.2 *Limits of dubbing translation in sitcom dialogues: the emergence of 'dubbese' as a 'lingua franca' variation*

Intonation, as well as accentual contrasts and pitch movements, however, are often missing in dubbed versions of television comedy. This may be due to the fact that the conventional dubbing technique cuts up the recording of the actors who dub into takes, which are thus dubbed individually to the detriment of the overall effect of spontaneous conversational intonation. Also the widespread use of the standard variety of the target language can contribute to the effect of a non-natural conversation which is normally absent in the original script where, instead, diatopic and diastratic varieties of the source language are often used to create a sense of naturalness of the situation. Herbst (1997) points out that dubbed texts usually contain a large amount of stylistic features typical of written registers or of formal spoken styles in the target language—such as, for instance, the use of subjunctive, subordinate clauses, participle constructions, pre-modification and nominalization. Also cohesion is often disregarded, especially when pro-forms and ellipsis are unfittingly employed to compensate for the timing of the original utterances and lip-synchronization. Another reason for the lack of naturalness in dubbed sitcoms is the extensive use of Anglicism (*ibidem*), meant as 'loan translations'—namely, the preference for words etymologically related to similar English words, but not appropriately used in the target language. Loan translations are not just restricted to lexicon, in fact they can affect also the syntactic level of sentence structure (where transfer from the typical English pre-modification, for instance, is very frequent), and even the pragmatic level of speech acts inappropriately used in the target language because they are derived from the source language. Obviously, such operations of 'transfer' (Selinker and Lakshmanan 1992) have the effect of unnaturalness on the target audience. In Herbst's (1997) view, the occurrence of loan translations is principally due to the fact that there are two main phases in the dubbing translation process—one aimed at the production of a rough translation of the script (often carried out by unprofessional and poorly paid translators, even without the support of the relevant audiovisual version), and the other regarding the actual dubbing which adapts the previous rough translation to the technical constraints of the visual version of the sitcom. Very frequently such adaptation is not carried out by professional dialogue adaptors, either, but by the dubbing directors themselves who modify the rough translation to fit better lip-synchronization (cf. Whitman-Linsen 1992). Furthermore, the adaptation of the rough translation is not made by considering the script and its context as a whole, but it is performed take-for-take, which diverts the attention from pragmatic meanings to focus principally on the mere denotative sense of words and sentences. This entails that pragmatic choices concerning target language naturalness or diatopic, diastratic, and even diachronic equivalence in translation are very rarely regarded as central to the process of film dubbing in general and, even more frequently, of sitcom dubbing in particular. Also Luyken *et al.* (1991) outline the awkward process of dubbing translation, with the translator producing a 'raw translation' which is subsequently adapted by the dubbing team to each film-chunk, called 'nucleus sync', identified according to actors' lip movements, intonation and gestures, as well as paratextual elements. Then, each 'nucleus sync' is transferred on a master copy reproducing a time-code allowing lip synchronization (or 'lip sync'). The choice of the teams of dubbing actors, however, is conditioned by the production budget, so the casting director has to choose between three categories of actors (A, B, and C), according to their experience and expertise, but also to the budget availability s/he can rely on. Once in the dubbing studio, actors may perform their dialogic turns as a group, or individually—in this latter case, each individual recording is then mixed with the others through a computerized multi-track system. Another dubbing technique consists in projecting the film onto a screen with the translated text reproduced at the bottom of the images, together with other symbols as 'directions', so that the actors can watch the film, and read and perform the translated lines simultaneously. The final mix and edit is carried out by the dubbing director, the editor and the dubbing mixer by using analogical and, today, also digital equipments (cf. Dries 1995). Gambier (2003: 173) remarks the fact that, differently from audiences of other nationalities, the Italian audiences focus more on the dubbing actors' performance rather than on lip-synchronization. This may be explained with the prevalence of monosyllabic words in English which does not correspond to the pervasiveness of polysyllabic words in Romance languages, like Italian. This lack of morpho-syntactic correspondence affects lip-synchronization in film dubbing (Chaume Varela 1998), but also favours the widespread habit of transferring calques of words, or whole clausal structures, from English to the target language (cf. Zabalbeascoa 1996a), thus contributing to the creation of an artificial variety of Italian that some scholars have defined as 'doppiaggese' (cf. Raffaelli 1994), or 'dubbese' (Pavesi and Perego 2006). Furthermore, dubbing actors often resort to typically Italian 'acting codes' marked by mannerisms, but also by consolidated gender stances which are reflected in pitch and tone of voices that often do not match with the original characters' personality (cf. Ulrych 1994). This preference for specific and recognizable acting methods may explain the choice of the same few dubbing actors 'lending' their voice to a large number of actors (cf. Dries 1995: 12), which means that the same actor ends up dubbing many foreign actors thus impeding any possibility for the audience to identify an actor by associating him/her with a specific voice—even when it is a dubbed one (cf. Camuzio 1993). Some dubbing practitioners, such as La Polla (1994), advocate the use of a 'creative dubbing' to characterize the personality of the dubbed actors by means of specific accents that would help Italian audiences identify particular foreign players. He also recommends the substitution of the culturally-marked source references with parallel ones in the target culture to enhance familiarity and identification in the audience and, as a consequence, the marketing success of a film or a TV comedy (with the resulting appreciation of its humour) (*ibidem*: 56-59). Indeed, from the perspective of the Italian dubbing practitioners, such a disregard for the original script seems to be the common trend. Also Lionello (1994) and Galassi (1994) claim that equivalence between source and target language and culture is not at all important in dubbing translation, the ultimate objective being the success of the audiovisual product. Their position is often supported by scholars in audiovisual translation (cf. Bovinelli and Gallini 1994; Agorni 2000) who defend 'localization' strategies in translation to the detriment of a 'foreignization' approach (Venuti 1995, 1998) that would respect, at least to a certain extent, the target culture and pragmatics. Paolinelli (2004), however, warns against the influence of marketing strategies on dubbing choices as they have reduced the quality of dubbed products in Italy, despite the many efforts made by the Italian Association of Dubbing Actors and Adaptors for the Cinema and Television (ADIAC) to keep production standards high. The 'adaptor', or 'script producer', is the expert who re-edits the 'raw translation' of the script to adapt it to the screen constraints. Yet, as Galassi (1994) remarks, an adaptor in Italy is unbelievably not required to know the source language and, thus, s/he is not expected to make reference to the original script in case of doubt—his/her only skill being just to manage to produce a script that 'can work successfully' on the screen. Such disappointing reality is corroborated by a research carried out by Pavesi and Perego (2006) on the professional skills of Italian adaptors. Their data reveal that a very limited number of adaptors work in Italy, they are mostly men, living in Rome, where the dubbing studios are located, and without a degree in foreign languages and translation as this is not deemed to be necessary for them. Furthermore, they work in isolation and under strict time limits, without sharing experience either with their colleagues or even with the teams of translators and dubbing actors. Predictably, the strict time limits they are allowed for the production of their dubbing script lead them to rely more and more on the 'raw translation' supplied by the team of translators. This may explain the persistence of 'dubbese' even in their 'revised' version for the dubbing. Pavesi and Perego (*ibidem*) report that adaptors are aware of 'dubbese' and they try to avoid it in their editing work by using slang, idiomatic and colloquial expressions in the target language, which render their final version of the script an instance of 'product localization'.

Indeed, the occurrence of the inappropriate uses of the target language outlined above, perceived as an unnatural 'dubbese' variation of Italian, is now influencing the syntactic, semantic and pragmatic structures of the native Italian language to the point that it is becoming an actual Italian 'lingua franca' variation adaptable to any formal and informal communicative situation. However, even the supporters of 'localization' strategies would admit that creating an analogy between, for instance, an American regional accent and an equivalent Italian one is almost impossible insofar as the visual context would not allow for such 'creative dubbing' (cf. Comuzio 1993) (although this is the case of an American sitcom to be analysed in this book, *Roseanne*, whose successful Italian version features characters living in the Mid-West speaking with a Neapolitan accent, thus representing an immigration context that is absent in the original script). In such cases, therefore, the solution may be—as Galassi (1994: 67) suggests, with reference to the film *Guys and Dolls*—to 'invent a jargon anew' which the target audience could perceive as diastratically marked in relation to the social status of the characters, and yet not diatopically identifiable. As for diatopic-variation equivalence, a possibility could be to use an accent in the target language that is as close as possible to the accent that a person living in the same place the fictitious character comes from would have when speaking Italian. This choice was not taken into consideration, for instance, in an episode from the sitcom *Dharma & Greg* (to be analysed in Chapter 5) where the diatopically-marked American accent of a character from a southern state was not rendered in dubbing through the accent that a real American from the same US state would use in speaking Italian—in fact, it was completely reinvented into a non-existent accent in the target language. More reasonably, when an accent is particularly marked in the original version, it would be advisable to have dubbing actors from the same national and ethnic provenance of the original actors (as well as with the same physical and age characteristics) so as to reproduce accents, pitches and intonations in a more realistically equivalent ways. Herbst's (1996: 107) following claim seems to come precisely in support of this view advanced here:

> "accents can be crucial for the interpretation of an utterance or be an integral part of the cohesive network of a text, and then, especially when

> explicit reference is made to a meaning element contained in the accent, they must be translated as well."

Dubbing creativity, however, needs to be systematically defined in both its theoretical and practical aspects. In the next chapter, therefore, the foundations of the sitcom dubbing-translation model proposed in this book will be set, which contends that sitcom dubbing translators as 'acting translators' should also 'embody' the language of the sitcom characters, making it 'their own' by physical, vocal and socio-cultural appropriation by acting the script out, possibly together with the other dubbing translators of their team, in order to understand the humorous dynamics of the dialogues. This embodiment would be achieved by means of specific acting techniques as well, based on the physical/psychological improvisation on characters' personality and the verbal communication they would use first in the source language of the original sitcom, and then in the target language in which the dubbing translation has to be produced. Through such 'embodiment' techniques (cf. Guido 1999), the dubbing translator would thus make the characters' personalities and language 'familiar' first of all to himself/herself, and then to the target audiences who receive their dubbing translations, and who would therefore experience the language of the translated scripts as 'natural'. This does not mean, however, that the socio-cultural and pragmalinguistic peculiarities of the original version are disregarded by the dubbing translator embodying characters, scripts and situations. In fact the risk would be that of assimilating the sitcom to the translator's own culture, leaving no space to most cultural references in the original sitcom. The dubbing translator's 'embodiment' advocated in this book would furthermore entail—in La Polla's (1994: 53) definition—the process of 'interpreting actors', since also the sitcom actors' embodiment of characters and their original language has to be 'incorporated' in the translator's own embodiment of the sitcom. The translator's consideration for the original voices and interpretation of the sitcom actors would thus set the grounds for the planning of an 'implied voice' in the dubbed version of the sitcom which, hopefully, would prevent the choice of dubbing actors whose professional and cultural backgrounds are quite dissimilar from the acting and personal history of the original actors.

2.3.3 *Inter-semiotic and transcultural issues in sitcom translation*

The sitcom, as a television genre, belongs to an inter-semiotic generic type, which means that only the verbal dimension of its structure can undergo translation, whereas the socio-culturally marked visual dimension remains unchanged. This lack of socio-cultural and pragmatic harmonization between the verbal and the visual dimensions often induces a distorted perception of the dubbed sitcom versions. Hence the need for the translator to become aware of the transcultural aspects of sitcom dubbing, taking into account the inter-semiotic process underlying the re-contextualization of the translated script within the visual dimension of the sitcom. Niemeier (1991) suggests that in the audiovisual dimension of a film, Peirce's (1992) cognitive semiotics cannot apply insofar as he views semiosis as a process occurring exclusively in a person's mind producing an image—or 'interpretant'—of the 'object' a specific word stands for. This justifies the process of 'endless semiosis' he advocates, due to the impossibility of achieving a definite interpretation of the object. Niemeier (*ibidem*), on the contrary, proposes Morris's (1964) semiotic theory as the most appropriate to analyze the audiovisual synchronization in a film since it accounts for the crucial dimensions of the 'interpreter' and the 'context', which are missing in Peirce's theory. Furthermore, Niemeier (*ibidem*: 147) points out Morris's fundamental dissection of Peirce's notion of the 'object' into two distinct dimensions – i.e., that of the 'designatum', that is the object a sign refers to, and that of the 'denotatum', that is the real object. Therefore, Niemeier concludes, since a film represents fictitious situations, it can only have 'designata' which refer to the socio-cultural context reproduced on the screen. Hence, if the spectator as interpreter has no clue of how to interpret the signs of an unfamiliar, foreign socio-cultural context, s/he will misinterpret them. To explain how convergence on an acceptable interpretation usually occurs in cross-cultural communicative situations, Morris also provides a new notion of the 'interpretant' which is different from the parallel notion advanced by Peirce, based on individuals' endless semiotic interpretations of the same sign, insofar as by 'interpretant' Morris (1964: 93) means a 'disposition' of the interpreter to respond to a sign-stimulus in ways which are shared by other interpreters since they are part of the same "response-sequences of some behaviour family". The task of the dubbing translator, therefore, is to help spectators-interpreters to converge on a particular interpretation of the signs 'designated' in a film so as to enable them to understand aspects of the foreign context represented in it which they may misunderstand. This, as Niemeier (1991: 148) points out, is only possible by emphasizing the pragmatic dimension of translation equivalence in film synchronization.

Pragmatics, however, in the context of a sitcom, has also to account for the humorous dimension of discourse, which is in itself culture-specific. This further dimension, indeed, makes dubbing translation even more complex as it has to encompass not only lip-movement synchronization and references to the original situational context to make it accessible to the target audience, but also—and crucially—original patterns of humorous discourse that have to be rendered into equivalent forms and functions in the target language and culture in order to be experienced by the target audience in the same way as the original audience is expected to experience them. In this sense, dubbing translation has to be 'transcultural' and, to achieve this aim, the translator needs to possess not only a deep knowledge of the original culture, language and patterns of humour underlying the original sitcom, but also a deep knowledge of the culture, language and humour of the target culture, so as to be able to 'embody' sitcom characters and their language in both inter-semiotic contexts, thus making their communicative styles 'his/her own' in order to produce a script translation that can be experienced as 'natural' and 'familiar' by the target audience. Obviously, as Niemeier herself (*ibidem*: 151) acknowledges, the dubbing translator shall encounter enormous difficulties in connecting target language and original visual context in his/her translation of a film script, which means that s/he often needs to introduce extra socio-contextual and even historical-geographical hints in dubbing translation that, in their turn, have not to interfere with lip synchronization. Such extra information is indeed often needed to make target audience overcome the sense of estrangement with 'designata'—i.e., the representation of foreign contexts, situations and behaviours in the sitcom—and then become familiar with them, thus activating in their mind an 'interpretant' shared with the original audience. Such hints are not simply meant as an addition of extra explicatory words and phrases uttered by off-camera characters in the dubbed version, but also as a search for pragmalectal accents which may be diatopically and diastratically equivalent to the original ones, as well as for cultural references which can be perceived as parallel to the source references in the original version without, however, distorting them. Yet often the major obstacle to equivalence is not language, but culturally-marked proxemics, voice pitch and intonation, which often differ significantly in the two languages involved in the dubbing-translation process (cf. Burgess 1980).

Regrettably, as Rowe (1960) points out, audiences generally focus more on lip-synchronization, than on translation quality, especially when television sitcoms are concerned, as they are prevalently filmed in close-up or medium close-up (Kilborn 1989: 425). Indeed, subtitling would be more respectful of the original than dubbing as it simply adds a written translation summary to the original dialogues, allowing audiences to appreciate the real voices of the actors. Moreover, subtitling is a far less expensive process than post-synchronization—which is the technical word for dubbing—and yet Gottlieb (1994: 102) claims that even subtitling lays itself bare to the criticism of those who understand both source and target languages and can object to semantic and even pragmatic equivalence choices in rendering a register that is originally of a spoken type into a—frequently inappropriate—written one in the target language, not to mention that subtitling can interfere with the audience's appreciation of the visual dimension of the film (cf. Voge 1977). A common shortcoming of dubbing, on the other hand, is disregarding 'voice personality' (Kilborn 1989: 425), that is—as pointed out above—the matching of the dubbing actor's voice timbre and tonal qualities with those of the original actor. However, preference for one or the other film-translation modality depends on how audiences are accustomed to view foreign films in their own countries (Italy, like France, Spain, England and Germany, opt for dubbing, whereas the Netherlands, Belgium and Scandinavia for subtitling), which indeed reveals the degree of sensitivity of a particular country to the different languages and cultures it engages with, even by means of a movie (although economic reasons, connected to the potential extent of film-audience's response, also play their part in this choice). Furthermore, there are historical reasons which have contributed to the preference for one option or the other. Post-war Italy, France, Spain and Germany promoted film dubbing as a strategy to assert their national identity and stem American ascendancy by creating the illusion that actors speak the target audience's language (Danan 1991: 612). Not only, but dubbing allowed these countries to manipulate original scripts which were considered as 'inappropriate' or 'offensive' to the target audience. This is the case with the Italian post-war dubbing policy which imposed a modification of the original names of Italian gangsters and criminals featuring in Hollywood films in order to make them sound as if they belonged to people of a different national origin (e.g., Johnny *Rocco* becoming Johnny *Rocky* in *Key Largo*, or Martino *Roma* becoming Martino *Rosky* in *Cry of the City*, both 1948 movies)—despite the inter-semiotic hints at the Italian opera and Neapolitan songs in the film soundtrack, as well as the landscapes with Vesuvio or Italian famous monuments in the background (Fink 1984). Changing the identity of negative Italian characters in American films was in fact part of the wider post-war Italian censorship policy of rejecting external offensive stereotypes of Italian people in order to promote a positive and self-assured reconstruction of their national identity. This also implied that Italian films belonging to the *Neorealismo* trend were considered with suspicion at home, despite their success abroad, as they portrayed the real dimension of poverty and corruption that Italian people wanted to ignore, especially when engaged in the escapist activity of 'going to the movies'. On the other hand, however, American films have often portrayed Italian negative characters grotesquely, and this characterization has principally been achieved through their use of a kind of pidgin Italian, or a funny dialectal accent and even a 'lack of articulateness' (*ibidem*: 218) which triggered a response of 'humorous disparagement' in the American audiences resulting offensive for the Italian sense of ethnic pride since no comic 'relief strategy' was applied to neutralize denigration. This indeed justified the post-synchronization policy of translating original Italian accents into standard Italian.

2.3.4 *Italian sociolects and back-transfer processes in sitcom translations*

The customary practice of preferring standard Italian in dubbing translation is another issue that has often triggered, also in sitcom translation, cognitive processes of 'back-transfer' (cf. Selinker and Lakshmanan 1992) from English to Italian, affecting syntactic, morphological, semantic and pragmatic patterns of the Italian language (cf. Paolinelli and Di Fortunato 2005; Perego 2005; Massara 2007; Petillo 2008). As Ross (1995) points out, this may be induced by the dubbing translator's task of keeping the same initial consonant sounds in the original words also in the translated version, since these are the sounds that are most visibly articulated through the actors' lip movements. The search for an equivalence simply confined to the initial sounds of words noticeably causes a loss in pragmatic equivalence. For instance, expressions like 'great!' is inappropriately translated as 'grande!' or 'grandioso!', rather than 'molto bene!' or 'benissimo!'. 'Hallo' is frequently rendered with the informal 'ciao', or the more unusual 'salve', in every occasion, rather than 'buon giorno' or 'buona sera', and 'sure' is translated as 'sicuro' (meaning 'secure', 'safe'), rather than 'sì', 'senz'altro' or 'certo'. Even worse, the expression 'absolutely' is now normally rendered as 'assolutamente' (meaning 'completely'), rather than 'proprio così', 'certamente' ('certainly'). Other examples of shift in meaning are represented by verbs like 'biasimare' (which has lost its original sense of 'disapprove' and 'censure' to adapt itself to the meaning of 'blame' that should instead be translated with the longer expressions 'dare la colpa', meaning 'to lay the blame', or 'ritenere responsabile', meaning 'to hold responsible'), and 'ritornare' (which, together with the original meaning of 'going back', has also acquired the sense of 'restituire' by calquing the English verb 'to return') (*ibidem*: 46-47). What is more, such inappropriate translation choices have become part of everyday Italian speech by means of a back-transfer process, modifying not only the semantics of such words, but also their pragmatic use (i.e., the 'dubbese as a lingua franca process' mentioned in *2.3.2*). Maraschio (1982) examines the unnaturalness of the Italian language used in film dubbing, a language which, as Pavesi (1994) points out, loses its diastratic dimension which, however, is recovered through lexical and morpho-syntactic choices. Hence, with reference to diastratic varieties employed by working-class characters, the preference goes, for instance, to the use of the indicative mood, rather than the subjunctive one, or to the prepositional accusative with the additional personal pronoun, as in 'a me non mi freghi' (*ibidem*: 133). The choice of informal, and even ungrammatical language to render a lower-class accent or dialect may in fact contribute to the naturalness of a dubbed character's speech without provoking socio-cultural clashes with the visual setting of the scene (see also Pavesi 2005). The consequence of this 'translation process' (cf. Widdowson 1979: 71), however, is often the construction of a new script whose 'deviations' from the original one trigger new interpretative discourses in the target receivers.

There is a number of translation scholars, however, who are sceptical about the possibility of preserving the source cultural references in translation (cf. Hickey 1999) and, more specifically, the source humour in the target language. Leppihalme (1996), for instance, claims that culture-bound allusive wordplays are untranslatable because of the particular references that the target audiences need to know in order to fully appreciate their comic effect. Also Chiaro (1992) expresses her reservations about the possibility of translating wordplays by keeping the linguistic equivalence in the target text and, at the same time, achieving the same pragmatic effect the original wordplays would prompt in the source audience. Lendvai (1996) actually demonstrates the untranslatability of specific categories of jokes that are based on linguistic synonymy, antonymy, or polysemy so as to play with ambiguity and introduce, through it, socio-cultural references. Other translation scholars obviously disagree with such discouraging views (cf. Leibold 1989; Hatim and Mason 1997). Popa (2005) suggests that the translation of humour crucially requires a respect for its original pragmatic intent and for the interpersonal functions it expects to establish with the audience—both representing the objective a translator has to try hard to achieve in rendering humour into a target language and culture. The practical difficulties inherent in such pragmatic approach, however, are many. Above all, in the attempt to reproduce on the target audience the same perlocutionary effect the original text produces on the source audience, a translator may need to adapt the source-culture references to the target culture, with the substitution of original references with new ones accessible to the target audience, or with the addition of extra explanatory information (cf. Leppihalme 1996). In his application of the General Theory of Verbal Humour to translation, Attardo (2002) defends the feasibility of translating humour despite the acknowledgement of the fact that it would, in any case, represent an approximate rendering of the original text. To this purpose, he points out the relevance of the 'six knowledge resources' advanced in his theory to the rendering of humour into another language and culture. In particular, Attardo advises translators to strive to preserve the linguistic equivalence but, if this is not be possible, they need to safeguard the original 'script opposition' (*ibidem*: 190) which would trigger, also in the target audiences' minds, the activation of the expected 'logical mechanism' bridging the gap between the two opposite scripts that produce the comic effect. Zabalbeascoa (2005), however, is critical of Attardo's application of the General Theory of Verbal Humour to translation practice since, he claims, in this way the translator's priority becomes only that of safeguarding the original formal structure of humour, rather than its equivalent comic effect on the target audience. Zabalbeascoa (1996a) in fact advocates his own translation theory of humour—applied precisely to sitcoms—which is more practical than Attardo's cognitive theory, although it shares with it the same objective, namely, to prove that the translation of humour is practicable and can be achieved by ensuring both commercial success to the comic product and pragmalinguistic equivalence between source and target scripts. To this purpose, he identifies the following six categories of jokes, each presenting peculiar translation problems to be solved: *(1)* "International or bi-national jokes" that can be understood cross-culturally and, therefore, their formal and pragmatic transfer into the target language and culture should not be problematic as the semantic and socio-cultural references, and the humorous implications, are assumed to be shared by the source and target audiences; *(2)* "National-culture-and-institutions jokes", conveying culture-specific references that may not be accessible to the target audience's background knowledge and, therefore, need some degree of cultural adaptation by retaining, at the same time, the implied pragmatic or ideological meaning; *(3)* "National-sense-of-humour jokes", usually having as a target specific stereotypical categories of people or of social groups whose disparagement is deemed to be funny only by source audiences. The translation strategy in this case is to substitute the original culture-bound stereotype with an equivalent one in the target culture; *(4)* "Language-dependent jokes", often based on idiomatic expressions or particular stylistic features that may need to be substituted with pragmatically equivalent ones in the target language; *(5)* "Visual jokes", entirely or partially based on visual elements that may convey culture-bound meanings in need of disambiguation (e.g., by the addition of explanatory written captions); *(6)* "Complex jokes", which may encompass all the other types of categories outlined so far and, therefore, the translator has to decide which problems to tackle first with reference to the target audience's assumed expectations.

Having outlined the main theories of humour translation, it becomes clear that a novel model of dubbing translation in general, and of dubbing translation for television comedy in particular, is much needed in order to cope with such equivalence issues (cf. also Zabalbeascoa 1996b). In the Acting Translator Model advanced in this book in the next chapters, the dubbing translator is crucially expected to encompass, together with his/her actual role of translator, also that of the adaptor and even the role of the actor 'embodying' the situation script and the characters. Furthermore, s/he has to recognize within the original script the addresser's intentionality clues that will guide him/her to interpret the script and then render it into the target language in ways that can be regarded as 'equivalent' to the originally intended ones. The question at this stage, however, is to identify such intentionality clues within the original script (i.e., its illocutionary force) so as to avoid the translator's top-down imposition of his/her own subjective experience of the script on his/her interpretation and translation of its language in context (due to the perlocutionary effects of the script upon him/her). Interpretation, in fact, has to account for a socio-culturally and pragmalinguistically marked interplay of implicatures, presuppositions and inferences to be recognized in the script and then conveyed through an equivalent and coherent dubbing translation. Translation, in its turn, also needs to be consistent with the visual context of the film as well as with its purpose which, in the case of the sitcom dubbing translation, coincides with the rendering of the original socio-cultural patterns of humour into equivalent comic modes.

At this point, the Acting Translator Model shall be discussed in the following chapter in order to illustrate the dubbing translator's process of 'embodiment' of the original sitcom script aimed at the achievement of an 'experiential equivalence' and 'pragmatic naturalness' in translation.

Chapter 3

The Acting Translator Model Applied to Humorous Conversation Analysis

3.1 The Acting Translator Model

3.1.1 *The theoretical grounds of the Model*

This chapter introduces the Acting Translator Model advanced in this book, by exploring it in connection with an approach to conversation analysis which fits the structural peculiarities of sitcom humorous dialogues. According to this Model, the dubbing translator is expected to 'embody' the dynamic patterns of such dialogues so as to make them his/her own, first in their original version and then in an equivalent version in the target language, aimed at reproducing an effect of naturalness in the dubbed dialogues. Indeed, as mentioned in the Introduction, the Acting Translator Model claims that sitcom dubbing translators, since their very first approach to the sitcom script, need to find ways to 'appropriate' sitcom humorous languages and characters into their own identity so as to 'embody' it through their own experience. By 'experience' it is here meant both a bilingual and bicultural experience that a dubbing translator has to develop and master in order to feel at ease within the two sociolinguistic contexts of the source and target cultures. This does not mean of course that a dubbing translator has to be a native speaker of both languages involved in the translation process, but it is necessary that s/he has developed a deep and specialized competence of the comedy genre in both languages and cultures. Only in this way can s/he 'embody' and 'dramatize' the script, thus becoming an Acting Translator capable of analysing and translating a humorous discourse by activating a process of interaction between his/her own subjective and socio-cultural background experience, or 'schemata', and the formal organization of the original sitcom script. The implication, as anticipated in the Introduction, is that schemata are not to be conventionally considered as 'mental', 'cognitive', but rather as 'bodily', on the assumption that it is through the body that human beings have started to experience and make sense of the world till developing from its physical experience the abstract parameters of its conceptualisation and logical reasoning (Guido 1999, 2005). Being aware of 'logical reasoning' means becoming conscious above all of the fact that its parameters are not universal but culture-bound, and that they can be continuously flouted, as its happens when the mechanism of Humour is activated. Humour, in particular, can emphasize precisely the bodily and emotional roots of schemata insofar as, by deroutinizing logical reasoning and its linguistic organization, it can reveal the extent to which the pragmatic use of language depends on physical actions and reactions. This justifies the definition of 'body/thought schemata' (*ibidem*) employed also in this book, meant to mark precisely the bodily aspects of schemata that, in everyday communication, are usually kept atrophied but that, instead, come to be revitalized precisely by the quality itself of a sitcom script that is written to be 'enacted' at the 'physical' and 'dramatic' levels of its humorous discourse. On a 'physical level', a sitcom script is designed to prompt receivers to embody the characters within the fictional situation that contextualizes their actions and words. In doing so, receivers—and translators among receivers—activate bodily responses and emotional, cognitive and affective reactions to the humorous language that characters use, thus feeling entitled to 'embody' them as if they were not just receivers (i.e., readers, or translators), but precisely the 'actors' who have to play the various characters' roles making their language and behaviours 'their own' at both physical, emotional and cognitive levels.

It is important to highlight at this point that Humour in a sitcom script is to be interpreted 'in action' (cf. Critchley 2002) as it essentially 'deviates' not only from the generic register of a 'written humour', principally grounded on language patterns of wordplays and puns, but also – and crucially – from any other use of language both at the phonological and prosodic levels and, consequently, at the semantic and textual levels of discourse. Humorous discourse deviations, in fact, by disrupting the conventional—expected and routinized—dialogic patterns of conversation scripts have the effect of revitalizing in the receivers' minds their defused body/thought schemata, prompting them to embody and enact their own interpretation of the humorous language not only through their own voice, but also through their whole body. The implication is that a particular linguistic and cognitive pattern of humour is inherently associated to the receivers' response to such a pattern since their first reading of the script—a response which would involve their subjective body/thought schemata. This means that a humorous pattern of an Arousal/Safety type, or of a Disparagement kind, may be interpreted differently by different receivers with different experiential body/thought schemata. The outcome of this is that such responses also diverge from any normal use of language in everyday situations where, instead, schema convergence is expected and, consequently, any deviation from the shared socio-cultural conversation norms is considered as an infringement of the accepted social codes of behaviour if it is not justified by a recognized humorous register. This being so because the humorous patterns of a sitcom script impede any normal interpretation of the situation in point because it cannot occur by reference to ordinary behavioural codes, or to common logical reasons. This is why receivers feel entitled to have different personal reactions to the humorous script. And yet, during the phase of translation, some interpretative convergence has to be achieved also in the interpretation of humorous discourse, which means that a search for pragmatic equivalence with the original humorous intentions of the scriptwriter should be one of the professional objectives of the dubbing translator of sitcoms. It is at this stage that the technique of 'dramatization' becomes crucial in the dubbing translation process, as the translator needs to explore the characters' 'voices' achieved within the language pattern of the sitcom script. In the course of this exploration, the translator is first of all a reader who, by becoming conscious of such 'textual voices', consciously or unconsciously feels the need to 'appropriate' them, 'embody' them, and ultimately 'enact' their dramatic potentialities as if s/he were on an actual stage, thus realizing that s/he interprets the humorous quality of such voices according to his/her own 'individual voice'. The notion of 'individual voice' involves the dubbing translators' own physical, emotional, intellectual and socio-cultural personalities—that is, their own schemata in their body/thought entirety—which, by interacting with the 'textual voices' of the sitcom script, allows translators to approach and familiarize with the characters' personalities and sense of humour. This is made possible by the fact that sitcom humour entails a 'direct speech-act' made up by 'humorous utterances'—which are locutions linguistically and cognitively built upon a typically ambiguous language that brings together two conflicting contexts—namely, an explicit context represented by the actual situation characters are involved in, and an implicit one. The assumption is that translators can recreate in space humorous ambiguous situations parallel to the sitcom original ones through a dramatic appropriation of the 'humorous voices' should occur within a real 'stage of enactment'. Within such parallel situations, dubbing translators, as a team, can give vent to their own imagination by improvising upon the explicit and implicit contexts of the original script by using both the source and the target languages. The translators' physical and vocal renderings of the 'humorous utterance' and their improvisation upon them can indeed be considered as expressions of their creative interpretations aimed at familiarizing with the characters' humorous language and with the fictional situations. This crucially entails the recognition of the physical and vocal dimensions of humour as a fundamental prerequisite for achieving pragmatic equivalence in dubbing translation. These dimensions, however, are often neglected in current research on the translation of humorous discourse in general, and on dubbing translation of comedy-movie genres in particular, as well as in the wider research fields of multimodal semiotics and intercultural communication studies applied to the audiovisual registers employed in the media. The basic assumption of this claim, thus, is that to be conceptually receptive to sitcom humorous language the dubbing translator needs to be physically prepared to be receptive to it.

The 'Acting Translator', therefore, will be here regarded as an empirical dubbing translator who 'physically' inhabits the original sitcom script and embodies the humorous discourse s/he achieves from it in such a way as to derive from it his own subjective 'dramatic' interpretations capable of enhancing his/her own imaginative apprehension of humour at all levels of experience. Therefore, by 'embodiment of the dramatic discourse of humour' it is here meant the continuous interplay of different effects the sitcom humour produces on the Acting Translator as s/he physically, emotionally, and mentally explores and interprets it in a 'real' space of enactment, thus creating, 'while acting', a kind of multi-modal, 'physical translation' consistent with the effects produced by the formal organization of the humorous script on his/her own body/thought schemata. It follows that translating sitcom humour involves five processes: *(1)* acting the source script out, *(2)* analyzing its effects, *(3)* improvising on it in the source and in the target languages, *(4)* viewing the related original sitcom episode, *(5)* translating its script for dubbing. The claim is that acting and improvising on sitcom scripts will be all the more effective if acting translators work in a team to produce a dubbing translation. This implies that an acting translator creates his/her own dramatic discourse and its effects which are followed by his/her own reflection upon them. Dubbing translation, in this way, is meant as the analysis of the acting translator's own 'body/thought' schematic responses to the humour patterns of the script, not as the translation of the script as such. The theory of the 'Acting Translator', in this perspective, can be ranked within the cognitive-linguistic field of the Experientialist approach to language (Johnson 1987; Sweetzer 1990; Langacker 1991), which raises objections against the typical mentalist view that dubbing translation is just a cognitive act of 'equivalence search' which, implicitly or explicitly, can only be 'mental'.

The practical demonstration of how to apply this model to the 'embodiment' of the conversation structure of a sitcom script shall inform the chapters that will follow in Part Two of this book. The attention shall be focused on the extent to which 'drama techniques' consistent with the Acting Translator theory can be worked out with the objective of encouraging dubbing translators to explore the culture-bound structure of the discourse of sitcom humour and the comic effects that such a structure can produce not only in the source culture, but also in the target culture the dubbing translation is aimed at. This justifies the pedagogic dimension of this study as this theory comes to be applied to university classes of Translation Studies and becomes actualised in the training of undergraduate Italian students of English Language and Translation. The aim of this principled training is not only attempting to open an innovative perspective on the nature of dubbing translation as a 'dramatic' use of language, but also showing the relevance of theory to the empirical experience of translation teaching. As such, it provides a subsequent discussion of pedagogic practice arising from the views expressed, whose effectiveness is demonstrated by a series of students/acting-translators' protocols illustrating the extent to which workshops devised to encourage the actual 'embodiments of meanings' in groups of students, carried out by using drama techniques, has indeed the potential for developing the students' awareness of the cognitive, linguistic and socio-cultural structure of the humorous sitcom language. In other words, drama techniques, in such pedagogic context, become useful procedures to help dubbing translators either access and become aware of the 'bodily dimension' of their own schemata, or realize the extent to which such a dimension is at the source of their physical, vocal, emotional and, subsequently, conceptual responses to the peculiar formal characteristics of the humorous language. The dubbing translator, therefore, is here assumed to hold a central position in the process of actualizing the dramatic 'voices'—intrinsic in the sitcom script—by 'embodying them' according to his/her own personality. The notion of 'voice' advanced here relies essentially on a continual, vital interaction between the acting translator's individual 'inner voice', which takes its origin from his/her own experience and personality (that is, from his/her own body/thought schemata), and the 'textual voices' s/he achieves within the sitcom script by dramatically accessing humorous language through his/her own 'inner voice'. This entails an interplay of three reading/translating strategies, each of which marks a phase of the present enquiry.

3.1.2 *Phase 1: top-down strategies*

This *Phase 1* is concerned with the acting translators' exploration of a 'top-down', affective and deconstructive strategy relying on their dramatic improvisation in both source and target languages and creative-writing retextualizations. A reading strategy of this type recognizes only a very low degree of textual constraint which would simply acknowledge the plot frame and the characters' main personality features so as to allow acting translators to get rid of the sense of estrangement they experience on their first approach to sitcom script and, thus, to become familiar with the unconventional pragmatic and formal patterns of the humorous text. The acting translators' process of 'familiarizing' with the sitcom script is brought about by superimposing their own 'voices' upon the initial dramatic discourses they achieve from the script. In doing so, they appropriate both the authorial, first-person stance, as well as the receivers' third-person stances since it is also crucial for dubbing translators to keep their distance from their own interpretation of the sitcom humour so as to be able to perceive it as if they were part of an audience. Such top-down appropriation process to be fully effective needs to occur in both languages involved in the dubbing-translation process.

However, there are serious limits to a possible misuse of this top-down approach to dubbing translation which would in fact disregard completely the humorous patterns of language and culture in the original script to make the dubbing translator's imaginative interpretation and schema background prevail over it. A blatant example of such a misuse is represented by the Italian dubbing translation of the British comic film *Monty Python and the Holy Grail*. In this case, the Bagaglino Company—an Italian vaudeville group of comedians (among whom there is the comedian, dubbing actor and translator Oreste Lionello) very famous on the Italian TV for their crass political satire that never seriously criticizes the party at the power—was entrusted with the task of producing a dubbing translation of the Monty Python film dialogues they had to dub, too. In fact, in their dubbing translation, it turned out that the typically British sophisticated nonsense humour which characterizes the Monty Python group of comedians was outrageously transformed into a gross farce with vulgar innuendos and the use of dialectal varieties of the Italian language —a mannerism of the Bagaglino Company characterizing their comedians but showing no equivalence at all with the Monty Python parallel script. This exercise of 'schematic imposition' of the dubbing translators' 'creativity' upon the original script indeed represents the extreme outcome of a merely top-down embodiment of the script, resembling in many ways the total creative rewriting of humorous video-game scripts in rendering them into another language—a process defined as 'transcreation' (Mangiron and O'Hagan 2006). The examples that follow are drawn from the parallel English and Italian scripts of the *Monty Python and the Holy Grail* movie (*Monty Python e il Sacro Graal*). This is a 1975 comic fantasy film based on the legend of Arthur, King of Britons, and his Knights of the Round Table (Sir Galahad, Sir Lancelot, Sir Bedevere and Sir Robin, all of them played by the Monty Python comedians) who are in quest of the Holy Grail, the legendary sacred cup in which Joseph of Arimathea collected the drops of Christ's blood. In their quest on imaginary horses (the squires following them imitate the noise of the horses' hooves by tapping coconut shells), King Arthur and his Knights finally find the Castle where the Holy Grail is held because a peasant (Dennis) gives them the right information (*Scene 1* below), then they meet some French guards who impede them to get in there (*Scene 2*), and a three-headed giant monster defending the Castle and threatening to kill them (*Scene 3*). Even a very quick glance at the parallel scripts of the three scenes that follow (the original one in English and the translated one in Italian) can reveal the radical changes that the dubbing translators have imposed upon the original text, not only at the pragmatic level, but also at the semantic and textual one, thus totally rewriting the whole text to fit the Bagaglino comedians' humour and mannerism. The following three scenes under consideration are reported in their original English version, their Italian dubbing translation, and a back-translation into Standard English:

Scene 1

Original English version	***Italian dubbing translation***	***Back-translation into Standard English***
ARTHUR: Old woman!	**ARTÙ:** Ehi, lei, plebeo! Come la si chiama?	**ARTHUR:** Hey you, plebeian, What's your name?
DENNIS: Man!	**BESTIA:** Bestia!	**BEAST:** Beast!
ARTHUR: Man. Sorry. What knight live in that castle over there?	**ARTÙ:** La senta, Bestia, di chi è quel castello laggiù?	**ARTHUR:** Listen, Beast, whose castle is that one over there?
DENNIS: I'm thirty-seven.	**BESTIA:** E daglie con le domande!	**BEAST:** There he goes again with the questions!
ARTHUR: I— what?	**ARTÙ:** Cosa?	**ARTHUR:** What?
DENNIS: I'm thirty-seven. I'm not old.	**BESTIA:** È chiuso. Si apre solo quando che piove.	**BEAST:** It's shut. It is opened only when it rains.
ARTHUR: Well, I can't just call you 'Man'.	**ARTÙ:** E perché solo quando piove?	**ARTHUR:** Why only when it rains?
DENNIS: Well, you could say 'Dennis'.	**BESTIA:** Se no fuori te bagni, ignorante.	**BEAST:** Because outside you get drenched, thickhead.
ARTHUR: Well, I didn't know you were called 'Dennis'.	**ARTÙ:** Ma il padrone dove vive?	**ARTHUR:** But where does the master live?
DENNIS: Well, you didn't bother to find out, did you?	**BESTIA:** Da 'ste parti, ma è difficile.	**BEAST:** In these parts, but it's difficult.
ARTHUR: I did say 'sorry' about the 'old woman', but from the behind you looked	**ARTÙ:** È difficile vivere su queste terre?	**ARTHUR:** Is it difficult to live in these lands?
DENNIS: What I object to is that you automatically treat me like an inferior!	**BESTIA:** No, standoci sopra tirava pure a campa', ma da sotto è difficile.	**BEAST:** No, when he was on them he was able to get by, but from below it's difficult.
ARTHUR: Well, I am king!	**ARTÙ:** Chi sono gli eredi?	**ARTHUR:** Who are the heirs?
DENNIS: Oh king, eh, very nice. And how d'you get that, eh? By exploiting the workers! By 'anging on to outdated imperialist dogma which perpetuates the economic and social differences in our society. If there's ever going to be any progress with the-	**BESTIA:** E questo ci insistisce con le domande. Oh, mica sei delle tasse, eh? Sai che te dico? Che se fai tante domande è capace che te ne accettano una e ti assumono a corte dove ti ingrassi senza lavora', e il lavoro invece è tutto...	**BEAST:** This one keeps on making requests. Oh, aren't you a taxman, are you? Because if you make so many requests maybe they will grant one of them and they will take you on at court where you can grow fat [and get rich] without working, whereas work is all...
WOMAN: Dennis, there's some lovely filth down here. Oh! How d'you do?	**DONNA:** Vai a lavora', Bestia! **BESTIA:** Mia moglie, 18 anni, un fiore. **DONNA:** E chi sei tu?	**WOMAN:** Go to work, Beast! **BEAST:** Meet my wife, eighteen years old, a beauty. **WOMAN:** And who are you?
ARTHUR: How do you do, good lady. I am Arthur, King of the Britons. Who's castle is that?	**ARTÙ:** Permetta che mi presenti. Sono Artù, re dei Bretoni. Desideravo un'informazione circa...	**ARTHUR:** May I introduce myself? I'm Arthur, King of the Britons. I'd need some information on...
WOMAN: King of the who?	**DONNA:** E 'ndò lavori?	**WOMAN:** Where do you work?
ARTHUR: The Britons.	**ARTU:** Io comando.	**ARTHUR:** I give orders.
WOMAN: Who are the Britons?		
ARTHUR: Well, we all are. We are all Britons, and I am your king.		

Scene 2

Original English version	***Italian dubbing translation***	***Back-translation into Standard English***
ARTHUR: Halt!	**ARTÙ:** Alt! C'è qualcuno? Oooh!	**ARTHUR:** Halt! Is anybody there? Oooh!
FRENCH GUARD: Allo! Who is it?	**SOLDATO:** Cu è?	**SOLDIER:** Who's there?
ARTHUR: It is King Arthur, and these are my Knights of the Round Table. Who's castle is this?	**ARTÙ:** Io sono il re Artù e questi sono i miei cavalieri di Camelot. Il castello di chi gli è?	**ARTHUR:** *(speaking with a Tuscan accent)* It is King Arthur, and these are my Knights of Camelot. Whose castle is this?
FRENCH GUARD: This is the castle of my master Guy de Loimbard.	**SOLDATO:** E a tia presentemente che te ne fotte? È di chi deve essere.	**SOLDIER:** *(speaking with a Sicilian accent)* Now, what business is it of yours? It belongs to whom it must belong to.
ARTHUR: Go and tell your master that we have been charged by God with a sacred quest. If he will give us food and shelter for the night he can join us in our quest for the Holy Grail.	**ARTÙ:** Vada dal suo padrone e gli riferisca che Dio mi ha incaricato di compiere una missione di molto prestigio, che consiste nella ricerca e nella conquista del Santo Graal.	**ARTHUR:** Go to your master and tell him that God has charged me with a highly prestigious mission, which consists in the quest and conquest of the Holy Grail.
FRENCH GUARD: Well, I'll ask him, but I don't think he'll be very keen. Uh, he's already got one, you see?	**SOLDATO:** Io vado a riferire, ma penso che non ci interessa, ehm, perché uno ce l'ave già.	**SOLDIER:** I'll go and tell him, but I think that he's not interested in it, um, because he's already got one.
ARTHUR: What?	**ARTÙ:** Ei che ci ha?	**ARTHUR:** Hey, what has he got?
GALAHAD: He says they've already got one!	**GALAHAD:** Dice che ne ha già uno.	**GALAHAD:** He says that he's already got one.
ARTHUR: Are you sure he's got one?	**ARTÙ:** Il Calice Santo ce l'ha qui?	**ARTHUR:** It's the Holy chalice that he's got here?
FRENCH GUARD: Oh, yes, it's very nice-a. (I told him we already got one.)	**SOLDATO:** E pure molto grazioso! Ci ho fatto credere che noi ne abbiamo un altro.	**SOLDIER:** And it's also very nice! I made him believe that we've got another one.
ARTHUR: Well, u— um, can we come up and have a look?	**ARTÙ:** Che, gli si potrebbe dare un'occhiatina?	**ARTHUR:** Is it possible to have a quick look at it?
FRENCH GUARD: Of course not! You are English types-a!	**SOLDATO:** Manco morto. Siete porci europei.	**SOLDIER:** Not on your life! You are rotten Europeans.
ARTHUR: Well, what are you then?	**ARTÙ:** Perché, voi che siete?	**ARTHUR:** Well, what are you then?
FRENCH GUARD: I'm French! Why do think I have this outrageous accent, you silly king-a?!	**SOLDATO:** Austriaci. È perché pensi che ci haio questo fituso accento. Lampo nei peri.	**SOLDIER:** We are Austrian. Why do you think I have this damned accent, blast it!
GALAHAD: What are you doing in England?	**GALAHAD:** E che volete qui nel Nord?	**GALAHAD:** What do you want here in the North?
FRENCH GUARD: Mind your own business!	**SOLDATO:** Fatti l'affari toi.	**SOLDIER:** Mind your own business!
ARTHUR: If you will not show us the Grail, we shall take your castle by force!	**ARTÙ:** Se non ci mostrate il Graal attaccheremo il castello con la forza.	**ARTHUR:** If you will not show us the Grail, we shall attack the castle by force!
FRENCH GUARD: You don't frighten us, English pig-dogs! Go and boil your bottom, sons of a	**SOLDATO:** Matri che paura che ruggisci, piecoro, ma comu criri ca mi spaventu. A mia. Mi spa-	**SOLDIER:** Goodness gracious, you scare me with your roaring, you sheep, what a shouting at me,

silly person. I blow my nose at you, so-called Arthur King, you and all your silly English k-nnnnniggets. Thpppppt! Thppt!	venta a mia. Mi fa tremare tuttu u pizzu da suttanedda. Iarruso. E testa di m- m-m-min-chia. Prrr! Prrr! Prrr!	it frightens me. At me. It frightens me. It makes all the lace of my underskirt shake. You puff. And dickhead. Thpppppt! Thppt!
GALAHAD: What a strange person.	**GALAHAD:** Questo dev'essere di Cefalù.	**GALAHAD:** This guy must be from Cefalù.

Scene 3

Original English version	***Italian dubbing translation***	***Back-translation into Standard English***
ALL HEADS: Halt! Who art thou?	**TRE TESTE:** Alt! Chi sei tu?	**THREE-HEADS:** Halt! Who are you?
MINSTREL: *[singing]* He is brave Sir Robin, brave Sir Robin, who—	**MENESTRELLO:** Questo è Mr. Robin, Mr. Robin, uh...	**MINSTREL:** This is Mr. Robin, Mr. Robin, uh...
ROBIN: Shut up! Um, n— n— n—nobody really, I'm j— j— j— ju—just um, just passing through.	**ROBIN:** Crepa! Eh... noi si passava, loro passavano qui per caso...	**ROBIN:** Drop dead! Um, we were passing through, they were just passing through...
ALL HEADS: What do you want?	**TRE TESTE:** Per che fare? **ROBIN:** Eh...	**THREE-HEADS:** To do what? **ROBIN:** Um...
MINSTREL: *[singing]* To fight and—	**MENESTRELLO:** Una strage!	**MINSTREL:** A massacre!
ROBIN: Shut up! Um, oo, a—nothing, nothing really. I, uh, j— j— just— just to um, just to p—pass through, good Sir Knight.	**ROBIN:** Ti prego. Eh... niente, niente, veramente, io vorrei soltanto passare, o no?	**ROBIN:** Please. Um... Nothing, nothing, really. I'd just want to pass, wouldn't I?
ALL HEADS: I'm afraid not!	**TRE TESTE:** In che categoria?	**THREE-HEADS:** into which rank [do you want to pass]?
ROBIN: Ah. W— well, actually I— I am a Knight of the Round Table.	**ROBIN:** Ah... io... sarei un cavaliere.	**ROBIN:** Ah... well.... I'm actually a knight.
ALL HEADS: You're a Knight of the Round Table?	**TRE TESTE:** Tu allora stai dalla parte dei padroni!	**THREE-HEADS:** Then you are on the masters' side!
ROBIN: I am.	**ROBIN:** È male?	**ROBIN:** Is that bad?
LEFT HEAD: In that case I shall have to kill you.	**I TESTA:** Hai la tessera dei sindacati?	**FIRST HEAD:** Have you got the union membership card?
MIDDLE HEAD: Shall I?	**II TESTA:** È un iscritto?	**SECOND HEAD:** Is he a member?
RIGHT HEAD: Oh, I don't think so.	**III TESTA:** Ma se se' un aristocratico.	**THIRD HEAD:** But he's an aristocrat!
MIDDLE HEAD: Well, what do I think?	**II TESTA:** Bisogna accettare tutti.	**SECOND HEAD:** We need to accept anybody.
LEFT HEAD: I think kill him.		
RIGHT HEAD: Oh, let's be nice to him.	**III TESTA:** Ma sono irrecuperabili.	**THIRD HEAD:** But they are hopeless.
LEFT HEAD: Oh shut up.	**I TESTA:** Oh, sta' zitto.	**FIRST HEAD:** Oh, shut up.
ROBIN: Perhaps I could—	**ROBIN:** Mentre che voi...	**ROBIN:** While you...
LEFT HEAD: And you. Oh, quick! Get the sword out. I want to cut his head off!	**I TESTA:** Fermo, noi dobbiamo offrire la massima apertura.	**FIRST HEAD:** Stop, we must offer the utmost overture.

RIGHT HEAD: Oh, cut your own head off!	**III TESTA:** No, perché poi ce la otturano.	**THIRD HEAD:** Not at all, because they will otherwise obstruct it.
MIDDLE HEAD: Yes, do us all a favor!		
LEFT HEAD: What?	**I TESTA:** Interpelliamo la base.	**FIRST HEAD:** Let's peck at this question with the shop floor.
RIGHT HEAD: Yapping on all the time.	**III TESTA:** Non ci si può basare sulla base.	**THIRD HEAD:** We cannot be floored by the shop floor.
MIDDLE HEAD: You're lucky. You're not next to him.	**II TESTA:** E allora su che cosa ci si deve basare?	**SECOND HEAD:** What then shall be pecked at?
LEFT HEAD: What do you mean?	**I TESTA:** Sulla bocca.	**FIRST HEAD:** At the mouth.
MIDDLE HEAD: You snore!	**II TESTA:** Mi no te baso.	**SECOND HEAD:** I will not peck your mouth!
LEFT HEAD: Oh, I don't. Anyway, you've got bad breath.	**I TESTA:** Oh, ma chi ti credi di essere? La principessa del pisello?	**FIRST HEAD:** Oh, who do you think you are? The princess on the pea?
MIDDLE HEAD: Well it's only because you don't brush my teeth.	**II TESTA:** Non mi sei neanche simpatico.	**SECOND HEAD:** I don't even like you.
RIGHT HEAD: Oh stop bitching and let's go have tea.	**III TESTA:** Basta così, noi dovemo tutelare le masse.	**THIRD HEAD:** Enough, we must protect the masses.
LEFT HEAD: Oh, all right. All right. All right. We'll kill him first and then have tea and biscuits.	**I TESTA:** Lo so, più potere d'acquisto, più potere occupazionale, più potere programmatorio.	**FIRST HEAD:** I know, more purchasing power, more occupational power, more planning power.
MIDDLE HEAD: Yes.	**II TESTA:** Il potere!	**SECOND HEAD:** The power!
RIGHT HEAD: Oh, not biscuits.	**III TESTA:** E le piattaforme?	**THIRD HEAD:** And the platforms?
LEFT HEAD: All right. All right, not biscuits, but let's kill him anyway.	**I TESTA:** Non mi parlare di piattaforme. Non ho mai capito le piattaforme. **II E III TESTA:** Nemmeno noi!	**FIRST HEAD:** Don't talk to me of platforms. I've never understood the platforms. **SECOND & THIRD HEADS:** Neither do we!
ALL HEADS: Right!	**TRE TESTE:** Morte ai padroni!	**THREE-HEADS:** Death to the masters!
MIDDLE HEAD: He buggered off.	**I TESTA:** È scappato. **II TESTA:** È scappato.	**FIRST HEAD:** He's fled. **SECOND HEAD:** He's fled.
RIGHT HEAD: So he has. He's scarpered.	**III TESTA:** Era un industriale.	**THIRD HEAD:** He was a tycoon.

The original film is a magnificent example of British nonsense humour which may actually cause problems in the search for translation equivalence when too 'culture-bound' lexical, literary and, above all, pragmatic features are met in the source text. But from finding solutions to such equivalence problems to completely distorting the original text in translation, in order to provide what is assumed to be a 'pragmatically equivalent'

Italian version, is really a too arrogant feat carried out by the Italian dubbing translators of this film. Indeed, such translators seem to have first 'acted' the script according to their own experience as farcical comedians and, then, 'translated' it by privileging a totally top-down, self-centred translation strategy accounting for: *(a)* Italian regional dialects and accents employed to render in translation the original dialogue in archaic English – thus flouting the principle of pragmatic equivalence, *(b)* entirely new dialogues, *(c)* cue additions—when the camera is away from actors' faces—and *(d)* completely unlike punch-lines which make the British film an utterly different one in its Italian version. This practice, however, is not to be regarded as a thorough 'acting translator' procedure, but only as the very first explorative part of the translator's top-down, creative improvisation on the original scripts. In fact, in this specific case, on the one hand the translators' aim was evidently to draw from their consolidated experience as comedians and thus to appeal to 'their own' Bagaglino's audience to make them laugh according to expected patterns of humour which, however, disrespect the original ones. The Italian producers' aim, on the other hand, may have been not to take too much risk in presenting a movie marked by a typically British humour which may meet the appreciation of only a small elitist audience and, thus, may turn out to be a box-office failure. Hence, in *Scene 1*, the peasant's unexpected and sudden shift of register from an everyday English to a cliché left-wing political, unionistic discourse ("Oh king, eh, very nice. And how d'you get that, eh? By exploiting the workers! By 'anging on to outdated imperialist dogma which perpetuates the economic and social differences in our society") is completely ignored and rewritten anew in the Italian version so as to convey a different sense, as evident in its Standard-English back-translation: "This one keeps on making requests. Oh, aren't you a taxman, are you? Because if you make so many requests maybe they will grant one of them and they will take you on at court where you can grow fat [and get rich] without working, whereas work is all". This total replacement of the original cues with different ones in Italian goes on for the rest of *Scene 1*. But also the Italian version of *Scene 2* has little to do with the original one. Here, for instance, the French guard defending the Castle claims that he is Austrian, but then he speaks with a strong Sicilian accent, whereas King Arthur, originally speaking Standard English, in the Italian version is made to speak with a Tuscan accent. Noticeably, not just the accents have been changed in the Italian version but, as expected, whole parts of the text have been rewritten to suit the Bagaglino's farcical slapstick humour. *Scene 3* represents the ultimate affront to the original film. In it, the political register omitted in *Scene 1* is inappropriately introduced here when, rather than rendering the original tiff started among the monster's three heads over trivial everyday issues regarding their being forced to live together (which reveals their conflicting personalities) the translators totally rewrite the dialogue in Italian by employing typical unionist clichés and eliminating the heads' divergent traits. This is evident, for instance, in the rapid exchange of cues among the three heads starting from the issue about what to do with Robin, the knight. The original version reads: "*Left Head:* Oh, quick! Get the sword out. I want to cut his head off! / *Right Head:* Oh, cut your own head off! / *Middle Head:* Yes, do us all a favor! / *Left Head*: What? / *Right Head:* Yapping on all the time. / *Middle Head:* You're lucky. You're not next to him. / *Left Head:* What do you mean? / *Middle Head:* You snore! / *Left Head:* Oh, I don't. Anyway, you've got bad breath. / *Middle Head:* Well it's only because you don't brush my teeth. / *Right Head:* Oh stop bitching and let's go have tea. / *Left Head:* Oh, all right. All right. All right. We'll kill him first and then have tea and biscuits." This exchange is completely transformed into the following unionist debate here reported in a back-translation that tries to reproduce the Italian wordplay pattern: "*First Head:* Stop, we must offer the utmost overture. / *Third Head:* Not at all, because they will otherwise obstruct it. / *First Head:* Let's peck at this question with the shop floor. / *Third Head:* We cannot be floored by the shop floor. / *Second Head:* What then shall be pecked at? / *First Head:* At the mouth. / *Second Head:* I will not peck your mouth! / *First Head:* Oh, who do you think you are? The princess on the pea? / *Second Head:* I don't even like you. / *Third Head:* Enough, we must protect the masses. / *First Head:* I know, more purchasing power, more occupational power, more planning power."

However, Oreste Lionello (1994) himself – as said before, one of the translators of this film script and a Bagaglino comedian – asserts that a movie script that is translated to be dubbed is only 'a fake' and, as such, it should not sound like the original version, but it has just to 'approach' it and have, in the case of humorous texts, as its principal aim to induce laughter in the target audience. This position is opposed by La Polla (1994) who, being a professional dubbing translator, argues instead that the formal, linguistic equivalence has to be preserved in the dubbing translation of a foreign film not only because the film language is closely related to its visual dimension, but also because it would be unethical to use a different wordplay in translation. This, in fact, would disconnect the language of the film from the original socio-cultural context that produced it and that, in the case of comedy, motivates a specific type of humour which represents that specific context.

Indeed, La Polla's remarks introduce the next *Phase 2* of the 'bottom-up' reading/translating strategies that, it is here argued, dubbing translators also need to explore in their process of becoming 'acting translators'.

3.1.3 *Phase 2: bottom-up strategies*

This *Phase 2* regards the acting translators' development of a 'bottom-up', cognitive and re-constructive strategy based on the 'actualization in space' of the sitcom script with its specific conversation patterns of dialogic move and acts. Such reading strategy is expected to have as its main effect to 'defamiliarize' acting translators from the humorous language of the script as they gradually focus on the textual form of the script and its constraints. Indeed, such defamiliarization process would allow acting translators to identify—and then, eventually, to embody—the 'voices' of addressers and addressees which, in the case in point, are represented by the voices of the characters within the script. Also this bottom-up strategy, however, may show its limits when it becomes the only procedure adopted by dubbing translators (cf. Pisek 1997). In fact, scrupulously searching for a formal equivalence in the dubbing translation of a script pattern may lead translators to overlook the pragmatic patterns of humour which, if translated literally, will not yield an equivalent effect in the translated version. This is the case, for instance, of the 1999 American comic movie set in the sixties *Austin Powers—The Spy Who Shagged Me* (Italian title: *Austin Powers—la spia che ci provava*), where the rapid sequences of quips and wordplays are frequently translated literally, thus making the comic effect rely almost always upon the clowning mimicry of the leading actor (Mike Myers). The following short extract is an instance of such bottom-up, 'defamiliarizing' translation, where attention to literal rendering spoils the search for an equivalent comic effect in Italian:

Original English version	***Italian dubbing translation***	***Back-translation into Standard English***
FELICITY: Austin Powers, I presume?	**FELICITY:** Austin Powers, se devo supporre?	**FELICITY:** Austin Powers, if I must presume.
AUSTIN: Powers by name, Powers by reputation.	**AUSTIN:** Sì, Austin di nome, Pop-powers per reputazione.	**AUSTIN:** Yes, Austin by name, Pop-powers by reputation.
FELICITY: Felicity Shagwell, CIA. Shagwell by name, Shag-very-Well by reputation.	**FELICITY:** Felicity Ladà, della CIA. Ladà di nome e La-Dà-molto-bene per reputazione.	**FELICITY:** Felicity Givesitaway, from CIA. Givesitaway by name, Gives-It-Away-very-well by reputation.

In this short exchange it is evident that the Italian dubbing translator has attempted to mitigate the original vulgar connotation of the term "shag" deictically attributed to the female protagonist, Felicity Shagwell - a mitigating strategy already present in the movie title "The spy who shagged me" translated into "La spia che ci provava", that is, in back-translation, "the spy who came on to me". However, the choice to translate her name into "Felicity Ladà", namely, "Felicity Givesitaway" signals the translator's attention to a rendering that could be conventionally acceptable for an Italian audience, predictably of young people, but that defamiliarizes them even from the Italian language as the expression "La-dà-molto-bene" ("Gives-it-away-very-well)—translating the original wordplay "Shag-very-Well"—not only sounds non-natural in Italian, but also ignores the linguistic structure of the pun with the insertion of "very" in the middle of Felicity's surname, which has sense in the original, but becomes a pointless and pragmatically artificial addition in the Italian translation ("La-Dà-molto-bene"—"Gives-it-Away-very-well"). In a classroom workshop on alternative dubbing translations of this comic movie, Italian undergraduate students of English Language and Translation suggested possible renderings of this pun that could work better pragmatically and humorously in Italian without missing the original structure. Some of such literal renderings are: *Felicity:* "Sbattebene di nome, Sbatte-molto-bene per reputazione"; or "Scopabene"; "Scopasuper"; "Scopa-davvero-Bene"; "Scopa-davvero-Super"; "Superbotta"; "Granbotta"; "davvero una Super/Gran Botta". Such alternatives, by playing with Italian vulgar terms that are equivalent to the English "shag" (i.e., the verbs "sbattere", "scopare" and the noun "botta"), succeed in keeping the pun structure as well as the comic effect of the original.

A similar bottom-up, pragmatic translation can be noticed in the rendering of the pun uttered by the male character, the secret agent Austin Power—a James-Bond-like, wannabe sex symbol. His original cue is: "Powers by name, Powers by reputation", hinting at his renowned sexual powers named as his "mojo" throughout the film—another translation challenge. This pun, impossible to be rendered into another language without translating also Austin's surname, went totally missed in the Italian translation where reference was made to the Pop atmosphere pervading the movie—hence the translation "Austin di nome, Pop-powers per reputazione". Possible alternative renderings of the original wordplay emerged during the same classroom workshop, some of them being: "Powers di nome, Sexy-Powers per reputazione", or "Sex-Powers", or "Super-Powers" which creates a parallelism with Felicity's possible surname "Scopasuper / Superbotta". However, the whole film is characterized by defamiliarizing mistranslations. For instance, there is no search for equivalence between the typical jargon terms used in the sixties in Britain (in the Swinging London era) and parallel terms used in the same period in Italy. (Incidentally, there is a strange lack of bilingual dictionaries providing diachronic equivalence in the lexis marking the jargon of a era, or a decade.) For instance, the term "groovy", used as an adjective, but often as an interjection, so trendy only in the sixties in the UK and recurring in this movie, is variously rendered in translation with Italian contemporary—indeed, 'dubbese'—expressions, such as: "grandioso", "fantastico", "divertente", whereas a possible translation consistent with that specific period could be "guappo!", "ganzo!" (as suggested by the parents of students participating in the workshop), or probably "forte!"—though this expression started to be used in a later period in Italy, but now become obsolete. Other interjections of that period, such as "behave!", "smashing", both unfathomably translated as "fallico!", and then "cracky!", translated as "cacchio!", may have deserved a translation more respectful of the period in which the film was set and less defamiliarizing for the audience since they are either expressions that have never been in use (i.e., "fallico"), or are too trivial to be appreciated as comic ("cacchio!"—meaning "damn!", but implying "fuck!"), whereas a large part of the humour in this film is in the revival of the jargon of the sixties. Possible alternative solutions came again from the inter-linguistic diachronic research carried out by the undergraduate students participating in the workshop, who proposed a rendering of "behave!" as "funziona!" ("it works!"), "alla grande!" (an interjection meaning "doing something in a big way"), "e vai!" ("go strong!"). "Smashing", a term popular at that time among drug-addicts, was translated into parallel terms used in Italy in the sixties, such as: "allucinante" ("hallucinating"), "da sballo" ("mind-blowing"), "tossico" ("junkie"), "che trip!" ("what a trip!"). "Cracky" (literally meaning "nutty", "crazy") was rendered into "pazzesco" ("crazy"), "da matti" ("raving"), and into "caspita!" ("crickey!") to respect lip-synchronization in close-up scenes. However, the possible lack of lip-synchronization does not seem to be a problem for the translator who literally rendered the interjection "ouch" as "se volevi ferirmi" ("if you meant to hurt me") and "wow" as "cavoli!" ("crickey!"). As mentioned above, a further translation challenge was offered by the term "mojo", an expression common in the sixties to refer to the male sexual energy metaphorically represented as an "amulet". In the film, Austin Powers has been deprived of his "mojo" by wicked Dr Evil and so he fights throughout the film to repossess it. Austin's moaning about his lost "mojo" often occurs in close-up shots, hence the search for lip-synchronization is crucial. The movie translator tries to solve this problem by providing, once again, another pragmatically unnatural solution—namely, he translates "mojo" into the expression "mai più moscio" ("never again limp"), with "moscio" ("limp") sounding like "mojo" and somewhat helping lip-synchronization (although the dubbing actor has to speed up on uttering the initial "mai più"), but not retaining the sense and conciseness of a word so typical of the sixties. Some students, during the same workshop, did not want to discard completely the translator's solution and thus proposed "anti-moscio" as a better equivalent translation which respected lip-synchronization by replacing an adjective phrase ("mai più moscio") with a noun ("anti-moscio") conveying the sense of an antidote against sexual impotence. Other students of course suggested different solutions, equally respectful of lip-movements by retaining the initial labial sound, as in "botto", "bum-bum" (both meaning "bang", "firework"), "birba", "monello" (both meaning "rascal"), "monile" ("jewel"), "martello" ("hammer"), "motore" ("engine") and finally "amuleto", the literal translation of "mojo".

So far, instances of totally top-down and bottom-up dubbing translation strategies have been analyzed, showing how they fail in rendering equivalent effects in humorous discourse. At this point, some interactive strategies will be explored.

3.1.4 *Phase 3: interactive strategies*

Phase 3 regards the acting translators' realization of an 'interactive', cognitive/affective strategy, based on their physical and emotional embodiment of the 'voices' that they achieve in the script as they make such 'textual voices' interact with their own personal, 'experiential voices'. Such 'interactive strategy' is expected to induce in acting translators a sort of reconciliation of the contrasting sensations of 'familiarity' and 'estrangement' respectively experienced during the previous two phases of script exploration. In addition, this strategy would predictably prompt in acting translators the need to 'embody' their own interpretation of the script and then to communicate it to the other acting translators of the dubbing team who, in their turn, should also feel the need for 'embodying' the script and communicating their own interpretation by inter-acting with the other fellow-translators of the team group. Such a process of embodiment and group interaction should occur 'in space', namely, in a kind of rehearsal room where the acting translators working as a team can actually share their interpretations by 'acting' them out and by 'inter-acting' with the others until an interpretative coherence and convergence on a shared version is achieved. Crucially, the interchange of familiarizing/defamiliarizing stances taking place in such a situation of interpretative interaction should allow acting translators to position themselves variably in relation to their perception of—and response to—their own dramatic representation of the humorous sitcom discourse. An 'acting translator', therefore, does not just look at the linguistic analysis of the script without any presupposition of the subjective performance. On the contrary, acting translators have to 'internalize' humour by 'acting it out' in order to sharpen their own perception as to what the cultural, sociopragmatic and pragmalinguistic features are in the original scripted text which allow them to assume the ways they interpret it. Therefore, acting translators first perform the humorous script by creating their own discourse and its effects—on themselves and on their listeners/observers as well in the team of co-workers—and then they go on reflecting on their own performance and analyzing those effects. In this way, acting translators become intercultural mediators negotiating meanings between the source and the target cultures to achieve an ultimate dubbing translation as 'cross-cultural transmediation'. Indeed, a sitcom-script reading cannot be an activity carried out silently and in isolation, or just in team reading, but it should instead involve groups of acting translators who, together, set up a workshop where imaginative, experiential and physical energies—in relation to the culturally-marked humorous language they explore—are constantly communicated. One of the most suitable situations for learning and realizing this approach to dubbing translation is certainly the translation classroom which, under such circumstances, resembles indeed the rehearsal room. On such basis, the subsequent work of adjusting the dubbing translation to achieve lip-synchronization would account for the translator's first-person experience of script embodiment which would prevent opting for equivalence solutions that would sound 'artificial' to the target audiences.

An excellent example of dubbing translation of a humorous film, which may be considered as the outcome of an interactive strategy of embodiment, is represented by the Italian dubbing translation of the Marx Brothers' movie *Horse Feathers*, superbly carried out by Sergio Jacquier. This is a 1932 mad-cap film set in an American college. Here the translator seems to be drawn in the script, feeling compelled to embody the fast-paced sequence of pun-filled and nonsensical humorous dialogue of this group of slapstick comedians, making their physical and linguistic dynamism contagious for him and, thus, paving the way for the new experience of becoming an 'acting translator'. Jacquier himself (1995: 262) said that the film could be introduced in Italy only by respecting the Marx Brothers' paradoxical and clownish humour which is, however, strongly marked by the American culture of their times. Separating the actors' clowning movements and absurd feats from the humorous quips and socio-cultural references is impossible and this, indeed, is often quite challenging for the translator who has to find witty equivalent solutions in rendering the comic cues into the target language without ignoring the visual dimension of the film (cf. Fuentes-Luque 2003). A case in point is represented by the scene in which Professor Wagstaff (Groucho Marx) wants to make a signed agreement official with a seal that he can't find on his desk and thus keeps saying "Where's the seal?" until Pinky (Harpo Marx) leaves the scene to return immediately afterwards delivering a live seal to his desk. The wordplay with "seal" supported by the image of the live animal was brilliantly rendered by Jacquer with the pun between the verb "focalizzare" ("to focus") and the image of the seal ("foca", in Italian) in the following cue: "Un momento, qua c'è un punto che va focalizzato! Focalizziamo! Focalizzamo! Fo-ca-li-zziamo! ("Let's focus on it!")" prompting the entrance of the seal, the "foca", and thus matching the translated cue with the visual image. A similar physical slapstick scene is the one in which Baravelli (Chico Marx) and Pinky (Harpo Marx) have to force open a door and, at Baravelli question whether Pinky has brought a "pick" with him, the dumb Pinky opens his bag and a small pig walks out of it, to which Baravelli complains with his Italian accent (pronouncing "pig" for "pick"): "That's a no pick [pig]. That's a hog. Don't you know what a hog is?"—"hog" mispronounced like "hug", prompts Pinky to extend his arms to hug Baravelli. This humorous physical/verbal exchange based on misunderstanding due to word assonance is rendered by Jacquier into Italian with a witticism where the assonance quip is absent: "*Baravelli:* Li hai portati i ferri? Dai, lascia il piede di porco. Il piede di porco! Noo, that's ... no, un piede, no un porchetto intero! Puoi aprire le porte?"—"have you brought the tools? Come on, keep the crowbar! (Italian literal translation: "pig's trotter") Noo, no, a trotter, not a whole piglet! Can you open the doors?" to which Pinky extends his arms like an opening door to hug Baravelli. During a physical workshop on dubbing-translation embodiment carried out with undergraduate students of English, a different and effective 'acting translation' of this pun emerged, in which the original visual/verbal association, and also the assonance, were respected in rendering the quip: "*Baravelli:* prendi il piede di porco… il piede di porco! No i maiali! Come entri? Voli? Ma hai le ali?"—"take the crowbar… the crowbar (literally "pig trotter")! Not the pigs! How would you get in? Do you fly? But have you got wings?") to which Pinky opens his arms as if he were opening his wings. The wordplay here is based on the assonance between the word "maiali" ("pigs") and the expression "ma hai le ali?" ("but have you got wings?) which makes this alternative rendering of such a pun quite witty, successful and also respectful of the cue timing.

The following extracts from this same movie represent two additional creative instances of interactive strategies in dubbing translation of humorous discourse. In *Scene 1*, Professor Wagstaff (who has assumed the presidency of Huxley College to take his student son, Frank, away from the 'college widow', a promiscuous young lady his son is infatuated with) asks Frank where he can recruit good football players for the College. Wagstaff dismisses with a pun Frank's reply that they can be met at the speakeasy but that it is unethical for him, as a College President, to go there and, then, at his son's question whether he has further requests, he replies revealing all his disappointment with him.

Scene 1

Original English version	***Italian dubbing translation***	***Back-translation into Standard English***
FRANK (*ZEPPO MARX*): It isn't right for a college to buy football players.	**FRANK:** Ma non puoi andarci, è contro l'etica, non è ammesso che un college compri dei giocatori.	**FRANK:** But you can't go there, it is unethical, it is not allowed that a college should buy players.
WAGSTAFF (*GROUCHO MARX*): It isn't, eh? Well, I'll nip that in the bud. How about coming along and having a nip yourself?	**WAGSTAFF:** Ah no, eh? Berrò l'amaro calice. Beh, vieni anche tu a farti un sorso. O meglio ancora aspetta qui.	**WAGSTAFF:** Ah it isn't, eh? I'll drink the bitter cup. Well, come along, you too, and have a drop of it. Or rather, wait here.
FRANK: Anything further, Father?	**FRANK:** C'è altro oltre a ciò?	**FRANK:** Is there anything further, besides this?
WAGSTAFF: Anything further, Father? That can't be right. Isn't it 'Anything Father, further?' The idea! I married your mother because I wanted children. Imagine my disappointment when you arrived.	**WAGSTAFF:** "C'è altro oltre a ciò?" L'avete sentito? Si dice "che oltre c'è inoltre?" Sarà vero? Io sposai tua madre perché volevo un bambino. Pensa allo strazio quando ti vidi.	**WAGSTAFF:** "Is there anything further, besides this?" Have you heard him? It should be said "What further there is furthermore?" Would that be true? I married your mother because I wanted a child. Think of my agony when I saw you.

In *Scene 2*, Professor Wagstaff arrives at the speakeasy with the intention of recruiting the football players but, at the door slot, Baravelli, a speakeasy worker, asks him the password, thus starting a sequence of gags based on nonsensical associations.

Scene 2

Original English version	***Italian dubbing translation***	***Back-translation into Standard English***
BARAVELLI (*CHICO MARX*): Who are you?	**BARAVELLI:** Chi sei?	**BARAVELLI:** Who are you?
WAGSTAFF *(GROUCHO MARX)*: I'm fine thanks, who are you?	**WAGSTAFF:** Io bene, grazie, e tu?	**WAGSTAFF:** I'm fine, thanks, and you?
BARAVELLI: I'm fine too, but you can't come in unless you give the password.	**BARAVELLI:** Sto buono anch'io ma qua nu se trasse senza parola d'ordine.	**BARAVELLI:** I'm good too, but here one can't come in without password.
WAGSTAFF: Well, what is the password?	**WAGSTAFF:** Qual è la parola d'ordine?	**WAGSTAFF:** What is the pass-word?
BARAVELLI: Aw, no! You gotta tell me. Hey, I tell what I do. I give you three guesses. It's the name of a fish.	**BARAVELLI:** Ah no, tu devi dire a me. Tu prova che indovi-ni, ti do tre volte. E' il nome di uno pesce.	**BARAVELLI:** Ah no, you must tell me. You try to guess, I give you three times. It's the name of a fish.
WAGSTAFF: Is it Mary?	**WAGSTAFF:** E' Marianna?	**WAGSTAFF:** Is it Marianna?
BARAVELLI: Ha-ha. That's-a no fish.	**BARAVELLI:** Ha ha, that's-a no pesce.	**BARAVELLI:** Ha-ha. That's-a no fish.
WAGSTAFF: She isn't, well, she drinks like one. Let me see. Is it sturgeon?	**WAGSTAFF:** No? perché non l'hai vista bere! Aspetta, allora, è l'aguglia?	**WAGSTAFF:** No? That's because you haven't seen her drinking! Wait, then, is it needlefish [*aguglia*]?
BARAVELLI: Hey you crazy! Sturgeon, he's a doctor cuts you open when-a you sick. Now I give you one more chance.	**BARAVELLI:** Ehi, you pazzo! 'A guglia sta n'copp'u campanile, non è pisce! Ora ti do n'altra chance	**BARAVELLI:** Hey, you crazy! The steeple (*guglia*) is on the top of the bell tower, it is not a fish! Now I give you one more chance.
WAGSTAFF: I got it! Haddock!	**WAGSTAFF:** Ci sono! Totano!	**WAGSTAFF:** I got it! Squid! (*totano*)
BARAVELLI: That's-a funny. I gotta haddock, too.	**BARAVELLI:** Tu scherzi! No scherza con il male!	**BARAVELLI:** You must be joking! Don't make light of evil!
WAGSTAFF: What do you take for a haddock?	**WAGSTAFF:** E il male che c'en-tra?	**WAGSTAFF:** And what's that got to do with evil?
BARAVELLI: Well-a, sometimes I take-a aspirin, sometimes I take-a Calamel.	**BARAVELLI:** Bè è una cosa che ci muori se non hai fatto l'anti-totanica.	**BARAVELLI:** Well, it is some-thing you die of if you don't get the anti-tetanus injection. (*anti-tetanica / anti-totanica*)
WAGSTAFF: Say, I'd walk a mile for a Calamel.	**WAGSTAFF:** Bah, io farei l'anti-teutonica.	**WAGSTAFF:** Mah, I'd get the anti-teutonic. (*anti-teutonica*)
BARAVELLI: You mean choco-late calamel. I like that too, but you no guess it. Hey, what-sa matter, you no understand English? You can't come in here unless you say 'swordfish.' Now I'll give you one more guess.	**BARAVELLI:** Tu non sai che pisci pigghiare. Ehi, what's the matter? Tu non capisci English? Non entri qua se non dici 'pisci-spada'. Indovina n'altra volta.	**BARAVELLI:** You are at a loss what to do (literally: *you don't know what fish to choose*). Hey, what's the matter (*in English*)? Don't you understand English? You can't get in if you don't say 'swordfish'. Try to guess again.
WAGSTAFF: (*to himself:* Swordfish. Swordfish) I think I got it. Is it 'swordfish'?	**WAGSTAFF:** (*A sé stesso:* Pescespada... pescespada...*)* ah, forse ci sono: è 'pescespada'?	**WAGSTAFF:** (*to himself:* Swordfish... swordfish) Ah, maybe I got it. Is it 'swordfish'?
BARAVELLI: Hah! That's-a it! You guess it!	**BARAVELLI:** Ah, that's-a it! Hai indovinato!	**BARAVELLI:** Hah! That's-a it! You guess it!

Scene 1 represents a typical example of incoherent dialogue where no predictable schema or script are accounted for since the pattern of this exchange is almost solely based on language quips made of meaningless labial/dental fricative alliterations, vowel assonance and word inversions ("*Frank:* Anything further, Father?—*Wagstaff:* Anything Father, further?"). Such sound-centred nonsense has been reproduced also in Jacquier's translation, obviously by opting for a different alliterative pattern of palatal fricatives and /ltr/ consonant clusters in a chiasmus structure ("*Frank:* c'è altro oltre a ciò? - *Wagstaff:* Che oltre c'è inoltre?"). And yet, a possible logical consistency was detected in the course of a physical embodiment workshop by the same group of students as 'acting translators' who, in rehearsing this exchange as a group felt 'bodily' and 'emotionally' that something 'further' might be hidden behind these cues and thus, by applying an interactive top-down/bottom-up strategy came to connect *(1)* Professor Wagstaff's initial alliterative pun and *(2)* his subsequent expression of disappointment at the birth of his son. The covert schema that the workshop revealed was in fact concerned with Wagstaff's doubting his paternity of Frank. Consequently, the following alternative translations were devised (alliterative patterns are emphasised):

Original English version	***Italian dubbing translation***	***Back-translation into Standard English***
(1)	*(1a)*	*(1a)*
FRANK: Anything further, Father?	**FRANK:** C'è di **più**, **p**adre?	**FRANK:** Is there anything more, father?
WAGSTAFF: Anything further, Father? That can't be right. Isn't it 'Anything Father, further?'	**WAGSTAFF:** "C'è di più, padre?" Non è per caso che "c'è più di un padre?"	**WAGSTAFF:** "Is there anything more, father?" Isn't that, by any chance, that "there's more than one father?"
	(1b)	*(1b)*
	FRANK: Nient'altro di **più**, **pap***à*?	**FRANK:** Anything else, dad?
	WAGSTAFF: "Nient'altro di più, papà?" Non vorrai dire "un altro papà in più?"	**WAGSTAFF:** "Anything further, dad?" Wouldn't you say "a further father?"
(2)	*(2)*	*(2)*
The idea! I married your mother because I wanted children. Imagine my disappointment when you arrived.	Che idea! Io sposai tua madre perché volevo un bambino. Immagina il mio disappunto quando arrivasti.	What an idea! I married your mother because I wanted a child. Imagine my disappointment when you arrived.

Another possible coherent schema underlying the exchange was also identified during the same workshop, connecting Wagstaff's disappointment with his son with the fact that Frank didn't support his father's believes, initiatives and actions. Hence the following alternative translation likewise respecting the alliterative pattern of the original pun:

Original English version	*Italian dubbing translation*	*Back-translation into Standard English*
(1)	*(1c)*	*(1c)*
FRANK: Anything further, Father?	**FRANK:** Va **b**ene così, **b**a**bb**o?	**FRANK:** Is it alright like this, daddy?
WAGSTAFF: Anything further, Father? That can't be right. Isn't it 'Anything Father, further?'	**WAGSTAFF:** "Va **b**ene così, **b**a**bb**o?" Non va bene! Perché non "babbo così vai bene?"	**WAGSTAFF:** "Is it alright like this, daddy?" That can't be right. Why not "daddy you're alright like this?"

Scene 2 (the 'password scene') is another instance of madcap scene based on puns and displaced cross-references. In the original version Baravelli's misunderstandings stem not simply from his naiveté, but precisely from his lack of proficiency in the English language. He is in fact represented as an Italo-American who speaks with a strong Italian accent and often intersperses what he says with Italian expressions marked by the typical Southern accent of the early Italian immigrants in the US. His difficulty in processing the meaning of American words by their standard sound is the main cause of misunderstanding. In fact, he misinterprets the fish names that Wagstaff pronounces in trying to guess the password by something else—hence "sturgeon" is misunderstood as "surgeon", "haddock" as "headache", prompting a sequence of misapprehension gags with Wagstaff. Conversely, in Jacquier's dubbing translation, Baravelli speaks broken Italian, with a recognizably Neapolitan accent, interspersed with American expressions, and it is precisely this lack of proficiency in standard Italian that makes him misunderstand by assonance the meaning of words—hence "aguglia" ("needlefish") is misunderstood as "guglia" ("steeple"), and "totano" ("squid") as "tetano" ("tetanus"), prompting Wagstaff's pun on "anti-tetanica/anti-teutonica" ("anti-tetanus/anti-teutonic" vaccine) marked by an evident racist humorous-disparagement pattern. In the course of the above-mentioned dubbing-translation workshop, undergraduate students were engaged on a top-down drama improvisation sessions on this 'password scene' which produced some valid bottom-up translation alternatives to the one proposed by Jacquier. Sketches were improvised on the assonance between "cefalo" ("grey mullet") and "cefalea" ("headache"); "cernia" ("gropper") and "ernia" ("hernia"); "aringa" ("herring") and "arringa" ("harangue"); and finally "occhiata" ("saddled bream") and "occhiata" ("glance"—which Wagstaff tries to take at the speakseasy from the door slot).

So far, some crucial strategies of top-don/bottom-up discourse processing have been introduced with reference to the discourse of humour. At this point, a further analytical method of conversation analysis will be explored as it represents an important approach that an acting translator needs to know in theory and apply in practice.

3.1.5 *Cognitive/affective variables in the applications of the Acting Translator Model*

In the context of the three phases outlined above, the conversational structure of the humorous language in a sitcom will be now explored from the point of view of the translators who have also to cope with the experiential and cross-cultural challenges that the interpretation and translation of such a language pose to them. The specific purpose of this approach is to allow dubbing translators to make the humorous sitcom script their own through dramatic interpretation so as to access, authenticate, and understand it better. More specifically, the focus shall be on *(a)* how acting translators manage to embody the 'textual voices' achieved in the sitcom script within the contexts of the source and target languages and cultures, and *(b)* how a team of acting translators eventually achieve a shared pragmatic and interactive embodiment of a humorous discourse in an actual space of dramatic sitcom representation. It will be also demonstrated that, although acting translators are here encouraged to act within imaginary, virtual situations, they share true feelings, thoughts, actions and re-actions to the humorous language. This is considered as an integral part of the communicative contexts generated by the interaction between the translators' imagination and the sitcom scripted text. The aim is to find out how the dubbing translator's cognitive/affective process of 'acting sitcom humour out' can be influenced by the following variables:

(a) the script itself—which the translator analyzes through the activation of purely bottom-up reading strategies as s/he focuses on the textual form;

(b) the author's meanings—which the translator believes s/he achieves from what s/he assumes the author's psycho-cultural schemata are;

(c) external factors—which are: different real socio-cultural contexts and situations in which interpretation and translation take place (objective stance); different virtual contexts dependent on individual imagination and psycho-cultural schemata (subjective stance); different virtual situations created by the team of acting translators while dramatically inter-acting and interpreting the humorous language of the script, also by improvising on it (collective stance). This is indeed a way to explore how that same sitcom language would work in physical contexts which can be different from the one suggested in the script, thus creating 'parallel scripts' to the original one;

(d) external ideas—which are achieved through the acting translators' top-down activation and 'public' disclosure of their own cognitive/affective schemata while physically interacting either with the sitcom script, or with the other acting translators' interpretation of it. In such collective context, the acting translator's first/second/third-person positioning in relation to the dramatic representation of humorous lan-

guage is crucial to the establishment of degrees of detachment and involvement in the stances s/he alternatively—or simultaneously—takes during the group interaction;

(e) internal motivations of the acting translator—which become conscious through the top-down 'private' physical, experiential and intellectual investment of the acting translator's own individual personality within the collective experience of sitcom dramatization.

These variables shall be investigated in relation to the acting translators' exploration of the sitcom conversation structure which represents the topic of the next section.

3.2 Conversation Analysis of Sitcom Scripts

3.2.1 *Sitcom dialogic patterns: reassessing conventional CA models*

In this section, a cross-cultural investigation will be carried out on the conversation patterns that, in Part Two of this book, will be identified in a number of episode-scripts from American sitcoms in their original English language as well as in their respective Italian dubbing translations. Here, more specifically, the methodological approach will be pointed out, to be subsequently applied to the case studies in the last three chapters of the book. One of the primary pedagogic objectives of the contrastive conversation analysis is to guide translation students not only to activate top-down, schema-based strategies of creative 'experiential embodiment', which would disregard the script structure in both versions of a sitcom, but to explore also more exacting and 'text-based' bottom-up processes of discourse analysis with the purpose of analyzing the conversation patterns of the selected sitcom scripts. In this section, the exploration shall be illustrated by focusing on four relevant speech acts—namely, expressions of 'requests', 'gratitude', 'complaints' and 'apologies' —which are here assumed to represent the 'structural backbone' of an American sitcom episode. Indeed, sitcom episodes normally start with a character advancing a 'request' which, when fulfilled by another character, is followed by an expression of 'gratitude'. Gratitude, however, is usually ensued by disappointment at the character's realization that the outcome of his/her request is not exactly the expected one. This is typically a misinterpretation of reality by the character who, the moment s/he realizes that s/he is wrong, immediately expresses his 'apologies' to the other 'offended' character. This is specifically reflected in the episodes from the five sitcoms selected for the analysis, representing instances of a novel Revelation/Negotiation pattern of humour which developed in the American sitcoms at the turn of the century as an adaptation of the conventional Arousal/Safety pattern to fit in the new social and conversational dynamics occurring among characters as members of unconventional and innovative family units—as it will be explored in-depth in Part Two of this book. Furthermore, because the visual dimension of the sitcom is the same in both the original and the translated script versions, this speech-act scheme is assumed to provide a kind of framework allowing acting translators to explore both versions by activating top-down improvisation strategies as well as a bottom-up conversation analysis so as to identify and 'embody' discourse similarities and differences in the American-English and Italian culture-bound use of humorous language, with reference to the pattern of such speech acts. Indeed, since translators are 'intercultural mediators', they are therefore expected to develop precise cross-cultural schematic representations of the social contexts informing the speech-act dynamics in the languages they deal with (cf. Bialystok 1996). Therefore, after a phase of top-down improvisation, a return to a more careful, bottom-up analysis of the script structure is therefore advocated here as acting translators come to focus on the speech-act pattern in the source and, subsequently, in the target versions of the sitcom scripts. To this purpose, two models of Conversation Analysis (CA) are here considered as guidelines for a rigorous analysis of the sitcom humorous conversation structure. The objective is to make acting translators reflect on the humorous construction of the dialogue not only at a linguistic level, but also at a cognitive, socio-cultural one. The two models taken into account are the Structuralist and the Ethnomethodological Models, both involving a discourse analysis that is particularly relevant to the study of spoken-discourse interaction as it is constructed and negotiated between participants. This would make dubbing translators aware of the socio-cultural conventions within which oral communication is carried out. In applying these two models of conversation to the analysis of sitcom dialogues it is crucial to point out that both of them were not originally devised for analyzing 'fictional', artificially-created conversations, as sitcom dialogues are, insofar as the Structuralist model proposes a frame for the analysis of naturally-occurring language, whereas the Ethnomethodological one enquires into spontaneous conversation as it unfolds in time. Despite the fact that they specifically focus on natural conversation, both models have however been criticized for keeping a too rigid, ethnocentric perspective on spoken interaction accounting for well-defined, culture-specific scripts. Hence the importance to explore the extent to which these two approaches to CA—respectively defined as the UK Structuralist Model and the US Ethnomethodological Model—are relevant to the cross-cultural analysis of sitcom conversation in its original and translated versions, or rather they need to be revised in the light of the humorous language of the sitcom genre in general, and of the specific 'new-family dynamics' in the American sitcoms under analysis in particular.

3.2.2 *The Structuralist Model of Conversation Analysis applied to sitcom scripts*

The UK Model of Conversation Analysis, introduced by a team of British text grammarians known as the Birmingham School of Discourse Analysis (Sinclair and Coulthard 1975; Coulthard and Montgomery 1981; Stubbs 1983; Coulthard and Brazil 1992), offers a frame for discourse analysis to be applied to naturally-occurring conversation which is regarded not as a randomly unfolding exchange, but as a type of discourse following pre-established patterns which, once identified, would greatly facilitate the analysts in their process of interpreting interactions. Conversely, the US Model of Conversation Analysis, developed by a group of American Ethnomethodologists (Firth 1957; Gumperz and Hymes 1964; Sachs *et al.* 1974), is grounded on the practice of collecting data of naturally-occurring conversations by tape-recording them, transcribing them into protocols, and then analyzing conversation transcriptions without imposing any rigid interpretative frame upon them. The comparison between the two models makes it evident the reason why the UK Model, which is based on Halliday's Systemic-Functional Grammar (cf. Halliday 1994), is conventionally ranked among the theories of Text Grammar, rather than of Discourse Pragmatics. When Sinclair and Coulthard (1975) first elaborated it—by applying it to the 'scripted' dialogue of classroom interaction before extending it to almost all areas of spoken conversation—they established two crucial levels of conversation pattern—namely, the level of 'Situation' (meant as social conventions, environment, and participants' shared knowledge and experience) and the level of 'Tactics' (meant as syntagmatically interdependent patterns of discourse). Upon these two levels, Sinclair and Coulthard (*ibidem*) grounded their conversation analysis on a predictable structure determining what participants consider permissible in a 'socially-scripted' spoken interaction. Such a conversational structure takes the form of a ranking frame within which every unit of each rank is composed by elements of the next smaller rank according to the following chain: Situation → Interaction → Transaction → Exchange → Move → Act. In this Structuralist CA Model, the smallest unit of discourse structure is therefore the 'Act'. Acts may be represented by clauses or single words, but they should not be confused with the 'pragmatic acts' in Speech-Act Theory (to be examined later in this chapter). In fact, Acts in this CA Model are not based on the speaker's intention, but they just mark a fixed position in a conventionally scripted discourse frame. Applied to a typical American sitcom script, such fixed position in the script could actually fit some types of humorous pattern, such as the Arousal/Safety or the Disparagement ones which account for a predictable conversation structure. In applying the UK model of conversation analysis, the most frequent types of Acts in sitcom discourse frames are the ones that follow (from Guido 2004: 343-344), here marked by their conventional use in Arousal (A), Safety (S), and Disparagement (D) humorous patterns:

(a) Marker. This (S)-Act is actualized by expressions such as: "Well/Okay/Good/Right/Alright", relieving the tension in Arousal/Safety patterns of humour and also marking the boundary of an Exchange by constituting the *Head* (or *Head Act*) of a Framing Move.

(b) Starter. This (A)-Act is realized by a statement/question/command triggering a state of tension within an Arousal/Safety pattern. It occurs in Opening Moves to 'provide information about' / 'direct attention to' some particular topic. It functions as *Pre-Head.*

(c) Elicitation. This is an (A)-Act realized by a question provoking 'tension arousal' and requesting an answer. It functions as *Head* in an Opening Move.

(d) Check. This (S)-Act is actualized by a series of questions requesting polar answers ("yes/no" answers) such as: "Finished?" "Ready?" or "Have you got problems/difficulties?", "Can you see/hear?", etc., usually aimed at mitigating tension.

(e) Directive. This (A)-Act is performed by a command, conventionally realized by an Imperative triggering tension, and requesting a non-linguistic response – i.e., the required action.

(f) Informative. This (D)-Act is realized by a statement, and its objective is to provide information, often aimed at humorous disparagement in some sitcom scripts.

(g) Prompt. This is an (A)-Act aimed at reinforcing Directive and Elicitation Acts, and it is realized by expressions like "Go on/Have a go/Come on/Quickly". Its use in humorous Arousal/Safety patterns is often to trigger tension.

(h) Clue. This (D)-Act is actualized by a statement, a command, or a question, and its aim is to provide additional information in a *Post-Head* position usually reinforcing a disparagement pattern of humour.

(i) Cue. This (A)-Act is realized by expressions like "Hands up!/Don't call out!", etc., its function being that of evoking an appropriate bid and generating anxiety arousal.

(j) Bid. This is an (A)-Act that signals the speaker's will to contribute to discourse, and it is realized by expressions like: "Jim!/Sir!/Miss!/Raise your hands!", etc. often initiating situations of humorous tension.

(k) Nomination. This (A)-Act is actualized by names (e.g., "Jim", "You", "Yes, Mary") or by more general expressions (e.g. "anybody"), used to call on, or give permission to the nominated person to contribute to the conversation. Also in this case, a 'nomination' may be used as a tension trigger.

(l) Acknowledge. This (S)-Act is performed by means of expressions like: "Yes/Okay/Wow/mmhm", as well as by means of non-verbal expressions. The aim is to show that what was just said has been understood. This Act occurs as either *Pre-Head* or *Head* in Answering Moves and it

functions as a 'safety' marker relieving tension.

(m) Reply. This (A)-Act is realized by a statement, a question, or nods, to provide an appropriate response to an Elicitation Act, often increasing tension in an Arousal/Safety pattern of humour. It occurs as *Head* in Answering moves.

(n) React. This has been categorized as a non-linguistic (A)-Act, providing an appropriate behaviour in reply to a Directive Act frequently enhancing tense situations through slapstick to provoke a humorous response.

(o) Comment. This (D)-Act is realized by a statement or a tag question aimed at exemplifying, expanding, justifying, or providing additional information frequently of a humorous disparagement kind. It is subordinated to the Head.

(p) Accept. This is an (S)-Act accomplished by expressions like: "Yes/No/Good/Fine" in *Pre-Head* position, showing that the participant in conversation has understood the correct information, thus creating a sense of relief in a comic Arousal/Safety pattern.

(q) Evaluate. This (D)-Act expresses an evaluation of what has been said, and it is realized by a statement, a tag question, or also expressions like: "Interesting!" and often employed in humorous disparagement.

(r) Silent Stress. This is an (A)-Act realized by a pause often aimed at creating disconcerting tension in Arousal/Safety patterns of humour, and it is aimed at framing Moves as Qualifier.

(s) Loop. This (A)-Act returns to the point before giving an answer, and it is signalled by expressions like: "Pardon?", "Say it again?" causing confusion and tension.

(t) Conclusion. This (S)-Act is meant to provide a summary of what has been said or done. It is signalled by expressions like: "So, what we've been doing is..." and it is frequently employed to mark a sense of safety and relief after tension.

These conversational Acts in the Structuralist CA Model are to be viewed as part of larger conversational units, i.e., the Moves. A 'Move' is the second smallest unit of the discourse structure in the Conversation Frames proposed by Sinclair and Coulthard (1975), Burton (1980), and Stenstrom (1994), and it corresponds to the basic functional unit of discourse, providing a primary structure to conversation. As such, it is realized by a Head Act, with optional Starter, Pre-Head, and Post-Head Acts. The basic Move types in a sitcom structure may be considered in the ones that are reported below and that may represent an actual framework for acting translators' top-down improvisation sessions aimed at the creation of parallel scripts to the original one. This top-down phase, however, has to be followed by a bottom-up one during which the pattern of conversation moves in a sitcom script will guide the acting translators to focus on the actual structure of the original humorous dialogue in order to search for equivalent choices in the target language that would sound 'natural', and not 'artificial' in the dubbing translation. Here are some frequent moves in sitcom scripts (from Guido 2004: 344-345) that, once revised in terms of Arousal/Safety and Disparagement humorous structures can help the dubbing translator understand the physical, 'embodied' pattern of the sitcom dialogue under analysis:

(a) Opening. This is the Move by which a participant initiates an exchange.

(b) Summoning. This Move is activated in order to attract the listener's attention, often marking an 'arousal' exchange.

(c) Backchannel. This Move signals the listener's attention and it is frequently employed to relieve tension and create a sense of 'safety' in the exchange.

(d) Eliciting. This Move is meant to provoke, stimulate, and induce a response and is often the cause of tension.

(i) Answering. This Move provides a response to a question which may be either of an 'arousal' or of a 'safety' type. Sometimes it can represent a 'humorous disparagement' marker.

(f) Informing. This is a Move by which information is provided, frequently involving 'humorous disparagement'.

(g) Focusing. This is a Move by which concentration on something/somebody is solicited. Again, this is often employed in 'humorous disparagement' patterns of comic discourse.

(h) Supporting. This Move is meant to uphold a previous statement. It is usually employed to emphasize a situation of tension in an 'Arousal/Safety' pattern.

(i) Challenging. This Move asks for or defies a previous statement arousing tension.

(j) Acknowledging. This Move recognizes and accepts a previous statement, thus marking relief and a sense of 'safety' after tension.

(k) Repairing. This Move is meant to hold up the exchange and, thus, it is again a 'safety' marker in humorous discourse.

(l) Directing. This Move requests an action and is often the cause of a state of tension.

(m) Closing. This is the Move by which a participant ends an exchange and often determines a sense of relief.

(n) Re-opening. This Move is employed to avoid concluding the exchange and thus it frequently marks a new state of tension.

Moves have many similarities with the pragmatic notion of Speech Acts insofar as Answering, Eliciting, Informing, and Directing Moves imply the use of specific Speech Acts (Searle 1969), whereas Framing, Opening, and Acknowledging Moves are metalinguistic Speech Acts employed to frame discourse. Challenging and Repairing are Moves that are frequently identified in the Speech-Act structure of Humour, in particular of an Arousal/Safety type, and they typically frame sitcom conversation Exchanges. An 'Exchange' represents a minimal group of

Moves (cf. Coulthard and Brazil 1992), specifically consisting of Initiating, Responding and Follow-up Moves. In Sinclair and Coulthard's (1975) Model, Exchanges are divided into two basic types: Organizational and Conversational Exchanges. An Organizational Exchange can be further divided into Boundary (constituted by Framing Moves) and Structuring Exchanges (constituted by Opening Moves). A Conversational Exchange, on the other hand, can be divided into Elicit, Inform and Direct Exchanges. Finally, there are two more types of Exchanges, Clarify and Repeat, which are bound to the conventional Exchange and are always initiated by an Eliciting Move. Both Organizational and Conversational Exchanges are crucial in the construction of a sitcom script. Even more important for the building of a sitcom story are the further rank units introduced by this UK Model (*ibidem*) in its Conversation Frame. One of them is the 'Transaction', which corresponds to a single topic-unit and consists of a Preliminary Exchange, a sequence of one or more Medial Exchanges, and an optional Terminal Exchange. The other one is the 'Interaction', which is the largest unit of this Conversation Frame consisting of a sequence of Transactions. For example, in a sitcom frame, the fact that a misunderstanding will precede a conflict, and a challenge will be followed by a repair act has to do with the comic structure of the represented situation informing the humorous language of the sitcom dialogues.

However, the examples of sitcom dialogues brought in support of this Model are all of a ritualistic kind, typical of the sitcom generic structure, which makes it easy for external participants (i.e., the audience) to predict the next Move. Prediction, in this case, is not determined by a conformity to the expected Moves in naturally-occurring conversations in everyday situations. Humour, indeed, typically requires a deviation from the common and shared socio-pragmatic rules of conversation since, as discussed in Chapter 1, it is grounded on the recognition of two simultaneous scripts, one that the audience expects and another that is unexpected and, thus, would be interpreted as an expression of humorous insubordination, ignorance, or as a sign that the participant (the sitcom character) is unaware of the double implications of his/her actions and words, as it often happens in miscommunication. In this sense, the UK Model may represent a useful tool for understanding the sitcom opposite and interacting scripts, but also the reasons why the interactions taking place in its script are perceived by sitcom participants (namely, the interacting characters, on the one hand, and the same characters interacting with the audience on the other) either as effective, collaborative, fair, or rather as challenging, disruptive and unfair until a Repair Move is enacted to trigger a sense of Relief that re-establishes a socio-emotional order. This Model, therefore, may be adopted by the conversation analyst and the translator who intend to focus on how a sitcom interaction is often managed in such a way as to maintain existing power structures and social differences by first challenging them and then reasserting them by means of a humorous sense of 'safety' (in an Arousal/Safety pattern of humour) at having escaped a stressful condition. However, one limitation of this Model is represented by the fact that it codes Acts and Moves only in terms of their effect on the discourse frame, not on the participants in that discourse (Francis and Hunston 1992). This, in many ways, represents the limit of Halliday's (1994) Functional Grammar applied to the analysis of discourse structure which, by advancing the possibility of putting an 'ordering frame' on the chaos of situational contexts of interactions, sets as its analytical focus to "describe the choices that are available to interlocutors at different points in the discourse process in the form of systems operating at different places in the discourse structure." (Tsui 1989a: 163). But this of course does not work in comic interactions where conventional scripts are constantly challenged for humorous effects. An example is represented by one participant's use of an 'indirect speech act' (cf. Searle 1975) in a socially scripted situation which is misinterpreted by the other participant who, instead, applies a different, unexpected script to the same situation:

(1) Expected script:
A: Doctor: Can you say ninety-nine?
B: Patient: (*says 'ninety-nine'*)

(2) Unexpected script:
A: Doctor: Can you say ninety-nine?
B: Patient: Sure.

Clearly, here A's Move is not an Elicitation (i.e., the Doctor's request for information about the Patient's 'ability to pronounce a phrase, maybe a tongue-twister') but it functions as a Directive (i.e., the Doctor's request for the Patient's verbal action of 'saying ninety-nine to check the functioning of his lungs'). However, in *(2)*, this Move distinction is not so clear since A's utterance functions both as an Elicitation (which is satisfied by B's answer supplying the required information) and a Directive (which is satisfied by B's action). On the one hand, therefore, in this Structuralist Model of Conversation each utterance may be classified in terms of its effect on the immediately following utterances. On the other hand, however, such a Model is largely presented—according to Roberts *et al.* (1992: 82)—as being about white, healthy, sexually straight, usually western and often middle-class speakers who are the participants in the conversations that have exemplified this model. In this way, it would deny precisely one of the most relevant characteristics of Halliday's Systemic-Functional Model of language analysis, which is the possibility of connecting language systems to semiotic cultural systems (cf. Fawcett *et al.* 1988). But it is precisely for this reason that it can describe the deviations from the conversation norms typical of sitcom humour. If, for instance, the Doctor's question "Can you say ninety-nine?" were addressed, for instance, to a dumb person who is disappointed because he cannot reply, or to a stammerer who stutters as he says the words, or to a foreigner who cannot understand the language, or even a monk who is observing the rule of silence, then the Doctor's utterance might be interpreted by the Patient as a request for information about the Patient's 'ability', or 'permission' to utter the phrase, or rather a Directive Move ignoring the patient's handicap, hence provoking hilarity in the viewers.

A conversation structure as the one outlined so far in relation to the UK Model of CA could be very useful to acting translators throughout the three phases of their sitcom-script exploration. Indeed, acting translators should keep in mind this conversation structure of Moves and Acts every time they start improvising on the sitcom script during the top-down phase. For instance, they may accomplish the creative task of *(a)* considering only the title, or the mere synopsis of a sitcom episode, *(b)* shaping the possible sequence of Acts and Moves that may structure the relevant episode script, and then *(c)* improvising possible dialogues upon such conversational sequence, being already acquainted with the personality of the sitcom characters. This top-down improvisation task requires from acting translators not only the physical embodiment of characters and situations, but also an actual challenge of the possible expected situational script since they need to apply the typical humorous structure of the two simultaneous (expected/unexpected) scripts, the unexpected script challenging the expected one and thus triggering laughter. Top-down improvisation sessions on a sitcom script would require from the acting translators remarkable skills as stand-up comedians, which is not so implausible as this should be an essential ability that a dubbing translator of comedy movies has to possess. However, if such top-down skills are regarded as necessary, they are not the only ones that the acting translator need to develop. In fact, once having improvised on the script to familiarize with comic situations and characters, during the bottom-up phase of their sitcom exploration, acting translators should then return to the original conversation structure of the script to find out an equivalent rendering of its humorous pattern into the target language. Finally, during the third, interactive phase, acting translators working together as a team on the dubbing translation of a sitcom can enact in group both the original and the translated versions to see if the latter, they have devised, does sound 'natural' and, thus, structurally and pragmatically 'equivalent' in the target language and culture.

As introduced at the beginning of this section, the structural UK model of conversation analysis is not the only model to be taken into consideration. In fact, also the US model of CA has interesting patterns that are relevant to sitcom analysis and translation.

3.2.3 *The Ethnomethodological Model of Conversation Analysis applied to sitcom scripts*

A more sophisticated way to analyze conversation by connecting language to semiotic, socio-cultural and pragmalinguistic systems is the strategy systematically explored by the so-called US Model of Conversation Analysis, the other trend in CA grounded on Ethnomethodology, meant as the study of how people use their knowledge to make sense of the social situations they are involved in (cf. Garfinkel 1967). Accordingly, this Model analyzes the structure of conversation by setting it within the specific sociolinguistic environments and behaviours in which it occurs, on the assumption that they are crucial in determining its meaning. This explains why this kind of analysis can also be applied successfully to the analysis of sitcom scripts and can also be useful in sitcom dubbing translation, insofar as it does not impose any pre-established interpretation frame on conversation as in the UK model of CA. In fact, this Ethnomethodological Model identifies conversational rules that participants apply in order to interact within the circumstances they find themselves in. Such rules are represented, on the one hand, by 'turn-taking' norms regulating the end of one participant's turn to speak in a conversation and the beginning of another participant's turn. Hence, when one participant 'A' speaks and then stops, another one, 'B', starts speaking and then stops. This turn-taking mechanism, in which speakers hold or pass the floor, produces the conversation stream A-B-A-B-A which is shared by all societies, although it may crucially vary in timing and overlapping segments across cultures and languages (Sacks *et al.* 1974), often producing misunderstandings in both intercultural communication (Guido 2008), as well as in dubbing translation when turn-taking timing, which is unfamiliar to the target pragmalinguistic culture, has to be retained in dubbing for reasons of lip-and-image synchronization. On the other hand, conversational rules are determined by 'adjacency pairs', which indicate a kind of turn alternation composed by two utterances, or dialogue cues, which are 'adjacent', since they are produced by different speakers, ordered as 'first cue' and 'second cue', and connected in such a way as that the second cue is in response to the first one. The second cue, however, can be of two types: an 'expected', or 'preferred' response, and an 'unexpected', or 'dispreferred' one. Usually a response is perceived as 'preferred' because it occurs more frequently in the socio-cultural environment in which the conversation takes place. Conversely, a response is perceived as 'dispreferred' because it is socio-culturally less common or less accepted. Predictably, the structure of adjacency pairs in a sitcom is mostly based on dispreferred responses deliberately devised for humorous effects, mainly of an Arousal/Safety type. An instance of adjacency pairs in Conversation Analysis (Levinson 1983) may, therefore, be described as follows:

Speaker A's First Cue	*Speaker B's Second Cue: Preferred*	*Speaker B's Second Cue: Dispreferred*
Offer	Acceptance	Refusal
Assessment	Agreement	Disagreement
Blame	Denial	Admission
Question	Expected Answer	Unexpected Answer

Sometimes, other 'insertion sequences' are embedded between these adjacency-pair sequences (Schegloff 1972), like the 'Hold/Accept' one, but also 'pre-sequences' represent other possible insertions of apparently nonessential turns in conversation (cf. Merritt 1976: 337; Atkinson 1979). Furthermore, the notion of 'Move' in Ethnomethodological Conversation Analysis is different from the one developed by the analysts of Structuralist CA frames examined above. For the ethnomethodologists, a Move is a stretch of talk that forms a unit in a functional relation to the conversation of which it is a part (cf. Labov 1972; Edmonson 1981). In this sense, Moves may coincide with adjacency pairs (Accept, Refuse, Agree, Disagree, Deny, Admit, Yes/No Answer, etc.). Goffman (1981), Moerman (1988), and Tsui (1989b), however, identify other types of Conversational Moves marking the socio-cultural structure of a conversation insofar as they directly relate to the sociopragmatic dimension of the exchange. These Moves are: Continuer, Downgrade, Misplacement Marker, Newsmark, Oh-Receipt, Passing Turn, Rejection Finalizer, Try-Marker, Upgrade. The following description of Ethnomethodological Moves (Guido 2004: 449-350) illustrates their possible roles in marking conversational turns in sitcom scripts:

(a) Continuer. This is a Move indicating that the speaker allows the other participant to continue holding the floor with his/her talk, by uttering expressions like: "uh hum"; "mmhm"; "yeah". This Move often represents a joke prompt when, at the end of the speaker's 'confident' cue after having being encouraged to continue his/her talk, the listener may in his/her turn reveal with a pun that s/he has misunderstood what the other participant has been saying.

(b) Downgrade. This Move is employed to weaken or mitigate a previous utterance (e.g., a request) in order to make it more acceptable (Moerman 1988: 164-165). This is a typical sitcom strategy aimed at inducing the other participants in a conversation to accept a point of view which was previously considered as unacceptable and that shall subsequently turn out to be mischievous.

(c) Misplacement Marker. This Move is used to indicate that a conversation turn is out of place (Tsui 1989b: 558-559) and it is often employed in sitcom scripts as an 'arousal' marker aimed at triggering a reaction of protest in the other participant whose talk was abruptly cut off.

(d) Newsmark. This is a Move that encourages further talk about a

previous utterance, considering its content as new information. Expressions of disbelief, like: "you don't say", or "you are kidding", usually signal this Move often employed for 'tall tales' recounted by sitcom characters for comic effects.

(e) Oh-Receipt. This is a Move introduced by the expression "oh", that signals the speaker's achievement of new information which modifies his/her previous expectation or knowledge. This is a Move performed by the sitcom character playing 'the trickster' to other 'innocent' participants in the humorous conversation who, in turn, accept the new information with a sense of surprise.

(f) Passing Turn. This Move indicates that the speaker has nothing further to say and so s/he passes the floor to another participant by uttering an expression such as "Okay", or "Alright". (Levinson 1983: 317).

(g) Rejection Finalizer. This Move marks the speaker's acceptance of a rejection (e.g., of an offer) by another participant. In this case, the conclusive "Okay" in the last turn is to be interpreted as a rejection finalizer (Tsui 1989b: 556).

(h) Try-Marker. This Move indicates the speaker's test to his/her addressee to assess whether s/he has recognized a referent (Moerman 1988: 35). A Try-Marker Move may be signalled by a rising intonation at the end of an utterance.

(i) Upgrade. This Move is intended to emphasize what has been previously said—e.g.: "Get in; the water's warm." (Moerman 1988: 76-77). In sitcom scripts, an 'upgrade move' is often the trigger of a pun introducing new, unexpected and incongruent information that prompts laughter in the audience.

By applying these Ethnomethodological Moves, a conversation analyst can therefore infer the private reasoning processes of the participants in a conversation from the Moves they employ in their joint construction of the interaction. That is why such Moves are particularly useful for the understanding of the dynamics of a sitcom conversation in its continuous breaking of the expected interactional conventions, especially when they are referred to scripted social settings, such as a courtroom, a restaurant, or doctor-patient/service-client relationships—to mention only some examples. In such settings, the analyst-translator can indeed realize how judgements about people crucially depend on what they say in interaction—namely, on the extent to which they conform to, or deviate from, the expected dialogic conventions. However, one of the risks of this approach is to take for granted that the reasoning processes interpreted by the analyst are actually the same as those used by the participants in the interaction. In situations of intercultural communication—like the one involved in the search for a pragmatic equivalence in the dubbing translation of a sitcom—this in fact may not be true. A Newsmark Move such as, for instance, "you don't say!" may, in a specific pragmatic context, be an expression of sarcasm, not of disbelief or surprise. Ethnomethodological

Moves, after all, are only discourse markers indicating a possible direction of the conversation outcome, with no implication of the participants' psychological motivations determining their intentions that may underlie their 'preference organization' of adjacency pairs. In order to explore intentionality underlying conversational turns it is in fact necessary to focus on the pragmatics of 'Speech Acts' (Searle 1983). It is possible, however, to integrate the Moves of the previous Structuralist Model with the Ethnomethodological Moves. In this way, the semantic meaning of the Moves setting a frame on discourse could be pragmatically adapted to the unpredictable unfolding of sitcom conversations.

3.2.4 *Cooperative Maxims and Speech-Act Theory in sitcom conversations*

When the pragmatic dimension of the sitcom conversation is involved, then, the dubbing-translators have to become aware of the dimensions of conversational cooperation, which indeed should mark the very beginning of their top-down processes of 'embodiment' of the sitcom meanings that would qualify them as 'Acting Translators'. In fact, even before considering the conversation pattern of Acts and Moves in a sitcom script, dubbing translators should reflect upon the degree of cooperation or cooperation-failure among the inter-acting sitcom characters – cooperation-failure being more frequent in comic dialogues as it is at the basis of humorous misunderstandings. Focusing on conversational cooperation, therefore, implies taking into account the notion of the 'Cooperative Principle' advanced by Grice (1975), who explores an interesting dimension of communication regarding the ways in which participants cooperatively contribute to the conversation they are involved in. In Grice's view, conversations are cooperative events organized around a principle of cooperation constituted by four 'conversational maxims' which are: 'Quality', 'Quantity', 'Relation', and 'Manner'. Participants who intend to cooperate in making their contribution to a conversation appropriate, relevant, and informative are thus expected to follow these maxims reported below in Grice's (*ibidem*) definition:

(a) Quantity—"Be informative: *(1)* Make your contribution as informative as is required (for the current purposes of the conversation). *(2)* Do not make your contribution more informative than is required."

(b) Quality —"Try to make your contribution one that is true: *(1)* Do not say what you believe to be false. *(2)* Do not say that for which you lack adequate evidence."

(c) Relation—"Be relevant".

(d) Manner—"Be perspicuous: *(1)* Avoid obscurity of expression. *(2)* Avoid unnecessary ambiguity. *(3)* Be brief (avoid unnecessary prolixity). (4) Be orderly."

Grice's Cooperative Maxims aim at achieving cooperation in conversation by enabling the speaker to convey his/her intention to the listener without any difficulty. These maxims, together with Lakoff's (1973) Maxims of Politeness (namely: "Don't impose", "Give options", "Make your receiver feel good"), reflect the main purpose in human relations, which is to act efficiently together with other people. Therefore they normally imply the existence of socio-cultural schemata shared by all the participants in a conversation, which would allow them to disambiguate any obscure meaning that could impede the inference of the intentionality encoded in what they say. According to Grice's notion of conversational cooperation, a speaker never doubts that his/her listener does not cooperate with him/her in inferring what s/he means and, in cooperating, the listener is assumed to always refer to such shared maxims. If the listener is uncooperative, this may be so only because s/he willingly 'flouts' these maxims, or 'opts out of' them but, in Grice's view, s/he is never assumed not to understand the speaker's intentionality. But misunderstanding on intentional grounds typically happens in sitcoms, due to schema confusion which constitutes a characteristic feature of its humour. Therefore, in his attempt to explain the principle regulating the cooperative construction of an interaction turn by turn, and to relate it to the processes of meaning inferencing, Grice misses the fact that the speaker's intention, and how it is interpreted by a listener, depends upon the social and situational context in which the interaction occurs. In addition, it depends upon the speaker's and listener's socio-cultural and experiential schemata which may not coincide, as often happens not only in intercultural communication, but also—and crucially in humorous dialogues—when cooperative and politeness strategies are used differently by the participants in the interaction, thus affecting its outcome and the judgements that participants make of each other. 'Politeness' in interaction, for instance, is used to 'preserve face' (i.e., 'to protect themselves') in all cultures (Lakoff 1973; Brown and Levinson 1987). This occurs by emphasizing what both participants have in common and minimizing social distance between each other—in other words, by showing each other a 'positive face' (Goffman 1967). Such a universal 'face-work' (*ibidem*), however, is differently actualized in different societies and groups according to different parameters of social distance, power and status which may—often involuntarily—cause 'face-threatening' in interaction (Brown and Levinson 1987), as it often occurs in sitcoms organized on Arousal/Safety patterns of humour. The principles of politeness and cooperation are not enough to provide the explanation for the inference of participants' intentionality. To do this, an analyst-translator also needs to make assumptions about the knowledge of the social and cognitive background of each participant in the interaction (that is, of each sitcom character). This, for acting translators, represents the very beginning of their process of 'embodiment' of sitcom characters.

An approach that can help the analyst and the translator to access such knowledge is represented by the Speech Act Theory, which was first formulated by Austin (1962) and further developed by Searle (1969, 1975). The assumption underlying Speech Act Theory is that people can do all sorts of things with words by means of speech acts, such as making requests or promises, asking questions, giving orders or thanks, offering apologies, etc. Moreover, almost any speech act may imply other acts, depending on the speaker's intention. Indeed, a speech act involves three fundamental communicative dimensions, which are *(a)* 'Reference', regarding the semantic patterning of propositions and their syntactic actualization into language to express the 'propositional content' of what the speaker says; *(b)* 'Force', regarding the intentionality that the speaker associates with what s/he says, or the 'illocutionary force' (i.e., the value assigned to an utterance when, by saying something, the speaker intends to inform, warn, request, promise, threaten, etc.); and *(c)* 'Effect', regarding the reactions of listeners to what the speaker says, or 'perlocutionary effect' (e.g.: reactions of surprise, fear, joy, persuasion, etc.). If speech acts succeed in producing the speaker's intended effects on listeners, it means that listeners have understood both the force and the content of what the speaker said and this cognitive achievement by listeners is what Austin defines as 'uptake'. In a sitcom context, however, failure in achieving an 'uptake' is one of the main features characterising humorous discourse based on misunderstanding. The notions of Reference, Force and Effect are to be associated with Austin's identification of three distinct levels of action, which are *(a)* the act of saying something, or 'Locutionary Act', *(b)* what one does in saying it, or 'Illocutionary Act', and *(c)* what one does by saying it, or 'Perlocutionary Act'. Such levels can be applied to the analysis of ambiguity in sitcom puns, which suggests that when a speaker performs a speech act, in particular an illocutionary act, s/he has got a specific intention to communicate. If listeners recognize that intention, then the speech act succeeds, and the speaker's intention is fulfilled. This occurs when speakers choose their words in such a way as to make their intentions easily recognizable. However, the speakers' utterances may not semantically encode their intentions—or, as in the case of humorous puns in sitcoms, two possible intentions can be encoded within the same semantic organization of the message, one of which is the normal, socially-expected intention, while the other is a totally different one which triggers the humorous effect. Often, to understand the speaker's intention, as well as the meaning of the illocutionary act s/he intends to convey, a listener does not have to decode it from what the speaker actually says, but rather he needs to 'recognize' it from 'how' the speaker says it. If this recognition occurs, then it succeeds at the illocutionary level (cf. Widdowson 1979).

Apart from conveying the speaker's communicative intentionality, however, speech acts may also function on other, more conventional, levels. In Austin's (1962) view, not all speech acts are acts of communication – in fact he does not take into account the actual communicative interplay between the speaker's intention and the listener's inference. Indeed, Austin assumes that the successful performance of an illocutionary act is a matter of 'convention', not 'intention', which justifies his interest in Performatives that explicitly 'perform the acts' named by the verbs denoting them (such as: nominating, declaring, appointing, absolving, sentencing, etc.) as, for instance:

> I *declare* the said person duly elected to Parliament.
> I *pronounce* that they be Man and Wife.
> I *sentence* you to death. / You are hereby sentenced to death.
> I *absolve* you from all your sins.
> I *name* this ship "Victoria".

The pragmatic function of Performatives, therefore, is not to communicate an intention, but to affect specific institutional circumstances. In this sense, Austin maintains, Performatives are neither 'true' nor 'false', since they can be only 'felicitous' or 'infelicitous'. The Felicity Conditions of the Performative Acts depend on the appropriate context in which the utterance is performed. For instance, a judge cannot address a criminal by saying: "I sentence you to death", if s/he performs this sentence in a country where there is no death penalty. In such a case, in fact, the felicity conditions for the judge's utterance would not be fulfilled. In the same way, a British citizen cannot just tell his wife: "I hereby divorce you", because he will not 'thereby get a divorce' since in the UK there is not such procedure whereby divorce is obtained by simply uttering this sentence. This condition, however, would be felicitous in some Muslim cultures where such a procedure is institutionalised. In this sense, Austin maintains, the use of a sentence with a certain illocutionary force encoded in it is 'conventional' insofar as it can be 'made explicit by the performative formula' (cf. Coulmas 1981). Austin, furthermore, points out that also the so-called Constatives are acts that apparently work like Performatives. A suggestion, for instance, or an assertion can be made by uttering expressions like "I suggest", "I assert"; an apology can be made by saying "I apologize for that", and a prediction by saying "I predict". Austin proposes a way to make a distinction between Constative and Performative Acts, that is Constative Acts 'say' what they mean, as in "I like the pink roses." (I state a personal preference for the pink roses); Performative Acts 'do' what they say, as in "I choose the pink roses." (I perform the act of choosing the pink roses). Moreover, Constative Acts can be either 'true' or 'false', which is an inappropriate consideration in reference to Performative Acts, as the following examples illustrate:

> *(a)* They are man and wife (*Constative*)
> *(b)* I now pronounce you man and wife (*Performative*)

The statement in example *(a)* represents a Constative Act that may be 'true' or 'false' (e.g.: "is what the speaker states true?"—Which implies:

"are they a married couple, or not?"). The declaration in example *(b)*, on the contrary, represents a Performative Act that may be 'felicitous' or 'infelicitous' (e.g.: "Does the speaker have the authority to officiate at a wedding?", If the answer is "yes", then the declaration is felicitous; if the answer is "no", it is infelicitous). One of the main discourse strategies of humour—especially of an incongruous type—is precisely to perform a 'conventional' speech act in an inappropriate context where it would normally be infelicitous but, in a comic situation, it is interpreted as if it were perfectly appropriate and felicitous. This is the typical humorous strategy adopted by comedians such us the Monty Python or the Marx Brothers, previously explored in this chapter. An instance of an infelicitous use of performatives can be observed in the Marx Brothers' movie *Horse Feathers* (1932) where the character of Professor Wagstaff (played by Groucho Marx) who will be assuming the presidency of Huxley College, begins his address to an audience of capped faculty colleagues and students by suddenly switching his inconsistent academic speech to unexpected utterances evoking completely inappropriate scripts, as when his address is suddenly turned into an auction scene:

> "Any questions? Any answers? Any rags? Any bones? Any bottles today? Any rags? Let's have some action around here. Who'll say 76? Who'll say 17 76? That's the spirit! 1776!"

Later on, during the same address, Professor Wafstaff makes another comic digression in his address by introducing once again an infelicitous performative completely inappropriate to the present situation—in fact, this time his academic discourse switches to the situation of a police control of the driving licence which, by a further infelicitous performative, unexpectedly becomes a 'marriage licence':

> "Pull over to the side of the road there and let me see your marriage license."

In the final scene of this film, furthermore, the characters played by the four Marx Brothers marry the same woman in the same wedding ceremony, all of them pronouncing simultaneously the words "We do" and, in doing so, producing another comic instance of infelicitous performative uttered in a context that would be socially impossible in reality.

The Monty Python comedians offer other instances of infelicitous performatives for humorous effects, as shown, for example, in their above-quoted 1975 film *Monty Python and the Holy Grail* in which infelicitous utterances were the result of a time-switch, signalled by a clashing difference of discourse style, as in the following exchange between the legendary King Arthur and a woman, his subject, who unexpectedly thinks and speaks as a modern person, thus making the King's 'Order' performative infelicitous:

> *Arthur:* Be quiet! I order you to be quiet!
> *Woman:* Order, eh? Who does he think he is? Heh.
> *Arthur:* I'm your king!
> *Woman:* Well, I didn't vote for you.

Finally, to remain in the context of infelicitous performatives in a 'wedding' context, here is another example provided by Monty Python in the same film:

> *Launcelot:* Hello.
> *Guest:* He killed my auntie!
> *Guests: (yelling)*
> *Father:* Please! Please! This is supposed to be a happy occasion! Let's not bicker and argue about who killed who. We are here today to witness the union of two young people in the joyful bond of the holy wedlock. Unfortunately, one of them, my son Herbert, has just fallen to his death.
> *Guests:* Oh! Oh no!
> *Father:* But I don't want to think I've not lost a son, so much as ... gained a daughter!

Strawson (1964) argues that Austin only accounts for utterances regarding institutional contexts and, thus, they should not be taken as a model of illocutionary acts in general. Searle (1969) tries to overcome this limitation in Austin's theory of 'conventional intentionality' encoded in Performative Acts when he re-elaborates his taxonomy by introducing the notion of 'Illocutionary Point' which presupposes a purpose in the speaker's mind as s/he produces an utterance within a specific socio-cultural context of interaction. This new focus on the speaker is extremely useful in the process of dubbing translation in that it may help the acting translator identify the hidden dialogic dynamics of a sitcom conversation where speakers' intentionality is not so obvious, expected and scripted. Strawson (1971), however, criticizes Searle's theory as it explains illocutionary forces by means of constitutive rules which are, again, just conventional 'force-indicating devices' (i.e., performative verbs) without which it is possible to perform exactly the same kinds of illocutionary acts. Differently from Strawson's view, the Austin/Searle speech-act taxonomy is instead a categorization of illocutionary acts that may be performed not by conforming to a 'performative convention', but by signalling a 'communicative intention' in the joint construction of a 'relational frame' in conversation (Coupland and Coupland 2000). The ways in which a communicative intention may account for socio-pragmatic, cognitive and cultural differences—as they frequently occur in the dubbing-translation process of intercultural transfer—can be explored by reference to two instances of speech acts which are frequent in sitcom structures, namely, Apologies and Requests.

3.2.5 *Apologies and Requests*

The Apology speech act is not just a structural act in a conversation pattern, but a communicative act to be interpreted by listeners as expressing the speaker's attitude of regret for some unexpected action or for the lack of an expected action. Obviously, a speaker can perform an Apology and implying, instead, a sarcastic remark, as in the case of the expression "I beg your pardon!", or rather—as in the case of the sitcom humour—a speaker can use this speech act to achieve a comic effect (e.g., while performing the Apology speech act doing unwittingly more damage, or uttering more offensive words). However, if the speaker uses the performative "I apologize", he would clearly make understanding easier for his/her listener insofar as communicative success is normally achieved when the speaker chooses his/her words in such a way that the listener will recognize his communicative intention.

Apart from explicit performatives, though, there are some pragmatic ways which speakers use in order to achieve their intentions, and these ways are typically 'culture-bound'. Faerch and Kasper (1984) introduce the notion of culture-bound knowledge of speech acts, focusing on how to put such a knowledge to practical use. More specifically, they claim that to realize speech acts within a real communicative situation, the participants in an interaction need to share two types of knowledge which, in Cognitive Psychology (cf. Anderson 1980), are defined as: *(1)* 'Declarative Knowledge', which is the knowledge of usage rules (cf. Widdowson 1978) reflected in: *(a)* the 'linguistic knowledge' of the phonological, morpho-syntactic, and lexical routine formulae (e.g.: "I'm sorry", "I apologize", etc.); *(b)* the 'speech-act knowledge', regarding the verbal acts occurring within a specific culture (e.g.: within a broad notion of 'western culture and society', the constitutive conditions of an Apology could be: 'S did x at a cost to H – hence: S assumes responsibility for causing x and wants to convey attitude of regret for x to H'); *(c)* the 'discourse knowledge', regarding the 'syntagmatic' (sequential) and 'paradigmatic' (alternative) characteristics of each speech act, determining coherence in discourse (e.g.: in the case of Apology, the syntagmatic sequence of acts is: Initiating → eliciting → 'paradigmatic alternative': accept/reject → request for explanation); *(d)* the 'socio-cultural knowledge', concerning social values, norms, and institutions in a given society (e.g.: again, in a broad notion of Western society, an Apology would be socio-culturally characterized by the 'degree of offence in relation to participants' status and socio-cultural roles'); *(e)* the 'context knowledge', regarding the context-determining factors of a given communicative situation; and *(f)* the 'knowledge of the world', concerning facts, objects, relations etc. of the world as it is expected to be schematically shared by the participants in an interaction; and *(2)* 'Procedural Knowledge', which is the knowledge of how to achieve an illocutionary goal by 'verbally planning' the actualization of the required speech act.

Particularly at this planning stage, the socio-cultural or ethnic background of the speaker plays a central role in the achievement of the goal.

By exploring the Apology speech act it will be possible to realize the extent to which Declarative and Procedural Knowledge of speech acts actually implies that the acting translators working in a sitcom-dubbing team have to possess a 'shared knowledge' of socio-cultural, contextual and cognitive frames (van Dijk 1977) belonging to each of the sitcom characters participating in the interaction. This shared knowledge can be tested and refined during the improvisation sessions on the sitcom scripts when acting translators 'embody' characters and situations. In fact, if these frames are not schematically shared by the team of acting translators, then the outcome of their improvised interaction shall be miscommunication and they will find it difficult to fully understand the sitcom interaction under analysis and its humorous language.

Blum-Kulka and Olshtain (1984) also explore the expression of the Request speech act by proposing the following sequence: *(a)* Address Term(s) → *(b)* Head Act (the nucleus of the speech act) → *(c)* Adjunct(s) to Head Act. Also in this case, the acting translators' improvisation workshops cannot ignore the procedural stage of 'verbally planning' a parallel script by incorporating the Request speech act which, in its turn, presupposes the translators' declarative knowledge of how to make use of this speech act within a specific linguistic and socio-cultural context in both source and target languages and cultures.

By starting from Austin's and Searle's early taxonomies which did not leave much space to ambiguity problems—which are instead typical of humorous discourse—in this chapter the discussion has moved on to more context-aware approaches to speech-act analysis. In the next Part Two of this book it will be explored how, by adjusting the illocutionary force of a speech act, it is actually possible to modify the potential perlocutionary effects that utterances can have on listeners. This is indeed an area of research in speech-act analysis known as Critical Discourse Awareness, focusing on the use of textual force to impose a manipulative, ideological view on receivers (Fairclough 1995; Tsohatzidis 1994; Ladegaard 1995). This would give acting translators the possibility of improvising parallel discourses on the original sitcom scripts not only by physically embodying sitcom characters and situations and inventing possible new dialogues, but also by 'verbally planning' such dialogues as they become 'critically aware' of their declarative and procedural knowledge applied to conversation structures and speech-acts so as to be properly used—or consciously misused for comic effects—in a socio-culturally marked situational context. This would allow acting translators to creatively reformulate the original conversations into different versions, thus exploring alternative expressions of the same locutionary content according to different illocutionary intents attributed to the sitcom characters and this is here contended to be a crucial top-down step towards a more conscious, bottom-up search for a 'natural' formal and pragmatic equivalence in dubbing translation, as reported in the next three practical chapters of Part Two.

PART TWO

Applying the Acting Translator Model to Source and Target Sitcom Scripts

Pictures: ensemble casts of *The Nanny; Roseanne; Dharma & Greg; Friends; Will & Grace.*

Chapter 4

Dubbing Translation as 'Product Localization': A Conversation Analysis of Source Script and Target Versions of *The Nanny* Sitcom

4.1 The Sitcom Corpus and the Revelation/Negotiation Pattern of Humour

4.1.1 *Focusing on turn-of-the-century 'transitional communities'*

This chapter starts the second part of the present book focused on the application of the Acting Translator Model, outlined so far, to a pedagogic approach to the dubbing translation of sitcom humour. Because of its introductory nature, this chapter will be more extensive than the other two ones that will follow. The sitcom corpus selected for the analysis to be carried out in this Part Two consists of episodes from five North-American sitcoms: *The Nanny, Roseanne, Dharma & Greg, Friends*, and *Will & Grace*, all of them aired at the turn of the century. The rationale underlying the choice of this corpus is that such sitcoms essentially represent a pre-9/11 period, that is, a time when there was still a vibrant sense of humour based on a hope for a 'new age'—which would allow new forms of enlarged affective communities undermining old family structures—and, crucial to this study, a novel sense of lightness encouraging an exploration of new forms of comedy that could ultimately defuse ethnic/racial and misogynist/homophobic patterns of humour. Racial humour at the turn of the century was in fact not yet perceived so racist and politically abusive as it is today, after the huge turn-of-the-century tragedy of the Islamic terrorists' attack to the World Trade Centre in New York on September, 9, 2001—affecting the world in general and the United States and the western world in particular. Indeed, since that ill-fated '9/11' date, in the western world humour has progressively been constrained and controlled by strict 'politically-correct' norms and precepts for fear of repercussions from religious radicalism and ideological dogmas—the Islamic ferocious censure on anti-Muslim comic cartoons issued in Europe being a case in point but not, by any means, the only disquieting example, as every humorous reference to any religious and cultural specificity has been stigmatized so as to keep a peaceful social status quo.

These five selected sitcoms, furthermore, introduce interesting instances of turn-of-the-century 'transitional communities' set in big

American cities—mainly New York—where fast life paces tend to alienate people, breaking traditional families and social groups which are thus replaced by 'new family organizations' that try to recover the lost affective bonds of the conventional family by continuously activating strategies of personality negotiation. Such 'transitional communities', on the increase in the United States in the pre-9/11 era, were constituted by groups of people bond to each other by friendly, affectionate relationships that replaced conventional family ties by allowing a greater freedom of thought and judgement also in reference to quite thorny social issued that, at the turn of the century, started to be viewed under a lighter, humorous perspective. However, after 9/11, these new atypical communities gradually disappeared to be replaced by the conventional and more dependable values of the traditional family unit grounded on more conventional, stable and reassuring beliefs. Such social change can be explained by means of Hofstede's (1991) five cultural dimensions and of Hall and Hall's (1990) perception of time and high-context/low-context models. According to Hofstede's model, the dimension of Individualism/Collectivism informs the search for interpersonal relationships and group harmony characterizing the pre-9/11 American attempts at establishing a new collectivist culture which is, however, not meant as a whole high-context national trend, as in Hall and Hall (*ibidem*), but as small social organizations relying more on in-group mutual support rather than on individual achievement characterizing the markedly low-context culture of the big American cities. As a consequence, the 'femininity' element in Hofstede's (1991) Femininity/Masculinity dimension prevails in such small collectivist organizations, promoting caring attitudes and cooperation among its members who, thus, feel strongly supported by their group to the point that they take the risk of flouting the dimension of Uncertainty Avoidance in order to try new, untraditional ways of organizing society and taking the consequent risks of behaving and expressing themselves unconventionally without fearing group stigmatization. Within such pre-9/11 groups, in fact, the dimension of Power Distance was constantly questioned and usually replaced by factual reasoning and short-term goals which, in turn, challenged the Long-Term Orientation dimension typical of traditional cultures. In such small-group organizations, the perception of time itself comes to be modified in reference to short-term goals, allowing flexibility in coping simultaneously with several tasks—typical of Polychronic cultures (cf. Hall and Hall 1990) – rather than with a task at a time—which is a dimension of Monochronic, traditional cultures (*ibidem*; Hofstede 1991).

In *Friends*, for instance, a sitcom which was aired before and immediately after 9/11, the protagonists are six young people, three men and three women, two of them being brother and sister, bound by a loving friendship and living in flats in the same condominium and neighbourhood in New York City. The affective and economic support they mutually guarantee to all the members of the small group allow each component to express his/her opinions freely also with reference to each other's behaviours without being judgmental and, by means of humour, overcoming situations of tension and disparagement. However, after 9/11, four of them become married couples, another one gets married too, while the last one, Joey, kept playing the bachelor in a spin-off—but less successful —series. Also in *Will & Grace*, Will, a gay attorney, and Grace, his bosom friend, live in the same flat in New York City while in the opposite flat on the same landing Jack, their gay friend, lives—or better, most of the time sleeps, as he normally dwells and has meals at Will's place, often with his bosom friend and Grace's secretary, the millionaire Karen. The same mutually-supportive group dynamics identified in *Friends* is also noticed in this sitcom. After 9/11, also Will and Grace find their respective stable partners and painfully (and rancorously too) part from each other to reunite only at the end of the series, as mature people. Although *Roseanne* and *Dharma & Greg* seem to mark a return to the traditional family unit, actually it is not so. In fact, Roseanne has an extended family which includes, together with her large family, also a boy she adopts, who will eventually become her teenage daughter's boyfriend and the father of her child. Dharma and Greg are a young married couple who, though close to their respective parents—coming from two very different socio-cultural backgrounds—are surrounded by a community of quite odd, but supportive, close friends. Also *The Nanny*, that is the sitcom to be analyzed in this chapter, is an example of situation comedy focused on one of such New-York untraditional family unit, composed by people from the most disparate socio-cultural backgrounds, and abounding with racial, sexist and class-conscious quips. This is not a surprise as it was aired from 1993 to 1999, hence in a period when 'experiments' were still permissible in the field of US humorous discourse.

Exploring 'transitional communities' in a sitcom plainly means devising a type of humour which undermines traditional socio-cultural values and taboos, including the 'politically incorrect' issues of racism, chauvinism and class-conscious social hierarchies, which are dealt with flippancy and without hypocrisy. Arousal/Safety and Humorous Disparagement patterns had been then at the service of the comic and irreverent construction of the sitcom dialogues until the epochal tragedy at the turn of the century banned every type of dangerous reference to races, religions, cultures and politics from the discourse of humour.[1] More specifically, the

[1] A tentative return to a kind of disrespectful humour attacking religious fanaticism can be detected only recently, in the British web-sitcom *Living with the Infidels* (livingwitheinfidels.com) in which a group of aspiring Islamic kamikazes residing in the UK are torn between their religious faith and the many temptations of the Western world (e.g., soccer, TV shows and young female neighbours).

episodes from these five sitcoms selected for the analysis are characterized by 'Revelation plots' dealing with young people emancipated from conventional views on social values who eventually decide to reveal (or, in one case, not to reveal) to other characters—i.e., parents, friends or elderly people attached to more traditional beliefs—certain truths that may disturb them. This entails the triggering of the 'Arousal' pattern often conveyed by the Request and the Apology Conversational Moves. The humorous quips that follow usually provide the Safety pattern of Relief in the sitcom dialogue, which is often achieved by the activation of an unconventional Negotiation move. In fact, the typical Arousal/Safety pattern of humour is here assumed to be insufficient to describe the unconventional dialogic and social dynamics represented in the conversations among the characters. This explains the introduction of the novel Revelation/ Negotiation pattern of humour, advanced in this book, as a development of the Arousal/Safety pattern to be applied to the conversation analysis of American sitcoms aired at the turn of the century. In the sitcom episodes under analysis, the Revelation plots are actualized into the ways in which, respectively, in *Will & Grace* Will, Grace and Karen encourage their gay friend Jack to reveal his homosexuality to his mother who, in turn, feels obliged to reveal an unpleasant truth to his son; in *Friends*, Joey reveals to his flatmate and friend Chandler that he wants to live on his own, Monica reveals to her parents that her new partner is much older than her and that he also happens to be their friend, and Phoebe reveals to her friend Rachel that, after having taken the decision to have themselves tattooed, she had not the courage to go through it. In *Roseanne*, Roseanne's teenage daughter Darleen and her boyfriend David reveal to her whole family that she is pregnant and that they are going to get married. In *Dharma & Greg*, Greg feigns a Southern accent for fun only to discover that the Federal Court Judge, with whom Greg has a motion he is hearing the following day, has heard him and believes he is actually from the South. Greg, this time, refuses to reveal him that he was just mocking his accent. Finally, in the episode from *The Nanny* (in this chapter), Fran, the nanny, reveals to Maxwell (her employer who secretly loves her) and, indirectly, to her mother, that her new boyfriend has proposed to her. In all these cases, Revelation is followed by a Negotiation act aimed at soothing conflict.

4.1.2 *Problems of equivalence in sitcom dubbing translation for the Italian TV*

Furthermore, the choice of the above-mentioned sitcoms was meant not only to represent novel and interesting socio-pragmatic and conversational dynamics set within new typologies of contemporary 'transitional' social and domestic communities in the United States at the eve and beginning of the new millennium. In fact, the selected sitcoms were also meant to be analysed in their translated versions for the Italian television with the purpose of identifying the textual choices operated by the dubbing translators in order to achieve pragmatic equivalence, as well as the marketing strategies operated by the sitcom producers which ultimately justified translation choices. Besides, the objective of the analysis was specifically pedagogical insofar as it principally aimed at making dubbing-translation students aware of their need to activate a 'first-person embodiment of textual meanings' by 'enacting' the sitcom script and 'dramatically improvising' upon it so as to make the sitcom dialogue pragmatically alive in both its source and target versions before analysing the textual and situational structure of the humorous script in detail. This pedagogic approach shall be illustrated in-depth in this and the following two chapters of this Part Two, which will focus respectively on episodes from the selected sitcoms with the purpose of carrying out also a comparative conversation analysis first on their original script and its translated version for the Italian television, and then on the dubbing translations produced by groups of Italian undergraduate students from two Italian Faculties of Foreign Languages majoring in Translation who, in the course of longitudinal case studies, were encouraged to apply the 'Acting Translator' model to their search for a pragmatic equivalence of an experiential, 'embodied' kind.

The comparative analysis between the source script and the 'official' dubbing translation was principally justified by the very peculiarities identified in the translations for the Italian television. Indeed, if on the one hand *Friends* and *Will & Grace* in their official Italian translation represent—as mentioned in the Introduction—instances of 'product globalization', or 'foreignization' (Venuti 1995, 1998; Shuttleworth and Cowie 1997) conveying both linguistic (lexico-semantic, pragmatic) and paralinguistic (intonation and rhythmical) features typical of the source American speech style, on the other hand, *The Nanny* and *Roseanne* represent instead instances of 'product localization', or 'domestication' (Venuti 1995, 1998; Shuttleworth and Cowie 1997; Martìnez-Sierra 2005b; Anderman and Diaz-Cintas 2009). For instance, in *The Nanny* the original comic dialogues are 'displaced' into a totally different schematic and socio-cultural context informed by 'regionalization' parameters that transform the Jewish conceptual and pragmatic background of the protagonist and her family into a parallel background typical of the Italian community of immigrants in New York. This is signalled by continuous humorous references to Italian schematic contexts whose aim seems to be that of triggering a sense of familiarity in the target audiences' minds despite the risk of deleting every culturally-marked specificity of the original version. Also *Roseanne* is a sitcom that, in its translated version for the Italian television, is characterized by a pragmalinguistic transfer of a standard Neapolitan variation with the aim of rendering the working-class Illinois accent into a diastratically equivalent Italian accent. The episode from *Dharma & Greg* selected for the comparative analysis may be considered, instead, as an example of 'product neutralization' insofar as in it an invented Italian diatopic/diastratic variety was devised to render the source Southern Tennessee accent into ways that were probably thought to be equivalent to the original one.

4.2 Processes of Sociopragmatic Transfer in the Dubbing Translation of *The Nanny* Sitcom

4.2.1 *Socio-cultural and pragmaliguistic dimensions of humour in* The Nanny

This chapter focuses on two main issues: the first one deals with a cross-cultural investigation of speech-act patterns in the original version of the American sitcom *The Nanny* (produced by Sterning & Fraser Ink, Inc. for CBS) and in its dubbing translation for the Italian television. The second issue aims to compare the outcome of such an enquiry with the results of a longitudinal case-study carried out with a group of Italian undergraduate students (from two Faculties of Foreign Languages) majoring in Translation. The objective of the investigation is to analyze the conversation patterns of some extracts from *The Nanny* sitcom by identifying discourse similarities and differences in American-English and Italian. Starting from the assumption that translators as intercultural mediators need to develop multicultural schematic representations underlying the pragmatic competence of the languages they deal with (Bialystok 1996), this chapter argues that, in the TV-translation of the dialogues in *The Nanny*, the Italian dubbing translators impose their own subjective, ethnocentric representations of contexts and pragmatic uses upon the original American-English conversation patterns of the scripts. Therefore, by adopting such purely top-down interpretative procedures, these translators actually behave as socio-cultural 'gatekeepers' (Barbe 1996)—rather than mediators—for the Italian audiences. Evidence of this will be supplied by the results of the contrastive conversation analysis carried out on parallel episodes—both in the source American-English language and in the target Italian one—from the sitcom series. In fact, analyzed data show that the dubbing translation of *The Nanny* (*La Tata* in the version for the Italian television) is characterized by a 'sociopragmatic transfer' of Italian social and conversational stereotypes into the American cultural, situational and pragmalinguistic patterns of the original version, a transfer that—as it will be demonstrated—ultimately determines a 'sociopragmatic failure' (Thomas 1984) in the audience's interpretative processes of the sitcom. This implies that several radical changes were carried out by the dubbing translator in the Italian sitcom scripts not only at the diatopic level of move-&-act realization, but also at the diastratic and even at the diaphasic levels (Trudgill 1983; Berruto 1987). In fact, in the Italian version of *The Nanny*, social-status and family-relation parameters are totally ignored and reinvented, as also the protagonist's characteristic New-York Jewish speech style (cf. Tannen 1981), as well as the socio-cultural references in conversation are completely transformed or neglected in translation. The outcome is a Nanny (a 'Tata') losing her Jewish origin to be turned into an Italian immigrant with her whole family relationships totally upturned and readapted to fit precise and socially-accepted Italian stereotypes.

What a translator needs to acquire in tackling this sitcom, therefore, is first of all a kind of schematic knowledge (cf. Rumelhart 1980) that is both socio-cultural—in the case in point, regarding the cultural contrasts between New York Jews and WASPs at the basis of the sitcom structure - and sociolinguistic—concerning a recognition of the diastratic variations of new York English used in *The Nanny*. Such a knowledge would thus enable the translator to embody the first-person perspective of this sitcom, that is a New York WASP's perspective from which the humorous disparagement targeting the Nanny's Jewish culture arises, marking the whole sitcom structure. The dubbing translator, however, before experimenting with his/her embodiment of the sitcom through acting, also needs to acquire a contextual knowledge which would allow him/her first to familiarize and 'inhabit' the physical setting of the sitcom—that is, the Manhattan upper-class WASP house where the Sheffield family lives—and then to 'embody' the participants in the sitcom, who are: Fran Fine, a New York Jewish 30-something woman employed as a Nanny in the WASP house; Maxwell Sheffield, a wealthy widower and Fran's WASP upper-class employer she secretly loves; Sylvia, Fran's stereotypical "Jewish mother"; Maxwell's children; Niles, Maxwell's British butler; C.C., Maxwell's business female partner who aims at marrying him. Finally, the dubbing translator needs to posses a steady systemic knowledge of the English language in all its semantic, syntactic, pragmatic and phonological dimensions—this last one regarding the ability to identify different accents. In brief, the original plot of *The Nanny* sitcom is this: Fran Fine, the protagonist, is a typical nasal-voiced, big-haired Jewish woman in her thirties of Polish origins (played by actress Fran Drescher) who comes from Flushing, Queens and, at the beginning of the series, has just been dumped by her boyfriend who also sacked her from her job as a bridal consultant at his shop. Fran, then, starts her new job as a door-to-door cosmetic salesperson and so she happens to ring at the doorstep of a wealthy British widower, the Broadway theatre producer Maxwell Sheffield. Maxwell by mistake thinks that Fran is applying for the position of a nanny to his three depressed children, Maggie, Brighton and Grace, recently bereaved of their mother, and hires her believing that she is perfect for taking care of them. The sitcom plot is evidently evocative of the musical movie *The Sound of Music* with an updated nanny (also resembling the female protagonist of the old sitcom *I Love Lucy* in her overacting through facial and gestural expressions) who soon reveals an unconventional—and often nonsensical—approach to educating the young children, which delights the Sheffield kids but also, and covertly, Maxwell. Fran, in fact, becomes quite fond of her employer's children and acts as if she were Mr. Sheffield's wife. The problem, indeed, is that Fran has a crush on Maxwell who, covertly again, reciprocates the feelings in a continuous unfolding of an 'Arousal/Safety' humorous scheme based on the disruption and restoration of social roles. Yet, also Maxwell's snobbish business partner C.C. Babcock has a crush on Maxwell and is jealous of Fran, trying all the time to get in her way by disparaging her by using sarcastic wit. Niles, the British household butler, keeps an eye on all that happens in this unconventional family and contributes to the development of the comic situations with his ironic, mocking sense of humour. He is friendly with Fran and fiercely sarcastic with the haughty C.C. However, what determines the 'Humorous Disparagement' pattern of this sitcom is the open 'Jewish quality' of the protagonist, Fran, and her family, at the source of most quips and jokes in the sitcom dialogues, and also reflected in the stereotypical (physical and gestural) dimension of the characters. This quality is above all identified in Fran's clichéd garish and gluttonous 'Jewish mother' Sylvia, a social climber determined to have her daughter 'marry money'. For instance, in the episode to be analyzed in this book (entitled *Dope Diamond*), Fran has a date with a wealthy, handsome and, crucially, Jewish medical doctor, Julius. When he proposes to her after only two weeks they met, Fran feels obliged to accept under Sylvia's pressures, threats and emotional blackmails. Yet, on buying Fran a very expensive engagement ring in an exclusive jewellery, Julius disappears taking the ring with him. In fact, he was just an experienced thief, so Fran finds herself dumped and deeply humiliated just because she felt compelled to take her mother's pressing advice. When CBS agreed on the airing of the series, sponsors actually had some reservations about the fact that actress Fran Drescher was playing the character of the Nanny as too deliberately 'Jewish' by emphasising her ethnic traits in language use, values and behaviour. Indeed, she was initially required to turn the Nanny into an Italo-American woman, but Drescher firmly refused to do so by explaining: "I said, there's no way this character is going to be Italian. It's not that, as an actress, I can't play Italian. But on TV, you have to work fast, and the most real, the most rooted in reality to me is Jewish. I wanted to do it closest to what I knew. I didn't want to compromise or apologize for it because corporate or middle America or the Sun Belt wouldn't embrace a Jewish character. And, in fact, they did first. Before New York and Los Angeles. They embraced her immediately."[2] The sitcom humour, as a consequence, is heavily characterized by a vocal Jewish quality which comes to be constantly challenged (indeed, 'humorously' belittled) by the opposite standoffish traits of the British humour embodied by Maxwell, Niles

[2] "I'm a Survivor". *Jewish Journal* (http://www.jewishjournal.com/home/preview.php?id=8435).

and, more sharply, by C.C.. The conveyance of a humorous disparagement, particularly with reference to the protagonist's attitudes deemed as typically 'Jewish'—such as her longing for material goods—occurs by means of a dialogic interplay of preferred/dispreferred conversational moves as in the two examples reported below from the episode entitled *Dope Diamond*. Here the situation is that in which the nanny's fiancé, Julius, the professional thief in disguise, says that he intends to buy Fran the engagement ring:

> *Julius:* Sweetheart, I want you to have the most beautiful engagement ring that money can buy (*Offer*).
> *Fran:* Oh, Julesy, I don't know if I can go through with this. (*Acceptance:* ambiguous reply - probably *Preferred*)
> *Julius:* Getting married? (*Question:* disambiguation - Fran's reply interpreted as *Preferred*)
> *Fran:* No. Buying retail. (*Answer: Dispreferred*)

> *Fran:* Now you know, Jules, I'm a simple girl with simple tastes, (*Pre-announcement*) just want a simple ring. (*Pre-request*) That's a nice little stone. (*Request*)
> *Jewellery Salesperson:* Madam, that's a crystal ashtray (*Answer: Dispreferred*).
> *Fran:* I was talking about the shape. Like the shape of that crystal pineapple over there. (*Hold*)
> *Jewellery Salesperson:* No. That's a ring (*Accept: Preferred*).
> *Fran:* Whip it out, honey. (*Request*)

More in general, the disparagement humour in *The Nanny* is built on the characters' misunderstandings of the Conversational Implicature in each other's dialogic turns—namely, an additional unstated significance that connects them, giving them a coherent contextual meaning (cf. Edmonson 1981; Bach 1994). Such misinterpretation is due to a lack of correspondence between the speaker's illocutionary intention in uttering his/her turn and the listener's perlocutionary interpretation of such a cue (Austin 1962) which is understood with reference to a schema and a script that are different from the ones intended by the speaker, thus deviating from audiences' expectations and triggering the comic effect. The following example, drawn from another episode of *The Nanny* (entitled *Nanny and the Professor*), represents a case in point:

> *Maxwell:* Well, it's 12:30. Where's this brother of yours, C.C.?
> *Fran:* Brother? There's a brother coming? Is he short, ugly, and married?
> *C.C.:* No. Why?
> *Fran:* Well, then I gotta change.
> *C.C.:* Nanny Fine, please, he is a full-time professor at Northwestern University.
> *Fran:* Well, I don't mind moving down south.

Here it is possible to notice that Fran and C.C. are not just stating unrelated things: the three utterances can be related by 'inferring', deducing the Conversational Implicature. Thus, Fran's request for information about C.C.'s brother is replied by C.C. by a request for disambiguation ("Why?") which Fran does not explicitly supply, but she replies with an apparently unrelated statement ("Well, then I gotta change"), that actually implicates her interest in him as a potential husband. C.C. this time understands Fran's implicature and replies by informing Fran of her brother's high social status (he is a professor at the prestigious Northwestern University), incompatible with the Nanny's lower status. To this Fran replies by flouting the maxim of Relation (Grice 1975) stating that, once married, she would not mind to move to the south where that university is located.

The same interplay of two different schemata and related scripts (one expected and the other unexpected) can be identified in the following example from *Dope Diamond* in which Fran scolds both her boyfriend Julius and her boss, Mr Sheffield, for competing in showing off their important social connections to make an impression on her, by saying: "*Fran:* I can't stand to see two grown men fight about who's got the biggest connection". In saying this, Fran is performing *(a)* the locutionary act of saying that the grown up men should not behave in a childish way, *(b)* the expected illocutionary act of scolding her receivers as if they were children, because of their silly competitive boasting about their respective influential social connections, and *(c)* the unexpected perlocutionary act of (unwittingly?) alluding to the children's game of competing over the size of their sex organs—which triggers the audience's laughter. Receivers, however, on the one hand can easily understand Fran's explicit illocutionary act of scolding them, as well as the implicit perlocutionary act of blaming her two suitors (Julius, the overt one, and Maxwell, still covert) for their competitive behaviour. Yet, her sexual innuendo may not have the same perlocutionary effect on the sitcom receivers (the audience), so their reactions could be diverse (e.g.: they may not understand this pun, or they may understand it and feel bothered by its vulgarity, or they may rather think it is only an easy, trivial pun, whereas some others may appreciate it as very humorous, and so on). Clearly, there is no association between the perlocutionary act of covertly inducing a further effect through the language used in the message and the words actually used in the message, which make no mention at all of sexual references. This indirect association is, therefore, 'inferential'—which is a characteristic of the humour of this sitcom.

As a whole, the comedy structure of *The Nanny* contains many jokes and witticisms based on characters' oppositions, each providing the stimulus for humorously disparaging the other. Hence the Maxwell/Fran opposition generates two-way jokes on class, gender, culture and ethnic differences; also the Niles/C.C. opposition is the source of class-conflict jokes, whereas the Fran/Sylvia opposition triggers jokes based on culture/generation differences and prejudices. Moreover, the characters' individual traits make them quite oddballs—which is stressed by the actors' skills in emphasizing their gags with caricatural facial expressions and physical slapstick. Maxwell, for instance, is obsessed about his rivalry with Broadway musical author and producer Andrew Lloyd Webber to the point that in the past he had discarded the opportunity of producing himself the Lloyd Webber's musical *Cats* which then, to his great disappointment, turned out to be a huge box-office success. Fran, in turn, is characterized by her habit of lying about her real age and by her stereotypically Jewish obsessions—that she shares with her simple-minded best friend Val—with getting a wealthy husband and material property before age makes such goals difficult to achieve, as well as with the garishly-dressed and eccentric singer Barbra Streisand to whom she makes reference as her model of style. Sylvia, Fran's mother, apart from her unrestrained love for junk food in excess and her habit of pushing Fran into finding a rich husband soon, before getting 'old', shares with her senile mother Yetta, Fran's grandmother, a weakness for handsome young men as well as for flashy clothes and exceedingly big hairstyles. Finally, C.C. is portrayed as a cynical, tough and cold-hearted character to the point of ignoring the names of Maxwell's children she actually takes no notice of.

4.2.2 *Target-culture dislocations in the Italian dubbing translation of* The Nanny

Despite such strong culture-centred construction of *The Nanny* sitcom, its dubbing translation for the Italian television (distributed by Mediaset Television Group) was definitely oriented towards a policy of 'product localization'. This is evident from the fact that the translation of this sitcom conveys a regionalization of contexts and dialogues capable of inducing a sense of familiarity in Italian audiences, which nullifies every sociolinguistic and cultural specificity of the original version. In this sense, the 'official translator' of this sitcom can be considered as an actual dialogist-adaptor who often creates dialogues and situations anew for the Italian audience, despite the culturally-marked visual dimension of the sitcom—a process very similar to the one defined by Mangiron and O'Hagan (2006) as 'transcreation' with reference to the 'localized' translation of humour in video games—a term meant "to explain the freedom granted to the translator, albeit within severe space limitations." (*ibidem*: 10). In fact, apart from the frequent linguistic distortions of *The Nanny* original script, the Italian translator actually subverts the whole family-relations structure of the sitcom in order to adapt them to the implied Italian receivers' schemata, meant—as stated in the Introduction—as a socially-recognized and experiential background shared by a speech community (cf.Rumelhart 1980; Carrell 1983). Hence, the Nanny protagonist of the sitcom, Fran Fine, becomes in the Italian version Francesca Cacace, a member of the Italo-American community in New York (cf. Ferrari 2011)—that is exactly the stereotypical role that the original production asked actress Fran Drescher to play and that she refused to perform. Also Fran's close friend Val is rendered in translation into an Italo-American, thus becoming Lalla. Most incredibly, Sylvia Fine, Fran's mother, does not exist anymore in the Italian version of the sitcom: in fact, the blond and corpulent middle-aged woman is made to assume the identity of 'Zia Assunta'—Aunt Assunta. Furthermore, Fran's absent and silent father, Mortie, occasionally seen from behind revealing a dreadful hairpiece, in the Italian adaptation of the sitcom becomes Uncle Antonio, Aunt Assunta's unresponsive husband. Yetta, Sylvia's mother and Fran's grandmother, becomes Zia Assunta's sister-in-law and Francesca's aunt. However, Yetta is the only character in Fran's family who, in the Italian adaptation, has retained her original name and the Polish origins. All the other characters belonging to Maxwell's family and entourage remain instead unchanged. The choice to turn the nanny's mother and grandmother into aunts in the Italian version might have been deemed necessary by the Italian film distributor because, according to the Italian 'family schema', mothers are not cognitively and culturally represented as middle-aged women who are still sex fanatic. By the same token, grandmothers are not assumed to be elderly women who spend the night in various men's beds, who take pleasure in fumbling about the rear of young men, and who long for getting married again. In a Catholic country like Italy, the stereotypical mother in the nineties was instead assumed to wish the best for her daughter and to hope that she may get married with the man she truly loves and makes her happy. Also fathers are not expected to be absent from their children's lives as Mortie is in Fran's life—this may have justified his transformation into the nanny's uncle. Nevertheless, the most significant modification occurred in the rendering the original script of *The Nanny* into its Italian version regards the religious and ethnic origins of the protagonist's family. Fran's family is markedly Jewish and of Polish origin, coming from the working-class neighbourhood of Flushing, Queens—yet, in the Italian adaptation, Francesca is Catholic and of Italian origins, precisely from Lazio, the region of Rome. This shift in the origin of the protagonist marks, as a consequence, the translator-adaptor's systematic and arbitrary flouting of any reference to the Jewish religion and culture. This is particularly striking in one of the last episodes when Fran finally marries Maxwell with a mixed Jewish/Anglican wedding rite which, in the Italian version, is turned into a Catholic marriage and—most incredibly—the rabbi is turned into the city major co-officiating with the priest at a joint civil and religious wedding ceremony. It was an idea of the late scriptwriter Guido Leone to carry out such changes in the Italian adaptation of *The Nanny*, and that perhaps was not just a choice dictated by the implied target audience's expectations—grounded on their supposedly shared socio-cultural schemata—ultimately conditioning the television industry and marketing strategies of the Italian distributors of this sitcom. In fact, the choice of avoiding any reference to the Jewish traditions was most likely dictated by the presence of a Jewish community in Italy that is still too vividly reminiscent of the Fascist and Nazi persecution against Jews and too painfully aware of today's fierce anti-Jewish racist trends in society to be able to tolerate disparagement-patterns of humour targeting Jews. In the States, instead, Jews have developed a more relaxed attitude towards anti-Semitic jokes as they have developed into a very wealthy and influential community in almost every domain of the intellectual/artistic, political and economic domains. This strong social position allows members of the American Jewish community in general, and of the New York intelligenzia in particular, to disregard the disparaging attacks they constantly receive for their culturally-marked attitudes, beliefs and practices. Indeed, whereas the Italian Jewish minority represents a close high-context society (cf. Hofstede 1991) with a homogenous set of values and taboos they strongly assert and for which they require full respect, the American Jewish community constitutes as a whole a self-confident low-context society (*ibidem*) more focused on the future achievements of its single members rather than on a backward mourning over their tragic past as a community. This has led American Jews to allow a derogatory, and even a self-derogatory humour targeting their cultural and religious peculiarities, which emerges not only in the entertainment industry but also in academic sociolinguistic studies. Deborah Tannen (1981), for instance, reports (not without some touch of self-disparagement humour!) a case study on the "New York Jewish conversation style" substantiating the negative stereotype of the "pushy New York Jew" that results "from discourse conventions practiced by some native New Yorkers of East European Jewish background" (*ibidem*: 133) as she herself is—being also one of the subjects of her case study. Tannen's 'entertaining' research is based on Labov's (1970) ethnographic work providing evidence of the lack of confidence experienced by middle-class Jewish New York women with regard to their accent evaluated as 'too aggressive' (cf. Erickson 1975), which induced them to start a process of correction whose result was a lack of spontaneity and authenticity in their speech style. One of the well-known risks is in fact to turn accent evaluation into personality evaluation of the speakers to the point that it may even affect employability judgements—as evident in the research conducted by Van Antwerp and Maxwell (1982) documenting New York Jewish women being assessed, on the sole basis of accent, as 'unable to articulate', 'disorganized and dull', till defining them as 'not very together'. Tannen (1981: 137-138) identifies four features characterizing the New York Jewish conversational style, which can be easily detected in the way the Jewish characters in

The Nanny interact with each other and with the other non-Jewish characters of the sitcom. They are: *(a) Topic*, marked by a preference for personal subjects, frequently shifted to a different one or introduced without hesitancy and reintroduced repeatedly if not immediately picked up; *(b) Genre*, marked by telling more stories based on the teller's emotional experience and dramatized, rather than lexicalized; *(c) Pacing*, marked by a fast rate of speech, overlap (with the often misinterpreted cooperative intent of showing enthusiasm and interest), fast turn-taking or avoidance of inter-turn pauses; *(d) Expressive Paralinguistics*, marked by expressive phonology and shifts in pitch, amplitude and voice quality. The effect of such 'abrupt' speech style on non-Jewish participants in the conversation is catching them off guard making them uncomfortable as they tend to perceive it as a rude lack of attention and respect towards what they want to say, rather than as enthusiastic interest (*ibidem*: 143). Tannen humorously admits that Jewish speakers "on hearing a taperecording of a conversation they thoroughly enjoyed in the process, they often feel critical of themselves and slightly embarrassed. They, too, believe that it is rude to interrupt, to talk loudly, to talk too much." (*ibidem*: 145). Tannen (*ibidem*: 147) concludes: "I suspect that the existence of this style represents the influence of conversational norms of East European Jewish immigrants"—which is exactly the origin of the Jewish characters in *The Nanny* and her peculiar speech style. How to render then such 'Jewish conversational style' into Italian? A solution—to be later advocated in this book (Chapter 5)—is to choose dubbing actors with the same ethnic or national/regional background as the original characters of the sitcom so as to reproduce, in Italian, their typical phonological and intonation features (cf. Salmon Kovarski 2000).

This respect for the socio-cultural, pragmatic and phonological patterns of the original sitcom has not occurred in the case of the Italian adaptation of *The Nanny*. Here, Francesca Cacace (i.e., the Italian name attributed to the nanny Fran Fine) and her family are Italian immigrants from Lazio, the region where Rome is located (more precisely, from Frosinone, a town in the rural area of Ciociaria) and, thus, their accent and speech style are quite different from the original Jewish way of speaking, and this is evident even in the protagonist's voice quality. Whereas Fran Fine speaks with a low-pitch, smooth and naughty intonation, Francesca Cacace is dubbed with a high-pitch, nagging intonation feigning naivety of the kind identified in the overacting performance by some Italian actresses of the fifties in Neorealist movies—Sophia Loren and Gina Lollobrigida being the international prototypes. This, however, entails trying to adapt to the target version also features of the Yiddish language still persistent in the Jewish variety of American English: a case in point is the typically Yiddish interjection 'oy!' which Goffman (1978) ranked among the 'response cries' aimed at building a rapport by unconsciously signalling a shared ethnic background to the other participants in a conversation (as, for instance, in showing empathy to someone who has just recounted some mishap s/he went through). This interjection occurs a number of times in *The Nanny* (also in the extract to be analyzed), but in the Italian translation it undergoes a process of 'cultural neutralization' being rendered into a 'oh' in an Oh-Receipt Move that, depending on the intonation, may signal acknowledgement, surprise, astonishment, or disappointment. In this last case, it has never rendered into the parallel Italian interjection 'ohi' which is typical of the South of Italy and may have fit perfectly with the origins of the nanny's family in the Italian version. The point is that, in this Italian version, the original humorous disparagement pattern comes to be transferred from the New-York Jewish culture to the uncultivated attitudes and beliefs of Italo-American people who came to the States from the poor provinces of Italy located in the South of Rome. Attacking Southern people with a low schooling level and speaking with a dialectal accent is, after all, an accepted pattern of the Italian disparagement humour. In their search for cross-cultural equivalence, dubbing translators can thus easily resort to their factual and procedural knowledge of the source and target language and culture to render a stereotype in the original comic script into an equivalent one in translation.

This shift in situational context also entails a process of adaptation of the various socio-cultural references in the source script to possible equivalent references in the target version. For instance, in the episode under analysis entitled *Dope Diamond*, Sylva asserts that she did the right thing in compelling Fran to go to the 'Hadassah hoedown', a feast celebrated every year by the Jewish community. In the Italian version, Zia Assunta's reference to this feast was turned into "ballo di famiglia ciociara"—"ball for the families from Ciociaria"—a dance party organized by families of immigrants from the same Italian area. In the same episode, Fran herself mentions a "Hebrew National Party" which, in the Italian adaptation, becomes "Festa nazionale della Ciociaria"—"Ciociaria National Feast". Even references to non-religious events, such as the Broadway celebration called "Renaissance Weekend", gathering all the most distinguished people in town (and from which Maxwell was excluded to his great disappointment), was misinterpreted by Fran as a "Renaissance Fair" and by Francesca, in the Italian version, as a Christmas Fair where people from her home town, Frosinone, make together "the living crib with Baby Jesus whose rebirth occurs every year at Christmas" ("il presepe vivente con il bambinello che rinasce ogni anno a Natale"—with a marked wordplay between 'rinascita' - 'rebirth'—and 'rinascimento' - 'renaissance'). Apart from these religious references, which abound in the whole sitcom, other kinds of cultural adaptation are systematically carried out. An instance may be considered the rendering of the titles of some famous American TV programme into equivalent Italian ones, such as, for example, the quiz show *Duds* that is rendered into *La Corrida di Corrado*, a famous Italian talent show hosted by the compere Corrado. Strange enough, references to films that are famous also in Italy were converted into something totally different, such as the hint at the movie *Dumb and Dumber*—which in Italy was literally translated into *Scemo e Più Scemo*—rendered instead into *La Settimana di Paperino* (*Donald Duck's Week*). Other references to Italian contexts are made even when they are not required. In the episode *Fran and the Professor*, Fran argues with Maxwell: "Oh, don't try and get on my good side, mister", which in Italian becomes "non è colpa mia se in casa non avete neanche una Fontana di Trevi" ("it's not my fault if at home you haven't even got a Trevi Fountain") and she continues: "we both know that I'm not as smart or cultivated as you are", which is rendered into "Lo so che sono solo una maestra elementare e che Frosinone non è New York e che quindi forse non ho la sua cultura" ("I know that I'm just a primary-school teacher and that Frosinone is not New York and that therefore maybe I haven't got your education"), and which is exceedingly too long to fit into the time lapse required to accomplish lip-synchronization in dubbing.

4.2.3 *The use of allocutions in the original and the dubbed versions of* The Nanny

Another feature characterizing the Italian of dubbed English movies is the non-natural pragmatic use of allocutions (Pavesi 1996). The fact that the English language does not grammaticalize allocution (as Italian instead does by means of the pronouns 'tu', 'lei', and 'voi', signalling different degrees of formality in interactions) means that the dubbing translator has to understand thoroughly the actual social relationships between the interacting characters within the original situational contexts in order to provide acceptable equivalent levels of formality in Italian. Indeed, English has a series of pragmatic strategies—such as titles, proper names, but also modalization, hedging, etc.—to make up for its shortage of allocution choices apart from the pronoun 'you', and often such strategies are adopted to signal power or solidarity relations between the participants in an interaction (cf. Brown and Gilman 1972; Braun 1988). Pavesi (1996: 12) identifies a widespread use of the informal second-person 'tu' in the Italian dubbing of English dialogues between working-class or young speakers, as well as a frequent use of a 'despising *tu*' in the dialogue between higher/lower-status speakers where the higher-status participant in the interaction (e.g., a policeman) addresses the lower-status one (e.g., a criminal) with the scornful second-person pronoun 'tu'. Also addressing a person only by his/her surname signals a higher/lower-status relationship in English, usually in contexts where a master addresses a servant. This happens in the sitcom *The Nanny*, in which the master of the house addresses his nanny (and, for humorous effects, also incongruously his close friend and the woman he secretly loves) by her surname, namely Miss Fine. The nanny, in her turn, addresses her master by using the complex allocution 'Mr. Sheffield', which is common in a British context to signal a lower-status speaker's social distance from—and respect for—a higher-status one (although in the sitcom she is flirtatious with him). But when it is literally reproduced in the Italian version of the sitcom (where the nanny addresses him as 'Signor Sheffield', not simply as 'Signore' or 'Dottore' as it would happen in Italian) this formal type of allocution conveys a distorted sense of deliberate detachment and even insolence (cf. Mazzoleni 1995: 398-399) which is absent in the original. Conversely, whereas in the original sitcom Mr. Sheffield formally addresses the nanny by her surname as 'Miss Fine', and sometimes as 'Nanny Fine', thus preserving the master/servant social roles in his attempts to distance himself from the nanny's romantic/sexual innuendos, in the Italian dubbed version, instead, he shifts to the more informal first name, 'Francesca', sometimes accompanied by the childish epithet 'Tata Francesca' which in Italian would convey a deeper sense of intimacy than in the English usage (cf. Pavesi 1996: 127). This entails altering the Arousal/Safety structure of humour of the original sitcom based on the reversal of the conventional and asymmetrical gender relations of dominance and subordination as they are 'constructed in interaction' (Tannen 1994: 10) in an ongoing process in which one participant's intentions are systematically misinterpreted by the other participant (Tannen 1993). Being aware of such socio-cultural subtleties—or sociolects—in both source and target languages also entails the dubbing translator's understanding of the world schemata which inform and justify their use and misuse in the humorous language of the sitcom. Such sociolects, in fact, are always integral to a system of kinesic, proxemic and intonation codes which give them a visual and auditory context, emphasizing social-status and power/solidarity relations between the interacting speakers. In the Italian version of *The Nanny*, for instance, Mr. Sheffield and the nanny address each other with the formal 'third-person-as-second-person' pronoun 'lei' which is inconsistent with the proxemic dimension of their relation revealing a high degree of restrained intimacy triggering the Arousal/Safety pattern of humour of the sitcom. This is not so pragmatically evident in the original English version where the reciprocal use of the neutral second-person address pronoun 'you' does not stress the humorous incongruity between the character's strife to keep the socially-asymmetrical conventions unaltered and their desire to break them signalled by proxemic and intonation strategies aimed at narrowing the social and emotional distance that separates them. Furthermore, in the original version of this sitcom, Mr. Sheffield addresses the nanny's mother by her first name, Sylvia, which in English is not always regarded so impolite as it would be perceived in Italian when used by a younger male speaker to address an elder woman. In fact, addressing an elderly person by name in English pragmatics would be perceived as a sign of the addresser's familiarity authorized by the addressee who is higher in status within an asymmetrical interaction. Sylvia, however, addresses her daughter's employer by using the formal address term 'Mr. Sheffield', hence the familiarity authorization is not reciprocal. In the Italian version of this dubbed American sitcom, Mr. Sheffield addresses Sylvia as 'Signora', thus re-establishing the social symmetry of the interaction (higher-status/elderly interacting people) by means of the formal dimension of the terms of address.

However, in consideration that two different cultural minorities (the Jewish and the South-Italian ones), and the relative pragmalinguistic ways of interacting, are respectively attacked and disparaged in the original and translated versions of this sitcom—and that the character who embodies the values, attitudes and linguistic expressions of such minorities is the protagonist, who also happens to be a woman—*The Nanny* may be considered as a sitcom in which humorous negotiation is vital for the comic style of its conversation which, otherwise, would be stigmatized as racist, sexist and class-conscious. Without a humorous negotiation, in fact, the 'Arousal' prompted by the indignation at the often outrageous puns would not be followed by the relief induced by the sense of 'Safety' at realizing that meanings are after all socially negotiable under the comic circumstances of the sitcom. Specific negotiating moves are therefore crucial in the context of this sitcom which, like the others under analysis in this book, represents an interesting example of socio-cultural and conversational strategies taking place within new typologies of family units. In the next section such negotiation moves shall be therefore explored.

4.3 A Comparative Conversation Analysis of *The Nanny* Script

4.3.1 *Intonation as 'move marker' in humorous conversation: Request, Apology and Negotiation Moves*

In a context like the one represented in *The Nanny*, involving a situation of actual 'intercultural and interethnic (mis)communication' in which the traditional social characters are challenged, a conversational Move (with its related Act) that could enhance mediation in situations of pressing Requests and unaccepted Apologies is a new one, never introduced in Conversation Analysis models so far—namely, the Negotiation Move (and the related Negotiate Act). By this Move, sitcom characters from different socio-cultural and ethnic backgrounds can in fact succeed in solving conflicts within Arousal/Safety and Disparagement patterns of humour, thus inducing the necessary sense of 'relief' in audiences and triggering the cathartic laughter.

There are, however, some 'negotiation maxims' (Myers Scotton 1983) that need to be respected in a sitcom conversation like this, marked by social and ethnic challenges. First of all, negotiation maxims in conversation have to acknowledge a certain degree of markedness determined by the participants' level of divergence from the accepted norms of their speech community (cf. Guido 2009). By speech community is here meant not simply a community speaking the same native language, but also sharing the same socio-cultural values codified in a set of pragmatic norms that are, thus, 'situated' within a specific context. If the participants in a conversation belong to two (or more) different speech communities, the level of divergence—and, thus, the degree of markedness—is obviously expected to be higher and, as a consequence, misunderstandings may be more frequent. Hence, it is necessary that participants come to a negotiation not only of their meanings, but also of their identities and values to achieve an agreement on the interpretation of their conversational implicatures (Bach 1994). It is a typical feature of humour, of course, the one that makes participants in a conversation go through a series of misunderstandings on how to interpret implicatures before coming to an agreement by negotiation – thus causing relief and laughter as a response to such humorous discourse. Differently from Grice's (1975) cooperative principle and its set of maxims focusing on the content of what is said, to make conversation efficient to the utmost, Myers Scotton's (1983: 116-117) negotiation principle deals with maxims depending on the choice of the linguistic register in which the content of what is said comes to be conveyed in conversation. The participants' respective conversational implicatures underlying their register choices, in fact, require their convergence on an interpretation, which also has to be 'salient' for them in order to make their exchange socially acceptable, efficient and successful. The achievement of an interpretative convergence on an interpretation, and the evaluation of its salience (cf. Guido 2001), can be possible only by means of the participants' joint process of negotiation of their social rights and obligations. Normally, in a conventionalised exchange, the societal norms are well defined and acknowledged by both participants, thus their rights and obligations in the unfolding of the exchange are recognized and unmarked. For instance, a Request Move in a conventionalised exchange will predictably receive the expected preferred response with the receiver's supply of the required goods or services. If the Request Move is not of a socially sanctioned type, then the expected response will be instead the speaker's dispreferred one. Yet, if this pragmatic mechanism works for conventionalised exchanges, it does not work at all with non-conventionalized exchanges where there is not any established agreement between the participants on the unmarked interpretation of the conversational content and its implicatures. Needless to say, this is the typical case of sitcom conversations characterized by the participants' marked exchanges flouting social rights and obligations to create situations of Arousal/Safety and Disparagement humour. In fact, whereas in conventionalised exchanges speakers interpret each other's implicatures by making reference to a shared pragmatic code and social norms that help them disambiguate the illocutionary force of what they intend to communicate, in non-conventionalized exchanges the disambiguation of the participants' intentions is not so automatic because the participants themselves interacting in the conversation tend to deviate (deliberately or unintentionally) from the set of sanctioned socio-pragmatic norms shared within the speech community the conversation takes place, thus making their exchange a 'marked' one, requiring therefore a reciprocal negotiation action aimed to cooperation. This explains the need for the participants in a marked exchange to be aware of the 'negotiation principle' (Myers Scotton 1983: 120) which would allow them to interpret each other's conversational implicatures in the correct way and to achieve mutual understanding. For instance, in a marked exchange, where shared social rights and obligations are disregarded by the participants, a Directive Move formulated in an indirect way can be misinterpreted as something else, for example, as a Request for information—as in this example from Sinclair and Coulthard (1975: 5): "*Father:* Is that your coat on the floor again?—*Son:* "Yes". If such a reply in an everyday conversation is considered as rude or, at best, unfocused, since it comes from a son answering his father and, in doing so, disrupting a normative 'power differential' between them (Goody 1978), in a comic situation the son's unexpected and dispreferred reply that misinterprets the illocutionary force of the father's implicature can provoke the audience's laughter as it produces a humorous trigger of an 'Arousal' type that disrupts the accepted social norms of behaviour regarding 'authority recognition and obedience'. In other terms, as Myers Scotton (1983: 121) remarks, "a powerful person's interrogative utterances have a general unmarked interpretation as directives, not requests for information". To re-establish the social order (which would prompt the sense of 'Relief' that the audience of a humorous discourse actually expects in order to resolve the tension caused by social disruption) a Negotiation Move, developed according to a specific negotiation principle, is necessary to achieve disambiguation. The Negotiation principle advanced by Myers Scotton (*ibidem*) can be seen as part of the 'accommodation theory' proposed by Giles and Powesland (1975), which explains in terms of 'speaker's motivation' the strategies of sociopragmatic-code divergence, convergence, or 'social-code exploration' adopted by a participant in a conversation while interacting with another higher/lower-status participant. Indeed, these strategies imply the speaker's activation of multiple identities for himself/herself as s/he explores and takes decisions about the ways in which s/he wants the conversation to unfold. This is what Myers Scotton (1983: 126-127) defines as 'the multiple-identity maxim' of the negotiation principle—namely, the most relevant maxim insofar as it allows a participant in a conversation to switch among different pragmalinguistic codes that evoke different sets of social rights and obligations in order to convey "the conversational implicature that [s/he] has multiple identities and [that such code switching] also offers [the other participant] options regarding the right-and-obligation set to be established for the exchange." If a participant decides to flout the established set of rights and obligations (RO set) to be followed in the exchange, then s/he intends to make a 'marked choice' that "generates the implicature that [the participant] is 'disidentifying' herself/himself with the unmarked RO set" and that, therefore, signals the participant's covert request for "a negotiation to establish a different RO set as unmarked" (*ibidem*: 127). The expected response from the other participants is an emotional one as the accepted status quo in that particular social context runs the risk of being disrupted. In a sitcom, the characters' emotional Moves in reply to another character's marked request for negotiation is, at the beginning, usually an expected Refusal - if not Disparagement - because the Negotiation Move is misinterpreted as a Challenge flouting both the cooperation (Grice 1975) and politeness (Brown and Levinson 1978) principles. But then, eventually, Relief arises, and generates the comic effect, when an agreement among the participants is reached and the intended illocutionary force of the request is disambiguated. To this, it usually follows an Apology Move which reveals the motivation behind the request for negotiation, thus making markedness unmarked.

However, sitcom scripts are not to be analyzed in their written form—indeed, conversational moves can be identified only by watching the actors' embodiment of the sitcom characters. This means that intonation is crucial as a marker of moves in humorous dialogue insofar as it helps disambiguating them. A humorous script is only in part a written text—in fact it is an unscripted spoken discourse co-constructed by the participants in the interaction to achieve their conversational goals (cf. Couper-Kuhlen and Selting 1996) but also "to jointly construct and negotiate verbal interaction" (Wichmann 2000: 125). Wichmann (*ibidem*) goes on arguing:

> "Conversational Analysis is concerned primarily with uncovering 'structures' in conversation—building blocks such as turn-taking rules and adjacency pairs, openings and closings etc. It is my view that these cannot be an end in themselves but are one step on the way to explaining interactional *meaning*, which relies crucially on an understanding of how these structures operate in a social context. The many approaches to the study of interpersonal meaning, broadly subsumed under the heading of 'pragmatics', rarely take intonation into account. The contribution of intonation to meaning still lurks unsatisfactorily under the 'paralinguistic' or 'attitudinal' label. This is a convenient but unenlightening way of accounting for what ultimately matters most in human interaction—what people mean."

Wichmann's contention highlights the notion of 'conversational routines' (Aijmer 1996), or 'discourse markers' (Schiffrin 1987), explaining them "in terms of how they are realized prosodically" as, for instance, pitch and tempo variations that mark the meaning of a "spoken utterance" (Wichmann 2000: 126). Within the boundaries of spoken utterances, Wichmann (*ibidem*: 130) identifies the conversational moves within what Ladd (1996) defines as a 'tonal space' created by variations in pitch range. This means that, for instance, a high pitch is more phatic as it tries to get the attention of the hearer and thus, it may be defined as 'hearer-oriented'. Conversely, a low pitch is more detached and proposition-oriented. Shifts in pitch have however to be negotiated to guarantee successful communication, hence negotiation may occur only by using larger units of discourse—namely, the conversational moves, whose meaning is crucially determined by intonation and the turn-taking system (cf. Cutler and Pearson 1986). In turn-taking, a 'downstep'—or low drop syllable (cf. Crystal 1969; Cruttenden 1986)—marks the falling contour (↓) of a Head Act in a Move and, thus, usually sounds final, determining the end of a turn (Cutler and Pearson 1986: 149). An 'upstep' (*ibidem*), instead, is a tonic syllable that marks the rising contour (↑) of an Act usually within Opening and Continuing Moves (cf. Wichmann 2000: 134), thus signalling that the speaker controls the topic and does not intend to cede the floor to other speakers. If this is almost the norm in spontaneous conversation, it may not be so in scripted sitcom conversations aiming at humorous effects. In such cases, flouting such intonation norms to obtain the opposite effect may be a strategy to prompt laughter in audiences. The process of 'talk negotiation' (cf. Couper-Kuhlen and Selting 1996: 31) by means of intonation is rather the sitcom norm to achieve humorous relief in an Arousal/Safety structure. The Arousal part of the pattern of humour is instead often conveyed by 'competitive interruptions' trying to steal the floor from the current speaker (cf. French and Local 1986) by activating loud rising pitch in types of challenging moves. But, again, intonation can modify the intentions of Moves that are semantically marked since they mean one thing whereas tone and pitch can make them mean the opposite. Whichmann (2000: 140) argues:

> "The orthographic transcription suggests supportive backchannels responses, but in fact they sound highly competitive. The word *right*, spoken with a rising tone, could be heard as encouragement meaning 'yes, I understand, please continue'. [...] [But, if] the speaker uses a falling tone (also spoken very rapidly) the effect is very different. The sense of closure conveyed by the way [...] [the word *right* is spoken] does not imply support. On the contrary, it suggests an attempt to end the current speaker's topic and turn."

Sometimes, as Wichmann (*ibidem*: 146) points out, the speaker's meaning implications may be intentional, thus generating 'prosodic implicature', or unintentional, thus prompting the receiver to draw his/her own 'inference' from what has been said. In any case, however, intonation conveys not simply the speaker's intention, but also his/her attitudes (or behaviours) and emotions (meant as feelings, beliefs and opinions) (*ibidem*: 145).

At this point, the theoretical aspects outlined so far shall be applied to the conversation analysis of an extract from an episode of *The Nanny*.

4.3.2 *Case study: a comparative conversation analysis of a script from* The Nanny *sitcom*

The novel model of comparative sitcom-conversation analysis introduced in this section intends to contribute to the recent, ongoing search for an effective and reliable approach to the multimodal transcription of audiovisual texts in script analysis and translation (cf. Thibault 2000; Chaume 2002, 2004; Baldry and Thibault 2006) by proposing a method aimed at identifying the interplay between:

(a) Moves (M) of Arousal *(A)*, Safety *(S)*, or Disparagement *(D)* types, and either 'preferred' or 'dispreferred' ones in terms of the receiver's social and individual expectations;

(b) Acts (A) of *Pre-Head, Head,* or *Post-Head* types;

(c) Intonation contours (falling ↓ and rising ↑ tones)

(d) Physical and spatial dimensions of the interaction, by possibly introducing relevant freeze frames or, rather, video extracts or, alternatively, accurate descriptions of each conversation exchange (cf. Coulthard and Brazil 1981), or—still more precisely—of each conversation turn (cf. Martin 2000) of the scene under analysis, better if turns are tagged with their duration in terms of seconds/minutes as this is useful for timing lip-synchronization in dubbing (not fully examined in the present analysis which does not focus specifically on timing and lip-synchronization, although this technical aspect of dubbing was explored in related classroom tasks).

The outcome of such conversational interplay would characterize the comic style of this sitcom dialogue. To contribute to this, the Negotiation Move has been introduced to mediate embarrassing situations, often covertly conveying humorous disparagement patterns. The comparative conversation analysis shall be carried out on the original version of the script and on its dubbing translation for the Italian television (*La Tata*), both tagged for their respective patterns of Moves, Acts and Intonation contours and numbered with reference to the turns progressively taken by various characters. This Italian version goes with its literal back-translation into Standard English. The selected script reproduces an instance of what has been here defined as a Revelation plot in which the classic Arousal/Safety pattern of humour comes to be interpreted according to a novel Revelation/Negotiation pattern fitting these specific sitcom situations. As outlined in *4.1.1*, in the following extract to be analyzed, drawn from the episode *Dope Diamond*, Fran, the Nanny, (Francesca, in the translated version), reveals to her employer Maxwell Sheffield (who is secretly in love with her and is secretly returned) and his children that Jules, the handsome and rich doctor she has dated for only two weeks, has proposed to her. Fran also reveals that she has not yet accepted the proposal, but her hesitation irritates her mother Sylvia (Aunt Assunta in the Italian version) with whom Fran has to start a negotiation since she fiercely pressurizes her into accepting to marry him by emotionally blackmailing her. Finally, Fran has to yield to her mother who also impedes her to negotiate with Maxwell trying to make Fran change her mind. Later in the same episode another shocking revelation occurs: Jules turns out to be a thief who steals in a jewellery the engagement ring chosen by Fran, who is thus deeply humiliated. This is the tagged script:

The Nanny (***La Tata***) episode #304 *Dope Diamond*
(*Giulio, aitante e brillante—Giulio, handsome and smart*)
Exchange 1: turns [1]-[4]; Exchange 2: turns [5]-[28]; Exchange 3: turns [29]-[40]

Original English version:	***Italian dubbing translation:***	***Back-translation into Standard English:***
[Int. Dining Room] *(Maxwell and his children are having supper)*	**[Int. Sala da pranzo]** *(Maxwell e i suoi figli stanno cenando)*	**[Int. Dining Room]** *(Maxwell and his children are having supper)*
[1] **MAXWELL: [a]** Please, Sylvia↓, **[b]** why - why don't you join us?↓ **[a. Open M*(A)*, Nomination A *Pre-Head* + b. Negotiation M*(D)*, Elicit A *Head*]**	***[1]*** **MAXWELL: [a]** Signora Assunta↑, **[b]** non vuole sedersi a tavola con noi?↑ **[a. Summon M*(A)*, Bid A *Pre-Head* + b. Negotiation M*(D)*, Invite A *Head*]**	***[1]*** **MAXWELL:** Signora Assunta *[approx. Mrs. Fine]*, won't you like to sit down to eat with us?
[2] **SYLVIA: [a]** Oh, no↓. **[b]** I just came over to see how Fran's date went↓. **[c]** Make like I'm not even here↓. **[a. Refusal M*(S)* *socially-dispreferred / receiver-preferred*, Reply A *Pre-Head* + b. Inform M/A*(S)* *Head* + c. Direct M*(A)*, Clue A *Post-Head*]**	***[2]*** **ZIA ASSUNTA: [a]** Oh no, **[b]** io sono qui solo per sentire da Francesca com'è andata oggi↑. **[c]** Mangi↑ **[d]** e faccia come se io non ci fossi↓. **[a. Refusal M*(S)* *socially-dispreferred / receiver-preferred*, Reply A *Pre-Head* + b. Inform M/A*(S)* *Head* + c. Direct M*(A)*, clue A *Head* + d. Upgrade M*(A)*, Clue A *Post-Head*]**	***[2]*** **AUNT ASSUNTA:** Oh, no. I'm here just to hear from Francesca how things were getting on today. Go on eating and make like I'm not here.
[3] **NILES:** Are you sure we can't offer you something?↑ **[Offer M*(S)*, Elicit A]**	***[3]*** **NILES:** È sicura che non possiamo offrirle qualcosa?↑ **[Offer M*(S)*, Elicit A]**	***[3]*** **NILES:** Are you sure we can't offer you something?
[4] **SYLVIA: [a]** Oh, no, thank you↓. **[b]** I had a yoplait this morning around 10:30↓. *(She takes a potato from Grace's dish)* **[c]** Oh↑, such a big potato for such a little girl↑. **[d]** Look at the time↑. **[e]** They must be having a ball↑. **[f]** I'm gonna go in the kitchen↓. **[g]** I need a meat to wash this down with↓. **[a. Refusal M*(S)* *socially-dispreferred / receiver-preferred*, Reply A *Pre-Head* + b. Inform M/A*(S)* *Head* + c. Focus M*(A)*, Comment A *Head* +**	***[4]*** **ZIA ASSUNTA: [a]** No, no, no grazie, **[b]** sono a dieta↓ **[c]** e sto morendo di fame↓, **[d]** ma voi mangiate tranquilli↓. *(Prende una patata dal piatto di Grace)* **[e]** Oh↑, una patata troppo grande per una bambina così piccola!↓ **[f]** Però, come tardano!↑ **[g]** Si vede che si divertiranno molto!↑ **[h]** Se non vi spiace vado in cucina↓, **[i]** ci vuole del manzo come contorno ad una grossa patata↓. **[a. Refusal M*(S)* *socially-dispre-***	***[4]*** **AUNT ASSUNTA:** No, no, no, thank you. I'm on diet and I'm starving, but please, go on eating easy. *(She takes a potato from Grace's dish)* Oh, a too big potato for such a little girl! Hey, how late they are! They must be having a very good time! *[idiom: they must be having a ball]* If you don't mind I'm going in the kitchen, some beef is required as a side dish for a big potato. *(Aunt Assunta leaves the dining room)*

d. Focus M*(A)* Cue A *Pre-Head* + e. Upgrade M*(A)*, Evaluate A *Head* + f. Inform M/A*(S)* *Pre-Head* + g. Upgrade M*(A)*, Evaluate A *Head*] *(Sylvia leaves the dining room)*	***preferred / receiver-preferred*, Reply A *Pre-Head* + b. Inform M/A*(S)* *Head* + c. Upgrade M*(A)*, Inform A *Adjunct to Head* + d. Direct M*(A)*, Clue A *Adjunct to Head* + e. Focus M*(A)*, Comment A *Head* + f. Focus M*(A)*, Evaluate A *Pre-Head* + g. Upgrade M*(A)*, Evaluate A *Head* + h. Inform M/A*(S)* *Pre-Head* + i. Upgrade M*(A)*, Evaluate A *Head*]** *(Zia Assunta esce dalla stanza)*	
***[5]* BRIGHTON: [a]** I don't know about you guys↓, but I like Jules↓, **[b]** and he has yet to beat me in chess↑. **[a. Negotiation M*(S)*, Evaluate A *Pre-Head+Head* + b. Upgrade M*(S)*, Comment A *Post-Head*]**	***[5]* BRIGHTON: [a]** Non so a voi↑, ma a me Giulio piace molto↓ **[b]** e non mi ha battuto neanche una volta a scacchi↓. **[a. Negotiation M*(S)*, Evaluate A *Pre-Head+Head* + b. Upgrade M*(S)*, Comment A *Post-Head*]**	***[5]* BRIGHTON:** I don't know if you do, but I like Giulio a lot and he has beaten me not a single time in chess.
***[6]* MAXWELL:** Oh, God, Brighton↓, he throws every game↑. **[Challenge M*(D)*, Evaluate A *Pre-Head+Head*]**	***[6]* MAXWELL:** Ma su, Brighton↓, è lui che vuole perdere!↓ **[Challenge M*(D)*, Evaluate A *Pre-Head+Head*]**	***[6]* MAXWELL:** Come on, Brighton, it's him who wants to lose!
***[7]* BRIGHTON:** Do you see how easy it is to bond?↑ **[Challenge M*(A)*, Elicit A]**	***[7]* BRIGHTON:** È così che si diventa amici↓. **[Challenge M*(A)*, Comment A]**	***[7]* BRIGHTON:** That's how people become friends!
***[8]* MAXWELL: [a]** Well, I wouldn't get too attached to the bloke if I were you↑. **[b]** We all know Miss Fine's relationships eventually end in disaster↓. **[a. Challenge M*(A)* Direct A *Head* + b. Blame M*(D)*, Comment A *Post-Head*]**	***[8]* MAXWELL: [a]** Guarda↓, **[b]** se fossi in te non mi ci affezionerei troppo a Giulio↓. **[c]** I rapporti di Francesca con gli uomini finiscono sempre in un disastro↓. **[a. Focus M/A*(A)* *Pre-Head* + b. Challenge M*(A)* Direct A *Head* + c. Blame M*(D)*, Comment A *Post-Head*]**	***[8]* MAXWELL:** Look, if I were you I wouldn't get too attached to Giulio. Francesca's relationships with men always end up in disaster.
(Fran enters) ***[9]* FRAN:** He asked me to marry him↑. **[Inform M/A*(A)*]**	*(Entra Francesca)* ***[9]* FRANCESCA: [a]** Ragazzi, **[b]** mi ha chiesto di sposarlo!↓ **[a. Summon M*(A)*, Bid A *Pre-Head* + b. Inform M/A*(A)* *Head*]**	*(Francesca enters)* ***[9]* FRANCESCA:** Guys, he asked me to marry him!
***[10]* NILES:** Right on the money as always↑, sir↑. **[Challenge M*(A)*, Comment A]**	***[10]* NILES:** Come sempre, signore↑, c'ha azzeccato↓. **[Challenge M*(A)* , Comment A]**	***[10]* NILES:** As always, sir, you guessed right.
***[11]* BRIGHTON:** That is so cool, Fran↓. Congratulations↓. **[Support M*(A)*, Evaluate A]**	***[11]* BRIGHTON:** Bene, brava Francesca! Congratulazioni↓. **[Support M*(A)*, Evaluate A]**	***[11]* BRIGHTON:** Well done, bravo Francesca! Congratulations.
***[12]* FRAN: [a]** I know, I know. **[b]** I can't believe it↓. **[c]** I'm so excited↓. I couldn't eat a - **[d]** oh, kielbasa↑, **[e]** sweet and sour cabbage↑. *(To Niles)* **[f]** Hit me again↓. *(She takes a corn from Grace's dish)* **[g]** Oh, such a big corn↓ for such a little girl↓. **[a. Agree M*(A)*, Acknowledge A *Pre-Head* + b. Upgrade M*(A)*, Inform A *Head* + c. Upgrade**	***[12]* FRANCESCA: [a]** Oh che bello!↑ Che bello!↑ **[b]** Non riesco a crederci!↑ **[c]** Sono così eccitata↑ che neanche ceno↓ – **[d]** uh↑, i salsicciotti↓, **[e]** oh e anche i cavoli in agrodolce↓, *(rivolta a Niles)* **[f]** gli dia dentro!↓ *(Prende una pannocchia dal piatto di Grace)* **[g]** È una pannocchia troppo grande per te↓.**[a. Upgrade M*(A)*, Comment A**	***[12]* FRANCESCA:** Oh, how marvelous! How marvelous! I can't believe it! I'm so excited that I couldn't even dine — uh, the sausages, oh, and also the sweet and sour cabbages, *(to Niles)* let's tuck in! *(She takes a corn from Grace's dish)* This is a corn too big for you.

M*(A)*, Inform A *Post-Head* + d. Oh-Receipt M*(S)*, Evaluate A *Pre-Head* + e. Upgrade M*(S)*, Clue A *Pre-Head* + f. Direct M/A*(A) Head* + g. Focus M*(A)*, Comment A *Head*]	***Pre-Head* + b. Upgrade M *(A)*, Inform A *Head* + c. Upgrade M*(A)*, Inform A *Post-Head* + d. Oh-Receipt M*(S)*, Evaluate A *Pre-Head* + e. Upgrade M*(S)*, Clue A *Pre-Head* + f. Direct M/A*(A) Head* + g. Focus M*(A)*, Comment A *Head*]**	
***[13]* MAXWELL:** He asked you to marry him?↑ **[Elicit M*(D)*, Check A]**	***[13]* MAXWELL:** Ma davvero le ha chiesto di sposarlo?↑ **[Challenge M*(A)*, Check A]**	***[13]* MAXWELL:** But, did he really ask you to marry him?
***[14]* FRAN:** Uh-huh↑. **[Answer M(A) *socially-preferred / receiver-dispreferred,* Reply A]**	***[14]* FRANCESCA:** Uh-uh. **[Answer M(A) *socially-preferred / receiver-dispreferred,* Reply A]**	***[14]* FRANCESCA:** Uh-huh.
***[15]* MAXWELL:** You've barely known the man for two weeks↓. **[Blame M*(D)* + Comment A]**	***[15]* MAXWELL:** Lo conosce solo da due settimane↓. **[Blame M*(D)* + Comment A]**	***[15]* MAXWELL:** You've barely known him for two weeks.
***[16]* FRAN: [a]** What?↑ **[b]** You think it's so hard to believe a man would fall in love with me that fast?↑ **[a. Challenge M*(A)*, React A *Pre-Head* + b. Elicit M/A*(D) Head*]**	***[16]* FRANCESCA: [a]** No, cosa significa?↑ **[b]** Un uomo ci deve sempre mettere anni per dire che è innamorato?↑ **[a. Focus M*(A)*, React A *Pre-Head* + b. Challenge M*(D)*, Elicit A *Head*]**	***[16]* FRANCESCA:** No, what does it mean? A man has to wait for years before telling that he is in love?
***[17]* GRACE: [a]** Yeah. **[b]** Todd and I knew each other three minutes before I got↑ a Pudding-Pack right in the eye↓. **[a. Acknowledge M/A*(S) Pre-Head* + b. Downgrade M*(S)*, Comment A *Head*]**	***[17]* GRACE: [a]** Giusto↓. **[b]** Todd, appena conosciuto↑, mi ha subito buttato il primo budino in faccia↓. **[a. Acknowledge M/A*(S) Pre-Head* + b. Downgrade M*(S)*, Comment A *Head*]**	***[17]* GRACE:** Right. Todd, as soon as I met him, threw the first pudding at hand on my face.
***[18]* FRAN:** There you go↑. **[Acknowledge M/A*(A)*]**	***[18]* FRANCESCA:** Ecco, ha sentito?↑ **[Acknowledge M/A*(A)*]**	***[18]* FRANCESCA:** There you go, have you heard that?
***[19]* MAXWELL: [a]** You know nothing about this man↓. **[b]** All right↓, so he's a doctor↓. **[c]** Is he a specialist?↑ **[a. Blame M*(D)*, React A *Head* + b. Acknowledge M*(A)*, Conclusion A *Pre-Head* + c. Challenge M(A), Elicit A *Head*]**	***[19]* MAXWELL: [a]** Oh, ragioni!↓ **[b]** Lei non sa niente di quest'uomo↓. **[c]** D'accordo, lei saprà che fa il medico↓. **[d]** Che medico?↓ Specialistico?↑ **[a. Direct M/A*(A) Pre-Head* b. Blame M*(D)*, React A *Head* + c. Acknowledge M*(A)*, Conclusion A *Pre-Head* + d. Challenge M(A), Elicit A *Head*]**	***[19]* MAXWELL:** Oh, be reasonable! You know nothing about this man. All right, you may know he's a doctor. What kind of doctor? A specialist?
***[20]* FRAN:** You ain't just whistling "Dixie,"↑ baby↑. **[Challenge M*(A)*, Clue A]**	***[20]* FRANCESCA: [a]** Lui è ultra specialisticissimo↓, **[b]** è molto bravo!↓ **[a. Challenge M*(A)*, Clue A + b. Upgrade M*(A)*, Evaluate A]**	***[20]* FRANCESCA:** He is very super-highly-specialized, he's very good!
***[21]* MAXWELL:** Oh, God↓. **[Oh-Receipt M*(A)*, React A]**	***[21]* MAXWELL:** Oh, la testa!↓ **[Oh-Receipt M*(A)*, React A]**	***[21]* MAXWELL:** Oh, the head!
***[22]* MAGGIE: [a]** Oh, this is so exciting↑. **[b]** So can I be a bridesmaid?↑ **[a. Acknowledge M*(S)*, Comment A *Pre-Head* + b. Elicit M/A*(S) Head*]**	***[22]* MAGGIE: [a]** Sono così contenta!↓ **[b]** Mi vuoi come damigella d'onore?↑ **[a. Inform M*(S)*, React A *Pre-Head* + b. Elicit M/A*(S) Head*]**	***[22]* MAGGIE:** I'm so happy! Do you want me as a bridesmaid?

(Sylvia enters behind Fran) *[23]* **FRAN: [a]** I know the doctor asked me to marry him↓, **[b]** but I didn't say yes↑. **[c]** This is delicious↓. **[a. Acknowledge M*(S)*, Reply A *Pre-Head* + b. Challenge M*(A)*, Clue A *Head* + c. Assess M*(S)*, Evaluate A *Post-Head*]**	*(Zia Assunta entra alle spalle di Francesca)* *[23]* **FRANCESCA: [a]** Aspetta, Maggie↓, **[b]** è vero che lui mi ha chiesto di sposarlo↓, **[c]** però io non gli ho detto di sì↑. **[d]** Oh, questo cavolo è delizioso!↓ **[a. Direct M/A*(A)* *Pre-Head* b. Acknowledge M*(S)*, Reply A *Pre-Head* + c. Challenge M*(A)*, Clue A *Head* + d. Assess M*(S)*, Evaluate A *Post-Head*]**	*Aunt Assunta enters behind Francesca)* *[23]* **FRANCESCA:** Hold on, Maggie, it's true that he asked me to marry him, but I didn't say yes to him. Oh, this cabbage is delicious.
(Sylvia falls to the floor behind Fran) *[24]* **SYLVIA:** Why don't you grab a knife and stick it straight through my heart↓. **[Challenge M*(A)*, React A]**	*(Zia Assunta cade al suolo alle spalle di Francesca)* *[24]* **ZIA ASSUNTA: [a]** Che le racconto adesso a mia sorella↑ **[b]** che poi è tua madre?↑ **[a. Focus M*(A)*, Elicit A *Head* + b. Upgrade M*(A)*, Inform A *Post-Head*]**	*(Aunt Assunta falls to the floor behind Francesca)* *[24]* **AUNT ASSUNTA:** What shall I say now to my sister, who is also your mother?
[25] **FRAN:** *(hinting at Grace)* **[a]** That was great↓. She sounded just like - **[b]** Ma! ↓ Ma ... Ma↓, **[c]** let go of my ankle↓. **[a. Assess M*(S)*, Evaluate A *Pre-Head+Head* + b. Summon M*(A)*, Bid A *Pre-Head* + c. Direct M/A*(A)* *Head*]**	*[25]* **FRANCESCA:** *(riferendosi a Grace)* **[a]** Ah ah ah ma che brava!↑ Sembri proprio Zia↑ As—ah! **[b]** Lasciami↓, lasciami la caviglia!↓ Lasciami la caviglia, **[c]** Zia Assunta!↓ **[a. Assess M*(S)*, Evaluate A *Pre-Head+Head* + b. Direct M/A*(A)* *Head* + c. Summon M*(A)*, Bid A *Post-Head*]**	*[25]* **FRANCESCA:** *(hinting at Grace)* Ah ah ah, how clever! You really sounded like Aunt As—ah! Let, let go of my ankle! Let go of my ankle, Aunt Assunta!
[26] **SYLVIA:** You better run↓. **[Challenge M*(A)*, Direct A]**	*[26]* **ZIA ASSUNTA:** Ti conviene scappare!↓ **[Challenge M*(A)*, Direct A]**	*[26]* **AUNT ASSUNTA:** You better run!
(Fran runs around the table chased by Sylvia) *[27]* **FRAN: [a]** Brighton, **[b]** is she taking off her shoe?↑ **[a. Summon M*(A)*, Bid A *Pre-Head* + b. Question M*(A)*, Check A *Head*]**	*(Francesca corre intorno al tavolo inseguita da Zia Assunta)* *[27]* **FRANCESCA: [a]** Brighton, **[b]** se l'è cavata una scarpa?↑ **[a. Summon M*(A)*, Bid A *Pre-Head* + b. Question M*(A)*, Check A *Head*]**	*(Francesca runs around the table chased by Aunt Assunta)* *[27]* **FRANCESCA:** Brighton, has she taken off her shoe?
[28] **BRIGHTON: [a]** No. **[b]** But she's gonna hurl the corn↑. **[a. Answer M/A*(A)* *Pre-Head, dispreferred* + b. Upgrade M*(D)*, Inform A *Head*]**	*[28]* **BRIGHTON: [a]** No, **[b]** però si è armata di pannocchia↓. **[a. Answer M/A*(A)* *Pre-Head, dispreferred* + b. Upgrade M*(D)*, Inform A *Head*]**	*[28]* **BRIGHTON:** No. But she's armed herself with a corn.
[Int. Kitchen]	**[Int. Cucina]**	**[Int. Kitchen]**
[29] **FRAN: [a]** Oy, oy, oy, oy. Ma↑, **[b]** put down the vegetable↑ and no one gets hurt↓. **[a. Summoning M*(A)*, Bid A *Pre-Head* + b. Direct M/A*(A)* *Head*]**	*[29]* **FRANCESCA: [a]** Oh, oh, oh, oh. Bada!↑ **[b]** O metti giù quella pannocchia↑ o apro l'acqua bollente↓. **[a. Challenge M*(A)*, Cue A *Pre-Head* + b. Direct M/A*(A)* *Head*]**	*[29]* **FRANCESCA:** Oh, oh, oh, oh. Mark! Put down that corn or I'll turn the hot water on.
[30] **SYLVIA: [a]** All right↓. **[b]** Help me to understand↑ which was the biggest turnoff↑ - **[c]** the fact that Jules was gorgeous↑, **[d]** rich↑, **[e]** or a doctor?↑ **[a. Finalizer M*(S)*, Accept A *Pre-Head* + b. Focus M*(A)*, Prompt A *Head* + c. Upgrade M*(A)*,**	*[30]* **ZIA ASSUNTA: [a]** Parliamo↑. **[b]** Vorrei solo che mi spiegassi↑ cos'è che ti ha spaventato così↓ — **[c]** il fatto che Giulio è stupendo↓, **[d]** ricco↓ **[e]** e anche medico?↓ **[a. Elicit M/A*(A)* *Pre-Head* + b. Focus M*(A)*, Prompt A *Head* + c. Upgrade**	*[30]* **AUNT ASSUNTA:** Let's talk. I'd only want you to explain to me what has scared you so much — the fact that Giulio is gorgeous, rich and also doctor?

Evaluate A *Post-Head* + d. Upgrade M*(A)*, Evaluate A *Post-Head* + e. Upgrade M*(A)*, Evaluate A *Post-Head*]	**M*(A)*, Evaluate A *Post-Head* + d. Upgrade M*(A)*, Evaluate A *Post-Head* + e. Upgrade M*(A)*, Evaluate A *Post-Head*]**	
***[31]* FRAN:** Did I mention he was Jewish?↑ **[Upgrade M*(A)*, Inform A]**	***[31]* FRANCESCA:** Ha un sudore che sa di pecora↓. **[Upgrade M*(D)*, Comment A]**	***[31]* FRANCESCA:** He has a sweat that smells of sheep.
***[32]* SYLVIA: [a]** Oh. Darling↑, **[b]** I only say this because I love you↓. **[c]** You're a glorified cleaning girl↓. **[d]** This could be your last chance↓. **[a. Summon M*(S)*, Bid A *Pre-Head* + b. Repair A*(S)*, Clue A *Pre-Head* + c. Assess M*(D)*, Evaluate A *Head* + d. Upgrade M(D), Evaluate A *Post-Head*]**	***[32]* ZIA ASSUNTA: [a]** Ma che cos'hai contro le pecore? ↓ **[b]** Tuo nonno ci ha fatto i milioni!↓ **[c]** E i soldi puzzano sempre↑ di qualcosa↓. **[d]** Questa forse è la tua ultima occasione!↓ **[a. Challenge M*(A)*, Prompt A *Pre-Head* + b. Focus M*(A)*, Comment A *Head* + c. Upgrade M*(A)*, Comment A *Post-Head* + d. Assess M*(D)*, Evaluate A *Post-Head*]**	***[32]* AUNT ASSUNTA:** But why are you so against the sheep? Your grandfather made money hand over fist with it! And money always smells of something. This maybe is your last chance.
***[33]* FRAN: [a]** Oh, Ma, **[b]** I didn't say no↑. **[c]** I just said I'd think about it↓. **[d]** Okay, I did↓. **[a. Summon M*(S)*, Bid A *Pre-Head* + b. Repair M*(S)*, Inform A *Head* + c. Negotiate M*(S)*, Inform A *Post-Head* + d. Conclude M*(S)*, Close A *Head*]**	***[33]* FRANCESCA: [a]** Ma guarda che non gli ho detto no!↓ **[b]** Gli ho detto soltanto↑ che volevo pensarci un po' su↑. **[a. Repair M*(S)*, Inform A *Head* + b. Negotiate A*(S)*, Inform A *Post-Head*]**	***[33]* FRANCESCA:** But, look, I didn't say no to him. I just said I'd want to think about it.
***[34]* SYLVIA:** You mean I do?↑**[Try Marker M*(A)*, Check A]**	***[34]* ZIA ASSUNTA:** Oh **[Oh-Receipt M*(S)*, Marker A]**	***[34]* AUNT ASSUNTA:** Oh
***[35]* FRAN:** Yeah↑. **[Expected Answer M*(S)* *preferred*]**	***[35]* FRANCESCA:** E adesso l'ho fatto. **[Conclude M*(S)*, Close A]**	***[35]* FRANCESCA:** And now I did.
***[36]* SYLVIA:** Oh. **[Oh-Receipt M*(S)*, Marker A]**	***[36]* ZIA ASSUNTA: [a]** Cioè, dirai di sì↑, **[b]** vero?↑ ?↑**[Try Marker M*(A)*, Elicit A *Head*, Focus M*(A)*, Check A *Post-Head*]**	***[36]* AUNT ASSUNTA:** This means that you'll say yes, won't you?
***[37]* FRAN: [a]** Ma, **[b]** you may kiss the bride↑. **[a. Summon M*(S)*, Bid A *Pre-Head* + b. Direct M/A*(S)* *Head*]**	***[37]* FRANCESCA: [a]** Sì!↑ **[b]** Puoi baciare la sposa↓, **[c]** Zia Assunta!↓ **[a. Expected Answer M*(S)* *preferred* + b. Direct M/A*(S)* *Head* + c. Summon M*(S)*, Bid A *Post-Head*]**	***[37]* FRANCESCA:** Yes, you may kiss the bride, Aunt Assunta!
***[38]* FRAN/SYLVIA:** Moi! Moi! Moi! Moi! Moi! **[Close M*(S)*, React A]**	***[38]* FRANCESCA/ZIA ASSUNTA:** Muà! Muà! Muà! **[Close M*(S)*, React A]**	***[38]* FRANCESCA/AUNT ASSUNTA:** Moi! Moi! Moi! Moi! Moi!
(Maxwell enters the kitchen) ***[39]* MAXWELL: [a]** You know, Miss Fine, **[b]** I think you're very wise↓ not to rush into this↓. **[c]** You're far too sensible a woman to marry a man you just - **[d]** Ow! **[a. Re-opening M*(A)*, Bid A *Pre-Head* + b. Support M*(A)*, Comment A *Head* + c. Upgrade M*(A)*, Acknowledge A *Post-Head* + d. Misplacement Marker M*(A)*, React A *Post-Head*]**	*(Maxwell entra in cucina)* ***[39]* MAXWELL: [a]** Guardi, Francesca↓, **[b]** penso che sia stata molto saggia↓ a non prendere una decisione così affrettata. **[c]** Lei è una donna troppo intelligente↓ – **[d]** Ohi! **[a. Re-opening M*(A)*, Bid A *Pre-Head* + b. Support M*(A)*, Comment A *Head* + c. Upgrade M*(A)*, Acknowledge A *Post-Head* + d. Misplacement Marker M*(A)*, React A *Post-Head*]**	*(Maxwell enters the kitchen)* ***[39]* MAXWELL:** Look, Francesca, I think you're very wise not to take a hasty decision. You're far too intelligent a woman - Ow!

[40] **SYLVIA: [a]** Oh, I'm sorry↓. **[b]** Did this fork accidentally puncture your tuchas?↑ **[a. Apology M/A(*D*) *Pre-Head*, + b. Challenge M(*D*), Check A *Head*]**	*[40]* **ZIA ASSUNTA: [a]** Oh, quanto mi dispiace!↓ **[b]** Per caso non volendo le ho bucato una delle due guance posteriori?↑ **[a. Apology M/A(*D*) *Pre-Head*, + b. Challenge M(*D*), Check A *Head*]**	*[40]* **AUNT ASSUNTA:** Oh, I'm so sorry! Have I by chance accidentally punctured one of your rear cheeks?

The comparative conversation analysis between the original and the translated versions of this sitcom scene reveals the crucial pragmatic differences between them. The first move in the original version is Maxwell's Open Move, in turn [1], by which he performs a pre-head Nomination Act addressing Sylvia with a falling tone of voice, marking disappointment at having her standing next to him as he and his family dine, and introducing an Arousal pattern of humour triggering laughter. The next move performed by Maxwell is a Negotiation one by which he tries to conceal the disparagement (however evident in his facial expression) he feels towards the peculiar behaviour of Fran's mother as he invites her to join them to supper by an Elicit Head Act. In the Italian dubbing translation of the same turn [1], Maxwell instead performs a straightforward Summon Move instantiated by a Bid Pre-Head Act and marked by a rising tone of voice as he utters the name of "Signora Assunta", the new Italian name and role (i.e., Fran[cesca]'s aunt) given to Sylvia. Also the subsequent Negotiation Move is instantiated differently, by an explicit Invite Head Act. Sylvia, in the original version, replies in turn [2] with a Refusal Move as a Reply Pre-Head Act which corresponds to the translated version and has the same 'preferred' effect on receivers (despite the fact that Refusal is a 'socially-dispreferred' move). However, the moves that follow the next move [b] of this turn—aimed at informing the others on why she was there ("I just came over to see how Fran's date went", imprecisely rendered into Italian as "io sono qui solo per sentire da Francesca com'è andata oggi" - "I'm here just to hear from Francesca how things were getting on today")—do not correspond at all in the two versions. In fact, in the original version, Sylvia concludes her turn [2] with a Direct Move through the Clue Post-Head Act "Make like I'm not even here", thus reinforcing the Arousal pattern of humour. In the translated version, instead, she, as Zia/Aunt Assunta, adds one more Direct Move rendered by the imperative "Mangi" - "Go on eating", before upgrading it with "e faccia come se io non ci fossi" - "and make like I'm not here". The addition of this move rendered by such blunt, one-word imperative, together with Zia Assunta's higher pitch and rising tone of voice (whereas, in the original, Sylvia utters this turn by keeping a low, nasal pitch and a falling tone of voice) make the character of this garish and elderly woman appear in the Italian version to be in more familiar terms with Maxwell than in the original version. This is particularly evident in her next turn [4], following butler Niles' turn [3] with his formal Offer Move eliciting her to have something to eat – literally reproduced in the Italian version. In [4], Sylvia replies again with a 'receiver-preferred' Refusal Move, followed by an Inform Move reinforcing the Safety pattern by letting people know with a final low tone of voice that she "had a Yoplait this morning around 10:10", indirectly hinting at the fact that she was on diet. Zia Assunta's translated Inform Move, instead, aims at strengthening the Arousal pattern of humour with her sequence of short utterances upgrading her explicit expression of personal physical and psychological reactions to her being on diet, ending with another explicit Direct Move: "sono a dieta e sto morendo di fame, ma voi mangiate tranquilli" - "I'm on diet and I'm starving, but please go on eating easy". The result is again a much vulgar character than the original, violating the socially-sanctioned status gap between her and Maxwell, Fran's employer. Sylvia's turn [4] continues with a Focus Move, literally reproduced in translation, and actualized by a Comment Act, addressed to Maxwell's younger daughter Grace ("Oh, such a big potato for such a little girl!") and accompanied by the greedy gesture of removing the potato from the girl's dish to bite it ravenously. What comes next in her turn, however, changes again the pattern of humour by modifying the sequence of moves and acts. Whereas in the original version Sylvia has a look at her watch and with a Focus Move performs the Cue Act "Look at the time" with a rising tone, Zia Assunta's Focus Move is rendered with a Comment Act explicitly referred to Francesca and her boyfriend being late: "Però, come tardano!" - "Hey, how late they are!". Sylvia's idiomatic expression that follows—"They must be having a ball"—upgrading her focusing on time with a rising tone is literally rendered in Italian as Zia Assunta's explicit and more vulgar "Si vede che si divertiranno molto"/"They must be having a very good time!". Sylvia's remarks on Fran's date may actually clarify the reasons why the Italian production chose to turn her character into that of Fran's aunt: Sylvia, in fact, is morally harmful to her daughter in her pressing attempts to make her daughter marry money and acquire social status and material goods even at the expense of her reputation, which is in contrast with the traditional view of "mother"—well established in Italy, at least till the end of the last century—as guiding her children to make ethical principles their own.

In the dialogue under analysis, Sylvia concludes her turn [4] by informing the others that she is going in the kitchen ("I'm gonna go in the kitchen"), thus introducing a Safety pattern of humour freeing the Sheffield family from her inconvenient presence, to introduce again Arousal by humorously upgrading what she has said with the paradoxical Evaluate Head Act "I need a meet to wash this down with". Zia Assunta, instead, utters her Inform Move in Italian with an apparently more obsequious tone, as if she were asking for permission ("Se non vi spiace vado in cucina" - "If you don't mind I'm going in the kitchen"), followed by the Upgrade Move conveying a less effective Evaluate Act: "ci vuole del manzo come contorno ad una grossa patata" - "some beef is required as a side dish for a big potato".

When Sylvia/Zia Assunta leaves the dining room, Brighton, Maxwell's younger son, introduces, in turn [5], a Negotiation Move as a Safety strategy to express his positive evaluation of Jules, Fran's fiancé, upgrading this with his Comment Post-Head Act "and he has yet to beat me in chess", almost literally rendered into Italian, with the difference only in the rising pitch of the dubbed version revealing the boy's covert request of consent from the others, whereas the original cue is uttered by Brighton with a more assertive falling tone of voice. In line with the dubbing policy of this sitcom, also the name of Fran's fiancé, "Jules", has been rendered into the Italian "Giulio".

To Brighton's comment, his father Maxwell replies, in turn [6], with a Challenge Move triggering a humorous Disparagement pattern in negatively evaluating both Brighton's naivety in judging Jules and Jules's compliant behaviour towards him as he loses every game on purpose ("Oh God, Brighton, he throws every game") marked by a spiteful rising pitch in his voice. In the Italian version, the Disparaging pattern of moves is the same as in the original, but the rendering of its meaning is more explicit ("Ma su, Brighton, è lui che vuole perdere!" - "Come on, Brighton, it's him who wants to lose!"), which Maxwell utters with a final falling tone of voice that does not allow any objections. But Brighton, instead, challenges his father in turn [7] with an Elicit Act in the original version—"Do you see how easy it is to bond?", emphasized physically by the gesture of crossing fingers and vocally by a rising tone of voice. In the dubbed version again any idiomatic innuendo is lost and, also in this case, Brighton explicitly states: "È così che si diventa amici" - "That's how people become friends!", with a falling tone that emphasizes the sense of the boy scolding his father. But another challenge comes in reply from Maxwell in turn [8], and this time he adopts an authoritative Direct Act addressed to his son: "Well, I wouldn't get attached to the bloke if I were you", literally reproduced in Italian with the only substitution of "bloke" with "Giulio" and the Focus Pre-Head Act "Guarda" - "Look". Also Maxwell's following Blame Move has been rendered almost literally into Italian, reproducing the final falling tone of voice of his bemused disparaging comment "We all know Miss Fine's relationships eventually end in disaster", thus stepping out of his official role of Fran's employer to unwittingly reveal his real character of her jealous lover. However, also in this case there are some crucial differences between the two versions. In the original one, Maxwell makes formal reference to the Nanny, in the presence of his children, as "Miss Fine", whereas in the Italian version he refers to her by her first name, "Francesca". Moreover, in the Italian translation there is the addition of the phrase "I rapporti di Francesca con gli uomini" - "Francesca's relationships with men", which makes Maxwell's remark—still in the presence of his young children—more vulgar than the original one.

At this point a coup de theatre occurs with Fran entering the room and exultantly informing everybody, in turn [9], that: "He asked me to marry him!", with the addition, in the Italian version, of a Summon Move addressing directly the Sheffield family with a Bid Pre-Head Act: "Ragazzi, mi ha chiesto di sposarlo!" - "Guys, he asked me to marry him!". Another difference lies in the intonation contour of this turn: in the original one, Fran utters this announcement, as she jumps and shakes her whole body, with a rising tone of voice revealing a sense of disbelief, whereas in the Italian dubbed version Francesca has a falling tone in her voice suggesting that the decision has already been taken—which, as made clear in the following turns, is not the case.

In the next turn [10], Niles steps out of his role of the butler—as he usually does—to hiss in Maxwell's ear one of his notorious witticisms, this one metaphorically referred to the betting jargon to imply that Maxwell's prediction was—predictably!—erroneous—"Right on the money as always, sir"—underscored by a rising, sarcastic tone that challenges Maxwell's previous guess. The Italian dubbing translation of this turn is less effective than the original as it loses its metaphorical innuendo to become a more literally explicit and final comment, as emphasized by the falling tone of voice—"Come sempre, signore, c'ha azzeccato" - "As always, sir, you guessed right". In considering the infringement of the conventional 'master/servant' relationship, the Italian translation thus renders Niles's typical one-upmanship attitudes towards Maxwell more insolent. Brighton, in turn [11], positively assesses Fran's news and, with a Support Move, keeps the Arousal atmosphere by congratulating her on the marriage proposal in an impersonal way—at least in the original cue ("That is so cool, Fran. Congratulations") whereas, in the Italian version, he uses a more direct way in evaluating Fran personally ("Bene, brava Francesca! Congratulazioni"—"Well done, bravo Francesca! Congratulations"). Fran's reply in the original turn [12] is actualized through an animated Agree Move by which she agrees with Brighton as a Pre-Head Act to upgrade her enthusiasm with a Head Act informing that she "can't believe it" with a falling tone of her low, nasal voice. With a further Upgrade Move Fran goes on informing everybody: "I'm so excited, I couldn't eat a -" interrupting her excitement as she realizes, with an Oh-Receipt Move that she immediately upgrades, the food the Sheffield family is eating and that she positively assesses with the Evaluate and Clue Pre-Head Acts briefly relieving the tension caused by such unexpected announcement. The following move is a Direct one introducing the Head Act by which Fran, addressing Niles at the sideboard, tells in a falling tone of voice: "hit me again" before focusing on the corn in Grace's dish and, by taking it out and starting eating it, comments: "Oh such a big corn for such a little girl", alarmingly reproducing her mother's previous words and thus showing how similar they are in their behaviour. In the translated version for the Italian television, Francesca's reply, in turn [12], to Brighton's congratulations on her marriage proposal is much more jubilant: she does not simply agree with

Brighton as in the original version, but she keeps underscoring what he has said by means of three Upgrade Moves introducing her overexcited comment and further information on how she feels, always keeping a high and loud tone of voice and a rising pitch suggesting bewilderment: "Oh che bello! Che bello! Non riesco a crederci! Sono così eccitata che neanche ceno-" - "Oh, how marvelous! How marvelous! I can't believe it! I'm so excited that I couldn't even dine-". The Oh-Receipt Move by which Francesca suddenly redirects the enthusiasm for the marriage proposal to the food on the table is rendered in the translated version by means of references to similar Italian food "uh, I salsicciotti, oh e anche I cavoli in agrodolce" ("uh, the sausages, oh and also the sweet and sour cabbages"). The Direct Move addressed to Niles contains a more greedy hint than the original: "gli dia dentro!" / "let's tuck in!" adding a marked gluttonous quality to Francesca making her very similar to her Aunt Assunta. Her subsequent focus on Grace's corn and its removal from her dish to eat it by uttering Aunt Assunta's similar lines (not the same ones, as in the original: "E' una pannocchia troppo grande per te" / "This is a corn too big for you") render Francesca a character that essentially differs from Fran. In fact Fran is represented as more cautious than Francesca in her reaction to the unexpected marriage proposal: her tone of voice, though excited, is lower, the pace of her utterances is slower and her pitch, in this turn [12] focusing on her Revelation, is almost always falling, thus signalling a certain degree of thoughtfulness. The Italian-speaking Francesca, instead, with her loud and squeaking tone of voice and with the high pitch by which she ends almost every phrase, is actually represented as a bimbo closely resembling the character of Peg, the mother in *Married ... with Children*—at least as it was rendered in the Italian dubbed version of that sitcom of the eighties.

In response to Fran's enthusiastic burst, Maxwell intervenes with turn [13] introducing a disparaging move meant to elicit Fran's confirmation of what she has just revealed in order to check its truth ("He asked you to marry him"). The corresponding translated turn shows a different conversational pattern with Maxwell contributing to the general atmosphere of Arousal challenging Fran with a Check Act: "Ma davvero le ha chiesto di sposarlo?" - "But did he really ask you to marry him?". Fran's non-linguistic positive reply ("uh-huh"), in turn [14], is perceived as 'dispreferred' by Maxwell who, thus, insists with his Disparagement mood by introducing a Blame Move as a final comment on Fran's behaviour, marked by a falling tone: "You've barely known the man for two weeks", this time rendered with its literal translation into Italian ("Lo conosce solo da due settimane" - "You've barely known him for two weeks"). To such derogatory attack, Fran reacts, in turn [16], with a Challenging Move, eliciting from Maxwell an explanation as a repair for having offended her with his comment ("What? You think it's so hard to believe a man would fall in love with me that fast?"). The Italian dubbing translation of

Francesca's turn [16] has a different React structure: it starts with a Focus Move ("No, cosa significa?" - "No, what does it mean?") and continues with a Challenge Move eliciting from Maxwell a reflection, rather than an explanation, on what he has just told to her ("Un uomo ci deve sempre mettere anni per dire che è innamorato?" - "A man has to wait years before telling that he is in love?"), sounding more like a covert reproach to Maxwell's hesitancy in declaring his love to her. Grace's interference with her turn [17] serves as a break for the atmosphere of tension fuelling the Arousal pattern of humour. With an Acknowledge Move, the little girl shows understanding for what Fran's has just said and contributes to re-establishing a Safety atmosphere by introducing a Downgrade Move with her naïve comment "Yeah. Todd and I knew each other three minutes before I got↑ a Pudding-Pak right in the eye". The Italian version sounds like a summary of the original turn: "Giusto. Todd, appena conosciuto, mi ha subito buttato il primo budino in faccia" - "Right. Todd, as soon as I met him, threw the first pudding at hand on my face". Fran briefly acknowledges what Grace has said ("There you go") which differs from the Italian more receiver-oriented and expanded rendering of the same turn ("Ecco, ha sentito?" - "There you go, have you heard that?") thus re-establishing the Arousal mood in conversation. Maxwell's reaction in turn [19] is still of blame: "You know nothing about this man" which, in the Italian version, explicitly becomes an attempt to make Francesca change her mind by introducing an additional Direct Move: "Oh, ragioni! Lei non sa niente di quest'uomo" - "Oh, be reasonable! You know nothing about this man". Maxwell concedes with an Acknowledge Move by concluding: "All right, so he's a doctor", but then, with a subsequent Challenge Move, he elicits: "Is he a specialist?" giving vent to his curiosity. The Italian version, again expands the linguistic rendering of such moves, making the pace of speaking faster and more frantic than the original, due to the timing and lip-synchronization limits visually imposed by the uttering of the turn ("D'accordo, lei saprà che fa il medico. Che medico? Specialistico?" - "All right, you may know he's a doctor. What kind of doctor? A specialist?"). Fran's challenging reply in turn [20] is rendered idiomatically as "You ain't just whistling 'Dixie,' baby" with a crooner-like rising and chanting tone of voice and a confidential attitude towards Maxwell who reacts, in turn [21], with an Oh-Receipt Move "Oh God". The reference in Fran's pun is to Dixie or Dixieland music, a forerunner of the Jazz style based on easy tunes improvised during jam sessions by bands playing brass and percussion instruments. In everyday use, the term Dixie may be derogatory as it refers to a lack of knowledge of music sloppily performed by amateurish players. This explains Fran's witty contention that her fiancé's high competence and specialization in his profession is something real and serious and not just feigned and improvised, to be metaphorically associated to a Dixie tune. This reference is, as expected, completely lost in the dubbing translation for the Italian television. Here, Francesca's turn [20], in reply to Maxwell's request for more information about her fiancé, is rendered into "lui è ultra specialisticissimo, è molto bravo!" - "he is very super-highly-specialized, he's very good!", which fills the time lapse of the original utterance with extra trivial words that reinforce the representation of Francesca as a not-conversant bimbo. Also Maxwell's Oh-Recept move in reply to Francesca's pun is different from the original: here, by referring to Maxwell's gesture of taking a hand to his forehead with an expression on his face that may be interpreted as pain, the translator makes him say: "oh, la testa!" - "oh, the [my] head!".

It is again one of Maxwell's children, Maggie, the character that introduces a Safety pattern in an atmosphere of humorous tension. In turn [22], the girl first enthusiastically acknowledges, with a rising tone of voice, Fran's exciting news ("Oh, this is so exciting"), and then she elicits from Fran a positive reply to her request ("so, can I be a bridesmaid?"). In the Italian version of turn [22], Maggie Pre-Head Act of commenting on Francesca's news does not occur any longer by means of an Acknowledge Move, but by an Inform Move introducing her subjective, personal reaction to such news: "sono così contenta!" - "I'm so happy!". Also Maggie's subsequent Elicit Move is made more personal than the original, involving directly Francesca's will: "mi vuoi come damigella d'onore?" / "do you want me as a bridesmaid?". To Maggie's covert offer Fran replies, in turn [23], with an Acknowledge Move ("I know the doctor asked me to marry me") which is also heard by her mother Sylvia returning into the dining room from the kitchen without being seen by her daughter who goes on revealing, with a new Challenge Move and a rising tone of voice, that although she received the marriage proposal she has not yet accepted it ("but I didn't say yes"). Sylvia's smile of satisfaction suddenly turns into an expression of anguish as she faints, unseen, behind her daughter who, unsuspectingly, enjoys the food she is eating: "this is delicious". In the Italian version of turn [23], Francesca starts with an additional Direct Move holding Maggie's excitement back ("Aspetta, Maggie" - "Hold on, Maggie") before acknowledging the fact that she has received a marriage proposal by conceding: "è vero che lui mi ha chiesto di sposarlo" - "it's true that he asked me to marry him", but then, with a Challenge move, she reveals her reservations about her possible acceptance ("però io non gli ho detto di sì" - "but I didn't say yes to him")—which makes Aunt Assunta (Sylvia) collapse behind her as she relishes the specific food she is eating (Oh, questo cavolo è delizioso!" - "Oh, this cabbage is delicious!").

While she is lying on the floor, Sylvia in the original version has a violent verbal reaction against her daughter Fran by challenging her in turn [24]: "Why don't you grab a knife and stick it straight through my heart?". Surprisingly, the Italian version of this turn is not a translation at all—in fact the whole turn has been totally substituted with a different one which makes Aunt Assunta elicit an answer from Francesca, soon upgrading it with new information that is completely redundant in this context as it simply aims at throwing light on the relations within Francesca's family: "Che le racconto adesso a mia sorella, che è poi tua madre?" - "What shall I say now to my sister, who is also your mother?". By this substitution, the Italian dubbing translator may have tried to justify Aunt Assunta's pressures on Francesca as a sense of responsibility she feels towards her sister (probably still living in Italy) who has placed her daughter, Fran, in the care of Assunta, her sister living in the States in the hope for a better future for her. Indeed, in dealing with such plot distortions, it becomes difficult to justify why the Italian production opted for such radical changes that sometimes, as in this case, seem to get out of the translator's control. In turn [25], Fran believes that these words have been uttered by Grace imitating her mother's voice and she positively evaluates it with an Assess Move addressed to the little girl: "That was great. She sounded just like-", but she suddenly realizes that those words did not come from Grace, but from Sylvia who, by increasing the Arousal atmosphere of tension, now grabs Fran's ankle from behind the table, impeding her daughter to run away from her. Hence Fran, with a Summon Move, bids her mother to let her go: "Ma ... Ma, let go of my ankle". The Italian translation this time does not substantially diverge from the original one, except for Francesca's reference to her aunt, rather than to her mother, summoning her at the end of her turn, rather than at the beginning as in the original: "Ah ah ah ma che brava! Sembri proprio Zia As -ah! Lasciami, lasciami la caviglia! Lasciami la caviglia, Zia Assunta!" - "Ah ah ah, how clever! You really sounded like Aunt As -ah! Let, let go of my ankle! Let go of my ankle, Aunt Assunta!". Sylvia's infuriated reply in turn [26] is a Challenge Move with a threatening Direct Act addressed to her daughter Fran: "You better run", literally translated into Italian: "Ti conviene scappare!". As Fran runs around the table in her attempt to escape her mother's reach, she summons Brighton in turn [27] asking him, with a Check Act: "Brighton, is she taking off her shoe?", translated into Italian as Francesca checking about an already performed action: "Brighton, se l'è cavata una scarpa?" - "Brighton, has she taken off her shoe?". Brighton's reply, in turn [28], contributes to turn Arousal into humorous Disparagement as he informs Fran about Sylvia's grotesquely violent behaviour: "No, but she's gonna hurl the corn", rendered even more ferocious into the Italian translation where Brighton uses a warlike metaphor: "No, però si è armata di pannocchia" - "No, but she's armed herself with a corn".

The scene at this point changes and Fran and her mother Sylvia, chasing her, move into the kitchen. As she runs away from her mother, Fran, in turn [29], utters repeatedly the typically Yiddish interjection "oy!" defined by Goffman (1978) a 'response cry' by which, in this context, Fran tries to convey a comic amplification of her feeling of fear for the possible consequences of her mother's threat, thus building a relation of empathy with the audience outside the play. Then, by turning her attention to the situation she is involved in, Fran, with a Summon move, addresses her mother ordering her, with a Direct Move and by pointing to her the hot-water pipe: "Ma, put down the vegetable and no one gets hurt!". The Italian version omits the Yiddish interjection, substituting it with a repetition of a neutral "oh"—whereas, probably, the rendering of the Yiddish interjection with the pragmatically equivalent Italian exclamation "mamma mia!" would have rendered the protagonist's sense of anguish not only better, but also more appropriate to the new context of the Nanny's Italian background. However, this sense of anguish becomes explicit in Francesca's expression of threat through a Challenge Move and unambiguous references: "Bada! O metti giù quella pannocchia o apro l'acqua bollente" / "Mark! Put down that corn or I'll turn the hot water on". When both women put down their 'weapons', Sylvia tries to establish an accommodating Safety pattern of discourse by starting her turn [30] with a Finalizer Move marked by a falling tone of voice and an Accept Pre-Head Act, "All right", apparently establishing a Safety environment. But then, with a Focus Move she brings Arousal back in conversation by employing a covertly uncompromising Prompt Head Act to pretend a collaborative exchange with her daughter: "Help me to understand which was the biggest turnoff". Sylvia's deceptive 'request for help' is soon upgraded with three moves introducing increasingly pressing Evaluate Acts – each emphasized by a higher pitch and a louder tone of voice – listing Jules's alleged qualities that Fran, instead, regards as 'turnoffs': "the fact that Jules was gorgeous, rich, or a doctor?". In the translated version of turn [30], Aunt Assunta does not even pretend a cooperative Safety atmosphere, in fact, she starts straightforwardly with an Elicit Move keeping the Arousal pattern of conversation and, with a rising tone of voice asks Francesca: "Parliamo". Then, with a Focus Move she prompts an explanation from Francesca: "Vorrei solo che mi spiegassi cos'è che ti ha spaventato così" - "I'd only want you to explain to me what has scared you so much", and continues with three Upgrade Moves each evaluating, with an incontestable falling tone of voice, the qualities of Francesca's fiancé: "il fatto che Giulio è stupendo, ricco e anche medico?" ("the fact that Giulio is gorgeous, rich also a doctor?"). Fran's reply in turn [31] further contributes, in the original version, to the Revelation plot of this scene as she introduces an Upgrade Move informing her mother about her fiancé's further crucial 'quality' which, at Sylvia's eyes, would make Jules incontestably eligible as Fran's husband as he belongs to her same community: "Did I mention he was Jewish?". In the Italian version of turn [31], instead, there is no Revelation enhancement since Francesca upgrades her aunt's list of Giulio's qualities not by adding another vital one—namely, his being 'Jewish' like her family, mentioned in the original —but by introducing a disparaging comment on him which cannot be considered at all as a translation: "Ha un sudore che sa di pecora" - "He has a sweat that smells of sheep". In the original version, in the next turn [32], Sylvia replies to Fran's new revelation by trying to start a negotiation with the aim of making her daughter change her mind. Sylvia, therefore, breaks the Arousal conversation pattern by introducing a Safety one first by means of a Summon Move through which she attempts to appease Fran ("Oh. Darling"), and then by starting a Repair Move introducing a Clue Pre-Head Act that emphasizes her apparent good disposition towards her daughter: ("I only say this because I love you"). But, suddenly, Sylvia re-establishes tension by introducing a Disparagement pattern of humour through an Assess Move that negatively evaluates Fran: "You're a glorified cleaning girl", which is immediately upgraded by a further Evaluate Act: "This could be your last chance", thus threatening and emotionally blackmailing her daughter. The Italian version of this turn [32], again, is not a translation of the original script. Here, it is Aunt Assunta the one who introduces in the dialogue the cultural context of Fran's family that, in the original version, was brought in by Fran with her mentioning the fact that Jules was Jewish. Aunt Assunta, instead, goes back to Francesca's comment on Giulio's sweat smelling of sheep first to challenge her, with a Prompt Pre-Head Act, by asking: "Ma cos'hai contro le pecore?" - "But why are you so against the sheep?", and then by focusing, with a Comment head act, on a related story of their Italian family: "Tuo nonno ci ha fatto i milioni!"—"Your grandfather made money hand over fist with it!", to upgrade such a comment with an Italian folk proverb: "E I soldi puzzano sempre di qualcosa" - "And money always smells of something". Finally, Aunt Assunta concludes her turn with the translation of Sylvia's last disparaging Evaluate Act: "Questa forse è la tua ultima occasione" - "This maybe is your last chance" which, said after what she has uttered so far, seems an unrelated, gratuitous insult against Francesca. It is up to Fran, at this point, to resume, in turn [33] of the original version, the Negotiation atmosphere initially introduced, and then flouted, by her mother. With a Summon Move she addresses her mother to inform her, by means of a Repair Move: "Oh, Ma, I didn't say no". At this point Fran activates an actual Negotiate Move aimed at restoring a Safety atmosphere by adding: "I just said I'd think about it"—which makes Sylvia smile with hope. After a brief pause, Fran concludes with a final Close Act uttered with a final falling tone of voice: "Okay, I did". In the corresponding turn [33] of the Italian translation, Francesca starts informing Aunt Assunta straightforwardly with the Repair Move, "Ma guarda che non gli ho detto di no!" ("But, look, I didn't say no to him"), to continue with the actual Negotiate move, "Gli ho detto soltanto che volevo pensarci un po' su" ("I just said I'd want to think about it"), but she doesn't add anything more about her having taken the decision, as in the original script. Sylvia's reply in turn [34] is in fact a Try-Marker Move checking positive confirmation from her daughter: "You mean I do?". In the corresponding translated version of turn [34], Aunt Assunta just acknowledges what Francesca has said with a simple "Oh", marking an Oh-Receipt Move. At Sylvia's question "You mean I do?", Fran enthusiastically replies in turn [35] with the preferred answer that her mother expected: "Yeah", which Sylvia happily acknowledges in turn [36] with an emotionally-overwhelmed Oh-Receipt Move ("Oh"). In the Italian version, instead, the order of the dialogic cues is still not coinciding with the original one. Francesca, in her turn [35], finally says what Fran has already said in turn [33], namely, "E adesso l'ho fatto" ("And now I did"), thus concluding, with a Close Act, her 'thinking about it'. In turn [36], Aunt Assunta fills the original time span of Sylvia's "Oh" by saying what Sylvia said in her turn [34], that is: "Cioè, dirai di sì, vero?" - "This means that you'll say yes, won't you?". After Sylvia's simply receiving her daughter's good news with a "oh", Fran, in turn [37] summons her mother and, with a Direct Move, asks Sylvia to rejoice with her: "Ma, you may kiss the bride". In the corresponding Italian turn [37], Francesca first finally replies to her aunt's question with the preferred positive answer, and then with the Direct Move and a subsequent Summon Move she invites Aunt Assunta to rejoice with her: "Sì! Puoi baciare la sposa Zia Assunta!" "- Yes! You may kiss the bride, Aunt Assunta!". The following turn [38], in both versions, represents a Close Move with the emotional reaction of both women affectionately simulating a sequence of kisses: "Moi! Moi! Moi! Moi! Moi!" ("in Italian: "Muà! Muà! Muà! Muà! Muà!"), thus establishing a Safety atmosphere of humorous relief. But Maxwell suddenly enters the kitchen and reinstates tension, with his turn [39], by supporting Fran's choice of not accepting Jules's marriage proposal. He thus intrudes into the two women's bliss and re-opens the dialogue—by directly addressing Fran, not Sylvia—in order to positively comment, with a categorical falling tone of voice, on her prudent decision, and also to upgrade it with what he was just about to say as an acknowledgement of Fran's judicious choice ("You know, Miss Fine, I think you are very wise not to rush into this. You're far too sensible a woman to marry a man you just—Ow!") before Sylvia brutally stops him by piercing his bottom with a fork. Maxwell's turn [39] in the Italian version is not dissimilar in its structure from the original one ("Guardi, Francesca, penso che sia stata molto saggia a non prendere una decisione così affrettata. Lei è una donna troppo intelligente -Ohi!" - "Look, Francesca, I think you're very wise not to take a hasty decision. You're far too intelligent a woman -Ow!"). Sylvia's final turn [40], emphasized by her gesture of raising the fork from behind Maxwell, is characterized by a formal Apology Move which soon becomes another Challenge Move as she checks, in quite vulgar terms, if she by chance has hurt him: "Oh, I'm sorry. Did this fork accidentally puncture your tuchas?"—this last word being an Yiddish term for 'buttocks'. Aunt Assunta's final turn [40] is only apparently less vulgar than the original with her consciously unnatural attempt to avoid foul language: "Oh, quanto mi dispiace! Per caso non volendo le ho bucato una delle due guance posteriori?" - "Oh, I'm so sorry! Have I by chance accidentally punctured one of your rear cheeks?".

The objectionable equivalence choices made by the dubbing translators of *The Nanny* for the Italian TV, and identified in the comparative conversation analysis carried out so far between the original and the translated versions of a script from this sitcom, will represent the starting point for the pedagogic work that shall follow, aimed at finding alternative renderings of the same script through the application of the Acting Translator Model.

4.4 Applying the Acting Translator Model to *The Nanny* Sitcom Script: The Three Explorative Phases

4.4.1 *Setting the scene for pedagogic action*

The equivalence failure persistently identified in the above-reported conversation analysis of *The Nanny* original and translated scripts is principally due to the fact that the 'official' dubbing translators (engaged by the Italian television channel producing this sitcom in the mid-nineties) applied a wholly top-down approach to the rendering of such situation comedy into Italian. In transferring native cultural patterns to the rendering of the sitcom script into the target language, the Italian production actually aimed at devising a 'marketable product' capable of appealing to the 'implied' Italian audience's shared expectations. Such expectations are referred to the socio-cultural and pragmatic behaviours of the sitcom characters, as well as to the humorous language they would use, and the comic situations they would be involved in. The underlying assumption is that to be 'humorous', language and situations need to be interpreted and accepted as such by the target audience, which can explain the decision of not reproducing, in the Italian version, socio-culturally marked patterns of comic behaviour that may be perceived as alien, disturbing and, thus, not comic at all.

Yet, a sitcom dubbing translator, being an intercultural mediator, has to find ways of conveying different social and pragmalinguistic patterns of behaviour from one culture to another in order to trigger actual 'learning experiences' in the target audiences, enabling them to appreciate different ways of 'being humorous'—which entails to discover different ways of interpreting, assessing and subverting reality by 'experiencing' it through mental/physical schemata that are different from the accepted and expected ones. On such grounds, the issue discussed in this section concerns the results of a longitudinal case study focused on a search for alternative dubbing translations of the previously-analyzed sitcom script from *The Nanny*. The translator's objective was not only to look for socio-pragmatic and pragmalinguistic equivalence to the original move-&-act realization patterns (cf. Niemeier 1991), but also to reproduce the spontaneity of the Italian natural conversational styles. The empirical investigation reported in this and in the following chapters was carried out in the Faculties of Foreign Languages and Literature of two Italian universities, respectively in an undergraduate course of Foreign Languages for Interpreters and Translators and in another undergraduate course of Intercultural and Interlingual Mediation, involving students with a post-intermediate/advanced competence of English as a foreign language. The case study was motivated by the pedagogic application of the Acting Translator Model, and the guidance given to students in interpreting and authenticating the sitcom humorous dialogues through first-person voice and bodily involvement was actualized through activities involving physical-theatre methods (Chekhov 1953; Stanislavski 1981a/b/c; Johnstone 1981), creative sitcom writing (cf. Rannow 2000; Blake 2005; Sedita 2005; Bull 2007; Sandler 2007; Smith 2009), and conversation analysis.

This process of sitcom authentication will be explored in this extended section through the analysis of the students' protocols (Ericsson and Simon 1984), which are both transcriptions of students' tape-recorded retrospective verbalizations of their experience of sitcom improvisation and dramatization, as well as first-person reports of their conversation analyses and subsequent dubbing translations. The protocol analysis will especially focus on the students-as-acting translators' (henceforth students/acting-translators) interpretations and renderings of the original script into the target language. The assumption justifying this ethnomethodological approach is that becoming aware of how students' minds work while bodily accessing a sitcom script is a fundamental condition for a successful pedagogic action. In this case, therefore, the researcher's and the teacher's perspectives come to coincide in the classroom implementation of such a principle.

The Italian university students participating in the case study were subdivided into two groups of about twenty-five students each: the first top-down phase of script exploration regarded only Group A (the experimental group) who was guided in the use of physical-theatre techniques to embody characters and improvise dialogues—both in Italian and English—on open-ended situations related to the topic and the prevailing speech acts of the episode under analysis. Such impro-conversations were also audio-taped and transcribed for subsequent analysis. Group B (the control group) did not receive such initial top-down treatment, but experienced only the subsequent bottom-up phase, together with Group A. The hypothesis was that Group B's bottom-up performance in conversation analysis and the following interactive enactment of translation would result less pragmatically spontaneous and appropriate than Group A's equivalent 'embodied realizations' achieved after the top-down impro-drama sessions on moves and acts that determine the sitcom humorous discourse. The difference, indeed, lies in the fact that the dubbing translators in Group A experienced first-hand the actual spatial, physical and auditory 'diamesic level' of sitcom communication which is not just a written text, but a text that is 'written to be spoken' in dialogic discourse.

4.4.2 *Applying the Acting Translator Model: the top-down phase*

This top-down phase of the Acting Translator process concerned exclusively the convenience sample of students/acting-translators in Group A. The objective was to explore possibilities of physical expression capable of freeing creativity and, then, refreshing also the intellectual experience of students as dubbing translators. 'To do, to observe, and to reflect' represented therefore the three steps of the students' cognitive process at this stage, which involved their own physical experience as a way of discovering new and unpredictable perspectives in reference to characters and situations of *The Nanny* sitcom. At the grounds of this top-down phase there is the view of the public and objective nature of the embodied schemata (meant as universally-shared gestalt structures conditioning the individual metaphorical and imaginative expression—cf. Lakoff 1987) that, in the intercultural-mediation context of the dubbing translation of television comedy, necessarily has to be put under discussion. This becomes evident, for instance, through the implementation of one of Chekhov's (1953) actor-training *etudes*, namely, the 'Psychological Gesture' (P.G.), a physical-theatre exercise capable of revealing that, although it is possible to share some conventionalized, given-for-granted gestalt patterns of meanings, people can actually discover their own personal connotations within them by 'inhabiting' their own 'embodied schemata'—or patterns of individual experience—by exploring them in-depth not only intellectually, but also and crucially physically, bodily. This is assumed to be the necessary first step for acting translators to develop an awareness of the source of their own socio-culturally and experientially-marked individual creativity before letting it being disturbed, dislodged, and finally deconstructed and reconstructed in the contact with other people's culturally different ways of expressing creativity—especially through humour. This would also constitute the basis for a different, emotional and physical kind of shared intercultural communication—which explains why at the very first, warm-up stages of the Acting Translator process, it is advisable to have initial text-free activities, totally based on self-exploration as a preparatory first step to the dubbing translators' actual encounter with the sitcom script which, already in its humorous construction, encourages a divergence from conventionalized thought. Michael Chekhov's (*ibidem*) drama technique of the Psychological Gesture is here assumed to be an appropriate method to prime students/acting-translators to undertake such 'personal quest' insofar as, in Chekhov's definition, the P.G. is a subjective "archetype" which "takes possession of our whole body, psychology and soul, entirely" (*ibidem*: 77). As an 'archetype', therefore, it can be considered as a structure of people's embodied schemata. The role of subjective 'archetypal myths' is not new in both Jungian approach and in Gestalt psychotherapy. Jung (1953), for instance, is primarily concerned with how people can discover those personal myths which lie unresolved underneath conscience, and yet they emerge through gestures and behaviours they are not aware of. Becoming conscious of one's own gestalt structures, therefore, was the objective of the enquiry at this stage. This, however, was by no means meant to be a solitary experiential exploration. Group-A students/dubbing-translators needed in fact to feel, since the beginning, that they were 'a group' whose aim was ultimately to co-create an equivalent Italian version of an American sitcom. Exploring one's own individual Psychological Gestures within the group was thus possible through a warm-up group-activity aimed at making students feel, physically and psychologically, in harmony with each other. The Psychological Gestures proposed for individual and group exploration were connected with the Arousal/Safety and Disparagement patterns of humour at the basis of the Request and Apology moves characterizing the sitcom episodes under analysis. To achieve psycho-physical relaxation within the group—so as to become more receptive towards the others—Group-A students started walking around the room establishing eye-contact with each other, smiling, and shaking hands saying "yes". Then, they started concentrating upon themselves as they were encouraged to go through different degrees of tension by embodying a number of archetypal experiential states, physically explored by means of a number of 'embodied schemata' referred to as: "Fighting Gravity", an experiential schema bodily representing the mental and physical sensation of 'feeling weary', inducing students to focus on the perception of their knees and legs as heavy, weak, impeding them to stand up or walk, triggering sadness, despair, but also self-disparaging emotions; "Mr. Cool", the archetype for 'feeling relaxed', prompting students to experience a sense of Safety; "Waiter with a Problem", the Arousal archetype for 'feeling worried' and having to solve problems though being in a lower-status condition, physically reflected in an alert state of mind and nervous movements; and finally "There is a Bomb!", the situational schema triggering a state of maximum tension, increasing Arousal and generating hectic—and often comic—reactions (cf. Guido 1992: 63). During this exercise, students had to find a gesture (actually, a P.G.) true to their feelings that should be felt as a physical extension of the image and emotions generated by the archetypal experiential states, helping them access their own personal embodied schemata. Chekhov (1953) suggests the addition of a sound while embodying the P.G., for example, by uttering the word that better expresses the mental, emotional state induced by the P.G. in the students' minds. Such embodiment procedure is in line with Paivio's (1969) explorations of the 'dual coding interpretations', based on the effects produced by highly 'imaging' words activating both verbal and visual codes. Such 'dual-code' patterns present in our mind are acknowledged also by Neisser (1967) who proves the existence of interrelated visual and auditory stores he defines as 'iconic' and 'echoic memory'. In the context of the present research it is contended that individual students can access their iconic-echoic memory not only through their own body, but also through the other students' parallel schematic embodiments and this is assumed to pave the way to the students/acting-translators' subsequent conscious experience of subjective artistic creation, as well as of the artistic creations produced by the other acting translators interacting in the same group (cf. Guido 1999: 223).

The physical-theatre activity that followed, likewise based on an exploration of Psychological Gestures and defined as "Archetypes and Psychological Gesture", was more specifically correlated with the archetypal essence of the characters in *The Nanny* sitcom. Indeed, sitcoms—like any type of narrative—is grounded on a number of archetypal characters representing universal dynamics of social/physical interaction (cf. Frye 1957, 1959). Here it is assumed that such narrative archetypes can be recovered directly within each individual's experiential schemata by means of Psychological Gestures. Group-A students, therefore, started exploring the archetypes of the Master, the Servant, the Innocent, the Trickster, and the Fool (cf. Guido 1992: 63-64) that can be identified in *The Nanny* sitcom (as well as in any comedy frame of the Italian *Commedia dell'Arte*, with each mask representing an archetype). Students' searching within their own selves for a P.G. that can encompass the archetypal essence of each sitcom character is the aim of this activity. Once identified, such P.G. was initially expressed through the students' bodies in an emphatic—though spontaneous—way, often by associating it with a vocal sound, before they internalized it and consciously made it their own. This activity was assumed to be useful for the students/acting-translators as it allowed them to develop a physical memory of the characters' archetypal essence to be reactivated later, when they had to work on the analysis and the dubbing translation of the script. So that, the Innocent was embodied as a person keeping an upright physical position, with wide-open eyes at discovering that everything is new and surprising to him/her. For the embodiment of the Trickster, students were encouraged to imagine a tiny rigid circle in one of their eyes which soon made them feel and appear as sneaky and deceitful. The Master was embodied holding his(her) head high and moving around with self-confidence, being aware that there is always a Servant ready to anticipate every will or wish the Master might have. Finally, the Fool—the archetype of the ironic, sarcastic character—was conventionally represented by some students through a P.G. expressing haughty, derisive physical energy, whereas others represented this character through an unexpected P.G. revealing the physical weakness and fatigue of a character whose only defence is bitter derogatory irony. In both cases, however, the Fool was represented as a physically bent human figure, with the latter 'weary' type having the full weight of his/her body rest on the knees. This difference in the embodiment of the Fool archetype is evident from the students' first-person feelings experienced at accessing such archetypal gestalts through the P.G., as they were tape-recorded immediately after the physical-theatre activity through the retrospective 'think-aloud technique' and, then, transcribed into protocols (Ericsson and Simon 1984)—as the two instances reported below, reproducing two different physical/emotional interpretations of the Fool:

> *Top-down protocol 1:* "I feel I'm tall, big, heavy, curved under the huge weight of my body filling all the space around me. I become bigger and bigger as I scorn the other little people surrounding me, they are so small and so mean, they laugh at me because I'm so big, but I don't care! They know that I can crush them completely, physically and psychologically, because they know my superiority".

> *Top-down protocol 2:* "I feel exhausted. I can't stand up, my legs are melting for weakness and I feel I can soon fall on the floor. I know that people deride me, they think I'm lazy, and I make them believe that it is so, I make them laugh, but I'm feeble and weak, I have no energy in my body, that's why I hate them, I despise all of them in my heart!"

It is evident here that the former P.G. for the Fool (protocol 1) represents an almost conventionalized schema of the bulky, out-of-shape clown despising people by deprecating their physical and moral meanness, and being feared—but also despised—by them in return. In the latter embodiment of the Fool P.G. (protocol 2), the student was experiencing the sensation of feeling physically inferior to the others and, consequently, of being perceived by the others as morally inferior, making them overtly laugh at him/her for this—which triggers in the Fool a covert disparagement for such shallow people who misattribute a low moral value to someone with a low physical energy.

Sitcoms, therefore, cannot rely completely on the traditional theory of 'prototypal characters', which so far has found applications to both narrative (Propp 1968, Frye 1957, Greimas 1983, Fowler 1977) and drama methods (Chekhov 1953). In Forster's (1966) terms, when 'flat characters' come to be imposed upon narrative, they actually 'flatten' the language, thus obliging it to re-compose itself around pre-defined, predictable constructs that Structuralism has defined as gestalt structures or 'semes' (Fowler 1977: 36) belonging to collectively shared schemata. This assumption of prototypal constructs applied to narrative is also close to Lakoff's (1987: 85) experientialist notion of 'social stereotypes' which "can be used to stand for a category as a whole [...] since they define cultural expectations, they are used in reasoning and especially in what is called 'jumping to conclusions'". Lakoff points at a series of social stereotypes ("the stereotypical politician is conniving, egotistical, and dishonest. The stereotypical bachelor is macho, dates a lot of women..." etc.) which indeed become 'prototypes' as they are shared categories applied "in certain situations to define expectations, make judgments, and draw inferences." (*Ibidem*: 86). The similarities between Lakoff's 'social stereotypes' and Forster's literary 'flat characters' (expected to use prototypal behaviours in particular situations) are evident. What is necessary to ensure is that students/acting-translators do not make use of such stereotypes to 'jump to conclusions' about the interpretation of sitcom characters' personalities. Such prototypal view, in fact, translated into acting practice, would actually lead to what Stanislavski (1981c: 70) labels as playing 'on tears', 'on laughs', 'on joy', 'on alarm', etc. He says:

> "The attitude of such actors toward human psychology and passions is naively one-sided and single-tracked: love is portrayed by love, jealousy by jealousy, hatred by hatred, grief by grief, joy by joy. There are no contrasts, no mutual relationships between inner nuances; all is flat and monotone. Everything is done in one color. The villains are all black, the benefactors all white. For each passion the actor has his own special color, the way painters paint a fence or children paint pictures. The result is acting 'in general'. Such actors love 'in general', they are jealous 'in general', they hate 'in general'. They portray the complex components of human passion by means of elementary and mostly external signs."

What Stanislavski advocates, instead, is the actor's search for the character's 'creative objectives'. He adds (*ibidem*: 54):

> "Conscious or unconscious objectives are carried out both inwardly and outwardly by both body and soul. Therefore they can be both physical and psychological."

Applied to the Acting Translator methodology, Stanislavski's suggestion can imply the students' achievement of the characters' objectives not by reference to pre-established social stereotypes, but, instead, 'within' the peculiar patterning of language of the sitcom script. To this purpose, the acting translator has to use his/her own embodied schemata to give life to the characters' intentions s/he infers from the textual organization. In other words, s/he has to let his/her own schemata be challenged by the humorous language of the sitcom as it diverges from social conventions. In *The Nanny* sitcom, for instance, none of the characters may be said to represent only one stereotypical archetype. In fact, the Master is often an Innocent; the Trickster and the Servant sometimes become the Master, and vice versa, but ultimately all the characters eventually turn into the Fool, thus determining the comic structure of the sitcom. The assumption is that in the construction of a sitcom dialogue, characters are made to deviate on purpose from the conventional and expected stereotypes since unpredictable behaviour can trigger a humorous response.

This view was also explored in the course of another activity of this top-down phase defined as "Playing with Status". In this case, students were encouraged to put such archetypes in relation with each other on stage by means of physical-improvisation exercises based on the 'status gap' between them, which marks the dominant (high status) and the subdued (low status) qualities of the characters. In pairs, therefore, students started improvising comic scenes—video-recorded and transcribed into protocols—in which:

(a) Both students embody subdued, low status characters. Both of them may be embodiments of the Servant type, or they could be instances of Master and Servant types whose unexpected behaviour can trigger the comic effect:

> *Top-down protocol 3:*
> *A:* Oh, excuse me, I think, er, I'm afraid that slice of cake is mine. Sorry again...
> *B:* Sorry, er... sorry, I thought it was a leftover cake... I didn't know it was yours...
> *A:* Oh, but no, no, please, have it ... I'll take another slice from the fridge.
> *B:* But, I'm sure there is no more cake in the fridge ... this is the last slice and it's yours...
> *A:* No... please. Er, don't worry about me, I... I'm going to make another cake...
> *B:* But there are no more ingredients in the cupboard, please ... eat it, it's yours
> *A:* I'll go out and buy them, no problem, please eat that slice...
> *B:* It's freezing outside... no, do eat this slice, please, I'll go and buy the ingredients for you...

(b) Both students embody dominant, high status characters. They may respectively be embodiments of a Master and a Servant, the latter stepping out from his role, thus creating the comic situation:

> *Top-down protocol 4:*
> *A:* You drank my vintage bottles of wine!
> *B:* Yes, I did!
> *A:* How dare you do this to me? That wine was excellent!
> *B:* And I wanted to drink it!
> *A:* I didn't give you the permission to drink my wine!
> *B:* Well? So what?

(c) One student is dominant (high status) and the other one is subdued (low status). If the high status one is the Servant (also playing the Trickster) and the low status one is instead the Master (also an Innocent), then the expected schema comes to be subverted, thus triggering a humorous effect:

> *Top-down protocol 5:*
> *A:* Why did you tell your friends that I'm your butler?
> *B:* Who? Me?

A: Yes, you! I'm talking to you!
B: I didn't say anything... sorry, I just asked you to serve our tea, sorry...
A: You mean! They didn't know I'm a butler, except you!
B: Yes, you are right, it was very mean of me to ask you for the tea! I should have gone myself to the kitchen and make it... sorry, I'm so sorry..
A: Now go and make tea for me! Hurry up!

(d) The initial dominant/subdued relationship (e.g., a Master/Servant relationship) is turned upside down in the course of the dialogue:

Top-down protocol 6:
A: Where are my children at this time of the night?
B: Er... sorry, I don't remember where I left them... I don't know... sorry...
A: You don't remember? You don't remember? You careless, absent-minded nanny! Find them and bring them home immediately!
B: Alright... don't worry, sir, I don't remember, really... maybe... maybe... I must have forgotten to pick them up from school...
A: You haven't picked them up from school? Are you crazy?
B: I always leave them somewhere, sir, before coming home, they are such a nuisance, I don't want to have them around at home, I need relax!
A: Oh, ... well, I see... yes, you're right... okay, then.
B: They are so noisy! They scream and cry all the time! If you want them back, tomorrow morning when the school opens, go and pick them up yourself!
A: Alright, fine, don't be furious with me now, I'm a quiet person, I've never disturbed you...

As evident from these protocols, such improvised comic scenes were based on a physical/emotional exploration of the two moves under analysis in the present study—namely, Requests and Apologies (or absence of expected apologies)—by means of gestalt archetypes of narrative characters.

After such an exploration, students in Group A were encouraged to write sitcom scripts (cf. Rannow 2000; Sedita 2005; Sandler 2007) with characters informed by such archetypes. The topics of these scripts were prompted by a magazine article and by a number of related guidelines meant to help students frame their scenes - and, crucially, to introduce, in a covert way, the themes of *The Nanny* sitcom episode to be analyzed in the subsequent phases of their exploration. The aim was to make students acquainted first-hand with the authorial role of the sitcom writer for, as translators, they would ultimately be required to become authors of the target version. The topic of the prompt magazine article is about situations of social and psychological discrimination against young women of different cultural and linguistic backgrounds living in an English-speaking country:

Caught in the Culture Gap (Adapted from: Hilary Burden, "Caught in the Culture Gap", *Cosmopolitan*, UK; partly quoted in Guido 2004: 46-47)
There are thousands of people in Britain who feel that they don't really belong here. They might look like everyone else. But by the very nature of their upbringing and their parents' origins, they are regarded by others as outsiders. Many of them see themselves as outsiders, too. Learning to live in a culture

that's in complete contrast to that of your upbringing can be fraught with self-doubt and confusion about who you are and where you belong. People who experience this are the victims of a culture gap.

Many of those who undergo this cultural chasm, particularly women, frequently refer to it as having a split personality. The conflict usually emerges because of the difference between what their parents instil and their peers expect. Recognizing and abiding by one set of rules can mean undermining, or quite often even abandoning, the other. [...]

English born Maria P. is a public relations officer and Androulla is her Greek Cypriot mother. Both mother and daughter communicate every day by phone, but Maria keeps a lot to herself. For a start, she could never elaborate on the perks she gets through work, or take her mother to the swish restaurants she frequents, or expect her to *really* understand or celebrate a promotion. It's become a source of sadness and sometimes guilt for Maria. Although she loves her parents, Maria feels she chose her job as a form of rebellion against her upbringing – a real career that had absolutely nothing to do with her background. The typical "good Greek girl" leaves home to get married, helps her parents in the home and attends church on Sundays. In contrast, Maria left home and bought her own flat, goes out regularly and saves Sunday as her own "mental health" day. "It's a feeling of being torn into two people," says Maria, "In Cyprus you're called 'Englesou' which means 'little English girl', and here you're a 'bubble' (Cockney rhyming slang—bubble and squeak, meaning Greek), so you can't win. I want to be Cypriot, but there's part of me that doesn't accept the suffocation and lack of ambition, especially as a woman". [...]

Sahera C. has a similar belief in the importance of self-reliance in overcoming cultural differences. An employment assistant at R. College, her cultural chasm became particularly apparent when her mother died four years ago. "Her death was a terrible thing for me because I saw it as having lost all connection with my Indianness, and worried I would be bulldozed into Englishness. (Her father left when she was very young.) But I've managed to overcome that panic by seeing it as my responsibility to create that Indianness for myself. It's now up to me. [...] Although I've spent most of my time with English people, I can't say I'm English. I don't have white skin and I'm not from this culture. If I said I was English I'd look a fool and it would be a betrayal of my heritage." Sahera confesses this is only a recent acknowledgment. She used to fantasise about having white skin and would never wear Indian clothes because people would treat her differently. "I sometimes feel that to fit in and avoid racist abuse I have to disguise myself. It's something I feel ashamed of and I'm trying to overcome." But equally she understands, when she sees communities of Indian women gathered together in the kitchen toiling for their men, that women in this country have come too far for her to feel totally comfortable with her culture. "I don't condemn arranged marriages, but mine wouldn't last more than a week! I don't put a condition on being Indian. I *am* Indian and that's it. It won't make me Indian just to have an arranged marriage. [...]

Like Sahera, Millie M.'s cultural chasm is perhaps greater than most because of her colour, but she's made a point of confronting her dual personality head on. Millie is the first black teenage author to be published in this country and often writes mixing Jamaican Creole and English "because that's me." [...] "I'm caught up in two different cultures," she says. "If someone asks me where I'm from, I say I'm English and my parents are Jamaican. But I think of myself as black British, even though many black people won't use that term as they don't want to be identified with Britain and the government's negative view of black people." [...]

In Sahera's words, "Internationalism is a good thing; it really *is* the source of peace. We should learn to understand and respect each other's differences and stop hurling abuse at one another."

This article was meant to contextualize the creative sitcom-writing activity that followed, whose characters were represented by the same young female subjects of the magazine survey. Also in this case, the interacting archetypal characters explored at the beginning were deemed to be useful to create situations of comic tension, mainly based on Arousal/Safety and Disparagement patterns of humour. The following frames were meant as prompts for the students' group-work creation of their sitcom dialogues:

Frame A: Maria and her Greek Cypriot mother Androulla are having a row about Maria's lifestyle in London.
This evening Maria is getting ready to go out to a swish restaurant with a male colleague.

Her mother Androulla (who has come over for a few days) is very worried about her daughter and she wants to know more about the man she's going out with, about her job, the real amount of her income (which would explain the fact that her daughter's clothes are so expensive), why she is dressing in such smart way, etc. So, she asks her daughter many questions, but then she has to base her judgements only on her own conjectures, because Maria is elusive in her answers.

In fact, Maria is kind to her mother, but quite firm in not telling anything about her life, because she is convinced that her mother wouldn't understand or appreciate her promotions at work, or her life-goals in general.
Androulla reminds her daughter of her Greek values, and the dangers she would have to face if she didn't follow them.

Frame B: Sahera is participating in a party at an Indian friend's place in London.
The party has been organized by an Indian community in Britain. Sahera's Indian girlfriends are busy with preparing nice food for their men. Sahera reminds them that women shouldn't try to 'please' their men every moment, as the Indian culture dictates.

But her girlfriends tease her, telling her she is losing all connections with her Indianness.

Then, the girlfriends inform Sahera that they are arranging a marriage for her with a nice Indian guy. They express their concern about the fact that she's still unmarried and that, since her mother's death, she has been alone, with nobody caring for her, or thinking about her future.
Sahera protests and asserts her own views, values and goals, which not all her Indian girlfriends can understand.

Frame C: Millie meets a British publisher.
Millie submits the manuscript of her new novel to a British publisher. She

explains that her novel is partly written in Jamaican Creole because, otherwise, if written completely in English it "wouldn't be her."

But the publisher tries to tell her tactfully that the British book-market is not interested in a novel written by a black about black people and in Jamaican Creole. He explains that this kind of books wouldn't sell in Britain. Millie protests and asserts her own views on the British government's social policy against blacks, trying to convince the publisher that issuing her novel in the U.K. would represent a crucial "political action."

Yet the publisher is firm in not accepting her novel for publication as it is, but he suggests some modifications.

The instances of sitcom creative writing reported below clearly show the students' development of their skills in devising a comic script by making archetypal characters interact within specific cognitive/textual patterns of humour to create comedy:

Top-down protocol 7 – Frame A:
(Maria is putting on some make-up before going out. Her mother Androulla enters and looks at her despisingly)
Androulla (with a Greek accent): Where do you want to go, dressed in this way?
Maria: On the road.
Androulla: (shocked) On the road?
Maria: Yeah, a new swish restaurant in Notting Hill.
Androulla: Ah! A restaurant! And who's coming with you?
Maria: Some colleagues...
Androulla: Really? Some colleagues or just one?
Maria: (after a pause) Mum, what a nice haircut! Have you changed your hairdresser?
Androulla: (getting angry) These tricks won't fool me! You're changing, your job has changed your life! All that money! How much do you earn? Tell me!
Maria: (amusingly) Enough to buy these smart clothes, Mum. Look! *(She opens her wardrobe full of stylish clothes)* Choose the ones you like for you, Mum! You're still a beautiful woman! *(She tries to hug her. Androulla is initially flattered by Maria's compliment, but then she soon recollects herself).*
Androulla: (wriggling out of Maria's arms) Shame on you! You have forgotten all your family values! If we were still in Cyprus you wouldn't behave like this!
Maria: Mum, I haven't forgotten anything. I still love my country, but life is different here in London.
Androulla: You should go back to Cyprus then, and marry Iannis. I'll go back too, along with you, to help you with the children.
Maria: Iannis? The one-brow man who looks after baboons at the zoo?
Androulla: Who do you think you are? Your granny looked after pigs!
Maria: And so should I? Looking after Iannis? I'm sorry, Mum, I miss Cyprus and its sea, but here I fulfil myself, I'm pleased with myself, Mum.
Androulla: You silly Englesou! You'll end up in tears! Then, you will remember my words! But it would be too late for you to find a remedy!
Maria: Oh, Mum, stop it, now! Tomorrow I'll take you to the Demis Roussos concert, okay? *(She sings softly his famous song)* "Rain and tears are the same...".

Top-down protocol 8 – Frame B:
(Sahera is at an Indian party in London. She wears smart western clothes. She enters the kitchen where her two girlfriends, Amisha and Priyanka – exhausted, but in elegant traditional Indian clothes – are preparing food. Sound of Indian music comes from the next room)
Sahera: (trying to move rhythmically at the sound of the music) Oh, there's no rhythm in this music! Hip-hop, hip-hop... no, it doesn't work. *(She realizes that her girlfriends are very busy with food preparation)* What the hell are you doing still in here?
Amisha: (with an Indian accent) Can't you see? We're preparing some delicious food for our men, over there.
Sahera: For your men? *(She opens the door and, in the next room, two fat young men in the foreground are dancing clumsily. Then, they turn their faces to the open door, smile and wave their hands to Sahera. She shuts the door with an expression of disgust)* You're stuffing them fat, like elephants! What's the use of huge balloons like them cluttering up the home?
Priyanca: So they won't move away! You see?
Sahera: (opens the door again) Look! They are dancing, enjoying themselves! And you're staying in here, shut into the kitchen, tired, cooking for them, why?
Amisha: (moving seductively) But we are women! And that's our task!
Sahera: They will eat you, too, some day! Women and food swallowed at once in one mouthful!
Priyanca: Sahera, you're losing your connection with your Indianness, and it's not good for you.
Amisha: You'll become a sour cake very soon!
*Priyanca:*We are worried about you. You are still unmarried, and now that your mother is no longer with you there is nobody to care for you and for your future.
Sahera: And so I came here to enjoy myself!
Priyanca: You surely will! That's why we asked you to come to the party. Because we want you to meet a guy...
Amisha: An *Indian* guy!
Sahera: What?
Priyanca: Here, tonight, at the party!
(Someone rings at the front door)
Amisha: Go! Go! Open the door!
Sahera: You're mad! *(She leaves the kitchen and goes to the front door to open it. A handsome, young man in traditional Indian clothes stands at the entrance, smiling)*
Young Man: Hi! Is the party here?
Sahera: (looks at his face and then at his hands, that are empty) No Martini, no party! *(She shuts the door – to open it again soon afterwards)* But I can make an exception for you! Come in! *(She pulls him in by grabbing his arm)* Come in!
Young Man: Okay! Okay!
Sahera: (goes back to the kitchen hastily) Oh my goodness! Who's that gorgeous man that I've just let in?
*Amisha:*Congratulations! That's your husband-to-be!
Sahera: What? Oh no! I'll find my man myself!
Priyanca: Don't be angry! We've just arranged it for your interest. Just give

him a chance with you – you might change your mind!
Sahera: No! You can't decide about my life! *(She glances at the handsome man again as he stands smiling in the next door)* Well... for once I can sacrifice myself...

Top-down protocol 9 – Frame C:
(Millie enters a British publisher's office)
Millie: Good morning, Mr. Smith.
Mr. Smith: Good morning, Millie. Please, have a sit!
Millie: Thanks.
Mr. Smith: Well, I've read your manuscript, Millie, and I must say that your narrative style is really good, lively, sparkling. Yet ... you know ... er ... there's a little, a little problem ... you'd better modify something, if you intend to submit it again to us ... But, believe me, your style is really good!
Millie: Oh ... I understand. I think *I know*.
Mr. Smith: Really? Well.
Millie: Is it the language, isn't it?
Mr. Smith: I'm afraid yes. ... Sorry ... it's quite innovative, I can see it, but would it sell here in Britain? I mean, a book that is not only about ... Jamaican culture in Britain, but also written ... partly written in Jamaican Creole ... you know?
Millie: I see ...
Mr. Smith: May I offer my advice?
Millie: Please ...
Mr. Smith: You might write in Standard English the same story of immigration and integration...
Millie: But that wouldn't be me! I mean, writing in Standard English ... I ...
Mr. Smith: I know, but ... do you want it published? Look, ... you see ... also the young female protagonist, longing for the job of her dreams for half of the book, to become what? A social worker...
Millie: She would help other black women become self-confident with their culture, help them assert themselves, by using their own language, their 'own English' ... it's really a 'political action'! I mean, it's a way to make our voice heard against the British government's social policy against blacks, ... and specifically against black women, living in Britain but with no hope for seeing their dreams fulfilled.
Mr. Smith: Oh yes, ... I see, ... right, ... well. What if the protagonist's dream job were becoming an actress, struggling with her female friends for success ... I mean, hard work to improve their accent ... and so you can include some Jamaican Creole in the process ... and their body, becoming glamorous ... you see? *This* would sell! It would even make a box-office hit as a Hollywood movie ... and you ... you would become rich! ... So? What do you think?
Millie: I'm ... I'm ... speechless!
Mr. Smith: You may even add a male character, some kind of blond, handsome, clever guy, who helps her achieve her goals, ... kind of Pygmalion, a remake of *My Fair Lady*, I mean. ... You see? In contexts like this you need to negotiate, and you've got the writing skills to make a success! ... And with your pretty face on the book cover, believe me, you would sell lots of copies! ... Just have your dreadlocks cut, ... I'm sure a good photographer can lighten your skin and soften your features ... some cleavage would add to the picture,

> you know? Eh? ... So? What would you say?
> *Millie:* I say ... goodbye!

As these sitcom-writing protocols illustrate, students in Group A were given the possibility of experimenting first-hand with their creative skills as original authors of comedy scripts, building characters cast in archetypal roles—e.g., Mr. Smith, in Frame C, represents the Trickster interacting with the Innocent Millie; two high-status 'Masters' interact in Frame A (i.e., Maria and Androulla), whereas another Innocent (Sahera) has to interact with a Master (Priyanca) and a Fool (Amisha) in Frame B.

Having explored sitcom characters dynamics in space and in writing, Group-A students were allowed to watch a number of original sitcom episodes of *The Nanny*, the episode under analysis included. Then, they were guided to embody the characters of this sitcom. This "Embodiment" activity was crucially meant as an exercise of dislocation into the fictional context of the sitcom—which corresponds to the experience of theatre where real time and space disappear as both actors and audiences are entirely absorbed by what is being dramatically represented on stage. Therefore, in order to develop the kind of mind-set for the students' dramatic interpretation of the sitcom, it was necessary to create conditions for them to dislocate their own body and their whole mind into imaginative dimensions. It is at this stage that students as dubbing-translators start becoming real 'acting translators' as they set in motion a process of 'authentication-by-embodiment' of the sitcom script, with its representation of characters and their language. The principled relationship between theory and practice, in this case, regards the connection between the cognitive/affective top-down strategies activated by the translator to access and familiarize with the sitcom script, and the way in which such strategies become pedagogically crucial in the classroom methodology proposed here for the acting translators' achievement of a dramatic representation of the sitcom. Indeed, there is an essential difference between *(a)* the above-analyzed stage concerning the individual student's original process of creative projection of his/her own embodied schemata through the drama techniques of the 'Psychological Gesture' and the 'Archetypes', and *(b)* the stage of the acting translator's creative process of embodiment of somebody else's (e.g., the sitcom author's) creative projections of his/her embodied schemata into the sitcom characters. The contention in this study is that the acting translator's process of dramatic authentication of the sitcom-author's characters is exactly as creative and 'original' as the process of physical representation of his/her own embodied schemata through the P.G. and the archetypes. Indeed, authenticating the sitcom-author's characters by embodying them is assumed to be a very powerful and challenging experience for the acting translator. In fact, s/he needs to activate within himself/herself a state of physical/emotional schematic openness and availability to access and accept the sitcom-author's projections of his/her own embodied schemata into characters. This process would lead the acting translator to a state of 'readiness in apprehension' (cf. Guido 1999: 228) as s/he allows the author's schematic projections to re-define and challenge his/her own embodied schemata which, as a result, are greatly widened and enriched. This process of sitcom embodiment represents what can be defined as the 'authorial' role of the acting translator insofar as s/he has to free himself/herself from the passive, silent role of a mere Receiver by appropriating both the Sender's (i.e., the sitcom author's) and the Addresser's (i.e., the sitcom characters') roles. It shall be practically illustrated, at this stage, how this process of 'appropriation' actually occurs by means of the acting translator's physical, emotional, and then, intellectual embodiment of the sitcom author's characters.

During the "Embodiment" activity, the acting translator cannot access his/her own schemata right away, as s/he did in the previous process of first-person embodiment of archetypal gestalt structures by means of the Psychological Gesture. In fact, as a translator, the student has to cope with a sitcom script, that is, the textualization of the author's representation of his/her own embodied schemata. The risk of becoming just a passive Receiver, or a submissive 'silent reader', is therefore very high if the translator does not intend to become physically and emotionally assertive upon the script—to become, in other words, an acting translator. As an acting translator, first of all, the student encounters the sitcom script, which is the textualization of the author's creative representations of his/her own embodied schemata projected into the sitcom characters. Furthermore, being an audiovisual text, the acting translator has also access to the original tape-recording of the sitcom script, played by the actors in specific culture-bound situational contexts. The viewing of the staged version of the sitcom is expected to trigger in the acting translator the activation of his/her own embodied schemata in order to access the author's illocutionary intentions, and also to overcome the sense of unfamiliarity that s/he may feel on his/her first approach to the sitcom. This entails that the acting translator has to physically 'appropriate' the sitcom characters and situations by accessing them by means of his/her own embodied schemata—thus inhabiting them, embodying them, and dramatically representing them by inferring his/her own meanings from the scripted and staged language in order to authenticate it as a discourse s/he feels familiar with. Such a process can actually go on endlessly and creatively, by having acting translators re-textualize their own embodiments of the author's characters and situations into brand new scripts. Actually, this is the first, playful top-down phase of sitcom-dubbing theory advocated in this book, which allows the acting translator to disrupt his/her own conventionalized schematic patterns and re-organize them according to the characters' behaviours and pragmaliguistic uses s/he achieves from the sitcom script.

As a practical illustration of this stage, the activity of "Embodiment" represented a possibility for the students/acting-translators to identify themselves with the sitcom characters. The very first question that they were encouraged to pose to themselves was: "What is the difference between me and this particular sitcom character?"—It is necessary that, at the beginning, students keep an objective stance on the characters in order not to impose their own opinions or feelings upon them. However, such initial distance from the characters would expand the students' feelings of experiential empathy towards the others. Then, by activating a state of creative concentration, students/acting-translators started imagining that, in the same space they occupied, there exist another body, the imaginary body of the character they intended to embody as their mind was progressively creating it. Such a body did not have to necessarily resemble that of the actor playing the character in the sitcom. Then, the next step was that of the students/acting-translators who 'put on' the character's body, giving it life and moving and speaking as if they were another person. This experiential process was the same as that of putting on a mask—or simply a new outfit—thus wearing something unusual that would influence one's own cognitive and emotive personality. In the case at hand, wearing the character's imaginary body started influencing not only the students' personality, but also their voice and physical aspect. At this point it was necessary for them to trust the character completely, in all his/her movements and reactions. For this reason, before making the character act within the contexts of the sitcom, using his/her own scripted words, students/acting-translators explored their character they embodied within different situations. The following initial questions, aimed at enlivening the image of the embodied character in action, served in fact this very purpose:

a. Close your eyes and concentrate on one character from *The Nanny* sitcom.
b. Now, imagine you are him/her.
c. Stand up, now, and walk or move like him or her.
d. Who are you? (I'm Fran; I'm Sylvia; I'm Maxwell; etc.)
e. Show me Fran: how would you enter a room? How would you look around?
f. Show me Maxwell: how would you open a window?
g. Val, your friend, is coming to visit you: welcome her.
h. Sylvia, how would you appear in despair? (In a happy mood? Etc.)

Starting from the emotional and mental states created through the embodiment of characters, students were guided to make their 'embodied characters' interact with each other within the group in space, thus improvising new situations and dialogues. This allowed students to 'hear' their characters speak, which meant that they chose the kind of language intonation characters would probably adopt in specific contexts (for instance, a slow, fast, quiet, light, cold, aggressive, sarcastic, vulgar tone, and so on). In this way, students emphasized what they believed to be the intrinsic qualities of the character they were embodying. Furthermore, they were encouraged to create also some 'auxiliary selves' of their characters, to be associated with their 'main self', and by embodying such 'split identities', students started exploring the possible obscure, unconscious sides of the sitcom characters, their fears, nightmares and desires —such as those described in above-examined magazine article (*Caught in the culture gap*) on the 'split identity' feelings experienced in a cultural context different from the native one.

The following next step was represented by an improvisation activity defined as "Push and Pull", whose aim was to establish an Arousal/Safety relationship between two sitcom characters on stage, thus developing in students embodying them a specific 'physical memory' useful in scenes based on tense dialogues of a victim/aggressor type. Before tackling the actual sitcom dialogues, students improvise exchanges having *The Nanny* characters as protagonists. The physical activity consisted in one student, embodying an 'aggressive' role, who uttered his cues (with a pressing Request Move) by pushing another student—who put up resistance—against the student embodying the 'victim' role, who in turn uttered her cues (with dispreferred Apology Moves) by trying hard to dodge the student pushed against her since she, at the same time, had to pull after herself another student sitting on the floor. The physical effort required from both students improvising the dialogue produced effects suited to their roles. The following protocols report two of such 'push-&-pull' impro-dialogues having as characters Fran (the Nanny) and, respectively, Sylvia (her mother) and Maxwell (her employer):

Top-down protocol 10 – Push-&-Pull:
Sylvia (*Push–aggressor*): Stop watching TV. Tonight you must go out with Judith's son, David. It's fixed.
Fran (*Pull–victim*): But ... Mum! There's a beautiful film on TV tonight with Barbra Streisand! I don't want to go out!
Sylvia (*Push–aggressor*): Hurry up! You're in a mess! You've just got two hours to become the most beautiful woman in the world!
Fran (*Pull–victim*): Mum ... I don't want to go out with David! He's a bore! I don't like him!
Sylvia (*Push–aggressor*): He is rich! That's enough for you to like him and convince him to marry you!
Fran (*Pull–victim*): I don't want to marry him!
Sylvia (*Push–aggressor*): So, you'll become a poor old beggar! Shame!
Fran (*Pull–victim*): Mum ... I'm sure ... he's gay!
Sylvia (*Push–aggressor*): So what? Marry him, and he won't notice you getting old and ugly!
Fran (*Pull–victim*): I want a husband I love!
Sylvia (*Push–aggressor*): Stupid old girl! Do I love your father? A husband must make money for you, that's all!
Fran (*Pull–victim*): I've got a job I love! I like being a nanny and I earn enough money for myself.

Sylvia (*Push–aggressor*): Ah! You'll be fired as soon as the kids grow up and you'll be jobless as kids don't love granny-nannies!
Fran (*Pull–victim*): Okay, Mum, okay. ... I'll go out with David.

Top-down protocol 11 – Push-&-Pull:
Maxwell (*Push–aggressor*): What are you doing, Miss Fine?
Fran (*Pull–victim*): Er... I'm just ... reading.
Maxwell (*Push–aggressor*): What are you reading? What's that piece of paper?
Fran (*Pull–victim*): It's your children's shopping list.
Maxwell (*Push–aggressor*): Really? Let me see it!
Fran (*Pull–victim*): No, er... it's not important.
Maxwell (*Push–aggressor*): Oh! What's the problem, then? Let me see it.
Fran (*Pull–victim*): I can't. ... It's a list of gifts for your birthday.
Maxwell (*Push–aggressor*): My birthday is in six months! Give it to me!
Fran (*Pull–victim*): No! It's ... it's a secret!
Maxwell (*Push–aggressor*): My children must have no secrets for their father! I order you to give it to me!
Fran (*Pull–victim*): Here. ... It's mine...
Maxwell (*Push–aggressor*): Oh! A love letter from David! He asks you to marry him! ... Who's David?
Fran (*Pull–victim*): Oh, ... just a gay friend!
Maxwell (*Push–aggressor*): A gay friend indeed! Listen, I don't want a married woman as a nanny for my children, she'll have her own kids and wouldn't care for mine.
Fran (*Pull–victim*): Okay, Mr. Sheffield, don't worry, I'll not marry this man.

After improvising on the sitcom characters, students applied this Push-and-Pull activity to the above-analyzed dialogue from *The Nanny* sitcom. In this way they realized that feelings are principally expressed through intonation, which is the result of the interaction between characters 'on stage', not simply 'on page'. Furthermore, sitcom humour itself is not simply a linguistic construction, but it crucially becomes alive once it is embodied by the characters within a real space of enactment.

At this point, students were ready to move on to the second phase of this Acting Translator approach to sitcom dubbing translation – namely, the bottom-up phase of script analysis.

4.4.3 *Applying the Acting Translator Model: the bottom-up phase*

From this bottom-up phase on, both groups of students (A and B) were involved in classroom activities. During this specific phase, students were guided to explore the original sitcom script and video of *The Nanny* episode under scrutiny, by analyzing its move-&-act conversation structure so as to identify in it the sociopragmatic patterns and cultural meanings that inform the characters' linguistic and non-linguistic behaviours (cf. Edmonson 1981; Pomerantz and Fehr 1997). Indeed, at this stage of the Acting Translator method, students were encouraged to analyze the script by imaginatively becoming simultaneously the voices of the Sender (the author) and the Addresser (the characters). In performing such an 'imaginative leap' into the virtual context of the sitcom, even the role of the Addressee becomes a conscious, 'authorial' choice of the student who, at the same time, still remains a Receiver by taking a third-person stance on his/her own interpretation of the script. The argument is therefore that, at this stage, the student/acting-translator pragmatically and imaginatively appropriates the two speech-act domains of—in Carter's (1989: 61) definition—'macro-' and 'micro-conversation'. In his view, 'macro-conversation' corresponds to the 'outer context' operating between the author (the Sender) and the reader (the Receiver), whereas 'micro-conversation' defines the 'inner context' of the text within which 'at least two speakers' (the Addresser and the Addressee) come to interact. Carter's distinction between these two conversational domains is indeed crucial to the further development of this bottom-up stage of the Acting Translator Model, because, as he asserts (*ibidem*: 66):

> "This adds an extra dimension to the nature of conversation in a [fictional] context. However direct and naturalistic the exchanges in the inner context may be, it should not be forgotten that this forms only a part of the total message [the author] communicates to his reader. The competent reader overhears this conversation [...] but he must be at the same time alert to the speech acts transmitted indirectly by the author himself. Much work has still to be done in this area of overlap between direct and indirect speech acts".

As already argued elsewhere (Guido 1999: 238), to a certain extent it is possible to agree with Carter on his distinction between a direct (more or less overt) conversation between Addresser and Addressee, and an indirect (almost covert) ongoing conversation between the Sender and the Receiver – a distinction he derives from Widdowson's (1975) 'dual-focus situation' in literary discourse represented as '/1 Sender /2 Addresser //2 Addressee //1 Receiver'. Yet, there are some arguable points in his definition, such as his attempt to delimit the scope of the Sender/Receiver communication in terms of 'the total message the author communicates to his reader'. In fact, applied to sitcom scripts (but this may be valid for any kind of fictional literature), this communication pattern simply accounts for the messages that the sitcom author encodes in his/her text for the reader (then also the viewer and, later, the dubbing translator) to retrieve them, whereas it should be considered as a form of communicative discourse that the reader/viewer/translator achieves from the script (first 'on page' and, later, 'on stage') by means of his/her own schemata. And since it has been argued here that schemata are 'bodily', then one of the most effective ways for the reader/viewer/translator to achieve his/her own interpretative discourse from a sitcom script is to engage his/her whole physical/mental personality in it, exactly as an actor would do. Instead, what Carter seems to suggest is rather a passive reader – namely, a reader who is 'competent' only to the extent of being "alert to the speech acts transmitted indirectly by the author himself" (Carter 1989: 66). Carter's view is also supported by Short (1989) who does not recognize the presence of a reader/viewer/translator as an active interpreter of a fictional dramatic text as, in his view, only one assumption can be valid, that is: "the canonical form of a communicative event is one in which one person addresses and gives information to another" (*ibidem*: 148). This is a traditional pragmatic position to be referred back to Jakobson's (1960) statement: 'The Addresser sends a Message to the Addressee'—a univocal transmission of a message that Short applies also to the dual-focus situation of dramatic discourse. In his view, the creative presence of an interpreter, or even of a mere actor, is totally neglected in favour of the author's direct transmission of a message to the Receiver – that is, from 'Addresser 1', as Short (1989: 149) defines the Sender (i.e., the playwright), to 'Addressee 1', as he defines the Receiver (i.e., the audience) in the macro-communication context. The same kind of one-way transmission is reproduced by Short also in the context of micro-communication where 'Addresser 2' (i.e., character A) transmits a message to 'Addressee 2' (i.e., character B). Applied to the sitcom context, Short's view entails that an acting translator embodying and interpreting the sitcom script (as well as an actor of such dramatic text) has no part to play either in the appropriation and interpretation of the Sender's role in macro-communication, or in the personal, original embodiment of the Addresser's voice/character in micro-communication. The conclusion is clear: the only message that the Receiver has to 'submissively' retrieve in the sitcom script is the message encoded in the text by the real author.

Contrary to Short's assumptions, an acting translator is never a passive Receiver—i.e., a silent reader as s/he appropriates both Sender's and Addresser's roles in the context of the dramatic discourse of the sitcom. In fact, by 'appropriating the Sender's role' it is here meant the empirical Receiver's (i.e., the acting translator's) schematic authentication of the Sender's 'authorial role' within the context of the sitcom macro-communication in which the Sender communicates with his/her implied Receiver. This entails that the acting-translator/Receiver 'infers' from the sitcom script what s/he believes the author/Sender's implied meanings (or 'implicatures') are as s/he achieves them from the patterns of moves and acts that s/he identifies in the script. As a consequence, the sitcom script itself becomes a locutionary act set on a representational dimension in which the acting translator plays both the Sender's role (by appropriating the illocutionary force of the characters' utterances according to his/her own schemata) and the Receiver's role (by simultaneously experiencing the perlocutionary effect of such utterances, principally in terms of comic effect). The interpretation of the humorous discourse, therefore, involves either the acting translator's first-person embodiment of the 'comic effect' as a Receiver, or his/her third-person realization of the scripted 'textual cause' for that effect. The acting translator's first-person authentication of such 'textual cause' as an illocutionary force in the context of a macro-conversation marks his/her embodiment of the Sender's role as well. In sum, then, the illocutionary force represents the Sender's conditions of intentions and propositional reference as achieved (inferred) by the acting-translator/Receiver while s/he appropriates the sitcom pattern of conversational acts and moves by enacting the authorial role.

The acting translator's subsequent close-up scrutiny on the linguistic organization of the sitcom script—involving, this time, the embodiment of the Addresser/Addressee micro-communication—represents the core of the bottom-up phase of his/her exploration of the humorous discourse. At this stage, the acting translator's focus shifts from the 'Sender/Receiver macro-communication' to the 'Addresser/Addressee micro-communication'. The acting translator's objective during this phase consists in pragmatically appropriating and embodying the 'Addresser's voice' (i.e., the 'speaking voice' of the sitcom characters), that is, the Addresser's own linguistic style from which it could be possible to derive his/her own (fictional) personality. To achieve this, the acting translator paradoxically has to distance himself/herself from the language of the text in order to take a third-person, more detached stance in his/her exploration of the linguistic structure. This is expected to bring the acting translator to realize that the characters/Addressers' voices are characterized in terms of stylistic choices that need to be subjectively interpreted through his/her own embodied schemata in order to give them life within the pattern of acts and moves to be identified in the sitcom script. The acting translator's appropriation and embodiment of this conversational pattern—which occur by means of his/her inference and decision-making strategies on 'implicatures' (Grice 1975)—entails that s/he may achieve personal interpretations of the humorous pattern of moves and acts in the characters' dialogic turns as they are processed through his/her own schemata. This indeed represents the acting translator's own imaginative interpretation of the character/Addresser's voice. Indeed, the sitcom characters' use of comic puns, wordplays, and even sound and rhythmical patterns, once filtered through the acting translator's embodied schemata, can reveal a great deal about the way s/he is interpreting moods, emotions, thoughts, temperaments, feelings and attitudes of the characters/Addressers.

At this point, therefore, it becomes interesting to examine how the students in both Groups A and B—the subjects of the present study—reacted to the task of embodying the author/Sender's role and interpreting the characters/Addressers' voices in the selected extract from *The Nanny* sitcom script. What follows is an instance of bottom-up protocols with the transcriptions of students' verbal reports while they were analyzing the move-&-act pattern of the sitcom script. Such ethnographic research method was chosen because it permitted the monitoring of the embodying/interpreting strategies that students developed in their minds as they focused on the textual and discursive levels as well as the socio-cultural dimensions of the sitcom conversations. This meant that while students analyzed the original scripts, they externalized their mental processes and associations on possible cross-cultural interpretations of the conversation pattern. Both groups were given access to the annotated taxonomies of moves and acts from both the so-called UK and the US models of conversation analysis introduced in Chapter 3 of this book. However, it became soon evident from an enquiry into the bottom-up protocols that students in Group A (who, unlike Group-B students, went through the previous top-down pilot phase) produced conversation analyses that were more creative than the conventional ones produced by students in Group B as they managed to 'weave a *canovaccio*' (literally a 'canvas' as in the Italian *Commedia dell'Arte*) upon which they represented the sitcom scenario with its interacting characters. Eventually, most students in Group B felt inadequate even in the autonomous description of the conversation frame of the sitcom script and therefore they needed a more specific 'structural guidance' to cope with their analytical task. This justified the introduction of a conversational framework under the form of a True/False exercise posing them a very simple problem-solving task for the identification of a set of basic Structuralist moves in the sitcom dialogue—as the frame reported below, referred to the above-analyzed script extract from *The Nanny*:

> *Conversational framework (Group B):*
> *True/False. Please decide if the following statements are true or false in reference to the above-reported sitcom script from* The Nanny*:*
> 1. Cue 1 is an Offer Move and Cue 2 is a dispreferred Refuse Move. [T/F]
> 2. Cue 3 is an Offer Move and Cue 4 is a dispreferred Refuse Move followed by a preferred Accept Move. [T/F]
> 3. Cues 5-6-7 are respectively Assess - (dispreferred) Disagree - Agree. [T/F]
> 4. Cue 8 is a Direct Move. [T/F]
> 5. Cue 9 is and Inform Move. [T/F]
> 6. Cue 15 is a Support Move. [T/F]
> 7. Cue 19 is an Answer Move and Cue 20 is an Acknowledge Move. [T/F]
> 8. Cue 30 is a Question and Cue 31 is a (dispreferred) Unexpected Answer. [T/F]
> 9. Cue 34 is a Question and Cue 35 is a (dispreferred) Unexpected Answer. [T/F]
> 10. Cue 39 is a Support Move and Cue 40 is a Challenge Move. [T/F]
>
> *Keys:*
> 1-T; 2-T; 3-F (Assess-Disagree-Disagree/Challenge); 4-T; 5-T; 6-F (Challenge); 7-F (Elicit-Acknowledge/Challenge); 8-T; 9-F (Question—(preferred) Expected Answer); 10-T.

Differently from Group B, Group A showed instead a greater degree of analytical autonomy to the point that some students suggested the introduction of new moves and acts which could better describe the humorous dynamics of the sitcom dialogue, thus simultaneously embodying *(a)* the authorial role of the Sender, the characters' roles of *(b)* Addressers and *(c)* Addressees in the fictional conversation, and *(d)* the role of the Receiver as reader/viewer (hence member of the audience) as well as analyst/translator. The following extract from a bottom-up protocol (Frascerra 2006: 39-44) represents an instance of such analytical creativity:

> *Bottom-up protocol 1 (Group A) – Conversation analysis of* The Nanny *script (italics added to student's creative proposals)*
> "This exchange is opened by Maxwell who addresses Sylvia calling her by name. He uses a Summoning Move in order to attract her attention. Its corresponding Act is Bid, that is the Act that signals the speaker's will to start a conversation. Mr. Sheffield goes on speaking, inviting Sylvia to dine with them, He employs an Offer Move, that is the Move used to make a proposal to someone. As this Move is realized in the shape of a question, the corresponding Act is Elicitation. Sylvia does not accept with a Refusal Move to which corresponds a Reply Act, that is the Act used to provide a response. She proceeds saying that she has just come over to see how Fran's date went. In this case the Move used is an Informing Move which serves to provide additional information. Consequently the corresponding Act is Informative. Sylvia concludes saying to them to continue eating. *Since this time it doesn't exist an appropriate Move among those provided by the two CA models, I have created a new one. I have named it Reassuring Move in order to express the function of Sylvia's utterance. Also the Act associated with this Move has been devised by me. Its name is Permission Act.* At this point Niles intervenes repeating the suggestion to join them to dinner. He uses an Offer Move corresponding to the Elicitation Act. Sylvia turns down again though she is very hungry. The Move used is Refusal and the Act is Reply. She thanks them for the invitation with a Finalizer Move. *Also in this case it has been necessary to use a new type of Act called Thank. Its function is to show gratitude to someone.* Again Sylvia says that she had a Yoplait at 10:30 in the morning. She uses an Informing Move by which she provides information and as a consequence the Act is Informative. Immediately afterwards Sylvia, seeing that Grace is eating a big potato, says that it is too big for such a little girl and she takes it away of her dish. *She uses a Downgrade Move whose function is to soften the tone of the conversation. Its corresponding Act is the new Downtoner Act created on the basis of the Move name and function. This Move represents a humour marker, in fact it produces a comic scene which provokes the laughter of the public.* [...]
>
> At this point Brighton intervenes affirming that he likes Jules. He uses an Assessment Move which serves to express an evaluation. Consequently the Act is Evaluate. The boy follows his cue with an Upgrade Move used to emphasize his previous statement. He, in fact, says that Jules hasn't yet beaten him in chess. *The Act used in correspondence to the Upgrade Move has been called by me Emphasize on the basis of the Move function.* Maxwell blames his son saying that Jules did it on purpose. *He uses a Blame Move to express his disaccord. I have called the corresponding Act Dissent, because in my opinion this is an appropriate name which reflects the Move function.* With

> a Downgrade Move Brighton makes a rhetorical question to his father. The Act used is Elicitation. Maxwell replies counselling him not to become fond of Jules. *I have named this Move Advise*, while the Act used is Comment since Mr. Sheffield is providing additional information and he is expressing his opinion about Jules. Maxwell continues with an Upgrade Move with which he is going to strengthen the reason for his advice. He, in fact, says that Miss Fine's relationships always end in disaster. *In my opinion in this case the corresponding Act is the new Disparagement Act because Mr. Sheffield wants to discredit Fran.* From Mr. Sheffield's comment about Jules we can observe how this character diverges from the role of Fran's employer to embody that of the jealous lover. [...]
>
> Sylvia wants to convince fran to marry Jules because he is handsome and rich and this could be her last opportunity. Also from this attitude by Sylvia emerges her negative role as a mother. At this point Fran captures her mother's attention with a Summoning Move corresponding to a Bid Act and then she tries to negotiate explaining to Sylvia that she didn't say 'no' but she would think about it. *In this occasion the Move used is one of the most relevant of the dialogue, that is the Negotiating Move by which the conflict between Fran and her mother ends. The Act associated has been called by me Mediation in order to mirror the Move function.* Sylvia asks her if she has decided to accept using an Eliciting Move and consequently an Elicitation Act. Fran replies in an affirmative way an Acceptance Move corresponding to the Accept Act. The scene closes with an acknowledging Move used by Sylvia through which she expresses her happiness for Fran's decision. The corresponding Act is Acknowledge. But then Maxwell enters the room and re-opens the dialogue [...]"

However naïve this student's conversation analysis may at times appear, it shows interesting elements of creativity in the appropriation of the Sender's authorial role not only in mapping the pragmatic unfolding of moves and acts in the sitcom dialogue, but also in identifying some unconventional ones—and labeling them anew—characterizing the sitcom humour. Moreover, from this dialogic structure the student also manages to identify some peculiarities of the sitcom characters as respectively Addressers and Addressees in the exchanges, thus interpreting the conversational script as a prompt for the subsequent character embodiment, play enactment and dubbing translation of the sitcom during the next Interactive Phase to be introduced in the following sub-section.

4.4.4 *Applying the Acting Translator Model: the interactive phase*

Having focused so far on the top-down and the bottom-up phases, the third, interactive phase of the Acting Translator Model shall be now explored, by examining how the procedures that were adopted by students to establish their 'presence' in the iconic context they derived from the sitcom script are now relevant to the establishment of 'presence' in a group interaction with the text. For assessment reasons, the activities performed by Group A and Group B, though similar, were kept separate.

During this final interactive phase of sitcom embodiment and translation, the student/acting-translator starts interacting not only with the sitcom script, interpreting and translating it, but also with the other students/acting-translators' drama interpretations-in-progress of it, as the group is expected to work in team. In this process, therefore, the acting translator comes to 'enter' the others' sitcom interpretations by absorbing their different artistic experiences within his/her own. This allows him/her to be, on the one hand, schematically activated by the others' embodiments s/he empathically appropriates. On the other, however, s/he can also take bodily action upon other acting translators' embodiments of the sitcoms characters 'in an actual space of enactment' (i.e., a classroom that becomes a real 'rehearsal room'), thus re-interpreting the same sitcom situation in a multiplicity of ways according to the imaginative conditions s/he creates by physically and emotionally interacting with the group. It is at this stage that students/acting-translators have to be guided to achieve that special 'artistic' quality of being able to speak, as it were, 'in many voices', which means not only in those voices they themselves embody within the macro- and micro-communication dimensions of the sitcom script, but also in the other acting translators' voices they recognize and appropriate by dramatically interacting with them. In this new interactive context, therefore, the acting translators consciously 'shed their own referential selves' in order to assume both the Sender/Receiver and the characters' Addresser/Addressee roles, and to move from one to the other at the same time, taking different, simultaneous perspectives before tackling the task of translating the original script into the target language for its dubbing version.

Indeed, this phase of the student/acting-translator's physical interaction with the other students/acting-translators 'on stage' is useful for his/her subsequent translation activity insofar as s/he can come to realize that, if in interacting only with the sitcom script during the bottom-up phase and by appropriating both the Sender's and the Addresser's 'voices' s/he can have a free scope in the 'choice' of the Addressee's and the Receiver's roles as "vacant identities for [him/her] to occupy" (Widdowson 1992: 187), now, by also dramatically interacting with the other acting translators' 'displaced selves on stage' s/he realizes that they are no longer 'vacant identities to occupy'. In fact, with their 'real, physical existence', the other students/acting-translators' 'embodied identities' in the sitcom frame are imaginatively challenging for the student/acting-translator insofar as s/he does not perceive them as projections of his/her own self, but rather s/he actually sees them as 'different' from himself/herself, and yet s/he comes to appropriate them as well according to his/her own interpretative schematic parameters. Furthermore, by appropriating and embodying the others' 'embodied identities' of the sitcom, the acting translator realizes that s/he has to put under discussion also his/her own 'embodied identities' at both macro- and micro-communication levels in order to accommodate them within a collective 'theatrical frame'. In such a context, therefore, the Sender's, the Addresser's, the Addressee's and the Receiver's voices become a matter of a collective and negotiable dramatic choice in group interpretation because, once an acting translator realizes another acting translator's second-person perspective in embodying a character (as an Addresser) or an authorial voice (as a Sender) in sitcom dramatic interaction, then s/he empathically absorbs it within his/her own first-person perspective by sharing it and negotiating it with his/her own embodiments within the group.

How the students/acting-translators' empathic shifting into the others' sitcom embodiments actually took place will be practically illustrated now, by also accounting for the data reporting the students' shifting perspectives as they allowed their sitcom embodiments to be physically, emotionally and intellectually absorbed into the other acting translators' embodiments during the collective and multiple rehearsals of the original sitcom script, until it came to be fixed into a shared 'performance'—i.e., a final set of pragmatic choices that were also recorded into video-protocols. In analyzing the students/acting-translators' collective performance of the sitcom script under scrutiny, three types of protocols were accounted for: *(a)* video-recordings of the performance in progress, thus taking a third-person objective stance; *(b)* students' first-person retrospective reports on their interpretation of the conversation structure of the script (thus playing the Sender's role) and on their embodiment of the sitcom characters interacting with other students' embodiments of other characters (thus playing the Addresser's role); *(c)* students' retrospective reports on their own response as Receivers (audience) of the other students' interpretations, and on their characters' response 'on stage' as second-person Addressees of other characters' cues. Data, in all these cases, were collected by means of the 'think-aloud technique' (Ericsson and Simon 1984) consisting in video/tape-recording, and transcribing into protocols, the students' retrospective reports. What follows is an instance of a first-person protocol *(b)* and a related second-person protocol *(c)* produced within Group A:

> *Interactive protocol 1 (Group A)—type (b) retrospective report: embodying Addresser (character) and Sender (author) roles:*
> "[*Embodying the Addresser*] In group performance I played Fran, the Nanny. I felt very much an innocent victim of the whole situation ... I mean, everybody wanted me to behave in a different way that didn't correspond to my real desires. I've tried to negotiate ... for example, by keeping a joyful atmosphere in the family, ... but my mother started attacking me ... violently ... and also Mr. Sheffield was awful with me, criticising and ... belittling me all the time. I realized that the tone my voice was becoming ... monotonous ... whining, after the first cues, as I was wounded inside by the reaction of the people around me ... even the kids! I thought they wanted me to remain with them ... perhaps, I hoped, to become their step mother ... but they were happy,

instead, for my wedding. ... I perceived my body that began to bend as the conversation went on ... although I still feigned cheerfulness. ... Then my mother attacked me ... even physically ... and at that point I really felt within me all my Jewishness ... I don't know ... I mean ... the sensation of belonging to a tradition of bullying and abuse. That's how I felt when I embodied Fran. ... [*Embodying the Sender*] And I think that also the author may have meant this ... I could read this in the structure of the dialogue ... Fran is always contradicted by the other people that should love her ... and by the events ... everyone and everything seems challenging her, she is a victim ... but this unfortunately determines the humour of this sitcom."

Interactive protocol 2 (Group A) – type (c) retrospective report: embodying Addressee (character)and Receiver (audience) roles:

"[*Embodying the Addressee*] As I played Sylvia to you, embodying Fran, I was not at ease. I thought that you would behave as a naughty young woman that doesn't want to hear her mother's advice. But I soon found that I was wrong and it was very difficult for me because I perceived that you were suffering inside ... but you were also tough ... and this made me furious ... physically and emotionally. ... I expected I had to deal with a Trickster, actually, but you were playing the Innocent to me, or even my Servant and I felt I was your Master ordering you what you had to do. [*Embodying the Receiver*] Your acting was perhaps too subtle to be perceived by the audience, I think ... because I could perceive your feelings as I was on stage with you, but the way you embodied your ... Jewishness, as you say ... may not reach the audience out there."

What is particularly interesting in the first "interactive protocol 1" is the way in which the Italian student playing Fran came to embody the character's Jewishness by relying upon the European deep-rooted and collective memory of the Shoah with the related perception of the Jew as a persecuted human being—which was the archetype stored in her socio-cultural and experiential schemata. This perception, however, has nothing to do with the view of contemporary New York Jewishness represented in *The Nanny*, retaining no traumatic experience of the Holocaust, being rather marked by a full and cheerful adherence to the advantages of material goods—which characterizes the disparagement humour of this sitcom. Nevertheless, the student embodying Fran was appropriating this character by activating her own schemata through a top-down process that was somehow corrected by the other student playing Sylvia to her, who by taking a second-person, bottom-up stance pointed out, first as the character/Addressee of Fran's cues, her uneasiness in having to cope with an unpredicted embodiment of Fran as an Innocent, rather than as a Trickster fooling her mother, as she expected, and then, as a Receiver, her reservations about the effectiveness of the subtleties played by the student embodying Fran in terms of communication with the audience. Such critical interaction within Group A was very useful indeed as it allowed further collective adjustments till reaching a final performance shared by all its components.

Differently from students in Group A, who applied their experience developed by going through both top-down and bottom-up phases of the Acting Translator approach, students in Group B, who went through only the second bottom-up phase, felt almost uncomfortable in having to 'perform' the sitcom in group before tackling the dubbing translation activity. In fact, they did not 'embody' the sitcom 'voices' in both macro- and micro-communication, but rather they limited themselves to reproduce, unimaginatively, the original sitcom acting slavishly—'impersonating'—the actors' gestures, facial expressions and intonations, rather than attempting an actual 'embodiment' by involving their own experiential body/thought schemata. The result can be epitomized in the following instance of first-person protocol *(b)*:

> *Interactive protocol 3 (Group B) – type (b) retrospective report: 'impersonating' the Addresser role:*
> "It's difficult for me to become Fran! I'm very different from her! ... I tried hard to move my hips like hers ... using a nasal voice and ... saying her cues with the same intonation. ... At the end I think I succeeded! ... I viewed the tape-recordings and I must say ... well ... there is not much difference between my performance and the performance of the actress Fran Drescher!"

What these few protocols can illustrate is how Group-A students' physical and emotional embodiment of the sitcom script actually involved their own identities in the process of identification with other human beings while they interacted with both the first-person 'voices' they achieved within the text and with the other students' embodiments of such voices while co-creating their collective interpretation. It was at this stage that students were deemed ready to start producing their dubbing translations.

4.5 Applying the Acting Translator Model to *The Nanny* Sitcom Script: The Dubbing Translation

4.5.1 *Collected data from the dubbing-translation workshop*

So far, the practical outline of the three phases of the Model have aimed at illustrating how students were guided towards an awareness that, as acting translators, they can experience a simultaneous and total embodiment of the first-, second- and third-person perspectives while appropriating the 'sitcom voices' with other acting translators in a dramatic context. Evidence of this has therefore been provided by means of protocols reporting the analysis they operated retrospectively on the interaction between their own and the others' dramatic interpretations-in-progress. At this point, students were encouraged to apply this awareness to their process of translating *The Nanny* sitcom script under analysis, so as to provide an alternative dubbed version to the 'official' one produced for the Italian television. In this way they could exploit the characters' motivations they achieved by embodying the script during the previous phases. Indeed, this dubbing-translation activity falls within the third, interactive phase of the Acting Translator Model insofar as this phase would create conditions for the students to embody sitcom 'characters' using a 'contextualized language', which entails four main objectives:

(1) enabling students/acting-translators to shift their own identities into virtual ones, exploring all their facets and perspectives by finding equivalent expressions in the target language;

(2) widening the scope of their identification by acknowledging other expressive dimensions of their embodiments;

(3) enhancing their powers of imaginative dislocation into different states of mind and sensitivities expressed, this time, by means of the target language;

(4) enhancing their powers of emotional/physical communication by negotiating the meanings they infer from the American script and translate into Italian with the other acting translators' subjective meanings and interpretations rendered into Italian.

In doing so, students were expected to justify their translation choices at both pragmalinguistic and socio-pragmatic levels of variability. The collected data of some of their translation choices are reported below as they were transcribed into protocols and analyzed in parallel with the original version. From such transcriptions it will become evident that the students in Group A, who went through the top-down pilot phase, produced translations with a more spontaneous conversation style in the target language, as they felt they identified themselves with the sitcom characters and 'embodied' their voices without diverging from the original script at both formal and pragmatic levels. In this way, they enacted a kind of 'self-elicitation' of a 'contextual' kind, thus giving instances of the equivalent linguistic choices they would normally make in a given context, like the one represented in the sitcom episode under analysis. Students in Group B, instead, produced translations in almost artificial dialogic tones, marked by pragmatically-biased transfer and reverse-transfer patterns, and often reproducing typical literary written styles. This was so because they principally activated a kind of 'conceptual self-elicitation', associating the dialogic cues of the sitcom script with the Italian words and structures that came more readily to their minds as equivalent to the original ones. This often meant that students in Group B did not mind too much about identifying contextualized instances of naturally occurring Italian language, but rather employed the language that was more readily available in their mind—usually—and critically—in such situations, conventionalized instances of artificial Italian 'dubbese'. What follows is the protocol analysis of Groups A and B parallel translation choices of *The Nanny* sitcom script under examination—the translated cues of the sitcom dialogue are subdivided into segments (approximately coinciding with the moves) to facilitate the parallel analysis between the versions proposed by students from the two respective groups.

The Nanny (***La Tata***) episode #304 *Dope Diamond*

A) Original English version ***B) Official Italian dubbing translation*** ***C) Back-translation into English***	***Group A - Italian dubbing translation***	***Group B - Italian dubbing translation***
[Int. Dining Room] *(Maxwell and his children are having supper)*	**[Int. Sala da pranzo]** *(Maxwell e i suoi figli stanno cenando)*	**[Int. Sala da pranzo]** *(Maxwell e i suoi figli stanno cenando)*
A) [1] **MAXWELL:** Please, Sylvia, why - why don't you join us? *B) [1]* MAXWELL: Signora Assunta, non vuole sedersi a tavola con noi? *C) [1]* MAXWELL: Signora Assunta *[approx. Mrs. Fine]*, won't you like to sit down to eat with us?	*[1]* **MAXWELL:** **(1)** (La) prego, Sylvia, perché — perché non si unisce a noi? **[9 occurrences]** **(2)** Prego, Signora, vuole — vuole unirsi a noi? **[2 occurrences]** **(3)** La prego, Sylvia, perché — perché non ci tiene compagnia? **(4)** Prego, Sylvia, perché — perché non si siede con noi?	*[1]* **MAXWELL:** **(1)** Per favore, Sylvia, perché — perché non si unisce a noi? **[7 occurrences]** **(2)** Assunta, perché non si siede con noi? **[3 occurrences]** **(3)** Per favore, Sylvia, perché non ti unisci a noi? **(4)** Ti prego, Sylvia, perché — perché non ti unisci a noi? **(5)** Dai, Sylvia, perché non ti unisci a noi? **[2 occurrences]** **(6)** Dai, Sylvia, perché non ti aggiungi anche tu? **(7)** Sylvia, perché non si unisce a noi? **[4 occurrences]** **(8)** Sylvia, perché non stiamo in compagnia? **(9)** La prego, Sylvia, si unisca a noi. **[2 occurrences]** **(10)** Prego, Sylvia, si sieda con noi. **(11)** Su, Sylvia, perché (perché) non si unisce a noi? **[2 occurrences]**
A) [2] **SYLVIA: {a}** Oh, no. I just came over to see how Fran's date went. **{b}** Make like I'm not even here. *B) [2]* ZIA ASSUNTA: **{a}** Oh no, io sono qui solo per sentire da Francesca com'è andata oggi. **{b}** Mangi e faccia come se io non ci fossi. *C) [2]* AUNT ASSUNTA: **{a}** Oh, no. I'm here just to hear from Francesca how things were getting on today. **{b}** Go on eating and make like I'm not here.	*[2]* **SYLVIA:** **(1) {a}** Oh, no. Sono venuta solo per sapere come è andato l'appuntamento di Fran. **[5 occurrences] {b}** Fate come se non ci fossi. **[20 occurrences]** **(2) {a}** Oh, no. Sono solo venuta per sapere com'è andato l'incontro di Fran. **(3) {b}** Fate pure come se non ci fossi. **[2 occurrences]** **(4) {b}** Fate finta che non ci sono. **[2 occurrences]** **(5) {a}** Sto qui soltanto per sapere dell'appuntamento di Fran. **{b}** Fate finta che non ci sia. **(6) {a}** Oh, no, sono venuta giusto per vedere com'è andato l'appuntamento di Fran. **[2 occurrences] {b}** fate pure come se non fossi qui. **[2 occurrences]**	*[2]* **SYLVIA:** **(1) {a}** No, grazie. Sono venuta a vedere soltanto come è andato l'appuntamento di Fran / Francesca. **[10 occurrences]** **{b}** Perciò fate come se io non ci fossi. **[2 occurrences]** **(2) {b}** Fate proprio come se non ci fossi. **(3) {b}** Fate finta di niente. **(4) {a}** Oh, no sto uscendo per vedere come è andato l'appuntamento di Francesca. **(5) {a}** Oh no, sto giusto andando a vedere come è andato l'appuntamento di Fran. **(6) {a}** Oh no. Sono solo venuta per vedere come è andata la giornata a Francesca. **(7) {a}** Oh no. Ero solo venuta a vedere come è andato l'appuntamento di Fran.

	(7) {a} Oh, no, sono solo / ero giusto passata per sapere com'è andato l'appuntamento di Fran / Francy. **[3 occurrences]** **(8) {a}** Ho giusto fatto un salto per sapere com'è andato l'appuntamento romantico di Fran. **(9) {a}** Oh, no. Sono venuta a trovarvi giusto per sapere com'è andato l'appuntamento galante di Fran.	**(8) {a}** Oh no, sono solo venuta a vedere come andavano le cose a Francesca. **(9) {a}** Oh no. Vado a vedere come è andato l'incontro di Fran. **(10) {a}** Oh no, grazie. Sono venuta solo per vedere come va a finire l'appuntamento di Fran. **(11) {a}** On, no grazie. Sono venuta giusto per vedere come sta andando l'appuntamento di Fran.
A) [3]* NILES:** Are you sure we can't offer you something? ***B) [3] NILES: E' sicura che non possiamo offrirle qualcosa? ***C) [3]*** NILES: Are you sure we can't offer you something?	***[3]* NILES:** **(1)** È sicura che non possiamo offrirle qualcosa? **[9 occurrences]** **(2)** Ma è sicura che non le possiamo offrire qualcosa? **[2 occurrences]** **(3)** E' proprio sicura di non gradire nulla / niente? **[2 occurrences]** **(4)** È sicura che non le possiamo offrire nulla / niente? **[4 occurrences]** **(5)** Davvero non gradisce qualcosa? **(6)** È sicura che non vuole prendere niente?	***[3]* NILES:** **(1)** Sei sicura che non possiamo offrirti qualcosa? **[2 occurrences]** **(2)** Siete sicura che non possiamo offrirvi qualcosa? **[2 occurrences]** **(3)** Sicura che non possiamo offrirle / offrirti nulla / qualcosa? **[3 occurrences]** **(4)** E' (proprio) sicura di non voler niente? **[3 occurrences]** **(5)** Sei sicura di non voler qualcosa? **(6)** Le posso offrire qualcosa? **[2 occurrences]** **(7)** Vuoi che ti offra qualcosa?
A) [4]* SYLVIA: {a}** Oh, no, thank you. I had a yoplait this morning around 10:30. **{b}** *(She takes a potato from Grace's dish)* Oh, such a big potato for such a little girl. **{c}** Look at the time. They must be having a ball. **{d}** I'm gonna go in the kitchen. I need a meat to wash this down with. *(Sylvia leaves the dining room)* ***B) [4] ZIA ASSUNTA: **{a}** No, no, no grazie, sono a dieta e sto morendo di fame, ma voi mangiate tranquilli. **{b}** *(Prende una patata dal piatto di Grace)* Oh, una patata troppo grande per una bambina così piccola! **{c}** Però, come tardano! Si vede che si divertiranno molto! **{d}** Se non vi spiace vado in cucina, ci vuole del manzo come contorno ad una grossa patata. *(Zia Assunta esce dalla stanza)* ***C) [4]*** AUNT ASSUNTA: **{a}** No, no, no, thank you. I'm on diet and I'm starving, but please, go on eating easy. **{b}** *(She takes a potato from Grace's dish)* Oh, a too big potato for such a little girl! **{c}** Hey, how late they are! They must be having a very good time! **{d}** If you don't mind I'm going in the kitchen, some	***[4]* SYLVIA:** **(1) {a}** Oh no, grazie. Ho (già) preso già uno yogurt questa mattina (intorno) alle / verso le 10:30. **[3 occurrences] {b}** Ma che patata grande per una bambina così piccola! **[2 occurrences] {c}** Ma ancora non tornano... si staranno divertendo! **[2 occurrences] {d}** Vado in cucina. Non riesco a mandar giù la patata senza un pezzo di carne. **(2) {a}** No, La ringrazio, ho già mangiato uno yogurt alle vitamine stamattina. **(3) {a}** grazie, no. Ho preso uno yogurt dietetico stamattina alle 10 e mezza. **(4) {a}** No grazie, ho mangiato uno Yomo / Iocca / dei fiocchi di latte verso le 10:30 stamattina. **(5) {a}** On no, grazie, Ho già preso uno yogurt leggero questa mattina verso le 10 e trenta. **(6) {b}** Ma questa è una patata troppo grande per una bimba così piccola! **(7) {b}** Oh, una patata così grande / grossa per una bimba / bambina così piccola. **[13 occurrences]** **(8) {b}** Oh, che patata grande per una bimba così piccola. **(9) {c}** Ma guarda l'orario! Si sta-	***[4]* SYLVIA:** **(1) {a}** Oh no, grazie. Ho preso uno yogurt questa mattina intorno alle 10:30. **[2 occurrences] {b}** Oh che grande patata per una così piccola bambina! **[4 occurrences] {c}** Guardi l'ora. Devono divertirsi molto. **{d}** Sto andando in cucina, ho bisogno di qualcosa di sostanzioso per mandarla giù. **[2 occurrences]** **(2) {a}** Oh no, grazie. Ho già preso un piatto allo yogurt questa mattina intorno alle 10:30. **[2 occurrences] {b}** Oh, una patata così grande per una così piccola ragazza. **{c}** Guarda che ore sono. Saranno ad un ballo. **[2 occurrences]** **(3) {b}** Oh una così grande patata per una così piccola bambina. **{c}** Guarda che ora è /sono. (Probabilmente / a quest'ora) staranno ballando. **[4 occurrences]** **(4) {b}** Ma che grande / grossa patata per una bimba così piccola. **[2 occurrences]** **(5) {b}** Una sventola di patata per uno scricciolo di ragazza! **(6) {b}** Oh, una patata così grossa per una ragazzina così

beef is required as a side dish for a big potato. *(Aunt Assunta leaves the dining room)*	ranno divertendo moltissimo! **(10) {c}** Guarda che ora si è fatta! Si staranno divertendo quei due! **[2 occurrences]** **(11) {c}** Guardate un po' che ore sono! Se la staranno spassando un mondo! **[3 occurrences]** **(12) {c}** (Ma) guardate l'ora! **[2 occurrences]** Se la staranno spassando. **[3 occurrences]** **(13) {c}** Guarda che ora! Devono essersi dati alla pazza gioia! / Si staranno dando alla pazza gioia **[3 occurrences]** **(14) {c}** Guarda un po' l'orario! Si staranno divertendo molto! **[3 occurrences]** **(15) {c}** Oh, si è fatto tardi. Di sicuro se la staranno spassando alla grande! **(16) {d}** Sto andando in cucina. Ho bisogno di una bella bistecca per annaffiare questa patata. **(17) {d}** Vado in cucina. Ho bisogno di una bistecca per mandar giù questa. **[2 occurrences]** **(18) {d}** Mi sposto in cucina. Vorrei della carne per mandar giù questa. **[4 occurrences]** **(19) {d}** Me ne vado in cucina. Ho bisogno di (una fetta di) carne per mandarla giù. **[6 occurrences]** **(20) {d}** Ora vado in cucina a mandar giù questa patata con della carne. *(Sylvia esce dalla stanza)*	piccola! **(7) {b}** Oh poveretta, una patata così grande per una bambina così piccina! **(8) {a}** Oh no, grazie, ho mangiato uno yogurt stamattina presto. **[2 occurrences]** **(9) {a}** No grazie. Ho fatto uno spuntino stamattina verso le / intorno alle 10:30. **[5 occurrences]** **(10) {a}** Oh no, grazie. Ho preso un frullato verso le 10:30. **[2 occurrences]** **(11) {a}** Oh no, grazie. Ho mangiato una peperonata alle 10:30 stamattina. **(12) {a}** Oh no, grazie. Ho già fatto fuori un piatto a base di yogurt stamattina intorno alle 10:30. **(13) {a}** Oh no grazie, ho preso uno Yoplait stamattina / stamane alle 10:30 circa. **[3 occurrences] {b}** Oh una patata così grande per una fanciulla così piccola. **{c}** Guarda l'ora, staranno giocando a palla. **[2 occurrences]** **(14) {c}** Oh, ma guardate l'ora. Staranno avendo molto di cui parlare! **(15) {a}** Oh no, grazie, ho mangiato uno Yoplait questa mattina verso le / intorno / attorno alle 10:30. **[4 occurrences] {b}** Oh, ma è una patata troppo / così grande per una ragazza così piccola. **[5 occurrences] {c}** Date uno sguardo all'orario. Devono starsi divertendo un mondo! **{d}** Sto andando in cucina. Ho bisogno di carne per digerire la patata. **(16) {d}** Vado in cucina. Mi ci vuole / Ho bisogno di qualcosa per digerire (la patata / ciò). **[3 occurrences]** **(17) {c}** A quest'ora dovrebbero essere al ballo. **(18) {a}** No, grazie. Questa mattina alle 10 e mezza ho mangiato un piatto a base di yogurt. **(19) {a}** Oh no, la ringrazio. Ho già mangiato un piatto di pasta questa mattina verso le dieci. **(20) {c}** Giusto in tempo. Si staranno divertendo. **{d}** Vado in cucina. Ho bisogno di una bistecca da mandar giù con questa. **(21) {c}** Guardando l'ora direi che starebbero ballando. **{d}** Beh, vado in cucina. Ho un conto in sospeso con la carne.

		(22) {d} Vado in cucina. Ho bisogno di un succo per berci su. **(23) {d}** Non riesco a mandare giù la patata senza carne. **(24) {d}** Ho bisogno di carne per trangugiare meglio questa. **(25) {d}** Ora vado in cucina. Ho bisogno di un pezzo di carne con cui annaffiare giù questa patata. **(26) {d}** Vado in cucina. Mi serve un po' /della carne per mandarla giù. **[2 occurrences]** **(27) {d}** Me ne vado in cucina. Devo berci su qualcosa. **(28) {d}** Sto andando in cucina. Ho bisogno di una fettina con cui mandare giù questa patata. **(29) {d}** Andrò in cucina. Ho bisogno di qualcosa come contorno per questo. **(30) {d}** Vado in cucina. Dovrò accompagnare con una bistecca questa patata, no? **(31) {d}** Allora vado in cucina. Devo prendere della carne da accompagnare con questo. *(Sylvia esce dalla stanza)*
A) [5]* BRIGHTON: {a}** I don't know about you guys, but I like Jules, **{b}** and he has yet to beat me in chess. ***B) [5] BRIGHTON: **{a}** Non so a voi, ma a me Giulio piace molto **{b}** e non mi ha battuto neanche una volta a scacchi. ***C) [5]*** BRIGHTON: **{a}** I don't know if you do, but I like Giulio a lot **{b}** and he has beaten me not a single time in chess.	***[5]* BRIGHTON:** **(1) {a}** Non so a voi, ragazzi, ma a me piace Jules. **[15 occurrences] {b}** E ancora deve battermi a scacchi. / E mi deve ancora battere a scacchi. **[11 occurrences]** **(2) {a}** Non so che ne pensate, ma a me Jules piace. **{b}** E non è ancora riuscito a battermi a scacchi. **[2 occurrences]** **(3) {a}** Non so voi cosa ne pensiate, ma a me piace Jules. **(4) {a}** Non so a voi, gente, ma a me Jules piace. **(5) {b}** e poi / e in più, non mi ha ancora battuto a scacchi. **[3 occurrences]** **(6) {b}** e non mi ha ancora / mai battuto a / agli scacchi. **[11 occurrences]**	***[5]* BRIGHTON:** **(1) {a}** Non so voi, ma a me piace Giulio, **[3 occurrences] {b}** deve ancora sconfiggermi a scacchi. **(2) {a}** Non so niente di ragazzi, ma Jules mi piace. **(3) {a}** Non so i tuoi figli, ma a me piace Jules. **{b}** soprattutto perché non mi ha ancora battuto a scacchi. **(4) {a}** Non vi conosco ragazzi, ma mi piace Jules. **{b}** e deve ancora vincermi a scacchi. **(5) {b}** vinco sempre contro di lui a scacchi. **(6) {b}** e ha ancora intenzione di battermi a scacchi.
A) [6]* MAXWELL: {a}** Oh, God, Brighton, **{b}** he throws every game. ***B) [6] MAXWELL: **{a}** Ma su, Brighton, **{b}** è lui che vuole perdere! ***C) [6]*** MAXWELL: **{a}** Come on, Brighton, **{b}** it's him who wants to lose!	***[6]* MAXWELL:** **(1) {a}** Mio Dio, Brighton, **{b}** bara per farti vincere. **(2) {a}** Oddio, Brighton, **{b}** è lui che vuole perdere! **(3) {a}** Suvvia, Brighton, **[2 occurrences] {b}** ma (se) perde apposta ogni volta! **[3 occurrences]** **(4) {a}** Oh Signore, Brighton, **{b}** (lui) perde apposta! **[6 occurrences]** **(5) {a}** Oh cielo, Brighton! **{b}** perde di proposito.	***[6]* MAXWELL:** **(1) {a}** Dio, Brighton! **{b}** Manda all'aria ogni partita! **(2) {a}** Oh Dio, Brighton, **{b}** manda all'aria ogni gioco. **(3) {a}** Oh Dio, Brighton, **{b}** lui getta via ogni gioco. **(4) {a}** Oh sciocco Brighton, **{b}** lo fa apposta a perdere. **[2 occurrences]** **(5) {a}** O Dio, Brighton, **{b}** lui fa vincere ad ogni gioco. **(6) {b}** lui butta ogni gioco. **(7) {b}** lui getta ogni partita.

	(5) **{a}** Oh cielo, Brighton! **{b}** perde di proposito. **(6)** **{a}** Santo cielo, / Oh cielo, Brighton! **[3 occurrences]** **{b}** La sua tattica è far vincere! **(7)** **{a}** Oh, per l'amor di Dio, Brighton! **{b}** Ti lascia vincere (di proposito) (ogni partita). **[6 occurrences]** **(8)** {a} Oh, ma che dici, Brighton, {b} si da sempre per vinto. **(9)** {a} Oh, ma per favore, Brighton, {b} ti fa vincere sempre!	**(8)** **{a}** Cielo, Brighton, **{b}** perde ad ogni gioco. **[3 occurrences]** **(9)** **{b}** lo fa apposta. **(10)** **{a}** Oh Dio, Brighton, **{b}** perde apposta ogni gioco. **(11)** **{b}** Ci rinuncerà! **(12)** **{b}** ha perso apposta!
A) [7] **BRIGHTON:** Do you see how easy it is to bond? ***B) [7]*** BRIGHTON: È così che si diventa amici. ***C) [7]*** BRIGHTON: That's how people become friends!	***[7]*** **BRIGHTON:** **(1)** Vedi come è facile farsi gli amici? **[2 occurrences]** **(2)** Vedi com'è facile diventare amici? **(3)** Vedi quanto è semplice diventare amici? **(4)** Vedi com'è facile fare amicizia? **[7 occurrences]** **(5)** Capisci (Vedi) com'è facile affezionarsi? **[3 occurrences]**	***[7]*** **BRIGHTON:** **(1)** Hai visto come è semplice legarsi? **(2)** Vedi come è facile essere suo amico? **(3)** Guarda com'è facile legare? **(4)** Vedi com'è facile / semplice legare? **[4 occurrences]** **(5)** Vedi come è facile legarsi? **(6)** Vedi come è facile legarsi a lui? **(7)** Ma è solo così che facilmente si diventa amici! **(8)** Vedi come è facile stabilire un legame? **(9)** Vedi come è facile da legare? **(10)** Vedi? Basta poco per legarsi a qualcuno. **(11)** Vedi quanto è facile fidanzarsi? **(12)** Vedi com'è semplice far colpo? **(13)** Vedi quanto è facile / come è semplice stare insieme? **[2 occurrences]** **(14)** Non capisci quanto è facile legare? **(15)** È così che ci si fa benvolere. **(16)** Vedi com'è facile vincere?
A) [8] **MAXWELL:** **{a}** Well, I wouldn't get too attached to the bloke if I were you. **{b}** We all know Miss Fine's relationships eventually end in disaster. ***B) [8]*** MAXWELL: **{a}** Guarda, se fossi in te non mi ci affezionerei troppo a Giulio. **{b}** I rapporti di Francesca con gli uomini finiscono sempre in un disastro. ***C) [8]*** MAXWELL: **{a}** Look, if I were you I wouldn't get too attached to Giulio. **{b}** Francesca's relationships with men always end up in disaster.	***[8]*** **MAXWELL:** **(1)** **{a}** Beh, se fossi in te non mi affezionerei così tanto / troppo a quel tipo / a lui. **[6 occurrences]** **{b}** Lo sappiamo tutti come le relazioni di Fran si concludano sempre in modo disastroso. **(2)** **{a}** Io non mi affezionerei troppo a quell'individuo, se fossi in te. **{b}** Sappiamo tutti che le relazioni della signorina Fran finiscono sempre in maniera disastrosa. **(3)** **{b}** Sappiamo tutti che le relazioni della Signorina Fine finiscono in un disastro! **[5 occurrences]** **(4)** **{a}** Se fossi in te non mi affezionerei troppo a quel tizio **{b}**	***[8]*** **MAXWELL:** **(1)** **{a}** Bene, io <u>non mi attaccherei</u> troppo a quel tipo se fossi te. **[11 occurrences]** **{b}** Sappiamo tutti che i rapporti di Francesca terminano in disastro. **(2)** **{a}** Bene, io non mi legherei troppo a quell'individuo se fossi in te. **[6 occurrences]** **{b}** Noi sappiamo tutti che le relazioni di Miss Fine finiscono sempre male. **[3 occurrences]** **(3)** **{a}** Se fossi in te non mi attaccherei troppo al tipo. **{b}** Lo sappiamo tutti che le relazioni di Francesca vanno sempre a rotoli! **(4)** **{a}** Se io fossi in te non mi legherei così fortemente/troppo

	anche perché sappiamo tutti chle relazioni della Tata si rivelano poi un disastro. **[2 occurrences]** **(5)** **{a}** Comunque non affezionerei troppo a quel tipo se fossi in te. **{b}** Sappiamo tutti come i grandi amori di Tata Francesca vanno a finire in disastro. **(6)** **{a}** Invece, se fossi in te, non mi appiccicherei così a quel tizio. **{b}** Sappiamo tutti che le storie (d'amore) della Tata finiscono sempre in un disastro! **[2 occurrences]** **(7)** **{b}** Tutti noi sappiamo che le relazioni della signorina Fine alla fine terminano in un disastro! **(8)** **{b}** Sappiamo tutti che le relazioni sentimentali della signorina Fine alla fine si rivelano un completo disastro. **(9)** **{b}** Sappiamo tutti che le relazioni amorose di Miss Fine finiscono sempre disastrosamente. **[2 occurrences]**	con/a quel tipo. **[2 occurrences]** **{b}** Sappiamo tutti che le storie della Splendida finiscono sempre male! **(5)** **{b}** Sappiamo tutti che le relazioni di Miss Finezza terminano sempre in modo disastroso. **(6)** **{b}** Sappiamo tutti che i rapporti della signorina Fine alla fine sono un disastro. **(7)** **{a}** Non rimarrei troppo attaccato all'uomo, se fossi in te. **{b}** Tutti sappiamo che le relazioni di Miss Fine alla fine finiscono in un disastro. **(8)** **{a}** Beh, non starei così attaccato al bello, se fossi in te. **{b}** Sappiamo tutti come vanno a finire le storie/relazioni di Miss Fine. **[2 occurrences]** **(9)** **{a}** Non voglio assolutamente schierarmi contro quel bellimbusto. **{b}** Ma sappiamo che le relazioni di Miss Fine finiscono sempre in un disastro. **(10)** **{a}** Umm ... Non vorrei che ti legassi troppo a quel tipo. **{b}** Si sa che le storie della signorina Fran finiscono sempre tragicamente. **(11)** **{b}** Tutti noi sappiamo che alla fine le relazioni della signorina Francesca finiscono male. **[2 occurrences]** **(12)** **{b}** Sappiamo tutti con che velocità le relazioni della signorina finiscono in disastro. **(13)** **{a}** Beh, non sarei così attaccato a quell'individuo se fossi in te. **{b}** Tutti sanno che le relazioni della Signorina Fine finiscono disastrosamente. **(14)** **{a}** Bene, fossi in te non ci spererei più di tanto. **{b}** Tutti sappiamo come vanno a finire tutte le relazioni di "Miss Impossibile Resistermi" - un disastro!
(Fran enters) ***A) [9]*** **FRAN:** He asked me to marry him. ***B) [9]*** FRANCESCA: Ragazzi, mi ha chiesto di sposarlo! *(Francesca enters)* ***C) [9]*** FRANCESCA: Guys, he asked me to marry him!	*(Entra Fran)* ***[9]*** **FRAN:** **(1)** Mi ha chiesto di sposarlo! **(2)** Mi ha chiesto di sposarloooo!!!	*(Entra Fran)* ***[9]*** **FRAN:** **(1)** Ha chiesto la mia mano! **(2)** Mi ha chiesta in moglie! **(3)** Mi ha fatto una proposta di matrimonio!
A) [10] **NILES:** Right on the money as always, sir. ***B) [10]*** NILES: Come sempre, signore, c'ha azzeccato. ***C) [10]*** NILES: As always, sir, you guessed right.	***[10]*** **NILES:** **(1)** Le ultime parole famose, signore! **[4 occurrences]** **(2)** Come sempre, signore, ha fatto la puntata giusta! **(3)** Signore, come sempre ha fatto centro! **[2 occurrences]**	***[10]*** **NILES:** **(1)** Preciso sui soldi / sul soldo come sempre, signore. **[6 occurrences]** **(2)** (Proprio) al momento giusto, come sempre, signore. **[8 occurrences]**

	4) Centrato in pieno, signore. **(5)** Proprio come ha detto lei, signore! **(6)** Un'altra ottima intuizione, signore. **(7)** Profetico come sempre, signore.	**(3)** Giusto in tempo come sempre, signore. **(4)** Puntuale come sempre, signore. **(5)** Tempismo perfetto come sempre, signore. **(6)** A proposito come al solito, signore. **(7)** Dritto ai soldi come sempre, signore. **(8)** Come non detto (signore)! **[2 occurrences]** **(9)** Giusto sul soldo, come sempre, sir. **(10)** Attaccata ai soldi, come sempre. **(11)** Giusto per i soldi, come sempre, signore. **(12)** Solo per i soldi, come sempre, signore.
A) [11] **BRIGHTON:** That is so cool, Fran. Congratulations. ***B) [11]*** BRIGHTON: Bene, brava Francesca! Congratulazioni. ***C) [11]*** BRIGHTON: Well done, bravo Francesca! Congratulations.	***[11]*** **BRIGHTON:** **(1)** Formidabile, Fran! Congratulazioni! **(2)** Che forte, Fran! Congratulazioni! **[3 occurrences]** **(3)** Figo, / Fighissimo Fran! Congratulazioni! **[4 occurrences]** **(4)** È strepitoso! Congratulazioni, Fran! **(5)** (È / Ma è) fantastico, Fran, congratulazioni! **[9 occurrences]** **(6)** (Ma) è fantastico, Fran, auguri! **[3 occurrences]** **(7)** (Ma) che bella notizia, Fran, Congratulazioni! **[2 occurrences]**	***[11]*** **BRIGHTON:** **(1)** È così / Che bello Fran. Congratulazioni! **[4 occurrences]** **(2)** Grande! Congratulazioni, Francesca! **[3 occurrences]** **(3)** Favoloso, Fran. Congratulazioni! **[2 occurrences]** **(4)** Splendido! Congratulazioni, Francesca! **(5)** È così fresco, Fran. Auguri! **(6)** E' così sfacciato, Fran. Congratulazioni! **(7)** (È) grandioso, Francesca, congratulazioni! **[3 occurrences]** **(8)** È meraviglioso, Fran, congratulazioni!
A) [12] **FRAN: {a}** I know, I know. I can't believe it. I'm so excited. I couldn't eat a — **{b}** oh, kielbasa, sweet and sour cabbage. **{c}** *(To Niles)* Hit me again. **{d}** *(She takes a corn from Grace's dish)* Oh, such a big corn for such a little girl. ***B) [12]*** FRANCESCA: **{a}** Oh che bello! Che bello! Non riesco a crederci! Sono così eccitata che neanche ceno — **{b}** uh, i salsicciotti, oh e anche i cavoli in agrodolce, **{c}** *(rivolta a Niles)* gli dia dentro! **{d}** *(Prende una pannocchia dal piatto di Grace)* È una pannocchia troppo grande per te. ***C) [12]*** FRANCESCA: **{a}** Oh, how marvelous! How marvelous! I can't believe it! I'm so excited that I couldn't even dine — **{b}** uh, the sausages, oh, and also the sweet and sour cabbages, **{c}** *(to Niles)* let's tuck in! **{d}** *(She takes a corn from*	***[12]*** **FRAN:** **(1) {a}** Lo so, lo so. Non riesco (ancora) a crederci. Sono così emozionata! **[11 occurrences]** Non potrei mangiare neanche un — **[3 occurrences] {b}** cos'è? Oh, salsicciotti alla polacca, cavoli in agrodolce! **{c}** Dammene ancora! **[2 occurrences] {d}** Oh, una pannocchia così grande / grossa per una bimba / bambina così piccola / piccina! **[14 occurrences]** **(2) {a}** Lo so, lo so, (io stessa) non ci credo, **[2 occurrences]** sono felicissima, non riuscirei neanche a mangiare — **[3 occurrences]** **(3) {a}** Lo so, lo so, sono così contenta, non potrei mangiare neanche — **(4) {a}** È vero, non posso crederci, sono così emozionata. Non riesco neppure a mangiare — **(5) {a}** ... non potrei mandar giù nient- —**{b}** Oh, c'è del kielbasa	***[12]*** **FRAN:** **(1) {a}** Lo so, lo so, non posso crederci. Sono così eccitata! **[16 occurrences]** Non riesco a mangiare nemmeno — **{b}** Oh i salsicciotti **[3 occurrences]**, cavoli in agrodolce, **{c}** Mi tentate di nuovo / ancora! **[10 occurrences] {d}** Oh che grande pannocchia per una così piccola bambina. **[2 occurrences]** **(2) {a}** Grazie, grazie, non ci posso credere. Sono così / troppo felice! Non mangerei nemmeno un **[4 occurrences]** — **{b}** Kielbasa dolce, aspro cavolo! **{c}** Dammi un'altra botta! **{d}** Guarda! / Ma guarda, **[3 occurrences]** una così grande pannocchia per una così piccola bambina. **[2 occurrences]** **(3) {a}** Lo so, lo so. Non ci credo. Sono così entusiasta. Non ce la faccio a mangiare un — **{b}** oh kielbasa, un cavolo dolce

Grace's dish) This is a corn too big for you.	**[4 occurrences]**, i cavoli in agrodolce! **{c}** Dacci sotto! **[2 occurrences]** **(6) {d}** ma che grande pannocchia / che pannocchia grande per una bimba così piccola! **[2 occurrences]** **(7) {a}** Ah ah, lo so, non posso crederci, / non ci posso credere, **[5 occurrences]** sono così emozionata che ho lo stomaco chiuso — **{b}** Oh, kielbasa, cavoli in salsa agrodolce! **[2 occurrences] {c}** Mi riempia / riempimi il piatto! **[2 occurrences]**	ed agro, **{c}** picchiami ancora! **{d}** Oh, un'enorme pannocchia per una fanciulla! **(4) {a}** Favoloso, lo so, non ci posso credere, sono così eccitata, non sto più nella pelle — non posso / non potrei / non potevo / non riuscirei neanche a mangiare un — **[4 occurrences] {b}** oh kielbasa, verza in agrodolce. **(5) {a}** ...non sono riuscita a mangiare un - **[4 occurrences]** **{b}** oh kielbasa, cavolo in agrodolce. **[5 occurrences]** **(6) {a}** ... non riuscivo neanche a mangiare — **{b}** Oh salsiccia e cavoli in agrodolce! **(7) {b}** Oh ma c'è salsiccia con patate! **(8) {a}** ... non ho neanche fame, **{b}** Oh, kielbasa, un cavolo agrodolce! **[2 occurrences]** **(9) {b}** Oh, kielbasa, cavoli in agrodolce e del succo! **(10) {b}** Oh, una salsiccia! Un cavolo dolce e aspro! **[2 occurrences]** **(11) {b}** Oh, salsicciotto, dolce e acido cavolo! **(12) {b}** Oh, guarda guarda, cavolo agrodolce! **(13) {b}** Oh, bistecca! Cavoli in agrodolce! **{c}** Mi tentano! **[2 occurrences]** **(14) {b}** Salsicciotto! Delizioso e aspro cavolo! **{c}** Colpiscimi di nuovo! **[3 occurrences]** **(15) {b}** Oh, salame! Cavoletti in agrodolce! **{c}** Ancora uno! **(16) {b}** Oh, una salsiccia e dei cavoletti di Bruxelles! **{c}** Mettili da parte! **(17) {b}** Oh, salsiccia affumicata, cavoli in agrodolce! **{c}** È una tentazione continua! **(18) {c}** Mi colpisce ancora. / Colpiscimi ancora. **[7 occurrences]** **(19) {c}** Dacci dentro! / Ci dia dentro! / Gli dia dentro! **[4 occurrences]** **(20) {c}** Quanto ben di Dio! **(21) {c}** Dammene un altro. **(22) {c}** Mi state tentando! **(23) {d}** Ma che pannocchia grande per una bimba così esile! **(24) {d}** Oh una così grande pannocchia per una ragazza così piccola. **[7 occurrences]** **(25) {d}** Oh, una pannocchia così grande per una ragazzina così piccola. **(26) {d}** Oh, una pannocchia così grossa per una bambina così piccola!

		(27) **{d}** e questa è una pannocchia troppo grossa per te. **(28)** **{d}** Oh che grande spiga per una ragazza così piccola. **(29)** **{d}** Oh, che pannocchia di grano così grande per una fanciulla così piccola. **(30)** **{d}** Pannocchia un po' grossa per una bambina così piccola.
A) [13] **MAXWELL:** He asked you to marry him? ***B) [13]*** MAXWELL: Ma davvero le ha chiesto di sposarlo? ***C) [13]*** MAXWELL: But, did he really ask you to marry him?	***[13]*** **MAXWELL:** **(1)** Le ha chiesto di sposarlo? **[10 occurrences]** **(2)** Allora le ha chiesto di sposarlo. **(3)** Così le ha chiesto di sposarlo.	***[13]*** **MAXWELL:** **(1)** Ti ha chiesto di sposarlo? **[8 occurrences]** **(2)** Le ha chiesto di sposarla? **(2)** Le ha chiesto la mano? **(3)** Ti vuole sposare? **(4)** E così ti avrebbe chiesto di sposarlo!
A) [14] **FRAN:** Uh-huh. ***B) [14]*** FRANCESCA: Uh-uh. ***C) [14]*** FRANCESCA: Uh-huh.	***[14]*** **FRAN:** **(1)** Uh-uh **(2)** Sì sì! **[3 occurrences]** **(3)** Ah ah! **[4 occurrences]** **(4)** Eh già. **(5)** Mm-mm	***[14]*** **FRAN:** **(1)** Esatto! **(2)** Sembra proprio di sì! **(3)** Sì. **(4)** Proprio così! **(5)** Oh-hoh
A) [15] **MAXWELL:** You've barely known the man for two weeks. ***B) [15]*** MAXWELL: Lo conosce solo da due settimane. ***C) [15]*** MAXWELL: You've barely known him for two weeks.	***[15]*** **MAXWELL:** **(1)** Lei quest'uomo lo conosce da appena due settimane. **[2 occurrences]** **(2)** Ma lo conosce sì e no da due settimane! **(3)** Ma lo conosce solo da / da appena due settimane. **[7 occurrences]** **(4)** (Ma se) lo conosce a malapena da due settimane! **[4 occurrences]** **(5)** Conosce quell'uomo da solo / appena due settimane! **[6 occurrences]** **(6)** Conosce a stento quell'uomo da due settimane. **(7)** Ma se lo conosce da appena due settimane!	***[15]*** **MAXWELL:** **(1)** Lo hai appena conosciuto da due settimane. **(2)** (Ma) lo conosci appena da due settimane. **[4 occurrences]** **(3)** Conosce quest'uomo a malapena da due settimane. **(4)** Lo conosce da appena due settimane. **[2 occurrences]** **(5)** Conosce appena l'uomo da due settimane. **(6)** Ma lo conosci e ci esci insieme da due settimane. **(7)** (Ma se) vi conoscete a malapena da / da appena due settimane. **[4 occurrences]** **(8)** Lo conosce da due settimane scarse.
A) [16] **FRAN:** What? You think it's so hard to believe a man would fall in love with me that fast? ***B) [16]*** FRANCESCA: No, cosa significa? Un uomo ci deve sempre mettere anni per dire che è innamorato? ***C) [16]*** FRANCESCA: No, what does it mean? A man has to wait for years before telling that he is in love?	***[16]*** **FRAN:** **(1)** Cosa? È tanto difficile per lei credere che un uomo si possa innamorare di me così in fretta / così in fretta di me? **[2 occurrences]** **(2)** E con ciò? Le è così difficile credere che un uomo cada ai miei piedi così presto? **(3)** E allora? Crede sia tanto difficile per un uomo innamorarsi di me così in fretta? **[6 occurrences]** **(4)** Cosa? Pensa sia così / tanto difficile che un uomo s'innamori di me così velocemente / in così poco tempo? **[6 occurrences]**	***[16]*** **FRAN:** **(1)** Cosa? Pensi sia così difficile credere che un uomo possa / potrebbe innamorarsi di me così velocemente? **[7 occurrences]** **(2)** Crede sia così difficile immaginare un uomo che si innamori di me così rapidamente? **(3)** Cosa? È così difficile per lei pensare che un uomo possa innamorarsi di me in così poco tempo? **(4)** Perché? Non è possibile che un uomo si innamori di me in così breve tempo? **(5)** Cosa? Pensa che sia così difficile da credere che un uomo

	(5) Che? Pensa sia improbabile che un uomo si innamori di me così alla svelta? **(6)** Cosa? Crede che sia difficile che un uomo possa innamorarsi così presto di me? **(7)** Beh? Pensa che non sia possibile che un uomo si innamori di me in così poco tempo? **(8)** E allora? Trova tanto difficile che un uomo s'innamori di me così rapidamente? **(9)** E dunque? Le sembra impossibile che un uomo si innamori di me così velocemente? **(10)** Che cosa? Pensa che sia così difficile che un uomo possa innamorarsi di me tanto rapidamente?	possa innamorarsi di me così velocemente? **[3 occurrences]** **(6)** Cosa? Ti riesce così difficile credere che un uomo possa innamorarsi di me così velocemente? **(7)** Ma perché è così difficile credere che un uomo si innamori rapidamente di me? **(8)** E allora? Credi dunque difficile che un uomo si innamori di me così velocemente? **[3 occurrences]** **(9)** Cosa? E' così difficile credere che un uomo si sia innamorato di me così velocemente? **(10)** Come? Crede sia così difficile innamorarsi di me così in fretta?
A) [17]* GRACE:** Yeah. Todd and I knew each other three minutes before I got a Pudding-Pack right in the eye. ***B) [17] GRACE: Giusto. Todd, appena conosciuto, mi ha subito buttato il primo budino in faccia. ***C) [17]*** GRACE: Right. Todd, as soon as I met him, threw the first pudding at hand on my face.	***[17]* GRACE:** **(1)** Proprio così. Todd ed io ci eravamo conosciuti solo tre minuti prima che mi arrivasse un pacchetto di budini dritto in un occhio. **[2 occurrences]** **(2)** Sì, io e Todd ci conoscevamo solo da tre minuti quando mi ha tirato una confezione di budini dritta nell'occhio. **[2 occurrences]** **(3)** Oh sì, Todd e io ci siamo conosciuti proprio tre minuti prima che io ricevessi un budino in faccia / negli occhi. **[4 occurrences]** **(4)** Sì sì, Todd e io ci conoscevamo solo da tre minuti prima che mi arrivasse una vaschetta di budino dritta nell'occhio. **(5)** Sì, Todd e io ci conoscevamo da soli tre minuti prima che mi lanciasse il budino (dritto) nell'occhio. **[2 occurrences]** **(6)** Sì, Todd e io ci eravamo conosciuti da soli tre minuti quando mi è arrivato il budino negli occhi. **(7)** E già. Todd ed io ci conoscevamo da tre minuti prima che mi lanciasse il budino nell'occhio.	***[17]* GRACE:** **(1)** Già, Todd ed io, tre minuti dopo che ci siamo conosciuti, avevo un budino negli occhi. **(2)** Infatti. Todd si innamorò di me tre minuti prima che mi schizzasse il budino dentro l'occhio. **(3)** Sì, Todd ed io ci conoscevamo tre minuti prima che avessi un Pudding Pack dritto nell'occhio. **[2 occurrences]** **(4)** Sì, io e Todd ci conoscevamo / ci siamo conosciuti tre minuti prima che mi ritrovassi un budino in faccia. **[3 occurrences]** **(5)** Sì, io e Todd ci conoscevamo da tre minuti quando iniziammo a fare a torte in faccia. **(6)** Sì, Todd e io ci siamo conosciuti 3 minuti prima di quando ho avuto un Pudding Pack dritto nell'occhio. **(7)** Infatti. Todd e io ci conoscemmo tre minuti prima che io ricevetti / presi un Pudding-Pack dritto nell'occhio. **[2 occurrences]** **(8)** Sì. Todd ed io ci siamo conosciuti tre minuti prima che io avessi un pezzo di budino dritto nell'occhio. **(9)** Sì. Todd ed io ci siamo conosciuti tre minuti prima che ricevessi un pasticcio di carne / una torta dritto in faccia. **[2 occurrences]** **(10)** Sì, io e Todd ci siamo conosciuti tre minuti prima che mi arrivasse un pacco nell'occhio. **(11)** Beh, io e Todd ci siamo

		conosciuti tre minuti prima che io prendessi un budino dritto in un occhio. **[2 occurrences]** **(12)** Certo. Todd ed io ci conoscemmo tre minuti prima che mi finisse una torta pachistana in faccia. **(13)** Todd ed io ci siamo conosciuti tre minuti prima di avergli tirato un budino nell'occhio. **(14)** Già, Todd ed io ci eravamo appena conosciuti la prima volta che mi ha tirato i capelli. **(15)** Già, Todd e io ci conoscevamo da tre minuti prima che io avessi un Pudding-Pack proprio nell'occhio. **(16)** Infatti. Io e Todd ci siamo conosciuti proprio tre minuti prima che io gli infilassi una bic dritta nell'occhio. **(17)** Infatti. Io e Todd abbiamo aspettato solo tre minuti perché scoccasse il colpo di fulmine. **(18)** Sì, io e Todd ci siamo conosciuti tre minuti prima che mi arrivasse un Pudding-Pack dritto nell'occhio.
A) [18] **FRAN:** There you go. ***B) [18]*** FRANCESCA: Ecco, ha sentito? ***C) [18]*** FRANCESCA: There you go, have you heard that?	*18]* **FRAN:** **(1)** Ecco qui! **[4 occurrences]** **(2)** Ecco, appunto! **[7 occurrences]** **(3)** Lo vede? **[3 occurrences]** **(4)** Ecco. **[2 occurrences]** **(5)** Vede? **(6)** È proprio così.	*[18]* **FRAN:** **(1)** Visto? **[5 occurrences]** **(2)** Come al solito. **(3)** Come volevasi dimostrare! **(4)** È così che è andata. **(5)** Giusto. **(6)** Esatto, piccola! **(7)** Ci risiamo! **(8)** Siamo alle solite. **(9)** E vai! **(10)** Pensa tu! **(11)** Ecco, <u>hai</u> visto?
A) [19] **MAXWELL: {a}** You know nothing about this man. **{b}** All right, so he's a doctor. Is he a specialist? ***B) [19]*** MAXWELL: **{a}** Oh, ragioni! Lei non sa niente di quest'uomo. **{b}** D'accordo, lei saprà che fa il medico. Che medico? Specialistico? ***C) [19]*** MAXWELL: **{a}** Oh, be reasonable! You know nothing about this man. **{b}** All right, you may know he's a doctor. What kind of doctor? A specialist?	*[19]* **MAXWELL:** **(1) {a}** Ma lei non sa nulla di quest'uomo! **[7 occurrences]** **{b}** Allora, sa che è un dottore. Cosa? Uno specialista? **(2) {a}** (Ma lei) non sa niente di quest'uomo! **[5 occurrences]** **{b}** Va bene, è un medico. È uno specialista? **[7 occurrences]** **(3) {a}** Non lo conosce affatto quest'uomo! **{b}** Va bene, dunque è un dottore. È uno specialista? **(4) {a}** Lei non conosce nulla di quest'uomo. **[3 occurrences]** **{b}** Bene, è un dottore. È uno specialista? **(5) {a}** Ma non sa niente di lui! **{b}** D'accordo, è un medico. Ed è uno specialista, anche? **(6) {b}** D'accordo, è un dottore.	*[19]* **MAXWELL:** **(1) {a}** Non <u>sai</u> niente di quest'uomo. **[7 occurrences] {b}** Ok, è un dottore. E' uno specialista? **[6 occurrences]** **(2) {a}** Non sa niente a proposito di quell'uomo. **{b}** Bene, così è un dottore. Uno specialista? **[4 occurrences]** **(3) {a}** <u>Tu</u> non sai nulla di quest'uomo. **[3 occurrences] {b}** Ok, è un dottore. E' uno specialista? **(4) {a}** Resta il fatto che non sa niente di lui. **{b}** Va bene, è un dottore. Ma sa se è uno specialista? **(5) {a}** Ma cosa sa di quest'uomo? Praticamente niente! **{b}** Ok, è medico ... ma è uno specialista? **[3 occurrences]**

	Ma è uno specialista?	**(6) {b}** Va bene, è un dottore – ma almeno è uno specialista? **(7) {a}** Se lo conosci appena! **{b}** Va bene che è un dottore — un ginecologo? **(8) {a}** Non conosci niente di quest'uomo. **{b}** D'accordo, così è un dottore: è uno specialista? **(9) {a}** Non sa niente di quest'uomo. **{b}** Solo che è un medico. È uno specialista? **(10) {b}** Va bene, è un dottore. È specializzato in qualcosa in particolare? **(11) {b}** A quanto pare è un dottore. È specialista?
A) [20] **FRAN:** You ain't just whistling "Dixie," baby. *B) [20]* FRANCESCA: Lui è ultra specialisticissimo, è molto bravo! *C) [20]* FRANCESCA: He is very super-highly-specialized, he's very good!	*[20]* **FRAN:** **(1)** Non stiamo qui a scherzare! **(2)** Un pezzo grosso, per l'esattezza! **(3)** Non si tratta di un tipo qualunque, baby! **(4)** Mica stiamo giocando, giovanotto! **(5)** Senta, stiamo mica parlando di sciocchezze? Eh? **(6)** Eh qui non canto quel motivetto che ti piace tanto! Dudu dudù. **(7)** Puoi / Può ben dirlo (ragazzino! / caro! / cocco)! **[9 occurrences]** **(8)** Può / puoi dirlo forte (amico) (amico mio)! **[5 occurrences]** **(9)** Non è certo una passeggiatina la sua professione! **(10)** Non stai certo giocando all'Allegro Chirurgo, bimbo bello! **(11)** E scusa se è poco, tesoro! **(12)** Eh, qui non si fischietta la canzoncina, caro, si canta l'Opera! **(13)** Jules non compone certo musica leggera, bello, scrive sinfonie! **(14)** Baby, non fischietto certo un motivetto, lui è specialista provetto!	*[20]* **FRAN:** **(1)** Non stai (solo) fischiettando "Dixie", dolcezza! / bello / baby! **[5 occurrences]** **(2)** Non stai solo fischiando "Dixie" ragazzo! **[2 occurrences]** **(3)** Non stai forse fischiettando "Dixie", eh, baby? **(4)** Hai appena fischiettato "Dixie", bella! **(5)** Non sta fischiettando solo una musichetta jazz! **(6)** Non starà per caso fischiettando un motivetto? **(7)** Geloso? **(8)** Sì, uno specialista per gelosi come lei! **(9)** Brutta cosa l'invidia, eh?
A) [21] **MAXWELL:** Oh, God. *B) [21]* MAXWELL: Oh, la testa! *C) [21]* MAXWELL: Oh, the head!	*[21]* **MAXWELL:** **(1)** Oddio! **(2)** Oh, Dio! **(3)** Oh, cielo! **(4)** Oh Signore!	*[21]* **MAXWELL:** **(1)** Cosa? **(2)** Oh, mio Dio! **(3)** Ma sentitela! **(4)** Oh Gesù! **(5)** Oh no.
A) [22] **MAGGIE: {a}** Oh, this is so exciting. **{b}** So can I be a bridesmaid? *B) [22]* MAGGIE: **{a}** Sono così contenta! **{b}** Mi vuoi come damigella d'onore? *C) [22]* MAGGIE: **{a}** I'm so happy! **{b}** Do you want me as	*[22]* **MAGGIE:** **(1) {a}** Oh, è (tutto) così emozionante! **[8 occurrences] {b}** Posso fare la damigella d'onore? **[2 occurrences]** **(2) {a}** Oh, che bello! **{b}** Posso farti da damigella? **[7 occurrences]**	*[22]* **MAGGIE:** **(1) {a}** E' (tutto) così eccitante! **[19 occurrences] {b}** Dunque posso essere la tua damigella? **[2 occurrences]** **(2) {a}** Sono così eccitata! **[2 occurrences]** **(3) {a}** Oh, è così divertente!

happy! **{b}** Do you want me as a bridesmaid?	3) **{a}** Oh che emozione! **{b}** Mi fai fare la damigella? **(4)** **{b}** Allora posso essere la tua damigella? **[6 occurrences]** **(5)** **{a}** Oh, è così entusiasmante! **[2 occurrences]** **{b}** Allora posso fare la damigella? **[2 occurrences]**	**(4)** **{a}** (Tata,) è fantastico! **[2 occurrences]** **{b}** Perciò posso essere la damigella d'onore? **(5)** **{b}** Posso fare la damigella? **[4 occurrences]** **(6)** **{b}** Così, posso essere una / la damigella? **[5 occurrences]** **(7)** **{b}** Posso essere una delle damigelle d'onore? **(8)** **{a}** Oh, ma è meraviglioso! **{b}** Così io sarò la damigella d'onore?
(Sylvia enters behind Fran) ***A) [23]*** **FRAN:** **{a}** I know the doctor asked me to marry him, but I didn't say yes. **{b}** This is delicious. *(Zia Assunta entra alle spalle di Francesca)* ***B) [23]*** FRANCESCA: **{a}** Aspetta, Maggie, è vero che lui mi ha chiesto di sposarlo, però io non gli ho detto di sì. **{b}** Oh, questo cavolo è delizioso! *(Aunt Assunta enters behind Francesca)* ***C) [23]*** FRANCESCA: **{a}** Hold on, Maggie, it's true that he asked me to marry him, but I didn't say yes to him. **{b}** Oh, this cabbage is delicious.	*(Sylvia entra alle spalle di Fran)* ***[23]*** **FRAN:** **(1)** **{a}** Sì, è vero, il dottore mi ha chiesto di sposarlo, ma io non ho detto di sì! **[6 occurrences]** **{b}** Mmm (questo/a) è (davvero) squisito/a! **[13 occurrences]** **(2)** **{a}** Ho detto che il dottore mi ha chiesto di sposarlo, ma non di aver risposto sì. **{b}** Questo/a è buonissimo/a! **[2 occurrences]** **(3)** **{a}** Capisco che il dottore mi abbia / ha chiesto di sposarlo, ma io non gli ho detto sì. **[2 occurrences]** **{b}** Veramente / Davvero ottimo! **[2 occurrences]** **(4)** **{a}** D'accordo, il dottore mi ha chiesto di sposarlo, ma non gli ho mica detto sì. **(5)** **{a}** Beh,(sai,) il dottore mi ha chiesto di sposarlo, però io non gli ho detto di sì. **[2 occurrences]** **(6)** **{a}** È vero che il dottore mi ha chiesto di sposarlo, ma io non gli ho detto di sì.	*(Sylvia entra alle spalle di Fran)* ***[23]*** **FRAN:** **(1)** **{a}** Aspetta, lui mi ha chiesto di sposarmi, ma non ho ancora detto sì! **[3 occurrences]** **{b}** Buona questa salsiccia! **(2)** **{a}** (Lo) so che il dottore mi ha chiesto di sposarlo, ma non gli ho detto di sì. **[8 occurrences]** **{b}** (Questo) è (così) delizioso! **[13 occurrences]** **(3)** **{b}** E' fantastico! **(4)** **{a}** Giulio mi ha chiesto di sposarlo, ma io non ho ancora detto di sì. **{b}** E' il caso che soffio un po'. **(5)** **{a}** Io conosco il dottore che mi ha chiesto di sposarlo, ma io non ho detto sì. **(6)** **{b}** (Questo) è delizioso. **[6 occurrences]** **(7)** **{a}** E' vero, il dottore mi ha chiesto di sposarlo, ma questo non vuol dire che abbia detto di sì. **(8)** **{a}** Il dottore mi ha chiesto di sposarlo, ma non gli ho detto sì. **[4 occurrences]** **{b}** E' buono il cavolo! **(9)** **{a}** So che il dottore vuole sposarmi, ma io non ancora. **(10)** **{a}** Mi ha chiesto di sposarlo, ma non ho detto di sì. **(11)** **{a}** Sì, il dottore mi ha chiesto di sposarlo, ma io gli ho detto di sì. **(12)** **{a}** So che il dottore si è fatto avanti, ma non gli ho detto di sì, ancora!
(Sylvia falls to the floor behind Fran) ***A) [24]*** **SYLVIA:** Why don't you grab a knife and stick it straight through my heart. *(Zia Assunta cade al suolo alle spalle di Francesca)* ***B) [24]*** ZIA ASSUNTA: Che le racconto adesso a mia sorella che poi è tua madre? *(Aunt Assunta falls to the floor*	*(Sylvia cade al suolo alle spalle di Fran)* ***[24]*** **SYLVIA:** **(1)** Facevi prima a conficcarmi un coltello nel cuore! **(2)** Perché (a questo punto) non afferri un coltello e mi trafiggi subito il cuore? **[2 occurrences]** **(3)** Bé, allora? Che aspetti a pugnalarmi? **(4)** Perché non afferri un coltel-	*(Sylvia cade al suolo alle spalle di Fran)* ***[24]*** **SYLVIA:** **(1)** Perché non prendi un coltello e lo ficchi / pianti dritto nel mio cuore? **[4 occurrences]** **(2)** Perché non afferrate un coltello e me lo ficcate dritto nel cuore. **(3)** Perché non mi uccidete lentamente con un coltello

behind Francesca) *C) [24]* AUNT ASSUNTA: What shall I say now to my sister, who is also your mother?	lo e me lo ficchi nel cuore? **(5)** Giacché, afferra un coltello e piantamelo dritto nel cuore, (eh)? **[2 occurrences]** **(6)** Perché non prendi un coltello e me lo conficchi (direttamente) nel cuore? **[3 occurrences]**	conficcandomelo nel cuore? **(4)** Perché non afferri /prendi un coltello e non lo conficchi nel mio cuore? / e me lo conficchi dritto nel cuore? **[9 occurrences]** **(5)** Perché non prendi un coltello e lo fai entrare nel mio cuore. **(6)** Prendi un coltello e trafiggimi il cuore! **(7)** Prendi un coltello e conficcamelo nel cuore. **(8)** Perché non prendi un coltello e lo infili dritto al cuore? **(9)** Perché non prendi un coltello e lo conficchi nel cuore? **(10)** Questo è peggio di una colpo al cuore! **(11)** Il mio povero cuore! Sta per venirmi un infarto! **(12)** Mi hai dato una pugnalata! **(13)** Oh, perché non afferri un coltello e me lo pianti dritto in petto?
A) [25] **FRAN: {a}** *(hinting at Grace)* That was great. She sounded just like - Ma! **{b}** Ma ... Ma, let go of my ankle. *B) [25]* FRANCESCA: **{a}** *(riferendosi a Grace)* Ah ah ah ma che brava! Sembri proprio Zia As—ah! **{b}** Lasciami, lasciami la caviglia! Lasciami la caviglia, Zia Assunta! *C) [25]* FRANCESCA: **{a}** *(to Grace)* Ah ah ah, how clever! You really sounded like Aunt As—ah! **{b}** Let, let go of my ankle! Let go of my ankle, Aunt Assunta!	*[25]* **FRAN:** *(riferendosi a Grace)* **(1) {a}** E' incredibile! Grace ha imitato benissimo la - Ma! **{b}** Mamma! Lasciami la caviglia! **[7 occurrences]** **(2) {a}** (Caspita) che brava! Sembrava proprio (come) la (voce di) — Ma! **[11 occurrences]** **{b}** Mamma! Molla la (mia) caviglia! **[4 occurrences]** **(3) {a}** Questa era / è bella! **[3 occurrences]** Sembrava la stessa voce di — Ma! **[2 occurrences]** **{b}** Mamma, Mamma, non tirare! Lasciami la caviglia! **(4) {a}** Wow, la voce sembrava proprio quella di Ma! — **{b}** Ma, Ma, lasciami la gamba! **[2 occurrences]** **(5) {a}** Proprio forte! Hai fatto identica la voce di Ma! — **[2 occurrences]**	*25]* **FRAN:** *(riferendosi a Grace)* **(1) {a}** Questo è fantastico / E' stato fantastico **[3 occurrences]**. Suona appena come - Ma! **{b}** Ma, staccati dalla mia caviglia! **[3 occurrences]** **(2) {a}** (E' stato) grandioso. **[3 occurrences]** Suonava proprio come — **{b}** Mamma, Ma! Ma, lascia andare la mia caviglia. **[5 occurrences]** **(3) {a}** (Che) strano! Sembrava (fosse) la voce di zi.. / Ma! **[4 occurrences]** **(4) {a}** E' fantastico, rassomiglia a — **[3 occurrences]** **{b}** Mamma! Mamma, lascia stare la mia caviglia. **[6 occurrences]** **(5) {a}** Quello era grande. **[3 occurrences]** Ella ha appena rimbombato come — **(6) {a}** È stato grande. Dà l'impressione come — **{b}** Ma! Ma ... togliti dalla mia caviglia! **(7) {a}** Era forte. Aveva l'aria come di — **(8) {a}** È una situazione troppo intrigante — **{b}** Zia, zia ... zia ti prego, lasciami stare! **(9) {a}** E' stato grandioso. Sembravi proprio — **{b}** Zia Assunta! Lascia la caviglia! **(10) {a}** Grande! Sembrava la voce di mia madr — Mamma! **[2 occurrences]** **(11) {a}** Sembrava come se stesse — Mamma! **(12) {a}** Stupendo! Sembrava come se —Ma!

		(13) {a} Sarebbe un'idea. Suonava proprio come — Ma! **(14) {a}** Era fantastico. / Fantastica! Sembrava che — **[2 occurrences] {b}** Ma, Ma ... Ma lascia la mia caviglia!
A) [26] **SYLVIA:** You better run. ***B) [26]*** ZIA ASSUNTA: Ti conviene scappare! ***C) [26]*** AUNT ASSUNTA: You better run!	***[26]*** **SYLVIA:** **(1)** Faresti bene / meglio a scappare! **[7 occurrences]** **(2)** È meglio che corri! **(3)** Comincia a scappare, è meglio per te! **(4)** È meglio se / che inizi a correre! **[2 occurrences]** **(5)** Scappa, che è meglio! / È meglio se scappi! **[2 occurrences]**	***[26]*** **SYLVIA:** **(1)** È meglio che ti metti a correre! **(2)** E' meglio che ti affretti. **(3)** Ma insomma cosa vuoi aspettare? **(4)** Faresti meglio / bene a correre! **[12 occurrences]** **(5)** Corri meglio! / Ma corri, meglio! **[2 occurrences]** **(6)** Inizia a correre.
(Fran runs around the table chased by Sylvia) ***A) [27]*** **FRAN:** Brighton, is she taking off her shoe? *(Francesca corre intorno al tavolo inseguita da Zia Assunta)* ***B) [27]*** FRANCESCA: Brighton, se l'è cavata una scarpa? *(Francesca runs around the table chased by Aunt Assunta)* ***C) [27]*** FRANCESCA: Brighton, has she taken off her shoe?	*(Fran corre intorno al tavolo inseguita da Sylvia)* ***[27]*** **FRAN:** **(1)** Brighton, si sta levando la scarpa? **[2 occurrences]** **(2)** Brighton, si è tolta la scarpa? **[8 occurrences]** **(3)** Brighton, si sta togliendo la scarpa? **[16 occurrences]** **(4)** Brighton, mi sta tirando una scarpa?	*(Fran corre intorno al tavolo inseguita da Sylvia)* ***[27]*** **FRAN:** **(1)** Brighton, si sta sfilando la scarpa? **(2)** Brighton, si sta togliendo le scarpe? **[4 occurrences]** **(3)** Brighton, ha tolto la / una scarpa? **[2 occurrences]**
A) [28] **BRIGHTON:** No. But she's gonna hurl the corn. ***B) [28]*** BRIGHTON: No, però si è armata di pannocchia. ***C) [28]*** BRIGHTON: No. But she's armed herself with a corn.	***[28]*** **BRIGHTON:** **(1)** No. Ma sta lanciando la pannocchia. **[5 occurrences]** **(2)** No, ma ti sta tirando la pannocchia! **(3)** No, ma (ti) sta per tirare / scagliare / lanciare/lanciarti la pannocchia. **[13 occurrences]** **(4)** No, ma sta per scagliarti contro la pannocchia. **[2 occurrances]** **(5)** No, ma ha impugnato la pannocchia!	***28]*** **BRIGHTON:** **(1)** No, ma si è armata di pannocchia. **(2)** No, ma sta attenta alla pannocchia! **(3)** Con l'intenzione di dartela in testa! **(4)** No, ma sta tirando la spiga. **(5)** No, però si sta lanciando sulla pannocchia. **(6)** No, ma sta gettando la pannocchia. **(7)** No, ma ha afferrato la / una pannocchia! **[2 occurrences]** **(8)** No, ma ha una pannocchia in mano! **[2 occurrences]**
[Int. Kitchen]	**[Int. Cucina]**	**[Int. Cucina]**
A) [29] **FRAN:** Oy, oy, oy, oy. Ma, put down the vegetable and no one gets hurt. ***B) [29]*** FRANCESCA: Oh, oh, oh, oh. Bada! O metti giù quella pannocchia o apro l'acqua bollente. ***C) [29]*** FRANCESCA: Oh, oh, oh, oh. Mark! Put down that corn or I'll turn the hot water on.	***[29]*** **FRAN:** **(1)** Oh, oh, oh. Ma, posa l'arma e nessuno rimarrà ferito. **(2)** Oh oh oh oh. Ma, metti giù la pannocchia e nessuno si ferirà. **[2 occurrences]** **(3)** Oh oh oh oh. Ma, posa quella pannocchia e nessuno si farà (del) male! **[7 occurrences]** **(4)** Oh oh oh oh. Mamma, metti giù la pannocchia e non ci sarà nessun ferito. **(5)** Oh oh oh oh. Mamma, metti	***[29]*** **FRAN:** **(1)** Oh, oh, oh. Mamma, metti giù il / quel vegetale e nessuno si farà male. **[11 occurrences]** **(2)** Oh oh oh oh. Mamma metti giù quell'affare e vedrai che nessuno ne uscirà ferito. **[3 occurrences]** **(3)** Oh oh oh oh, Zia, metti via gli oggetti contundenti o celebreremo un funerale! **(4)** Oh oh oh oh. Ma, metti giù / posa / lascia la / quella verdura e

	giù quell'ortaggio e nessuno si ferisce. **[4 occurrences]** **(6)** Oh oh oh. Ehi, Mamma! Metti giù quel coso prima che qualcuno si faccia male. **(7)** Ma, molla la pannocchia e nessuno si farà male!	e nessuno si farà male / si ferirà. **[5 occurrences]** **(5)** Oh oh, Ma, metti giù la spiga e che nessuno si faccia male. **(6)** Oh oh oh oh. Mamma, metti giù quell'affare e nessuno si farà del male.
A) [30] **SYLVIA: {a}** All right. Help me to understand which was the biggest turnoff — **{b}** the fact that Jules was gorgeous, rich, or a doctor? ***B) [30]*** ZIA ASSUNTA: **{a}** Parliamo. Vorrei solo che mi spiegassi cos'è che ti ha spaventato così — **{b}** il fatto che Giulio è stupendo, ricco e anche medico? ***C) [30]*** AUNT ASSUNTA: **{a}** Let's talk. I'd only want you to explain to me what has scared you so much — **{b}** the fact that Giulio is gorgeous, rich and also doctor?	***[30]*** **SYLVIA:** **(1) {a}** Bene. Fammi capire qual era il suo punto debole — **[4 occurrences] {b}** il fatto che Jules è uno schianto, perché è ricco, o perché è un dottore? **(2) {a}** Va bene. Aiutami a capire cosa ti ha scoraggiata — **{b}** il fatto che Jules fosse / sia bellissimo, ricco, o un dottore? **[5 occurrences]** **(3) {a}** D'accordo. Ma aiutami a scoprire qual era la cosa più fastidiosa – **(4) {a}** Ok. Spiegami però qual è il difetto. **(5) {a}** Va bene. Fammi allora capire qual è stata la pecca, **{b}** il fatto che è bello, ricco, o che è un dottore? **(6) {a}** Ok. Fammi capire qual è la cosa più repellente: **{b}** il fatto che Jules era magnifico, ricco, o un dottore? **(7) {a}** D'accordo. Però spiegami cosa ti ha fatto cascare le braccia — **{b}** il fatto che Jules fosse affascinante, ricco, o un dottore? **[2 occurrences]** **(8) {a}** Va bene. Ma fammi capire qual è la cosa che più non ti piace — **[2 occurrences]** **(9) {a}** Va bene. Ma fammi capire cos'è che / cosa non va in lui — **(10) {a}** D'accordo. Ma mi devi spiegare qual è la cosa che più ti ripugna in lui — **(11) {a}** Va bene, ma fammi capire cos'è che non va — **[3 occurrences]** **(12) {a}** Va bene. Ma spiegami cos'è che non andava stavolta — **{b}** il fatto che Jules fosse molto bello, che fosse ricco, o che fosse medico?	***[30]*** **SYLVIA:** **(1) {a}** Ok. Aiutami però a capire qual è il problema. **[5 occurrences]** — **{b}** il fatto che Giulio sia bello, ricco, o un dottore? **(2) {a}** Va bene. Aiutami a capire qual è stato il problema più grande: **[3 occurrences] {b}** il fatto che Giulio / Jules sia fantastico, ricco, o un dottore? **[5 occurrences]** **(3) {a}** Va bene. Aiutami a capire quale è stato il più grande errore, **[3 occurrences] {b}** quello che Giulio era bellissimo, ricco, o un dottore? **(4) {a}-{b}** Ma insomma, è praticamente perfetto, magnifico, ricco e anche medico! **(5) {a}** Giusto. Aiutami a capire quale era il grandissimo / il più grande difetto, **[2 occurrences] {b}** il fatto che Jules era stupendo, ricco o un dottore? **[5 occurrences]** **(6) {a}** Va bene. Spiegami qual è la cosa più disgustosa, **{b}** il fatto che sia bello, o ricco, o il fatto che è un dottore? **(7) {a}** D'accordo. Aiutami a capire quale è stato il motivo più grande / principale: **[2 occurrences] {b}** il fatto che Jules fosse meraviglioso, ricco o un dottore? **(8) {a}** D'accordo, aiutami a capire qual è la cosa che ti ha fatto rifiutare — **(9) {a}** Bene. Fammi capire che cosa ti ha spinto a dirgli di no. **{b}** Il problema è che è bello, ricco, o che è un dottore?
A) [31] **FRAN:** Did I mention he was Jewish? ***B) [31]*** FRANCESCA: Ha un sudore che sa di pecora. ***C) [31]*** FRANCESCA: He has a sweat that smells of sheep.	***[31]*** **FRAN:** **(1)** (Ti / te l') ho (mai) detto / Ti avevo già detto che è / era ebreo? **[18 occurrences]** **(2)** Non ti avevo detto che era anche ebreo? **(3)** Ho dimenticato di dirti che è anche ebreo?	***[31]*** **FRAN:** **(1)** Ti ho detto che ha l'alito pesante? **(2)** Ha un alito che uccide. **(3)** Ti ho (mai) detto (menzionato) che è un ciociaro? **[5 occurrences]** **(4)** Oltre che napoletano? **(5)** Te l'ho detto che è italiano?

		(6) Ho reso noto che era ebreo? (7) Ho dimenticato che è ebreo? (8) Ti ho già detto che è un pecoraro?
A) [32] **SYLVIA:** **{a}** Oh. Darling, I only say this because I love you. **{b}** You're a glorified cleaning girl. **{c}** This could be your last chance. ***B) [32]*** ZIA ASSUNTA: **{a}** Ma che cos'hai contro le pecore? **{b}** Tuo nonno ci ha fatto i milioni! E i soldi puzzano sempre di qualcosa. **{c}** Questa forse è la tua ultima occasione! ***C) [32]*** AUNT ASSUNTA: **{a}** But why are you so against the sheep? **{b}** Your grandfather made money hand over fist with it! And money always smells of something. **{c}** This maybe is your last chance.	*[32]* **SYLVIA:** **(1) {a}** Oh. Senti, Cocca! Te lo dico per il bene tuo. **{b}** Tu sei solo una servetta montata / che si dà arie **{c}** e questa può essere la tua ultima occasione. **[10 occurrences]** **(2) {a}** Ma cara, se lo dico è perché ti voglio bene. **{b}** Sei solo una ragazza delle pulizie (ben) tirata su. **[2 occurrences]** **(3) {a}** Cara mia, io te lo dico solo perché ti voglio bene. **{b}** (In fondo) sei soltanto / solo una cameriera abbellita. **[5 occurrences]** **(4) {a}** Oh. Bella mia, ti ho detto così perché ti voglio bene. **{b}** Sei una donna delle pulizie / cameriera che si sforza di essere signorile. **[2 occurrences]** **(5) {b}** Sei solo un po' più di una donna delle pulizie. **(6) {b}** Tu sei una donna delle pulizie esaltata che cerca di essere altro. **(7) {b}** Tu sei solo una cameriera tirata a lucido.	*[32]* **SYLVIA:** **(1) {a}** Oh tesoro, ma è proprio grazie a persone come lui che il commercio delle mentine sopravvive. È da apprezzare. Lo dico per te! **{b}** Sei una ragazza delle pulizie **{c}** e questa potrebbe essere la tua ultima spiaggia. **(2) {a}** Oh cara. (Ti) dico questo soltanto perché ti voglio bene. **[11 occurrences] {b}** Sei una donna delle pulizie. **{c}** Questa potrebbe essere la tua ultima opportunità. **[2 occurrences]** **(3) {a}** Ma tesoro, io lo dico per il tuo bene. **[6 occurrences] {b}** Ricorda che hai una certa età. **{c}** potrebbe essere la tua ultima chance! **[5 occurrences]** **(4) {a}** Oh tesoro. L'ho detto / lo dico / ti dico questo solo perché ti voglio bene. **[8 occurrences] {b}** tu sei una nota donna delle pulizie. **{c}** Questa potrebbe essere la tua ultima possibilità. **[13 occurrences]** **(5) {a}** Oh, amore. Lo dico solo perché ti voglio bene. **{b}** Tu sei una ragazza delle pulizie fatta sembrare più importante. **(6) {b}** Tu sei soltanto una bella ragazza delle pulizie. **(7) {b}** Sei una così bella ragazza delle pulizie. **(8) {b}** Tu sei una ragazza pura. **(9) {b}** Sei un'ottima padrona di casa. **{c}** Potrebbe essere la tua ultima carta da giocare! **(10) {b}** Tu sei un'appariscente donna delle pulizie. **(11) {a}** Oh mia cara, io l'ho solo detto / lo dico solo perché ti amo. **[2 occurrences] {b}** Tu sei un'esaltata donna delle pulizie. **(12) {b}** Sei una ragazza delle pulizie sollevata. **(13) {b}** Tu sei una contessina mancata. **(14) {b}** Hai solo questo magnifico lavoro da tata. **(15) {a}** Oh cara, te lo dico perché ti voglio bene. **{b}** sei una colf D.O.C. **(16) {b}** ricordati che sei solo una governante / una tata. **[4 occurrences]** **(17) {b}** Sei un'adorabile casalinga. **(18) {b}** tu sei una stupenda / magnifica donna delle pulizie. **[3 occurrences] {b}** Sarebbe la tua ultima speranza.

A) [33] **FRAN:** **{a}** Oh, Ma, I didn't say no. **{b}** I just said I'd think about it. **{c}** Okay, I did. *B) [33]* FRANCESCA: **{a}** Ma guarda che non gli ho detto no! **{b}** Gli ho detto soltanto che volevo pensarci un po' su. *C) [33]* FRANCESCA: **{a}** But, look, I didn't say no to him. **{b}** I just said I'd want to think about it.	*[33]* **FRAN:** **(1) {a}** Mamma! Io non ho detto no! **[9 occurrences]** **{b}** Ho solo detto che ci pensavo! **{c}** Ok, l'ho fatto. **[3 occurrences]** **(2) {a}** Oh, Ma, non ho detto di no. **[7 occurrences]** **{b}** Ho solo detto che mi piacerebbe rifletterci su. **(3) {a}** Ma io non ho detto di no, **{b}** solo che devo pensarci un po' su. **(4) {a}** Ma mica gli ho detto no, **[2 occurrences]** **{b}** gli ho detto che ci avrei pensato (un po') (su). **[10 occurrences]** **(5) {b}** Ho solo detto che ci devo pensare. **(6) {b}** Ho detto solo che ci avrei pensato (su). **[7 occurrences]** **(7) {b}** Ho solo detto che ci dovevo pensare. **(8) {c}** Va bene, / Ok, (ora) l'ho fatto. **[17 occurrences]** **(9) {c}** E l'ho fatto. **[2 occurrences]** **(10) {c}** Fatto! / Ok, fatto. **[5 occurrences]**	*33]* **FRAN:** **(1) {a}** Ma io non ho detto proprio no. **{b}** Ho solo detto che ci avrei pensato. **[6 occurrences]** **{c}** Ok. L'ho fatto. **(2) {a}** Oh mamma, non gli ho detto di no. **[4 occurrences]** **{b}** Ho soltanto detto che devo pensarci. **{c}** Ok, ci ho pensato! **[2 occurrences]** **(3) {a}** Oh Zia, non ho detto no, **{b}** voglio solo pensarci un po'. **(4) {b}** ho solo detto che dovrò pensarci. **(5) {c}** Okay, l'ho detto. **(6) {a}** Mamma, non ho detto di no. **{b}** Ci avrei pensato su. **{c}** E va bene, ho pensato. **(7) {a}** Dai, Mamma, non gli ho detto di no. **{b}** Gli ho solo detto di lasciarmi il tempo per pensare. **{c}** Ma gli dirò di sì.
A) [34] **SYLVIA:** You mean I do? *B) [34]* ZIA ASSUNTA: Oh *C) [34]* AUNT ASSUNTA: Oh	*[34]* **SYLVIA:** **(1)** Vuoi dire / Vuol dire che lo fai / farai? **[4 occurrences]** **(2)** Vuoi dire, 'lo faccio'? **[2 occurrences]**	*[34]* **SYLVIA:** **(1)** Vuoi dire, c'ho ripensato? **(2)** Intendi, lo fai? **(3)** Intendi di sì? **(4)** Dirai di sì? **(5)** Vuoi dire, lo fai? **[2 occurrences]** **(6)** Allora ti sposi? **(7)** Vuoi dire che (gli) dirai di sì? **[3 occurrences]** **(8)** Vuol dire un sì? **(9)** Significa sì? **[2 occurrences]** **(10)** Vuoi dire che ce l'ho fatta [a convincerti]? **(11)** Vuoi dire (di) sì? **[5 occurrences]** **(12)** Vuoi dire che dovrò... **(13)** E allora? **(14)** Vuol dire che accetti? **(15)** Dici sul serio? **(16)** Vuoi dire che— **(17)** Vuoi dire che posso? **(18)** Cosa, gli hai detto di sì? **(19)** È come penso io?
A) [35] **FRAN:** Yeah. *B) [35]* FRANCESCA: E adesso l'ho fatto. *C) [35]* FRANCESCA: And now I did.	*[35]* **FRAN:** **(1)** Sì!	*[35]* **FRAN:** **(1)** Già! **[2 occurrences]** **(2)** Certo! **(3)** Gli dirò di sì. **(4)** Esatto. **(5)** Proprio.
A) [36] **SYLVIA:** Oh.	*[36]* **SYLVIA:** **(1)** Oh.	*[36]* **SYLVIA:** **(1)** Oh, bene! **[2 occurrences]**

B) [36] ZIA ASSUNTA: Cioè, dirai di sì, vero? *C) [36]* AUNT ASSUNTA: This means that you'll say yes, won't you?		
A) [37] **FRAN:** Ma, you may kiss the bride. *B) [37]* FRANCESCA: Sì! Puoi baciare la sposa, Zia Assunta! *C) [37]* FRANCESCA: Yes, you may kiss the bride, Aunt Assunta!	*[37]* **FRAN:** **(1)** Mamma, puoi baciare la sposa! **(2)** Ma, ora puoi baciare la sposa! **(3)** Puoi baciare la sposa, mamma!	*[37]* **FRAN:** **(1)** Zia, puoi baciare la sposa! **[4 occurrences]** **(2)** Mamma, tu puoi baciare la sposa. **(3)** Dovresti baciare la sposa! **(4)** Mamma / Zia, devi baciare la sposa! **[2 occurrences]** **(5)** Mamma, puoi baciare la tua futura sposa! **(6)** Mammina, puoi baciare la sposa!
A) [38] **FRAN/SYLVIA:** Moi! Moi! Moi! Moi! Moi! *B) [38]* FRANCESCA/ZIA ASSUNTA: Muà! Muà! Muà! *C) [38]* FRANCESCA/AUNT ASSUNTA : Moi! Moi! Moi! Moi! Moi!	*[38]* **FRAN/SYLVIA:** **(1)** Muà! Muà! Muà!	*38]* **FRAN/SYLVIA:** **(1)** smack smack smack **[5 occurrences]** **(2)** Moi moi moi **(3)** Evvivaaaaa!!!!
(Maxwell enters the kitchen) *A) [39]* **MAXWELL: {a}** You know, Miss Fine, I think you're very wise not to rush into this. **{b}** You're far too sensible a woman to marry a man - Ow! *B) [39]* MAXWELL: **{a}** Guardi, Francesca, penso che sia stata molto saggia a non prendere una decisione così affrettata. **{b}** Lei è una donna troppo intelligente – Ohi! *C) [39]* MAXWELL: **{a}** Look, Francesca, I think you're very wise not to take a hasty decision. **{b}** You're far too intelligent a woman – Ow!	*(Maxwell entra in cucina)* *[39]* **MAXWELL:** **(1) {a}** Sa, Fran, penso sia stata molto intelligente a non gettarsi a capofitto in questa storia. **[5 occurrences] {b}** E' una donna troppo previdente per sposare un uomo — Ohi! **(2) {a}** Sa, Signorina Fine, penso sia stata molto saggia a non precipitarsi in questa situazione. **(3) {a}** Sa, Signorina Fine, è stata molto saggia a non prendere una decisione avventata. **(4) {a}** Lo sa, Miss Fine, penso che lei sia stata molto saggia a / nel non affrettarsi in tutto questo. **[5 occurrences]** **(5) {a}** Sa, Fran, penso che lei sia una persona davvero molto saggia per prendere decisioni affrettate. **(6) {b}** Lei è una donna troppo ragionevole per sposare un uomo — Ahio! **[5 occurrences]** **(7) {b}** Lei è una donna troppo giudiziosa per sposare un uomo — Ohi! **[2 occurrences]** **(8) {a}** Sa, signorina, penso che lei sia proprio saggia a non affrettarsi / a non affrettare le cose. **[2 occurrences] {b}** Lei è una donna molto prudente per decidere così di sposare uno — Ahi! **(9) {a}** Sa, Signorina Fran, penso sia stato molto saggio da parte	*(Maxwell entra in cucina)* *[39]* **MAXWELL:** **(1) {a}** Sa Francesca, credo che lei sia molto saggia per non precipitarsi in questa avventura. **{b}** Lei è una donna troppo sensibile per sposare un uomo...Ow! / Ahi! **[18 occurrences]** **(2) {a}** Sa, Miss Fine, lei è molto saggia a non precipitarsi in questa cosa. **(3) {b}** Lei è una donna troppo sensibile per un tipo come quel — Ow! **(4) {a}** Sai, Francesca, io penso che lei sia molto saggia a non precipitarsi. **{b}** Lei è una donna di gran lunga sensibile per sposare un uomo — **(5) {a}** Ascolti, signorina Francesca. Io penso che lei sia troppo saggia per affrettarsi così tanto. **(6) {a}** Lo sa, signorina Fine, che penso che lei sia tanto saggia da non tuffarsi a capofitto in questa situazione. **(7) {a}** Tata Francesca, sono sicuro che lei sia abbastanza saggia da non fare stupidaggini. **{b}** Bisogna avere un certo coinvolgimento per sposare un uomo — Ahi! **(8) {a}** Sai, Miss Finezza, io credo sia molto saggio da parte tua non tuffarti a capofitto su questa occasione. **{b}** Tu sei una donna fin troppo sensibile per

	sua non aver preso una decisione così affrettata. **{b}** Lei è di gran lunga una donna troppo previdente per sposare un uomo — Ohi!	sposare un uomo — Ow! **(9) {a}** Lo sai, Splendida, saresti troppo astuta per precipitare le cose. **{b}** Sei una donna troppo sensibile per sposare un uomo — Ow! **(10) {a}** Sa Signorina Fran, penso che lei sia molto saggia a non gettarsi precipitosamente in questo. **{b}** È una donna troppo sensibile per sposare un uomo per i soldi — Ow! **(11) {a}** Miss Fine, penso che lei sia molto istruita per non fare questo. **(12) {a}** Sa, Miss Fine, penso che non si dovrebbe gettare a capofitto in questo matrimonio. **(13) {a}** Sa, signorina Fine, credo che lei sia abbastanza matura da non buttarsi a capofitto in una cosa del genere. **(14) {a}** Sa, signorina Fine, credo che lei sia abbastanza saggia da non avere fretta. **(15) {a}** Sa, Miss Fine, credo che sia molto intelligente per non farlo. **{b}** Lei è troppo ponderata per sposare un uomo — Ahio! **(16) {a}** sa signorina Fine, penso che non sia molto saggio affrettarsi in questo. **{b}** È una donna troppo razionale per sposare un uomo — Ow! **(17) {b}** Lei è una donna molto cosciente per sposare un uomo — Ahi! **(18) {a}** Sa, signorina Fran, penso che sia stata molto saggia a non affrettarsi nel prendere una decisione. **{b}** Lei è una donna troppo intelligente per sposarsi — Ow! **[2 occurrences]** **(19) {b}** Lei è troppo sensibile come donna per sposare un uomo — Ow! **(20) {a}** Signorina, penso che lei sia una persona davvero molto ragionevole per prendere decisioni affrettate. **{b}** Lei è una donna molto responsabile per sposare un uomo — Ahi! **(21) {a}** Penso che sarebbe saggio da parte sua non affrettarsi, signorina Fine. **{b}** Non è ancora una donna così matura da poter sposare un uomo — Ahi! **(22) {a}** Sai, "Miss Impossibile Resistermi", penso proprio che sei stata molto saggia a non precipitarti. **{b}** Le donne, si sa, diventano sensibili quando si tratta di sposarsi, beh! **(23) {a}** Lo sa, signorina Fine, non penso che sia prudente che si affretti in questo modo. **{b}** Lei è

		una donna davvero troppo sensibile per sposare un uomo — Ahi!
A) [40] **SYLVIA: {a}** Oh, I'm sorry. **{b}** Did this fork accidentally puncture your tuchas? ***B) [40]*** ZIA ASSUNTA: **{a}** Oh, quanto mi dispiace! **{b}** Per caso non volendo le ho bucato una delle due guance posteriori? ***C) [40]*** AUNT ASSUNTA: **{a}** Oh, I'm so sorry! **{b}** Have I by chance accidentally punctured one of your rear cheeks?	***[40]*** **SYLVIA:** **(1) {a}** Oh, mi dispiace! **{b}** Questa forchetta ha per caso punto il suo fondoschiena? **(2) {b}** Questa forchetta le ha punto accidentalmente le natiche / chiappe? **[5 occurrences]** **(3) {a}** Oh, mi spiace. **{b}** Questa forchetta ha accidentalmente pizzicato le sue chiappe? **[3 occurrences]** **(4) {b}** Forse questo forchettone ha punto per sbaglio le sue chiappe? **(5) {b}** E' stata per caso questa forchetta a pungere il suo sederino? **(6) {b}** Accidentalmente questo forchettone ha punto il suo didietro? **(7) {b}** Questo forchettone ha forse, accidentalmente, punto il suo didietro? **(8) {b}** Questa forchetta ha per caso (involontariamente) infilzato le sue chiappe? **[3 occurrences]** **(9) {b}** Questa forchetta ha accidentalmente punto le sue chiappe? **(10) {b}** Per caso questa forchetta ha punto il suo sederino?	***[40]*** **SYLVIA:** **(1) {a}** Oh, mi dispiace. **{b}** E' stato punto accidentalmente da questa forchetta? **(2) {a} {a}** Oh (mi) scusi. **[9 occurrences] {b}** Questa forchetta le ha accidentalmente punto il didietro? **(3) {b}** Oggi questa forchetta va da sola! **(4) {b}** Questa forca incidentalmente ha punto il tuo fondoschiena? **(5) {a}** Oh, mi perdoni. **[2 occurrences] {b}** Questo forchettone le ha per caso punto / infilzato le natiche? **[2 occurrences]** **(6) {b}** Questa forchetta ha accidentalmente bucato le tue chiappe? **(7) {b}** come ha potuto questa forchetta pungere accidentalmente questo sedere? **(8) {a}** Sono spiacente. **{b}** Per caso una forchetta le ha punto il sedere? **(9) {b}** Questa forchetta ti ha punto per sbaglio? **(10) {b}** Le ho per caso punto il sedere? **(11) {b}** Non ho idea di come questa forchetta sia finita nelle sue chiappe! **(12) {b}** Questa forchetta ti ha punto il sedere accidentalmente? **(13) {b}** Per caso questa forchetta ti ha accidentalmente punto il sedere? **(14) {b}** Le ho per caso infilzato accidentalmente il sedere? **(15) {b}** E' stata la forchetta a infilzarvi le chiappe?

4.5.2 *Dubbing-translation data analysis*

Before analyzing the translation choices of the two groups of students it is necessary to point out that, although both Groups A and B were made up of about twenty-five students each, students in Group B mostly proposed individual versions of the Italian translation of the scene, whereas students in Group A, who had experienced the initial top-down phase, came up with shared solutions they achieved through collective rehearsals, which were also timed against the duration of each cue in the video. This explains why there are more translation alternatives in 'Group-B' slots than in 'Group-A' ones. In general, however, students in Group A produced translations with a more spontaneous conversation style in the target language, as they confidently identified themselves with the sitcom characters and spontaneously 'embodied' their voices, still in respect of the socio-cultural frame of visual references and background given by the sitcom. Students in Group B, instead, produced Italian translations in a kind of non-natural, mannered dialogic style, closer to literary modes of writing rather than to spontaneous speaking, often characterized by processes of pragmalinguistic and structural transfer from the source language to the target one, determining the typical 'dubbese' varieties of Italian that, once become part of people's everyday linguistic use, are then re-transferred into the 'Italian-English varieties' they eventually develop which would further affect the Italian language again, thus paradoxically generating processes of reverse transfer also in translation, making the target language sound even more artificial and stilted.

One of the most noticeable flaws in Group B's translation options in this scene is the persistent, inappropriate use of allocutions. This is evident since turn [1], when Maxwell addresses Fran's mature mother, Sylvia (sometimes addressed to as Assunta, in line with the 'official' translation) by her first name and by using the informal second-person pronoun 'tu'. This is a literal translation from the original dialogue which does not sound socially improper at all according to the English pragmatic code, but it is perceived as ethically unacceptable and socially disrespectful according to the Italian politeness principles insofar as, however lower Sylvia's social status may be in comparison with Maxwell's one, a young person, like Maxwell, is expected to address an aged person by using the formal 'lei' (if not 'voi') and Ms., Mr., ('Signore', 'Signora'), or titles added before their names or surnames. This is especially true when a young man addresses a mature woman that is not one of his relatives. Students in Group A seem to be very well aware of this interactional rule in Italian as they always make use of 'lei' when Maxwell addresses Sylvia (sometimes referred to as "Signora"—approximately corresponding to "Mrs. Fine" in English—a code which is also respected in the official translation where Maxwell addresses Sylvia/Assunta as "Signora Assunta"). The sense of annoyance revealed by Maxwell's body movements and facial expression at having Sylvia standing next to him while he is dining and looking hungrily into his dish, is further emphasized in the translation occurrences by students in Group B when they render "Please Sylvia"—a formal English invitation (to join Maxwell's family for dinner)—into "Per favore, Sylvia", or "Ti prego, Sylvia" (literal back translation: "Do me a favour, Sylvia" and "I beg you, Sylvia") implying an annoyed request for putting an end to an irritating behaviour. Other solutions proposed by students in Group B—such as the informal and convivial "(6) Dai, Sylvia, perchè non ti unisci a noi?", "(11) Su, Sylvia, perché non si unisce a noi?" (both literally rendered as "C'mon, Sylvia, why don't you join us?") and "(8) Silvia, perché non stiamo in compagnia?" ("Sylvia, why don't we keep each other's company?") - are obviously incongruent with the characters' roles and not supported by Maxwell's body movements and facial expression.

Sylvia's reply in turn [2] is rendered by students in Group A in ways that are pragmatically equivalent to the original humorous construction of Sylvia's kindly refusing Maxwell's offer (a socially-expected move, in this case) by downplaying the reasons for her being at Maxwell's home at dinner time ("{a} Oh no. I just came over to see how Fran's date went") and thus marking a Safety pattern of humour only to create, soon afterwards, a displacing sense of tension (marking an Arousal pattern of humour) at not showing any intention to leave ("{b} Make like I'm not even here."). In Group-A students' Italian translation alternatives, Sylvia kindly replies with the same gentle "Oh no", explaining in most of the occurrences: "(1) (2) (9) Sono venuta [a trovarvi] solo per sapere com'è andato l'appuntamento [romantico / galante] / l'incontro di Fran" ("I came over [to see you] just to know how Fran's date [romantic rendezvous] / meeting went"), "(5) Sono qui soltanto per sapere dell'appuntamento di Fran" ("I'm here just to know about Fran's date"), "(7) (8) Oh no, sono solo / ero giusto passata / ho giusto fatto un salto per sapere com'è andato l'appuntamento di Fran" ("Oh no, I just called in / I just popped round to know how Fran's date went"). Then, also in Group-A students' translation, Sylvia establishes an Arousal pattern as in the original version by showing her determination not to leave: "(3) Fate [pure] come se non ci fossi" ("Make like I'm not even here"), or the more informal "(4) (5) "Fate finta che non ci sono / che non ci sia" ("Pretend I'm not even here"). Most students in Group B, instead, represented Sylvia replying to Maxwell in a quite blunt, even rude way with her initial, sharp "No, grazie." ("No, thanks.") that is present in many occurrences and that actually modifies the original illocutionary force of the cue—as she immediately marks an Arousal situation of tension—and, consequently, also modifies the possible perlocutionary effect of this cue on the target audience. Moreover, Group-B students sometimes produced very elaborate dialogic cues that actually exceed the lip-synch timing of each shot and therefore are useless in the dubbing process—as in "(10) No grazie. Sono venuta solo per vedere come va a finire l'appuntamento di Fran." ("No thanks. I just came over to see how Fran's date is turning out") and in "(8) Oh no, sono solo venuta a vedere come andavano le cose a Francesca." ("Oh no, I just came to see how things were going for Francesca."). Some other times, students in Group B produced actual mistranslations, due to a lack of attention to the plot structure as well as to the contextual signals coming from the visual frame of the sitcom. This is the case with cues such as: "(3) {b} Fate finta di niente" ("Pretend not to notice")—a too generic expression which does not clarify that Sylvia is specifically referring to her presence in Maxwell's dining room; or "(4) Oh, no sto uscendo per vedere come è andato l'appuntamento di Francesca." ("Oh, no I'm going out to see how Francesca's date went.") and "(5) Oh no, sto giusto andando a vedere come è andato l'appuntamento di Fran." ("Oh no, I'm just going to see how Fran's date went."), both of them not corresponding to Sylvia's actions on stage—in fact, she is not going anywhere, nor does she show any intention to leave the house.

In turn [3], Niles, the household butler, formally offers Sylvia something to eat ("Are you sure we can't offer you something?"). Group-A students keep the same level of formality also in translation, taking into consideration the predictable culturally-marked and stereotypical role of the 'British butler' behaving according to expected—and scripted—physical and pragmalinguistic codes of behaviour. Hence, Niles, in Group-A students' translations, always uses the formal second-person pronoun 'lei' in addressing Sylvia ("(1) È sicura che non possiamo offrirle nulla?", almost literally rendering the original cue), often accompanied with 'politeness boosters' such as the adversative 'ma' / 'but' ("(2) Ma è sicura che non le possiamo offrire qualcosa?" - "But are you sure we can't offer you something?), or 'proprio' and 'davvero'—both rendered as 'really' ("(3) Èproprio sicura di non gradire nulla?" - "Are you really sure you wouldn't like something?"; "(5) Davvero non gradisce qualcosa?" - "Are you really sure you wouldn't like something?"). Differently from Group A, students in Group B once again disrupt the culture-bound formality pattern of the exchange and put Niles, the butler, and Sylvia, the nanny's mother, on the same social level, irrespective of the fact that Sylvia is however a guest in Maxwell's house (though self invited) and that Niles at the moment of speaking is in charge of his role as a butler. In most of Group-B students' translations, Niles addresses Sylvia with the informal second-person allocution 'tu' and organizes the structure of his cue on such a pragmatic choice ("(1) Sei sicura che non possiamo offrirti qualcosa?" (untranslatable into English where there is no difference between the allocutions 'tu' and 'lei' both rendered into 'you') up to the brisk "(7) Vuoi che ti offra qualcosa?" - "Do you want me to offer you something?"). But in few cases, students in Group B opt for the opposite choice by making Niles's cue overformal by even using the plural second-person pronoun 'voi' in addressing Sylvia ("(2) Siete sicura che non possiamo offrirvi qualcosa?"—once again untranslatable into the limited system of allocutions in English).

In turn [4], Sylvia replies to Niles's offer with another polite refusal move, once again hoped for and welcome by the Sheffield family at dinner and therefore perceived as 'preferred' ("{a} Oh no, thank you. I had a yoplait this morning around 10:30."). In the dubbing translation for the Italian TV, Assunta (Sylvia's recreated character) actually flouts Grice's (1975) conversational maxim of Quantity by adding information that is absent in the original version and thus 'making her contribution to the conversation more informative than is required' ("No, no, no grazie, sono a dieta e sto morendo di fame, ma voi mangiate tranquilli" - "No, no, no, thank you. I'm on diet and I'm starving, but please go on eating easy").

Students in Group A, instead, opted for translation alternatives which could be more pragmatically equivalent to the original. The first difficulty encountered in this cue in fact is the translation of the culturally-marked reference to a dietetic product—i.e., the 'Yoplait', a brand of yogurt well known in the international market except in Italy, where it was advertised only in 1992 but with little success, so in 1999 the product was finally withdrawn from the Italian market. This is also the period when *The Nanny* sitcom was aired in Italy, so the reference to Yoplait also in the Italian version of the sitcom could have been made and understood. But brands cannot be mentioned in Italian TV programs, unless they are the program sponsor, and so the reference had however to be replaced. Group-A students produced a series of equally valid equivalent options. The most literal one is "(1) Oh no, grazie. Ho già preso uno yogurt questa mattina verso le 10:30", just substituting 'Yoplait' with 'yogurt'. Other dubbing alternatives that do not exceed cue timing consider the addition of relevant attributes to the noun 'yogurt': "(2) uno yogurt alle vitamine" ("a vitamin yogurt"); "(3) uno yogurt dietetico" ("a diet yogurt"); "(5) uno yogurt leggero" ("a light yogurt"), or the reference to a brand become in Italy a synonym of the product, as in "(4) ho mangiato uno Yomo / uno Iocca / dei fiocchi di latte verso le 10:30 stamattina." ("I ate a Yomo / Iocca / some milk flakes [Iocca] at about 10:30 this morning."). Also some students in Group B opted for the more generic 'yogurt' to render 'Yoplait', but surprisingly, some other Group-B students produced a translation that they must have perceived as literal on the sole basis of assonance – hence, 'yoplait' was interpreted as 'a plate of yogurt' and rendered as "(2) Ho già preso un piatto allo yogurt questa mattina" ("I already had a plate of yogurt this morning") and "(12) Ho già fatto fuori un piatto a base di yogurt questa mattina" ("I already polished off a yogurt dish this morning"). Group-B students are not however short of other (often bizarre, but not equivalent) alternatives to 'yoplait', such as "(9) ho fatto uno spuntino" ("I had a snack"), "(10) ho preso un frullato" ("I had a milk shake") and even "(11) ho mangiato una peperonata" ("I ate a 'peperonata' [sliced peppers cooked with oil, tomatoes and onions]"), and "(19) ho mangiato un piatto di pasta" ("I ate a plate of pasta"), till resorting to leaving the same original reference with no explanation whatsoever "(13) ho preso uno Yoplait stamattina" ("I had a Yoplait this morning").

Sylvia's original turn [4] continues with this hungry woman stealing a potato from Grace's dish (Maxwell's youngest child) and commenting with an oxymoron-like sentence: "Oh, such a big potato for such a little girl" also respected in the translation for the Italian TV: "Oh, una patata troppo grande per una bambina così piccola" ("Oh, a too big potato for such a little girl!"). Group-A students offer Italian versions of this sentence that are more structurally equivalent to the original one than the 'official' translation. For instance: "(1) Ma che patata grande per una bambina così piccola!" ("But what a big potato for such a little girl!"), "(6) Ma questa è una patata troppo grande per una bimba così piccola!" ("But this is a too big potato for such a little girl!"), "(7) Oh, una patata così grande / grossa per una bimba / bambina così piccola." ("Oh, such a large / big potato for such a little girl."). A number of students in Group B disregarded the oxymoron-based structural parallelism and opted for, respectively, an almost stilted literal translation with an English→Italian transfer of the adjectives position placed before—rather than after—the nouns, as in "(1) Oh che grande patata per una così piccola bambina!" (in English sounding like the strange "Oh what a potato so big for such a girl so little!"). Some other students in the same control group produced a chiasm-like structure with adjectives in the former clause following the noun and in the latter preceding it, as in "(2) Oh, una patata così grande per una così piccola ragazza" ("Oh, a potato so big for such a little girl"). In other cases, the choice of 'ragazza' ('teenage girl') rather than 'bambina' ('little girl') is replaced by 'fanciulla' (13), a more archaic alternative meaning 'young girl' or 'maiden'. In (7), Sylvia even addresses Grace as 'Oh poveretta" ("Oh, poor thing") before uttering her comment on the potato she is lifting form the girl's plate, whereas in (5) the sentence is rendered not without a certain oddity, as it is: "(5) una sventola di patata per uno scricciolo di ragazza!" (literally: "such towering potato for a shrimp [a jenny wren] of a girl!").

Then, after glancing at the watch, Sylvia remarks "{c} Look at the time. They must be having a ball." which in the Italian TV version is rendered into "Però, come tardano! Si vede che si divertiranno molto!" ("Hey, how late they are! They must be having a very good time!"). This indeed represents the idiomatic expression that caused the main problems during the translation workshop, and not simply when it was not understood, but also when students intended to keep the idiomatic quality of the expression also in the target language. Students in Group A, for instance, provide solutions that range from the literal "si staranno divertendo moltissimo" ("they must be having a great time!") to the more colloquial "se la staranno spassando un mondo" ("they must be having the time of their life") up to the idiom "si staranno dando alla pazza gioia!" (literally: "they must be yielding to a wild joy", namely, "they must be having a high old time", or "they must be living it up"). In Group B, instead, students were not encouraged to search for contextual meanings and cross-cultural equivalent renderings of idiomatic expressions. Indeed, the 'working conditions' they were required to respect during the experiment were very similar to the ones actually occurring in the real workplace where dubbing translators are normally given random scripts of sitcom episodes, often not arranged into a chronological sequence and even without any audiovisual support, since the final work of dialogue adaptation and lip-synchronization is normally carried out later (often by unprofessional people), during the dubbing sessions. This explains why, also in this case, Group-B students often produced odd mistranslations of

Sylvia's expression "they must be having a ball" mostly based on literal interpretation as, for instance, in "(2) saranno ad un ballo" ("they must be dancing in a ballroom"), or in "(13) staranno giocando a palla" ("they must be playing ball"), but also in "(14) staranno avendo molto di cui parlare!" ("they must be having a lot to talk about!").

Sylvia concludes her turn [4] by informing the Sheffield family that she is moving in the kitchen: "{d} I'm gonna go in the kitchen. I need a meat to wash this down with", which, in the Italian TV translation is rendered into "Se non vi spiace vado in cucina, ci vuole del manzo come contorno ad una grossa patata" ("If you don't mind I'm going in the kitchen, some beef is required as a side dish for a big potato"). Students in Group A, during the interactive physical rehearsals, found it difficult to identify an equivalent Italian alternative to the expression "to wash this down with" referred to two solid types of food (i.e., meat and potato). Hence they produced the following options: "(1) Vado in cucina. Non riesco a mandar giù la patata senza un pezzo di carne." ("I'm going in the kitchen. I can't swallow this potato without a piece of meat."); "(16) (17) Ho bisogno di [una bella] bistecca per annaffiare questa [patata]." ("I need a [nice] steak to wash this [potato] down with."; "(18) Vorrei della carne per mandar giù questa." ("I'd like some meat to swallow this."). Students in Group B produced translations that mostly disregarded the humorous effect of 'washing a potato down with a steak' as they tried to focus on the implied literal meaning of each word contributing to the sense of the sentence. Hence the solutions, from the more plain: "(1) Sto andando in cucina. Ho bisogno di qualcosa di sostanzioso per mandarla giù." ("I'm going in the kitchen. I need something substantial to swallow this."), "(15) Ho bisogno di carne per digerire la patata" ("I need some meat to digest this potato."), "(23) Non riesco a mandare giù la patata senza carne." ("I don't manage to swallow the potato without meat.") to the more fanciful ones: "(21) Ho un conto in sospeso con la carne." ("I have a score to settle with the meat"); "(22) Ho bisogno di un succo per berci su." ("I need a juice to drink on it!"); "(24) Ho bisogno di carne per trangugiare meglio questa." ("I need some meat to better bolt this down."); "(30) Dovrò accompagnare con una bistecca questa patata, no?" ("I must match with a steak this potato, mustn't I?").

When Sylvia leaves the dining room, Brighton starts his turn [5] with his remark: "{a} I don't know about you guys, But I like Jules, {b} and he has to beat me in chess." (In the dubbing translation for the Italian TV: "Non so a voi, ma a me Giulio piace molto e non mi ha battuto neanche una volta a scacchi."—" I don't know if you do, but I like Giulio a lot {b} and he has beaten me not a single time in chess."). Group-A students provide translation options that are more respectful of the lip-synch time span than the 'official' translation—as, for instance: "(1) {a} Non so a voi, ragazzi, ma a me piace Jules. {b} E ancora deve battermi a scacchi." ("I don't know about you, guys, but I like Jules. And he has still to beat me in chess."), and "(2) {a} Non so che ne pensate, ma a me Jules piace. {b} E non è ancora riuscito a battermi a scacchi." ("I don't know what you think about it, but I like Jules. {b} And he hasn't yet succeeded in beating me in chess.", or the more informal "(4) {a} Non so a voi, gente, ma a me Jules piace." "(5) (6) e poi non mi ha ancora / mai battuto a scacchi." (I don't know about you, folks, but I like Jules. And he hasn't yet / he has never beaten me in chess."). Surprisingly, Group-B students produced a series of mistranslations mostly due to a lack of situational knowledge, as in "(2) Non so niente di ragazzi, ma Jules mi piace." ("I know nothing about guys, but I like Jules."), or "(3) Non so i tuoi figli, ma a me piace Jules." ("I don't know about your children, but I like Jules."), or even "(4) Non vi conosco ragazzi, ma mi piace Jules." ("I don't know you guys, but I like Jules.") to conclude with "(6) e ha ancora intenzione di battermi a scacchi." ("and he has still the intention of beating me in chess"), often using 'warlike' metaphors, such as "deve ancora sconfiggermi" ("he has still to vanquish me") or "vincermi a scacchi" ("to defeat me in chess").

Maxwell's reply, in turn [6], is aimed at disparaging his son for his naivety: "{a} Oh, God, Brighton, {b} he throws every game."—in the Italian TV translation: "{a} Ma su, Brighton, {b} è lui che vuole perdere!" ("{a} Come on, Brighton, {b} it's him who wants to lose!"). The main difference between the solutions proposed respectively by students in Group A and B is prevalently pragmatic. In Group A the prevailing interpretation is that of Maxwell trying to wake his naïve son up and make him see reality, as in "(1) Mio Dio, Brighton, bara per farti vincere." ("My God, Brighton, he cheats to make you win."), or in "(3) (4) (5) Suvvia, Brighton, perde apposta / di proposito ogni volta!" (C'mon, Brighton, he loses on purpose / deliberately every time!"), or "(7) (9) Ti lascia vincere sempre / ogni partita." ("He always lets you win / every game.") and "(8) si da sempre per vinto." ("he always gives in."). In Group B, instead, students came up with interpretations mostly stressing Maxwell's sense of annoyance at his son's naivety, hence his comment at Brighton's remark is often rendered into a sharp tone, as in: "(1) (2) Dio, Brighton, manda all'aria ogni gioco / ogni partita!" ("God, Brighton. He upsets every game!") which, this time, is perhaps more pragmatically equivalent to Maxwell's original cue.

In turn [7], Brighton replies to his father with a challenge: "Do you see how easy is to bond?"—translated for the Italian TV with a quick-witted statement: "È così che si diventa amici." ("That's how people become friends!"). In Group A, students came up with solutions that aimed to disambiguate the implications of the English verb 'to bond' with reference to the situation under analysis. Hence, they opted for a translation choice similar to the one made by the 'official' translators of the sitcom – namely, the overt reference to 'making friends with someone'. This is evident in "(1) (2) (3) (4) Vedi come è facile / semplice farsi gli amici? / diventare amici? / fare amicizia?" ("Do you see how easy / simple is to make friends [with someone]? / to become friends?"). Few other students in the same group, however, produced a different, yet acceptable, alternative: "(5) Vedi (Capisci) com'è facile affezionarsi?" ("Do you see [understand] how easy is to grow fond / attached [of / to someone]?"). The solutions proposed by students in Group B did not show the same efforts towards disambiguation, therefore some of their translation options still retain a certain degree of interpretative obscurity, as in: "(1) (4) (5) Hai visto / Non capisci come è semplice / facile legarsi / legare?" (literal back-translation: "Have you seen / Don't you understand how simple / easy is to bind / to bind oneself"). Other alternatives, though clear, are rendered through long and stilted sentence-structures exceeding the lip-synch timing of the cue, as in "(7) Ma è solo così che facilmente si diventa amici!" ("But it is only in this way that people easily become friends!"); in "(8) Vedi come è facile stabilire un legame?" ("Do you see how easy is to establish a bond?"); in "(10) Vedi? Basta poco per legarsi a qualcuno." ("Do you see? A little is enough to bind oneself to someone."); and in "(15) E' così che ci si fa benvolere." ("That's how people make themselves liked"). In other cases, the alternatives proposed by some students in Group B are just misinterpretations, as in: "(9) Vedi come è facile da legare?" ("Do you see how easy is to bind it?"); "(11) Vedi quanto è facile / semplice fidanzarsi?" ("Do you see how easy is to get engaged [to someone]?"); "(12) (13) (16) Vedi com'è semplice / facile far colpo? / stare insieme? / vincere?" ("Do you see how simple /easy is to impress? / to be together? / to win?").

The Arousal pattern of humour runs on to the following turn [8] with Maxwell challenging his son by replying: "{a} Well, I wouldn't get too attached to the bloke if I were you. {b} We all know Miss Fine's relationships eventually end in disaster." In the translation for the Italian television, the further specification of the kind of relationships Miss Fine has been involved in ("with men") add a touch of vulgarity to Maxwell's words uttered in front of his young children, casting him out of his standard role as an English gentleman. Students in Group A, having embodied the character of Maxwell (and of the other protagonists of the sitcom) during the physical improvisation workshops and the drama rehearsals, managed to avoid stepping out of his role and kept the sense of disparaging amusement at making predictions about the expected development of Fran's new date. First of all, the verb group 'to get attached' has almost always been translated as 'affezionarsi' ('to grow fond of somebody'), but for one case in which Maxwell is made to address his young son as if he were a little child by using the verb 'appiccicarsi' ('to cling'): "(6) Invece, se fossi in te, non mi appiccicherei così a quel tizio." ("Well, if I were you, I wouldn't cling that much to the bloke."). In line with Maxwell's character speaking with his young children, also the word 'relationships' has often been rendered into soft terms which would not immediately suggest any direct sexual involvement on the part of the nanny, as in: "(5) (6) Sappiamo tutti come i grandi amori / le storie d'amore / le relazioni sentimentali / le relazioni amorose di Tata Francesca vanno a finire in disastro." ("We all know how Nanny Francesca's great loves / love stories / romantic attachments / love affairs end up in disaster."). Students in Group B did not seem to mind too much to such subtleties connected with the character's role and thus they went on translating almost literally and casually Maxwell's cues in this turn. Thus, the verb group 'to get attached' is literally translated as 'attaccarsi' (literal back-translation: 'to become attached') which, however, is closer to the Maxwell's original expression, but that in Italian acquires the slightly negative implication of 'becoming unhealthily attached to someone', especially when Maxwell is made to refer to Jules as 'l'uomo' ('the man') as in "(7) Non rimarrei troppo attaccato all'uomo, se fossi in te." ("I wouldn't stay too attached to the man, if I were you"), or as "(8) bello" ('the beauty'), or "(9) bellimbusto" ('fop'). The noun 'relationships' is always literally rendered into 'relazioni' that, also in this case, when referred to love affairs, acquires the negative implication of some sort of 'clandestine love affair'. Then, also the expression 'to end in disaster', referred to the usual conclusion of Fran's relationships, is rendered differently by group-B students, as in: "(2) (4) finiscono sempre male." ("always come to a bad end"); "(3) vanno sempre a rotoli!" ("end up from bad to worse / downhill"); and even "finiscono sempre tragicamente." ("always end up tragically."). Misinterpretations include the literal translation of the nanny's name, Miss Fine, as "(5) Miss Finezza" ("Miss Refinement / Miss Finesse"), or rather its rendering into "(4) la Spledida" ("the Scrumptious"), or even into "(14) Miss Impossibile Resistermi" ("Miss It's-Impossible-to-Resist-Me").

It is at this point that, with turn [9], Fran bursts into the dining room announcing: "He asked me to marry him.", literally rendered in translation by students in Group A ("Mi ha chiesto di sposarlo(ooo)!"), whereas some students in Groups B proposed some minor—and unnecessary -variations, such as "(1) Mi ha chiesto la mano!" ("he asked for my hand!"), "(2) Mi ha chiesta in moglie!" ("He asked me in marriage!"), "Mi ha fatto una proposta di matrimonio!" ("He made me a proposal of marriage!"). To such news, Niles, stepping for a moment out of his butler role, whispers in Maxwell's ear "Right on the money, as always, sir.", translated for the Italian television into "Come sempre, signore, c'ha azzeccato." ("As always, sir, you guessed right"). Group-A students tried to find pragmatically equivalent expressions in Italian so as to render into a target quip Niles's humorous mix of insolence and friendship towards Maxwell —so, for instance, they came up with an analogous reference to the betting jargon in "(2) Come sempre, signore, ha fatto la puntata giusta!" ("As always, sir, you've placed the right bet!"), or with another metaphorical reference to the target shooting jargon, as in "(3) Signore, come sempre ha fatto centro!" ("Sir, as always you hit the mark!"), and in "(4) Centrato in pieno, signore." ("Right on the mark, sir."). Some of the students also adopted the idioms "(1) Le ultime parole famose, signore!" ("The famous last words, sir!") and "(7) Profetico come sempre, signore!" ("Profetic [words], as always, sir!", whereas some others preferred unidiomatic expressions, as in "(5) Proprio come ha detto lei, signore!" ("(5) Exactly as you said, sir!") and "(6) Un'altra ottima intuizione, signore." ("Another excellent intuition, sir."). Students in Group B, in contrast, not understanding the quip—or, probably, not finding an equivalent expression in Italian—opted for literal translations which often turned into mistranslation. For instance, literal translations of Niles's original pun may result meaningless, as in "(1) Preciso sui soldi come sempre, signore." ("Precise on the money, sir."), or "(7) Dritto ai soldi come sempre, signore." ("Straight to the money as always, sir."), and "(9) Giusto sul soldo, come sempre, signore." (literally: "Just on money, as always, sir."). Other alternatives in Group B regarded misinterpretations of the very sense of the expression, understood as Niles's remarks on the perfect timing of Maxwell's comments on the truthfulness of facts that, right away, give him the lie, as in "(3) Giusto in tempo come sempre, signore." ("Just in time as always, sir."), and "(4) Puntuale come sempre, signore." ("Punctual as always, sir."). Three very similar alternatives, instead, totally misinterpreted Niles's quip as a disparaging remark on Fran's attachment to money – which may even be interpreted as a derogatory, racist comment on a stereotypical trait of Jewishness. Hence, Niles is made to say: "(10) Attaccata ai soldi, come sempre." ("[She's] attached to money, as always."), or "(11) (12) Giusto per i soldi / Solo per i soldi, come sempre, signore." ("Just / Only for money, as always, sir."), thus implying that Fran is accepting the marriage proposal only for financial interest, not for love.

Brighton immediately supports Fran by saying in turn [11]: "That is so cool, Fran. Congratulations.", translated for the Italian TV into "Bene, brava Francesca! Congratulazioni!" ("Well done, bravo Francesca! Congratulations!"). The translation issue in this case is the rendering into Italian of the term 'cool' finding an equivalent expression that an Italian boy of Brighton'a age and status would use. Group B mainly produced random translation choices such as "(3) Favoloso", "(4) Splendido", and "(8) Meraviglioso", without reflecting on the fact that an Italian boy would not normally employ them as an exclamation, being rather emphatic expressions normally used by girls. Other easy solutions advanced by Group-B students are those ones directly transferred from English and become part of the so-called 'dubbese' variety of Italian which does not actually exist in reality. In this specific case, the translation of 'cool' is rendered into "(2) Grande!", "(7) Grandioso!" that are not pragmatically equivalent to the original expression. Finally, Group B misread the expression by translating it literally into "(5) È così fresco" ("it's so fresh/cool"). Group-A students, instead, having embodied the adolescent Brighton during the acting rehearsals and impro-workshops, developed a physical memory of how this boy would speak—even in communicative contexts that are parallel to the sitcom ones—and so they proposed alternative translations that are more appropriate to an Italian boy of

Brighton's age such as, for instance, "(1) Formidabile", "(2) Che forte", "(3) Figo / Fighissimo", (all of them untranslatable into English, yet representing appropriate male-teenage renderings of the expression 'cool'), and "(5) (6) Ma è fantastico" ("But that's fantastic").

Fran's acknowledgement in the original turn [12] is: "I know, I know. I can't believe it. I'm so excited. I couldn't eat a -", inappropriately rendered for the Italian TV into: "Oh che bello! Che bello! Non riesco a crederci! Sono così eccitata che neanche ceno -" (back-translation: "Oh, how marvelous! How marvelous! I can't believe it! I'm so excited that I couldn't even dine -"). Students in Group A preferred in most cases to keep the literal translation ("Lo so, lo so"—"I know, I know")—but for one case in which they opted for a less effective "(4) È vero" ("True")—and, alongside with the literal translation of "I can't believe it" ("(4) Non posso crederci"—which is itself a transfer from English, now become common usage in Italian), they proposed the more realistic Italian rendering "(1) Non riesco (ancora) a crederci" (literally, "I [still] fail to believe it"). The other translation challenge in this turn [12] is the clause "I'm so excited". Most Group-B students opted for the English transfer "Sono così eccitata" which in Italian may have diverse implications, from 'agitated' to 'aroused', whereas students in Group A preferred the rendering "(1) (4) Sono così emozionata" ("I'm so thrilled"), together with "(2) Sono felicissima" ("I'm so, so happy!"), and "(3) Sono così contenta" ("I'm so delighted"). In the same turn, another translation problem with cultural implications is represented by the expression "oh, kielbasa, sweet and sour cabbage", translated for the Italian TV into "uh, i salsicciotti, oh e anche i cavoli in agrodolce" ("uh, the sausages, oh, and also the sweet and sour cabbages"). The word "salsicciotti" to translate "kielbasa" is a too generic term that disregards the reference to the protagonist's origins. Kielbasa, in fact, is a type of Polish sausage, one of the main dishes in the Polish cuisine, mainly made of pork meat with the addition of spices such as garlic, marjoram and pepper, often served with cabbage soup or stew, sauercrauts, or pickles and traditionally served at Polish weddings (cf. Webb 2002: 227-228). And Polish are also Fran's origins, which may explain her enthusiasm at the sight of a dish from her homeland and—what's more—reminiscent of pleasant celebrations that can be related to her marriage-to-be. But whereas kielbasa is a dish very well know also in the multiethic cuisine of the United States, it is almost unknown in Italy—hence the need felt by Group-A students to find ways to keep at least the reference to Polish culinary culture, as most of them did by choosing a 'foreignization' process, thus retaining the Polish word 'kielbasa' and leaving to video-images the task of disambiguating the nature of such food, while another solution was to render it into "(1) salsicciotti alla polacca" ("Polish sausages"). No reference, though, was possible to its being a typical well-wishing wedding food in Poland. Also some of Group-B students opted for keeping the original word 'kielbasa', whereas others preferred the cultural neutralization of the term into 'salsiccia' and 'salsicciotto', with only two of them choosing the 'domestication' process by rendering 'kielbasa' into "(15) salame" ("salami"), "(6) salsiccia con patate" ("sausage and potatoes") and even "(13) bistecca" ("steak"). Strangely enough, some of Group-B students found it difficult even to translate into Italian the phrase "sweet and sour cabbage" which shows no equivalence difficulty in Italian, being the 'sour and sweet' coooking method a very well known one, especially because of the popularity of the Chinese cuisine in Italy. And yet, sometimes the reference was omitted, as in (1), or the two adjectives were respectively attributed to 'kielbasa' and 'cabbage', as in "(2) kielbasa dolce, aspro cavolo" ("sweet kielbasa, sour cabbage"), in the latter reference not respecting the normal Italian collocation of the adjective after the related noun, or in "(3) un cavolo dolce e agro" ("a sweet and bitter cabbage") where the Italian adjectival collocation 'agro dolce' ('sour sweet') is not respected, as also in "(14) delizioso e aspro cavolo" ("cabbage delicious and tart"), where adjectives are placed before the noun, rather than following the correct collocation after it, or still in "(4) verza in agrodolce" ("sweet and sour savoy"), and even "(16) cavoletti di Bruxelles!" ("Brussels sprouts!"). Then, an exclamation that posed semantic and pragmatic problems in translation was "Hit me again" by which Fran addresses Niles who, smiling, starts serving her dinner. The Italian TV translation has rendered it into "gli dia dentro!" ("let's tuck in!"), but students in Group A tried to find a pragmatic equivalent which would retain the sense of Fran as a gluttonous young woman but also preserve her loveliness which went missing in the harsh order she gives Niles in the TV translation. Hence, students came up with solutions from the more literal rendering "(7) Mi riempia il piatto" ("Fill my plate up"), where Fran uses the formal third-person allocution in addressing Niles with an imperative—a distance that makes the same-status butler/nanny relatioship funny—to the more metaphorical "Dacci sotto!" ("Put your back into it"), with a second-person allocution which represents their relationship as informal and suggests the image of Niles working hard at filling Fran's plate with food. Group-B students mostly misread this exclamation, probably because they had not built a physical representation of the characters by embodying them as 'acting translators', making them 'their own' by empathic appropriation, so they misread this expression as, for instance, "(1) (22) mi tentate / state tentando ancora / di nuovo" ("you are tempting me again"), or "(16) mettili da parte!" ("keep them aside!"), till coming to such literal renderings as "(2) dammi un'altra botta!" ("gimme another hit!"), "(3) picchiami ancora!" ("beat me again!"), "(14) colpiscimi di nuovo!" ("strike me again!") up to the almost vulgar "(19) Dacci dentro!" ("knock it!"). Finally, Fran's exclamation parallel to her mother's previous one: "Oh, such a big corn for such a little girl.", uttered as she takes a corn from Grace's dish—rendered for the Italian TV into "E' una pannocchia troppo grande per te." ("This is a corn too big for you."), shows a sloppiness in Group-B students' translations of the same kind as the one found in their translations of Sylvia's analogous clause, which mainly consists in disregarding the Italian conventional collocation of adjectives after the related noun by putting them, instead, before the noun, directly transferring the English collocation to Italian and thus making the oxymoron structure 'big corn / little girl' sound stilted and unnatural, as in "(1) (2) Oh che grande / una così grande pannocchia per una così piccola bambina." (in English sounding like "Oh what a corn so big for such a girl so little"). Other misreadings of this clause found in Group-B translations are the translation of 'little girl' into the archaic term "(3) fanciulla" ("maiden") and "(24) ragazza" ("teenage girl / yound woman").

Maxwell's question in turn [13], "He asked you to marry him?", was literally rendered by most of Group-A students through the formal second-person address pronoun ("Le ha chiesto di sposarlo?"), which was in contrast with most Group-B students who opted for the informal and patronizing second-person pronoun, as in "(1) Ti ha chiesto di sposarlo?". The exception in Group A was represented by two cases in which the question was turned into a request for confirmation "(2) (3) Allora /così le ha chiesto di sposarlo." ("So he asked you to marry him."). To this, Fran replies in turn [14] with a "uh-huh' of confirmation, representing for jealous Maxwell a dispreferred answer creating a situation of tension. In some of Group-A translations, Fran's mere mumble was disambiguated by the use of actual words of affirmation "(2) Sì sì!" ("yes yes!") and "(4) Eh già!" ("Oh yeah [he did]."), a process that was also adopted by some students in Group B who, however, did not consider the lip-synch time span (actually, Fran's mumble was due to the fact that she was replying while eating) and so they produced longer and more articulated clauses than the original, as in: "(2) Sembra proprio di sì!" ("It seems just so!"), or "(4) Proprio così!" ("Quite so!"). In turn [15], Maxwell's irritated reprimand "You've barely known the man for two weeks", was translated by Group-A students into pragmatically equivalent expressions, slightly changing only in the rendering of the adverb 'barely': "Ma lo conosce da appena / sì e no da / solo da / a malapena da / a stento da due settimane!" ("But you've barely known this man / for about / just for / scarcely for / only just for two weeks!"), always keeping the formal allocutory pronoun 'lei' in addressing Fran. In Group-B students' translations, instead, the informal and condescending second-person form 'tu' prevails in Maxwell addressing Fran. Fran's piqued reaction to Maxwell's offensive criticism, in turn [16] ("What? You think it's so hard to believe a man would fall in love with me that fast?"), is rendered in the Italian TV version more impersonal—as there is no direct reference to herself—and through the addition of a concealed, witty attack to Maxwell's long-lasted hesitation at disclosing his love for her ("No, cosa significa? Un uomo ci deve sempre mettere anni per dire che è innamorato?" - "No, what does it mean? A man has to wait for years before telling that he is in love?"). In both groups, the choice was to keep the original structure of the sentence, but when reproduced literally, as in many translations by Group-B students, the language would sound unnatural and stilted, with a long and convoluted sentence-structure, as, for instance, in Group-B option "(5) Pensa che sia così difficile da credere che un uomo possa innamorarsi di me così velocemente?" ("Do you think that it is so difficult to believe that a man can fall in love with me so rapidly?"). Students in Group A, instead, tried to find solutions that could sound natural and genuine in spoken Italian—thus omitting in translation the verb phrase "You think" that would have rendered the expression artificial in Italian—as in: "(1) (2) Le è tanto / così difficile credere che un uomo si possa innnamorare di me così in fretta?" ("Is it so hard for you to believe a man could fall in love with me that fast?"). Other Group-A equivalent solutions are represented by: "(3) Crede sia così / tanto difficile che un uomo si innamori di me in così poco tempo?" ("You believe it's so hard a man would fall in love with me in such a little time?"), or "(5) (7) (9) Le sembra impossibile / Pensa che non sia possible / che sia improbabile che un uomo si innamori di me così alla svelta?" ("It seems impossibile to you / You think it's impossible / not possible / improbabile that a man would fall in love with me so quickly?").

Grace's turn [17] represented another translation challenge in both syntactic and pragmatic terms. The young girl, in support of Fran's reaction, offers the example of her own experience of 'fast falling in love' and says: "Yeah. Todd and I knew each other three minutes before I got a Pudding-Pack right in the eye", which, for the Italian television, was translated as "Giusto. Todd, appena conosciuto, mi ha subito buttato il primo budino in faccia." ("Right. Todd, as soon as I met him, threw the first pudding at hand on my face."). Most students in Group A left the sentence impersonal as it is in the original version, since they did not clearly specify the agent who performed the action of throwing the pudding-pack at Grace's face, thus focusing the attention on the girl's passive process of getting it "right in the eye". Translation solutions in this sense are "(1) (3) (4) Todd ed io ci eravamo conosciuti solo / ci siamo conosciuti solo da tre minuti prima che io ricevessi / che mi arrivasse / quando mi è arrivato un pacchetto di budini / una confezione di budini / un budino dritto in un occhio / negli occhi." ("Todd and I knew each other only / by only three minutes before I received / before / when a pack of puddings / a pudding pack / a pudding got me right in the eye"). Students in Group B met difficulties prevalently in the translation of 'Pudding Pack', oddly written with capital letters and therefore mistaken for a food brand. For this reason, in some occurrences, students opted for a 'foreignization process' and left the phrase in its original wording, as in (3) (6) (7) (15) (18), whereas other students preferred a 'neutralization process' and chose the generic word 'budino' ('pudding'), as in the majority of Group-B students' translations. Finally, some students in the same group attempted a 'domestication process' by rendering 'pudding pack' into "(9) pasticcio di carne" ("meat pie"), or "(5) (9) torta in faccia" ("custard pie right in the face")—with an evident mistranslation in "(12) torta packistana" ("Pakistani [Paki] pie", due to the 'Pack/Paki' assonance) playing with - and even "(14) (16) (17) Todd ed io / ci eravamo appena conosciuti la prima volta che mi ha tirato i capelli / ci siamo proprio conosciuti tre minuti prima che io gli infilassi una bic nell'occhio / abbiamo aspettato solo tre minuti perchè scoccasse il colpo di fulmine." ("Todd and I / had just met the first time he pulled my hair / knew each other just three minutes before I poked a Bic pen right in his eye / waited for just three minutes for love at first sight to strike"), where the impersonal construction is not the preferred one as the agent doing the action is specified and alternatively identified with Todd, Grace herself, and the abstract entity 'love at first sight' (literally 'lightning strike'). Fran's acknowledgement of Grace's childish exemplification, in turn [18], "There you go"—translated for the Italian TV into "Ecco, ha sentito?" ("There you go, have you heard that?")—had variable renderings in both groups, with Group-A students opting for short equivalent interjections to fit the lip-synch time-span, whereas students in Group B sometimes employed Italian clichés, often in the form of longer sentences, such as "(3) Come volevasi dimostrare!", a mathematical expression meaning QED (from Latin: "quod erat demonstrandum"), or "(7) Ci risiamo!" ("Here we go again!"), "(8) Siamo alle solite" ("it's the same old story!"), "(10) Pensa tu!" ("Just imagine!").

In turn [19], Maxwell resumes his previously interrupted reprimand first by uttering a disparaging comment ("You know nothing about this man"—with the emphatic addition of the imperative "Oh ragioni!" ["Oh, be reasonable!"] in the version for the Italian TV), and then by asking a direct question to Fran ("All right, so he's a doctor. Is he a specialist?"), implying a derogatory judgment of her fiancé and thus expecting from her a 'preferred' answer confirming his negative predictions. Group-A students opted for a literal translation, sometimes with the addition of the adversative "ma" ("but") at the beginning of Maxwell's turn and always with the use of the formal allocution 'lei' in addressing Fran. Students in Group B often employed the informal allocution 'tu' as Maxwell addresses Fran and also added more emphatic elements in their translations, making sentences longer than the original and, thus, not fitting the lip-synch time-span—such as "(2) Non sa niente a proposito di quell'uomo" ("You know nothing in connection with that man"), or "(4) Resta il fatto che non sa niente di lui" ("The fact remains that you know nothing about him"), and "(5) Ma cosa sa di quest'uomo? Praticamente niente!" ("But what do you know about this man? Practically nothing!"), "(6) (10) Va bene, è un dottore—ma almeno è uno specialista? / è specializzato in qualcosa in particolare?" ("All right, he is a doctor - but at least is he a specialist? / is he specialized in something in particular?"). Maxwell's originally covert derogatory judgments were also made explicit and sarcastic in some of Group-B translations with the addition of extra words and phrases that actually distort the original tone of the turn, such as the vulgar implication in: "(7) Va bene che è un dottore – un ginecologo?" ("It's okay that he is a doctor - a gynecologist?"), or the defamatory suspicion in "(11) A quanto pare è un dottore." ("So it seems that / So apparently he is a doctor").

Fran's proud reply in turn [20] actually aims at mocking Maxwell's disbelief in the professional qualifications of her fiancé and so, to Maxwell's utmost annoyance, she teasingly chants for him a one-liner referred to a jazz song ("You ain't just whistling 'Dixie,' baby.") with the counterpoint of the audience's (canned?) loud laughter. In the Italian version for the TV, this turn was naïvely translated into "Lui è ultraspecialisticissimo, è molto bravo" ("He is very super-highly-specialized, he's very good!"). Students in Group B felt insecure about how to render this quip into equivalent Italian ways and most of them came to the decision of leaving it as it is in the original, with the obvious loss of comic effect on Italian audiences, as for instance in "(1) (2) (5) Non stai solo / forse fischiettando / 'Dixie' / una musichetta jazz, dolcezza! / baby!" ("You ain't just / maybe whistling 'Dixie' / a jazz tune, sweetie / baby!"), where a bottom-up, foreignization process prevails. In the same group, however, there were also some instances of top-down translation processes of domestication, where more creative—but by no means equivalent—solutions were proposed, as in "(7) Geloso?" ("Jealous?"), "(8) Sì, uno specialista per gelosi come lei!" ("Yeah, a specialist for jealous guys like you!"), and "(9) Brutta cosa l'invidia, eh?" ("How nasty envy is, isn't it?"). Also some misreading can be detected in this group, as the translation of 'whistling' into "(2) fischiando" ("hissing"), and the mistranslation in "(4) Hai appena fischiettato 'Dixie', bella!" ("You've just whistled 'Dixie', gorgeous lady!"). Within Group A, students instead felt that they had to find an equivalent that could render also in Italian the humorous sense of Fran's getting her own revenge on Maxwell who was trying to humiliate her and her boyfriend by belittling his professional competence. At the same time, they wanted to keep a formal and cultural equivalence between the original one-liner chanted by Fran, while getting physically closer to Maxwell, and a parallel one in Italian, thus activating an 'intermediation' process between the two comic constructions and cultures. Hence, they came up with various valid solutions, from the more literal ones, aimed at implicature disambiguation, such as: "(1) Non stiamo qui a scherzare!" ("We are not joking, here!"), "(2) Un pezzo grosso, per l'esattezza!" ("A big shot, to be precise!"), "(3) Non si tratta di un tipo qualunque, baby!" ("It's not about an ordinary bloke, baby!"), "(4) Mica stiamo giocando, giovanotto!" ("We are not playing at all, young man!"), and "(5) Senta, stiamo mica parlando di sciocchezze? Eh?" ("Listen, aren't we talking nonsense at all? Are we?"), to the more idiomatic, chiché ones, such as: "(7) (8) Puoi ben dirlo / Puoi dirlo forte ragazzino! / caro! / cocco! / amico!" ("You can say that again, boy! / darling! / dearie! / friend!"), "(11) E scusa se è poco, tesoro!" ("If that's worthless I beg your pardon, darling!"), "(9) Non è certo una passeggiatina la sua professione!" ("Surely it's not a picnic his profession!"), but also "(10) Non stai certo giocando all'Allegro Chirurgo, bimbo bello!" ("You ain't hardly toying with the Amateur Surgeon, pretty baby!"), in this specific case by making reference to a famous battery-operated board game of the sixties—namely, *Operation*—in Italy renamed *L'Allegro Chirurgo* (literally, *The Merry Surgeon*) and more recently revived as an online game under the name of *Amateur Surgeon*.[3] Then Group-A students also tried to propose solutions that could be more formally and culturally equivalent to the original cue that referred to a popular jazz music—namely, Dixie tunes. These are the translation options they proposed: "(6) Eh qui non canto quel motivetto che ti piace tanto! Dudu dudù." (literally, "Eh, I'm not singing here that little tune that you like so much! Doodoo doo doo."), a rhyming line from a famous funny swing song that in the forties was played in Italy by the vocal trio and orchestra conducted by Pippo Barzizza and was based on a 1934 song by Dan Caslar-Galdieri. This may be considered an appropriate choice since this swing tune is well known in Italy as it was also employed in the sixities as a famous jingle for a brand of candies and, in this specific context, it stands for something light and trivial (as Dixie tunes stand for in the original version) which denotes exactly the opposite of what Jules's medical specialization represents, in Fran's view. Other similar variants are: "(12) Eh, qui non si fischietta la canzoncina, caro, si canta l'Opera!" ("Eh, here that's not a light song that is being whistled, dear - Opera is being sung!"), "(13) Jules non compone certo musica leggera, bello, scrive sinfonie!" ("Jules surely doesn't compose pop music, cutie, he does write symphonies!"), and finally the rhyming oneliner based on assonance "(14) Baby, non fischietto certo un motivetto, lui è specialista provetto!" (literally, "Baby, I'm not whistling a light tune, he is a practised specialist!").

Maxwell's reaction to Fran's mocking tone is, in turn [21], a whispered "Oh God", translated for the Italian TV into "Oh, la testa!" ("Oh, the head!"), as he brought the hand to his head which suggested a tension-induced headache. Translations in Group A were almost equivalent—"(1) (2) Oddio / Oh Dio" ("Oh God!"), "(3) Oh cielo!" ("Good heavens!"), "(4) Oh Signore!" ("Oh Lord!"), whereas in Group B, students opted for non-literal renderings which sometimes turned out to be mistranslations, as in

[3] This board game (initially produced by Milton Bradley and later by Hasbro) consisted of a plastic operating table with the picture of a funny patient lying on it, whose body had various openings containing some human organs represented through humorous plastic forms and amusing names (e.g., 'Adam's apple' an apple standing for the thyroid in the throat, 'broken heart' in the chest, etc.). If the tweezers used to remove the sick organ touched the metal edge of the opening, the red-bulb of his nose lit up and a buzzing noise informed children at play that their operation failed.

"(1) Cosa?" ("What?"), "(3) Ma sentitela!" ("Listen to that!"), and "(5) Oh no". Maggie, Maxwell's eldest child, in her turn [22], reacts differently from her father, and with enthusiasm she comments: "Oh, this is so exciting.", and then asks Fran: "So can I be a bridesmaid?". The dubbing translation for the Italian television turns Maggie's impersonal comment into a self-referential one: "Sono così contenta!" ("I'm so happy!") and adds a reference to Fran's decisional authority in saying: "Mi vuoi come damigella d'onore?" ("Do you want me as a bridesmaid?"). Here the most predictable translation issue is the one identified also in Fran's turn [12] and regards the term 'exciting' in "this is so exciting", which most of Group-B students translated into its 'almost-false' friend 'eccitante' ("Ècosì eccitante!"), with all the ambiguous implications outlined above with reference to Fran's expression "I'm so excited". Group-A students, on the contrary, reflected on renderings that could sound more natural in Italian, and so they proposed "(1) (5) Oh, è così emozionante! / entusiasmante! " (literally: "Oh, it's so emotionally-charged! / thrilling!", and "(2) (3) Oh che bello! / che emozione!" (literally: "Oh, how marvellous! / what an emotion!", obviously sounding more natural in Italian than in English). Also 'so', connecting the two clauses, is mistranslated by some Group-B students into 'così' ('therefore'), which in Italian denotes a logical consequence that is not implied in the original version, whereas Group-A students opted for the link-word 'allora' ('well') introducing a proposal (i.e., 'to be a bridesmaid').

Fran's reply in turn [23] apparently introduces an anticlimax in the conversation as she concedes (while her mother Sylvia enters the dining room behind her chair): "I know the doctor asked me to marry him" (and Sylvia happily smiles at Fran's back), but then Fran reveals her reservations: "but I didn't say yes." (and Sylvia, disappointed, faints to the floor behind Fran who is unaware she is there). Fran, then, absent-mindedly appreciates the food she is eating: "This is delicious". The dubbing translation for the Italian TV introduces an extra allocutory form, "Aspetta, Maggie" ("Hold on, Maggie") which puts emphasis on her reservations, but omits the reference to Jules as "the doctor" (which does stress his social status), to mention him just by the corresponding pronoun "lui" ("he"). The first translation issue that students in Group A had to solve was how to render into an appropriate Italian the concessive expression "I know". Some of them translated it into "(1) (2) [Sì,] è vero [che]" ("[Yes,] it's true [that]"), others opted for "(2) Ho detto che" ("I said that"), or "(3) Capisco che" ("I understand that"), and other students preferred the expressions of acknowledgment "(4) D'accordo" ("All right") and "(5) Beh, [sai]" ("Well, [you know]"). Most students in Group B, instead, produced literal translations that do not sound natural in Italian, such as: "(2) (9) (12) [Lo] so che" ("I know that"), also producing a blatant mistranslation in "(5) Lo conosco il dottore che mi ha chiesto di sposarlo" ("I know the doctor who asked me to marry him"). Even Fran's revelation of her reservation, literally translated by most Group-A students as "(1) (3) (5) (6) ma / però io non [gli] ho detto di sì" ("but I didn't say yes [to him]"), shows difficulties in Group-B students' attempts at rendering it into Italian as they oddly opted for more complex sentence-structures that often produced mistranslations, as in: "(4) (9) (12) ma io non ho ancora detto di sì" ("but I haven't yet said yes"), which may presuppose that she is keeping Jules on tenterhooks but that, eventually, she will accept his marriage proposal, or in "(7) ma questo non vuol dire che abbia detto di sì" ("but this doesn't mean that I said yes to him"), which keeps the options open without revealing her answer: she may have already said yes, or rather she may have declined the proposal.

Sylvia, out of sight because lying on the floor after having fainted at the bad news from her daughter, remarks sarcastically in her metaphorical turn [24]: "Why don't you grab a knife and stick it straight through my heart?". This turn was utterly 'transcreated' (cf. Mangiron and O'Hagan 2006) in the Italian version for television, where Sylvia is transformed into Fran's aunt Assunta who claims: "Che le racconto adesso a mia sorella che poi è tua madre?" ("What shall I say now to my sister, who is also your mother?"), thus introducing some contextual information about the new family relations devised in the Italian version of the sitcom. No student in both groups opted for such 'creative' top-down mistranslations - yet, in Group-B translations some flaws can be detected, as in the recurring use of the possessive adjective "mio" ("my") before "cuore" ("heart"), which is syntactically required in English but, transferred into Italian, it is perceived as an unusual and artificial structure. Another flaw is the use of the second-person plural pronoun—which, differently from Italian, in English is always 'you' in both singular and plural forms: "(2) (3) Perché non afferrate un coltello e me lo ficcate nel cuore. / Perché non mi uccidete lentamente con un coltello conficcandomelo nel cuore?" ("Why don't you [plural] grab a knife and stick it straight through my heart. / Why don't you [plural] kill me slowly with a knife by driving it into my heart?"). This use of the second-person plural pronoun in Sylvia's words may be interpreted as her charging her daughter, together with the Sheffield family, with a plot against her, aimed at subverting her plans for Fran's future. A further flaw is represented by the use of the imperative in "(6) (7) Prendi un coltello e trafiggimi il cuore! / Prendi un coltello e conficcamelo nel cuore." ("Take a knife and stab my heart! / Take a knife and drive it into my heart."), which removes the original sense of Sylvia considering her violent murder on the same level as 'Fran's not accepting Jules's proposal right away'. Other top-down alternatives offered by Group-B students often turned out to be non-equivalent translations in terms of textual form and pragmatic effect, such as: "(10) Questo è peggio di un colpo al cuore!" ("This is worse than a heart failure"), "(11) Il mio povero cuore! Sta per venirmi un infarto!" ("My poor heart! I'm going to have a heart attack!"), and "(12) Mi hai dato una pugnalata!" ("You stabbed me!"). Students in Group A, on the contrary, were aware of the comic potential of the hyperbolic resemblance that Sylvia sees in the devastating effects that both Fran's rejection of Jules's marriage proposal and a heart attack can have on her. Hence, students in this group tried to make such correlation clear also in Italian by using a number of semantic link-words emphasizing the logical cause-effect implicature, as in: "(1) Facevi prima a conficcarmi un coltello nel cuore!" ("It would have taken you less than expected to stick a knife straight through my heart!"), "(2) Perchè a questo punto non afferri un coltello e mi trafiggi subito il cuore?" ("Why at this point don't you grab a knife and stab my heart right away?"), or "(5) Giacché, afferra un coltello e piantamelo dritto nel cuore, eh?" ("While you're at it, grab a knife and stick it straight through my heart, uh?"), till suggesting a formally deviating, but pragmatically equivalent alternative: "(3) Bé, allora? Che aspetti a pugnalarmi?" ("Well, then? Stab me, what are you waiting for?").

In turn [25] Fran is still unaware of the presence of her mother in the dining room (precisely lying close to her feet) and so she believes that Grace is mockingly making an impersonation of Sylvia by imitating her voice. She appreciates the perfect imitation and says: "That was great. She sounded just like -", but then she suddenly realizes that her mother is there and shouts: "Ma! Ma ... Ma, let go of my ankle." In the Italian dubbing translation for television, Fran(cesca) addresses Grace directly, by using the second-person form, and congratulates with her: "Ah ah ah ma che brava! Sembri proprio -" ("Ah ah ah, how clever! You really sounded like -") before she realizes that her aunt Assunta (Sylvia's Italian identity) is there: "Zia As -ah! Lasciami, lasciami la caviglia! Lasciami la caviglia, Zia Assunta!" ("Aunt As -ah! Let, let go of my ankle! Let go of my ankle, Aunt Assunta!"). Students in Group A, having practiced as 'acting translators', took into account the strict correlation between bodily movents, quick change of emotions and words marking the humour in this turn, so they tried to render it into Italian by employing expressions that would sound natural and unaffected to the target audience, also retaining the same humorous effect as in the original version. Hence, the very first exclamation "That was great. She sounded just like -", was equivalently rendered into "(1) E' incredibile! Grace ha imitato benissimo la -" ("That's incredible! Grace has imitated perfectly well my -"); "(2) Caspita che brava! Sembrava proprio la voce di -" ("Goodness, how clever! It just sounded like the voice of -"); "(3) (4) Questa è / era / bella! / Wow / sembrava la stessa voce di - / la voce sembrava proprio quella di -" ("That's /was / funny! / Wow / it just sonde like the same voice as - / The voice just sounded like my -"), and finally, by directly addressing Grace: "(5) Proprio forte! Hai fatto identica la voce di -" (literally: "That's just amazing! You've imitated in exactly the same way the voice of -"). Then, as she tries to wriggle free from her mother's hold, Fran says: "(2) (3) Mamma, Mamma, molla la caviglia / non tirare, lasciami la caviglia!" ("Mummy, Mummy, don't pull, let go of my ankle!"). Differently from the translation options proposed by students in Group A, most students in Group B submitted almost stilted translations in 'dubbese', often bordering mistranslation, as in: "(1) (4) (14) Questo è fantastico, suona appena come – Ma! Ma, staccati dalla mia caviglia!" ("This is fantastic, it hardly sounds like – Ma! Ma, pull away from my ankle!"), or in "(2) (6) (9) (10) È stato grande / grandioso", representing the typical way of translating 'great' into a 'dubbese' variation which is not frequent at all in actual spoken Italian. Another transfer from the English language can be detected in "(2) Suonava proprio come", a literal translation of the verb 'to sound', implying the sound of music, not a resemblance to the voice of somebody else. And then, also in this case, some mistranslation instances have been identified in the solutions found by some students in Group B, probably due to a lack of contextual knowledge, though it is difficult to justify such bad renderings into Italian as the following ones: "(5) Ella ha appena rimbombato come -" ("She ['Ella' formal third-person pronoun] has just boomed like -"); "(8) E' una situazione troppo intrigante -" ("It's a too intiguing situation -"); and "(13) Sarebbe un'idea. Suonava proprio come -" ("That could be an idea. It just sounded like -").

In turn [26], Sylvia's angry reply at Fran's request for letting go of her ankle is sharp: "You better run.", literally transalted into the Italian version for the TV ("Ti conviene scappare!"). But, whereas students in Group A tried to render Sylvia's threat into Italian by translating the word 'run' into 'scappare' ('escape', 'run away' from Sylvia's menace of physical aggression), students in Group B rendered 'run' into 'correre' (meant as 'hurry up'), which turns Sylvia's threat into a mere simulation of aggression in which she only plays the part of the furious mother and, what is more, she urges her daughter to play in turn her part as the threatened one. This is evident in renderings like: "(2) E' meglio che ti affretti." ("You'd better hurry up."), or "(1) (6) È meglio che ti metti a correre! / Inizia a correre." ("You'd better start running!" / "Start running."), and "(3) Ma insomma cosa vuoi aspettare?" ("Then, well, what do you want to wait for?"). As Fran starts running around the table, chased by Sylvia, she anxiously asks Brighton in turn [27]: "Brighton, is she taking off her shoe?". Students in Group A reproduced the dynamics of the feared-for action, originally represented through a process in the continuous aspect, by likewise using verb forms that in Italian are equivalent to the continuous aspect, and with verbs that allow a visualization of Sylvia's action, such as: "(1) (3) Brighton, si sta levando / togliendo la scarpa?" ("Brighton, is she taking off her shoe?") or, more aggressively, "(4) Brighton, mi sta tirando la scarpa?" ("Brighton, is she hurling a shoe at me?"), or rather, focusing on a probably already occurred action: "(2) si è tolta la scarpa?" ("has she taken off her shoe?"). In Group B, students opted for the same forms, except for some cases of mistranslation, such as: "(1) Brighton, si sta sfilando la scarpa?" ("Brighton, is she slipping off her shoe?"), where the verb 'sfilare' ('slip off') entails a slower movement that is incompatible with the tumult of the moment. Also "(2) si sta togliendo le scarpe?" ("is she taking off her shoes?") may be considered a case of mistranslation as it implies that Sylvia is taking off both her shoes to run faster after Fran, which is not the actual sense of the scene. In fact, this sense is disambiguated not just by the images of the action, but also by Brighton's words, who, in turn [28], answers Fran's question: "No. But she's gonna hurl the corn". This turn, in the Italian TV version, was translated with a 'war metaphor': "No, però si è armata di pannocchia." ("No, but she's armed herself with a corn"). In Group A, most students preferred a literal translation respecting the original continuous form capable of representing linguistically the rapid development of the action, as in: "(1) (2) (3) (4) No. Ma sta lanciando / Ma ti sta tirando / Ma ti sta per tirare / lanciare / scagliare la pannocchia." ("No, but she's going to throw / hurl the corn at you"). In one case, a student in this group proposed a translation containing a 'war metaphor' (cf. Lakoff and Johnson 1980): "(5) No, ma ha impugnato la pannocchia!" ("No, but she has seized the corn!"). In Group B, again some top-down non-equivalent translations and even some odd mistranslations can be identified. For instance, "(2) No, ma sta attenta alla pannocchia!" ("No, but beware of the corn!") and "(2) Con l'intenzione di dartela in testa!" ("With the intention to hit your head with it!") are not exactly equivalent to the original turn as they both disambiguate the covert implication in Brighton's warning, thus diminishing the comic effect. Mistranslation instances may be considered instead the following ones: "(4) No, ma sta tirando la spiga." ("No. but she's going to hurl the ear"); "(5) No, però si sta lanciando sulla pannocchia." ("No, yet she's throwing herself on the corn") – in this case, probably misinterpreting it as Sylvia's greedy act of being distracted from what she was doing (i.e., chasing Fran) by the sight of food that, actually, seems to make her change the direction of her mind and movement—and also "(6) No, ma sta gettando la pannocchia" ("No, but she's throwing away the corn"), a mistranslation due to a diatopic use of the Italian verb 'gettare' (literally: 'throw away') with the intending meaning of 'lanciare' ('throw').

At this point there is a change of scene as mother and daughter move into the kitchen—Sylvia, still furious, chasing Fran and brandishing the corn, and Fran, as she runs trying to escape her rage, repeats short of breath, a sequence of 'oy' that reveal her distress. When she reaches the sink, Fran turns to her mother and, by grabbing the mixer tap and pointing it against Sylvia, threatens her by saying, in turn [29]: "Ma, put down the vegetable and no one gets hurt." The translation for the Italian TV disambiguates Fran's intentions, thus diminishing the comic effect of the pun on the target audience: "Bada! O metti giù quella pannocchia o apro l'acqua bollente." ("Mark! Put down that corn or I'll turn the hot water on"). In Group A, only one student produced the literal translation of 'vegetable': "(4) Mamma, metti giù quell'ortaggio" (Mummy, put down that vegetable"), which may sound comic just because it is an unusual 'technical' word in common Italian. Most students in the same group, instead, solved the problem of rendering this word into everyday spoken Italian by making explicit reference to the type of vegetable Fran refers to - namely, the corn ('pannocchia'), as in: "(2) (3) (4) (7) Ma, metti giù / posa / molla la pannocchia" ("Ma, put down / release the corn"). Exceptions are to be found in "(6) Ehi, Mamma! Metti giù quel coso prima che qualcuno si faccia male!" ("Ehi, Mummy, put down that doodah before someone gets hurt!"), and in "(1) Ma, posa l'arma" ("Ma, put down the weapon"), which extends the 'war metaphor' Brighton used in the previous turn ("No, ma ha impugnato la pannocchia!"—"No, but she has seized the corn!"). The same 'war metaphor' can be identified also in the students' use of the verb phrase 'rimanere ferito' ('to get injured') to translate 'to get hurt', as in: "(1) (2) (4) (5) Ma, metti giù la pannocchia e nessuno si ferirà / si ferisce / e non ci sarà nessun ferito." ("Ma, put down the corn and non one gets injured / and there will be no injured"). In Group B, some transfer from the English language produced unnatural translations, as in the literal rendering of the word 'vegetable' into "(1) (4) Mamma, metti giù quell vegetale / quella verdura e nessuno si farà male." ("Mummy, put down that plant [vegetable] / those vegetables [in Italian an uncountable singular noun, 'verdura'] and no one gets hurt"). In two cases this word was translated into the generic 'affare' ('whatsit', as in "(2) (6) Mamma, metti giù quell'affare" ("Mummy, put down that whatsit"), in one case 'corn' was again mistranslated into 'spiga' ('ear') and in another case a top-down 'creative' mistranslation was produced: "(3) Zia, metti via gli oggetti contundenti o celebreremo un funerale!" ("Aunt, put away the dangerous objects or we shall take part in a funeral service! / or a funeral service will take place!").

Sylvia, realizing Fran's distress, tries to soothe her daughter by suddenly becoming sympathetic and saying, in turn [30], "All right. Help me to understand which was the biggest turnoff—the fact that Jules was gorgeus, rich, or a doctor?". In the translation for the Italian TV, 'Aunt Assunta' says: "Parliamo. Vorrei solo che mi spiegassi cos'è che ti ha spaventato così - il fatto che Giulio è stupendo, ricco e anche medico?" ("Let's talk. I'd only want you to explain to me what has scared you so much—the fact that Giulio is gorgeous, rich and also doctor?"). Differently from students in Group B who, in the majority of cases, operated a transfer from the English language by translating the expression "help me to understand" literally into "Aiutami a capire"—another instance of Italian 'dubbese' variety still sounding unnatural in common spoken Italian—most students in Group A opted for a more natural Italian translation of this expression, such as: "(1) (6) (8) (9) (11) Fammi capire" ("Let me understand"), "(4) (7) (10) (12) Però spiegami / Ma spiegami / Ma mi devi spiegare" ("But explain to me / But you must explain to me"), and when the verb 'to help' is retained, the clause structure is not made to conform to the English one, but it takes a more spontaneous form in Italian: "(3) Ma aiutami a scoprire" ("But help me to discover"). The other problematic point in this turn is the dubbing translation of the phrase 'the biggest turnoff', which needs to be rendered effectively into everyday spoken Italian by trying, at the same time, to respect the original timing of the cue as it is uttered by the character of Sylvia in the film. Group-B students solved this issue by choosing, in the majority of cases, the neutral and plain term "il problema (più grande)" ("the [most serious] problem"). Others, in the same group, opted for a similar alternative, namely, "il più grande errore" ("the biggest mistake"). Students in Group A, instead, rather focused on pragmatic equivalence as well as on preserving the comic effect of the phrase, so they rendered it into various forms, more or less idiomatic and, in general, all of them effective in the humorous construction of the turn. For instance, they translated this phrase into: "(1) qual era il suo punto debole" ("which was his weak point"), "(2) cosa ti ha scoraggiata" ("what has discouraged you"), "(3) qual era la cosa più fastidiosa" ("which was the most irksome thing"), (4) qual è il difetto" ("what's the fault"), "(5) qual è stata la pecca" ("which was the failing"), "(6) qual è la cosa più repellente" ("which is the most repellent thing"), the idiomatic clause "(7) cosa ti ha fatto cascare le braccia" ("what has made your heart sink [literally: what has made your arms fall down]"), "(8) qual è la cosa che più non ti piace" ("which is the thing that you don't like"), "(10) qual è la cosa che ti ripugna in lui" ("what is the thing that revolts you"),"(9) (11) cos'è che non va in lui" ("what's wrong with him"), and the covert reproach in "(12) ma spiegami cos'è che non andava stavolta" ("but explain to me what was wrong this time"). Students in Group B also translated the attributes that Sylvia ascribes to Jules ("the fact that Jules was gorgeous, rich, or a doctor") into adjectives that are not normally used in Italian, especially the one in reference to the good looks of a man ('gorgeous'), such as "(2) fantastico" ("fantastic") or "(7) meraviglioso" ("marvellous"). In this context, students in Group A produced more pragmatically appropriate translations, such as "(1) uno schianto" ("gorgeous"), or "(7) affascinante" ("charming").

In turn [31], Fran shyly adds another relevant quality possessed by Jules that she has omitted to reveal to her mother until now: "Did I mention he was Jewish?". But any reference to Fran's Jewishness was in fact removed from the translation for the Italian television, as discussed before, and so this turn was rendered into Fran's vulgar comment "Ha un sudore che sa di pecora" ("He has a sweat that smells of sheep"), thus making reference to the peasant origins of her Italian family. Whereas all students in Group A decided to preserve the original reference to Jules's Jewishness and the original sentence-structure, most students in Group B advanced some proposals of top-down 'transcreations' (cf. Mangiron and O'Hagan 2006) which, in point of fact, betrayed the original sense of the quip and, thus, turned out to be actual mistranslations, such as: "(1) (2) Ti ho detto che ha l'alito pesante? / Ha un alito che uccide." ("Have I told you that he's got a foul breath? / He's got a breath that kills"), "(3) (5) (8) Ti ho già / mai detto che è ciociaro? / italiano? / pecoraro?" ("Have I already / ever told you that he's from Ciociaria? / Italian? / a shepherd?"), "(4) Oltre che napoletano?" ("Apart the fact that he is Neapolitan?"). In all these cases, Group-B students had been influenced by the dubbing translation for the Italian TV, so there was nothing actually creative in their proposals.

Sylvia's disappointment is evident in her turn [32], when she attempts to make Fran reflect on her real hopeless condition, disguising her deprecation as sympathetic advice to her daughter: "Oh. Darling, I only say this because I love you. You're a glorified cleaning girl. This could be your last chance." In the Italian TV production of this sitcom, this turn was transformed into something totally different from the original, so 'Aunt Assunta' is made to say: "Ma che cos'hai contro le pecore? Tuo nonno ci ha fatto i milioni! E i soldi puzzano sempre di qualcosa. Questa forse è la tua ultima occasione!" ("But why are you so against the sheep? Your grandfather made money hand over fist with it! And money always smells of something. This maybe is your last chance"). In Group B, some students attempted a similar 'transcreation' as a reply to Fran's previous mentioning that Jules has a foul breath. Sylvia, thus, is made to reply: "(1) Oh tesoro, ma è proprio grazie a persone come lui che il commercio delle mentine soprevvive. E' da apprezzare. Lo dico per te!" ("Oh Darling, but it's just thank to people like him that the peppermint business survives. That should be appreciated. I'm saying this for you!"). Apart from this peculiar instance (not totally original though, as it was inspired by the Italian TV version of this episode), all the other translation proposals in both groups were attempts at finding ways of rendering this turn into a pragmatically appropriate Italian equivalent. Students in Group A, for instance, considered the issue of equivalence since the beginning, as came across the very first allocution in this turn, "darling", conventionally translated into 'dubbese' as "tesoro", which is not a natural, spontaneous choice in everyday spoken Italian, as it normally sounds rather pretentious and artificial. Regrettably, such 'dubbese' choice is evident in most of the translation options made by Group-B students. Students in Group A, instead, having developed in their physical memory the experience of character embodiment, tried to find more naturally-occurring alternatives to this translation which could fit not only the pragmatic situation, but also the way a character like Sylvia would express herself in Italian, and thus they came up with a number of solutions from the more sympathetic towards Fran, as in "(2) Ma cara, se lo dico è perchè ti voglio bene." ("But darling, if I say so it's because I love you."), to the more intolerant towards her daughter's reluctance to marry Jules, implying various degrees of impatience disguised as indulgent advice, as in "(3) Cara mia, io te lo dico solo perchè ti voglio bene." ("My dear, I say this to you only because I love you."), and in "(4) Oh. Bella mia, ti ho detto così perché ti voglio bene." ("Oh. My darling, I told you so because I love you."), up to the recommendation disclosing a repressed irritation, as in: "(1) Oh. Senti, Cocca! Te lo dico per il bene tuo." ("Oh. Listen, poppet! I say this to you for your own good"). Also the derogatory epithet "glorified claning girl", by which Sylvia defines Fran, caused quandaries in both groups on how to render it equivalently and humorously in the Italian dubbing translation. Students in Group A found semantically and pragmatically equivalent solutions which could still retain a comic effect and fit, at the same time, the lip-synch time span, such as: "(1) Tu sei solo una servetta montata / che si dà arie" ("You're just a swollen-headed servant girl / who gives herself airs"), "(2) Sei solo una ragazza delle pulizie ben tirata su." ("You're just a well-groomed clearing girl"), "(3) (7) In fondo sei soltanto una cameriera abbellita / tirata a lucido", ("After all you're just an embellished / a natty housemaid"). Other solutions, instead, though effective, do not fit the timing allowed by the moving image, as in: "(4) Sei una donna delle pulizie che si sforza di essere signorile" ("You're a cleaner who makes every effort to be ladylike"), "(5) Sei solo un po' più di una donna delle pulizie" ("You're just a little more than a cleaner"), "(6) Tu sei solo una donna delle pulizie esaltata che cerca di essere altro" ("You're just a cleaner who tries to be somebody else"). Group-B students also produced translation solutions to this epithet, but with less convincing effects. For instance, in order to respect the lip-synch time span, some of them gave up the possibility of finding a pragmatic and comic equivalent in Italian and translated it just as "(2) (4) (6) (7) (10) (11) (18) Sei una nota / (così) bella / appariscente / esaltata / stupenda / magnifica donna delle pulizie." ("You are a popular / [so] beautiful / flashy / hot-headed / stupendous / magnificent cleaner"). Other 'creative' alternatives advanced in this group aimed at disambiguating too much what Sylvia meant in disparaging her daughter, thus diminishing the comic effect, such as "(3) Ricorda che hai una certa età." ("Remember that you're getting on in years"), "(14) Hai solo questo magnifico lavoro da tata." ("You've only got this wonderful job as a nanny"), "(16) Ricordati che sei solo una governante / una tata." ("Remember that you're just a governess / nanny"), "(15) sei una colf D.O.C." ("You're a quality help"). Other options in this same group were stilted literal renderings or obvious mistranslations, such as: "(5) Tu sei una ragazza delle pulizie fatta sembrare più importante" ("You're a cleaning girl made to appear more important [than she is]"), and "(8) Tu sei una ragazza pura" ("You're a pure girl"), "(9) Sei un'ottima padrona di casa" ("You're an excellent lady of the house"), "(12) Sei una ragazza delle pulizie sollevata" ("You're an uplifted cleaning girl"), "(13) Tu sei una contessina mancata" ("You're a young countess manqué"), and "(17) Sei un'adorabile casalinga" ("You're an adorable housewife"), till translating "because I love you" said by a mother to a daughter into a declaration of romantic love, rather than of parental affection. Also the final comment (a covert threat, indeed): "This could be your last chance", had different realizations in each group—Group-A students converging on the more frequently used term 'occasione' ('opportunity', 'chance', not 'occasion'), whereas Group-B ones opting for various and not always equivalent renderings, such as the metaphorical and idiomatic ones: "(1) (9) Questa potrebbe essere la tua ultima spiaggia / la tua ultima carta da giocare /la tua ultima speranza" ("This could be your last resort / your final trump to play / your last hope").

Fran, apparently tamed by her mother's threats, replies submissively in turn [33]: "Oh, Ma, I didn't say no. I just said I'd think about it. Okay, I did." The Italian version for television totally dissociates what the characters say from their original turns, as illustrated in *4.3.2*, and therefore its realization into the target language will not be considered at this stage as relevant for the comparative analysis. Students in Group A offered translations that were formally and pragmatically equivalent to the original. This was also the case with students in Group B, though some of them showed again a tendency to add unnecessary extra words as emphasis, as in "(1) Ma io non ho detto proprio no" ("But I didn't say exactly no"), or in "(2) On mamma, non gli ho detto di no" ("Oh Mummy, I didn't say no to him"). And yet few other students in Group B produced misreadings, as in the rendering of "Okay, I did" as "(5) Okay, l'ho detto" ("Okay, I've said so") and "(7) Ma gli dirò di sì" ("But I'll say yes to him"). Sylvia's hopeful question asking for confirmation in turn [34], "You mean I do?", is almost unanimously translated by Group-A students into "(1) (2) Vuoi dire / Vuol dire che lo fai? / lo farai? / 'lo faccio'?" ("You mean that you do it? / you'll do it? / 'I do it'?"). In Group B, students did not agree on a few convergent solutions, in fact they tended as usual to disambiguate the character's implications, which are part of the comic construction, and offer their own interpretation, rather than an equivalent transaltion, as in: "(1) Vuoi dire, c'ho ripensato?" ("Do you mean, I've changed my mind?"), "(6) Allora ti sposi?" ("So, are you getting married?"), "(7) Vuoi dire che gli dirai di sì?" ("You mean you'll say yes to him?"), "(10) Vuoi dire che ce l'ho fatta a convincerti?" ("You mean that I've succeded in convincing you?"), "(12) Vuoi dire che dovrò..." ("You mean I have to..."), "(14) Dici sul serio?" ("Are you serious?"), "(17) Vuoi dire che posso?" ("You mean I can?"), "(18) Cosa, gli hai detto di sì?" ("What, did you say yes to him?"), "(19) È come penso io?" ("Have I thought the same thing?"). As Fran replies with a loud "Yeah" in turn [35], Sylvia lets out a sigh of relief in turn [36], "Oh". This quick exchange (containing both an Arousal pattern if viewed from Fran's stance as she is induced to capitulate to her mother's wish, and a Safety one if instead viewed from Sylvia's stance as she finally sees her daughter conform to her plans) is literally rendered into Italian by all students in Group A: "*Fran:* Sì! – *Sylvia:* Oh.", but variously translated by students in Group B. In this group, for instance, "yeah" was rendered into a typical 'dubbese' equivalent: "(1) Già!", but also into pragmatically improbable "(2) Certo!" ("Sure!"), "(4) (5) Esatto / Proprio"

("Exactly"), adding an unnecessary emphasis to Fran's reply, till disambiguating her implicature in "(3) Gli dirò di sì" ("I will say yes to him"). Even Sylvia's reply is rendered redundant by some students in Group B: "Oh, bene!" ("Oh, very well"). Fran's inviting her mother to 'kiss the bride', in turn [37], is even mistranslated into illogical Italian by one student in Group B: "(5) Mamma, puoi baciare la tua futura sposa!" ("Mummy, you may kiss your future wife!"). The onomatopoeic sounds produced by Fran and Sylvia as they kiss in turn [38], "Moi moi moi", are phonetically transcribed by students in Group A ("Muà! Muà! Muà!), whereas in Group B they are written in the original spelling, whereas, in 5 occurrences, onomotopoeias are oddly rendered into a conventional written cartoon form ("smack smack smack") neglecting the fact that this script is written to be spoken on stage. The alternative of "(3) Evvivaaaa!!!!" ("hurrah!!!") is obviously to be considered as a mistranslation.

At this point, Maxwell enters the kitchen and, in turn [39], addresses Fran by saying: "You know, Miss Fine, I think you're very wise not to rush into this. You're far too sensible a woman to marry a man -Ow!". In the version for the Italian television, this turn was translated almost literally: "Guardi, Francesca, penso che sia stata molto saggia a non prendere una decisione così affrettata. Lei è una donna troppo intelligente - Ohi!" ("Look, Francesca, I think you're very wise not to take a hasty decision. You're far too intelligent a woman – Ow!"). Students in both groups provided different but in all cases acceptable translation alternatives as for the first part {a} of this turn. The only difficulties in this part only concerned the use of allocutions in the way Maxwell addressed Fran, sometimes by using the informal second-person pronoun 'tu' and calling her by her first name, Fran, and some other times by employong the formal allocution 'lei', calling her as 'Signorina Fine' ('Miss Fine'). As seen before, there are also peculiar ways by which Maxwell addressed Fran in some of Group-B students, such as: "(8) Miss Finezza" ("Miss Finesse") and "(9) Splendida" ("Splendid"), which are just out-of-place mistranslations meant to be comic but actually casting characters outside their roles. Problems of equivalence and appropriateness, however, arose principally in part {b} of the turn, this being particularly due to the rendering of the adjective "sensible", which does not correspond to the Italian similar word 'sensibile', meaning 'sensitive'. In fact, this utterance (abruptly interrupted by Sylvia pricking Maxwell's bottom with a fork to prevent him making more comments that could induce Fran to change her mind) was rendered by students in Group A into pragmatically equivalent ways, as: "(1) (9) È (di gran lunga) una donna troppo previdente per sposare un uomo – Ohi!" ("You're [far too] provident a woman to amrry a man – Ow!"), "(6) (7) Lei è una donna troppo ragionevole / giudiziosa per sposare un uomo – Ohi!" ("You're a woman too reasonable / judicious [sensible] to marry a man – Ow!"), "(8) Lei è una donna molto prudente per decidere così di sposare uno – Ahi!" ("You're an over-cautious woman to decide this way to marry a – Ouch!"). The mistranslation of the adjective "sensible" into its Italian 'false friend' "sensibile" ("sensitive") yet represents the first choice for the majority of students in Group B. Furthermore, two students of the same group also produced three quite bizarre top-down mistranslations: "(7) Bisogna avere un certo coinvolgimento per sposare un uomo – Ahi!" ("It is necessary to feel a certain involvement to marry a man – Ouch!"), "(21) Non è ancora una donna così matura da poter sposare un uomo – Ahi!" ("You're still not such mature woman to marry a man – Ouch!"), and "(Le donne, si sa, diventano sensibili quando si tratta di sposarsi, beh!" ("Women, of course, become sensitive when getting married is involved, well!").

At Maxwell's exclamation of pain, Sylvia raises a bif fork from behind his back and, in turn [40], says: "Oh, I'm sorry. Did this fork accidentally puncture your tuchas?". This impersonal sentence, with the inanimate fork becoming the animate agent of the action, is turned into a first-person admission of non-deliberate agency in the Italian TV translation, as Sylvia/Aunt Assunta apologises: "Oh, quanto mi dispiace! Per caso non volendo le ho bucato una delle due guance posteriori?" ("Oh, I'm so sorry! Have I by chance accidentally punctured one of your rear cheeks?"). The impersonal structure of the utterance is kept by all the students in Group A, placing the 'fork' as the animate subject of the sentence performing the process of 'puncturing' Maxwell's 'tuchas'. These two words, actually, caused some discussion in this group as for how to render them in translation. 'Fork', in the related image, is not normal-size, but a very big one suddenly materialized in Sylvia's hand . For this reason, together with the common word "forchetta", also "forchettone" ("carving fork") appears in translation. As for the vulgar term "tuchas"—an Yiddish word originally standing for 'underneath' and entered the American English with the meaning of 'buttocks', 'butt', or 'ass'—Group-A students realized that it was impossible to find an equivalent in Italian that could retain the reference to Sylvia's Jewish background and so they opted for parallel terms with very different pragmatic implications, from the neutral and polite "fondoschena" ("posterior") and "didietro" ("backside"), to the childish term of endearment "sederino", up to the vulgar "chiappe" ("buttocks"). In all their translations, however, students in this group made Sylvia address Maxwell by the formal allocutory pronoun 'lei', marking the social distance between them despite the familiarity and the bodily proximity with which Sylvia interacts with Maxwell, even in quite physically aggressive ways, as in this case. In Group B, students instead moved freely from the informal allocutory pronoun 'tu' to the more formal 'lei' up to the very formal 'voi' by which Sylvia addresses Maxwell, as in (15). Also the apology clause "Oh, I'm sorry" finds an unusual realization in this group, deviating from the expected "mi dispiace" to be transferred from the English construction to the Italian as in "(8) sono spiacente". Problems of mistranslation were again present in this group: "fork", for instance, was in one case translated as "(4) forca" ("pitchfork") and, more generally, in their attempt to be 'creative', students sometimes deviated from the original sense and humour of the turn to produce translations such as "(7) Come ha potuto questa forchetta pungere accidentalmente questo sedere?" ("How could this fork puncture accidentally this behind?"), or the quite naughty remark: "(11) Non ho idea di come questa forchetta sia finita nelle sue chiappe!") ("I have no idea of how this fork has ended up in your buttocks!").

4.5.3 *Conclusions*

In this lengthy chapter, the analysis carried out on the sitcom *The Nanny* has been very extensive and detailed because it was meant to be fully illustrative of the application of the Acting Translator Model to the process of translating the cognitive and pragmatic dimensions of humour aimed at the dubbing practice. The work carried out by students in Group A, who experienced the three phases outlined in the Model, represents indeed an instance of dubbing translation meant as the acting translators' interactive process of 'transmediation' between two different sets of socio-cultural values, trying to negotiate between them by using 'natural occurring' instances of the target language without obliterating the socio-pragmatic peculiarities of the source language and culture. Indeed, the outcome of the comparative analysis between Group-A translations and the dubbing translation for the Italian TV has evidenced a higher frequency of cross-cultural 'natural' discourse equivalence in the patterns realized by Group-A students than in the 'official' dubbed patterns.

The chapters that follow will not be so analytically detailed as the present one, since they are meant just to be illustrative of some meaningful aspects of the enquiry that have not been dealt with so far. However, the translation of *The Nanny* script by a student taking part in the just-described translation workshop introduces a peculiar dubbing translation process of 'localization', or domestication, that shall be analyzed in the next chapter with reference to the sitcom *Roseanne*. In the translation that follows, the student rendered the original script into a South-Italian accent (namely, the Sicilian variety), diatopically different but diastratically similar to the sitcom characters' original Jewish one, without modifying the semantic and pragmatic meanings of the various dialogic turns—as it occurred, instead, in the version of *The Nanny* for the Italian TV. This is the result of such creative work (in the back-translation provided, the Sicilian accent has been retained following the phonetic-transcription conventions and the use of original lexical items typical of the well-known screenplay of Mafia movies, such as *The Godfather*):

The Nanny **(*La Tata*)** episode #304 *Dope Diamond*

A) Original English version:	***Italian dubbing translation:***	***Back-translation into English:***
[Int. Dining Room] *(Maxwell and his children are having supper)*	**[Int. Sala da pranzo]** *(Maxwell e i suoi figli stanno cenando)*	**[Int. Dining Room]** *(Maxwell and his children are having supper)*
[1] **MAXWELL:** Please, Sylvia, why - why don't you join us?	*[1]* **MAXWELL:** Prego, Rosalia, perché non si unisce a noi?	*[1]* **MAXWELL:** Please, Rosalia, why don't you join us?
[2] **SYLVIA: {a}** Oh, no. I just came over to see how Fran's date went. **{b}** Make like I'm not even here.	*[2]* **ROSALIA: {a}** Nno grazie, venuta sono solo per sapere come è andato ll'appuntamento di Carmela. **{b}** Fate come se non ci sono.	*[2]* **ROSALIA: {a}** Nno. I came over just to know how Carmela's ddate went. **{b}** Make like I'm not even here.
[3] **NILES:** Are you sure we can't offer you something?	*[3]* **NILES:** È proprio sicura che non possiamo offrirle qualcosa?.	*[3]* **NILES:** Are you quite sure we can't offer you something?
[4] **SYLVIA: {a}** Oh, no, thank you. I had a yoplait this morning around 10:30. **{b}** *(She takes a potato from Grace's dish)* Oh, such a big potato for such a little girl. **{c}** Look at the time. They must be having a ball. **{d}** I'm gonna go in the kitchen. I need a meat to wash this down with. *(Sylvia leaves the dining room)*	*[4]* **ROSALIA: {a}** Nno grazie, sono a ddieta. Ho mangiato un ccannolo questa mattina, verso le dieci e mmezzo. **{b}** *(Prende una patata dal piatto di Grace)* Minghia, una patata così grande per una bbambina così ppiccina! **{c}** Vediamo l'ora ... di sicuro stanno ballando. **{d}** Vado in cucina, ho proprio bbisogno di una bistecca per digerire lla patata. *(Rosalia esce dalla stanza)*	*[4]* **ROSALIA: {a}** Nno, grazie. I'm on diet. I ate a cannolo this morning around 10:30. **{b}** *(She takes a potato from Grace's dish)* Minghia [shit], a potato so big for a girl so piccina! **{c}** Let's see the time. They must be ddancing. **{d}** I'm gonna go in the kitchen. I really need a steak to digest the potato. *(Rosalia leaves the dining room)*
[5] **BRIGHTON: {a}** I don't know about you guys, but I like Jules, **{b}** and he has yet to beat me in chess.	*[5]* **BRIGHTON: {a}** Non so voi, ragazzi, ma a me piace Jules, **{b}** e non mi ha ancora battuto a scacchi.	*[5]* **BRIGHTON: {a}** I don't know about you guys, but I like Jules, **{b}** and he has yet to beat me in chess.
[6] **MAXWELL: {a}** Oh, God, Brighton, **{b}** he throws every game.	*[6]* **MAXWELL: {a}** Ma dai, Brighton, **{b}** ti lascia vincere ogni volta.	*[6]* **MAXWELL: {a}** Come on, Brighton, **{b}** he lets you win every time.
[7] **BRIGHTON:** Do you see how easy it is to bond?	*[7]* **BRIGHTON:** Vedi com'è facile farsi un amico?	*[7]* **BRIGHTON:** Do you see how easy it is to make friends?
[8] **MAXWELL: {a}** Well, I wouldn't get too attached to the bloke if I were you. **{b}** We all know Miss Fine's relationships eventually end in disaster.	*[8]* **MAXWELL: {a}** Beh, io non mi legherei troppo a quel tipo, se fossi in te. **{b}** Sappiamo tutti che le relazioni sentimentali della signorina Canicattì alla fine si rivelano un completo disastro.	*[8]* **MAXWELL: {a}** Well, I wouldn't get too attached to the bloke if I were you. **{b}** We all know Miss Canicattì's romantic relationships eventually end in complete disaster.
(Fran enters) *[9]* **FRAN:** He asked me to marry him.	*(Entra Carmela)* *[9]* **CARMELA:** Mi ha chiesto di sposarlo!	*(Carmela enters)* *[9]* **CARMELA:** He asked me to marry him!
[10] **NILES:** Right on the money as always, sir.	*[10]* **NILES:** Giunge proprio al momento giusto, come sempre, signore.	10] **NILES:** You arrive precisely at the right time, as always, sir.
[11] **BRIGHTON:** That is so cool, Fran. Congratulations.	*[11]* **BRIGHTON:** Sei forte, Carmy! Congratulazioni!	*[11]* **BRIGHTON:** You're so cool, Carmy! Congratulations!

[12] **FRAN:** **{a}** I know, I know. I can't believe it. I'm so excited. I couldn't eat a — **{b}** oh, kielbasa, sweet and sour cabbage. **{c}** *(To Niles)* Hit me again. **{d}** *(She takes a corn from Grace's dish)* Oh, such a big corn for such a little girl.	*[12]* **CARMELA:** **{a}** Sì, lo so. Non riesco proprio a crederci. Troppo emozionata sono. Non posso mangiare un — **{b}** minghia, cosa vedono i miei occhi, melanzane che annegano nel pecorino! **{c}** *(rivolta a Niles)* Mi volete tentare? **{d}** *(Prende una pannocchia dal piatto di Grace)* E che ci fa una pannocchia così grande con una bambina così piccina?	*[12]* **CARMELA:** **{a}** Yeah, I know. I just can't believe it. Too excited I am. I couldn't eat a — **{b}** minghia, what am I seeing with my own eyes, eggplants drowing in the pecorino cheese! **{c}** *(To Niles)*You want to tempt me? **{d}** *(She takes a corn from Grace's dish)* And what is it doing a corn so big with a girl so piccina?
[13] **MAXWELL:** He asked you to marry him?	*[13]* **MAXWELL:** Ti ha chiesto di sposarlo?!	*[13]* **MAXWELL:** He asked you to marry him?!
[14] **FRAN:** Uh-huh.	*[14]* **CARMELA:** Sicuro! Prima la verità dissi!	*[14]* **CARMELA:** Sure! Before the truth I said!
[15] **MAXWELL:** You've barely known the man for two weeks.	*[15]* **MAXWELL:** Conosci quel-l'uomo a malapena da due settimane.	*[15]* **MAXWELL:** You've barely known the man for two weeks.
[16] **FRAN:** What? You think it's so hard to believe a man would fall in love with me that fast?	*[16]* **CARMELA:** Cosa? Pensi che così difficile è per un uomo innamorarsi della sottoscritta in così poco tempo?	*[16]* **CARMELA:** : What? You think that so hard it is for a man to fall in love with me the undersigned in such a little time?
[17] **GRACE:** Yeah. Todd and I knew each other three minutes before I got a Pudding-Pack right in the eye.	*[17]* **GRACE:** Giusto, Todd e io ci conoscevamo solo da tre minuti prima che prendessi il suo budino in faccia.	*[17]* **GRACE:** Right. Todd and I knew each other three minutes before I got his pudding right in the face.
[18] **FRAN:** There you go.	*[18]* **CARMELA:** Ecco la testimonianza!	*[18]* **CARMELA:** Here is the testimony!
[19] **MAXWELL:** **{a}** You know nothing about this man. **{b}** All right, so he's a doctor. Is he a specialist?	*[19]* **MAXWELL:** **{a}** Non sai nulla di quest'uomo! **{b}** Sai soltanto che è un dottore. È uno specialista?	*[19]* **MAXWELL:** **{a}** You know nothing about this man! **{b}** You only know he's a doctor. Is he a specialist?
[20] **FRAN:** You ain't just whistling "Dixie," baby.	*[20]* **CARMELA:** Puoi dirlo bbene, picciotto!	*[20]* **CARMELA:** You can say that again, picciotto!
[21] **MAXWELL:** Oh, God.	*[21]* **MAXWELL:** Oh, mio Dio!	*[21]* **MAXWELL:** Oh, my God!
[22] **MAGGIE:** **{a}** Oh, this is so exciting. **{b}** So can I be a bridesmaid?	*[22]* **MAGGIE:** **{a}** Wow, è così eccitante! **{b}** Posso farti da damigella d'onore?	*[22]* **MAGGIE:** **{a}** Wow, this is so exciting! **{b}** So can I be your bridesmaid?
(Sylvia enters behind Fran) *[23]* **FRAN:** **{a}** I know the doctor asked me to marry him, but I didn't say yes. **{b}** This is delicious.	*(Rosalia entra alle spalle di Carmela)* *[23]* **CARMELA:** **{a}** Ehi, un momento, il dottore mi chiese di sposarlo, ma io ho non dissi di sì. **{b}** Mmm, buono!	*(Rosalia enters behind Carmela)* *[23]* **CARMELA:** **{a}** Hey, one moment, the doctor asked me to marry him, but I ddidn't say yes. **{b}** Mmm, buono!
(Sylvia falls to the floor behind Fran) *[24]* **SYLVIA:** Why don't you grab a knife and stick it straight through my heart.	*(Rosalia cade al suolo alle spalle di Carmela)* *[24]* **ROSALIA:** Perché non prendesti una zappa e mme la conficcasti dritta nel cuore?	*(Rosalia falls to the floor behind Carmela)* *[24]* **ROSALIA:** Why ddidn't you grab a hoe and stuck it straight through my heart?
25] **FRAN:** **{a}** *(hinting at Grace)* That was great. She sounded just like - Ma! **{b}** Ma ... Ma, let go of my ankle.	*[25]* **CARMELA:** **{a}** *(riferendosi a Grace)* Però ... sembrava proprio la voce di — **{b}** Mamma! Ma, lla caviglia lasciami!	*[25]* **CARMELA:** **{a}** *(hinting at Grace)* Hey ... it sounded just like the voice of - Mamma! **{b}** Ma, let go of my ankle!

[[26] **SYLVIA:** You better run.	*[26]* **ROSALIA:** Se corri è meglio!	*[26]* **ROSALIA:** If you run it's better!
(Fran runs around the table chased by Sylvia) *[27]* **FRAN:** Brighton, is she taking off her shoe?	*Carmela corre intorno al tavolo inseguita da Rosalia)* *[27]* **CARMELA:** Braitenne, lla scarpa si sta togliendo?	*(Carmela runs around the table chased by Rosalia)* *[27]* **CARMELA:** Brightenne, the shoe is she taking off?
[28] **BRIGHTON:** No. But she's gonna hurl the corn.	*[28]* **BRIGHTON:** No, ma sta per lanciarti la pannocchia.	*[28]* **BRIGHTON:** No. But she's gonna hurl the corn against you.
[Int. Kitchen]	**[Int. Cucina]**	**[Int. Kitchen]**
[29] **FRAN:** Oy, oy, oy, oy. Ma, put down the vegetable and no one gets hurt.	*[29]* **CARMELA:** Oh oh oh oh, Mamma, metti giù quell'ortaggio e nessuno si fa male.	*[29]* **CARMELA:** Oh, oh, oh, oh. Mamma, put down that vegetable and no one gets hurt.
[30] **SYLVIA:** **{a}** All right. Help me to understand which was the biggest turnoff — **{b}** the fact that Jules was gorgeous, rich, or a doctor?	*[30]* **ROSALIA:** **{a}** Va bbene, ma capire voglio che cosa ti ha ammosciato — **{b}** il fatto che è bellissimo, ricco, o che è un dottore?	*[30]* **ROSALIA:** **{a}** All right. But understand I want, what dampened you — **{b}** the fact that he is gorgeous, rich, or that he's a doctor?
[31] **FRAN:** Did I mention he was Jewish?	*[31]* **CARMELA:** Al pecorino devo rinunciare! Ti dissi che allergico è ai latticini?	*[31]* **CARMELA:** The pecorino cheese I have to give up! Ddid I tell you that he's allergic to milk products?
[32] **SYLVIA:** **{a}** Oh. Darling, I only say this because I love you. **{b}** You're a glorified cleaning girl. **{c}** This could be your last chance.	*[32]* **ROSALIA:** **{a}** Oh, Carmela. Ti dissi questo perché io ti voglio bbene. **{b}** Tu sei una pastorella abbellita. **{c}** Questa può essere lla tua ultima occasione.	*[32]* **ROSALIA:** **{a}** Oh. Carmela, I said this to you because I love you. **{b}** You're an embellished young shepherdess. **{c}** This can be your last chance.
[33] **FRAN:** **{a}** Oh, Ma, I didn't say no. **{b}** I just said I'd think about it. **{c}** Okay, I did.	*[33]* **CARMELA:** **{a}** Oh, Mamma, non gli ho ddetto di no. **{b}** Ho ssolo detto che ci pensavo. **{c}** Okkey, llo fatto.	*[33]* **CARMELA:** **{a}** Oh, Mamma, I ddidn't say no. **{b}** I just ssaid I'd think about it. **{c}** Okay, I ddid.
[34] **SYLVIA:** You mean I do?	*[34]* **ROSALIA:** Vuoi dire che llo sposi?	*[34]* **ROSALIA:** You mean you'll marry him?
[35] **FRAN:** Yeah.	*[35]* **CARMELA:** Sicuro!	*[35]* **CARMELA:** Sure!
[36] **SYLVIA:** Oh.	*[36]* **ROSALIA:** Oh.	*[36]* **ROSALIA:** Oh.
[37] **FRAN:** Ma, you may kiss the bride.	*[37]* **CARMELA:** Mamma, puoi baciare la sposa!	*[37]* **CARMELA:** Mamma, you may kiss the bride!
[38] **FRAN/SYLVIA:** Moi! Moi! Moi! Moi! Moi!	*[38]* **CARMELA/ROSALIA:** Muà, muà, muà, muà.	*[38]* **CARMELA/ROSALIA:** Moi moi moi moi.
(Maxwell enters the kitchen) *[39]* **MAXWELL:** **{a}** You know, Miss Fine, I think you're very wise not to rush into this. **{b}** You're far too sensible a woman to marry a man - Ow!	*(Maxwell entra in cucina)* *[39]* **MAXWELL:** **{a}** Sa, signorina Canicattì, penso che sia saggio non affrettarsi in questo genere di cose. **{b}** Lei è una donna molto intelligente per sposare un uomo — Ow!	*(Maxwell enters the kitchen)* *[39]* **MAXWELL:** **{a}** You know, Miss Canicattì, I think it's very wise not to rush into this kind of things. **{b}** You're a too intelligent woman to marry a man - Ow!
[40] **SYLVIA:** **{a}** Oh, I'm sorry. **{b}** Did this fork accidentally puncture your tuchas?	*[40]* **ROSALIA:** **{a}** Oh, mmi scusasse. **{b}** Forse questa forchetta ha punto per caso il suo ddiddietro?	*[40]* **ROSALIA:** **{a}** Oh, I'm ssorry. **{b}** Maybe this fork accidentally punctured your bbehind?

Though representing an interesting instance of humorous domestication process, this translation typology has indeed particular flaws that deserve a specific enquiry—as it will be illustrated in the next chapter with reference to the American sitcoms *Roseanne* and *Dharma & Greg*.

Chapter 5

Dubbing Translation as 'Product Localization and Neutralization': Applying the Appraisal Framework to a Sitcom-Humour Analysis of *Roseanne* and *Dharma & Greg* Source and Target Scripts

5.1 Culturally-marked Comic Script and its 'Domesticated' Translation in *Roseanne* Sitcom

5.1.1 *Displacing* Roseanne *sitcom into a target-culture context*

In this chapter two scripts from the *Roseanne* and *Dharma & Greg* sitcoms shall be analyzed in both their original and translated versions. The Appraisal Framework (Martin and White 2005) will be applied to the conversation analysis in order to investigate how humorous language is constructed to create sitcom characters and to shape their stances and interpersonal positionings. The dubbing translations for the Italian television shall be examined in parallel with the original versions of the selected sitcom scripts, and then in comparison with the dubbing translations produced by the students in Group A (i.e., the 'acting translators') and in the 'control' Group B.

The first American sitcom to be analyzed in this chapter is *Roseanne*, which was produced by Carsey and Werner and aired from 1988 to 1997 on ABC with the title role conceived and played by the famous stand-up comedian Roseanne Barr—who gave her own name to the main character. The sitcom is about an economically-disadvantaged working-class family, the Conners, living in a small town in Illinois. The 'family boss' bossing all the other family members with caustic witticism and sarcastic humour is the mother, Roseanne, an overweight and yet self-assured woman who struggles to scrape a living while her husband Dan (played by the likewise overweight actor John Goodman) frequently changes jobs as he is frequently fired. The three Conner children represent three different typologies of adolescent kids: the eldest daughter Becky is a rebel girl attracted by boys and fashion, Darlene, the middle daughter, is a kind of tomboy teenager, cheeky and interested in male sports. D.J. is a little boy, indeed a child at the beginning of the sitcom, developing into a typical teenage kid. Other important components of the family are

Roseanne's muddled-up sister Jackie and, to a lesser extent, Roseanne's nutty mother Bev. Although apparently this sitcom seems to conform to the standard family-life television comedy, actually it is not so, as the Conner family is almost atypical, always having to cope with problems related to some of the most serious issues in today's western society, from drug and alcohol addiction to poverty, unemployment, teenage rebellion against parental authority, teenage pregnancy, abortion, birth control, sexual dysfunction, mental and physical illness, breast surgery, domestic abuse, and discrimination due to race, homosexuality, social class and obesity. The novelty of this sitcom, indeed, is precisely to be found in turning into triggers for comic effect such huge problems which, what is more, eventually come to affect the components of the same family. Furthermore, the fact that the Conner family is dominated by a very strong mother figure introduces a feminist stance in the whole sitcom, with Roseanne who even decides to enlarge her family by adopting Darlene's family-abused boyfriend David. Being a strong character, Roseanne is also judgmental about everything that happens around her, fiercely trying to redirect people's actions and situations to fit her plans and values. And it is exactly this ongoing conflict between strong and weak characters that determines the Arousal/Safety pattern of humour in this turn-of-the-century American sitcom.

The dubbing translation strategy adopted in *Roseanne* for the Italian television (i.e., for one of Mediaset commercial channels) is evident since the rendering of its title into *Pappa e Ciccia*, an idiomatic stock phrase metaphorically corresponding in meaning to being 'hand in glove', and whose literal translation into Italian—'pap and fat'—recalls the quite corpulent build of the main characters who, as the stock phrase suggests, are also a very close family. This translation strategy, therefore—as evident from the title—is aimed at a 'domestication' of the culturally-marked characteristics of this sitcom. As such, it consists first of all, of a top-down 'pragmalinguistic transfer' of a pseudo Neapolitan variation of Italian (traditionally adopted in telling disparaging jokes set in this socio-economically depressed part of South Italy) to the dubbing translation of the original working-class Illinois pragmalect spoken by the sitcom characters. The outcome is that such diatopic and diastratic dislocations towards the target Italian culture frequently alter the original socio-culturally marked humour of the sitcom because, although the rendering of the various dialogic turns into such Neapolitan variation is often semantically and syntactically equivalent, it is not so pragmatically because the socio-cultural, experiential and discursive implications are obviously different (cf. Anderman and Dìaz-Cintas 2009). This lack of pragmatic equivalence can indeed produce a 'pragmalinguistic failure' (Thomas 1983) in the Italian audience's reception processes—namely, a displacing sense of experiencing a socio-cultural familiarity with the language of the dubbed sitcom and, at the same time, a situational estrangement due to the incongruence of such Italian variation with the visual 'socio-semiotic' context of the sitcom. The idea—conceived by the same Italian producers of *The Nanny / La Tata*—was once again to represent a family of Italian immigrants who, this time, were not from Ciociaria, but from another southern area, Campania, the region where Naples is located. Indeed, the Neapolitan accent has always been associated in the Italian culture with comic theatre (from Eduardo De Filippo's plays set in Naples to Massimo Troisi's more recent comedy pieces) and, more generally, with comedians who have no scruples in using their native accent—or even imitating such accent (with the unnatural effects to be found also in *Roseanne*)—to denigrate their local culture and the general state of poverty of people living in that area just to make audience laugh at their ignorance and disgrace (and, what is worse, make economic profit out of it). Strangely enough, as in *The Nanny,* also in this sitcom Roseanne's mother, Bev, is turned into the character of her aunt, Palmira, although Bev is a marginal character in this comedy and her behaviour has nothing so indecorous as to be compared to Fran's mother, Sylvia, turned into Aunt Assunta in the Italian dubbed version (presumably because in the nineties, in Italy, an undignified character like Sylvia's was deemed to be unacceptable as a 'mother' character). The very character of Roseanne must have represented a challenge—a risky business indeed—for the Italian script adaptors trying to accommodate her original cues to the culture of the implied target audience. Roseanne, in fact, contradicts the deeply-rooted Italian stereotype of the mother who is an angelic, beautiful, sweet and caring figure, as she is rather an aggressive, apparently unmotherly woman, often harsh in her cynical criticism against the members of her own family—from which, however, a deep compassion transpires. In the Italian dubbed version, such strong personality was rendered linguistically through the Neapolitan accent in order to emphasize the character's sarcastic tone by associating it with the stereotypical figure of the vehement and fiery Neapolitan woman, a common humorous character in the traditional Italian comedy and conventionally accepted by the Italian audience as part of their comic culture. The process of adaptation in the Italian version of this sitcom involves also the names of Roseanne's original family members migrating to the US from Italy: thus, not only has Bev, her mother, turned into Palmira, but also Roseanne is turned into Annarò (Annarosa), or Rosy, and her sister's name, Jackie, into Giacomì (Giacomina). This linguistic adaptation, as mentioned before, has also economic motivations: both Roseanne and Jackie, together with Roseanne's husband Dan, represent the very stereotypes of the factory workers who, eventually, lose their job to become day labourers for a while and then unemployed – thus forced to reinvent their jobs by becoming self-employed before failing again. This situation of job insecurity is very close to the precarious economic situation of people living in the depressed area of Naples, where Roseanne's family is made to originate in the Italian version of the sitcom. This also explains the choice of the Neapolitan accent which is strictly connected with the typical Neapolitan humour, traditionally characterized by an attempt at defusing dramatic and hopeless socio-economic situations through sarcastic witticism but also a sad sense of fatalism. Moreover, the dubbing translators' main concern in this Italian version of the sitcom seems to be trying to overcome the cultural differences that the Italian audience may perceive between the parallel source and target situational contexts, since a working-class family of the American Midwest acts and reacts (proxemically as well as prosodically) in ways that are different from the corresponding Italian ones and this is assumed to induce in the audience a sense of cultural estrangement and psychological distance from the sitcom humour. This explains the choice of 'domesticating' it by 'localizing' not only the characters' diatopic and diastratic accent, but also their pragmatic expression filtered through a different phonetic and prosodic communicative code. In this way, the main sitcom characters are adapted to discursive modes of expression that are assumed to be socio-culturally consistent with the target audience's schemata. The translation strategy adopted in cases like this by the dubbing translators consists in rendering the effects that the source text produces on the translator's sensibility into stylistically equivalent forms that are consonant with his/her own culture. This would allow the translator to 'appropriate' the source text authenticating it through sociolinguistic and cultural experiences that are not exactly those conveyed by the original script but that are nevertheless deemed to be parallel and equivalent to them, though they belong to the translator's own cultural and experiential background. Such exclusively top-down strategy, however, only relies upon the translator's schemata through which s/he assigns meanings to every aspect of reality and, in this specific case, to every aspect of the 'sitcom reality', thus often misrepresenting it.

5.1.2 *Instances of target-culture dislocations*

A case in point can be considered the episode #919 from *Roseanne* entitled *Springtime for David*. In it, David—Darlene's boyfriend adopted by the Conner family—finds a job in an amusement park, the Edelweiss Gardens, a sort of Disneyworld adapted to a Heidi-like Swiss setting. In one of the first scenes of this episode, Roseanne, her sister Jackie and Dan accompany David to the park on the day he has to take up his job and are welcomed by David's roommate with an apparently enthusiastic, yet affected tone: "Oh, well, hi everyone! It's great to have you here," but immediately afterwards he warns—indeed, intimidates—them: "but you should know, in the future, there are no visitors allowed in the men's residence". To this, Roseanne reacts by redirecting her sarcasm at David, not at his roommate, as expected, by replying disparagingly: "Oh, well, you don't have to worry about that, David's not very popular." In the Italian translation, Roseanne's sarcasm is defused and not directly addressed to David, which makes her cue almost obscure. This is the exchange between the roommate and Roseanne rendered into its Italian TV version: "*Roommate:* Sono felice di conoscervi. Felice e onorato. Ma in avvenire ricorda che ai visitatori non è concesso l'ingresso in stanza." (Back-translation: "I'm delighted to meet you. Delighted and honoured. But in the future remember that to visitors admission in the residence is not allowed")—*Roseanne:* "Uh, non ti preoccupare. Lo abbiamo già visto abbastanza negli ultimi anni." ("Uh, don't worry about that. We've already seen enough of it over the last years"). Finally, the advice Roseanne gives David before parting—though apparently playful because she does not want to embarrass him before a stranger with her warning—contains the gloomy forecast of what she feels his experience is going to be: "Uh ... well, remember to write us everyday. And, uh ... don't forget to include a photo of yourself holding up that day's newspaper." This humorous cue based on the incongruity between the 'residential job' schema and the 'hostage's prison' one becomes even more marked in the version for the Italian TV, with an explicit reference to the Southern-Italy criminal practice of sending pictures of Mafia hostages holding a newspaper with its date in the foreground: "Allora ciao. Mi raccomando, ricordati di scriverci tutti i giorni e con le lettere mandaci sempre una tua foto con il quotidiano in mano e metti la data bene in primo piano." ("Well, bye. Mind you don't forget to write us every day, and with the letters always send us a picture of yours with the newspaper in your hand and put its date quite in the foreground"). A similar trigger for the translator to render an original sitcom cue into a hint to a stereotypical Italian criminal behaviour is represented, in the same episode, by Roseanne pushing Dan, her husband, who is busy filling job-application forms, to find less legal ways to get a job. If this cue is seen within the original context of the sitcom, though quite harsh because expressed through an imperative, it may appear just as one of Roseanne's spiteful, yet candid jokes: "Hey, I heard something on the news about these government contractors getting all these kickbacks, y'know. Find out how that works." But if this cue is set in the new context of Italian immigrants coming from a traditional Mafia area, Annarò's remark may appear, to the Italian audience, not so much as a joke, but rather as a cheery—yet sly—suggestion to be taken seriously, as in the following translation for the Italian television: "Oggi al telegiornale dicevano che alcuni appaltatori statali stanno prendendo delle grosse tangenti. Hai capito? Perchè non vedi come funziona?" ("Today, on the news, they said that some government contractors are getting big kickbacks. Do you understand? Why don't you find out how that works?").

But the Conners' generosity, despite their indigence, is however out of question, as evident in the scene from the same episode when Roseanne is worried about David's economic situation—which induced him to accept a dehumanizing job at the Edelweiss Gardens—and so she suggests Dan that they should help him, but her husband replies: "No, we gotta let go. He's over eighteen and remember, as much as we love David, he's not really our son." To which Roseanne remarks: "Well, not according to our last tax returns." In the dubbed version, the pragmatic equivalence has been adapted to the Italian idiomatic expressions and socio-cultural references: "*Dan:* No, dobbiamo lasciarlo in pace. E' maggiorenne e anche se gli vogliamo bene lui non è nostro figlio." —"*Annarò:* Però nella dichiarazione dei redditi risulta a carico." ("*Dan:* No, we must leave him in peace. He is of age and even though we love him, he's not our son."—"*Annarò:* But in the income-tax return he appears to be dependent on us."). Also Roseanne's deep sense of individual liberty and freedom of speech, movement and thought, becomes evident when she returns to the Edelweiss Gardens to rescue David, who is morally subjugated by the dictatorial policy of the entertainment park where he works. So she tries to stir him up by saying: "Wake up, David. This place wants to be Disney World, but it's just some creepy fascist copy. I mean, today, it's 'Hi, I'm Hans the Hare, welcome to the park', and tomorrow it's 'I was only following orders'". In the translation for the Italian TV, the reference to Fascism as a totalitarian regime strangely disappears (maybe not to 'hurt' the political sensibility of some 'extreme right-wing' components of the audience, or just not to make reference to a quite painful period of the Italian history) to be replaced with the non-equivalent reference to the concentration camps of the Nazi period, where the consequence was not so simply a loss of freedom, but indeed the very loss of life—which is an almost inappropriate simile in this case in point: "Che aspetti a svegliarti. Questo posto vorrebbe essere Disney World ma assomiglia sempre più ad un campo di concentramento. Oggi dici 'Ciao, sono Hans la lepre, benvenuti'. E domani dirai 'Io stavo solo eseguendo gli ordini'." ("What are you waiting for to wake up? This place would like to be Disney World, but it looks more and more like a concentration camp. Today you say 'Hi, I'm Hans the hare, welcome. And tomorrow you'll say 'I was just carrying out orders'."). Then, Roseanne's outburst of pride at being a free citizen of the United States of America suddenly follows like an election address to the Nation, as she fiercely attacks with her stern sarcasm the park managers who train young employers, like David, to become slaves of a degrading code of behaviour imposed by their job: "You say they have freedom. But do they really? Are they free, after work, to go sit and have a beer, and trash their boss, like you can on any other job? No! And yet this place claims to represent what America stands for. Well, my America stands for more than five dollars to park, thirty dollars to get in and five dollars tasteless bunny-shaped hamburgers. Now, if you excuse us, David and I are going get in my crappy car, drive along that polluted river, where we could get car jacked, or forced off the road by a drunk, pull up in front of our house and run in before we are robbed. Because that, Mister, is my America. And I thank God we're free to enjoy it." The translated version of this speech for the Italian TV is not exactly equivalent from both semantic and, thus, pragmatic perspectives. In it, Annarò is made to say: "Lei sostiene che i suoi impiegati sono liberi. Ma di quale libertà parla? Avanti, sono forse liberi, dopo il lavoro, di andarsi a bere una birra e di sparlare del capo come si fa negli altri posti di lavoro? No! E avete la faccia tosta di dire che in questo posto regnano la libertà e i valori dell'America? L'America dove io ho deciso di vivere vale molto più dei cinque dollari per il parcheggio, dei trenta dollari per l'ingresso e dei cinque dollari per uno schifoso hamburger fatto a forma di lepre. Adesso, col vostro permesso, noi togliamo il disturbo, saliremo sulla mia macchina scassata e andremo a casa passando vicino a un fiume inquinato. Forse incontreremo due drogati, sbanderemo per colpa di un ubriaco e speriamo di arrivare a casa prima di venire derubati. Però, caro signore, è questa la mia America. E ringrazio il cielo di potermela godere così com'è." ("You claim that your employees are free. But what freedom are you talking about? Come on, are they free, after work, to go and have a beer and backbite their boss, as it's common in the other workplaces? No! And you have the cheek to say that in this place freedom and the American values reign!? The America where I decided to live is worth much more than the five dollars for a parking place, the thirty dollars for admittance and the five dollars for a yucky hare-shaped hamburger. Now, with your permission, we're going to be off, we're going to get in my beat-up car and go home driving along a polluted river. Maybe we'll run into a couple of drug-addicts, we'll skid because of a drunk and let's hope we come home before we are robbed. Yet, dear sir, this is my America. And I thank heavens I can enjoy it as it is."). In this translation it is clear that some crucial points have been modified: first of all, the employers Roseanne blames are not indirectly addressed as in the original script ("And yet this place claims to represent what America stands for."), but they are directly attacked by means of a second-person address term (in back-translation: "And you have the cheek to say that in this place freedom and the American values reign?"). Then, whereas in the original version Roseanne makes reference to "my America", in the translated version, the immigrant Annarò crucially refers to "the America where I decided to live". From this point on, all her hints at the decayed state of America acquire, in the Italian version, a baffling additional meaning as Annarò may appear to find in such a squalor a familiar parallel with the degraded social and environmental situation so endemically typical of the southern area of Italy she comes from, namely, Campania, the region of Naples, a town with everlasting criminality and uncollected-rubbish problems. Moreover, not all the references correspond in translation. For instance, the clause "where we could be car jacked", an American slang expression meaning 'to be mugged while still in the car', has been misinterpreted as a reference to the popular meaning of the verb phrase 'to jack (oneself) up', meaning 'to be on drugs'. Hence the mistranslation into "we'll run into a couple of drug-addicts", which is really out of place in a sitcom that in a very liberal and non-judgmental way faces up to serious social problems, one of which being crucially drug-addiction. Finally, in Roseanne's reference to America, the addition in the translated version of "And I thank heavens I can enjoy it *as it is.* [emphasis added]") (thus diverging from the original "And I thank God we're free to enjoy it"), implies that she would accept—and indeed approve of—all such social evils of her nation unconditionally—which is not the case with the original version and, more specifically, with Roseanne continuously struggling against the social and moral problems of her country.

In the last part of this same episode, there is another monologue by Roseanne where the addition of new phrases in the Italian translation makes a critical difference in terms of semantic and pragmatic equivalence with the original version. In it, Roseanne warns David: "Let me tell you a little something about Edelweiss Gardens. It's mediocre food and mediocre fun, at best. And you know why I know that, David? Because I am an expert on what is mediocre." With this, Roseanne clearly means to say that she can recognize and judge mediocrity—but here is the Italian translation: "E poi ti voglio dire qualcosa che non sai su Edelweiss Gardens. E' mediocre. Il cibo e il divertimento sono mediocri. E sai come faccio a saperlo? Perché so riconoscere la mediocrità. *E la so riconoscere perché sono una mediocre anch'io.* [emphasis added]" ("And then I want to tell you something you don't know about Edelweiss Gardens, It's mediocre. Food and fun are mediocre. And do you know how I know that? Because I know how to recognize mediocrity. *And I know how to recognize it because I'm mediocre too.*"). Such gratuitous self-disparaging remark is not in line with the self-confident, assertive character of Roseanne who would never, ever use such derogatory expressions to refer to herself. On the contrary, the illocutionary claim in her original cue seems to be exactly the opposite, namely, from the standpoint of her self-acknowledged moral superiority, and despite her low status in society, Roseanne knows very well how to recognize what is ethically and functionally mediocre. This sense of proletarian superiority in passing judgement on everyone and everything is even more emphasized in Roseanne by the lower-class, Midwest variety of English she uses, characterized, for instance, by phoneme elisions (as in "I bought 'em", "We're eating 'em", "y'kow", "That'd be darn well worth it") and non-standard syntactic structures (as in "I think you better just calm down!", "You sure you just don't want to...", "I thought I was don filling out forms"). In the Italian version, instead, Annarò's self-denigration seems to be even emphasized by the diatopic and diastratic quality of her Neapolitan variety, characterized, for instance, by the inappropriate use of verbs, such as 'tenere' ('to keep') instead of 'avere' ('to have') as in the expression 'avere famiglia' (to have a family', namely, 'to have a wife and children') turned into 'tenere famiglia' ('to keep a family'), or the interjection 'mò', literally meaning 'now' and used instead of 'well' when a change of topic is introduced. But more than the structural characteristics of this variety, the very phonological quality of the Neapolitan accent represents the linguistic feature that conventionally triggers in comedy audiences a negative judgement of value attributed to its speakers. Such a phonological quality is marked by wide open-indeed, gaping—vowel sounds (/æ/ and /o/ in particular), and a fricative /ʃ/ consonant sound replacing the sibilant /s/—a slackened accent traditionally associated to a kind of derogatory humour directed against southern Italian people represented—through the 'chewing' sound of their voice—as lazy, sly and, ultimately, shifty and dishonest.

This incongruence between the original assertive, judgmental character of Roseanne and its rendering into the dubbing translation for the Italian television can be indeed investigated in parallel by applying the Appraisal Framework (Martin and White 2005) to the analysis of a scene from the sitcom, where another 'revelation plot' is featured.

5.2 Applying the Appraisal Framework to the Analysis of *Roseanne* Sitcom

5.2.1 *Evaluative use of language in* Roseanne *dialogic situations*

The application of the Appraisal Framework (*ibidem*) to the dialogic analysis of a script from this specific sitcom, *Roseanne*, can be very useful as this is an approach aimed at investigating how language is employed by speakers to express their stances, establish relationships with other participants in an interaction and, ultimately, construct their own identities through discourse. Indeed, this last point becomes crucial when the creation of sitcom characters' identities through language is involved, as it entails that their peculiar attitudes, judgements and emotional responses—either explicitly expressed or implicitly assumed—are all constructed linguistically through precise discourse choices that must also involve the planning of a comic effect in accordance with the personality of such sitcom characters.

Being a 'judgmental character', Roseanne lends herself to being examined through the application of this analytical framework as it would enquire into the linguistic ways by which she passes judgements on the other sitcom characters as well as on the critical situations they all eventually find themselves involved in. Indeed, the very word 'Appraisal' suggests an analytical focus on the evaluative use of language in dialogic situations during which the participants' value stances may be accepted by other participants, or rejected, or—as it happens in most cases—negotiated. In fictional situations dialogically constructed to produce a comic effect, the expression of such stances takes place on two incongruent schematic dimensions, i.e., one which is expected and another one that is instead unexpected, the latter triggering the audience's humorous response. In socially-grounded sitcoms, such as *Roseanne*, the comic effect often coincides with an overt/covert critique of socio-cultural and ethical problems. This entails that, although the 'Arousal/Safety' pattern is still very frequent, the language of humour typically involves a 'Disparagement' pattern through which negative judgmental positionings are expressed, usually through a sarcastic tone, as if disparagement was a praise. What is more, usually disparagement occurs when characters are shown to be on the verge of a 'fall' into an even more problematic state, from which they eventually manage to escape. In this sense, therefore, the sitcom characters' 'attitudinal positioning' becomes crucial in the analysis. This is especially true when they behave as Roseanne does, for her actual 'blaming' and 'praising' do make the difference in the development of the sitcom action and, as a consequence, in the actions and reactions of the other characters who are conditioned by her judgement – as it is not usually expressed as an individual stance, but rather as a 'community concern' she gives voice to. In this respect, the use of hedging, boosting, modality, evidentiality represents a discourse strategy employed by the characters of this sitcom to try to 'manage' or 'negotiate' Roseanne's judgments when they disagree with them. In such cases, in the attempt to disagree with Roseanne's authoritative evaluations, the other 'weaker' characters (i.e., almost all the members of her family) often resort to the discourse strategy of 'intertextual positioning', consisting in making reference to the judgments of others in support to their own against Roseanne's one. Such references are all positive and 'endorsed', as the participants in a conversation explicitly indicate their reliable source, thus representing what they claim as true, shared, and convincing. The comic effect may be achieved in such situations of 'Arousal' when the intertextual positioning makes reference to a judgment that is actually 'disendorsed', and therefore it represents a weak and unreliable claim because participants, the very moment they state its value, actually distance themselves from it by taking no responsibility for the truth or reliability of what they assert.

The principal parameter to be taken into account in the application of the Appraisal Framework to the analysis of *Roseanne* is, therefore, that of 'attitudinal positioning', or 'Attitude' which includes three sub-types: 'emotional', or 'Affect'—here tagged for the subsequent analysis as [Aff]—'ethical', or 'Judgement' [Judg], and 'aesthetic', or 'Appreciation' [App] positionings of the speaker as s/he takes the responsibility for expressing a positive (+) or a negative (-) evaluation. A positive attitude can be expressed by the participant straightforwardly, by means of single words and phrases (mainly adjectives/adverbs and adjectival/adverbial phrases) conveying a favourable evaluation, or in a more complex way which involves the sense of a whole utterance. In this latter case, context plays a crucial part in the speakers' conveyance of their attitudes as well as in the receivers' interpretation processes. In a sitcom, in fact, the speakers' expression of intentionality and its understanding by receivers is not so unproblematic at it is expected to be in normal communication as the very structure of a sitcom is built on the ambiguity of, at least, two simultaneous and incongruent schemata (and related scripts) by which an utterance can be likewise interpreted—and indeed such an interpretative duality does trigger the comic effect. This means that in a sitcom, the speaker's Attitude is not so much overtly stated, or 'explicit' (Exp), as rather it is covertly unstated or 'implicit' (Imp).

5.2.2 *Sitcom characters' Attitude positionings of Affect, Judgement, and Appreciation*

In applying to sitcom analysis the first sub-type of Attitude positionings—namely, Affect [Aff]—it is necessary to consider that, though in conventional communication it involves the speaker's expression of positive or negative emotional states aimed at being clearly recognized as such by receivers, in the incongruous world of the sitcom, the speakers' conveyance of their emotions are not, in general, assumed to be immediately interpreted in the correct way by receivers - in fact, such discrepancy between the speaker's illocutionary intention and the receiver's perlocutionary interpretation is meant to trigger the humorous effect. Affect, therefore, can be explicitly or implicitly expressed by means of precise semantic and syntactic choices which, in the construction of the sitcom, may even assume the opposite pragmatic meaning in that, for instance, the explicit expression of a positive emotion may actually entail the implicit conveyance of a negative one. Typical semantic and syntactic choices employed to communicate Affect are: verbs of Mental Processes of Affection and Emotion (Halliday 1994: 112-119), adjectives of emotional states, nominalizations of such verbs and adjectives, adverbs of manner. Every emotional evaluation made by a speaker contains in its very formulation his/her Attitude positioning in terms of Affect—that is, his/her emotional response to the person, thing or event s/he is assessing. Such emotional evaluation may be straightforwardly expressed by the speaker who used the first-person pronoun and thus takes the 'authorial' responsibility for his/her value assessment, or rather it may be expressed by the speaker indirectly, by using the second- or third-person pronoun and thus declining his/her responsibility in his/her emotional evaluation. In 'Authorial Affect' [(Aut)Aff] Attitude, the speaker asserts his/her own subjective and emotional evaluation stance in an interaction and, in doing so, s/he expects from his/her receivers to fully understand it, judge it as valid and relevant to the conversation topic and, ultimately, agree with it. In a sitcom like the one in point, the character who better embodies this Authorial Affect Attitude is precisely Roseanne, whose emotional reactions are rarely kept covert and 'implicit' and, even in such cases—as it will be soon demonstrated in the analysis—she eventually makes them overtly 'explicit'.

On the other hand, a 'Non-Authorial Affect' [(Non-Aut)Aff] Attitude regards instances in which the speaker does not take the responsibility for his/her own expression of emotion, either positive or negative, and thus s/he attributes it to other people through the use of the second- or third-person pronoun, as if s/he were merely reporting somebody else's emotional reactions to some behaviours or events. This kind of Non-Authorial Affect Attitude is typically expressed in a sitcom by characters with a weak personality and a lower status who are not allowed—or rather fear—to express their own emotional stances in the first-person. This is, however, also typical of cowardly, or uncommitted characters who prefer not to expose themselves openly by making their emotional positioning manifest, or liable of other characters' negative judgment or criticism, hence they prefer to attribute their own emotional stance to others in order to explore the receivers' reactions before stating it in the first person.

The second sub-type of Attitude positionings to be applied to this sitcom analysis is Judgement [Judg], regarding a positive or a negative attitudinal evaluation of human behaviour with reference to the norms of a shared social code determining what is moral, legal, or proper and what is not (Martin and White 2005). Positive and negative judgements, therefore, embody the collective evaluation of the community that has sanctioned such norms and, thus, is in charge of assessing 'normal', 'competent', or 'constructive' behaviours against their negative counterparts. As such, a Judgement is always shaped by cultural and ideological forces —as well as by individual, experiential ones—that determine the illocutionary intention of the speaker formulating it. On the other hand, the same forces affect the perlocutionary interpretations of the receivers of a Judgement, who may not share the speaker's judgemental positioning, or rather may misinterpret it by filtering it through their own different socio-cultural, ideological, and experiential schemata. This situation of schema incongruence, where a character formulates a Judgement which is misinterpreted by its receivers, represents a very common trigger of comic effect in a sitcom—and, indeed, it is a recurring Arousal-pattern of humour in *Roseanne* where the main character playing the title role insistently expresses Judgements about the behaviour of people around her who often feel hurt and thus misinterpret her constructive intentions. However, the receivers' correct interpretation of a Judgement (namely, congruent with the speaker's intentionality) is crucially affected by the degree of 'implicitness' or 'explicitness' of the Judgement itself. An 'Explicit Judgement' [(Exp)Judg], in fact, is signalled by lexical choices (mainly adverbs, adjectives, and verbs) that clearly convey the sense of a positive (+) or a negative (-) judgement on a human behaviour. An 'Implicit Judgement' [(Imp)Judg], instead, is not formulated straightforwardly, but can be rather 'evoked' by an apparently objective description of facts which covertly lead receivers to share with the speaker a positive or a negative judgement, as in Roseanne's negative Judgement of David's behaviour in performing his new job at the Edelweiss Gardens: "I mean, today, it's 'Hi, I'm Hans the Hare, welcome to the park', and tomorrow it's 'I was only following orders'." In between an Explicit Judgement and an Implicit one there is the Provoked Judgement [(Pro)Judg] which uses evaluative language not to explicitly state, but to 'provoke' in receivers a specific Judgemental response. An instance of this type is represented by Roseanne's endorsed remarks to her unemployed husband Dan looking for a new job: "Hey, I heard something on the news about these government contractors getting all these kickbacks, y'know. Find out how that works", where she apparently keeps a neutral stance on this 'remunerative job', but actually provokes a negative judgement on it in her husband who may be tempted to turn to dishonesty only to find any job to scrape a living. Differently from Affect which involves the speaker directly and emotionally in evaluation (usually by means of the first-person pronoun —i.e., "I hate this place", but also by means of a third-person stance—i.e., "Everyone hates this place"), Judgement is instead a more objective evaluation of a fact (usually expressed by means of a third-person subject—i.e., "this place is awful"). Affect and Judgement, however, are not to be confused with the third sub-type of Attitude positioning—namely, Appreciation.

Appreciation [App] concerns the speaker's positive (+) or negative (-) assessment of processes, events, states of facts, places or objects (but not human behaviours) with no affective involvement on the side of the speaker. Usually Appreciation is related to the aesthetic dimensions of things, but also of human beings, without any assessment of the appropriateness or inappropriateness of their behaviours. However, Appreciation can also involve a favourable or disapproving evaluation of some ideological construction, again, with no direct affective or judgmental involvement of the speaker. An example of this type can be represented by Roseanne's comment on the Edelweiss Gardens where David works: "Wake up, David. This place wants to be Disney World, but it's just some creepy fascist copy." In this case, the speaker's subjective affective and judgmental involvement is not overtly stated, but it may be seen as just implied in her negative appreciation of the totalitarian ideology underlying the policy of David's workplace. In fact, the emotional reaction ("creepy") and the judgmental stance ("fascist") have been respectively dissociated from the speaker's disturbing experience ([(-)Aff]) and from human beings' negative behavioural performance ([(-)Judg]), and related instead to the place being evaluated, as if they were its intrinsic and objective qualities. In other words, the evaluation has been made objective by shifting from the speaker's negative affective stance and from her judgment on the behaviour of people in charge of the management of such a place to focus on her negative Appreciation ([(-)App]) of the quality of the place as the harmful 'product' of people's behaviour.

5.3 Applying the Appraisal Framework to a Comparative Analysis of a Script from *Roseanne* Sitcom

5.3.1 *Method and tagged data*

The 'Attitude' categories that will be applied to the analysis of a scene from *Roseanne*, in sum, are:

(1) 'Affect' [Aff] – positive (+), or negative (-) – to be classified into 'Authorial Affect' [(Aut)Aff] and 'Non-Authorial Affect' [(Non-Aut)Aff] attitudinal positionings;

(2) 'Judgement' [Judg] – positive (+), or negative (-) – to be classified into 'Explicit Judgement' [(Exp)Judg], 'Implicit Judgement' [(Imp)Judg], and Provoked Judgement [(Pro)Judg] positionings;

(3) 'Appreciation' [App] – positive (+), or negative (-).

It must be noticed, however, that these Attitude categories, normally shared and implicitly understood in the course of a normal conversation taking place within a homogeneous speech community, do not entirely apply to the atypical circumstances represented in a sitcom where what is said usually implies a different schematic interpretation that triggers the comic effect. Such categorial incongruity is particularly true when applied to *Roseanne*, where the protagonist's expressions of negative Affect, Judgement and Appreciation positionings normally are not to be interpret as derogatory stances, but as covertly sympathetic and positive ones. Indeed, the humorous disparagement in Roseanne's sarcastic cues is principally aimed at creating circumstances of comic 'Arousal' to awaken in the other characters the awareness of a critical situation and, thus, to encourage them to solve it in order to achieve 'Safety' and comic relief. The tagging for such ambiguous utterances will be (+/-) or (-/+), respectively indicating: in the former tag, an apparent positive evaluation (signalled by an initial +/) implying a negative one (signalled by the following /-) and, in the latter tag, an apparent negative evaluation (signalled by an initial -/) implying a positive one (signalled by the following /+).

The episode under analysis highlights Roseanne's peculiar judgmental character since its title, *Another mouth to shut up* (Italian title: *Sedotti e ... sposati – Seduced and ... married* [plural]). In it, Darlene – Roseanne's teenage daughter—introduces another 'revelation plot' as she feels obliged to disclose to her family the fact that she is pregnant and that she intends to marry her boyfriend David (which means that another component of Roseanne's poor and numerous family is coming—namely, 'another mouth to feed' that, with a humorous schematic shift referred to Roseanne's domineering temperament, becomes 'another mouth to shut up'. The scene to be analyzed, by adapting the Appraisal Framework to the humorous language of the sitcom, is precisely the one in which Darlene is induced by Roseanne's sarcastic remarks to reveal her secret in front of her whole family dining in the kitchen. Both the original English version and the dubbed one for the Italian television are tagged for the characters' attitudinal positionings. The possible interpretation of such positionings will be then discussed in order to identify the dialogic construction aimed at the achievement of a comic effect. An English back-translation of the Italian version is also provided.

***Roseanne* (*Pappa e Ciccia*)** episode #920 *Another mouth to shut up* (*Sedotti e ... sposati – Seduced and ... married*)
Exchange 1: turns [1]-[16]; Exchange 2: turns [17]-[44]

Original English version	***Italian dubbing translation***	***Back-translation into Standard English***
[Ext. Porch - Night]	**[Esterno, Portico - Sera]**	**[Ext. Porch - Night]**
[1] **DAVID:** Pregnant, you mean like, pregnant? **[(-) (Imp)Judg]**	*[1]* **DAVID:** Incinta? Vuoi dire, incinta? **[(-) (Imp)Judg]**	*[1]* **DAVID:** Pregnant, you mean, pregnant? **[(-) (Imp)Judg]**
[2] **DARLENE:** Yes, David, you've knocked me up. **[(-/+) (Imp) Judg]**	*[2]* **DARLENE:** Sì, David, sono proprio rimasta incinta. **[(-/+) (Imp)Judg]**	*[2]* **DARLENE:** Yes, David, I've really got pregnant. **[(-/+) (Imp)Judg]**
[3] **DAVID:** How? When? **[(-) (Pro)Judg]**	*[3]* **DAVID:** Come? Quando? **[(-) (Pro)Judg]**	*[3]* **DAVID:** How? When? **[(-) (Pro)Judg]**
[4] **DARLENE:** When? Disney World. **[(+) (Imp)Judg]**	*[4]* **DARLENE:** Quandò? A Disney World! **[(+) (Imp)Judg]**	*[4]* **DARLENE:** When? At Disney World! **[(+) (Imp)Judg]**
[5] **DAVID:** Oh, my god! You mean that night after the fireworks? **[(-/+) (Pro)Judg]**	*[5]* **DAVID:** Oh, cavolo! È successo quella notte dopo i fuochi d'artificio? **[(-/+) (Pro)Judg]**	*[5]* **DAVID:** Oh, gee! Did it happen that night after the fireworks? **[(-/+) (Pro)Judg]**
[6] **DARLENE:** Well, either that **[(-) (Imp)Judg]**, or it truly is a Magic Kingdom. **[(-) App]**	*[6]* **DARLENE:** O è successo allora **[(-) (Imp)Judg]**, o è veramen- mte un bel mistero. **[(-) App]**	*[6]* **DARLENE:** Either it happened then **[(-) (Imp)Judg]**, or it is truly quite a mystery. **[(-) App]**
[7] **DAVID:** Wow. What are we gonna do? **[(-) (Aut)Aff]**	*[7]* **DAVID:** Wow. E adesso che facciamo? **[(-) (Aut)Aff]**	*[7]* **DAVID:** Wow. What are we gonna do now? **[(-) (Aut)Aff]**
[8] **DARLENE:** Oh, don't worry. You know, getting married and having a baby can't change things that much. **[(+) (Pro)Judg]**	*[8]* **DARLENE:** No, non ti preoccupare. In fondo sposarsi e avere un bambino non ti cambia drasticamente la vita. **[(+) (Pro)Judg]**	*[8]* **DARLENE:** No, don't worry. After all, getting married and having a baby don't change your life drastically. **[(+) (Pro)Judg]**
[9] **DAVID:** I kinda wanted a dog first. **[(+/-) (Aut)Aff]**	*[9]* **DAVID:** Preferivo avere prima un cane. **[(+/-) (Aut)Aff]**	*[9]* **DAVID:** I would have preferred to have a dog first. **[(+/-) (Aut)Aff]**
[10] **DARLENE:** Oh, it'll be okay. I'm still gonna finish school. And by getting married I can get on your health coverage, our car insurance will go down, we'll be in line for married student housing ... I mean, it just makes sense, you know. **[(+) (Exp)Judg]**	*[10]* **DARLENE:** Andrà tutto bene. Io devo ancora finire la scuola. Se ci sposiamo potrò usufruire della tua assistenza sanitaria e inoltre ci assegneranno una casa per i giovani sposi. Si sistemerà tutto, vedrai. **[(+) (Exp)Judg]**	*[10]* **DARLENE:** It'll be okay. I'm still gonna finish school. If we get married I can get on your health coverage and, furthermore, we will be assigned a house for young married couples. Everything shall right itself, you'll see. **[(+) (Exp)Judg]**
[11] **DAVID:** ...Wouldn't have to be a big dog. **[(+/-) (Non-Aut)Aff]**	*[11]* **DAVID:** Non doveva essere un cane grande. **[(+/-) (Non-Aut)Aff]**	*[11]* **DAVID:** It wouldn't have to be a big dog. **[(+/-) (Non-Aut)Aff]**

[12] **DARLENE:** Come on. Let's go tell everybody inside and get this over with. **[(-/+) (Aut)Aff]**	*12]* **DARLENE:** Vieni, andiamo a dare la bella notizia a tutta la famiglia. **[(+/-) (Aut)Aff]**	*[12]* **DARLENE:** Come on. Let's go tell the whole family the good news. **[(+/-) (Aut)Aff]**
[13] **DAVID:** Whoa, whoa, slow down. **[(-) (Exp)Judg]** You mean, tell everyone in there? **[(-) (Imp)Judg]** Look, Darlene, couldn't we wait a few months? **[(-) (Pro)Judg]** I mean, then they would just think you were getting fat - they gotta be expecting that **[(-) App]**. So then, when we do tell them, they'll just go, "Oh, good she's not getting fat!" **[(+) App] / [(-) (Imp)Judg]**	*[13]* **DAVID:** Ehi, ehi, aspetta. **[(-) (Exp)Judg]** Hai intenzione di dare la notizia a tutti adesso? **[(-) (Imp)Judg]** Oh Darlene, non potremmo, non potremmo aspettare qualche mese? **[(-) (Pro)Judg]** All'inizio penseranno tutti che ti sei ingrassata un po' troppo, **[(-) App]** a quel punto, quando glielo diremo commenteranno 'oh che bello! Allora non è ingrassata!' **[(+) App] / [(-) (Imp)Judg]**	*[13]* **DAVID:** Ehi, ehi, wait. **[(-) (Exp)Judg]** Do you mean to tell everyone the news now? **[(-) (Imp)Judg]** Oh Darlene, couldn't we wait, couldn't we wait a few months? **[(-) (Pro)Judg]** At the beginning they all will think that you are getting a bit too fat, **[(-) App]** so then, when we do tell them, they'll comment, "Oh, how marvelous! Then she's not getting fat!" **[(+) App] / [(-) (Imp)Judg]**
[14] **DARLENE:** Alright, we don't have to tell them yet. Now take a deep breath and try not to look so pasty. **[(-) App]**	*[14]* **DARLENE:** D'accordo, non glielo dobbiamo dire subito. Ora fai un bel respiro e cerca di non sembrare così sconvolto. **[(-) App]**	*[14]* **DARLENE:** Alright, we don't have to tell them soon. Now take a deep breath and try not to look so pasty. **[(-) App]**
[15] **DAVID:** We'll just, we'll tell them the movie we just saw affected me profoundly. **[(-) (Exp)Judg]**	*[15]* **DAVID:** Possiamo, possiamo dire che il film che abbiamo visto mi ha colpito profondamente. **[(-) (Exp)Judg]**	*[15]* **DAVID:** We can, we can tell them the movie we just saw affected me profoundly. **[(-) (Exp)Judg]**
[16] **DARLENE:** Okay, let's go inside. You ready? After you ... Daddy. **[(+) (Imp)Judg]**	*[16]* **DARLENE:** Va bene, andiamo dentro, sei pronto? Dopo di te ... paparino. **[(+) (Imp)Judg]**	*16]* **DARLENE:** Okay, let's go inside. You ready? After you ... Daddy. **[(+) (Imp)Judg]**
[Int. Kitchen]	**[Interno, Cucina]**	**[Int. Kitchen]**
[17] **D.J.:** What the hell are those? **[(-) (Pro)Judg]**	*[17]* **D.J.:** Ma che diavolo sono! **[(-) (Pro)Judg]**	*[17]* **D.J.:** What the hell are those? **[(-) (Pro)Judg]**
[18] **ROSEANNE:** They're cornish game hens. I, uh, bought 'em off this guy that was selling them off the back of his truck down at the, uh, gas station parking lot. It's the very same guy that I bought our stereo speakers from last week. **[(-) (Imp)Judg]** *(Darlene and David enter from the living room)* Hey you guys just in time for dinner. **[(+) (Exp)Judg]** Grab a plate. Sit down here, David.	*[18]* **ANNARO':** Sono galletti ruspanti di campagna. Davvero, li ho comprati da un tizio con un turbante in testa che ha un allevamento vicino a una discarica dei rifiuti naturali. Tu lo sai che senza mangiare le bottiglie di plastica questi polli pesano quasi la metà? **[(+/-) (Imp)Judg]** *(Darlene e David entrano dal soggiorno)* Ehi, siete arrivati in tempo per cena. **[(+) (Exp)Judg]** Prendetevi un piatto. Siediti qua, David.	*[18]* **ANNARO':** They're country farmyard chickens. Really, I bought them from a guy with a turban on his head who has a chicken farm near an organic-waste dump. Do you know that without eating plastic bottles these chickens are almost half heavy? **[(+/-) (Imp)Judg]** *(Darlene and David enter from the living room)* Hey, You've just arrived in time for dinner. **[(+) (Exp)Judg]** Get a plate. Sit down here, David.
[19] **DAVID:** ...Next to you? **[(-) (Imp)Judg]**	*[19]* **DAVID:** Accanto a Lei? **[(-) (Imp)Judg]**	*[19]* **DAVID:** ...Next to you? **[(-) (Imp)Judg]**
[20] **ROSEANNE:** Yeah, come tell me about your, uh, new job as a graphic artist, there. **[(+) App]**	*[20]* **ANNARO':** Sì, raccontami qualche cosa del tuo nuovo lavoro di grafico, mi interessa. **[(+) App]**	*[20]* **ANNARO':** Yeah, tell me about your new job as a graphic artist, I'm interested in it. **[(+) App]**
[21] **JACKIE:** David, congratulations on the job. Is it on a computer, or do you just draw by hand? **[(+) App]**	*[21]* **GIACOMI':** Ah David, a proposito, congratulazioni per il tuo nuovo lavoro. Fai tutto con il computer, o disegni a mano? **[(+) App]**	*[21]* **GIACOMI':** Ah David, by the way, congratulations on your new job. Do you do everything on the computer, or do you draw by hand? **[(+) App]**
[22] **DAVID:** Uh, thanks, I'm fine. **[(+/-) (Aut)Aff]**	*[22]* **DAVID:** Oh, grazie, sto bene. **[(+/-) (Aut)Aff]**	*[22]* **DAVID:** oh, thanks, I'm fine. **[(+/-) (Aut)Aff]**

[23] **DAN:** I guess you're pretty excited about moving to Chicago, huh? **[(+) (Exp)Judg]**	*[23]* **DAN:** Scommetto che siete entusiasti di trasferirvi a Chicago, eh? **[(+) (Exp)Judg]**	*[23]* **DAN:** I bet that you both are excited about moving to Chicago, eh? **[(+) (Exp)Judg]**
[24] **DAVID:** Uh, uh-huh. Course it means I'll have to move to Chicago. **[(+/-) (Exp)Judg]** ... Oh, I'm so confused... **[(-) (Aut)Aff]**	*[24]* **DAVID:** Oh, oh, questo significa che mi trasferirò a Chicago. **[(+/-) (Exp)Judg]** ... Oh, sono così confuso. **[(-) (Aut)Aff]**	*24]* **DAVID:** Oh, oh, this means I'll move to Chicago. **[(+/-) (Exp) Judg]** ... Oh, I'm so confused... **[(-) (Aut)Aff]**
[25] **D.J.:** Oh, they're some kind of tiny chickens. We didn't know what they were either. **[(-) App]**	*[25]* **D.J.:** Oh, sì, questi polli sono minuscoli, non li conoscevamo neanche noi. **[(-) App]**	*[25]* **D.J.:** Oh, yes, these chickens are tiny, we didn't know them either. **[(-) App]**
[26] **ROSEANNE:** No, I don't think that's it D.J., David's just a little excited about his new job. Isn't that right David? **[(+/-) (Exp)Judg]**	*[26]* **ANNARO':** No, io dico che si tratta di qualche altra cosa e che David è assai eccitato per questo nuovo lavoro, ho ragione o mi sbaglio? **[(+/-) (Exp)Judg]**	*[26]* **ANNARO':** No, I say that it is about something else and that David's very excited about this new job. Am I right of wrong? **[(+/-) (Exp)Judg]**
[27] **DAVID:** The movie affected me profoundly. **[(-) (Aut)Aff]**	*[27]* **DAVID:** Quel film mi ha colpito profondamente. **[(-) (Aut)Aff]**	*[27]* **DAVID:** That movie affected me profoundly. **[(-) (Aut)Aff]**
[28] **DARLENE:** Uh, David, why don't you let me sit there. You've been hogging Mom long enough. **[(-) (Exp)Judg]**	*[28]* **DARLENE:** Eh David perché non mi fai sedere là? Hai scocciato mamma a sufficienza. **[(-) (Exp)Judg]**	*[28]* **DARLENE:** Eh, David, why don't you let me sit there? You've been bothering mom long enough. **[(-) (Exp)Judg]**
[29] **DAVID:** Okay, good, here. **[(+/-) (Imp)Judg]**	*[29]* **DAVID:** Oh certo, siediti. **[(+/-) (Imp)Judg]**	*[29]* **DAVID:** Okay, sure, sit here. **[(+/-) (Imp)Judg]**
[30] **DARLENE:** Uh, but you should sit somewhere, you know. **[(-) (Imp)Judg]**	*[30]* **DARLENE:** Ah, devi comunque sederti da qualche parte. **[(-) (Imp)Judg]**	*[30]* **DARLENE:** Ah, you should however sit somewhere. **[(-) (Imp)Judg]**
[31] **ROSEANNE:** What's up? I smell fear. I love that smell. **[(-) (Aut)Aff]** But what's up? **[(-) (Exp)Judg]**	*[31]* **ANNARO':** Che ti piglia? Sento odore di paura, è un odore che riconosco subito, **[(-) (Aut) Aff]** ma che avete combinato? **[(-) (Exp)Judg]**	*[31]* **ANNARO':** What's the matter with you? I smell fear. It's a smell I immediately recognize, **[(-) (Aut)Aff]** But what are you up to? **[(-) (Exp)Judg]**
[32] **DARLENE:** Nothing's up. God! **[(+/-) (Exp)Judg]** ... Hey, D.J., that's a great shirt. Where'd you get it? **[(+) App]**	*[32]* **DARLENE:** Non abbiamo combinato niente. **[(+/-) (Exp) Judg]** Ehi D.J. che bella camicia, dove l'hai presa? **[(+) App]**	*[32]* **DARLENE:** We are up to nothing. **[(+/-) (Exp)Judg]** Hey, D.J., what a nice shirt, Where did you get it from? **[(+) App]**
[33] **D.J.:** My closet. **[(-) App]**	*[33]* **D.J.:** Nel mio armadio. **[(-) App]**	*[33]* **D.J.:** From my closet. **[(-) App]**
[34] **ROSEANNE:** Oh no, I think something is up. **[(-) (Exp)Judg]** Uh, yeah, I've seen enough of that "Murder She Wrote" to figure that out. **[(-) (Imp)Judg]** ... Let's see here, David is pale and kind of weak kneed and all nervous. So, there's no clues there. **[(-) (Exp)Judg]** ... But Darlene wants to sit next to me, and she said something nice to her brother. **[(+/-) (Exp)Judg]** Eeww, I wonder. I know, you're pregnant! **[(-) (Imp)Judg]** *(All laugh except Darlene and David. Then everyone stops laughing)* That was my joke guess! **[(-) (Imp)Judg]**	*[34]* **ANNARO':** Eh no, qua c'è qualcosa che non mi quadra. **[(-) (Exp)Judg]** Eh, forse ho visto troppi episodi della "Signora in Giallo", ma non mi fregate. **[(-) (Exp)Judg]** Esaminiamo gli indizi: David è pallido, gli tremano le ginocchia ed è molto nervoso e fin qui stiamo nella normalità. **[(-) (Exp)Judg]** Però Darlene si vuole sedere vicino a me e tratta suo fratello quasi come un essere umano. **[(+/-) (Exp)Judg]** Uuuuu, gatta ci cova! Ho capito, aspetti un bambino! **[(-) (Imp)Judg]** *(Tutti ridono eccetto Darlene e David. Poi tutti smettono di ridere)* L'ho detto solamente per farci quattro risate! **[(-) (Imp)Judg]**	*[34]* **ANNARO':** Eh no, there's something fishy here. **[(-) (Exp)Judg]** Eh, maybe I've seen too many episodes of "Murder She Wrote" , but you don't cheat on me. **[(-) (Exp)Judg]** Let's examine the clues: David is pale, his knees are shaking and he's very nervous and so far we are within the normality. Yet Darlene wants to sit next to me and she treats her brother as a human being! **[(+/-) (Exp)Judg]** Eeww, there's something fishy going on here. I've got it, you're pregnant! **[(-) (Imp)Judg]** *(All laugh except Darlene and David. Then everyone stops laughing)* I've only said that just for the laugh of it! **[(-) (Imp)Judg]**

[35] **DAVID:** We're also getting married. **[(-) (Pro)Judg]**	*[35]* **DAVID:** E abbiamo deciso di sposarci. **[(-) (Pro)Judg]**	*[35]* **DAVID:** And we've decided to get married. **[(-) (Pro)Judg]**
[36] **ROSEANNE:** Well! I'm, I'm excited for you guys. **[(+/-) (Aut)Aff]** I think it's great? **[(+/-) (Exp)Judg]** ... Dan, we're gonna getting grandparents! Isn't that great. **[(+/-) (Pro)Judg]** I'm getting one of those sweatshirts that says "World's Greatest Grandma" on it, you know. And you can go out and get yourself, I dunno, like a cane something. **[(+/-) (Imp)Judg]**	*[36]* **ANNARO':** Bene! Io sono molto, sono molto felice, **[(+/-) (Aut)Aff]** una notizia stupenda, **[(+/-) (Exp)Judg]** Dan! Tra un po' avremo un nipotino, non fai salti di gioia? **[(+/-) (Pro)Judg]** Io mi compro subito una di quelle magliette con la scritta "Questa è la nonna più pazza del mondo" e tu invece ti potresti comprare, che so, un bel bastone per andare a passeggio. **[(+/-) (Imp)Judg]**	*[36]* **ANNARO':** Well! I'm very, I'm very happy, **[(+/-) (Aut)Aff]** wonderful news, **[(+/-) (Exp)Judg]** Dan! We will soon have a grandchild, don't you jump for joy? **[(+/-) (Pro)Judg]** I'm soon getting one of those sweatshirts that says "This is the World's Craziest Grandma" on it and you instead could get yourself, I dunno, a nice cane to stroll around. **[(+/-) (Imp) Judg]**
[37] **DAN:** Yeah. Oh boy. Good, good, good, good, good. **[(+/-) (Imp)Judg]**	*[37]* **DAN:** Già. Oh mamma. Bene, bene, nonni, nonni. **[(+/-) (Imp)Judg]**	*[37]* **DAN:** Yeah. Oh dear me. Good, good, grandparents, grandparents. **[(+/-) (Imp)Judg]**
[38] **DAVID:** Wow, thanks, Mrs. Conner. that wasn't the reaction I was expecting. **[(+) (Exp)Judg]**	*[38]* **DAVID:** Wow, grazie signora Conner, non era certo la reazione che mi aspettavo. **[(+) (Exp)Judg]**	*[38]* **DAVID:** Wow, thanks, Mrs. Conner. Certainly that wasn't the reaction I was expecting. **[(+) (Exp)Judg]**
[39] **DARLENE:** Yeah, me neither. **[(+) (Exp)Judg]** *(to David)* I guess you peed your pants for nothing. **[(-) (Imp)Judg]**	*[39]* **DARLENE:** già, nemmeno io. **[(+) (Exp)Judg]** *(rivolta a David)* Te la sei fatta nei pantaloni per niente. **[(-) (Imp)Judg]**	*[39]* **DARLENE:** Yeah, me neither. **[(+) (Exp)Judg]** *(to David)* You did it in your pants for nothing. **[(-) (Imp)Judg]**
[40] **ROSEANNE:** Dan! Dan! **[(-) (Pro)Judg]**	*[40]* **ANNARO':** Dan! Dan! **[(-) (Pro)Judg]**	*[40]* **ANNARO':** Dan! Dan! **[(-) (Pro)Judg]**
[41] **DAN:** What? Oh, I'm just trying to figure out how to go about eating this thing. **[(-) App]**	*41]* **DAN:** Che vuoi? Ah, stavo solo cercando di capire come si fa a mangiare questo galletto. **[(-) App]**	*[41]* **DAN:** What do you want? Ah, I was just trying to figure out how to go about eating this chicken. **[(-) App]**
[42] **JACKIE:** Well, I think it's good. That Darlene is getting pregnant, 'cause she's getting married 'cause she's has to— That's just what I did. **[(+/-) (Exp)Judg]**	*[42]* **GIACOMI':** Bé, è una notizia stupenda! Che Darlene è rimasta incinta e che sta per sposarsi perché deve perché è rimasta incinta e che... proprio come è successo a me. **[(+/-) (Exp)Judg]**	*[42]* **GIACOMI':** Well, that's wonderful news! That Darlene has got pregnant and that she's getting married 'cause she's has to 'cause she's got pregnant and that — That's just what happened to me. **[(+/-) (Exp)Judg]**
[43] **DAVID:** D.J., stop staring at me. **[(-) (Exp)Judg]**	*[43]* **DAVID:** D.J. smettila di fissarmi. **[(-) (Exp)Judg]**	*[43]* **DAVID:** D.J., stop staring at me. **[(-) (Exp)Judg]**
[44] **D.J.:** Babies having babies. **[(-) (Exp)Judg]**	*[44]* **D.J.:** bambini che fanno bambini. **[(-) (Exp)Judg]**	*[44]* **D.J.:** Babies making babies. **[(-) (Exp)Judg]**

5.3.2 *Appraisal Framework applied to the analysis of source and target scripts*

As evident from the tagging of the two parallel versions of the scene (the original and the translated ones), the 'attitudinal positioning' pattern of the conversation almost coincides. The difference, therefore, lays more in the diatopic/diastratic choice of the accent attributed to the main character, Roseanne, and in a mitigation of the almost vulgar expressions uttered by Darlene, the tomboy, which marks a change in the perception of humour in the target audience.

The first exchange between David and Darlene starts at the entrance of Darlene's house, in the porch, with David's reaction, in turn [1], to Darlene's unexpected revelation of her pregnancy which introduces an Arousal pattern of humour. David's expression of bewilderment (literally rendered into the translation for the Italian television) may conceal an implicit, negative judgement towards Darlene, a reaction to her probable misbehaviour in planning a pregnancy without his knowing and, thus, putting him in a spot by confronting him with a fait accompli. Darlene's reply in turn [2] apparently returns the implicit negative judgement to David, this being especially evident in the original version of the dialogue where she straightforwardly accuses her boyfriend of having put her in a prejudicial situation by using a direct second-person Blame Move and a popular—and quite vulgar—American expression ("Yes, David, you knocked me up"). This accusation, however, is evidently ironic as Darlene smiles while speaking, trying to replace a Safety pattern of humour in the conversation, which reveals that her judgment on David's scared reaction is actually positively sympathetic. The Italian version instead renders her turn impersonal, probably self-blaming, with no implied accusation towards David, but just a hint at her apparently sharing David's implicit negative judgement: "Sì, David, sono proprio rimasta incinta" (English back-translation: "Yes, David, I've really got pregnant"). David's state of bewilderment increases in turn [3] (and, with it, the humorous Arousal pattern), where he tries to induce Darlene to share with him a negative 'provoked judgment' by asking her "How? When?" (literally translated into Italian) thus attempting to disclaim his being involved in 'the fact'. Darlene – this time through a positive 'implicit judgement' clearly visible on the gleeful expression on her face—replies "When? Disney World" (also this time, almost literally translated into Italian). David's disbelief in turn [5] is made manifest by the interjection "Oh, my god!" (mistranslated into Italian with the almost unemotional and non-natural 'dubbese' exclamation "Oh, cavolo!"—roughly corresponding to "Oh, gee!"). This is followed by another negative 'provoked judgement' (which can be just apparent, since it may imply a possible positive and self-congratulating evaluation of his own 'feat') aimed at eliciting from Darlene a judgmental response of confirmation: "You mean that night after the fireworks?" (more unequivocally rendered into Italian as "E' successo quella notte dopo i fuochi d'artificio?" - "Did it happen that night after the fireworks?"). Darlene, in turn [6], seems to confirm only the negative 'implicit judgment' on David's 'performance', upgrading it with her negative appreciation of the 'event' by means of a fairy-tale metaphor related to the Disney-World context: "Well, either that, or it truly is a Magic Kingdom". The version for the Italian television makes Darlene's implicit negative judgment more clearly related to David's inferred poor sexual performance, followed by an openly disparaging comment where the original metaphor has disappeared to leave space to its literal paraphrase: "O è successo allora, o è veramente un bel mistero"—"Either it happened then, or it is truly quite a mystery"). David's 'authorial affective' attitude expressed in turn [7]—and rendered almost literally into the Italian translation—aims at emotionally involving Darlene in a jointly agreed decision to be taken for the future: "Wow. What are we gonna do?". In turn [8] it becomes evident that Darlene alone has already taken the final decision without waiting for David's consent—in fact, she uses the evaluative language of a positive 'provoked judgement' to induce David to share her views: "Oh, don't worry. You know, getting married and having a baby can't change things that much" (rendered into an almost equivalent way also in Italian). In turn [9], a still bewildered David keeps manifesting an 'authorial affective' attitude positioning which may appear positive for its humorous incongruous tone ("I kinda wanted a dog first"), but that actually may reveal his emotional negative evaluation of the unexpected situation he finds himself involved in. The Italian translation of this turn shows a less spontaneous tone which renders the utterance almost non-natural: "Preferivo avere prima un cane" ("I would have preferred to have a dog first"). Darlene, in turn [10], goes on with her optimistic description of their future as a family and explicitly expresses her positive judgement of how they will manage the new situation: "Oh, it'll be okay. I'm still gonna finish school. And by getting married I can get on your health coverage, our car insurance will go down, we'll be in line for married student housing ... I mean, it just makes sense, you know". The translation for the Italian television respects Darlene's positive 'explicit judgement', but omits the part concerning the 'car insurance' (probably for timing reasons) and renders the original cue "I mean, it just makes sense, you know" into "Si sistemerà tutto, vedrai" ("Everything shall right itself, you'll see") suggesting a kind of forced accommodation of events rather than a logical, meaningful and natural positive outcome. David, in turn [11], is still shocked and, despite his comic cue directly linked to turn [9] may suggest a positive 'non-authorial affect' attitude aimed at self-mocking ("...Wouldn't have to be a big dog"), he may actually well be expressing a negative emotional attitude affecting his self image of 'pet-loving boy' suddenly obliged to become adult to cope with untimely fatherhood. In turn [12], Darlene even goes so far as to ask her boyfriend to join her inside her house (which hosts also David) to reveal her family the fact and put an end to it: "Come on. Let's go tell everybody inside and get this over with". In saying so, Darlene, on the one hand, apparently adopts a negative 'authorial affect' attitude in showing her intention to go immediately through the problems related to her family's expected reactions to her teenage pregnancy. On the other, however, she may instead suggest a positive affect attitude in revealing her plans as an adult woman to her family, and involving David in them. In the Italian translation of Darlene's turn [12], this positive 'authorial affect' attitude emerges first, with a possible negative affect attitude and sarcastic implication to be identified in the expression "bella notizia" ("good news"): "Vieni, andiamo a dare la bella notizia a tutta la famiglia" (Come on. Let's go tell the whole family the good news"). David, in turn [13], stops Darlene with an explicit negative judgement on her impulsive behaviour and an implicit negative one addressed to her family's possible condemnatory reactions: "Whoa, whoa, slow down. You mean, tell everyone in there?". The translation for the Italian television is not exactly equivalent: David tells Darlene to 'wait' ("Ehi, ehi, aspetta")—not, instead, to 'slow down'—in her rash pursuing of her intentions, so the verb 'wait' is directly linked to the adverb 'now', stressing Darlene's hasty behaviour: "Hai intenzione di dare la notizia a tutti adesso?" ("Do you mean to tell everyone the news now?). In the original version of this turn, David subsequently introduces the verb 'wait' to advance a negative 'provoked judgement' trying to convince Darlene to agree with his suggestion that they should be prudent: "Look, Darlene, couldn't we wait a few months?"—this time almost literally translated into Italian. He then adds a negative appreciation of Darlene's possible future bodily changes as her family may eventually interpret it: "I mean, then they would just think you were getting fat—they gotta be expecting that". This last derogatory consideration that David makes on Darlene's prospect as an obese woman, like her mother and father (who would thus expect such physical change in her), is omitted in the Italian version: "All'inizio penseranno tutti che ti sei ingrassata un po' troppo" ("At the beginning they all will think that you are getting a bit too fat"), which diminishes the original disparaging comic effect. Then, David concludes his turn by introducing his quip built on the relief that Darlene's family shall experience at realizing that she is not getting fat like her parents, but she is just pregnant: "So then, when we do tell them, they'll just go, 'Oh, good, she's not getting fat!'" (rendered almost literally into Italian). This pun is produced by making two different attitudes coincide —on the one hand, David's ironic report of the positive appreciation expected from Darlene's family as a reaction at discovering that she is not fat but only pregnant and, on the other, his implicit negative judgment of the whole absurd situation he finds himself unwillingly involved in, which triggers his disparaging humour. Darlene, in turn [15], acknowledges his boyfriend's fears and agrees with David: "Alright, we don't have to tell them yet", thus establishing a certain degree of Relief in the tense conversation. Then she introduces her negative appreciation of David's countenance, apparently cheering him up, but actually disparaging him for his cowardice: "Now take a deep breath and try not to look so pasty" (almost literally translated into Italian). David, in turn [15], tries to collaborate with Darlene in concealing the fact to her family and, thus, he invents a justification for his 'pasty' countenance by negatively and explicitly judging it as the effect of a movie that 'affected profoundly' his overemotional sensibility: "We'll just, we'll tell them the movie we just saw affected me profoundly" (almost literally translated into Italian). In turn [16], Darlene appears more relaxed and ironic as in her words an implicit positive judgment towards David can be detected: "Okay, let's go inside. You ready? After you ... Daddy" (this last affective address term rendered into Italian with the childish—and mocking—equivalent "paparino").

The next exchange takes place in the kitchen of Darlene's house, where her mother Roseanne, her father Dan, her little brother D.J. and her aunt Jackie are starting their dinner. D.J. opens the conversation with his turn [17]—"What the hell are those?" (literally translated into Italian)—by trying to induce the others to share his negative 'provoked judgement' on the tiny chickens (cataphorically referred to) they are going to eat. Roseanne, in turn [18], replies with an implicit negative judgement based on two opposite scripts triggering disparaging humour that tries to mask her fierce criticism of today's hopeless lack of biological food. Hence, on the one hand she defined the chickens as wholesome and unprocessed "cornish game hens". On the other, however, she says she bought them from "this guy that was selling them off the back of his truck down at the, uh, gas station parking lot", a place very different from the expected biological farmyard. Furthermore she adds, by upgrading her incongruous information, that "it's the very same guy that I bought our stereo speakers from last week"—hence, the seller is implicitly represented as a very untrustworthy guy who lives by his own wits and, thus, by no means can he guarantee the organic quality of the hens as Roseanne initially asserts. In the dubbed version for the Italian television, Roseanne/Annarò's implicit judgement seems to be more optimistic and apparently positive than the original one, though it may still conceal a negative evaluation. Her cue, in fact, was not translated, but totally reinvented into the following comment: "Sono galletti ruspanti di campagna. Davvero, li ho comprati da un tizio con un turbante in testa che ha un allevamento vicino a una discarica dei rifiuti naturali. Tu lo sai che senza mangiare le bottiglie di plastica questi polli pesano quasi la metà?" ("They're country farmyard chickens. Really, I bought them from a guy with a turban on his head who has a chicken farm near an organic-waste dump. Do you know that without eating plastic bottles these chickens are almost half heavy?"). In this version of turn [18], Annarò mentions a farm which—in line with the spirit of the contemporary corrupted times—is expectedly close to a waste dump. Yet, unexpectedly, since it is an 'organic' waste dump, far from being dangerous to people's health, it appears to be perfect for chicken-farming which, in Annarò's words, normally takes place nearby waste dumps where 'plastic bottles' eaten by chicken make them fatter. The entrance of Darlene and David in time for dinner is assessed by Roseanne with an explicit positive judgement (literally translated into Italian) and with her inviting David to sit next to her. In his turn [19], David's scared reply, "...Next to you?" (translated into Italian with the formal second-person address term, 'lei', rather than the informal 'tu' in rendering 'you') clearly entails a negative implicit judgement. Roseanne, in turn [20], unaware of David's alarmed reply, confirms her invitation and asks him nonchalantly: "come tell me about your, uh, new job as a graphic artist, there", thus asking a conventional, yet almost detached, question that, by performing a suitably kind positive appreciation, actually belittles David's new job. In the Italian version of this turn, yet, Annarò makes an addition which renders her question and positive appreciation less detached and condescending, which clashes with the video-image of a quite indifferent and absent-minded Roseanne: "Sì, raccontami qualche cosa del tuo nuovo lavoro di grafico, mi interessa." ("tell me about your new job as a graphic artist, I'm interested in it."). In turn [21], Roseanne's sister Jackie intervenes to congratulate David on his new job and, by taking a positive appreciation stance, she shows him her interest in knowing if, as a graphic artist, he will draw on a computer or by hand. David, still in a daze, in turn [22] inconsistently replies: "Uh, thanks, I'm fine", thus expressing an apparently positive—but actually negative—first-person authorial affect positioning, disclosing his state of emotional confusion. To this, Dan, Roseanne's husband, replies in turn [23] with a scornful raspberry, but then he mitigates his spontaneous mocking reaction at David's inconsistent reply by making an explicit positive judgment justifying him: "I guess you're pretty excited about moving to Chicago, huh?". If in these last turns the translation for the Italian television was quite literal, in this turn it shows some ambiguities: in his original cue, Dan seems to refer the second-person pronoun 'you' to David only, using it in the singular sense. In the Italian version, instead, he uses it in the plural sense, thus implying that David and Darlene are already an acknowledged couple and that they would move together to Chicago—which is not the case: "Scommetto che siete entusiasti di trasferirvi a Chicago, eh?" ("I bet that you both are excited about moving to Chicago, eh?"). As a reply, in turn [24], David again shows his state of confusion by confirming—through another explicit and apparently positive judgement—the fact that he has to move to Chicago, which is not the expected answer to Dan's question on whether he was excited about moving to another town. In fact, David's judgement is actually negative, considering his unexpected condition as father-and-husband-to-be: "Uh, uh-huh. Course it means I'll have to move to Chicago", but then, at seeing the others quite puzzled at his incongruous words, he takes a negative authorial affect stance: "Oh, I'm so confused...". In the Italian version, David's ambiguous positive/negative explicit judgement is not expressed as the original confirmation of the fact that he has to move, but as a sudden realization of this fact: "Oh, oh, questo significa che mi trasferirò a Chicago" ("Oh, oh, this means I'll move to Chicago"). The state of humorous Arousal at this point is set, everybody looks at David with bafflement, so D.J., Roseanne's young son, in turn [25], tries to relieve tension by giving his explanation of David's confusion, laying the blame on the small dimension of the chickens that he negatively appreciates: "they're some kind of tiny chickens. We didn't know what they were either" (almost equivalently translated into Italian). Roseanne— who throughout the exchange so far has been silent with puzzlement—now starts to speak and, in turn [26], she tries to give her apparently positive explicit judgement on David's inconsistent behaviour —which she actually judges negatively: "No, I don't think that's it D.J., David's just a little excited about his new job. Isn't that right David?". Her ambivalent positive/negative judgement is rendered slightly differently in the Italian TV version where Annarò does not address D.J. and, with her Neapolitan accent and reformulated cue, rather appears a bit more aggressive than the original character: "No, io dico che si tratta di qualche altra cosa e che David è assai eccitato per questo nuovo lavoro, ho ragione o mi sbaglio?" ("No, I say that it is about something else and that David's very excited about this new job. Am I right or wrong?"). At this point David, put on the spot, in turn [27] tries to come out of such jeopardizing situation by resorting to the negative 'authorial affect' formula he and Darlene agreed on: "The movie affected me profoundly". It is Darlene, at this stage, that feels compelled to help David out of such embarrassing state and, in turn [28], she makes a suggestion under the form of an explicit negative judgement: "Uh, David, why don't you let me sit there. You've been hogging Mom long enough". Darlene's negative judgement of David's behaviour, in the Italian version, becomes stronger, taking the form of an actual reproach: "Hai scocciato mamma a sufficienza" ("You've been bothering Mom long enough"). David stands up immediately to leave the seat for Darlene and, in turn [29], makes an apparently positive implicit judgement on Darlene's request which conceals an actual negative one on the whole embarrassing situation (equivalently rendered into Italian). David, however, does not find another seat for himself and oddly keeps standing up at Darlene's back, which makes all the others even more puzzled in their attempt to judge his strange behaviour. Darlene, therefore, is obliged to perform an implicit negative judgement on David's demeanour and so, in turn [30], she remarks: "Uh, but you should sit somewhere, you know".

Roseanne, at this point, with an inquisitive tone, starts her examination in turn [31], first by expressing her negative 'authorial affect' stance: "What's up? I smell fear. I love that smell", and then by an explicit negative judgement: "But what's up?". The version for the Italian television keeps the same evaluation pattern but modifies its rendering into the target language which, because of Annarò's more direct Neapolitan idioms and pragmatic phonology, appears more aggressive and directly addressed to David and Darlene: "Che ti piglia? Sento odore di paura, è un odore che riconosco subito, ma che avete combinato?" ("What's the matter with you? I smell fear. It's a smell I immediately recognize, but what are you up to?"). As evident, also the affective process expressed by the verb 'to love' is substituted in translation with a cognitive process, 'to recognize', which makes Annarò's enquiry more detached and 'technical' than Roseanne's original one. Darlene, in turn [32], promptly tries to dismiss her mother's suspicions by impatiently replying with a seemingly positive—but actually negative—explicit judgement: "Nothing's up. God!", translated into Italian with a more distracted and final expression: "Non abbiamo combinato niente" ("We are up to nothing"). Then, by suddenly turning to her brother D.J. in an attempt to divert the others' attention to something else, and thus change the conversation topic, Darlene makes an overenthusiastic and totally out-of-place positive appreciation of her brother's shirt: "Hey, D.J., that's a great shirt. Where'd you get it?" (almost equivalently rendered into Italian). D.J., with an impassive look returns her sister's keen compliment by an unemotional and implied negative appreciation: "My closet". Roseanne now cannot refrain from expressing her negative judgement about this ambiguous situation and so, in turn [34], she goes on with her investigation. First, her negative judgement is explicitly stated: "Oh no, I think something is up"—which, in the Italian version, is rendered into the more idiomatic and popular expression: "Eh no, qua c'è qualcosa che non mi quadra" (the equivalent in English of: "Eh no, there's something fishy here"). Then, her negative judgement becomes implicit when she refers to her solid experience of 'mystery solver' developed by watching assiduously the famous TV detective series *Murder She Wrote* (featuring an elderly lady who, being a writer of mystery stories, always finds herself involved in real crimes that she eventually solves): "Uh, yeah, I've seen enough of that *Murder She Wrote* to figure that out". In the Italian version, Annarò's reliance on such indirect, TV-mediated experience seems to be less decisive than her own keen intuition, as made clear by her use of the hedge "forse" ("maybe") in opposition to the strong—and quite vulgar—claim "non mi fregate" ("you don't cheat on me"): "Eh, forse ho visto troppi episodi della *Signora in Giallo* (*The Lady in Yellow*—the Italian translation of the title of the above-mentioned series—'yellow' being the colour of the cover of a famous Italian series of detective-story books in the seventies), ma non mi fregate" ("Eh, maybe I've seen too many episodes of *Murder She Wrote*, but you don't cheat on me"). Roseanne, in the original version, now starts her investigation by examining the clues and expressing her explicit judgements. Initially her judgement on David's behaviour is overtly negative: "Let's see here, David is pale and kind of weak kneed and all nervous. So there's no clues there". Then, her explicit judgement of Darlene's unusual kindness is only apparently positive as Roseanne actually judges negatively her daughter's blatant deceptiveness: "... But Darlene wants to sit next to me, and she said something nice to her brother". The logical conclusion she finally arrives at is thus expressed by means of another apparently positive—but actually negative - explicit judgement: "Eeww, I wonder. I know, you're pregnant!"—a deduction that triggers the laughter of everybody in the room except Darlene and David who know that this is not a joke, but the truth. When all the others realize that they are not joining in the general hilarity, they suddenly stop laughing and become more and more disconcerted, especially Roseanne who looks at both of them increasingly anxious and, when she realizes that Darlene is actually pregnant, she produces an implied negative judgement by shouting fretfully: "That was my joke guess!", thus reaching the climax of humorous Arousal in this scene. In the dubbing translation for the Italian television, though keeping the same Judgement pattern as in the original version, Annarò's enquiry follows, since the beginning, the register of the detective investigation ("Esaminiamo gli indizi" - "Let's examine the clues"), supported by an inquisitive tone of voice, but often shifting to the use of everyday and idiomatic expressions that are emphasized, for comic effects, by her Neapolitan accent: "Esaminiamo gli indizi: David è pallido, gli tremano le ginocchia ed è molto nervoso e fin qui stiamo nella normalità. Però Darlene si vuole sedere vicino a me e tratta suo fratello quasi come un essere umano. Uuuuu, gatta ci cova! Ho capito, aspetti un bambino! ... L'ho detto solamente per farci quattro risate!" ("Let's examine the clues: David is pale, his knees are shaking and he's very nervous and so far we are within normality. Yet Darlene wants to sit next to me and she treats her brother as a human being! Eeww, there's something fishy going on here. I've got it, you're pregnant! ... I've only said that just for the laugh of it!"). To increase the tension of the scene even more, David, in turn [35], prompts in the others a negative 'provoked judgement' on the situation by adding: "We're also getting married" which, in David's tone of voice, sounds like a kind of forced wedding—and which, in the Italian translation, acquires a more explicit, ultimate significance with the emphasis on the couple's final decision already taken: "E abbiamo deciso di sposarci" ("And we've also decided to get married"). At this announcement, all the members of Darlene's family hold their breath in a state of disbelief mixed with panic at Roseanne's impending explosion of anger, clearly visible in her facial expression. Indeed, in turn [36], she explodes with an infuriated "Well", immediately subsided to leave space to a totally opposite positive 'authorial affect' positioning which, from her strained tone of voice and restless bodily posture, is obviously only feigned since, in fact, her emotional stance about the situation is utterly negative: "I'm, I'm excited for you guys". To strengthen this, she also adds an apparently positive—but actually negative—explicit judgement on the young couple's behaviour: "I think it's great?". Roseanne, however, is left alone to deal with such unexpected event as the others are still struck dumb. So in an attempt to induce her husband Dan to take the control of the situation and act as a strict father, Roseanne expresses a 'provoked judgement' which is ostensibly positive but, actually, it is aimed at making her husband share her deeply negative evaluation: "... Dan, we're gonna getting grandparents! Isn't that great". At Dan's prolonged gawking silence, Roseanne feels obliged to go on with her fake enthusiasm concealing, under an apparent implicit positive judgement, a tangible negative one: "I'm getting one of those sweatshirts that says 'World's Greatest Grandma' on it, you know. And you can go out and get yourself, I dunno, like a cane something". In the Italian version, the evaluation pattern is not altered, though the way Annarò expresses her astonishment changes in terms of diatopic and diastratic style variations. In expressing the 'provoked judgement' addressed to her husband, for instance, Annarò's apparent positive enthusiasm is evidently marked by a negative sarcasm in her description of the exaggerated reactions that are socially expected at the news of becoming grandparents: "Dan! Tra un po' avremo un nipotino, non fai salti di gioia? Io mi compro subito una di quelle magliette con la scritta 'Questa è la nonna più pazza del mondo' e tu invece ti potresti comprare, che so, un bel bastone per andare a passeggio" ("Dan! We will soon have a grandchild, don't you jump for joy? I'm soon getting one of those sweatshirts that says 'This is the World's Craziest Grandma' on it and you instead could get yourself, I dunno, a nice cane to stroll around."). Dan, having being addressed to directly, in turn [37], still with his blank expression, manages to utter only "Yeah. Oh boy. Good, good, good, good, good", thus implicitly conveying a positive judgement on the situation, which is instead obviously negative. The Italian version does not provide a literal translation of Dan's turn, in fact he is represented as more conscious of his new state as a grandparent than in the original version: "Già. (A typical unnatural mistranslation into 'Italian dubbese' of the English 'yeah') Oh mamma. Bene, bene, nonni, nonni" ("Yeah. Oh dear me. Good, good, grandparents, grandparents"). Despite the humorous Arousal pattern, due to the mounting tension triggered by Roseanne's attempts at prompting Dan's explicit negative judgement and consequent pragmatic reaction, David takes her words at their face value believing that they would reinstate a sense of relief and so, in turn [38], he thanks Roseanne expressing an explicit positive judgement at her understanding: "Wow, thanks, Mrs. Conner. That wasn't the reaction I was expecting". In the version for the Italian television, however, the addition of the adverb "certo" ("certainly") makes David's relief stressed by a further, subtler and covert criticism to the way Annarò would usually react: "Wow, grazie signora Conner, non era certo la reazione che mi aspettavo" ("Wow, thanks, Mrs. Conner. Certainly that wasn't the reaction I was expecting"). Also Darlene, in turn [39], shares with David the same sense of relief by expressing her explicit positive judgement at her mother's apparent open-mindedness: "Yeah, me neither", to express, immediately afterwards, an implicit negative judgement at David's timorous behaviour by means of a tomboyish smutty expression: "I guess you peed your pants for nothing"—which, in the Italian version is mitigated by indirect exophoric reference: "Te la sei fatta nei pantaloni per niente" ("You did it in your pants for nothing"). Yet, in turn [40], Roseanne still makes a desperate attempt at stirring up Dan's negative 'provoked judgement' by prompting his reaction: "Dan! Dan!". Finally, in turn [41], Dan awakens from his freezed state of bewilderment only to give Roseanne a dispreferred answer focused on a negative appreciation of the chicken he is going to eat: "What? Oh, I'm just trying to figure out how to go about eating this thing". In the Italian dubbing translation, Dan's reply to Annarò is more discourteous: "Che vuoi?" ("What do you want?") and includes an explicit reference to the chicken which is no longer defined as "this thing". An effort to appease the atmosphere is then made, in turn [42], by Roseanne's sister Jackie who, too, suddenly awakens from her state of bewilderment and awkwardly gives her explicit positive judgement on Darlene—which, however, as she speaks, clearly and inadvertently turns into a negative one as she identifies many similarities with parallel events in her own life: "Well, I think it's good. That Darlene is getting pregnant, 'cause she's getting married 'cause she's has to - That's just what I did.". The Italian version of Jackie/Giacomì's cue is more explicit in its references than the original one: "Bé, è una notizia stupenda! Che Darlene è rimasta incinta e che sta per sposarsi perché deve perché è rimasta incinta e che... proprio come è successo a me." ("Well, that's wonderful news! That Darlene has got pregnant and that she's getting married 'cause she's has to 'cause she's got pregnant and that - That's just what happened to me."). Jackie's intervention, meant to restore a humorous Safety pattern, actually increases the state of comic tension. David, in turn [43], realizing that D.J. is looking intently at him with a clear expression of accusation, addresses him with an explicit negative judgement: "D.J., stop staring at me". To this, in turn [44], D.J. replies with another explicit negative judgement as he comments in a condescending tone: "Babies having babies".

So far, the Appraisal Framework has been applied to a comparative analysis of the original script of a scene from one of the *Roseanne* episodes and its dubbing translation for the Italian television. At this point, some different realizations carried out by students in Group A (acting translators) and Group B (the control group) will be examined together with their top-down, bottom-up, and interactive processes of physical and psychological embodiment of the sitcom characters.

5.4 Embodying the Appraisal Framework in *Roseanne* Sitcom Script

5.4.1 *Applying the Acting Translator Model: the improvisation phase*

The above-reported comparative analysis of the script from *Roseanne* shows an almost constant equivalence between the original and the translated versions in the characters' expression of their Attitude stances. A divergence, instead, can be identified in the rendering of the characters' personalities, with a particular reference to the main character of Roseanne who is turned into a more aggressive woman due to her snappy tone of voice in a Neapolitan accent. Hence, also in this case, the 'official' dubbing translators for the Italian version of this sitcom (produced by the same commercial TV channel that in Italy aired the mistranslated version of *The Nanny*) opted for a prevalently top-down approach to the rendering of the original characters into another language and culture.

The challenge for students/acting-translators participating in the longitudinal case study was, therefore, to search for pragmatically equivalent ways of conveying the original culture-bound behaviours of the sitcom characters to the Italian target audience—ways that could preserve the Attitude pattern that organize the scripted dialogue without distorting the original humour and characters' personalities. Also in this case, the students involved in the empirical investigation were the same ones from the Faculties of Foreign Languages and Literature of two Italian universities and with a post-intermediate/advanced competence of English as a foreign language. The case study was similarly grounded on the application of the Acting Translator Model aimed at the students/acting-translators' authentication and embodiment of the characters' attitudes and humour through top-down physical-theatre methods (Chekhov 1953; Johnstone 1981), and bottom-up conversation analysis informed, this time, by the Appraisal Framework (Martin and White 2005). The acting-translators' embodiment process will be investigated through the analysis of protocols (Ericsson and Simon 1984) reporting transcribed improvisations and retrospective verbalizations tape-recoded during the workshop. Also in this case, two groups of students were involved: Group A (the experimental group of students/acting-translators) who adopted top-down physical-theatre techniques of character embodiment and English/Italian dialogue improvisation—thus experiencing first-hand the diamesic dimension of the sitcom conversation—and Group B (the control group), who did not experience such initial top-down phase, but only the subsequent bottom-up one, joining Group A in applying the Appraisal Framework to the conversation analysis and translation.

During the top-down phase, students/acting-translators in Group A explored the characters in the *Roseanne* sitcom by embodying them 'physically' on a real stage of enactment where improvisation processes were performed in order to discover novel perspectives on their personalities. One of the physical-theatre *etudes* carried out at this stage was "Eye Contact", focused on Roseanne's domineering personality marking the humour of this sitcom. In pairs, each student/acting-translator was required to fix his/her eyes on the other student's eyes: in some cases, one of them, eventually, would look away from the other student's gaze, unable to stare him/her out and, thus, putting on an air of submission. In other cases, one would rather accept the challenge and, in return, keep staring the other student out trying to dominate him/her. Then, Group-A students were asked to move around the room and say 'hallo' to each other every time their eyes met: some of them were asked to stare the others out for a further few seconds, whereas others were asked to look away at once from the others' stares. At the end of the *etude*, the former reported that they had felt domineering, whereas the latter revealed they had felt subservient. Then, another physical-theatre *etude* based on improvisation was introduced to further explore the high/low status relationship between the dominant character of Roseanne and the other members of her family. Indeed, the *etude*, named "A Coffee for the Queen", was meant to explore the 'maximum status gap' between the dominant participant in the interaction and the submissive one by exploring a hierarchy of individuals starting from the Queen, on her throne, down to the humblest of her servants. Orders and reproaches had to move down through this hierarchy of people, whereas apologies and problems had to move back up to the opposite direction. Each individual could deal only with the one immediately superior or inferior to him/her, but the status difference between the two of them was however huge. The improvised exchange enacted by students in Group A, arranged in a row, was video-recorded and transcribed into the following protocol:

> *Queen:* Number one!
> *Servant 1:* Yes, your Majesty!
> *Q.:* A coffee!
> *S.1:* You shall be obeyed.
> *(to Servant 2)* Number Two! A coffee!
> *S.2:* Yes Sir.
> *(to Servant 3)* Number Three! A coffee for the Queen!
> *S.3: (to Servant 4)* Number Four! Get a coffee!
> *S.4:* Yes Sir.
> *Q.:* Where's my coffee?
> *S.1: (to Servant 2)* What's happening?
> *S.2:* I'll just check, Sir.
> *(to Servant 3)* Where's the coffee?
> *S.3:* Number Four is making it, Sir.
> *S.4:* I ... I ... am sorry. ... There's no coffee in the kitchen.
> *S.3:* No coffee in the kitchen??
> *(to Servant 2)* He can't find any coffee!
> *S.2:* How dare you address me without kneeling?
> *(to Servant 1)* Sir, I'm afraid there's no coffee left.
> *S.1:* No coffee? Send someone out to buy it!
> *S.2:* But it's night, Sir.
> *S.1:* How dare you contradict me? Send someone to steal it somewhere!
> *S.2:* Yes, Sir [...]

The aim of this improvisation task was to make students/acting-translators aware of the role and the related attitude of the sitcom characters on stage.

Another top-down task that Group-A students carried out was similarly based on improvisation and on the emotional embodiment of the sitcom characters' "conscious and unconscious" sides. The fact that the characters of the *Roseanne* sitcom overtly express positive or negative judgements and affective attitudes while they often covertly entail the opposite stances clearly emerges from the conversation analysis on the scene reported in *5.3.1* Such 'split attitude positioning' is also evident in Roseanne's words a few scenes later in the same episode, when her fierce negative judgements on Darlene's and David's behaviour, hardly held off, turn into more lenient—yet still cynical—evaluations. For instance, Roseanne comments on Darlene's pregnancy with her husband Dan in the kitchen, after dinner, and she judges her daughter sarcastically though she compassionately empathizes with her: "Well, no, actually I think we are making a little progress in this family. Becky got married when she was seventeen. I was only eighteen. At last a Conner woman is mature enough to put it off 'til she's nineteen years old." (The version for the Italian television is more sarcastic in its diatopic lexical choices: "No, anzi, stiamo facendo dei piccoli progressi in questa famiglia. Becky si è sposata quando teneva diciassette anni. Io ne avevo diciotto. Finalmente una Conner è abbastanza matura da sposarsi alla veneranda età di diciannove anni" - "No, on the contrary, we are making a little progress in this family. Becky got married when she was seventeen. I was only eighteen. At last a Conner woman is mature enough to get married at the venerable age of nineteen"). Then, Roseanne criticizes David, too, for his weak and unmanly nature but, indeed, she is positively appreciating him for his caring personality: "Well, I don't know. I can't think of a better mother for a child than David" (which, reformulated for the Italian television version, becomes: "Beh, non lo so. Un bambino non potrebbe avere una madre migliore di ... David" - "Well, I don't know. A child couldn't have a better mother than ... David"). The "Conscious vs. Unconscious" improvisation task aims precisely at making students/acting-translators aware of the dissociation between the characters' conscious and unconscious minds—what they say, in fact, may not correspond to what they really think or feel. For this task, students were arranged in pairs, sitting shoulder to shoulder. In a pair, both students embodied the same character but only one of them read his/her original turn, thus representing the character's conscious side. The other student in the pair, instead, was required to improvise in Italian on what s/he believed was going on in the character's mind at that moment, thus representing his/her unconscious side. For instance, in dealing with the 'dinner scene' (exchange 2), while some students read the 'conscious' script through, overtly embodying the characters saying something 'expected' and 'conventional' in response to the unexpected situation, some other students improvised on the characters' 'unconscious judgements and affective attitudes', particularly as they held their breath in disbelief and panic at Roseanne's possible furious reactions after Darlene's and David's revelation. Also in the initial 'porch scene' (exchange 1), when Darlene reveals her pregnancy to a dismayed David, students explored their unconscious sides as Darlene covertly judges in negative and disparaging ways David's anxious reaction to her news, and David, in his turn, covertly judges with contempt Darlene's unfair framing him. This entails that, during this task, students/acting-translators' deep concentration was crucial as they needed to identify themselves totally with the roles. What follows is the transcription into a protocol of the video-recording of one of these improvisation tasks: 'column 1' reproduces the characters' turns read from the original script by the 'conscious-side' students in the pairs; 'column 2' reports some instances of the characters' thoughts and feelings going on in their minds as they were involved in the dialogue, subjectively inferred and formulated by various 'unconscious-side' students in the pairs through improvisation in the Italian language. Italian was used at this stage to encourage students/acting-translators to produce a language that could be 'true' to the character they respectively 'embodied' as this would facilitate them in making 'natural' and familiar choices in Italian once they were required to translate the original script for dubbing. 'Column 3' offers an English back-translation of the Italian improvisation choices made by students.

Roseanne (***Pappa e Ciccia***) episode #920 *Another mouth to shut up*
Exchange 1: turns [1]-[16]; Exchange 2: turns [17]-[44]

1. Characters' CONSCIOUS side (original English version)	***2. Characters' UNCONSCIOUS side (Italian improvisation)***	***3. Characters' UNCONSCIOUS side (back-translation into Standard English of Italian improvisation)***
[Ext. Porch - Night]	**[Esterno, Portico - Sera]**	**[Ext. Porch - Night]**
[1] **DAVID:** Pregnant, you mean like, pregnant? **[(-) (Imp)Judg]**	*[1]* **DAVID: [a]** Ma che sta dicendo? Incinta? Lo sapevo! Mi voleva incastrare e c'è riuscita! **[b]** Incinta? Ha fatto tutto sola! Non potevo decidere pure io? Pensa di essersi sistemata, ma si sbaglia! **[c]** Incinta? E chi lo vuole 'sto figlio? Io no di certo!	*[1]* **DAVID: [a]** What is she saying? Pregnant? I knew! She wanted to catch me and she's succeeded! **[b]** Pregnant? She did all by herself! Couldn't I take the decision as well? She's sure she's settled down, but she's wrong! **[c]** Pregnant? And who wants this child? I certainly don't!
[2] **DARLENE:** Yes, David, you've knocked me up. **[(-/+) (Imp)Judg]**	*[2]* **DARLENE: [a]** Stupido vigliacco, te la vuoi svignare, ma ormai è fatta! **[b]** Caspita! Ha paura! Non è che non lo vuole il figlio? E io che faccio? **[c]** Non è colpa mia, capisci? Tu mi hai messo incinta e mo' che fai, non ti prendi la responsabilità? **[d]** Adesso stai nel panico, ma poi quando ti riprendi sarai felice!	*[2]* **DARLENE: [a]** Silly coward, you want to slink away, but, well, it's done now! **[b]** Gosh! He's scared! Does this mean that he doesn't want the child? And what shall I do? **[c]** I'm not to blame, do you understand? You made me pregnant and now, what are you doing, wouldn't you assume responsibility for this? **[d]** Now you're panic-struck, but then, when you pull yourself together you will be happy!
[3] **DAVID:** How? When? **[(-) (Pro)Judg]**	*[3]* **DAVID: [a]** Ma che stai dicendo? Io ho sempre preso le mie precauzioni! **[b]** Mi prendi in giro? Ma quando mai siamo stati davvero insieme?	**DAVID: [a]** But what are you saying? I've always taken my precautions! **[b]** Are you fooling me? Whenever have we actually been together?

[4] **DARLENE:** When? Disney World. **[(+) (Imp)Judg]**	*[4]* **DARLENE: [a]** E' così imbranato che non si è neanche reso conto che abbiamo fatto sesso! **[b]** Possibile che per lui non sia stato memorabile? **[c]** Vedi come sono superfertile? È bastato davvero poco!	*[4]* **DARLENE: [a]** He's so clumsy that he didn't even realize that we had sex! **[b]** Is it possible that for him that was not memorable? **[c]** Do you see how super-fertile I am? The little we did was enough indeed!
[5] **DAVID:** Oh, my god! You mean that night after the fireworks? **[(-/+) (Pro)Judg]**	*[5]* **DAVID: [a]** Ehi! Sono proprio un vero macho! Son bastati pochi secondi e ta-ta l'ho messa incinta! **[b]** Ma come è possibile? È stato velocissimo, non è quasi successo nulla!	*[5]* **DAVID: [a]** Ehi! I'm really a true macho! Few seconds were enough and ta-ta, I made her pregnant! **[b]** But how is it possible? It was very quick indeed, nothing – or so – really happened!
[6] **DARLENE:** Well, either that **[(-) (Imp)Judg]**, or it truly is a Magic Kingdom. **[(-) App]**	*[6]* **DARLENE: [a]** Oh, che inetto! È come un bambinone! Beh, in effetti si è trattato solo di una sveltina! **[b]** E hai ragione, imbranato! È stato tutto così deludente che solo la magia di quel posto mi ha fatto restare incinta!	*[6]* **DARLENE: [a]** Oh, he's so inept! He's like a big baby! Well, actually, that was only a quicky after all! **[b]** And you are right, you gawky guy! It was all so disappointing that only the magic of that place made me get pregnant!
[7] **DAVID:** Wow. What are we gonna do? **[(-) (Aut)Aff]**	*[7]* **DAVID: [a]** Povero me! Povero me! Come farò adesso a caricarmi un figlio? Una famiglia? **[b]** E mo' che faccio? Me ne scappo via? La mando subito al diavolo, lei col suo bambino! Che mi doveva capitare!	*[7]* **DAVID: [a]** Poor me! Poor me! How can I manage now to burden myself with a child? With a family? **[b]** And now, what shall I do? Shall I run away? I'll tell her immediately to go to hell, and with her baby too! What had to happen to me!
[8] **DARLENE:** Oh, don't worry. You know, getting married and having a baby can't change things that much. **[(+) (Pro)Judg]**	*[8]* **DARLENE: [a]** Che penoso! Non sa prendersi le sue responsabilità! **[b]** Lo devo rassicurare, poveretto! La notizia lo ha sconvolto!	*[8]* **DARLENE: [a]** What a pathetic guy! He doesn't know how to assume responsibility for what he's done! **[b]** I must reassure him, poor thing! The news has upset him badly!
[9] **DAVID:** I kinda wanted a dog first. **[(+/-) (Aut)Aff]**	*[9]* **DAVID: [a]** Io... io non sono pronto a diventare padre! Io potrei solo accudire un cucciolo di cane, non un neonato! **[b]** Io sono un bambino, io voglio ancora tante cose prima di diventare adulto, io voglio un cane... un cane non richiede responsabilità così grandi...	*[9]* **DAVID: [a]** I'm... I'm not ready to be a father! I'm just a boy! I could just look after a puppy, not a baby! **[b]** I'm a child, I still want so many things before becoming adult, I want a dog... a dog is not such a big responsibility...
[10] **DARLENE:** Oh, it'll be okay. I'm still gonna finish school. And by getting married I can get on your health coverage, our car insurance will go down, we'll be in line for married student housing ... I mean, it just makes sense, you know. **[(+) (Exp)Judg]**	*[10]* **DARLENE: [a]** Idiota! Tu non vuoi diventare adulto, eh? Sentimi, adesso! Dobbiamo fare esattamente come ti dico! **[b]** Non riesci a capire che non ci sono proprio problemi! Al contrario! Le cose saranno più facili... almeno per me! Sarò più indipendente, grazie ai vantaggi che otterrò come giovane madre e moglie!	*[10]* **DARLENE: [a]** You idiot! You don't want to become an adult, uh? Listen to me now! We must do exactly what I'm saying! **[b]** You can't just see that there's no problem at all! On the contrary! Things will become easier... for me, at least! I'll be more independent, thanks to the advantages I'll get as a young mother and bride!
[11] **DAVID:** ...Wouldn't have to be a big dog. **[(+/-) (Non-Aut)Aff]**	*[11]* **DAVID: [a]** Mannaggia! Mi sta incastrando! Voglio scappare via da qui! Girerò per il mondo senza meta, libero, col mio cane come unico amico! **[b]** No! No! No! Non voglio tutto questo! Voglio	*[11]* **DAVID: [a]** Damn! She's framing me! I want to run away from here! I'll wander around the world free, with my dog as my only friend! **[b]** No! No! No! I don't want all this! I just want to

	solo essere un bambino e giocare col mio cagnolino!	be a child and play with my doggy!
[12] **DARLENE:** Come on. Let's go tell everybody inside and get this over with. **[(-/+) (Aut)Aff]**	*[12]* **DARLENE: [a]** Non puoi sfuggire adesso! Devi dire a tutti che adesso ti sei compromesso con me e che mi sposerai! **[b]** Poterebbe sentirsi sollevato se dice a tutti di questa cosa, perché gli altri si congratulerebbero con lui e lui si sentirebbe rassicurato.	*[12]* **DARLENE: [a]** You can't escape, now! You must tell everybody that now you've committed yourself with me and you'll marry me! **[b]** He may feel relieved if he tells everybody about this, because the others would congratulate with him and he would feel reassured.
[13] **DAVID:** Whoa, whoa, slow down. **[(-) (Exp)Judg]** You mean, tell everyone in there? **[(-) (Imp)Judg]** Look, Darlene, couldn't we wait a few months? **[(-) (Pro)Judg]** I mean, then they would just think you were getting fat - they gotta be expecting that **[(-) App]**. So then, when we do tell them, they'll just go, "Oh, good she's not getting fat!" **[(+) App] / [(-) (Imp)Judg]**	*[13]* **DAVID: [a]** Oddio! Vuole dirlo a tutti! No! Dobbiami inventarci... se lei si ingrassa non è a causa del bambino... Diventerà grassa come sua madre! E io ora sono legato a lei per sempre! **[b]** Devo fermarla! È pazza! E diventerà pure brutta e grassa come i suoi genitori! Oh, come posso liberarmi di tutto questo? **[c]** Non sono pronto! Mi deve rispettare! Io non ho ancora preso una decisione su che cosa voglio fare con questo bambino! Deve aspettare, adesso!	*[13]* **DAVID: [a]** Gosh! She wants to tell everyone! No! We must invent... if she gets fat it is not because of the baby... She will become fat like her mother! And I'm now tied to her for ever! **[b]** I must stop her! She's mad! And she will become ugly and fat like her parents, too! Oh, how can I get rid of all this? **[c]** I'm not ready! She must respect me! I haven't yet made up my mind on what I want to do with this baby! She must wait, now!
[14] **DARLENE:** Alright, we don't have to tell them yet. Now take a deep breath and try not to look so pasty. **[(-) App]**	*[14]* **DARLENE: [a]** Ok, non posso forzarlo! Adesso è troppo sconvolto! Aspetto qualche altro giorno. **[b]** Idiota! Va bene, aspettiamo! Stai per svenire! **[c]** Tu pensi che cambierò idea sul tenermi il bambino, lo so, ma ti sbagli di grosso! Vedrai! **[d]** E' un poverino! Ora non è pronto, non posso forzarlo, deve ancora accettare l'idea di diventare papa. Presto gli piacerà, ne sono sicura.	*[14]* **DARLENE: [a]** Okay, I can't push him! He's too shocked now! I'll wait for some more days. **[b]** You idiot! Alright, let's wait! You're going to faint! **[c]** You think I'll change my mind about keeping this baby, I know, But you're very wrong! You'll see! **[d]** He's a poor thing! He's not ready now, I can't force him, he has still to accept the idea he is a dad. He'll like it soon, I'm sure.
[15] **DAVID:** We'll just, we'll tell them the movie we just saw affected me profoundly. **[(-) (Exp)Judg]**	*[15]* **DAVID: [a]** Si è calmata! Che sollievo! **[b]** E' rinsavita! Bene, adesso dobbiamo inventarci una scusa nel caso la sua famiglia sospetta qualcosa.	*[15]* **DAVID: [a]** She cooled down! What a relief! **[b]** She's returned to reason! Well, now we must invent an excuse if her family suspects anything.
[16] **DARLENE:** Okay, let's go inside. You ready? After you ... Daddy. **[(+) (Imp)Judg]**	*[16]* **DARLENE: [a]** Mò basta e inizia ad accettare la tua nuova condizione! **[b]** Ok, devo trattarti come un bambino, invece adesso sei un 'papino', lo capisci?	*[16]* **DARLENE: [a]** Now stop, and start accepting your new condition! **[b]** Okay, I have to treat you like a baby, but you're a 'daddy' now, do you understand?
[Int. Kitchen]	**[Interno, Cucina]**	**[Int. Kitchen]**
[17] **D.J.:** What the hell are those? **[(-) (Pro)Judg]**	*[17]* **D.J.: [a]** Sto morendo di fame e questi polli sono minuscoli! **[b]** Questi devono essere uccellini! Mannaggia! Ho fame!	*[17]* **D.J.: [a]** I'm starving and these chicken are so tiny! **[b]** These must be little birds, not chicken! Damn! I'm hungry!

[18] **ROSEANNE:** They're cornish game hens. I, uh, bought 'em off this guy that was selling them off the back of his truck down at the, uh, gas station parking lot. It's the very same guy that I bought our stereo speakers from last week. **[(-) (Imp)Judg]** *(Darlene and David enter from the living room)* Hey you guys just in time for dinner. **[(+) (Exp)Judg]** Grab a plate. Sit down here, David.	*[18]* **ROSEANNE: [a]** Sto facendo mangiare spazzatura alla mia famiglia! Mi sento in colpa, ma non ho soldi da spendere in cibo sano. Ah, stanno arrivando altri due! Dove lo trovo dell'altro cibo per loro? **[b]** Beh? Che c'è? Mangiate e state zitti! Siete fortunati che avete ancora qualcosa da mangiare! Ecco che arrivano altri due da sfamare! **[c]** Sì, sono davvero trascurata, non m'importa dove lo compro il cibo e se è buono o no! Ma sono così stanca, mi sento così pesante e gonfia che dopo che faccio la spesa in fretta non vedo l'ora di tornare a casa e riposarmi!	*[18]* **ROSEANNE: [a]** I'm making my family eat rubbish! I feel guilty, but I have no money to spend in healthy food. Ah, two more of them are coming! Where shall I find extra food for them? **[b]** Well? What's the matter? Eat and shut up! You're lucky you still have something to eat! Here come too more guys to feed! **[c]** Yeah, I'm really careless, I don't mind where I buy food and if it's good or not! But I'm so tired, I feel so heavy and swollen that after shopping hastily I really look forward to coming back home and relax!
[19] **DAVID:** ...Next to you? **[(-) (Imp)Judg]**	*[19]* **DAVID: [a]** Che? Vuole che mi sieda accanto a lei? E' una strega! Capirà immediatamente come mi sto sentendo adesso! **[b]** Accanto a lei? Mi leggerà nel pensiero e quando vedrà che sono spaventato di diventare padre e sposare sua figlia mi ucciderà!	*[19]* **DAVID: [a]** What? She wants me to sit next to her? She's a witch! She'll understand immediately how I'm feeling now! **[b]** Next to her? She'll read my mind and, when she sees that I'm scared of becoming a father and marrying her daughter she'll murder me!
[20] **ROSEANNE:** Yeah, come tell me about your, uh, new job as a graphic artist, there. **[(+) App]**	*[20]* **ROSEANNE: [a]** Non solo sono esausta, devo pure intrattenere conversazione con questo tizio sul suo nuovo lavoro! **[b]** Non ho ancora chiesto nulla sul nuovo impiego di David! Sono davvero una sconsiderata! Lui deve essere emozionato e a me non me ne importa!	*[20]* **ROSEANNE: [a]** Not only am I worn-out, I have also to entertain a conversation with this guy on his new job! **[b]** I haven't yet asked anything about David's new job! I'm so thoughtless! He must be excited and I don't care!
[21] **JACKIE:** David, congratulations on the job. Is it on a computer, or do you just draw by hand? **[(+) App]**	*[21]* **JACKIE: [a]** A nessuno importa del nuovo lavoro di David! Che schifo! Devo chiedergli io qualcosa, altrimenti tutti pensano ai fatti propri! **[b]** Vorrei saperne di più del suo lavoro! Non ne parla troppo! E' un lavoro misterioso! Voglio saperne di più, ma devo stare attenta a non pressarlo troppo con le domande.	*[21]* **JACKIE: [a]** Nobody cares about David's new job! Too bad! I must ask him something, otherwise everyone minds one's own business! **[b]** I'd like to know more about his job! He doesn't talk too much about it! It's a mystery job! I want to know more, but I must be careful not to be too pushy with my questions.
[22] **DAVID:** Uh, thanks, I'm fine. **[(+/-) (Aut)Aff]**	*[22]* **DAVID: [a]** Che? Mi ha chiesto qualcosa? Ha scoperto che sono stravolto? **[b]** Eh? Forse mi ha chiesto come sto. O che?	*[22]* **DAVID: [a]** What? Has she asked me anything? Has she discovered that I'm upset? **[b]** Eh? Maybe she's asked me how I am. Or what?
[23] **DAN:** I guess you're pretty excited about moving to Chicago, huh? **[(+) (Exp)Judg]**	*[23]* **DAN: [a]** Che rimbambito! Sei talmente ottuso che non riesci a concentrarti sulle domande! Ma forse è agitato per via delle novità nella sua vita... **[b]** È davvero sconvolto! Il nuovo lavoro e il trasferimento a Chicago lo hanno ridotto allo stato confusionale.	*[23]* **DAN: [a]** You dumb! You're so dull-witted that you don't manage to focus on questions! But perhaps he's excited about his new life... **[b]** He's quite dazed! His new job and moving to Chicago have confused him.

[24] **DAVID:** Uh, uh-huh. Course it means I'll have to move to Chicago. **[(+/-) (Exp)Judg]** ... Oh, I'm so confused... **[(-) (Aut) Aff]**	*[24]* **DAVID: [a]** Ma... ma... che domanda! Non lo sa che devo trasferirmi a Chicago? Ma... era questa la domanda? Oddio! **[b]** Che? Perché continuano a farmi domande? Che sta dicendo? Chicago? Sì, devo trasferirmi lì...	*[24]* **DAVID: [a]** But... but... what a question! Doesn't he know that I have to move to Chicago? But... was this his question? Oh my God! **[b]** What? Why are they keeping on asking me questions? What is he saying? Chicago? Yes, I'll have to move there...
[25] **D.J.:** Oh, they're some kind of tiny chickens. We didn't know what they were either. **[(-) App]**	*[25]* **D.J.: [a]** È davvero sconcertato per via di questi polli minuscoli! Chissà che pensa che sono!! Eh eh! **[b]** David è sconvolto perché non capisce che cosa gli stiamo dando da mangiare! Sembrano gattini... sì! Adesso gli dico che sono gattini! Bé, no, sarebbe proprio una cattiveria!	*[25]* **D.J.: [a]** He's really confused by these tiny chickens! I wonder what he thinks they are!! Eh eh! **[b]** David is dazed as he doesn't understand what we are giving him to eat! They look like kittens... yeah! Now I tell him they are kittens! Well, no, it's too bad!
[26] **ROSEANNE:** No, I don't think that's it D.J., David's just a little excited about his new job. Isn't that right David? **[(+/-) (Exp)Judg]**	*[26]* **ROSEANNE: [a]** D.J. è un sempliciotto. No, questo tipo qui è molto strano stasera, è stordito e io voglio scoprire perché. **[b]** D.J. filtra le cose dal suo punto di vista bambinesco, ma qui c'è qualcosa di sospetto in David che io voglio capire. **[c]** No, D.J. non coglie il problema, naturalmente. Qualcosa sta andando male col nuovo impiego di David... voglio saperne di più.	*[26]* **ROSEANNE: [a]** D.J. is a simpleton. No, this guy here is quite strange tonight, he's dazed and I want to discover why. **[b]** D.J. filters things from his childish point of view, but here there's something fishy with David that I want to understand. **[c]** No, D.J. doesn't catch the problem, of course. Something is going wrong with David's new job... I want to know more.
[27] **DAVID:** The movie affected me profoundly. **[(-) (Aut)Aff]**	*[27]* **DAVID: [a]** M'ha beccato! Sì, è astuta, è vicina alla verità... capirà prestissimo... ma che sto dicendo? **[b]** Oddio, oddio! Ha capito! ... la scusa del film, sì, la scusa del film... oh, che penoso!	*[27]* **DAVID: [a]** She's caught me! Yeah, she's cunning, she's close to the truth... she'll understand very soon... but what am I saying? **[b]** Oh my God, oh my God! She's understood! ... The movie excuse, yes, the movie excuse... oh, how pathetic!
[28] **DARLENE:** Uh, David, why don't you let me sit there. You've been hogging Mom long enough. **[(-) (Exp)Judg]**	*[28]* **DARLENE: [a]** Idiota! Idiota! Idiota! E idiota! La sta facendo insospettire! Inizierà a fare domande... e lui non saprà come gestirla! Devo intervenire! **[b]** Oh, oh, David è davvero terrorizzato, è incapace di controllare la mamma, e lei ha quasi capito tutto, non smetterà di fare domande, vuole arrivare alla verità! David non dovrebbe starle così vicino!	*[28]* **DARLENE: [a]** Idiot! Idiot! Idiot! And idiot! He's making her suspicious! She will start to ask... and he won't know how to manage her! I must intervene! **[b]** Oh, oh, David is really frightened, he's unable to control Mom, and she's almost understood everything, she won't stop asking questions, she wants to get to the truth! David shouldn't stay so close to her!
[29] **DAVID:** Okay, good, here. **[(+/-) (Imp)Judg]**	*[29]* **DAVID: [a]** Oh, sì, buona idea! Credo che sto per svenire! **[b]** Oh, che? Sì, sì... Darlene sta tentando di salvarmi... dove vado? Dove? **[c]** Sì, giusto... vorrei scappare via... ma sono inchiodato qui, paralizzato... non riesco a muovermi... non riesco a pensare a nulla... ho bisogno di aiuto...	*[29]* **DAVID: [a]** Oh, yeah, good idea! I think I'm going to faint! **[b]** Oh, what? Yes, yes... Darlene's trying to save me... where shall I go? Where? **[c]** Yeah, right... I'd like to run away... but I'm stuck here, paralyzed... I can't move... I can't think of anything... I need help...

[30] **DARLENE:** Uh, but you should sit somewhere, you know. **[(-) (Imp)Judg]**	*[30]* **DARLENE: [a]** Oh mio Dio! Se ne sta lì in piedi come un idiota! La mamma ha già capito tutto adesso! **[b]** Sono terrorizzata! Ora sono in uno stato di confusione totale... David sta lì in piedi, spaventato, senza fare nulla e sta per collassare...	*[30]* **DARLENE: [a]** Oh my God! He's standing there like an idiot! Mom has understood everything now! **[b]** I'm frightened! I'm in a state of total confusion, now... David's standing there, scared, doing nothing and he's going to collapse...
[31] **ROSEANNE:** What's up? I smell fear. I love that smell. **[(-) (Aut)Aff]** But what's up? **[(-) (Exp)Judg]**	*[31]* **ROSEANNE: [a]** Sono spaventata... sto per avere brutte notizie... non sono sicura di volerle sapere... perché queste cose brutte devono accadere sempre a me? **[b]** Deve essere successo qualcosa di molto brutto... sono terrorizzata... non sono sicura di poterlo affrontare... che hanno fatto? **[c]** Ah... li ho scoperti... Immaginavano che non mi sarei accorta che c'era qualcosa che non andava, ma io sono in gamba, e ora scoprirò tutto!	*[31]* **ROSEANNE: [a]** I'm scared... I'm very close to bad news... I'm not sure I want to know... why should these bad things have to happen always to me? **[b]** Something very bad must have happened... I'm frightened... I'm not sure I can cope with this... what have they done? **[c]** Ah... I've caught them... They imagined I wouldn't realize that something was up, but I'm clever, and now I'll discover everything!
[32] **DARLENE:** Nothing's up. God! **[(+/-) (Exp)Judg]** ... Hey, D.J., that's a great shirt. Where'd you get it? **[(+) App]**	*[32]* **DARLENE [a]** Ha capito! Siamo in trappola! Devo distrarre la loro attenzione da noi... la camicia di D.J., forse... **[b]** No no no no, non può sapere adesso, ci uccide! Non sono pronta, ora cambio argomento, concentro la loro attenzione su... su... D.J.!	*[32]* **DARLENE: [a]** She's understood! We're caught up! I must turn their attention away from us... D.J.'s shirt, maybe... **[b]** No no no no, she can't know now, she'll kill us! I'm not ready, now I'll change topic, I'll focus their attention on... on... D.J.!
[33] **D.J.:** My closet. **[(-) App]**	*[33]* **D.J.: [a]** Bè? Mm... non mi fido di lei... sta per dirmi qualcosa di odioso! **[b]** Che le succede? Vuole che faccia qualcosa per lei... sì, altrimenti non mi direbbe cose gentili...	*[33]* **D.J.: [a]** Well? Mm.. I don't trust her... she's going to say something nasty to me! **[b]** What's the matter with her? She wants me to do something for her... yes, otherwise she wouldn't tell me nice things...
[34] **ROSEANNE:** Oh no, I think something is up. **[(-) (Exp)Judg]** Uh, yeah, I've seen enough of that "Murder She Wrote" to figure that out. **[(-) (Imp)Judg]** ... Let's see here, David is pale and kind of weak kneed and all nervous. So, there's no clues there. **[(-) (Exp)Judg]** ... But Darlene wants to sit next to me, and she said something nice to her brother. **[(+/-) (Exp)Judg]** Eeww, I wonder. I know, you're pregnant! **[(-) (Imp)Judg]** *(All laugh except Darlene and David. Then everyone stops laughing)* That was my joke guess! **[(-) (Imp)Judg]**	*34]* **ROSEANNE: [a]** Sono sicura che voglio sapere? Perché voglio sempre scoprire la verità? Perché devo sempre andare in cerca di sofferenza?... Ma è incinta? **[b]** David forse ha bisogno di aiuto... e pure Darlene... ma non parlano... sono spaventati... devo scoprire di cosa hanno bisogno... forse Darlene è incinta... **[c]** Ah, pensano di sfuggirmi! Ma non lo faranno! Devo sapere che stanno combinando! Non mi si può nascondere nulla! Sono molto astuta io! Potrei perfino scoprire che Darlene è incinta, eh eh eh **[d]** Darlene è incinta... ora ho capito... David è spaventato e non parlano... può essere così? No! E' solo la mia fantasia... Vediamo che sta succedendo... *(Tutti ridono eccetto Darlene e David. Poi tutti smettono di ridere)* **DARLENE:** Ci ha scoperti! Povera me!	*[34]* **ROSEANNE: [a]** Am I sure I want to know? Why do I always want to discover the truth? Why shall I always have to seek suffering?... But, is she pregnant? **[b]** David maybe needs help... and Darlene too... but they don't talk... they are scared... I must find out what they need... maybe Darlene is pregnant... **[c]** Ah, they think they can escape me! But they don't't! I must know what's up! Nothing can be hidden from me! I'm so clever! I may even discover that Darlene is pregnant, eh eh eh **[d]** Darlene is pregnant... now I understand... David is scared and they don't speak... could it be so? No! It's just my fantasy... Let's see what's going on... *(All laugh except Darlene and David. Then everyone stops laughing)*

	DAVID: Oddio! Oddio! È la fine! Mi devo rassegnare, ormai! **DAN:** Oh, che ridere! Ma t'immagini che disastro se era vero? **JACKIE:** Bè, spero che questo non succeda mai! Darlene non merita il mio destino miserabile. **D.J.:** Sììì, impossibile! Mia sorella e David sono due tonti! Non sanno nemmeno come fare i bambini! **ROSEANNE:** Per fortuna che non è così! Ero terrorizzata per niente... oh no? O no? Oh no! E' davvero incinta! Sì! Oh mio Dio! Che? **DAN:** Oh, ma che? Allora... è vero? E' vero? Sì, è vero, è vero! Come affronteremo tutto questo? **JACKIE:** Oh no! Oh no! Darlene è incinta! Oh poverina! E' tanto, tanto giovane! **D.J.:** Stanno facendo un bambino... bè perché sono tutti preoccupati per questo? Forse io sono felice, ma non darò questa soddisfazione a mia sorella!	**DARLENE:** She caught us! Poor me! **DAVID:** Oh God! Oh God! This is the end! I must give in, at this point! **DAN:** Oh, how funny! But do you imagine what a disaster if it were true? **JACKIE:** Well, I hope this would never happen! Darlene doesn't deserve my same miserable destiny. **D.J.:** Yeah, impossible! My sister and David are two dupes! They don't even know how to have babies! **ROSEANNE:** Luckily it's not so! I was frightened for nothing... or not? Or not? Oh no! She's really pregnant! Yes! Oh my God! What? **DAN:** Oh, but what? So... is it true? Is it true? Yes, it's true, it's true! How can we cope with all this? **JACKIE:** Oh no! Oh no! Darlene is pregnant! Oh poor thing! She's so, so young! **D.J.:** They're having a baby... well, why are they worried about this? Maybe I'm happy, but I will not give my sister this satisfaction!
[35] **DAVID:** We're also getting married. **[(-) (Pro)Judg]**	***[35]*** **DAVID:** **[a]** Diciamogli tutto adesso, diciamogli tutto... questa è anche responsabilità mia. **[b]** Devono sapere tutto adesso che sono scioccati! O saranno ancora più scioccati dopo, quando vengono a sapere di più... **[c]** Stanno per attaccare Darlene... non posso lasciarla sola!	***[35]*** **DAVID:** **[a]** Let's tell everything now, let's tell everything... this is also my responsibility. **[b]** They must know all now that they are shocked! Or they would be even more shocked again later, when they'll come to know more... **[c]** They're going to attack Darlene... I can't leave her alone!
[36] **ROSEANNE:** Well! I'm, I'm excited for you guys. **[(+/-) (Aut)Aff]** I think it's great? **[(+/-) (Exp)Judg]** ... Dan, we're gonna getting grandparents! Isn't that great. **[(+/-) (Pro)Judg]** I'm getting one of those sweatshirts that says "World's Greatest Grandma" on it, you know. And you can go out and get yourself, I dunno, like a cane something. **[(+/-) (Imp)Judg]**	***[36]*** **ROSEANNE:** [a] Sono furiosa... ma non posso essere sempre io quella che s'infuria per le cretinate che fa questa famiglia... nessun altro dice nulla... si aspettano che io esploda... ma devo trattenermi... **JACKIE:** Sta per saltare in aria! **DAN:** Sta per deflagrare... bene, non sarò io quello che se la deve vedere con questa faccenda. **D.J.:** Farà un massacro! **DARLENE:** S'infurierà, ma poi dovrà accettarlo. **DAVID:** Sta per menarmi... devo scappare... perché non riesco a scappare via da qui... **ROSEANNE:** **[a]** Dan è un vigliacco... se ne sta zitto! Zitto! Lascia tutta questa faccenda tremenda a	***[36]*** **ROSEANNE:** **[a]** I'm furious... but I can't always be the one who's furious for the foolish things this family does... nobody else is saying anything... they expect me to explode... but I must refrain... **JACKIE:** She's going to blow up! **DAN:** She's going to flare up... good, I won't be the one who has to deal with this matter. **D.J.** : She'll make a massacre! **DARLENE:** She'll get angry, but then she must accept it. **DAVID:** She's going to hit me... I must run... why can't I run away from here... **ROSEANNE:** **[a]** Dan's a coward... he's silent! Silent! Leaving

	a me!... Com'è possibile che non riesco a smuoverlo? È del tutto sbalordito! **[b]** Ma perché non m'aiuta? Perché? Non riesce a capire le conseguenze? Quelle negative? Nemmeno quelle positive? Nemmeno una reazione! Perché è senza parole? Perché non m'aiuta?	all this awful matter with me!... How is it possible that I can't wake him up? He's totally flabbergasted! **[b]** But why doesn't he help me? Why? Can't he see the consequences? The negative ones? Neither the positive ones? No reaction at all! Why is he speechless? Why doesn't he help me?
[37] **DAN:** Yeah. Oh boy. Good, good, good, good, good. **[(+/-) (Imp)Judg]**	***[37]*** **DAN: [a]** Perché si rivolge sempre a me? Perché non mi lascia in pace? **[b]** Stai zitta! Non voglio sentire! Non so che vuole da me... io non vado cercando altri guai!	***[37]*** **DAN: [a]** Why is she addressing me all the time? Why doesn't she leave me in peace? **[b]** Shut up! I don't want to hear! I don't know what she wants from me... I don't look for more troubles!
[38] **DAVID:** Wow, thanks, Mrs. Conner. that wasn't the reaction I was expecting. **[(+) (Exp) Judg]**	***[38]*** **DAVID: [a]** È così gentile! Così gentile! Riesce a vedere il lato bello di tutta questa storia! È proprio rassicurante! Non sarò da solo in questa avventura! **[b]** Che donna affettuosa! È così comprensiva! ¡È così felice per noi e per il bambino! Vedo le cose proprio sotto una luce diversa, positiva, adesso!	***[38]*** **DAVID: [a]** She's so nice! So nice! She can see the beautiful side of all this! This is really reassuring! I won't be alone in this adventure! **[b]** What a lovely woman! She's so understanding! And so happy for us and the child! I'm really seeing things under a different, positive light now.
[39] **DARLENE:** Yeah, me neither. **[(+) (Exp)Judg]** *(to David)* I guess you peed your pants for nothing. **[(-) (Imp)Judg]**	***[39]*** **DARLENE: [a]** Mia mamma è davvero speciale! Mi sorprende sempre! Mo David capirà quanto è buona! **[b]** Davvero non mi aspettavo che mia madre reagisse così a questa notizia! E' davvero eccezionale! Pure David ne sarà sorpreso!	***39]*** **DARLENE: [a]** My Mom is really special! She always surprises me! Now David shall know how kind she is! **[b]** Indeed, I didn't expect my mother reacting like this to this news! She's really exceptional! David shall be surprised too!
[40] **ROSEANNE:** Dan! Dan! **[(-) (Pro)Judg]**	***[40]*** **ROSEANNE: [a]** Maledizione! Mi stanno fraintendendo! Com'è possibile? Non capiscono che sono furiosa? Dan non riesce a capirmi? Che rimbambito! **[b]** Dan vigliacco! Li sta lasciando credere che sono veramente felice per tutto questo! Dovrebbe essere lui quello che reagisce rabbioso! Ma se ne sta lì, con l'espressione imbambolata, e mi lascia sola ad affrontare tutto!	***[40]*** **ROSEANNE: [a]** Damn! They're misunderstanding me! How is it possible? Can't they see I'm furious? Can't Dan understand me? What a sucker! **[b]** Coward Dan! He's letting them believe that I'm really happy for all this! He should be the one that reacts badly! But he's standing there, with his blank expression, leaving me alone to cope with everything!
[41] **DAN:** What? Oh, I'm just trying to figure out how to go about eating this thing. **[(-) App]**	***[41]*** **DAN: [a]** Insiste a rivolgersi a me! Non capisco perché non mi lascia in pace! Dopotutto stavamo parlando di questi polli strani! **[b]** Non me ne posso stare più per conto mio! E' una rottura! Perché non dice qualcosa di odioso a nome di tutti noi e fa saltare in aria quei due una volta per tutte?	***[41]*** **DAN: [a]** She insists on addressing me! I wonder why she doesn't leave me in peace! After all we were talking about these strange chicken! **[b]** I can't be on my own any longer! She's a nuisance! Why doesn't she say something nasty on behalf of us all, blasts the two of them once and for all?
[42] **JACKIE:** Well, I think it's good. That Darlene is getting pregnant, 'cause she's getting	***[42]*** **JACKIE: [a]** Devo intervenire per salvare Darlene... è in pericolo più di quanto possa	***[42]*** **JACKIE: [a]** I must intervene to save Darlene... she's in danger more than she can

married 'cause she's has to— That's just what I did. **[(+/-) (Exp)Judg]**	immaginare! Io lo so per esperienza diretta! È vero, deve sposarsi perché è incinta e ha bisogno di protezione e questa deve passare come una cosa buona! **[b]** Non posso lasciare sola Darlene adesso... Devo difenderla! E questo bambino deve pur essere il benvenuto in famiglia, come lo è stato il mio!	realize! I experienced this myself! It's true, she must get married 'cause she's pregnant and she needs protection, and this must pass as a good thing! **[b]** I can't leave Darlene alone, now... I must defend her! And this baby has to be welcome in the family, too, as mine was!
[43] **DAVID:** D.J., stop staring at me. **[(-) (Exp)Judg]**	***[43]*** **DAVID: [a]** Le cose non sono così positive come speravo! Veramente, come immaginavo, sua madre sta per esplodere di rabbia! E questo scemo di ragazzino continua a fissarmi con l'espressione di rimprovero! **[b]** Mi sbagliavo! Come mi aspettavo non stanno prendendo per niente bene tutta questa cosa! Perfino questo piccolo idiota mi sta giudicando negativamente, riversando la colpa su di me!	***[43]*** **DAVID: [a]** Things are not so positive as I hoped! Indeed, as I imagined, her mother's going to explode with rage! And this silly boy keeps staring at me reproachfully! **[b]** I was wrong! As expected they are not taking the whole thing well at all! Even this little idiot is judging me negatively, laying all the blame on me!
[44] **D.J.:** Babies having babies. **[(-) (Exp)Judg]**	***[44]*** **D.J.: [a]** Sono più adulto io di questi due tipi! Io non sarei così irresponsabile da fare bambini così giovane! **[b]** Mia sorella adesso è stata messa con le spalle al muro e i miei genitori di sicuro pensano che io sono più saggio di lei e del suo fidanzato cretino! Io sono davvero superiore a loro e loro devono percepire tutto il mio disprezzo!	***[44]*** **D.J.: [a]** I'm more grown up than these two guys! I wouldn't be so irresponsible as to make children so young! **[b]** My sister is now in a corner and my parents certainly think that I'm wiser than her and her silly boyfriend! I'm really superior to them and they have to feel all my despise!

The ultimate purpose of this "Conscious vs. Unconscious" improvisation task is to encourage Group-A students/acting-translators to embody the sitcom characters' personalities in order to explore their spontaneous 'Italian voices'. This is assumed to make their dubbing translation process a personal experience of giving characters the possibility of expressing themselves in Italian through natural and authentic pragmatic ways, not only according to the context of the sitcom, but also according to the characters' explicit and implicit 'Attitude' patterns of 'Affect', 'Judgement' and 'Appreciation' that construct the humour of this sitcom. In performing this task it is evident that Group-A students mainly emphasized the covert, 'unconscious' 'judgmental' and 'affective' positioning of this sitcom characters who, in quite intense ways, react emotionally and evaluate sternly each other's behaviours.

The success of such improvisation tasks explored so far is in fact evident in the subsequent phase of the embodiment process when students in both Groups A and B were required to provide their dubbing translation of the set scene of this sitcom.

5.4.2 *Applying the Acting Translator Model: the dubbing-translation phase*

After the first top-down phase carried out only by the students in Group A (i.e., the experimental group of acting translators), students in both Groups A and B (the latter being the control group with no input informed by the Acting-Translator Model) were asked to perform a dubbing translation of the above-analyzed sitcom scene from *Roseanne*. In the course of this task it was noticed that Group-A students still retained the 'physical memory' of the Italian language that would be 'naturally used' by the sitcom characters they had embodied in the previous improvisation stage. This meant that students adopted an 'interactive' (top-down/bottom-up) approach to the search for equivalent pragmatic choices that would be true to the characters' personalities as students had previously explored them. The implication in this case was that students respected the semantic and pragmatic layout of the script by activating a bottom-up analysis of the actual sense and meaning of the dialogue cues, but at the same time, they activated also a top-down process of seeking out in their physical memory the communicative style that each character would use if his/her language was Italian. The prevalent 'interactive' procedure of Group A as a whole, therefore, was to rehearse the ongoing translated script together as a 'company of players on stage', and the spontaneous choices that naturally emerged were not diatopically and diastratically marked by specific Italian accents, but were rather grounded on particular inflections and tones of their voices as if characters were 'possessing' the acting-translators' bodies and were speaking 'through them'. In this sense, the Group-A students/acting-translators brought to life the characters in the *Roseanne* sitcom neither by modifying the sense and the syntax of the script just to appeal to the target audience's familiar patterns of discourse (as it happened in the 'localized' version of *The Nanny* for the Italian TV), nor by imposing upon the characters any alien Italian accent that would typify them as members of a precise social class coming from a specific Italian geographical place (as it happened in the likewise 'localized' version of *Roseanne*). On the contrary, unmarked interactive choices were instead made—as, for instance, in the following case with Darlene's cue [10], where a spontaneous 'teenage' variation of Italian was employed, characterized by the use of colloquial terms (e.g., "macchina" rather than "automobile"), the present simple (*indicativo presente*) to refer to a future considered as certain, and by the use of a form of present continuous to indicate an action still in progress—without altering the Attitude pattern of the character's discourse. Here is Darlene's cue [10] followed by its literal back-translation into standard English: "Oh, andrà tutto bene. Io sto ancora finendo la scuola. Da sposati posso usufruire della tua assicurazione sanitaria, la nostra assicurazione della macchina diminuisce e siamo in regola per le case per studenti sposati. Vedi come tutto quadra?" (Literal back-translation: "Oh, everything will be okay. I'm still finishing school. As a married couple I can benefit from your health coverage, our car insurance goes down and we are in line for married student housing. Can you see how everything adds up?"). An alternative dubbing translation of the same cue [10] is: "È tutto ok. Io devo ancora finire la scuola e col matrimonio io sono coperta dalla tua assicurazione sanitaria, il costo dell'assicurazione dell'auto deve scendere e noi dobbiamo avere l'alloggio per studenti sposati... insomma, siamo a posto, sai?" (Literal back-translation: "Everything's okay. I must still finish school and with marriage I'm covered by your health insurance, the cost of the car insurance must go down and we must get the married student housing... in short, we're settled, you know?"). This alternative translation choice is likewise true to the resolute character of Darlene and reproduces the same present-simple pattern as the previous one, with the addition of the deontic modal verb "dovere" ("must") pointing to the incontestable series of favourable conditions – principally for her, and possibly for David, too. Other interesting solutions proposed by Group-A students are represented, for instance, by David's cue [13], here reproduced through a series of appropriate Italian alternatives (separated by slashes): "Ehi, ehi, vai piano! / Ferma, ferma, aspetta! – Intendi dirlo a tutti lì dentro? / Vuoi dire, dirlo a tutti di là? – Senti Darlene, non possiamo aspettare qualche mese? – Cioè / Voglio dire – che poi pensano solo che sei diventata grassa / così credono che stai solo ingrassando – devono aspettarselo / se lo aspettano / tanto se lo aspettano / e se lo aspettano – così poi quando glielo diciamo loro dicono / faranno solo "Oh meno male / Oh grazie a Dio / Ah bene! – non sta ingrassando! / non sta diventando grassa! / non è diventata grassa!" (Literal back-translation: "Ehi, ehi, slow down! / Stop, stop, wait! – You mean to tell everyone in there? / You mean, tell everyone over there? – Listen Darlene, can't we wait a few months?—I mean – that then they just think you've become fat / so they believe that you're getting fat – they must expect that / they expect that / after all they expect that / and they do expect that – so when we tell them they say "Oh thank goodness / Oh thank God / Ah good! – she's not getting fat! / she's not becoming fat! / she hasn't become fat!"). Also in this cue, the prevalent use of the present simple instead of the future tense or the conditional mood is the typical choice made by Italian teenagers and it was reproduced in the dubbing translation. Translating literally the original conditional forms would have made the style adopted by the two teenage characters too formal and unnatural in Italian. However, the original pattern of explicit, implicit and provoked judgements as well as the pattern of positive/negative appreciation were respected also in the translation options proposed by Group-A students.

The dubbing translation of Roseanne's cues was more challenging. Since this character shows a complex Attitude pattern made up of often contradictory implicit and explicit judgement positionings, the rendering of such complexity into a pragmatically equivalent Italian translation for dubbing was particularly difficult. Group-A students tried to solve it with the choice of a plain style with no specific dialectal accent. What emphasized the interplay of implicit/explicit judgement positionings in these students' Italian translation was instead Roseanne's inflection and tone of voice, which betrayed her repressed emotional response to her disquieting perception of an impending shocking revelation. For instance, in Roseanne's cue [34], when she pretends to be funny as she plays the detective role and uses the register of police investigations, her tone of voice fits the apparently amused expression of Roseanne's face, but the tone and pitch of her voice, progressively becoming louder as in the original version, suggests a mounting anxiety and a covert desire for exorcising her tension with the sense of humour. The example that follows shows a number of options (separated by slashes), pragmatically appropriate to the original Attitude pattern, that Group-A students proposed for cue [34]: "Oh no, secondo me è successo qualcosa. / Eh no, penso che sta succedendo qualcosa. / No, credo che è successo qualche cosa. / No no, qui c'è sotto qualcosa. *[(-) (Exp)Judg]* – Bé sì, ho visto già tante puntate della *Signora in Giallo* che capisco tutto. / Ho visto abbastanza *Signora in Giallo* per capire certe cose. / Ho visto così tante volte *La Signora in Giallo* che posso dire con certezza che c'è sotto qualcosa. / Eh sì, ho visto abbastanza di quella *Signora in Giallo* per capire che è così. *[(-) (Imp)Judg]* – Vediamo un pò: David è pallido, con le ginocchia tremolanti e tutto teso. Quindi lì nessun indizio… / Vediamo: David è pallido, le ginocchia sono molli e gli tremano perché è nervoso. Dunque, niente di strano… / Procediamo: David è pallido, ha le ginocchia molli ed è tutto agitato. Fin qui, niente di anormale… *[(-) (Exp)Judg]* – Ma Darlene si vuole sedere accanto a me e si è rivolta in modo gentile al fratello. / Ma Darlene vuole sedersi affianco a me e ha detto una cosa carina a suo fratello. / Ma Darlene vuole sedersi vicino a me e ha fatto un complimento a suo fratello. *[(+/-) (Exp)Judg]* – Quindi… ho capito! Sei incinta! / Bé, credo… ci sono! Sei incinta! / Eh, fammi pensare… sì! Sei incinta! *[(-) (Imp)Judg]* *(All laugh except Darlene and David. Then everyone stops laughing)* – Stavo tirando a indovinare per scherzo! / Stavo giocando a indovinare! / Era solo una battuta! / Stavo scherzando! *[(-) (Imp)Judg]*". (Literal back-translation: "Oh no, in my opinion something has happened. / Eh no, I think that something is up. / No, I believe that something has happened. / No no, here there's something behind this. *[(-) (Exp)Judg]* – Well, yeah, I've already seen so many episodes of *Murder She Wrote* that I figure out everything. / I've seen enough of *Murder She Wrote* to figure out such things. / I've seen so many times *Murder She Wrote* that I can say with certainty that there's something behind this. / Eh yeah, I've seen enough of that *Murder She Wrote* to figure out that it's so. *[(-) (Imp)Judg]* – Now let's see: David is pale, with trembling knees and all tense. So, no clues there… / Let's see: David is pale, his knees are weak and wobbly because he's nervous. So, nothing strange… / Let's proceed: David is pale, his knees are weak and he's all agitated. So far, nothing abnormal…

[(-) (Exp)Judg] – But Darlene wants to sit next to me and she addressed her brother kindly. / But Darlene wants to sit next to me and she said something nice to her brother. / But Darlene wants to sit near me and she paid a compliment to her brother. *[(+/-) (Exp)Judg]* – So... I've got it! You're pregnant! / Well, I believe... I've got it! You're pregnant! / Eh, Let me think about it... Yes! You're pregnant! *[(-) (Imp)Judg] (All laugh except Darlene and David. Then everyone stops laughing)* – I was just venturing a guess as a joke! / I was playing a guessing game! / I only meant it as a joke! / I was only joking! *[(-) (Imp)Judg]*").

Differently from Group-A students/acting-translators, students in control Group B did not adopt an interactive approach to dubbing translation since they could not ground their choices on the 'physical memory' of the characters' bodies and voices that Group-A students had instead developed during the previous top-down improvisation phase. As a result, the translation procedure that Group-B students mainly opted for was the traditional one of 'product localization', aimed at an exclusively top-down approach 'domesticating' the sitcom language according to the patterns humour that students assumed to be shared by the implied target audience. The objective, in this case, was to make the target audience familiar with the foreign context and the discourse practices of the American sitcom. More precisely, Group-B students' 'domestication' process entailed the use of Italian idiomatic expressions which, contrary to the expected sense of familiarity, could actually produce a sense of estrangement in the target sitcom viewers since they may instead perceive as incongruous such culturally-marked Italian expressions precisely because they are made to be uttered by American sitcom characters.

Some instances of an inappropriate use of Italian idiomatic expressions are represented by the following options to some of the cues (also literally back-translated into standard English): *(a)* Roseanne's cue [34]: "David sta come uno straccio e trema come una foglia / David è pallido, ha le ginocchia che gli fanno Giacomo-Giacomo / Ho capito! Sei in dolce attesa! / Era solo un indovina indovinello! (literal back-translation: "David looks like a rag and tremble like a leaf / David is pale, he has knees that are shaking under him like jelly [literal idiom rendering: "he has shaking knees that sound like 'James-James'"] / I've got it! You're expecting! [literally: 'you're a sweet expecting mother!'] / It was just my guessing the guess!"); *(b)* Darlene's cue [14]: "cerca di non sembrare così moscio." ("try not to look so down [literally: 'flabby']"); *(c)* Roseanne's cue [31]: "Che c'è? Sento puzza di bruciato. Mi piace questa puzza." ("What's up? I smell something burning [meaning: 'there's something fishy here']. I like this smell"); *(d)* Darlene's cue [28]: "Ehi David, perché non mi fai sedere là, sei stato mammone troppo a lungo. / sei stato tartassato da mamma abbastanza a lungo." ("Hey, David, why don't you let me sit there. You've been a mama's boy long enough. / You've been grilled by Mom long enough."); *(e)* Dan's cue [41]: " Sto solo provando a immaginare come ingoiare la faccenda." ("I'm just trying to imagine how to swallow this matter"). In all these instances of metaphorical use of the target Italian language, not only Group-B students seemed to disregard the actual time-span—and also the lip-synch—allowed by the sitcom video for each cue, but they also very often provided a mistranslation of the original cues just to make the target audience perceive them as familiar expressions.

Mistranslation, on the other hand, was indeed very frequent in Group-B students' rendering of the original script. This was mainly due to the students' wholly top-down choice of adopting a target-culture-oriented 'localization' in their translation of the conversation cues since they were often interpreted in detachment from the whole original sitcom context—as it usually happens in the normal practice of Italian TV dubbing translators. What follows is a series of mistranslation instances produced by Group-B students, together with their literal back-translations: *(a)* David's cue [1]: "Un bambino? Cioè... un bambino?" ("A baby? ... You mean, a baby?"); *(b)* Darlene's cue [2]: "Non vedi David che sono con il pancione?" ("Can't you see David that I'm with the big tummy?" [but the video clearly shows that Darlene has not yet got any 'big tummy']); *(c)* Darlene's cue [10]: "Io devo prima finire la scuola." ("I must first finish school."); *(d)* Dan's cue [37]: "Oh ragazzo! Bravo, bravo, bravo, bravo. / Dai ragazzi! Bene, bene, bene." (Oh, boy! Well done, well done, well done, well done. / Come on, guys! Very well, very well, very well."); *(e)* D.J.'s cue [44]: "I bambini avranno dei bambini!" ("The babies will have babies."); *(f)* Roseanne's cue [34]: "Ho visto *Jack lo Squartatore* troppe volte per poter immaginare. / Ho visto talmente tante volte *L'Ispettore Derrick* da poter affermare con certezza che qui c'è sotto qualcosa. / Guardiamo qui, David è pallido per esempio ginocchia tremanti e tutto nervoso. Quindi là non c'è traccia. / Eh, mi meraviglio. Ho capito, sei incinta!" ("I've seen *Jack the Ripper* too many times to be able to imagine. / I've seen so many times *Detective Inspector Derrick* to be able to declare with confidence that here there's something behind this. / Let's look at here, David is pale for example trembing knees and all nervous. So there's no trace. /Eh, I'm surprised. I've got it, you're pregnant!"); *(g)* Jackie's cue [42]: "Questo è solo quello che volevo dire. / È solo quello che pensavo." ("This is just what I wanted to say. / It's just what I thought."); *(h)* D.J.'s cue [25]: "Oh, sono una specie di minipolli. Non sappiamo cosa fossero prima." ("Oh, they'are some kind of mini chicken. We don't know what they were before."). In all these cases, mistranslation seems to be principally due, on the one hand, to the translators' top-down attempt to impose their own voice upon the characters' one by modifying the original cues in order to be 'authorially original' (as in instances *(a)*, *(b)*, and in *(f)*, for example, where the reference to Jack the Ripper—the nineteenth-century English killer murdering prostitutes—is totally inappropriate, and where the other reference to Derrick, a TV-fiction detective as famous as the original female protagonist of *Murder She Wrote*, has no apparent motivation justifying substitution). On the other hand, mistranslation may be due to the students' actual misunderstanding of the contextual, and even co-textual, elements of the sitcom script that give semantic sense and pragmatic meaning to the cues—as in the case with Dan's cue [37], in *(d)*, which is misinterpreted twice as his congratulating with David and then also with Darlene for what they have done.

Another common practice of Group-B students (and apparently in contrast with the previous top-down 'localization' practice) was to resort to 'dubbese'—namely, the 'unnatural' Italian variation that has developed from the bottom-up process of transferring lexical, structural and pragmatic features from English to Italian, often by resorting to inappropriate calque and false-friend choices. This practice is probably due to the short period of time that the Italian film productions normally grant to translators in order to carry out their dubbing translations—yet, the use of 'dubbese' is so popular in the Italian dubbing-translation practice that it has even become an actual variation affecting everyday language. Instances of 'dubbese' may be considered the following adjectives and adverbial interjections, as in: *(a)* Darlene's cue [39]: "*Yeah*, me neither" – with "Yeah" usually translated by the calque "Già" based on assonance ("*Già*, neanch'io"); *(b)* David's cue [38]: "Wow", an interjection of wonder directly transferred into Italian exactly as it is; *(c)* Roseanne's cue [36]: "I think it's *great*?" and Darlene's cue [32]: "Hey, D.J., That's a *great* shirt.", both representing the well-known instance of 'dubbese' referred to the interjection/adjective "great", conventionally translated into: "grandioso", by assonance, but also into the emphatic "fantastico / meraviglioso / favoloso / stupendo / perfetto / magnifico", whereas the more natural option would rather be "bellissimo"); *(d)* David's cue [24]: "Uh, uh-huh. *Course* it means I'll have to move to Chicago", with "course" – like "sure", in dubbese – conventionally rendered into the pragmatically inappropriate "sicuro", originally meant as 'safe', in Italian, and not 'sure', whose appropriate Italian translation would be 'certo'; *(f)* the adjective "excited" represents another case in point frequently mistranslated in dubbese and here used in Roseanne's cue [26] and Dan's cue [23] with reference to David, and in Roseanne's cue [36] with reference to her reaction to the unexpected news. All Group-B students adopted the dubbese false-friend mistranslation "eccitato", which actually means "aroused" in Italian, whereas Group-A students/acting-translators opted for more pragmatically appropriate solutions in Italian, such as "emozionato", or "agitato", "entusista", and "contento".

Dubbese has also an influence on dubbed sentence-structures, which are usually rendered in translation into very long and complex semantically equivalent ones. This obviously entails a disrespect not only for the characters' original conversation style, but also for the time-span allowed for dubbing the sitcom cues. A case in point is David's cue [9] "I kinda wanted a dog first", rendered by Group-B students into: "Io volevo piuttosto prima un cane." / "Avrei voluto prima avere un cane." ("I wanted rather first a dog / I would have liked first to have a dog"), with an unusual collocation of the adverb ("prima" / "first") among the three elements of the verb phrase in the former, and using a third-type conditional sentence of 'impossibility' which is almost obsolete among Italian youngsters. The preferred solution in this case would probably be: "io veramente volevo un cane prima" ("I actually wanted a dog first"). Another example of this kind is David's cue [11]: "...Wouldn't have to be a big dog", translated into the complex clause "Non sarebbe dovuto essere un gran cane" ("It shouldn't have been a big dog"), whereas a better option could be: "Non doveva essere un cane grosso" – same English back-translation as before, but more informal in style with the use of the Italian 'imperfect' tense, instead of the more formal Italian conditional mood, and the adjective "grosso" ("big") more naturally collocated after the noun. One more example is represented by Roseanne's cue [18]: "I, uh, bought 'em off this guy that was selling them off the back of his truck down at the, uh, gas station parking lot." rendered into the complex and stilted: "Li ho comprati da un tipo che li stava vendendo nella parte posteriore del suo camion, al parcheggio al distributore della benzina." ("I bought them from a guy who was selling them in the rear part of his truck, in the parking area of the gas station").

Also some chunk expressions were translated by Group-B students into Italian forms that sounded rather 'artificial'. For instance Roseanne's cue [36]: "World's Greatest Grandma" was literally rendered into "La Nonna più Grande del Mondo", whereas the sense of this statement on Roseanne's sweatshirt would rather, more appropriately, be: "La Nonna più Famosa del Mondo" ("World's Most Famous Grandma"). Allocutions represent another area of mistranslation due to pragmatic inappropriatateness. For instance: David's cue [19] "Next to you?", referred to Roseanne, Darlene's mother, was rendered with the informal second-person pronoun "te" ("vicino a te?") rather than with the formal equivalent "lei". Also David's cue [38]: "thanks Mrs Conner." Was inappropriately translated into "grazie signora Conner", reporting Roseanne's surname which is inappropriate in Italian, its equivalent rather being the simple "grazie signora" ("thanks madam"), or "grazie signora Roseanne", with the elder person first name preceded by the allocution "signora" ("Mrs", "madam").

Finally, a student in Group B provided a translation into the Italian diatopic and diastratic variety of "Sicilian dialect"—an extreme form of 'localization' choice which goes far beyond the choice of the Neapolitan accent made by the translators of the Italian edition and which is reported below in an extract (with no back-translation as the original script has been literally rendered):

> "ROSEANNE [34]: Santuzza mia! Pinzu cà successi quarchi cosa. Sì, vitti assai 'A Signura in Giallo' pi mmagginarimi. Lassatimi taliari cà, David avi

> a facci bianca e i ginocchia cà ci tramano e ie tuttu nirvusu. E finu a cà un ci su tracci. Ma Darlene se voli assittari allatu ammì, e dissi quarchi cosa di simpaticu a so frati. Eehh, mi dumannu. Ndovinasti, si 'ncinta! ... Avà, stavamu schirzannu!"

This instance of 'strict dialect' localization is indeed opposite to the 'neutralization' choice made by the 'official' dubbing translators of an episode from another American sitcom, *Dharma & Greg*, to be analyzed in the next section.

5.5 'Neutralized' vs. 'Naturalized' Dubbing Translations in *Dharma & Greg* Sitcom

5.5.1 *Method and tagged data*

In the dubbing translation for the Italian TV concerning the episode from *Dharma & Greg* selected for this study, the dubbing-translators' top-down invention of an Italian accent which does not exist in reality actually modifies and neutralizes the pragmalinguistically-marked implications of the original script. Also in this case, the protocol analysis of the dubbing-translation students embodying the sitcom characters' attitudes, achieved from the scripted cues, before producing their dubbing translation, shows that it is possible to develop more natural and equivalent alternative versions in Italian by applying the 'Acting Translator' method.

Dharma & Greg is another turn-of-the-century American sitcom based on a young couple who fell in love at first sight and got married on their first date despite the apparently irreconcilable cultural and status differences between the two of them and their respective families and friends – who eventually all together found new ways of contributing to a new model of an enlarged and integrated family. The sitcom was created by Dotty Dartland and Chuck Lorre and aired by ABC from 1997 to 2002, but already since 2001, immediately after the Twin-Tower Islamic attack, its ratings started declining as American people turned to more traditional and mono-cultural family standards which were perceived as more reliable and reassuring than the emerging new-age modes of multicultural and cross-class family/friend units that could not be trusted any longer after that tragic event. The plot of this sitcom was about Dharma Finkelstein (played by Jenna Elfman), a young yoga teacher who received an unconventional education by her hippie parents based on trust in all human beings and in her natural feelings, and her husband Greg Montgomery (played by Thomas Gibson), a young lawyer who was instead raised in an upper-class family who had high aspirations for him and gave him the chance for an excellent education at Harvard and then at the Stanford Law School. Despite their being total opposites, they married immediately on their first date and so their marriage had to rely completely on their true love to survive. Humour in this sitcom is therefore based on Arousal/Safety and Disparagement patterns triggered by the cultural contrast between lower/upper class origins of the characters, who also happen to be the protagonists of a series of revelation plots. Such plots initially create a state of socio-cultural tension within their respective families, who keep expressing overtly their disparagement against each other till reaching at the end of each episode, thanks to the mediation of Dharma and Greg, a certain state of accommodation and relief. With the exception of Dharma and Greg, the other leading roles of this sitcom are stereotypical 'flat' characters. Dharma's family is composed by her mother Abby, an ex flower child and an uncompromising vegan, and her father Larry, a typical radical activist of the sixties who believes he is still wanted by the FBI. On the other hand, Greg's family is represented by his mother Kitty, an upper-class calculating socialite, and his father Edward, Head of the Montgomery Industries, who keeps his distance from his family, and from his wife in particular. Jane is Dharma's 'gothic' friend with a predilection for the 'dark' side of people and events. Pete is Greg's friend and colleague who got his degree at the Law School in Barbados; he is an indolent and incompetent lawyer and eventually he married Jane not to spend the Valentine Day alone.

The sitcom episode #2ABD14 selected for this study is entitled *Dharma and Greg on a Hot Tin Roof* (literally translated into *Dharma e Greg sul tetto che scotta*) mocking the title of Tennessee Williams's play *The Cat on the Hot Tin Roof* not only through a pun referred to the co-protagonist, Judge Harper from the State of Tennessee, but also because Dharma and Greg, just for fun, while they are in a golf shop, put on a fake Southern accent, which is the accent of the characters in Williams's play, whose plot is entirely constructed on mendacity and deceit. And deceit is indeed the subject of this sitcom episode under analysis: in the golf shop where they pretend to be Southerners, Greg and Dharma meet Judge Harper who speaks with the southern accent of Tennessee and before whom Greg must plead the following day. In order not to disappoint the Judge, who believes the couple shares his same annoyance for the Yankees disparaging the Southerners and their accent, Greg and Dharma decide to go on with their deception without revealing their real accent to the Judge so as to avoid prejudicing the case Greg is arguing the next day —and, more worriedly, Greg's own career. Hence, they are on tenterhooks, as if they were, metaphorically, 'on a hot tin roof', refusing to jump down for fear of hurting themselves, like the protagonist of Williams's play (Maggie, whose nickname was 'the cat').

This episode, therefore, is permeated with a humour triggered by a feeling of 'Arousal' as the two protagonists decide against setting in motion the ethically expected revelation plot not to jeopardize their reputation. This 'revelation denial' can be analyzed by applying the Appraisal Framework (Martin and White 2005) to investigate the characters' covert self-attribution of responsibility for the dishonest way they behave and, at the same time, their overt dialogic positioning in terms of false 'endorsement' of perspectives that are not their own, and of their degrees of 'engagement' in such perspectives. The tense situation of falsity the two protagonists find themselves involved in does in fact distort the expected outcome of a dialogue as what they claim and endorse in the course of the conversation with Judge Harper does not correspond to their actual perspectives on the topics they deal with—and yet they refuse to disengage from what they claim for fear of losing their privileged status in the eyes of their interlocutor. Hence Greg and Dharma decide to take the whole responsibility for the deceitful situation they have started out. In doing so, however, they create their own 'split selves', thus counterfeiting for themselves two new personae who represent the personalized source of their claims, marked in terms of 'grouping' (Southern people) and 'status' (people disparaged for the diatopic variation of Tennessee pragmalect they speak). Yet, covertly, Dharma and Greg do not identify themselves with their counterfeit personae insofar as they still embody the perspective of the two young people of different socio-cultural backgrounds from San Francisco (which is the sitcom perspective, too). Furthermore, there is also the suspicion that they also covertly share the same disparaging stance on the southern accent which is indeed a direct reflection of their implied disparagement for the southern culture. Hence, in negotiating their positioning in conversation, Dharma and Greg shift their attribution of responsibility from their counterfeit personae, by means of what Martin and White (*ibidem*) define as an 'extra-vocalization' process, to themselves by means of an 'intra-vocalization' process that gives voice to their inner selves and personal stances. The incongruity between extra-vocalization (expressed through their fake southern accent) and intra-vocalization (expressed through their own Californian accent—as well as their bodily and facial expressions) represents a source of humour in this sitcom episode.

In the dubbed version of this episode for the Italian television (still Mediaset Television Group), translators put such incongruity in the background to give more emphasis to their device of turning the southern accent into an invented Italian variation meant to represent in an equivalent way not the actual accent, but rather the disparaging stance that Dharma and Greg take on the southern accent that they clearly perceive as grotesque. This entails a process of 'product neutralization' insofar as translators did not look for parallel accents in the Italian language that could be diatopically and diastratically equivalent to the Tennessee accent (as it happened with the Italian version of *Roseanne*, turning the Midwest accent into a Neapolitan one), but they devised a fake one anew, whose main characteristic was to distort the pronunciation of words producing a grotesque effect. Such accent invention actually modified the original socio-culturally marked implications of this sitcom episode to privilege a gross kind of humour based on a nasty disparagement for people who, despite their professional status, are still stigmatized for their ignorance of the fundamental rules of their mother-language phonology and morphology. What follows is an extract from the episode under analysis with the official Italian dubbing translation and a back-translation into Standard English. The original cues uttered by Dharma and Greg are tagged for their extra- *[EXTRA]* and intra- *[INTRA]* vocalization implications.

Dharma & Greg episode #2ABD14 *Dharma and Greg on a hot tin roof* (*Dharma e Greg sul tetto che scotta*)
Exchange 1: turns [1]-[39]; Exchange 2: turns [40]-[51]; Exchange 3: turns [52]-[87]

Original English version:	***Italian dubbing translation:***	***Back-translation into Standard English:***
[Int. Golf Store - Day]	**[Int. Negozio di articoli da golf - Giorno]**	**[Int. Golf Store - Day]**
(Greg and Dharma enter) ***[1]* DHARMA:** Okay. Go ahead. ***[INTRA]***	*(Entrano Greg e Dharma)* ***[1]* DHARMA:** Avanti. ***[extra cue 1a]*** **GREG:** No. ***[extra cue 1b]*** **DHARMA:** Dai, coraggio!	*Greg and Dharma enter)* ***[1]* DHARMA:** Go ahead. ***[extra cue 1a]*** **GREG:** No. ***[extra cue 1b]*** **DHARMA:** Come on, come on!
[2]* GREG:** Dharma, I can't do this. The sales guy'll never believe I'm from the South. ***[INTRA]	***[2]* GREG:** No, Dharma, non ci riesco, il commesso non crederà che vengo dal sud.	***[2]* GREG:** No, Dharma, I can't do this. The salesman will never believe I'm from the South.
[3]* DHARMA:** So then he'll think you're crazy. It's more fun shopping as a crazy person anyway, and sometimes they give you free stuff just to get rid of ya. Go on. ***[INTRA] *(Dharma nudges Greg toward the salesperson.)*	***[3]* DHARMA:** Crederà che sei svitato!È divertente fare compere fingendosi matti, ti regalano la roba per liberarsi di te. *(Dharma spinge Greg verso il commesso)*	***[3]* DHARMA:** He'll think you're crazy! It's funny to go shopping pretending to be a mad person, they give you free stuff just to get rid of you. *(Dharma nudges Greg toward the salesperson.)*
[4]* GREG:** *(in a southern accent)* Excuse me, son. ***[EXTRA]	***4]* GREG:** *(con un accento non identificato)* Salve ghiovino.	***[4]* GREG:** *(in a non-identified accent)* Hallo, young man.
***[5]* SALESPERSON:** Yes.	***[5]* COMMESSO:** Sì?	***[5]* SALESPERSON:** Yes?
[6]* GREG:** *(in a southern accent)* I'm lookin' for a nan ion. ***[EXTRA]	***[6]* GREG:** *(con un accento non identificato)* farro namero nave.	***[6]* GREG:** *(in a non-identified accent)* A number-nine iron.
***[7]* SALESPERSON:** Non on?	***[7]* COMMESSO:** Cosa ha detto?	***[7]* SALESPERSON:** What did you say?
[8]* DHARMA:** *(in a southern accent)* Uh, what my husband means to say is that he is in need of a nan ion. ***[EXTRA]	***[8]* DHARMA:** *(con un accento non identificato)* Mio ghiovino, quello che mio mareto voleva sapare è dove è che stanno i ferri nomero nove.	***[8]* DHARMA:** *(in a non-identified accent)* My young man, what my husband wants to know is that where the number-nine irons are.
[9]* GREG:** *(in a southern accent)* Yeah. I'm looking for a new, uh, nan ion. ***[EXTRA]	***[9]* GREG:** *(con un accento non identificato)* I farri namero nave, ho det-, namero nove.	***[9]* GREG:** *(in a non-identified accent)* Number-nine irons, I say, number nine.
***[10]* SALESPERSON:** I'm sorry.	***[10]* COMMESSO:** Ah, io non capisco... eh?	***[10]* SALESPERSON:** Ah, I don't understand... eh?
***[11]* GREG:** *(in A southern*	***[11]* GREG:** *(con un accento non*	***11]* GREG:** *(in a non-identified*

accent) You know, a non on, six, seven, eight, nan ion. ***[EXTRA]***	*identificato)* Namero nave, dai, satte, atto, nave.	*accent)* Number nine, come on, seven, eight, nine.
***[12]* SALESPERSON:** Oh, a nine iron.	***[12]* COMMESSO:** Oh, cerca il numero nove, ah, certo!	***[12]* SALESPERSON:** Oh, you look for a number nine, ah, sure!
[13]* GREG:** *(in a southern accent)* Nan ion. ***[EXTRA]	***[13]* GREG:** *(con un accento non identificato)* Namero nave.	***[13]* GREG:** *(in a non-identified accent)* Number nine.
***[14]* SALESPERSON:** Yes. They're right over there.	***[14]* COMMESSO:** Ah ecco, sono là in fondo.	***[14]* SALESPERSON:** Ah that's it, They're right over there.
[15]* GREG:** *(in a southern accent)* Thank you. *(to Dharma)* Damn Yankees. ***[EXTRA]	***[15]* GREG:** *(con un accento non identificato)* Graz— *(rivolto a Dharma)* Maledetti Yankie!	***[15]* GREG:** *(in a non-identified accent)* Thank— *(to Dharma)* Damn Yankees.
(Dharma and Greg walk past Judge Samuel Harper.) ***[16]* JUDGE HARPER:** I know what you're saying. It's impossible to understand these people.	*(Dharma e Greg passano accanto al Giudice Samuel Harper)* ***[16]* GIUDICE HARPER:** Ha raghione! E' impotsibile capire questi comme parlano!	*(Dharma and Greg walk past Judge Samuel Harper.)* ***[16]* JUDGE HARPER:** *(from now on he will always speak in a non-identified accent)* You are right! It's impossible to understand how these people talk.
[17]* GREG:** *(laughs) (in a southern accent)* That's true. ***[EXTRA]	***[17]* GREG:** *(ride) (con un accento non identificato)* Eh, sì è vero!	***[17]* GREG:** *(laughs) (in a non-identified accent)* Eh, that's true.
***[18]* JUDGE HARPER:** Where y'all hail from?	***[18]* GIUDICE HARPER:** Di dove tziete voialtri?	***[18]* JUDGE HARPER:** Where do you come from?
[19]* DHARMA:** *(in a southern accent)* Memphis. Where the hell you from? ***[EXTRA]	***[19]* DHARMA:** *(con un accento non identificato)* Di Mamphis. Lei invece di dove?	***[19]* DHARMA:** *(in a non-identified accent)* From Memphis. Where are you from, instead?
***[20]* JUDGE HARPER:** Oh, hail from, very good. Uh, well, we're pert'near neighbors. I'm from Knoxville.	***[20]* GIUDICE HARPER:** Oh, di Mamphis, per forza! Tziamo quazi vicini di caza, io vengo da Knoxville.	***[20]* JUDGE HARPER:** Oh, from Memphis, of course! We're almost neighbors. I'm from Knoxville.
[21]* DHARMA:** *(in a southern accent)* Is that right? Did you hear that, Stinkbug? This man is a Knoxidian. ***[EXTRA]	***[21]* DHARMA:** *(con un accento non identificato)* Dice davvero? Hai zentito vecchio mio. Quezto signore è un knoxvillano!	***[21]* DHARMA:** *(in a non-identified accent)* Really? Did you hear that, old boy? This man is a Knoxvillain!
[22]* GREG:** *(in a southern accent)* Yeah. ***[EXTRA]	***[22]* GREG:** *(con un accento non identificato)* Ah, ah.	***[22]* GREG:** *(in a non-identified accent)* Ah, ah.
***[23]* JUDGE HARPER:** Born and raised. What part of Memphis are you from?	***[23]* GIUDICE HARPER:** Nato e cresghiuto. E di quale parte di Mamphis?	***[23]* JUDGE HARPER:** Born and raised. What part of Memphis are you from?
[24]* GREG:** *(in a southern accent)* Well, uh, what part of Memphis would a man such as myself be from? ***[EXTRA]	***[24]* GREG:** *(con un accento non identificato)* Bé, ecco, bé, lei vuole, vuol, vorrebbe sapere da quale parte di Mamphis vengo io, ecco, dico bane signore?	***[24]* GREG:** *(in a non-identified accent)* Well, uh, well, you want to know what part of Memphis I come from, uh, am I right, sir?
***[25]* JUDGE HARPER:** Exactly.	***[25]* JUDGE HARPER:** Esatti!	***[25]* JUDGE HARPER:** Exactly.
[26]* GREG/DHARMA:** *(in unison) (in a southern accent)* Exactly! ***[EXTRA]	***[26]* GREG/DHARMA:** *(all'unisono) (con un accento non identificato)* Esatti!	***[26]* GREG/DHARMA**: *(in unison) (in a non-identified accent)* Exactly!
***[27]* JUDGE HARPER:** Allow me to introduce myself. I'm Judge Samuel Harper.	***[27]* GIUDICE HARPER:** Permettete che mi prezanti, io sono il ghiudice Samuel Harper.	***[27]* JUDGE HARPER:** Allow me to introduce myself. I'm Judge Samuel Harper.

[28] **GREG:** *(in a southern accent)* Judge Samuel Harper ... the new Federal Court Judge. ***[INTRA]***	*28]* **GREG:** *(con un accento non identificato)* Il Giudice Samuel Harper ... il nuavo ghiduce della Carte Fedarale.	*[28]* **GREG:** *(in a non-identified accent)* Judge Samuel Harper ... the new Federal Court Judge.
[29] **JUDGE HARPER:** Guilty and charged. How did you know that?	*[29]* **GIUDICE HARPER:** Reo e confasso. Come fa a saparlo?	*[29]* **JUDGE HARPER:** Pleased guilty. How did you know that?
[30] **GREG:** *(in a southern accent)* I'm — I'm with the U.S. Attorney's Office. I believe I have a motion you're hearin' in the mornin'. ***[INTRA]/EXTRA]***	*[30]* **GREG:** *(con un accento non identificato)* Bé, io lavoro con il Procuratore Distrettuale. Se non sbaglio avremo un'udienzia con Vostro Onore domani mattina.	*[30]* **GREG:** *(in a non-identified accent)* Well, I work with the District Attorney. If I'm not wrong we are having a hearing with Your Honor tomorrow morning.
[31] **JUDGE HARPER:** Is that so? And your name is?	*[31]* **GIUDICE HARPER:** Sul sario? Como si chioma lei?	*[31]* **JUDGE HARPER:** Really? What's your name?
[32] **GREG:** *(in a southern accent)* My name? ***[EXTRA]***	*[32]* **GREG:** *(con un accento non identificato)* Como mi chiomo?	*[32]* **GREG:** *(in a non-identified accent)* What's my name?
[33] **DHARMA:** Tell him your name. Butterbug. ***[EXTRA]***	*[33]* **DHARMA:** Dì como ti chiomi bel ghiovino.	*[33]* **DHARMA:** Tell him what your name is, young man.
[34] **GREG:** *(in a southern accent)* My name is, uh, Gregory Montgomery. ***[INTRA]/EXTRA]***	*[34]* **GREG:** *(con un accento non identificato)* Mi chiomo Gregory Montgomery.	*[34]* **GREG:** *(in a non-identified accent)* My name is Gregory Montgomery.
[35] **JUDGE HARPER:** *(laughs)* Well, it's nice to meet you, Mr. Montgomery. And this lovely flower is?	*[35]* **GIUDICE HARPER:** *(ride)* Ah ah piacere di conoscerla signor Montgomery. E questo fiore delizioso è?	*[35]* **JUDGE HARPER:** *(laughs)* Ah ah nice to meet you, Mr. Montgomery. And this lovely flower is?
[36] **GREG:** *(in a southern accent)* Uh, Dharma. ***[INTRA/ EXTRA]***	*[36]* **GREG:** *(con un accento non identificato)* Dharma.	*[36]* **GREG:** *(in a non-identified accent)* Uh, Dharma.
[37] **DHARMA:** Dharma Jean. ***[EXTRA]***	*[37]* **DHARMA:** Dharma Jean.	*[37]* **DHARMA:** Dharma Jean.
[38] **JUDGE HARPER:** Dharma Jean. You're a very lucky man sir.	*[38]* **GIUDICE HARPER:** Dharma Jean. Lei è un uomo molto fortunoto.	*[38]* **JUDGE HARPER:** Dharma Jean. You're a very lucky man.
[39] **GREG:** *(in a southern accent)* Yes sir, I am. And it is at moments like this I am made keenly aware of just how lucky I am. ***[INTRA/EXTRA]***	*[39]* **GREG:** *(con un accento non identificato)* Sì, signore, lo so bene, ed è proprio nei momenti come questo che ho la prova concreta di quanta fortona io abbia!	*[39]* **GREG:** *(in a non-identified accent)* Yes sir, I know that well, and it is just at moments like this I have the concrete evidence of how much luck I have.
[Int. Dharma and Greg's apartment - Night.]	**[Int. Appartamento di Dharma e Greg - Notte.]**	**[Int. Dharma and Greg's apartment - Night.]**
(Dharma and Jane sit on the couch talking.) *[40]* **DHARMA:** ... so then it turns out he has to appear before this judge tomorrow morning. ***[INTRA]***	*(Dharma e Jane siedono sul divano a parlare)* *[40]* **DHARMA:** Così scopriamo che domattina dovrà presentarsi proprio davanti a quel giudice.	*(Dharma and Jane sit on the couch talking.)* *[40]* **DHARMA:** So then it turns out he has to appear before this judge tomorrow morning.
[41] **JANE:** He seems to be takin' it pretty well.	*[41]* **JANE:** vedo che l'ha presa abbastanza bene!	*[41]* **JANE:** He seems to be takin' it pretty well.
(Greg sits in a chair hugging his knees, rocking.) *[42]* **DHARMA:** He's been rocking like that since we got home. ***[INTRA]***	*(Greg siede su una sedia stringendosi le ginocchia e dondolandosi)* *[42]* **DHARMA:** E' da quando siamo tornati che si dondola in quel modo.	*(Greg sits in a chair hugging his knees, rocking.)* *[42]* **DHARMA:** He's been rocking like that since we got home.
[43] **JANE:** You think he'll stay that way?	*[43]* **JANE:** E continuerà a farlo?	*[43]* **JANE:** And he'll stay that way?

[44] **DHARMA:** I don't know. ***[INTRA]***	*[44]* **DHARMA:** Non lo so.	*[44]* **DHARMA:** I don't know.
[45] **JANE:** I'm gonna go get my camera. *(Jane exits.)*	*[45]* **JANE:** Vado a prendere la telecamera. *(Esce Jane)*	*[45]* **JANE:** I'm gonna go get my camera. *(Jane exits.)*
[46] **DHARMA:** Honey, you wanna talk about it now? ***[INTRA]***	*[46]* **DHARMA:** Tesoro, ti andrebbe di parlarne?	*[46]* **DHARMA:** Darling, you wanna talk about it?
[47] **GREG:** No. ***[INTRA]***	*[47]* **GREG:** No.	*[47]* **GREG:** No.
[48] **DHARMA:** You know, it's not that big a deal. You just have to get there like five minutes early and just explain to him that — ***[INTRA]***	*[48]* **DHARMA:** Non è successo niente di grave in fondo, dovrai solo andare lì cinque minuti prima e spiegargli che —	*[48]* **DHARMA:** It's not that big a deal, you know, you just have to get there like five minutes early and just explain to him that —
[49] **GREG:** I was mocking him and his entire culture? ***[INTRA]***	*[49]* **GREG:** Che ho preso in giro lui e tutta la sua cultura?	*[49]* **GREG:** I was mocking him and his entire culture?
[50] **DHARMA:** You weren't mocking. You were making believe. ***[INTRA]***	*[50]* **DHARMA:** Non l'hai preso in giro, stavi solo fingendo.	*[50]* **DHARMA:** You weren't mocking him. You were making believe.
[51] **GREG:** Okay. And after he destroys me in court, I can make believe I still have a career. Hi, Greg Montgomery, attorney at law. These two gentlemen are my clients. *(Dog barks)* Okay. Were my clients. ***[INTRA]***	*[51]* **GREG:** Certo, e dopo che mi avrà distrutto in tribunale potrò fingere di avere ancora un lavoro. Sono Greg Montgomery, avvocato, e i signori sono i miei clienti. *(Il cane abbaia)* E va bene. Erano i miei clienti.	*[51]* **GREG:** Sure, and after he destroys me in court, I can make believe I still have a job. I'm Greg Montgomery, attorney at law, and these two gentlemen are my clients. *(Dog barks)* Okay. Were my clients.
[Int. The Court - Day.]	**[Int. Il tribunale - Giorno.]**	**[Int. The Court - Day.]**
Greg sits at the Attorneys' table. Dharma sits behind him in the Gallery.) *[52]* **DHARMA:** Just tell him the truth. I'm sure he'll get a kick out of it. ***[INTRA]***	*(Greg siede al tavolo dei procuratori. Dharma siede dietro di lui nella sala)* *[52]* **DHARMA:** È meglio che tu gli dica la verità, di sicuro si farà una risata.	*(Greg sits at the Attorneys' table. Dharma sits behind him in the Gallery.)* *[52]* **DHARMA:** You'd better tell him the truth, surely he'll have a good laugh.
(Pete enters) *[53]* **PETE:** What are you talking about? What truth?	*(Entra Pete)* *[53]* **PETE:** Che cosa? Che verità?	*(Pete enters)* *[53]* **PETE:** What? What truth?
[54] **GREG:** Uh, don't worry about it. As soon as I get a chance, I'll ask for a sidebar. ***[INTRA]***	*[54]* **GREG:** Em, non ti preoccupare, appena sarà possibile chiederò di parlargli.	*[54]* **GREG:** Ehm, don't worry about it. As soon as I get a chance, I'll ask to talk to him.
[55] **PETE:** What's it about?	*[55]* **PETE:** Di che stai parlando?	*55]* **PETE:** What are you talking about?
[56] **GREG:** It's not important. ***[INTRA]***	*[56]* **GREG:** Niente di importante.	*[56]* **GREG:** Nothing important.
[57] **PETE:** Is it about me? Are you gonna tell the judge I went to a Caribbean law school?	*[57]* **PETE:** Si tratta di me? Vuoi dire al giudice che ho studiato legge ai Caraibi?	*[57]* **PETE:** Is it about me? Are you gonna tell the judge I studied law at the Caribbean?
[58] **GREG:** No, now just cool it. ***[INTRA]***	*[58]* **GREG:** No, non ti preoccupare.	*[58]* **GREG:** No, don't worry.
[59] **PETE:** Why won't you tell me what the sidebar's about?	*[59]* **PETE:** Di che diavolo gli vuoi parlare allora?	*[59]* **PETE:** What the hell do you want to talk to him about?
[60] **GREG:** Because it has absolutely nothing to do with the case. ***[INTRA]***	*[60]* **GREG:** Ti assicuro che non ha niente a che fare con il caso.	*[60]* **GREG:** I assure you that it has nothing to do with the case.

[61] **PETE:** Well, then, I might know somethin' about it.	*[61]* **PETE:** A maggior ragione vorrei saperne qualcosa.	*[61]* **PETE:** All the more reason why I'd like to know somethin' about it.
[62] **BAILIFF:** All rise.	*62]* **UFFICIALE GIUDIZIARIO:** Tutti in piedi.	*[62]* **BAILIFF:** All rise.
(Judge Harper enters) *[63]* **JUDGE HARPER:** Sit down. I'm not the Queen. Good mornin', Counselors.	*(Entra il Giudice Harper)* *[63]* **GIUDICE HARPER:** Seduti, non sono una Reghina. Buon ghiorno, avvocati.	*(Judge Harper enters)* *[63]* **JUDGE HARPER:** Sit down. I'm not the Queen. Good morning, Counselors.
[64] **MR. MILLER:** Howdy, Judge.	*[64]* **AVVOCATO MILLER:** Ehilà, giudice!	*[64]* **MR. MILLER:** Hey there, Judge.
[65] **JUDGE HARPER:** How's that?	*[65]* **GI UDICE HARPER:** Che cosa?	*[65]* **JUDGE HARPER:** How's that?
[66] **MR. MILLER:** Howdy, Your Honor?	*[66]* **AVVOCATO MILLER:** Ehilà, Vostro Onore.	*[66]* **MR. MILLER:** Hey there, Your Honor?
[67] **JUDGE HARPER:** Howdy? Howdy? What are you implying, that I'm some sort of ignorant Southerner who doesn't understand proper English? If you wish to address me, say "hello".	*[67]* **GIUDICE HARPER:** Ehilà? Ehilà? Acchidenti, che mi sta forse trattando come un povero ignorante del sud? Che non sa parlare se non il proprio dialatto? Se vuole salutarmi mi dica, dica "buongiorno".	*[67]* **JUDGE HARPER:** Hey there? Hey there? Damn, are you perhaps treating me as a kind of poor ignorant Southerner who can speak only his own dialect? If you wish to address me, say "good morning".
[68] **MR. MILLER:** Yes, sir, Your Honor, Hello.	*[68]* **AVVOCATO MILLER:** Sì, Vostro Onore, buongiorno.	*[68]* **MR. MILLER:** Yes, Your Honor, good morning.
[69] **JUDGE HARPER:** The one thing I will not tolerate is the ridiculing of the melodic speech patterns of my people. Don't you agree, Mr. Montgomery?	*[69]* **GIUDICE HARPER:** Se c'è una cosa che non tollero è chi mette in ridicolo la particolare melodica parlata della mia ghente. Condivide, Avvocato Montgomery?	*[69]* **JUDGE HARPER:** If there is one thing I will not tolerate is the ridiculing of the particular melodic way of speaking of my people. Do you agree, Mr. *[Counselor]* Montgomery?
[70] **GREG:** *(in a southern accent)* Sho' 'nuff, Ya Honor. ***[EXTRA]***	*[70]* **GREG:** *(con un accento non identificato)* Com' no, Vostro Onore.	*[70]* **GREG:** *(in a non-identified accent)* 'v course, Your Honor.
[71] **PETE:** *(quietly)* Sho' 'nuff? What the hell you doin'?	*[71]* **PETE:** *(sottovoce)* Greg, ma come parli? Ma che sta succedendo?	*[71]* **PETE:** *(quietly)* Greg, How do you speak? What's happening?
[72] **JUDGE HARPER:** Now, the defense has, uh, made a motion here for a change of venue. Does the United States have any response to this motion?	*[72]* **GIUDICE HARPER:** La difesa ha presentato rischiesta di rìnvio della causa ad altra Corte. Che cosa ha da dire lo Stato in risposta alla rischiesta suddetta?	*[72]* **JUDGE HARPER:** The defense has made a motion for a change of venue. What does the State says in response to this motion?
[73] **GREG:** *(in a southern accent)* Yes, Your Hona, uh, I've examined counsel's motion and I find it spurious. Uh, it clearly does not meet the requirements of eighteen U.S.C. thirty-four. ***[EXTRA]***	*[73]* **GREG:** *(con un accento non identificato)* Ecco, Vostro Onore, io ho esaminato la richiesta dell'avvocato, ma secondo me è ìmpropria. E' che è schiaramente in contrasto con i requisiti rischiesti dalla diciotto trenta quattro.	*[73]* **GREG:** *(in a non-identified accent)* Well, Your Honor, uh, I've examined counsel's motion but, in my view, it is spurious. It clearly does not meet the requirements of eighteen U.S.C. thirty-four.
[74] **JUDGE HARPER:** So what you're saying, Mr. Montgomery, is that dog won't hunt?	*[74]* **GIUDICE HARPER:** Sarebbe come dire, Avvocato Montgomery, che il segugio non sa cacciare?	*[74]* **JUDGE HARPER:** That would mean, Mr. *(Counselor)* Montgomery, that the hound doesn't know how to hunt?

[75] **GREG:** *(in a southern accent)* No, sir, that dog is a ... vegetarian. ***[EXTRA]***	*[75]* **GREG:** *(con un accento non identificato)* No, signore, quel cane è ... un vegetariano.	*[75]* **GREG:** *(in a non-identified accent)* No, sir, that dog is a ... vegetarian.
[76] **JUDGE HARPER:** Vegetarian. Very good. *(chuckles)*	*[76]* **GIUDICE HARPER:** Ah ah un vegetariano, ma certo! *(ridacchia)*	*[76]* **JUDGE HARPER:** Ah ah a vegetarian, but of course! *(chuckles)*
[77] **PETE:** *(tugs on Greg's coat)* What are you doin'?	*[77]* **PETE:** *(tira Greg per la giacca)* Che stai facendo?	*[77]* **PETE:** *(tugs on Greg's coat)* What are you doin'?
[78] **GREG:** Well, maybe they didn't teach you this at the Bob Marley School of Law, but sometimes you have to butter up the judge. ***[INTRA]***	*[78]* **GREG:** Bé, forse non te l'hanno insegnato alla Bob Marley Facoltà di Legge, ma certe volte bisogna anche compiacere il giudice.	*[78]* **GREG:** Well, maybe they didn't teach you this at the Bob Marley Faculty of Law, but sometimes you have to humour the judge.
[79] **JUDGE HARPER:** Continue, Mr. Montgomery.	*[79]* **GIUDICE HARPER:** Continui pure, avvocato.	*[79]* **JUDGE HARPER:** Please continue, Counselor.
[80] **GREG:** *(in a southern accent)* Well, if I might, uh, beg the court's indulgence, but as it is unseasonably warm in here, I was wonderin' if there'd be any objection to my continuin' in my shirtsleeves? ***[EXTRA]***	*[80]* **GREG:** *(con un accento non identificato)* Ma veramante io mi appello all'indulghienzia della Corte, ma dato che fa incredibilmente caldo qui dantro chiederei di poter scontinuare il dibattimanto in maniche di camicia.	*[80]* **GREG:** *(in a non-identified accent)* Well, actually I beg the court's indulgence, but as it is incredibly warm in here, I'd like to ask if I may continue the hearing in my shirtsleeves.
[81] **JUDGE HARPER:** I don't see as how that can affect the dignity of these proceedin's.	*[81]* **GIUDICE HARPER:** Non vedo come questo possa offendere la dignità di questo procedimento.	*[81]* **JUDGE HARPER:** I don't see as how that can affect the dignity of these proceedings.
[82] **GREG:** Thank you, Your Hona. ***[EXTRA]***	*[82]* **GREG:** Grazie, Vostro Onore.	*[82]* **GREG:** Thank you, Your Honor.
[83] **PETE:** *(to Dharma)* Will you tell me what's goin' on?	*[83]* **PETE:** *(rivolgendosi a Dharma)* Dharma, mi spieghi che diavolo succede?	*[83]* **PETE:** *(to Dharma)* Dharma, will you tell me what's going on?
[84] **DHARMA:** What? ***[EXTRA]***	*[84]* **DHARMA:** Cosa?	*[84]* **DHARMA:** What?
[85] **PETE:** The accent.	*[85]* **PETE:** Come parla?	*[85]* **PETE:** How does he speak?
[86] **DHARMA:** What accent? ***[EXTRA]***	*[86]* **DHARMA:** Come parla?	*[86]* **DHARMA:** How does he speak?
[87] **GREG:** *(in a southern accent)* The learned attorney for the defense has presented us with a motion that is filled with all kinds of hoo-hah — prejudicial this, fair trial that. Frankly, when I read the thing, I was more mixed up than a basketful of puppies on a Ferris wheel. ***[EXTRA]*** *(Judge Harper laughs. Greg looks at Dharma surprised)*	*[87]* **GREG:** *(con un accento non identificato)* L'avvocato incaricato della difaisa ha presentato una mozione che potrei definire un guazzabuglio di incomprensibili termini legali — pregiudizievole qua, processo equo di là. Francamente, dopo averlo letto, mi sono sentito più sconvolto di una cesta di cuccioli sulla ruota di un battello! *(Il Giudice Harper ride. Greg guarda Dharma sorpreso).*	*[87]* **GREG:** *(in a non-identified accent)* The attorney in charge of the defense has presented us with a motion that I may define as a tangle of unintelligible legal terms — prejudicial this, fair trial that. Frankly, after having read it, I felt more mixed up than a basketful of puppies on a Ferris wheel. *(Judge Harper laughs. Greg looks at Dharma surprised)*

5.5.2 *Appraisal Framework applied to the analysis of source scripts and target 'neutralized' and 'naturalized' versions*

From the interplay of intra- and extra-vocalization in the original cues by Greg and Dharma it is possible to realize how, in the deceitful situation they set off just for fun, they feel obliged to activate an extra-vocalization process to endorse perspectives that are not entirely their own. Such perspectives are expressed by their respective counterfeit personae through a southern accent and by means of a degree of engagement that is very high at the beginning, when Dharma and Greg still feel safe as they believe they have started a playful game, and then becomes lower and lower since the moment they realize that the man with a southern accent they are mocking and mimicking is Judge Harper, who can have a decisive influence on Greg's career and reputation. In cues [30], [34], [36], and [39], Greg's endorsement of the false claims he is making through extra-vocalization starts vacillating towards intra-vocalization (*[INTRA/EXTRA]*) and he seems to be ready to reveal his pretence to Judge Harper, but Dharma carries on the deception, thus actually impeding Greg to tell the truth. In the second exchange taking place in their apartment, Greg's state of dejection is evident and expressed through intra-vocalization. Dharma, this time, encourages him to abandon his counterfeit persona and to reveal his pretence to the Judge, but Greg opportunistically evaluates the pros and cons of being sincere and then decides against it for the sake of his career. In the third exchange taking place in the Court, then, Greg has already made up his mind and he even seems to enjoy being deceitful by using his counterfeit persona through extra-vocalization, thus finding favour and partiality with Judge Harper despite his friend Pete's condemning remarks for his misleading behaviour.

The actual victim of such fraud is Judge Harper who, overtly, is ridiculed for his Southern accent and, covertly, for his culture. In the Italian version of this episode, however, the dubbing translators go far beyond such sociolinguistic implications of the Judge's accent to render his language into a mishmash of morphologically, phonologically and even prosodically distorted words and phrases which mark him as an unrealistic and grotesque caricature of the uneducated, unschooled person. Such a distortion is only partially evident in the dubbing translation reported in column B above, which only readers with a competence in the Italian language can read as it is not possible to achieve equivalence by rendering it into a similarly distorted English back-translation (just as an example, Greg's Italian cue [28], "Il Giudice Samuel Harper ... il nuavo ghiduce della Carte Fedarale..", could be phonetically rendered into something like "Judge Samuel Harper ... the neaw Fadaral Cart Gewdge"—thus representing a non-existent accent). Hence, rather than opting for a 'product localization' by identifying a diatopically and diastratically equivalent Italian accent (as actually expected, considering that the Italian TV production, Mediaset, was the same one that produced *Roseanne*), the Italian dubbing translators chose to bring about a 'product neutralization' by deactivating the sociocultural force of the original script.

During the first top-down phase of script exploration, Group-A students/acting-translators (the only group that was admitted to this phase) had to tackle such sociocultural force conveyed by the script of this episode and find ways to render it into Italian. In doing this, they almost immediately excluded the possibility of 'localizing' the script by 'domesticating' the Judge's accent into an equivalent Italian one, also because the very visual dimension of the situation excluded any possibility of interpreting it as set in a context of Italian immigrants. Dharma, for instance, wears a typical Nashville Country outfit which, at the end of the episode, her whole family shall wear to welcome at home for dinner Judge Harper and his illustrious guest from Tennessee, namely, the US vice-President Al Gore (played by an impersonator), that the Judge brings with him to meet Greg as a reward for his hospitality—and as an opportunity for his career. Students in Group A were then encouraged to explore the possibility of respecting the original setting of the script and, at the same time, retaining the difference in the accent used. The solution that Group-A students finally found was to involve in the process of character embodiment and dubbing translation a university language assistant who was precisely from Tennessee, could speak with Judge Harper's accent as a native speaker and, what is more interesting, spoke Italian with the South-American accent of his place of origin. The language assistant was therefore cast in the role of Judge Harper and students started learning his Italian inflection in order to play the roles of Dharma and Greg with a fake South-American accent. The rationale underlying such a choice is that Group-A students/acting-translators preferred to activate a process of 'naturalization' of original accents transferred to the target dubbed version rather than taking into consideration the same process of accent 'neutralization' adopted in the dubbed version for the Italian television. This rationale can be also applied to situations in which, for instance, the voices and accents in the original versions belong to actors of different nationalities, or different ethnic groups, who are conventionally dubbed in Italian by using 'generic' voices of Italian actors. In fact, there is no reason why an Asian actor cannot be dubbed by another Asian actor speaking Italian with an Asian accent, rather than by an Italian actor faking his accent, or neutralizing it. The same may be said with Afro-American actors in the original versions of movies, whose phonetic and phonatory characteristics should not be neutralized by the voice of any Italian actor but, rather, Afro-Italian actors should be employed to reproduce similar 'black' timbres of voices. It is here claimed, therefore, that 'domestication' and 'neutralization' as dubbing-translation processes should be replaced with 'plausibility' and 'naturalization' as processes more likely to achieve formal and pragmatic equivalence in the target version of the movie.

Obviously, reproducing equivalent accents, timbres, and phonological markers is not enough when students/acting-translators come to interpret characters and embody their feelings, attitudes and behaviours in relation to the situations they are made to interact. This is a dimension of the dubbing translation process that acting-translators need to be aware of since, as Couper-Kuhlen (1986: 185-187) points out, there is a distinction to be perceived in intonation contours between 'emotional or expressive intonation' prosodically indicating the speaker's feelings and states of mind, and 'attitudinal intonation' indicating a type of behaviour only partially conveyed through the voice, as the speaker's facial expression or bodily gestures may change the pragmatic meaning of what is said. This entails that attitudinal intonation often encompasses also 'emotional, expressive intonation'. An instance of attitudinal intonation is represented by Greg's cue [39] in response to Judge Harper paying a compliment to Dharma, the actual initiator of the pretense, when Greg seems to appreciate the Judge's flattering remark (through extra-vocalization overtly addressed to the Judge) but actually, from his frowning face and his disappointed tone of voice (covertly addressed to Dharma through intra-vocalization), it is evident that he means the exact opposite: "it is at moments like this I am made keenly aware of just how lucky I am". A further complication conveyed by attitudinal intonation may occur when humour is involved, insofar as an expected meaning may be interpreted differently because intonation conveys a specific prosodic implicature unintentionally triggering an unexpected inference of meaning in the receiver, as in the case with the exchange between Judge Harper and Mr. Miller, a Court lawyer who affably greets the Judge by using the Southern way of saying 'hello' which instead irritates the Judge: "[64] *Mr. Miller:* Howdy, Judge. / [65] *Judge Harper:* How's that? / [66] *Mr. Miller:* Howdy, Your Honor? / [67] *Judge Harper:* Howdy? Howdy? What are you implying, that I'm some sort of ignorant Southerner who doesn't understand proper English? If you wish to address me, say "hello". / [68] *Mr. Miller:* Yes, sir, Your Honor, Hello. / [69] *Judge Harper:* The one thing I will not tolerate is the ridiculing of the melodic speech patterns of my people. Don't you agree, Mr. Montgomery?".

Another dimension of the humour employed in this sitcom episode is represented by the type of Disparagement pattern constructed around the gullible Judge Harper by Greg and Dharma who, eventually, realize that mocking the Judge's accent is not just fun as they initially believed, but it is an act that, if found out by the Judge, would deeply offend him, which makes them feel guilty for what they have started and for the fact that they have opportunistically chosen to go on with the pretense. This dimension of falsity of the episode deserved an exploration by embodiment that Group-A students/acting-translators carried out during the first top-down phase of script improvisation when they were asked to perform, as a group, a series of physical-theatre exercises to develop an 'intonational memory' of the characters' attitudes and emotions through their use of voice, to be exploited during the subsequent 'interactive (i.e., top-down/bottom-up) phase of rendering the original script into a dubbing translation.

The first exercise directly involved the American language assistant from Tennessee, who embodied Judge Harper by acting out his cues of complaint first in their original version, and then translated into Italian with his South-American accent: "[67] Howdy? Howdy? What are you implying, that I'm some sort of ignorant Southerner who doesn't understand proper English? If you wish to address me, say 'hello'. / [69] The one thing I will not tolerate is the ridiculing of the melodic speech patterns of my people." While he uttered such cues, repeating them over and over again with his southern accent, the other students/acting-translators surrounded him and, by mimicking his accent, moved round him shouting mockingly at him all their despise: "Howdy, Judge?"; "Where y'all hail from?"; "Did you hear that, Stinkbug?"; "This man is a Knoxidian"; "Well, we're pert'near neighbors"; "Tell me your name, Butterbug!"; "Sho' 'nuff, Ya Honor". The 'crowd of people' insulting Judge Harper was meant to remain deep in the physical memory of the acting translator who embodied the Judge, to be exploited during the next 'interactive' dubbing-translation phase in order to find the most spontaneous equivalent words to express his anger and humiliation in Italian. The 'physical memory of the scornful crowd' was also meant to be appropriated and stored in the mind of the acting-translators playing Dharma and Greg since, at the beginning of the episode, these two characters covertly shared the same disparagement overtly expressed by 'the crowd' in this exercise and, indeed, the 'crowd' in this physical-theatre activity, in addressing Judge Harper, employed various expressions that Dharma and Greg themselves use in the script. Such 'physical memory' was also meant to be useful to the students/acting-translators playing Dharma and Greg in the course of the subsequent 'interactive' phase when they were required to develop their own dubbing translation by relying on their top-down physical experience of embodiment of the characters' attitudes and emotions, as well as on their bottom-up interpretation of the language in the script.

The second physical-theatre exercise concerned the Court scene: here, the American language assistant playing Judge Harper sat in the middle of the room and addressed his cue [72] to Greg, the US attorney, sure that he would be pleased and amused with the reply of a person from his same speech community: "Now, the defense has, uh, made a motion here for a change of venue. Does the United States have any response to this motion?". While Judge Harper uttered this cue [72], a number of students/acting-translators playing Greg moved again and again around him, using a fake southern accent and a hypnotic, chanting tone of voice in answering the Judge by means of the extra-vocalization of cue [73] ("Yes, Your Hona, uh, I've examined counsel's motion and I find it spurious. Uh, it clearly does not meet the requirements of eighteen U.S.C. thirty-four."). When the students playing Greg moved at the back of Judge Harper, not seen by him they made faces at him, whereas once before his sight they pretended to smile at him deferentially. The exercise went on with the American language assistant playing Judge Harper addressing his cues to Greg, and eventually improvising on them by inventing puns while the students/acting-translators playing Greg replied with Greg's cues containing silly puns (or inventing new ones) meant to make the well-disposed Judge laugh. Once again, when students playing Greg moved behind Judge Harper, they made sneering faces at him: [74] *Judge Harper:* "So what you're saying, Mr. Montgomery, is that dog won't hunt?" / [75] *Greg: (in a southern accent)* "No, sir, that dog is a ... vegetarian." / [76] *Judge Harper:* "Vegetarian. Very good. *(chuckles)*" / [79] *Judge Harper:* "Continue, Mr. Montgomery." / [87] *Greg: (in a southern accent)* The learned attorney for the defense has presented us with a motion that is filled with all kinds of hoo-hah—prejudicial this, fair trial that. Frankly, when I read the thing, I was more mixed up than a basketful of puppies on a Ferris wheel. / *(Judge Harper laughs)*". After repeating these cues for some time in English, in order to strengthen their physical memory of the deceiver (Greg) and the deceived (Judge Harper), students/acting-translator and the American language assistant (who at this stage was considered as an acting translator like the other Group-A students to all intents and purposes) moved to the next 'interactive' phase of the actual dubbing translation. At this stage, they switched to the Italian language to repeat the dialogic cues so as to find equivalent and natural emotional/attitudinal intonations, thus avoiding any artificial rendering of the legal language used by Greg.

This second phase of dubbing translation on *Dharma & Greg* involved also the students in Group B (i.e., the control group) who—differently from the students/acting-translators in Group A—did not experience the first phase of top-down script improvisation and embodiment. Therefore, they started dealing with the translation of the script straight away, without having the possibility of relying on a 'physical memory' developed during the previous top-down phase and, as expected, without taking into consideration any possibility of respecting, also in Italian, the Judge's original American accent. Group-B students' dubbing translation, in fact, generally showed characteristics of a 'product localization' which today marks the 'domestication' trend in the translation for the Italian TV (*Roseanne* being a case in point).

One of the most extreme domestication choices made by a team of students/dubbing-translators within Group B was that of rendering Judge Harper's accent and tone of voice into an impersonation of the voice of the famous Italian Judge Antonio Di Pietro, a fierce adversary of political corruption in the nineties (in the well-known "Mani Pulite"—"Clean Hands"—trial). The parallelism between the real Judge Di Pietro and the fictitious Judge Harper lays in the fact that Di Pietro (now a MP) has often been caricatured by his political opponents as a man from a poor southern region and a humble family who, despite his higher education and his professional role as a Judge, still speaks with his southern accent, often using dialectal idioms and, for this reason, he is believed to be totally ignorant about the 'standard' grammar and pronunciation of the Italian language. Obviously, a choice of this kind, however ingenious, totally disconnects the spoken dialogue from the visual dimension of the sitcom episode set in the United States with some characters wearing traditional Tennessee outfits.

Another inconsistent translation choice originating, also this time, from Group-B students' exclusively top-down inventiveness was to typify characters as Russian, or related to Russians. Once again, the discrepancy between the visual dimension of the sitcom episode and the translated cues do not tally at all. This is an extract from such dubbing translation regarding the first exchange (noticeably set in a golf store, a crucial detail that was, instead, completely neglected in this dubbing translation):

Original English version:	***Italian dubbing translation:***	***Back-translation into Standard English:***
[4] **GREG:** *(in a southern accent)* Excuse me, son.	*[4]* **GREG:** *(con un accento russo)* Mi scusi raguazzo.	*[4]* **GREG:** *(in a Russian accent)* Excuse me, young man.
[5] **SALESPERSON:** Yes.	*[5]* **COMMESSO:** Sì?	*[5]* **SALESPERSON:** Yes?
[6] **GREG:** *(in a southern accent)* I'm lookin' for a nan ion.	*[6]* **GREG:** *(con un accento russo)* stuo cercando della vuotka.	*[6]* **GREG:** *(in a Russian accent)* I'm looking for some *vuotka*.
[7] **SALESPERSON:** Non on?	*[7]* **COMMESSO:** vu-otka?	*[7]* **SALESPERSON:** vu-otka?
[8] **DHARMA:** *(in a southern accent)* Uh, what my husband means to say is that he is in need of a nan ion	*[8]* **DHARMA:** *(con un accento russo)* Mio muarito vuoleva dire che ha bisuogno di vuotka.	*[8]* **DHARMA:** *(in a Russian accent)* My husband wanted to know that he needs *vuotka*.
[9] **GREG:** *(in a southern accent)* Yeah. I'm looking for a new, uh, nan ion.	*[9]* **GREG:** *(con un accento russo)* Già, ho bisuogno di vuotka.	*[9]* **GREG:** *(in a Russian accent)* Yeah, I need *vuotka*.
[10] **SALESPERSON:** I'm sorry.	*[10]* **COMMESSO:** Non capisco.	*[10]* **SALESPERSON:** I don't understand.
[11] **GREG:** *(in a southern accent)* You know, a non on, six, seven, eight, nan ion.	*[11]* **GREG:** *(con un accento russo)* Alluora, whisky, gin, rum, vuotka.	*[11]* **GREG:** *(in a Russian accent)* So, whisky, gin, rhum, *vuotka*.
[12] **SALESPERSON:** Oh, a nine iron.	*[12]* **COMMESSO:** Oh, la vodka.	*[12]* **SALESPERSON:** Oh, vodka.
[13] **GREG:** *(in a southern accent)* Nan ion.	*[13]* **GREG:** *(in un accento non identificato)* vuotka.	*[13]* **GREG:** *(in a Russian accent) vuotka.*
[14] **SALESPERSON:** Yes. They're right over there.	*[14]* **COMMESSO:** si trova proprio laggiù.	*[14]* **SALESPERSON:** It's right over there.
[15] **GREG:** *(in a southern accent)* Thank you. *(to Dharma)* Damn Yankees.	*[15]* **GREG:** *(con un accento russo)* Gruazie. *(rivolto a Dharma)* Dannati capitalisti.	*[15]* **GREG:** *(in a Russian accent)* Thanks. *(to Dharma)* Damn capitalists.
(Dharma and Greg walk past Judge Samuel Harper.) *[16]* **JUDGE HARPER:** I know what you're saying. It's impossible to understand these people.	*(Dharma e Greg passano accanto al Giudice Damuel Harper)* *[16]* **GIUDICE HARPER:** *(con un accento russo)* So cosa vuolete dire. È impuossibile capire gli Americani.	*(Dharma and Greg walk past Judge Samuel Harper.)* *[16]* **JUDGE HARPER:** *(in a Russian accent)* I know what you mean. It's impossible to understand Americans.
[17] **GREG:** *(laughs) (in a southern accent)* That's true.	*[17]* **GREG:** *(ride) (con un accento russo)* è vero.	*[17]* **GREG:** *(laughs) (in a Russian accent)* that's true.

[18] **JUDGE HARPER:** Where y'all hail from?	*[18]* **GIUDICE HARPER:** *(con un accento russo)* da duove venite?	*[18]* **JUDGE HARPER:** *(in a Russian accent)* Where do you come from?
[19] **DHARMA:** *(in a southern accent)* Memphis. Where the hell you from?	*[19]* **DHARMA:** *(con un accento russo)* Russia. Non suarete una spia?	*[19]* **DHARMA:** *(in a Russian accent)* Russia. Would you be a spy by any chance?
[20] **JUDGE HARPER:** Oh, hail from, very good. Uh, well, we're pert'near neighbors. I'm from Knoxville.	*[20]* **GIUDICE HARPER:** *(con un accento russo)* Oh, non preoccupatevi. Ho lavuorato lì per trent'anni e ho spuosato una russa.	*[20]* **JUDGE HARPER:** *(in a Russian accent)* Oh, don't worry. I've been working there for thirty years and I married a Russian woman.
[21] **DHARMA:** *(in a southern accent)* Is that right? Did you hear that, Stinkbug? This man is a Knoxidian.	*[21]* **DHARMA:** *(con un accento russo)* Davvuero? Hai sentito compuagno? Quest'uomo ama la Russia.	*[21]* **DHARMA:** *(in a Russian accent)* Really? Did you hear that, comrade? This man loves Russia.
[22] **GREG:** *(in a southern accent)* Yeah.	*[22]* **GREG:** *(con un accento russo)* Già.	*[22]* **GREG:** *(in a Russian accent)* Yeah.

Apart from the unacceptable incongruity between the dialogic cues and the visual dimension, this instance of dubbing translation reproduces most of the typical inappropriate characteristics of 'dubbese'. For instance, the conventionalized translation of "yeah" as "già" (meaning "of course"), very rarely used in everyday spoken Italian with the meaning of "yes", or the literal translation of the Saleperson's cue [14], "si trova proprio laggiù" ("It's right over there"), which is a formal choice that would rarely occur in an Italian everyday conversation (especially the archaic adverb "laggiù"—literally: "down there"), whereas a more informal equivalent would have being "sta di là" ("it's over there"), or "guardi, sta di là" ("look, it's over there").

To conclude, this chapter has explored the two conventional processes of 'product localization' and 'product neutralization' in the field of dubbing translation and, by applying the Acting Translator Model to case studies carried out in a pedagogic context, has proposed an approach based on 'product naturalization' aimed at the respect of the socio-cultural and pragmalinguistic patterns of the original version by encouraging students/acting-translators to 'embody' the sitcom characters and their language and humour. The chapter has therefore ultimately attempted to redefine the notion of intercultural communicative competence in the field of dubbing translation, meant as a cognitive process by which the acting translator develops sociopragmatic and pragmalinguistic representations of both source and target cultures underlying the use of speech in the sitcoms. In the next chapter, another conventional approach to the dubbing translation of sitcoms will be analyzed—namely, 'product globalization'—and, then, some alternative solutions based on the acting translators' process of embodiment will be explored.

Chapter 6

Dubbing Translation as 'Product Globalization': Applying Humour Constructs to the Analysis of *Friends* and *Will & Grace* Source and Target Scripts

6.1 Reverse Transfer as a 'Foreignization' Process in the Dubbing Translation of *Friends*

6.1.1 *Socio-cultural dimensions of* Friends *sitcom*

Chapters 4 and 5 respectively introduced an analysis of *The Nanny* and *Roseanne* sitcoms as instances of dubbing translation as 'product localization', or 'domestication' (Venuti 1995, 1998). The dubbing translation of *The Nanny* (*La Tata*) for the Italian television was seen to convey an extreme regionalization of contexts which totally distorted the original dialogues in the attempt to adapt them to the newly devised situations for the target version, despite the often sharp contrast with the visual dimension of the sitcom denoting the characters' different socio-cultural background. The dubbing translators' objective, in this case, seems to have been that of inducing a sense of familiarity in Italian audiences, which however eradicates every sociolinguistic and cultural specificity of the source version. For instance, many radical adaptations were carried out by the dubbing translators in the Italian script at both diatopic and diastratic levels insofar as neither social/status and family-relation parameters, nor the typical New York Jewish speech style and socio-cultural references were respected. Instead, dubbing translators preferred a sociopragmatic transfer of Italian stereotypes (i.e., the family of immigrants from the Italian rural area of Ciociaria) to the original American interethnic context. Also in the dubbing translation of *Roseanne* (*Pappa e Ciccia*) for the Italian TV, the option was for a pragmalinguistic transfer of a standard Neapolitan variation to the Italian translation in order to render into equivalent ways the original working-class Illinois pragmalect used by the characters. In this case, diatopic and diastratic dislocations towards the target Italian culture actually affected and often modified the original culturally-marked humor of this sitcom. The other sitcom under analysis in Chapter 5 was *Dharma & Greg*, whose Italian dubbing translation was regarded as an example of 'product neutralization' with reference to a specific episode were dubbing translators for the Italian TV proposed an invented Italian variation to render the southern Tennessee accent. Such accent invention, however, modifies the original pragmalinguistic implications of this episode. In this sense, therefore, the notion of 'neutralization' as used here with reference to accent invention has not the same implications of 'neutralization' meant as a translation strategy aimed at substituting a culture-specific term in the source culture with a common term in the target one (cf. Ramière 2006: 156). Indeed, the discussion on the results of analysis upon the corpora of sitcom dubbed conversations shows how, in all these examined cases, the dubbing translators' processes of authenticating sitcom original voices, far from showing creativity within textual constraints (Chaume-Varela 1998) actually turn into strategies of re-authoring dialogues in their Italian versions by taking rigid ethnocentric and top-down stances.

Differently from the previous three cases under scrutiny, representing top-down instances of dubbing translation as 'product localization' and 'neutralization', in this chapter two more sitcoms aired at the turn of the century will be investigated—i.e., *Friends* and *Will & Grace*—as bottom-up instances of 'product globalization', or 'foreignization' (Venuti 1995, 1998). In this section, in particular, *Friends* will be analyzed in its source version and its respective target one for the Italian TV, which represents an example of sociopragmatic and pragmalinguistic 'reverse transfer' (Selinker and Lakshmanan 1992) of the American conversational styles and idiomatic expressions (socio-culturally marking the original sitcom) to the Italian version. As the untranslated title anticipates, the 'official' dubbing translators often render literally both the formal and the pragmalectal aspects of the American-English speech-act realizations so as to reproduce the 'foreign flair' of the original sitcom episodes. To achieve this aim, the dubbing translators of *Friends* (as well as those ones of *Will & Grace*, as it will be examined later in this chapter) strictly operate a text-based, bottom-up rendering of the original script, trying to carry out a literal translation at the syntactic, semantic and pragmatic levels, also respecting the timing of each spoken cue. Furthermore, in *Friends*, they have kept unmodified the original personalities of American characters and their names. Indeed, the dubbing translation of *Friends* for the Italian television does convey semiotic aspects typical of the source culture, which makes it close to the lexical-semantic construction and to the spoken rhythm and intonation of the American speech, thus triggering a sense of 'dislocation' towards the source culture in the target audience's reception and understanding. In fact, the dubbing translators of *Friends* frequently produce unnatural stylistic distortions upon the Italian dialogues, which also affect the spoken rhythms and intonations of the dubbed version. Yet, the Italian language they devise cannot be identified with any of the corresponding variations and jargons used by real groups of Italian youngsters (cf. Titone 1995), as it is rather a variant of the artificial 'Italian dubbese' characterizing the dubbing translation of most Anglo-American audiovisual products adapted for Italian audiences.

However, the pragmatic effect of such stylistic displacement on the Italian audience may be an impression of watching the sitcom as if it were in its original American version (cf. Kilborn 1989).

Starting from this preliminary enquiry—that, once again, stresses the lack of principled and systematic theoretical frameworks to be applied to the study of audiovisual translation (cf. Díaz Cintas 2004)—then, the Acting-Translator Model advanced in this book will be applied to longitudinal case studies implemented with reference to the episodes under analysis with the aim to investigate the possibility of developing new dubbing translations which, differently from the 'official' ones for the Italian TV, could instead provide an appropriate sociopragmatic and pragmalinguistic equivalence to the original move-&-act patterns and, at the same time, still retain the spontaneity of the Italian natural conversational styles (cf. Niemeier 1991; Bialystok 1996). Such dubbing-translation process, here defined as 'transmediation', aims at the achievement of a 'product naturalization' meant as a balance between the 'globalization' and 'localization' trends till reaching a kind of 'glocalized' rendering of the original sitcom into another language and culture. Such longitudinal case studies were once again implemented with a convenience sample of research subjects represented, as in the previous cases, by the same groups of Italian undergraduate students from two Italian Faculties of Foreign Languages majoring in Translation, arranged into Group A of students/acting-translators and Group B as a 'control group' of traditional dubbing translators.

The first step of the analysis, however, is represented by the identification, at a sociolinguistic level, of the conformities and differences in the characters' linguistic expressions in both versions. In particular, the analysis shall focus on which types of expressions have been respected in the version for the Italian TV, and in which way other types of 'specifically American' expressions have been translated and rendered into dubbing. This kind of enquiry aims at investigating both original and dubbed dialogues at the levels of adaptations, intonations, accents, tones and timbres of voices, with the purpose of establishing how they 'build' the characters in both versions (cf. Stanislavski 1981b), and to which extent the characters in the Italian version are faithful to their 'original' counterparts. The objective is to examine, through the comparative analysis of the pragmalinguistic strategies in the original dialogue and in its corresponding Italian dubbed version, the interaction between two different linguistic and socio-cultural structures (i.e., the American and the Italian ones) in two parallel groups of speakers of the same age—namely, the group of American young people that identify themselves with the dialogic style used by the protagonists in the original version of the sitcom, and the group of Italian young people that identify themselves with the same protagonists of the sitcom who, in this case, are made to interact through the use of the Italian language in the dubbed version. As mentioned above, the young protagonists of the Italian version of *Friends* do not in fact speak like the 'real' Italian youngsters as they do not possess any specific regional or dialectal intonation, their phonetics is not socio-culturally marked, and also their colloquial speech style cannot be identified with any of the youth jargons used in Italy since it reproduces almost faithfully the original American style and the idiomatic forms (with the exceptions of a certain 'neutralization' of vulgar expressions—not too many, however, in this sitcom—not allowed by RAI, namely, Italy's Public Broadcaster that aired this sitcom). On the contrary, considering the huge popularity of *Friends*, the Italian speech style of its protagonists contributed to the creation of a new colloquial register in the Italian young people who identified themselves with the protagonists' American lifestyle.

The *Friends* lifestyle has indeed had a huge socio-cultural impact on the younger generations all over the world at the turn of the century (precisely from 1994 to 2004) (cf. McCarroll 2004). *Friends* was created by David Crane and Martha Kauffman for NBC with the purpose of featuring a new atypical family nucleus which was becoming widespread in that period - a nucleus composed by young people in their mid-twenties who are, in the authors' own words, "in a time of your life when everything's possible. And it's about friendship because when you're single and in the city, your friends are your family." (Lauer 2005). Indeed, as Ross (1998: 92) points out, much of the success of *Friends* is due to the fact that this sitcom distances itself from the traditional notion of family to explore new social organizations based on mutual, loving support. The same may be said with the other sitcom to be analyzed in this chapter: *Will & Grace.* It is not by chance if both sitcoms start with one of the female protagonists (Rachel and Grace, respectively) literally leaving their husbands-to-be at the altar, still with their wedding gown on, to start a new life with the group of caring friends, thus deciding not to conform to the standards of the conventional family. The 'friends' in this sitcom are six young people—hree women and three men—experimenting life together in Manhattan, New York City. The tree young women are: Monica Geller (played by Courteney Cox), a chef and a former obese child who is the 'mother figure' of the group, featured as a perfectionist, also obsessed with orderliness and tidiness, and who eventually dates for a while Dr. Richard Burke (Tom Selleck), one of her father's friends, 20 years her senior; Rachel Green (Jennifer Aniston), Monica's best friend since high school, a frivolous and spoilt fashion-addict, yet somewhat clumsy, who lives in Monica's apartment after having dumped her fiancé, and who works first as a waitress at the coffee house Central Perk (in the ground floor of their building, a place where the group of friends usually meet), and then as a shop assistant at Bloomingdale's; Phoebe Buffay (Lisa Kudrow), a bizarre and illogical New-Age young woman who became homeless as a girl and then reinvented herself as a street-stylish masseuse and a peculiar musician and singer at

Central Perk, who lives in her own apartment although she spends much of her time at Monica's home. The three young men are: Ross Geller (David Schwimmer), Monica's brother, a naive palaeontologist, eventually becoming a lecture at New York University, who lives in his own apartment in a nearby block of flats—and so he spends most of his time at his sister's home—and who is intermittently involved in a romantic relationship with Rachel (despite having been married twice and being the father of a child from his first ex-wife who turned out to be a lesbian); Chandler Bing (Matthew Perry), a statistician for a multinational corporation first, and then a copywriter at an advertising agency, who is sarcastic and yet shy and insecure, unpopular with women, and who eventually falls in love and marries his friend Monica; Joey Tribbiani (Matt LeBlanc), an uncomplicated womanizer and a struggling actor, who eventually gets a role in the fictionalized version of the soap opera *Days of Our Lives*, and who shares with Chandler an apartment on the same landing as Monica's, where they usually dine and spend much of their time, thus becoming, together with the other friends—in the authors' own words (*ibidem*)—"new, surrogate family members". Indeed, the cast members also became very close friends off screen, even after the end of the series as they declared that they had become an actual family (Wild 2004). *Friends* became the most popular sitcom of its time to the point that when the series closed in 2004 some critics even predicted the end of the sitcom genre (cf. Shales 2004) to be replaced in popularity by the reality shows. However, after the terrorist attacks on September 11, 2001, *Friends* story-plots progressively developed towards more conventional forms of family to comply with bewildered people's search for comfort in tradition (cf. Carter 2002). This explains why the characters in *Friends* were made to opt for marriage and marriage-like relationships: Monica and Chandler got married and adopted two twins, Phoebe married her fiancé Mike (after having previously been an anti-conformist and controversial surrogate mother of three twins for her half brother and his wife), and Rachel and Ross decided to become a stable couple after the birth of their child Emma. Only Joey stayed single, but in *Friends* spin-off series, *Joey*, his character declined into a pathetic and lonely broken man.

6.1.2 *Instances of source-culture dislocations*

The scriptwriters of this sitcom, as expected, in representing a group of young American people living in Manhattan at the turn of the century, emplyed a typical speech style and comic register fitting their age, place, and peer relationship. The multinational company that produced this sitcom—i.e., the Warner Bros.—specifically required that the dubbing translation of *Friends* throughout the world had to respect the original speech style and humour of the characters, with a minimum freedom left to translators' 'creativity', since the title that had to be left unchanged.

Initially, this title was in fact rendered into the Italian equivalent, *Amici*, but then it was soon replaced with its original *Friends* by injunction (personal communication by Warner Bros. Italy). The choice of 'foreignization', thus, was actually dictated by production guidelines, rather than by specific choices made by the national TV broadcaster. This entailed, however, that dubbing translators had to cope with the problem of idiomatic language to be rendered faithfully into the target language not only at the pragmatic level, but even at the semantic one. The dubbing translators of the version for the Italian TV seem to have solved this quandary by opting for a literal translation of the original American-English language and for the neutral standard variety of Italian void of marked colloquialisms and dialectal or sociolectal inflections. The end-product, therefore, is a kind of 'dubbese' as a register of its own, that is not simply influenced by Anglicisms and calques of original idiomatic phrases, but it is also accurately deprived of any equivalent colloquialism in Italian at both phraseological and phonological levels. The protagonists of *Friends* are in fact dubbed by actors' voices that seem to be deliberately 'performing' dialogic cues (often overacting by emphasizing diction and intonation pitch)—if not actually 'reading them aloud' like 'word-runs' in play rehearsals—thus inducing in listeners the sensation that the actors themselves are feeling 'estranged' from the characters they are dubbing well before producing the same effect on the target audiences. Indeed, audiences are actually required to activate a 'suspension of disbelief' in order to accept the dialogues they listen to as spoken in an appropriate 'natural' and 'everyday' Italian. The aim of a dubbing translator, instead, should be that of achieving a 'natural equivalence' between source and target languages at both the semantic and pragmatic levels or, more specifically, in Fodor's (1976) terms, at the levels of phonetic, character, and content synchrony. In this sense, as argued throughout this book, the dubbing translator needs to become an 'acting translator' who not only encompasses the professional competences so far ascribed to different experts – namely: the script translator, the script adaptor accommodating the received translation to the timing and synchronization of the original screened dialogue, the dubbing director, and the dubbing actors. In fact, an acting translator also needs to 'embody' the characters within the sitcom contexts, their speech style, and their humour by means of acting strategies—such as top-down improvisation and bottom-up stylistic analysis—in order to 'appropriate' them (indeed, 'become' them), which is here argued to be the only way to render their original language 'naturally' into the target language.

What can be noticed in the dubbed speech style of the Italian TV version is the frequent, sudden shift from an informal style to a formal one within the same cue of a character, which has a disconcerting effect on audiences who are unable to establish, on the one hand, his/her actual personality through the speech style s/he uses and, on the other, the interpersonal 'tenor' relationship (Halliday 1973) that this character establishes with his/her interlocutors in the exchange they are involved as participants. A case in point is represented by the translation of "I'm sorry" into the formal "sono spiacente"—rather than the more natural and informal "mi dispiace", or "scusa/mi scusi"—which sounds unnatural in Italian when the young characters interact as peers and close friends. The effect of an Italian language that is unnatural and even stilted may in fact trigger disconcerting feelings in the audiences with the risk of making them miss the comic prompt. Furthermore, as far as the socio-cultural content is concerned, in the version of *Friends* for the Italian TV many literal dislocations from the original script to the target one may likewise undermine the humorous effect of the punch lines. For instance, in the episode *The One Where Joey Moves Out* (*Joey cambia casa*), Joey makes reference to Captain Crunch, an American brand of corn flakes (with the face of this 'captain' on its package), which is left as it is in the translated version, but then, the American idiomatic expression opening his cue "Man, this is weird. You ever realize Captain Crunch's eyebrows are actually on his hat?" is strangely omitted in translation: "Ti eri mai accorto che Capitan Crunch ha le sopracciglia sul cilindro?" (Back-translation: "Have you ever realized that Captain Crunch has his eyebrows on his top hat?"), though an appropriate natural equivalent could have been: "Guarda, che strano!" (Look, how weird!"). A case of literal translation of an idiomatic expression rendered into an 'artificial' Italian—and thus failing to convey the comic effect—is represented by a cue uttered by Monica's mother. In a conversation between Mrs. Geller and a friend about their mutual friend, Richard Burke, dating a much younger woman, Mrs. Geller, not knowing that this young woman is her daughter Monica, comments sarcastically: "We just know she's got the IQ of a napkin"—an expression that is left the same in Italian: "Io scommetto che avrà l'intelligenza di un tovagliolo" ("I bet she'll have the intelligence of a napkin"). In a Group-A workshop, instead, an alternative translation that was proposed was "intelligenza di una gallina" ("a hen's intelligence"), which is a natural pragmatic equivalent in Italian (cf. Matuella 2000). Similar choices can be detected throughout the same episode under analysis. For instance, in an exchange between Monica's parents, Mr. Geller asks his wife: "Have you seen my Harmon Kilerbrew bat?", mentioning an American brand of baseball bats that has been retained also in translation though with a spelling mistake: "hai visto la mia mazza Killbrew?". Soon afterwards, Mr. Geller mentions the movie *Cocoon* with reference to Richard's new lease of life: "He's like a new man. It's like a scene from *Cocoon*". This teen-movie is very well known also in Italy, although its connotative reference to the freshness of youth is overstressed in translation: "Sì, sembra ringiovanito, neanche fosse uscito da una scena di *Cocoon*" ("Yeah, he looks rejuvenated, as if he had come out of a scene from *Cocoon*"). In another scene, Ross breaks in the apartment of Chandler and Joey and asks them dejectedly if they have ever been laughed at by their girlfriend, and Chandler answers: "Yeah, but uh, it was 1982 and my flock of seagulls haircut was tickling her chin". This culture-bound reference to a typical haircut of the eighties has been kept in the Italian version although this was not the way such a hairstyle was defined in Italy, hence the audience's possible lack of immediate understanding may undermine the comic effect: "Sì, ma era l'82 e il mio ciuffo stile 'gabbiano' le faceva il solletico" ("Yeah, but it was 1982 and my seagull-style forelock was tickling her"). Another example of unmodified reference is represented by the scene in which Chandler and Joey, after having phoned for pizzas, decide to cancel part of the order and Chandler says: "I'll cancel the sodas". In the Italian version the term "soda" is strangely kept although it is not in use, not even in youth jargons: "Meglio disdire le sode" ("Better to cancel the sodas"). In a Group-A workshop the suggestion was to render this term into the normal and widespread "bibite" ("drinks") (*ibidem*). Another unmodified reference is markedly represented in episode #20 where Chandler and Joey identify themselves, respectively, with Mr. Peanut and Mr. Salty – the former being the image of a brand of snacks representing a peanut elegantly dressed with a monocle, a top hat, white gloves and a cane; the latter being the image of another brand of snacks in a sailor dress. In this exchange, Chandler says: "I can't believe you would actually say that. I would much rather be Mr. Peanut than Mr. Salty", to which Joey replies: "No way! Mr. Salty is a sailor, all right, he's got to be, like, the toughest snack there is". These culturally-marked references to typically North-American food brands are directly transferred from the source language to the target one: *Chandler:* "Non posso credere che tu dica sul serio. Io preferirei essere Mr. Peanut che Mr. Salty." *Joey:* "Scherzi? Mr. Salty è un marinaio, giusto? E quindi deve essere lo snack più da duri che ci sia!" (Back-translation: *Chandler:* "I can't believe you are serious about this. I'd rather be Mr. Peanut than Mr. Salty." *Joey:* "Are you kidding? Mr. Salty is a sailor, right? And so he must be the top snack for tough guys there is!"). In the workshop with Group-A students, a possible solution, aimed to overcome the cultural estrangement of the target audience, with the consequent lack of comic effect, was to translate the original names into "l'elegante Mr. Nocciolina" and "Mr. Salatino" (literally: "the elegant Mr. Peanut" and "Mr. Pretzel", with the addition of the adjective "elegant" to make up for the lack of information in the text on the characteristics of Mr. Peanut, which is instead given for Mr. Salty, the sailor). Some other times, however, cultural references in the original version were omitted in the dubbing translation, as in the case of Joey's mentioning the show that employed him as an actor: "Huh? *Days of Our Lives* picked up my option" which was omitted: "Vero? Festeggio la mia conferma in TV!" ("Really? I'm celebrating my confirmation in TV!"), on the assumption that Italian audiences would not know this real American TV serial that is fictionalized in *Friends*. The same may be said for the omission of the sports programme *Green Acres* in Chandler's enthusiastic appreciation of two recliners that Joey bought to celebrate his being confirmed in the TV show: "Now we can finally watch *Green Acres* the way it was meant to be seen", rendered into Italian as: "Adesso possiamo finalmente vederci la Partita come in tribuna d'onore!" ("Now we can finally watch the Football Match as in the VIP stand!")—an acceptable solution, considering that some Group-B students had suggested the 'domestication' choice of turning *Green Acres* into the corresponding Italian TV sports programme *La Domenica Sportiva*.

Regrettably, cases of mistranslation due to the interference of false-friend terms have also been noticed in the dubbing translation of *Friends* for the Italian TV, as in the scene when Monica and Phoebe are at Richard's home for his party and he remarks: "Yeah, since the divorce, when anybody asks me how I am, it's always with a sympathetic head tilt". In the Italian version the idiomatic expression is rendered in this way: "Sì, da quando ho divorziato, le persone che mi chiedono come sto fanno sempre un simpatico 'inclinamento'", thus mistranslating "sympathetic"—in Italian "compassionevole" ("compassionate")—with "simpatico" ("nice"). Also the informal "inclinamento"—rather than "inclinazione"—("tilt") is a partial translation of "head tilt", but Richard mimes the movement with his head and disambiguates it. However, examples of culture-bound expressions in the original version which, though they have already entered the Italian language, have not been kept in translation are frequent. An instance of this type can be found in Joey's cue with reference to one of his colleagues: "He's having a brunch", which is rendered into "Dà una festa" ("He's having a party"). "Brunch"—defined by the Oxford Dictionary as "a meal that you eat in the late morning as a combination of breakfast and lunch"—may have been left as it is in Italian, or—as suggested within Group-A students—could have been rendered into "rinfresco" ("refreshments") or "buffet" (*ibidem*). In other cases, literal translations work when there is a cultural equivalence also in the target language, as in the example from an exchange between Phoebe and Monica, at Mr. Geller's birthday party, where Phoebe offers to help as a waitress for Monica's mother and Monica replies: "Really Phoebs? Because, you know, you'd have to be an actual waitress. This can't be like your 'I can be a bear cub' thing", which has been rendered into "Attenta, dovrai avere lo 'stile' della cameriera! Non potrai atteggiarti a 'tenero orsacchiotto'" ("Beware, you should have the 'style' of the waitress! You can't pose as a 'sweet teddy bear'"). What is to be noticed in this case is that the infantile image of a 'teddy bear cub' finds a denotative and connotative equivalent in both source and target cultures and thus it is retained in translation. On the contrary, the original sarcastic tone used by Monica to clarify what her mother actually expects from a waitress, which Phoebe candidly does not seem to understand or take seriously, is turned into Monica's straightforward and discourteous warning to her friend. Another instance of equivalence can be found in the same episode, during a conversation between Phoebe and Rachel about the possibility of having themselves tattooed, when Phoebe attacks Rachel for her fear that Ross, her boyfriend, may not accept a tattoo on her body: "I don't believe this. Ross equals boss."—literally rendered into Italian as "Non ci posso credere. Ross uguale a boss?" because it is possible to retain the same alliterative wordplay. In the same scene, however, when Joey asks Phoebe what kind of tattoo she is going to get, the translator found it impossible to render into Italian another wordplay in Phoebe's answer: "Um, I'm getting a lily for my Mom. 'Cause her name's Lily", which was instead translated as: "Io un piccolo giglio. Per mia madre, perché lei li adorava." ("I, a small lily. For my mother, because she adored them"). Group-A students attempted a translation of the wordplay: some proposed the Latin word for "lily"—i.e., "lilium"—also in use in Italy as a technical term, and then rendered the utterance into: "Mi faccio un lilium per mia mamma, perché si chiama Lilia" ("I'm getting a lilium for my Mom, 'cause her name's Lilia"); some other students proposed the less effective wordplay "giglio/Gigliola": "voglio un giglio per mia madre, perché si chiama Gigliola" ("I want a lily (giglio) for my mother, because her name's Gigliola").

An instance of successful rendering of a wordplay in the 'official' dubbing translation of *Friends* is a scene from the episode *The One Where Rachel and Ross... You Know* (*Finalmente Ross e Rachel...*), when Chandler and Joey in their apartment, are sprawled on their new black leather recliners entirely taken up with watching TV and Ross, Monica and Phoebe are with them. Eventually Phoebe says: "I can't believe two cows made the ultimate sacrifice so you guys could watch TV with your feet up", and Chandler replies: "Well, they were chair-shaped cows. They never would have survived in the wild"—which, almost literally rendered into Italian, becomes: "*Phoebe:* È incredibile. Hanno 'immolato' due mucche per farvi stare con I piedi in aria a vedere la TV!", "*Chandler:* Erano due mucche-poltrone! Non sarebbero sopravvissute al pascolo!" ("*Phoebe:* "That's incredible. The have 'immolated' two cows to make you stay with your feet up in the air to watch TV!", "*Chandler:* "They were two lazy-cows [but also "chair-shaped cows"]! They wouldn't have survived out to pasture!"). In this case, the Italian version has created with the expression "mucche-poltrone" a wordplay into a wordplay, namely, the expected literal "chair ["poltrone"-Noun]-shaped cows" and the new "lazy ["poltrone"-Adjective] cows". A case of unidiomatic utterance rendered through an Italian idiomatic expression is represented by Phoebe's statement occurring later in the same episode, when she looms up in front of Joey and Chandler, still sprawled on their recliners watching TV, and says: "We have got to get you lazy boys out of these chairs". This is rendered into Italian as: "Oh, ma come si fa a 'schiodarvi' da quelle poltrone, pigroni?" ("Oh, but what can be done to get your backside off these chairs [Italian metaphor: "to unnail"], lazy boys?"). Probably, an effective wordplay suggested by some Group-A students would have been the literal one using the same omophony between the Noun "poltrone"/"chairs" and the Adjective "poltroni"/"lazy": "Vi dobbiamo far alzare da quelle poltrone, poltroni" ("We have got to get you out of these armchairs, lazy boys"). An instance of dubbese which could instead have been rendered into Italian through an appropriate socio-cultural and linguistic equivalent is represented by Chandler's exclamation at seeing the two recliners for the first time: "Sweet mother of all that is good and pure!". The reference here is religious as it implies a quotation from a prayer to the Virgin Mary, Mother of Jesus, which may sound unexpected when said by an American young man like Chandler, but it may have sounded less unusual to the Italian target audiences living in a traditionally Roman-Catholic country if it had been translated literally. Instead, in the translation for the Italian TV it was rendered into a pragmatically artificial Italian: "Per tutte le coccole della mamma, che meraviglia!" ("For all Mum's cuddles, how wonderful!"), an expression that an Italian young man would never ever use. An appropriate Italian equivalent, instead, could have been one that makes reference to the litanies to the Virgin Mary, which belong to the Italian cultural heritage and have by now become of common use in everyday speech. Hence some possible translations of this interjection could be: "Madre purissima causa della nostra gioia" ("Purest Mother cause of our joy!"), or "Madre purissima della grazia divina!" ("Purest Mother of the divine grace!") which, in both cases, refer to a fusion of two litany lines. Some Group-B students, instead, persisted in opting for dubbese, choosing to render this interjection into an utterly improbable Italian: "Wow, caspita! Sono grandiose!" ("Wow, crickey! The are grand!") (*ibidem*). Another missed opportunity for playing with words in the Italian dubbing translation is represented by Phoebe's words to her friend Monica who has fallen in love with Dr. Richard Burke but she does not want to acknowledge it. Phoebe remarks: "You are so smitten. Oh, you are so much the smitten kitten". The reference here is to a metaphorical expression common in the English language which associates the experience of 'secretly falling in love' to the physical, painful one of 'being smitten', enlarged to the metaphor of the 'smitten kitten' referred to the inexperienced girls secretly and painfully falling in love for the first time. In Italian, this emotional experience is not metaphorically associated to the physical one of 'being smitten', but rather to the – likewise painful – experience of 'being cooked', a sensation of having a high temperature to be enlarged to the image of a 'kitten in heat'. Hence, a possible translation could have been: "Sei bella cotta, Oh, sembri proprio una gattina in calore." (Literally: "You are so cooked. Oh, you are so much the kitten in heat"). In the dubbing translation for the Italian TV, this metaphorical parallelism was not taken into consideration as the translator opted for a literal rendering of the wordplay, thus cancelling it: "Ti sei presa una bella cotta. Oh, hai l'aria di una gattina in amore!" ("You've got a good crush. Oh, you look like a kitten in love!").

In sum, *Friends* is the sitcom that, among the others that have been analyzed so far, has respected the original script in its 'official' Italian translation in order to convey as much as possible all the references to the American culture and lifestyle, and this was so mainly because of a specific policy of 'product globalization' required by Warner Bros, with the aim of spreading, through television and the movies, a 'made-in-USA' culture. The 'exotic' effect of estrangement produced on target audiences is, therefore, also part of the producers' intentions. At this point, then, an analysis of the dialogic construction of this sitcom conversation is needed before moving to the workshop performed by the students/acting-translators.

6.2 A Comparative Conversation Analysis of the Act-pattern in a Script from *Friends*

6.2.1 *Method and tagged data*

The application of the patterns of Acts (Sinclair and Coulthard 1975; Burton 1980; Stenstrom 1994) to the analysis of the conversation in a script from *Friends* and in its dubbing translation for the Italian television is meant to reveal the way humorous discourse dynamics occur in this sitcom. As introduced above, the peculiarity of this sitcom is that, similarly to the others selected for this study, it represents interesting social and conversational dynamics occurring within new types of family contexts. These sitcoms, indeed, stage instances of modern 'transitional communities' at the turn of the century, constituted by groups of people whose close relationships substitute the traditional family ties. Three of the sitcoms selected for this study are set in New York, a multicultural city whose alienating life pace tends to disintegrate the conventional family routines, thus encouraging the emergence of new community organizations that try to make up for values and affective bonds of the conventional family. It is not by chance that the main set of all the selected sitcoms is not the workplace, but the home (usually the living room and the kitchen—often merged in the same room of a small apartment) that characters share at any hour of the day and night, even if some of them have another home-place elsewhere.

The episode of *Friends* selected for the analysis is #457316, *The One Where Joey Moves Out*, initially translated literally as *Joey cambia casa*, but then turned by the copyeditor into *I tatuaggi*, thus focusing on a different storyline of the episode (personal communication from Warner Bros. Italy). Here, the six young protagonists are in fact involved in three storylines, each containing a 'revelation plot': in one of them, Joey and Chandler argue because Joey has been forced to reveal to Chandler that he is thinking about leaving the apartment he shares with him to move to an apartment on his own. Another storyline is focused on Monica, who eventually feels compelled to reveal to her parents her relationship with their friend Richard, a man much older than her. The other storyline is about Phoebe who convinces Rachel to get tattooed together, but only Rachel has the tattoo done, whereas Phoebe quits just before doing it for panic and now she is obliged to reveal this unpleasant news to Rachel. Since these storylines are all about 'revelation plots', the main dynamics of the conversation is conflict followed by attempts at negotiation. Hence humour is constructed on an Arousal/Safety pattern where Arousal is often introduced by Disparagement. The conversational acts that shall be focused on in the analysis, therefore, are those ones involved in conflict arousing tension, often by denigrating the interlocutor, as well as those ones involved in negotiation aiming at a shared solution and, thus, at a sense of relief and 'safety'—as outlined in *3.2.2*. Yet, for the description of these dialogic exchanges, it will be necessary to introduce novel Acts in order to better describe the characters' complex emotional response at each other's cues. Indeed, frequently the rapid sequence of different Acts within a character's turn makes it necessary to identify them with labels that are normally used for whole Moves in order to describe the quick shift from a state of mind to another—often contradictory—one. In particular, a specific 'Negotiate Act' needs to be introduced precisely to stress the efforts made by the characters to appease challenges and achieve a mutual understanding of different behaviours and an accommodation of divergent socio-cultural stances. In this sense humour in 'transitional-community' sitcoms is a means to solve the conflicts of an affective nature at the source of the characters' judgements on causes of tension, which is eventually solved by witty strategies of negotiation inducing relief (Guido 1997).

What follows is a comparative conversation analysis of the original and the dubbed versions of an extract from the above-mentioned episode from *Friends*. The enquiry shall be carried out by focusing on the interplay of Acts that build the Arousal/Safety pattern of humour. In particular, the pattern of Acts (A) of *Pre-Head, Head,* or *Post-Head* types, marked for Arousal *(A)*, Safety *(S)*, or Disparagement *(D)* humour-triggers, shall be explored to investigate the negotiation dynamics in tense interpersonal discourse.

Friends episode #457316 *The One Where Joey Moves Out (I tatuaggi – The Tattoos)*
Exchange 1: turns [1]-[15]; Exchange 2: turns [16]-[60]; Exchange 3: turns [61]-[72]

Original English version:	***Italian dubbing translation:***	***Back-translation into Standard English:***
[Chandler and Joey's apartment]	**[Appartamento di Chandler e Joey]**	**[Chandler and Joey's apartment]**
(Chandler and Joey are returning from their brunch at the place of Joey's co-star who's moving and renting his apartment) ***[1]* JOEY: [a]** Can we drop this? **[b]** I am not interested in the guy's apartment. **[a. Prompt**	*(Chandler e Joey sono di ritorno da una colazione a casa di un collega di Joey che sta trasferendosi ed affitta il suo appartamento)* ***[1]* JOEY: [a]** Vuoi smetterla adesso? **[b]** Ti ho già detto che non mi interessa quell'apparta-	*(Chandler and Joey are returning from their brunch at the place of Joey's co-star who's moving and renting his apartment)* ***[1]* JOEY:** Would you come off it, now? I've already told you that I'm not interested in that apartment.

A*(A) Pre-Head* + b. Informative A*(S) Head*]	mento. **[a. Prompt A*(A) Pre-Head* + b. Informative A*(S) Head*]**	
***[2]* CHANDLER: [a]** Oh please, **[b]** I saw the way you were checking out his mouldings. **[c]** You want it. **[a. Blame A*(D) Pre-Head* + b. Evaluate A*(A) Head* + c. Comment A*(A) Post-Head*]**	***[2]* CHANDLER: [a]** Oh, per favore, **[b]** ho visto come guardavi tutte le rifiniture. **[c]** Tu lo vuoi. **[a. Blame A*(D) Pre-Head* + b. Evaluate A*(A) Head* + c. Comment A*(A) Post-Head*]**	***[2]* CHANDLER:** Oh please, I saw the way you were looking at all its mouldings. You want it.
***[3]* JOEY: [a]** Why would I want another apartment, huh? **[b]** I've already got an apartment that I love. **[a. Check A*(S) Pre-Head* + b. Informative A*(S) Head*]**	***[3]* JOEY: [a]** E perché mai dovrei volerlo? Eh? **[b]** Io ho già un appartamento che mi piace. **[a. Check A*(S) Pre-Head* + b. Informative A*(S) Head*]**	***[3]* JOEY:** Why should I want it? I've already got an apartment that I like.
***[4]* CHANDLER: [a]** Well **[b]** it wouldn't kill you to say it once in a while. **[a. Challenge A*(A) Pre-Head* + b. Blame A*(D) Head*]**	***[4]* CHANDLER:** Perché non dici la verità una volta tanto? **[a. Challenge A*(D) Head*]**	***[4]* CHANDLER:** Why don't you say the truth, once in a while?
***[5]* JOEY: [a]** Alright, **[b]** you want the truth? **[c]** I'm thinkin' about it. **[a. Marker A*(A) Pre-Head* + b. Challenge A*(A) Pre-Head* + c. Revelation A*(A) Head*]**	***[5]* JOEY: [a]** D'accordo, **[b]** vuoi la verità? **[c]** Ci sto pensando. **[a. Marker A*(A) Pre-Head* + b. Challenge A*(A) Pre-Head* + c. Revelation A*(A) Head*]**	***[5]* JOEY:** Alright, you want the truth? I'm thinkin' about it.
***[6]* CHANDLER:** What? **[Elicitation A*(A) Head*]**	***[6]* CHANDLER:** Cosa? **[Elicitation A*(A) Head*]**	***[6]* CHANDLER:** What?
***[7]* JOEY: [a]** I'm sorry. **[b]** I'm 28 years old, **[c]** I've never lived alone, **[d]** and I'm finally at a place where I've got enough money **[e]** that I don't need a roommate anymore. **[a. Apologize A*(S) Pre-Head* + b. Negotiate A*(S) Pre-Head* + c. Upgrade A*(S) Pre-Head* + d. Upgrade A*(A) Pre-Head* + e. Informative A*(A) Head*]**	***[7]* JOEY: [a]** Mi dispiace. **[b]** Chandler, **[c]** ho quasi ventotto anni, **[d]** non ho mai abitato da solo **[e]** e finalmente guadagno abbastanza **[f]** da potermi permettere di prendere una casa per conto mio. **[a. Apologize A*(S) Pre-Head* + b. Nomination A*(S) Pre-Head* + c. Negotiate A*(S) Pre-Head* + d. Upgrade A*(S) Pre-Head* + e. Upgrade A*(A) Pre-Head* + f. Informative A*(A) Head*]**	***[7]* JOEY:** I'm sorry Chandler, I'm almost 28 years old, I've never lived alone, and I finally earn well enough to be able to afford renting a house on my own.
***[8]* CHANDLER: [a]** Whoah, whoah, whoah. **[b]** I don't need a roommate either, **[c]** OK? **[d]** I can afford to live here by myself. **[e]** Ya know, **[f]** I may have to bring in somebody once a week to lick the silverware. **[a. React A*(A) Pre-Head* + b. Challenge A*(A) Head* + c. Check A*(A) Post-Head* + d. Informative A*(A) Head* + e. Cue A*(A) Pre-Head* + f. Challenge A*(D) Head*]**	***[8]* CHANDLER: [a]** Aspetta un attimo, **[b]** guarda che io ho sempre potuto permettermi un appartamento tutto mio come questo **[c]** dove far venire chi voglio a leccarmi l'argenteria. **[a. React A*(A) Pre-Head* + b. Informative A*(A) Head* + c. Challenge A*(D) Post-Head*]**	***[8]* CHANDLER:** Wait a minute, look, I've always been able to afford an apartment on my own like this where I can make anyone I want come to lick my silverware.
***[9]* JOEY: [a]** What're you gettin' so bent out of shape for, huh? **[b]** It's not like we agreed	***[9]* JOEY: [a]** Scusa, **[b]** ma vuoi dirmi perché ti scaldi tanto? **[c]** Noi non ci siamo mica sposati,	***[9]* JOEY:** Excuse me, but will you tell me why you are getting so heated? We are not married, I

to live together forever. **[c]** We're not Bert and Ernie. **[a. Blame A*(D) Pre-Head* + b. Challenge A*(A) Head* + c. Upgrade A*(D) Post-Head*]**	mi sembra. **[d]** E non siamo Tom e Jerry. **[a. Apologize A*(S) Pre-Head* + b. Blame A*(D) Pre-Head* + c. Challenge A*(A) Head* + d. Upgrade A*(D) Post-Head*]**	think. And we are not Tom and Jerry.
***[10]* CHANDLER: [a]** Look, you know what? **[b]** If this is the way you feel, **[c]** then maybe you should take it. **[a. Challenge A*(A) Pre-Head* + b. Acknowledge A*(A) Pre-Head* + c. Prompt A*(A) Head*]**	***[10]* CHANDLER: [a]** Lo sai che ti dico? **[b]** Se è così che la pensi, **[c]** allora dovresti andartene. **[a. Challenge A*(A) Pre-Head* + b. Acknowledge A*(A) Pre-Head* + c. Prompt A*(A) Head*]**	***[10]* CHANDLER:** You know what? If this is the way you think, then maybe you should go away.
***[11]* JOEY: [a]** Well **[b]** that's how I feel. **[a. Challenge A*(A) Pre-Head* + b. Upgrade A*(A) Head*]**	***[11]* JOEY:** È così che la penso. **[Challenge A*(A) Head*]**	**[11] JOEY:** That's how I think.
***[12]* CHANDLER: [a]** Well **[b]** then maybe you should take it. **[a. Challenge A*(A) Pre-Head* + b. Upgrade A*(A) Head*]**	***[12]* CHANDLER:** E allora vattene! **[Challenge A*(A) Head*]**	***[12]* CHANDLER:** And so go away!
***[13]* JOEY: [a]** Well **[b]** then maybe I will. **[a. Challenge A*(A) Pre-Head* + b. Upgrade A*(A) Head*]**	***[13]* JOEY:** Me ne andrò di sicuro. **[Challenge A*(A) Head*]**	***[13]* JOEY:** I will surely go away.
***[14]* CHANDLER:** Fine with me. **[Challenge A*(A) Head*]**	***[14]* CHANDLER:** Ne sono felice. **[Challenge A*(A) Head*]**	***[14]* CHANDLER:** I'm happy with it.
***[15]* JOEY: [a]** Great. **[b]** Then you'll be able to spend more quality time with your real friends, the spoons. **[a. Evaluate A*(D) Pre-Head* + b. Comment A*(D) Head*]**	***[15]* JOEY: [a]** Grazie! **[b]** Così finalmente potrai goderti in santa pace i tuoi veri amici, i cucchiai! **[a. Evaluate A*(D) Pre-Head* + b. Comment A*(D) Head*]**	***[15]* JOEY:** Thanks! So you'll be finally able to enjoy in peace your real friends, the spoons!
[Mr Geller's birthday party]	**[Festa di compleanno del Signor Geller]**	**[Mr Geller's birthday party]**
(Mr and Mrs. Geller enter the living room looking particularly refreshed. Monica follows looking rather pale) ***[16]* MR. GELLER:** Who's drink can I freshen? **[Offer A*(S) Head*]**	*(Il Signore e la Signora Geller entrano nel soggiorno e appaiono particolarmente ritemprati. Poi entra Monica che appare piuttosto pallida)* ***[16]* SIG. GELLER:** Chi vuole ancora vino? **[Offer A*(S) Head*]**	*(Mr and Mrs. Geller enter the living room looking particularly refreshed. Monica follows looking rather pale)* ***[16]* MR. GELLER:** Who wants more wine?
***[17]* MRS. GELLER:** Almost time for cake. **[Comment A*(S) Head*]**	***[17]* SIG.RA GELLER:** È quasi ora della torta! **[Comment A*(S) Head*]**	***17]* MRS. GELLER:** It's almost time for cake.
***[18]* ROSS: [a]** Mon, Mon, **[b]** are you OK? **[a. Bid A*(A) Pre-Head* + b. Check A*(A) Head*]**	***[18]* ROSS: [a]** Scusa... **[b]** Monica, **[c]** ma che ti succede? **[a. Apologize A*(S) Pre-Head* + b. Bid A*(A) Pre-Head* + c. Check A*(A) Head*]**	***[18]* ROSS:** Excuse me... Monica, what's wrong with you?
***[19]* MONICA:** You remember that video I found of mom and dad? **[Elicit A*(A) Head*]**	***[19]* MONICA:** Ricordi quella cassetta di mamma e papà che avevo trovato? **[Elicit A*(A) Head*]**	***[19]* MONICA:** Do you remember that videotape I found of mom and dad?
***[20]* ROSS:** Yeah. **[Reply A*(A) Head*]**	***[20]* ROSS:** Sì? **[Reply A*(A) Head*]**	***[20]* ROSS:** Yeah?

[21] **MONICA: [a]** Well, **[b]** I just caught the live show. **[a. Starter A*(A) Pre-Head* + b. Informative A*(D) Head*]**	*[21]* **MONICA: [a]** Bè, **[b]** adesso li visti dal vivo. **[a. Starter A*(A) Pre-Head* + b. Informative A*(D) Head*]**	*[21]* **MONICA:** Well, I just saw them in the live show.
[22] **ROSS:** Eww. **[React A*(A) Head*]**	*[22]* **ROSS:** Oh. **[React A*(A) Head*]**	*[22]* **ROSS:** Oh.
(Monica and Richard are alone in the kitchen). *[23]* **MONICA:** Hey there. **[Summon A*(A) Head*]**	*(Monica e Richard sono soli in cucina).* *[23]* **MONICA:** Ciao. **[Summon A*(A) Head*]**	*(Monica and Richard are alone in the kitchen).* *[23]* **MONICA:** Hi.
[24] **RICHARD:** What? **[Reply A*(A) Head*]**	*[24]* **RICHARD:** Che c'è? **[Reply A*(A) Head*]**	*[24]* **RICHARD:** What's the matter?
[25] **MONICA: [a]** Nothing, **[b]** I just heard something nice about you. **[a. Downgrade A*(S) Pre-Head* + b. Informative A*(S) Head*]**	*[25]* **MONICA: [a]** Niente, **[b]** ho sentito una cosa carina su di te. **[a. Downgrade A*(S) Pre-Head* + b. Informative A*(S) Head*]**	*[25]* **MONICA:** Nothing, I just heard something nice about you.
[26] **RICHARD: [a]** Humm, **[b]** really? **[a. React A*(A) Pre-Head* + b. Elicitation A*(A) Head*]**	*[26]* **RICHARD: [a]** Umm, **[b]** davvero? **[a. React A*(A) Pre-Head* + b. Elicitation A*(A) Head*]**	*[26]* **RICHARD:** Humm, really?
(Mrs. Geller and Ross both enter) *[27]* **MRS. GELLER: [a]** Richard. Richard. **[b]** Your son isn't seeing anyone **[c]** is he? **[a. Bid A*(A) Pre-Head* + b. Elicitation A*(A) Head* + c. Check A *(A) Post-Head*]**	*(Entrano la Signora Geller e Ross)* *[27]* **SIG.RA GELLER: [a]** Richard! Richard, **[b]** tuo figlio non ha una ragazza fissa, **[c]** vero? **[a. Bid A*(A) Pre-Head* + b. Elicitation A*(A) Head* + c. Check A *(A) Post-Head*]**	*(Mrs. Geller and Ross both enter)* *[27]* **MRS. GELLER:** Richard! Richard. Your son hasn't a steady girlfriend, has he?
[28] **RICHARD: [a]** Uhh, **[b]** not that I know of. **[a. React A*(A) Pre-Head* + b. Reply A*(A) Head*]**	*[28]* **RICHARD: [a]** No, **[b]** non che io sappia. **[a. React A*(A) Pre-Head* + b. Reply A*(A) Head*]**	*[28]* **RICHARD:** No, not that I know of.
[29] **MRS. GELLER: [a]** Well, **[b]** I was thinking, **[c]** why doesn't he give Monica a call? **[a. Marker A*(A) Pre-Head* + b. Evaluate A*(A) Pre-Head* + c. Directive A *(A) Head*]**	*[29]* **SIG.RA GELLER: [a]** Bè, **[b]** stavo pensando, **[c]** perché non gli dici di chiamare Monica. **[a. Marker A*(A) Pre-Head* + b. Evaluate A*(A) Pre-Head* + c. Directive A *(A) Head*]**	*[29]* **MRS. GELLER:** Well, I was thinking, why don't you tell him to give Monica a call.
[30] **RICHARD: [a]** That - **[b]** that's an idea. **[a. React A*(A) Pre-Head* + b. Evaluate A*(A) Head*]**	*[30]* **RICHARD: [a]** Certo, certo, **[b]** è un'idea. **[a. React A*(A) Pre-Head* + b. Evaluate A*(A) Head*]**	*[30]* **RICHARD:** Sure, sure, that's an idea.
[31] **MONICA: [a]** Well, actually, **[b]** I'm already seeing someone. **[a. Challenge A*(A) Pre-Head* + b. Revelation A*(A) Head*]**	*[31]* **MONICA: [a]** Ecco, in realtà **[b]** io ho già qualcuno. **[a. Challenge A*(A) Pre-Head* + b. Revelation A*(A) Head*]**	*[31]* **MONICA:** Well, actually, I have already someone.
[32] **MRS. GELLER:** Oh? **[React A*(A) Head*]**	*[32]* **SIG.RA GELLER:** Oh? **[React A*(A) Head*]**	*[32]* **MRS. GELLER:** Oh?
[33] **RICHARD:** Oh? **[React A*(A) Head*]**	*[33]* **RICHARD:** Oh? **[React A*(A) Head*]**	*[33]* **RICHARD:** Oh?
[34] **ROSS:** Ohh. **[React A*(A) Head*]**	*[34]* **ROSS:** Ohh. **[React A*(A) Head*]**	*[34]* **ROSS:** Ohh.

[35] **MRS. GELLER: [a]** She never tells us anything. **[b]** Ross, **[c]** did you know Monica's seeing someone? **[a. Blame A*(D) Head* + b. Bid A*(A) Pre-Head* + c. Elicitation A*(A) Head.***	*[35]* **SIG.RA GELLER: [a]** Lei non ci dice mai niente. **[b]** Ross, **[c]** lo sapevi che Monica aveva un ragazzo? **[a. Blame A*(D) Head* + b. Bid A*(A) Pre-Head* + c. Elicitation A*(A) Head*]**	*[35]* **MRS. GELLER:** She never tells us anything. Ross, did you know Monica has a boyfriend?
[36] **ROSS: [a]** Mom, **[b]** there are so many people in my life. **[c]** Some of them are seeing people and some of them aren't. **[d]** Is that crystal? **[a. Bid A*(A) Pre-Head* + b. Negotiate A*(A) Head* + c. Upgrade A*(A) Post-Head* + d. Check A*(A) Post-Head*]**	*[36]* **ROSS: [a]** Mamma, **[b]** ci sono tanti di quei ragazzi al mondo! **[c]** Ah! Alcuni di questi hanno una ragazza e altri no. **[d]** Questo è vero cristallo? **[a. Bid A*(A) Pre-Head* + b. Negotiate A*(A) Head* + c. Upgrade A*(A) Post-Head* + d. Check A*(A) Post-Head*]**	*[36]* **ROSS:** Mom, there are so many boys in the world! Ah! Some of them have a girlfriend and some others haven't. Is that real crystal?
[37] **MRS. GELLER: [a]** So, **[b]** who's the mystery man? **[a. Marker A*(A) Pre-Head* + b. Elicitation A*(A) Head*]**	*[37]* **SIG.RA GELLER: [a]** Allora, **[b]** chi è il fortunato? **[a. Marker A*(A) Pre-Head* + b. Elicitation A*(A) Head*]**	*[37]* **MRS. GELLER:** So, who's the lucky one?
[38] **MONICA: [a]** Well, uh, **[b]** he's a doctor. **[a. Marker A*(S) Pre-Head* + b. Informative A*(S) Head*]**	*[38]* **MONICA: [a]** Ecco, eh, **[b]** è un dottore. **[a. Marker A*(S) Pre-Head* + b. Informative A*(S) Head*]**	*[38]* **MONICA:** Well, uh, he's a doctor.
[39] **MRS. GELLER:** A real doctor? **[Challenge A*(D) Head*]**	*[39]* **SIG.RA GELLER:** Un vero dottore? **[Challenge A*(D) Head]***	*[39]* **MRS. GELLER:** A real doctor?
[40] **MONICA: [a]** No, a doctor of meat. **[b]** Of course he's a real doctor. **[c]** And he's handsome, **[d]** and he's sweet, **[e]** and know you'd like him. *(She puts her arm around Richard).* **[a. React A*(A) Pre-Head* + b. Repair A*(S) Head* + c. Clue A*(S) Post-Head* + d. Upgrade A*(S) Post-Head* + e. Negotiate A*(A) Post-Head*]**	*[40]* **MONICA: [a]** No, un dottore finto! **[b]** Ma certo che è un dottore vero! **[c]** Ed è affascinante, **[d]** è dolcissimo **[e]** e so che ti piace da morire. *(mette un braccio attorno a Richard).* **[a. React A*(A) Pre-Head* + b. Repair A*(S) Head* + c. Clue A*(S) Post-Head* + d. Upgrade A*(S) Post-Head* + e. Negotiate A*(A) Post-Head*]**	*[40]* **MONICA:** No, a fake doctor! Of course he's a real doctor. And he's charming, he's very sweet, and I know you adore him. *(She puts her arm around Richard).*
[41] **MRS. GELLER: [a]** Well **[b]** that's wonderful... **[c]** I **[a. Accept A*(S) Pre-Head* + b. Evaluate A*(S) Head* + c. Silent Stress A*(A) Post-Head*]**	*[41]* **SIG.RA GELLER: [a]** Ah, **[b]** mi fa piacer.. **[c]**.. **[a. Accept A*(S) Pre-Head* + b. Evaluate A*(S) Head* + c. Silent Stress A*(A) Post-Head*]**	*[41]* **MRS. GELLER:** Ah, I'm pleas..
[42] **MONICA: [a]** Mom, **[b]** it's OK. **[a. Bid A*(S) Pre-Head* + b. Negotiate A*(S) Head*]**	*[42]* **MONICA: [a]** Mamma, **[b]** respira adesso. **[a. Bid A*(S) Pre-Head* + b. Directive A*(S) Head*]**	*[42]* **MONICA:** Mom, get your breath back now.
[43] **RICHARD:** It is, Judy. **[Negotiate A*(S) Head*]**	*[43]* **RICHARD:** Stiamo insieme. **[Informative A*(A) Head*]**	*[43]* **RICHARD:** We are together.
[44] **MRS. GELLER: [a]** Jack. **[b]** Could you come in for a moment? **[c]** NOW! **[a. Bid A*(A) Pre-Head* + b. Directive A*(A) Head* + c. Upgrade A*(A) Post-Head*]**	*[44]* **SIG.RA GELLER: [a]** Jack! **[b]** Potresti venire un momento qui? **[c]** Subito! **[a. Bid A*(A) Pre-Head* + b. Directive A*(A) Head* + c. Upgrade A*(A) Post-Head*]**	*[44]* **MRS. GELLER:** Jack. Could you come in for a moment? NOW!
[45] **MR. GELLER:** *(enters with his bat)* Found it. **[Informative A*(A) Head*]**	*[45]* **SIG. GELLER:** *(Entra con la mazza da baseball)* L'ho trovata! **[Informative A*(A) Head*]**	*[45]* **MR. GELLER:** *(enters with his bat)* Found it.
[46] **ROSS: [a]** I'll take that **[b]**	*[46]* **ROSS:** La prendo io questa	*[46]* **ROSS:** I'll take this *(grabs the*

dad *(grabs the bat)*. **[a. Cue A*(A)* *Head* + b. Bid A*(A)* *Post-Head*]**	*(gli toglie la mazza dalle mani)*. **[Cue A*(A)* *Head*.** ***[extra cue 1]*** **SIG. GELLER:** Ma cosa...**[Elicitation A*(A)* *Head*]**	*bat)*. ***[extra cue 1]*** **MR. GELLER:** But, what...
[47] **MRS. GELLER:** It seems your daughter and Richard are something of an item. **[Blame A*(D)* *Head*]**	***[47]*** **SIG.RA GELLER:** Sembrerebbe che tra tua figlia Monica e il tuo amico Richard ci sia del tenero. **[Blame A*(D)* *Head*]**	***[47]*** **MRS. GELLER:** It would seem your daughter Monica and your friend Richard are sweet on each other.
[48] **MR. GELLER: [a]** That's impossible, **[b]** he's got a twinkie in the city. **[a. Challenge A*(A)* *Pre-Head* + b. Evaluate A*(D)* *Head*]**	***[48]*** **SIG. GELLER: [a]** Impossibile, **[b]** lui ha già un'amichetta in città. **[a. Challenge A*(A)* *Pre-Head* + b. Evaluate A*(D)* *Head*]**	***[48]*** **MR. GELLER:** That's impossible, he's already got a fancy girl in the city.
[49] **MONICA: [a]** Dad, **[b]** I'm the twinkie. **[a. Bid A*(A)* *Pre-Head* + b. Revelation A*(A)* *Head*]**	***[49]*** **MONICA:** Sono io l'amichetta. **[Revelation A*(A)* *Head*]**	***[49]*** **MONICA:** I'm the fancy girl.
[50] **MR. GELLER:** You're the twinkie? **[Elicitation A*(A)* *Head*]**	***[50]*** **SIG. GELLER:** Sei tu l'amichetta? **[Elicitation A*(A)* *Head*]**	***[50]*** **MR. GELLER:** You're the fancy girl?
[51] **RICHARD:** She's not a twinkie. **[Challenge A*(A)* *Head]***	***[51]*** **RICHARD:** Non è un'amichetta. **[Challenge A*(A)* *Head*]**	***[51]*** **RICHARD:** She's not a fancy girl.
[52] **MONICA: [a]** Al-alright, **[b]** l-look you guys, **[c]** this is the best relationship I've been in... **[a. Marker A*(S)* *Pre-Head* + b. Bid A*(S)* *Pre-Head* + c. Negotiate A*(S)* *Head*]**	***[52]*** **MONICA: [a]** va bene, **[b]** questa è la relazione più bella che abbia— **[a. Marker A*(S)* *Pre-Head* + b. Negotiate A*(S)* *Head*]**	***[52]*** **MONICA:** Alright, this is the most beautiful relationship I've had...
[53] **MRS. GELLER: [a]** Oh please, **[b]** a relationship. . **[a. Blame A*(D)* *Pre-Head* + b. Evaluate A*(D)* *Head*]**	***[53]*** **SIG.RA GELLER: [a]** Per favore, **[b]** adesso si chiama relazione? **[a. Blame A*(D)* *Pre-Head* + b. Evaluate A*(D)* *Head*]**	***[53]*** **MRS. GELLER:** Please, now this is named relationship?
[54] **MONICA: [a]** Yes, **[b]** a relationship. **[c]** For your information **[d]** I am crazy about this man. **[a. Challenge A*(A)* *Pre-Head* + b. Evaluate A*(A)* *Head* + c. Cue A*(A)* *Pre-Head* + d. Informative A*(A)* *Head*]**	***[54]*** **MONICA: [a]** Certo! **[b]** Una relazione! **[c]** Per tua informazione **[d]** io sono pazza di questo dottore. **[a. Challenge A*(A)* *Pre-Head* + b. Evaluate A*(A)* *Head* + c. Cue A*(A)* *Pre-Head* + d. Informative A*(A)* *Head*]**	***[54]*** **MONICA:** Yes! A relationship. For your information I am crazy about this doctor.
[55] **RICHARD:** Really? **[Check A*(S)* *Head*]**	***[55]*** **RICHARD:** Davvero? **[Check A*(S)* *Head*]**	***[55]*** **RICHARD:** Really?
[56] **MONICA:** Yes. **[Acknowledge A*(S)* *Head*]**	***[56]*** **MONICA:** Sì. **[Acknowledge A*(S)* *Head*]** ***[extra cue 2]*** **RICHARD:** Bene... **[Evaluate A*(S)* *Head*]**	***[56]*** **MONICA:** Yes. ***[extra cue 2]*** **RICHARD:** Well...
[57] **MR. GELLER:** Am I supposed to stand here and listen to this on my birthday? **[Blame A*(D)* *Head*]**	***[57]*** **SIG. GELLER:** E io dovrei ascoltare tutte queste idiozie nel giorno del mio compleanno? **[Blame A*(D)* *Head*]**	***[57]*** **MR. GELLER:** And I should listen to such foolish things on my birthday?
[58] **MONICA: [a]** Dad, dad **[b]** this is a good thing for me. **[c]** Ya know, **[d]** and you even said yourself, **[e]** you've never seen Richard happier. **[a. Bid A*(A)* *Pre-Head* + b. Evaluate A*(S)* *Head* + c. Clue A*(S)* *Post-Head***	***[58]*** **MONICA: [a]** Papà, **[b]** dovresti essere contento per me. **[c]** L'hai detto tu stesso **[d]** che non l'avevi mai visto così felice. **[a. Bid A*(A)* *Pre-Head* + b. Challenge A*(A)* *Head* + c. Negotiate A*(S)* *Pre-Head* + e.**	***[58]*** **MONICA:** Dad, you should be happy for me. You said yourself that you've never seen Richard happier.

d. **Negotiate A*(S)* *Pre-Head* + e. Evaluate A*(A)* *Head*]**	**Evaluate A*(A)* *Head*]**	
***[59]* MR. GELLER:** When did I say that? **[Challenge A*(A)* *Head*]**	***[59]* SIG. GELLER:** E quando l'avrei detto? **[Challenge A*(A)* *Head*]**	***[59]* MR. GELLER:** And when should I've said that?
***[60]* MONICA: [a]** Upstairs in the bathroom **[b]** right before you felt up mom. **[a. Informative A*(A)* *Head* + b. Upgrade A*(D)* *Post-Head*]** *(Everyone else enters and all start singing "Happy Birthday")*	***[60]* MONICA: [a]** Di sopra, in bagno, **[b]** appena prima di buttarti sulla mamma! **[a. Informative A*(A)* *Head* + b. Upgrade A*(D)* *Post-Head*]** ***[extra cue 3]* ROSS:** Venite avanti. **[Directive A*(D)* *Head*]** *(Entrano tutti gli altri e cominciano a cantare "Tanti Auguri")*	***[60]* MONICA:** Upstairs in the bathroom right before you jumped at mom. ***[extra cue 3]* ROSS:** Come this way. *(Everyone else enters and all start singing "Happy Birthday")*
[Tattoo parlor]	**[Salone dei tatuaggi]**	**[Tattoo parlor]**
(Rachel is showing Phoebe her tattoo) ***[61]* PHOEBE: [a]** Oh **[b]** that looks so good, **[c]** oh I love it. **[a. React A*(S)* *Pre-Head* + b. Evaluate A*(S)* *Head* + c. Upgrade A*(S)* *Post-Head*]**	*(Rachel mostra a Phoebe il suo tatuaggio)* ***[61]* PHOEBE: [a]** Oh, **[b]** è veramente carino! **[c]** Mi piace da morire! **[a. React A*(S)* *Pre-Head* + b. Evaluate A*(S)* *Head* + c. Upgrade A*(S)* *Post-Head*]**	*(Rachel is showing Phoebe her tattoo)* ***[61]* PHOEBE:** Oh it's really cute! oh I'm mad about it!
***[62]* RACHEL: [a]** I know, **[b]** so do I. **[c]** Oh Phoebe, **[d]** I'm so glad you made me do this. **[e]** OK, **[f]** lemme see yours. **[a. Acknowledge A*(S)* *Pre-Head* + b. Evaluate A*(S)* *Head* + c. Bid A*(S)* *Pre-Head* + d. Express-Gratitude A*(S)* *Head* + e. Marker A*(A)* *Pre-Head* + f. Directive A*(A)* *Head*]**	***[62]* RACHEL: [a]** Anche a me, **[b]** sai? **[c]** Grazie per avermi convinta. **[d]** Dai, **[e]** fammi vedere il tuo. **[a. Evaluate A*(S)* *Head* + b. Clue A*(S)* *Post-Head* + c. Express-Gratitude A*(S)* *Head* + d. Prompt A*(A)* *Pre-Head* + f. Directive A*(A)* *Head*]**	***[62]* RACHEL:** Me too, you know? Thanks for having convinced me. Come on, let me see yours.
***[63]* PHOEBE: [a]** Ahh. **[b]** OK, **[c]** let's see yours again. **[a. React A*(A)* *Pre-Head* + b. Marker A*(A)* *Pre-Head* + c. Directive A*(A)* *Head*]**	***[63]* PHOEBE: [a]** Oh, **[b]** va bene, **[c]** rivediamo il tuo. **[a. React A*(A)* *Pre-Head* + b. Marker A*(A)* *Pre-Head* + c. Directive A*(A)* *Head*]**	***[63]* PHOEBE:** Oh, Okay, let's see yours again.
***[64]* RACHEL: [a]** Phoebe **[b]** we just saw mine, **[c]** let me see yours. **[a. Bid A*(A)* *Pre-Head* + b. Clue A*(A)* *Pre-Head* + c. Directive A*(A)* *Head*]**	***[64]* RACHEL: [a]** L'abbiamo appena visto. **[b]** Ora fammi vedere il tuo. **[a. Clue A*(A)* *Pre-Head* + b. Directive A*(A)* *Head*]**	***[64]* RACHEL:** We just saw mine, now let me see yours.
***[65]* PHOEBE: [a]** Oh **[b]** OK. *(pulls over her shirt and shows a bare shoulder)* **[c]** Oh no, **[d]** oh it's gone, **[e]** that's so weird, **[f]** I don't know how-where it went. **[a. React A*(A)* *Pre-Head* + b. Marker A*(A)* *Head* + c. React A*(A)* *Pre-Head* + d. Express-Surprise A*(S)* *Head* + e. Upgrade A*(A)* *Post-Head* + f. Disclaim A*(A)* *Post-Head*]**	***[65]* PHOEBE: [a]** Come vuoi. *(Abbassa la camicia e scopre una spalla senza traccia di tatuaggi)* **[b]** Oh no! **[c]** Oh, santo cielo! **[d]** È scomparso! **[e]** Non ho veramente idea di dove sia finito! **[a. Agree A*(S)* *Head* + b. React A*(A)* *Pre-Head* + c. Express-Surprise A*(S)* *Pre-Head* + d. Upgrade A*(A)* *Head* + e. Disclaim A*(A)* *Post-Head*]**	***[65]* PHOEBE:** As you like. *(pulls over her shirt and shows a bare shoulder)* Oh no! Oh, good heavens! It has disappeared! I really have no idea where it's gone!
***[66]* RACHEL:** You didn't get it? **[Blame A*(D)* *Head*]**	***[66]* RACHEL:** Non te lo sei fatto? **[Blame A*(D)* *Head*]**	***[66]* RACHEL:** You didn't get it?
***[67]* PHOEBE:** No. **[Revelation A*(A)* *Head*]**	***[67]* PHOEBE:** No. **[Revelation A*(A)* *Head*]**	***[67]* PHOEBE:** No.

[68] **RACHEL:** Why didn't you get it? **[Elicitation A*(A) Head*]**	*[68]* **RACHEL:** Perché hai cambiato idea? **[Elicitation A*(A) Head*]**	*[68]* **RACHEL:** Why did you change your mind?
[69] **PHOEBE:** I'm sorry, I'm sorry. **[Apologize A*(A) Head*]**	*[69]* **PHOEBE: [a]** Scusa, **[b]** ma non ne ho avuto il coraggio! **[a. Apologize A*(A) Pre-Head* + b. Clue A*(A) Head*]**	*[69]* **PHOEBE:** Sorry, but I didn't have the nerve!
[70] **RACHEL: [a]** Phoebe, **[b]** how would you do this to me? **[c]** This was all your idea. **[a. Bid A*(A) Pre-Head* + b. Elicitation A*(A) Head* + c. Blame A*(D) Post-Head*]**	*[70]* **RACHEL: [a]** Phoebe, **[b]** ma come hai potuto farmi questo? **[c]** Era stata tua l'idea! **[a. Bid A*(A) Pre-Head* + b. Elicitation A*(A) Head* + c. Blame A*(D) Post-Head*]**	*[70]* **RACHEL:** Phoebe, but how would you do this to me? This was all your idea!
[71] **PHOEBE: [a]** I know, I know, **[b]** and I was gonna get it **[c]** but he came in with this needle and **[d]** uh di-, did you know they do this with needles? **[a. Blame A*(D) Pre-Head* + b. Informative A*(A) Head* + c. Clue A*(A) Post-Head* + d. Negotiate A*(A) Head*]**	*[71]* **PHOEBE: [a]** Sì. Lo so, lo so, **[b]** avrei voluto farlo, **[c]** ma quando ho visto l'ago – **[d]** ma lo sapevi che i tatuaggi si fanno con gli aghi? **[a. Blame A*(D) Pre-Head* + b. Informative A*(A) Head* + c. Clue A*(A) Post-Head* + d. Negotiate A*(A) Head*]**	*[71]* **PHOEBE:** Yes, I know, I know, I would have liked to get it, but when I saw the needle — but did you know tattoos are done with needles?
[72] **RACHEL: [a]** Really? **[b]** You don't say, **[c]** because mine was licked on by kittens. **[a. React A*(D) Pre-Head* + b. Newsmark A*(D) Pre-Head* + c. Blame A*(D) Head*]**	*[72]* **RACHEL: [a]** Ma davvero? **[b]** Non mi dire! **[c]** E allora perché il mio lo hanno fatto con i gessetti? **[a. React A*(D) Pre-Head* + b. Newsmark A*(D) Pre-Head* + c. Blame A*(D) Head*]**	*[72]* **RACHEL:** Really? You don't say! So why was mine done with crayons?

6.2.2 *Analysis of the Act-patterns of Humour in source and target versions*

Exchange 1 of this extract opens with a situation of conflict between the two friends and flatmates Joey and Chandler. Chandler assumes that Joey intends to leave their shared apartment to move into an apartment on his own. In turn [1], Joey rebuts this assumption with a Prompt Pre-Head Act aimed at 'dropping' the question, and a subsequent Informative Head Act stating that he is not interested in his colleague's apartment for rent. In the dubbing translation for the Italian television, Joey's turn [1] is less indirect than the original as it addresses Chandler straightforwardly, first with the Prompt Act specifically asking Chandler to come off it, thus omitting the less harsh "drop" metaphor also in use in Italian ("lasciar cadere una questione"—literally, "to let a question drop"). Then, translators have Joey make anaphoric reference—absent in the original—to something he said to Chandler before ("Ti ho già detto che" - "I've already told you that") to introduce the Informative Act stating his lack of interest in his colleague's apartment. In turn [2], Chandler replies with a disparaging Blame Pre-Head Act ("Oh please") that introduces his Evaluative Head Act negatively judging his flatmate's behaviour in "checking out" the "mouldings" in his colleague's apartment, and concluding with a Comment Post-Head Act accusing Joey: "You want it". The Act-pattern is respected in translation and, this time, also its rendering into Italian is almost literal, as in

Joey's subsequent turn [3], too. Here, with a Check Pre-Head Act, Joey addresses Chandler with a louder tone of voice asking him why he should want another apartment since, as he adds with the subsequent Informative Head Act, he has already got one that he loves. In turn [4], Chandler defies Joey by a Challenge Pre-Head Act ("Well") which introduces his Blame Head Act accusing Joey of being false, as usual. In the translated version, the Pre-Head Act has been omitted and Chandler attacks his flatmate straightaway with his Blame Act, but without rendering into Italian the original " kill" metaphor, thus defusing the comic effect by making his disparagement almost direct and dramatic ("Perché non dici la verità una volta tanto?" - "Why don't say the truth, once in a while?"). At this point Joey, in his turn [5], decides to be frank with Chandler and performs the Revelation Head Act by telling him: "I'm thinking about it". This admission is preceded by two Pre-Head Acts—namely, a Marker one ("Alright"), signalling the change of his attitude, and a Challenge one, preparing his flatmate to the disclosure of the truth ("You want the truth?"). The same Arousal pattern of Acts is also respected in the literal translation of this turn for the Italian TV, as well as in the following turn [6] when Chandler expresses his surprise with an Elicitation Act ("What?" - "Cosa?"). In turn [7], seeing that his friend has been shocked by the news, Joey attempts a mediation by performing first an Apologize Pre-Head Act ("I'm sorry"), and then introducing the subsequent Negotiate and two Upgrade Pre-Head Acts to create an atmosphere of Safety in order to prepare Chandler to the even harsher truth, stated through the Informative Head Act: "I don't need a roommate anymore". The Italian version is not so callous as the original one, as Joey does not make direct reference to a "roommate" that he does not need anymore, but simply to the fact that he "finally earn enough money to be able to afford renting a house" on his own ("e finalmente guadagno abbastanza da potermi permettere di prendere una casa per conto mio"). Chandler's bewildered response in turn [8] is rendered by an initial React Pre-Head Act ("Whoa, whoa, whoa"), followed by a Challenge Head Act ("I don't need a roommate either"), and a Check Post-Head Act to make sure that Joey understands the importance of what he is saying. In trying to raise to the same high and autonomous status played by Joey in this exchange, Chandler continues with an Informative Head Act aimed at asserting his economic and affective independence from his flatmate ("I can afford to live here by myself"). Finally, he introduces through a Cue Pre-Head Act ("Ya know") a new Challenge Head Act aimed at disparaging Joey's repulsive habit of licking the used cutlery before putting them back in the cupboard drawers as if they were clean ("I may have to bring in somebody once a week to lick the silverware"). In the Italian version of turn [8], Chandler reacts less impulsively than in the original ("Aspetta un attimo" – "Wait a minute"), and then he stresses his superiority in a less emotional and childish way, without making any reference to the fact that he does not need a roommate and that he can afford to live in that same apartment by himself. On the contrary, he emphasizes the Informative Head Act by pointing out that "ho sempre potuto permettermi un appartamento tutto mio come questo" ("I've always been able to afford an apartment on my own like this"), which highlights his higher financial status than Joey's, stressed even more by the Challenge Post-Head Act where he boasts "dove posso far venire chi voglio a leccarmi l'argenteria" ("where I can make anyone I want come to lick my silverware"). At this point, it is Joey's turn to denigrate his flatmate for his overemotional reaction. Hence, in turn [9], Joey attacks Chandler with a disparaging Blame Pre-Head Act, referred to Chandler's fretting and writhing movements, through the use of the effective physical metaphor "What're you gettin' so bent out of shape for, huh?"—Then, he goes on offending his friend with a Challenge Head Act arousing the tension: "It's not like we agreed to live together forever", to conclude with a disparaging Upgrade Post-Head Act ("We're not Bert and Ernie"), making reference to Bert and Ernie, the comic duo of puppet characters in *The Muppets Show* (aired from 1969 on), who are friends despite their differences. Bert is boring, clean and tidy and is annoyed at the fact that his roommate, Ernie, is not – exactly as Chandler is annoyed by Joey's unhygienic habits, like licking the cutlery. Bert and Ernie are featured as living together in a Sesame Street apartment, sharing a bedroom but sleeping in separate beds and arguing all the time, yet they are never represented according to the stereotype of the gay couple (on some occasions, Bert woos female characters and hints at his girlfriend). Joey, indeed, does not imply in any way a gay relationship in his offensive remark, just a reference to the two famous puppets sharing an apartment. In the Italian dubbing translation of turn [9], instead, Joey apparently seems to establish a Safety pattern with an Apologize Pre-Head Act ("Scusa" - "Excuse me"), and he does not even use a Blame Pre-Head Act so offensive as the original one aimed at ridiculing Chandler's wiggling movements, rather opting for the conventional 'rage/boil' metaphor of "getting heated" ("ma vuoi dirmi perché ti scaldi tanto?" - "but will you tell me why you are getting so heated?"). But then, in the next Challenge Head Act, Joey attacks Chandler with quite vulgar derogatory terms, by making explicit reference to a possible homosexual inclination in Chandler's relationship with him as he says: "Non ci siamo mica sposati, mi sembra" ("We are not married, I think.") to conclude by turning the original hint at Bert and Ernie into "Tom and Jerry". This change is actually inappropriate, insofar as the Hanna & Barbera cartoon duo does not represent an equivalent to Bert and Ernie, nor are they depicted as a gay couple. Tom and Jerry are, respectively, a house cat and a mouse that happen to live in the same house and that are engaged in a never-ending rivalry, often involving a much criticised cartoon violence as they enjoy tormenting each other. Probably the choice to render "Bert and Ernie" into "Tom and Jerry" is due to the fact that today the rights of this cartoon duo belong to Warner Bros.—namely, the producers of *Friends*—which would make employing their reference legally unproblematic. Turn [10] shows a much offended Chandler who, with a Challenge and an Acknowledge Pre-Head Acts introduces his taking note of Joey's stance ("if this is the way you feel") before suggesting, with a Prompt Head Act, that maybe he should take the apartment. In the Italian version, Chandler does not acknowledge Joey's affective processes (i.e., "the way you feel"), but his cognitive ones ("se è così che la pensi" - "if this is the way you think") and he does not suggest that Joey should take the apartment, but that he should "go away". To this, Joey replies, in turn [11] of the original version, with a Challenge Pre-Head Act ("Well") and an even more challenging Upgrade Head Act ("that's how I feel"). In the Italian version, only the Head Act has been retained, which makes the challenge less mediated (by the introductory "well") and more harshly straightforward and focused on Joey's cognitive, rather than affective processes: "E' così che la penso" ("That's how I think"). Chandler, in the next original turn [12], introduces the same and parallel Challenge Pre-Head Act ("Well") before reinforcing it with an Upgrade Head Act defying his flatmate, though using some modal hedging ("maybe" and "should") as softeners: "then maybe you should take it". In the Italian version of turn [12], instead, the Pre-Head "Well" is omitted again and Chandler makes a quite violent and rude use of the imperative: "E allora vattene!" ("And so go away!") with a loud and peevish tone of voice and wriggling arm movements. In turn [13] of the original version, Joey replies with another parallel "Well" signalling a Challenge Pre-Head Act, followed by an Upgrade Head Act marking his statement of intention, though modulated by the hedge "maybe" ("then maybe I will"). In the dubbing translation of turn [13], Joey omits the Pre-Head "Well" once again and directly introduces his Challenge Head Act with no modulating hedging, but rather by strongly asserting his intention: "Me ne andrò di sicuro" ("I will surely go away"). In the original version of turn [14], Chandler replies sternly with a Challenge Head Act: "Fine with me". In its Italian version, Chandler seems to overreact to Joey's final decision by saying: "Ne sono felice" ("I'm happy with it"). In the original turn [15], Joey replies to his flatmate's firm acceptance of his decision with a negative Evaluate Pre-Head Act ("Great"), before introducing his derogatory Comment Head Act attacking Chandler's fixation for tidiness: "Then you'll be able to spend more quality time with your real friends, the spoons". In the translated version of this turn [15], Joey's negative assessment of his flatmate's apparent relief for his moving out is expressed by means of a different Evaluate Pre-Head Act: "Grazie!" ("Thanks!"), sarcastically showing appreciation for Chandler's happiness, to continue insulting him with his Comment Head Act, slightly different from the original one: "Così finalmente potrai goderti in santa pace I tuoi veri amici, I cucchiai!" ("So you'll be finally able to enjoy in peace your real friends, the spoons!").

The second exchange of this extract opens with Mr. Geller, the father of Monica and Ross, entering the room where his birthday party is going on after having had sex with his wife, Mrs. Geller, in the bathroom where Monica happened to be hidden after meeting her boyfriend Richard, in a previous scene. On his entrance, Mr. Geller (who in the stage directions is described as "looking particularly refreshed") with an Offer Head Act in turn [16] invites his guests to freshen their drink. Mrs. Geller enters after him, with Mr. Geller's same "refreshed look' and remarks in turn [17], through a Comment Act, that it is "almost time for cake". Both turns are rendered literally in the Italian version. Monica enters following them "looking rather pale". Ross notices her sister's discomfort and, in turn [18], addresses her with a Bid Pre-Head Act and then, with a Check Head Act, asks her if she is OK. In the Italian translation, Ross is given an extra Apologize Pre-Head Act as he excuses himself for leaving the guest he is talking to and then he addresses Monica with a Bid Pre-Head Act to add a more specific Check Head Act: "ma che ti succede?" ("what's wrong with you?"). In her original turn [19], Monica addresses her brother Ross with an Elicit Act aimed at raising tension—"You remember that video I found of mom and dad"—referring to an old home-made videocassette of their parents making love that Monica was seen to find by chance in a previous scene. The Italian translation of this turn is literal, as well as Ross's reply in turn [20] ("Yeah" – "Sì?") which functions as a Continuer Move in that it encourages Monica to go on, so that, in turn [21], she begins with a Starter Pre-Head Act aimed at raising tension ("Well") to explain with an Informative Head Act "I just caught the live show", translated into Italian as: "adesso li ho visti dal vivo" ("I just saw them in the live show"). In turn [22] Ross performs a React Head Act, "Eww", rendered into Italian as "Oh".

The perspective on this scene changes as Monica enters the kitchen where Richard, her elderly boyfriend, is alone. She addresses him in turn [23] with a Summon Act, "Hi there", rendered into Italian with "Ciao" ("Hi"). To this, Richard, in turn [24], answers with a Reply Act enquiring into Monica's evident intention to reveal him something: "What?", rendered more explicitly into Italian: "Che c'è?" ("What's the matter?"). Monica replies in turn [25] with a Downgrade Pre-Head Act ("Nothing") aimed at relieving tension, to continue with an Informative Head Act: "I just heard something nice about you", translated into Italian with the literal "ho sentito una cosa carina su di te". In turn [26], Richard performs a React Pre-Head Act ("Humm") to add an Elicitation Head Act "Really?", introducing a certain tension and literally translated into Italian. At this point, Mrs. Geller enters the kitchen with Ross and, in turn [27], she addresses Richard with a Bid Pre-Head Act to continue with an almost intrusive Elicitation Head Act: "Your son isn't seeing anyone", and to conclude with a pushy Check Post-Head Act which increases the atmosphere of tension: "is he?". In the translated version for the Italian television, Mrs. Geller is even more nosy and explicit: "tuo figlio non ha una ragazza fissa, vero?" ("Your son hasn't a steady girlfriend, has he?"). In turn [28], Richard answers first with a React Pre-Head Act ("Uhh"), and then with a Reply Head Act ("not that I know of"), literally rendered into the Italian version. To this expected answer, Mrs. Geller launches her impertinent proposal, in turn [29], first introduced by a Marker and a Evaluate Pre-Head Acts, "Well, I was thinking,", mitigating what she is going to say, and then expressed through a Directive Head Act under the form of a question: "Why doesn't he give Monica a call?", which, in the Italian version, is rendered into an explicit direction to Richard: "perché non gli dici di chiamare Monica" ("why don't you tell him to give Monica a call"). In turn [30], Richard replies first with a React Pre-Head Act ("That -"), translated into Italian as "Certo, certo" ("Sure, sure"), and then with an Evaluate Head Act ("that's an idea"), literally translated into Italian. At this point, Monica, with her turn [31], introduces with a Challenge Pre-Head Act ("Well, actually,") her Revelation Head Act, disclosing to her mother that "I'm already seeing someone", thus contributing to arouse tension. Mrs. Geller, in turn [32], replies to such unexpected revelation with an Oh-Receipt Move, corresponding to a React Act ("Oh?") which also represents Richard's and Ross's responses in turns [33] and [34], respectively (yet, in their cases, with a different implication, not of surprise—as in Mrs. Geller's case—but of incredulity at Monica having revealed her 'atypical' relationship to her mother). In turn [35], Mrs. Geller straightforwardly introduces her Blame Head Act disparaging Monica for her silence so far ("She never tells us anything"), literally translated into Italian. Then, by turning to Ross with a Bid Pre-Head Act, Mrs. Geller asks him with an Elicitation Head Act: "did you know Monica's seeing someone?". In Italian, such an elicitation is even more explicit: "lo sapevi che Monica aveva un ragazzo?" ("did you know that Monica has a boyfriend?"). In his turn [36], Ross's reply to his mother is quite vague. He starts with a Bid Pre-Head Act ("Mom"), to continue with a Negotiate Head Act ("there are so many people in my life"), and to conclude with an Upgrade Post-Head Act trying to reinforce his negotiation ("Some of them are seeing people and some of them aren't."). His final quip, "Is that crystal?" uttered while removing a crystal glass from his mother's hand is a Check Post-Head Act aimed at increasing tension and provoke a humorous response at predicting what may have happened to that glass in the course of this tense conversation. The Italian translation of Ross's turn [36] is not literal as expected: the dubbing translator in fact opts for a less vague Negotiate and Upgrade Acts than the original: "ci sono tanti di quei ragazzi al mondo! Ah! Alcuni di questi hanno una ragazza e altri no" ("there are so many boys in the world! Ah! Some of them have a girlfriend and some others haven't"). Also the concluding quip is slightly different in its emphasis: "Questo è vero cristallo?" ("Is that real crystal?"), with the addition of the adjective "real" and of the deictic pronoun "questo" which is normally omitted as redundant in equivalent Italian sentences with a visual support. Mrs. Geller now goes on with her investigation and, in turn [37], she introduces her question with a Marker Pre-Head Act ("So"), and then she asks Monica with an Elicitation Head Act increasing tension: "who's the mystery man?". This reference term is modified in the Italian translation: "chi è il fortunato?" ("who's the lucky one?"), which is less consistent with the situation of Monica who, so far, has kept keeping her boyfriend hidden and 'mysterious'. Monica, in her turn [38], uses another Marker Pre-Head Act to hesitate ("Well, uh,") before revealing, with an Informative Head Act aimed at soothing her mother's tension, that "he's a doctor". In turn [39], Mrs. Geller provokes her daughter with a straightforwardly disparaging Challenge Head Act ("A real doctor?"), doubting the fact that the man Monica dates is a genuine doctor. Monica's reaction in turn [40] is initially almost annoyed, as evident in the React Pre-Head Act "No, a doctor of meat", a derogatory metaphor literally rendered into Italian as "No, un dottore finto!" ("No, a fake doctor"). But then she moderates her tone and addresses her mother with a Repair Head Act aimed at relieving her tension: "Of course he's a real doctor". A sequence of Post-Head Acts follows, the first two ones—Clue ("And he's handsome") and Upgrade ("and he's sweet")—meant to enhance the sense of satisfaction in Mrs. Geller (and non-literally rendered into Italian as: "ed è affascinante" - "And he's charming", "è dolcissimo" – "he's very sweet"). Monica's last Negotiate Post-Head Act, instead ("and know you'd like him"—matched to Monica's gesture of putting her arm around Richard), though aimed at mediating with her mother who is going to discover the identity of her boyfriend, actually makes tension arouse even more when Mrs. Geller, with turn [41], at first performs a satisfied Accept Pre-Head Act ("Well"), followed by a positive Evaluate Head Act, "that's wonderful" (rendered into Italian through the less enthusiastic "mi fa piacer.." - "I'm pleas.."), but then, as she swings round, she suddenly realizes that her young daughter's boyfriend is actually her friend Richard and, as she stays dumbfounded staring at them, she performs a high-tension Silent Stress Post-Head Act. Monica, in turn [42], tries to reassure her mother by addressing her directly with a Bid Pre-Head Act ("Mom") and then adding the Negotiate Head Act "It's OK"—mistranslated into Italian with the disrespectful expression "respira adesso" ("get your breath back now"). Richard, in his turn [43], referring back to what Monica has said before to reassure her mother, performs another Negotiate Head Act by adding "It is, Judy". The Italian version mistranslates this turn by making Richard redundantly state what is already evident: "Stiamo insieme" ("We are together") by means of an Informative Head Act. At this point, Mrs. Geller calls her husband out with a Bid Pre-Head Act ("Jack"), and then she adds a Directive Head Act "Could you come in for a moment?", further emphasized by a loud Upgrade Post-Head Act ("NOW!", in capital letters in the original script to mean 'shouting'), literally translated into Italian. Mr. Geller enters the kitchen with his bat and, in turn [45], with an Informative Head Act announces: "Found it". Ross, in his turn [46], says, through a Cue Head Act and by grabbing the bat, "I'll take that", humorously overstressing the possible violent use that Mr. Geller may make of it once he realizes what is going on in that kitchen, and then softening his gesture with a Bid Post-Head Act "dad"—which is instead omitted in the Italian version, where an extra cue by Mr. Geller is added under the form of an Elicitation Head Act: "Ma cosa..." ("But, what..."). Mrs. Geller, in turn [47], sternly announces with a Blame Head Act aimed at disparaging her daughter's behaviour: "It seems that your daughter and Richard are something o fan item". This idiomatic expression has obviously not rendered literally into the Italian version where another parallel idiomatic choice was made: "Sembre-rebbe che tra tua figlia Monica e il tuo amico Richard ci sia del tenero" (approximately back-translated into: "It would seem your daughter Monica and your friend Richard are sweet on each other"), which has not exactly the same pragmatic implications as the original one where hints at 'tenderness' or 'sweetness' in Monica's affair are absent—in fact, other equivalent idiomatic solutions in Italian would have been possible —as pointed out in the next section. In turn [48], Mr. Geller replies with a Challenge Pre-Head Act positively stating that "That's impossible", since, as he adds in his following negative Evaluate Head Act, "he's got a twinkie in the city", thus disparaging Richard's young girlfriend, not yet realizing that she is precisely his daughter, by defining her as "twinkie"—literally, the name of an American sponge cake filled with vanilla cream, manufactured by Hostess, here used as a disparaging epithet for a 'young girlfriend'. In the Italian TV version, the idiomatic expression "twinkie" has not been translated into another idiomatic equivalent in Italian, but it was rather rendered into its euphemistic literal meaning, namely "amichetta", a diminutive of "amica" ("girlfriend") approximately corresponding to the English expression "fancy girl". Also in this case, other possible equivalent and idiomatic solutions could have been found in Italian to render this epithet more appropriately (as explored in the next section). Monica, in her turn [49], actually offended by her father's unaware reference to her, alerts Mr. Geller with a Bid Pre-Head Act, "Dad" (omitted in the Italian version), to introduce abruptly her Revelation Head Act "I'm the twinkie" (in Italian rendered into "Sono io l'amichetta" - "I'm the fancy girl"). In turn [50], Mr. Geller unbelievably asks through an Elicitation Head Act which has the effect of arousing tension: "You're the twinkie?", to which Richard replies piqued, in his turn [51], "She's not a twinkie". At this point Monica intervenes, in turn [52], trying to soothe the tense atmosphere first with a Marker Pre-Head Act ("Al-alright"), attempting to put an end to this discussion by attracting the attention of all the present people with a Bid Pre-Head Act ("l-look you guys"), and then with a Negotiate Head Act as she tries to explain that "this is the best relationship I've been in...". The Italian TV translation omits the Bid Pre-Head Act and renders the Negotiate Act into the more romantic "questa è la relazione più bella che abbia -" ("this is the most beautiful relationship I've had.."). Mrs. Geller, in turn [53], cuts short her daughter's enthusiastic description of her relationship with Richard through a Blame Pre-Head Act ("Oh please"), followed by a negative Evaluate Head Act ("a relationship..."). The Italian TV translation has rendered this disparaging remark by Mrs. Geller into a more explicit and sarcastic observation: "adesso si chiama relazione?" ("now this is named relationship?"). Monica, even more offended, in turn [54], vigorously defends her relationship with a Challenge Pre-Head and an Evaluate Head Acts, to add a Cue Pre-Head Act ("For your information") introducing a tension-provoking Informative Head Act: "I'm crazy about this man" (literally translated into Italian). Richard, in turn [55], responds encouragingly to such gratifying compliment with a Check Head Act ("Really?") and Monica, in turn [56], confirms it with an Acknowledge Head Act ("Yes"). Mr. Geller, instead, in turn [57], protests with a Blame Head Act disapproving of the whole situation ("Am I supposed to stand here and listen to this on my birthday?"), which is rendered even more disparagingly into the Italian TV translation - and with a belittling, offensive word choice absent in the original version: "E io dovrei ascoltare tutte queste idiozie nel giorno del mio compleanno?" ("And I should listen to such foolish things on my birthday?"). To this, Monica retorts, in turn [57], first with a Bid Pre-Head Act (Dad, dad"), announcing a tension arousal, but then she chooses a positive Evaluate Head Act to assess her relationship ("this is a good thing for me"). Then, she introduces a Clue Post-Head Act meant to soothe the tense atmosphere ("Ya know"), and a Negotiate Pre-Head Act aimed at involving her father directly ("and you even said yourself"), to finally give away what she overheard from him: "you've never seen Richard happier". In the Italian version, the degree of her father's involvement in Monica's Pre-Head Acts is more emphasized: "Papà, dovresti essere contento per me" ("Dad, you should be happy for me"). In turn [59], Mr. Geller soon rejoins with a Challenge Head Act, "When did I say that?", rendered into Italian by the use of the conditional ("E quando l'avrei detto?" - "And when should I've said that"), absent in the original, which stresses Mr. Geller's doubting of what her daughter is attributing to him. In turn [60], Monica replies aggressively with an Informative Head Act ("Upstairs, in the bathroom"), and increases the tension by adding the disparaging Upgrade Post-Head Act: "right before you felt up mom"—which is rendered into Italian with the more colloquial and vulgar "appena prima di buttarti sulla mamma" ("right before you jumped at mom"). At this point, while Mr. and Mrs. Geller are struck dumb, an extra cue is added in the Italian version uttered by Ross who, as the guests enter the kitchen with the birthday cake, tells them "Venite Avanti" ("Come this way"), and then all start singing 'Happy Birthday' in front of a dazed Mr. Geller.

In the third exchange of this extract, the two friends Rachel and Phoebe are in a tattoo parlour and Rachel is showing Phoebe her tattoo that she has just got following Phoebe's insistent advice. In turn [61] Phoebe, with a React Pre-Head Act ("Oh") introduces her Evaluate Head Act enthusiastically assessing her friend's tattoo ("that looks so good"), to subsequently emphasize it with an Upgrade Post-Head Act ("oh I love it"), thus creating a pleasant atmosphere of relief. In the version for the Italian TV, the translation of this turn is not exactly equivalent, as it renders "good" into "carino" - "cute" ("è veramente carino" - "it's really cute"), and "love" with the overemphatic and non-lip-synchronized "Mi piace da morire!" ("I'm mad about it!" - literally: "I like it, to die for!"). Rachel, in turn [62], agrees with her friend with an Acknowledge Pre-Head Act and a positive Evaluate Head Act, and then, by addressing Phoebe with a Bid Pre-Head Act she thanks her with an Express-Gratitude Head Act ("I'm so glad you made me do this"), thus strengthening the sense of joyful serenity. The Italian version does not respect the original Act pattern as Rachel starts her turn with an Evaluate Head Act ("Anche a me" - "Me too") and a Clue Post-Head Act ("sai?" - "you know?"). But suddenly, introduced by a Marker Pre-Head Act ("OK"), Rachel performs a Directive Head Act provoking tension as she asks Phoebe: "lemme see yours". In the Italian version, the Marker Act is substituted by a more peremptory Prompt Act ("Dai" - "Come on"). In the next turn [63] (literally translated into Italian, this time), Phoebe responds to Rachel's request with a tense React Pre-Head Act ("Ahh"), but then she suddenly performs a Marker Pre-Head Act to divert her friend's attention away from herself ("OK"), and thus asks Rachel with an unexpected Directive Head Act: "let's see yours again". Rachel, in turn [64], appears perplexed as she addresses Phoebe with a Bid Pre-Head Act (absent in the Italian version), and then protests through a Clue Pre-Head Act ("we just saw yours") to finally perform a Directive Head Act: "let me see yours". In turn [65], tension arouses as Phoebe appears to be in a tight corner. She first performs a React Pre-Head Act ("Oh") and then, introduced by a Marker Head Act and according to the stage directions, "she pulls over her shirt and shows a bare shoulder". This prompts her to perform another React Pre-Head Act ("Oh no"), followed by an Express-Surprise Head Act ("oh, it's gone"), emphasized by an Upgrade Post-Head Act ("that's so weird"), to conclude with a Disclaim Post-Head Act ("I don't know how-where it went"), making it clear that she is lying. Again, also in this case the Italian version does not respect the original Act pattern as Phoebe initiates her turn with an Agree Head Act ("Come vuoi" - "As you like") and, after revealing the absence of tattoos on her bare shoulder, she continues with a React and an Express Surprise Pre-Head Acts ("Oh no! Oh santo cielo!" - "Oh no! Oh, good heavens!"), introducing the Upgrade Head Act ("È scomparso!" - "It has disappeared!"), to conclude with the Disclaim Post-Head Act ("Non ho veramente idea di dove sia finito!" - "I really have no idea where it's gone!"). The dubbing translation of this turn [65] shows a typical example of 'foreignization' of the Italian 'movie language' rendered into a variant of stilted 'dubbese' where none of the expressions used by the dubbed sitcom character correspond to spontaneous stylistic choices that an Italian person of the same age and gender as the character would normally opt for in naturally-occurring conversation. In the following turn [66], Rachel shown her annoyance through a Blame Head Act: "You didn't get it?", to which Phoebe replies, in turn [67], with a stern Revelation Head Act: "No". Rachel, even more exasperated, keeps asking her with an Elicitation Head Act: "Why didn't you get it?", incorrectly translated into Italian as "Perché hai cambiato idea?" ("Why did you change your mind?"). Phoebe's reply, in turn [69], through an Apologize Head Act ("I'm sorry, I'm sorry") is expanded in the Italian version to include a Clue Head Act: "Scusa, ma non ne ho avuto il coraggio!" ("Sorry, but I didn't have the nerve!"). In turn [70], Rachel scolds her friend first by addressing her directly through a Bid Pre-Head Act, and then asking her by means of an Elicitation Head Act: "how would you do this to me?", concluding with a disparaging Blame Post-Head Act ("This was all your idea"). In this case, the Italian version of turn [70] has been rendered literally. Phoebe replies, in turn [71] with a self-disparaging Blame Pre-Head Act ("I know, I know") introducing an Informative Head Act ("I was gonna get it") to which she adds a Clue Post-Head Act ("but he came in with this needle and"). Then she suddenly performs an implausible Negotiate Head Act in an attempt to gain her friend's sympathy ("uh di-, did you know they do this with needles?"). The Italian version of this turn, though respecting the original Act pattern, renders Phoebe's words slightly differently—thus, for instance, the Informative and the Clue Acts now become "avrei voluto farlo, ma quando ho visto l'ago -" ("I would have liked to get it, but when I saw the needle-"), whereas the Italian version of the Negotiate Act shows a redundant reference to the 'tattoos' ("ma lo sapevi che I tatuaggi si fanno con gli aghi?" - "but did you know tattoos are done with needles?"). Rachel, in turn [72], becomes even more irritated with Phoebe's deceptiveness, so she bursts into a reproach with a React Pre-Head Act ("Really?"), strengthened by a disparaging Newsmark Pre-Head Act ("You don't say!") leading to a sarcastic Blame Head Act ("because mine was licked on by kittens"). This final figurative expression is differently rendered into Italian through another image which is not exactly equivalent in both semantic and pragmatic terms: "E allora perché il mio lo hanno fatto con i gessetti?" ("So why was mine done with crayons?").

Having analyzed the original and the translated version of this extract from *Friends*, it is necessary at this point to explore how students belonging to Groups A and B tackled the dubbing-translation problems posed by this sitcom.

6.3 Achieving 'Dialogic Naturalization' by Applying the Acting Translator Model to *Friends*

6.3.1 *Becoming aware of Humour constructs in source and target scripts*

The comparative analysis between the original and the dubbed version of the exchanges from *Friends* examined above shows evidence of how the main interpersonal dynamics between the sitcom characters is marked by stressful relationships. The task students participating in the longitudinal case study were asked to carry out was therefore to explore possibilities of rendering the conflicting turns of the interacting characters into ways that could sound 'natural' in Italian, though respecting the original metaphoric, idiomatic and cultural references that determine the humour in this sitcom conversation. The university students engaged in the dubbing-translation workshop on *Friends* (and, later in this chapter, on *Will & Grace*) were the same ones who took part in the previous sitcom workshops reported in the earlier chapters of this book. Also in this case, two groups of students were involved: the experimental Group A who applied the Acting Translator Model and thus was initially prompted to adopt top-down physical-theatre techniques of character embodiment and English/Italian dialogue improvisation, and the control Group B who was not given the possibility of approaching dubbing translation through the Acting Translator Model and so they did not experience such initial top-down phase, but only the subsequent bottom-up one, joining Group A in carrying out the dubbing translation.

During the top-down phase, therefore, students/acting-translators in Group A explored physical possibilities of 'internalizing' such tense conversation dynamics between interacting characters in order to make it become part of their inner experience. Stressful relationships in this sitcom, however, are also exploited by each character to make the other characters aware of his/her personal problems that they refuse—consciously or unconsciously—to acknowledge, hence the ultimate objective of the 'tension-arousal' pattern in conversation is to achieve negotiation aimed at mutual sympathetic acceptance, reconciliation, and relief. The physical-theatre task that Group-A students carried out at this stage was therefore intended to be employed by each participant in a conversation to 'awaken' the other participant so as to make him/her see the truth s/he does not want to acknowledge. Hence, in pairs, students/acting-translators were asked to perform the turns characterized by tense interpersonal dynamics in the above-analyzed exchanges. Each turn uttered by each student embodying a sitcom character was accompanied by his/her throwing of a little paper ball against the other student embodying another character, striking him/her. The other student, in his/her turn, replied with the throwing of another little paper ball against his/her interlocutor, striking him/her. The aim of this physical-theatre task was to help students/acting-translators build in their mind a physical memory of the words and phrases that have 'struck' his/her character, making him/her aware of a 'painful' problem. Moreover, the physical effort made by each character in throwing the little paper ball also affected their tone of voice which became strained while uttering turns full of tension. The exchanges were first performed in the original English version and then translated extempore into Italian while performing them through the paper-ball throwing. This impromptu translation while students were involved in this 'physical performance' was meant to make them choose spontaneously more natural equivalent forms in Italian.

This first top-down phase was performed only by the students/acting-translators in the experimental Group A, but, in the case of this specific sitcom, the second bottom-up phase kept students in Groups A and B separated since, differently from the previous sitcom workshops, here they received a different guidance. Thus, whereas students in the control Group B were asked to provide their dubbing translation of the sitcom exchanges solely on the basis of their conventional training as translators, students in Group A at this stage were required to become aware of relevant theoretical models of Humour in Cognitive Linguistics, such as schema incongruence, or 'script opposition' (Raskin 1985; Attardo and Raskin 1991; Attardo 1994, 2001) applied to the dubbing translation of the humorous sitcom conversation. The first problem to tackle for Group-A students, therefore, regarded the rendering into Italian of the socio-cultural references in the original humorous puns in order to trigger a parallel comic effect in the target audience (cf. Bovinelli and Gallini 1994; Aixela 1996; Leppihalme 1997; Ramière 2006). In particular, they were required to achieve semantic and pragmatic equivalence in the translation of those socio-cultural references that are only specific of the source culture since they have no correspondence in the target one, rather than to achieve an easy equivalence in translating the so-called 'transcultural' references which are familiar to both cultures (Leppihalme 1997: 66). The use of cultural references to induce humour is a conventional comic strategy aimed at producing incongruity between the expected contextual script the reference normally hints at, and the unexpected script the comic situation alludes to (*ibidem*: 40-42). Hence, Group-A students needed, first of all, to identify the 'logical mechanism' (Attardo *et al.* 2002: 18) by which two opposite scripts come to be juxtaposed for humorous effects. Nida and Taber (1969) provide a taxonomy of domains that mark scripts socio-culturally and help categorize references, which they broadly classify into: 'material', referred to everyday objects or concepts (as in the references, reported above, to the product brands of 'Mr. Salty', Mr. Peanut', or 'Captain Crunch', left unaltered in the TV Italian translation); 'social', referred to shared cultural notions or knowledge (as in the simile reported above "she's got the IQ of a napkin", literally rendered into Italian); 'ecological', related to places and their physical characteristics; 'religious', associated with any public or private expression of faith (e.g., rituals, prayers, etc., as in Chandler's religious allusion in his exclamation "Sweet mother of all that is good and pure!", quoted above, not rendered, this time, into Italian); 'linguistic', referred to the expression of attitudes connected with the previous domains through language. Leppihalme (1997) points out the difficulty in rendering such culturally-marked references in translation, suggesting that, in the case of a lack of familiarity with them, a translator needs to replace them—in her own words, by 'recreating' them (*ibidem*: 106-107)—with other references that are familiar to the target audience, thus actually implementing a 'domestication' process, also defined by Hervey and Higgins (2001: 132-135) as 'cultural transplantation". Contrary to this view, Antonopoulou (2004) argues that at least socio-culturally marked proper names need to be retained in translation as they are an integral part of the humorous message to be conveyed—which is almost unavoidable in audio-visual translation since the referent is often clearly visible on the screen. Yet, the problem of rendering the comic effect into the target language and culture still remains to be solved. Facing such quandaries meant for Group-A students having to decide which strategy would render the original reference and comic effect better—whether a direct transfer of the original reference (as it frequently happens in the dubbed translation of *Friends* for the Italian TV), or its substitution by another reference belonging to the source culture or, rather, to the target culture, or by recreating the reference anew, or by neutralizing it by opting for a corresponding common noun, or even by omitting it altogether (which often means removing along with it also the 'canned laughter' that highlights the related pun) (cf. Ramière 2006). The Acting Translator Model, however, postulates that a dubbing translator should attempt to achieve an effect of 'naturalization' also in rendering a culture-specific reference into another language and culture, which means that s/he has to strive to be faithful to the source culture by providing a semantic and pragmatic equivalence that would be perceived as 'natural', and not 'affected', by the target audience, also in its comic implications. Therefore, a principled awareness of theoretical issues for Group-A students/acting-translators was advocated, particularly in relation to the rendering into the target language of one of the most difficult areas of humorous discourse—namely, puns.

In exploring the structure of puns, Attardo (1994: 133) highlights the fact that they entail two opposing senses respectively related to two different scripts. Such 'script opposition' is assumed to prompt in receivers the perception of an incongruity that can be resolved only by activating a 'logical mechanism' (*ibidem*: 144-145) bringing the two opposing senses together by what Raskin (1985: 114) defines as 'script-switch trigger'. Just because procedural scripts are involved in this Incongruity/Resolution process, Hempelmann (2004) argues that puns are not simply about conflicting semantic senses, but rather about divergent pragmatic meanings to be inferred from the play of words in conversation (cf. Nash 1985; Norrick 1993). This means that Group-A students/acting-translators, in solving the problem of rendering puns into the target language, needed to explore the pragmatic scripts evoked by the two opposing senses involved in the wordplay, which can be expressed through a series of formal strategies that Delabastita (1996: 128) summarizes into four categories: *(1)* 'homonymy', entailing a play of words with the same sound and spelling; *(2)* 'homophony', or playing with words with the same sound but different spellings; *(3)* 'homography', or play of words with different sounds but the same spelling; and *(4)* 'paronymy', involving a play of words with minor differences in sound and spelling. The scripts that such opposing words trigger in the receivers' mind can be interconnected, on the one hand, by a paradigmatic (or vertical) association, when one of the two words is not explicitly stated in the pun (e.g., "wedding belles" —*ibidem*) and thus has to be inferred by the receiver on the basis of his/her background knowledge (i.e., the homophonic "wedding bells"), and, on the other, by a syntagmatic (horizontal) association, when both opposing words are present in the pun, thus making inference almost unnecessary (e.g., the homographic "How the US put us to shame" —*ibidem*). Delabastita (*ibidem*: 134) also suggests a number of translation strategies ranging from 'foreignization' to 'domestication' (Venuti 1995, 1998), which respect Attardo's (2002) application of the knowledge resource of 'script opposition' to humorous translation and which students/acting-translators may consider while taking their rendering decisions. Such strategies are: *(a)* 'pun→pun', the typical 'foregnizing' choice of rendering verbatim the pun into the target language; *(b)* 'pun→non-pun', a foregnization choice that opts for translating the pun so as to render only its semantic sense, not the original wordplay; *(c)* 'pun→related rhetorical device', a choice meant to substitute the pun with a rhetorical device, such as parody, paradox, etc., in order to approximately convey the original effect; *(d)* 'pun→zero pun', the choice to omit the pun completely from translation; *(e)* 'ST-pun→TT-pun', a typical domestication choice substituting a pun in the source text with an equivalent one in the target text; *(f)* 'non-pun→pun', adding a completely new pun in the target text often to compensate for previous pun omissions; *(g)* 'zero→pun', meant as the gratuitous addition of new puns in the target text without any compensatory justification; *(h)* 'editorial technique', such as the addition of explanatory notes, regarding written texts only. Indeed, the translation of idioms with their predetermined forms and formulae is extremely complicated, if not utterly impossible (cf. Baker 1992: 63)—although, as Moon (1998) points out in her study on 'fixed expressions and idioms', some minor variations may be feasible with the aim of achieving a comic effect (*ibidem*: 170). Such variations, Moon (*ibidem*: 163) asserts, are made possible by the recognition of an underlying and unifying "idiom schema" that allows divergent realizations from the "idiom canonical form", though the 'lexical nucleus' of the idiom remains invariable. The possibility of variable realizations of the same idiom within the same language becomes therefore a facilitation strategy also in rendering an idiom from a source language into a target one as it would simply require the acknowledgment of the underlying fixed 'idiom schema', which would allow a certain flexibility in translation. Veisbergs (1997) analyzes specifically such 'idiom transformations' and their possible translation. To this purpose, he first focuses on the cognitive structure of the idiom which evokes not just a univocal schema, but a kind of schema incongruity—or 'script opposition' in Attardo's (1994) definition —that allows its "dual actualization" (Veisbergs 1997: 158) into both a literal interpretation and a figurative, idiomatic one. Indeed, he claims that, to achieve a comic effect, the idiom can be flexibly 'actualized': *(a)* in its literal interpretation only; *(b)* in its idiomatic interpretation expanded into its reformulation (by additions, substitutions, or ellipsis); *(c)* in the literal interpretation of only some of its lexical components; *(d)* in the interpretation of incongruous situational scripts inferred from the literal meaning of some lexical components of the idiom. As instances of such 'dual actualization' of idioms, Veisbergs produces extracts from the nonsense humour of Carroll's surrealist novels on 'Alice's in Wonderland', but Group-A students/acting-translators were required, on the one hand, to interpret the double actualization of idioms within the specific socio-cultural context of the sitcom under analysis and, on the other, to find equivalent ways to render it into the target language of the dubbing translation. Veisbergs (*ibidem*: 164-171) also provides a taxonomy of strategies aimed at conveying the perception of the 'dual actualization' of an idiom also in translation, which may be viewed as complementary to Delabastita's (1996) similar taxonomy for pun translation outlined above. Veisbergs identifies idiom-translation strategies of: *(a)* 'equivalent idiom transformation', which is possible only when both source and the target languages share the same idiom (e.g., 'play with fire' – 'giocare col fuoco' in Italian); *(b)* 'loan translation', a foreignization strategy based on the literal translation of the idiom into the target language, thus producing an effect of 'cultural estrangement' in receivers who, for instance, may not understand its idiomatic implications if only one of the two opposing scripts is made explicit; *(c)* 'Extension', another foreignization strategy which involves the literal translation of an idiom with the addition of an explanation; *(d)* 'Analogue idiom transformation', a strategy between foreignization and domestication based on the rending of the original idiom into another one in the target language that is equivalent in form and meaning; *(e)* 'Substitution', entailing the choice of an idiom in the target language which is equivalent in meaning but different in form; *(f)* 'Compensation', a domestication strategy that introduces an idiom in the target text where there was none in the source text; *(g)* 'Omission', consisting in the complete deletion of an idiom in the source text, or in its substitution with its implied meaning; *(h)* 'Metalinguistic comments', regarding the use of notes and parentheses (that obviously cannot be used in audio-visual translation). Dore (2010) illustrates Veisbergs's translation strategies precisely by reference to some idiom-based puns in the dubbing translation of the sitcom *Friends* for the Italian television. For example, she identifies an instance of complete 'Omission' in an exchange from episode #13 in which Rachel is furious about the fact that Chandler accidentally glanced at her bare breasts, so Ross suggests an equitable settlement: *Ross:* "Alright, alright. We're all adults here, there's only one way to resolve this. Since you saw her boobies, I think, uh, you're gonna have to show her your peepee."—*Chandler:* "Y'know, I don't see that happening?" —*Rachel:* C'mon, he's right. Tit for tat." —*Chandler*: "Well, I'm not showing you my 'tat'." In the context of this exchange, the idiom 'tit for tat' becomes a humorous pun as the term 'tit' is also a colloquial way to refer to women's breasts – here representing the core of the argument going on between Rachel and Chandler. The Italian translation totally omits this wordplay: *Ross:* "D'accordo, siamo tutti adulti. C'è solo un modo per risolvere la cosa. Visto che tu hai guardato le sue tette, credo che tu dovresti farle vedere il tuo pisellino." —*Chandler:* "Sai, non credo sia possibile." —*Ross (extra cue):* "Eh sì!" —*Rachel:* "Andiamo, ha ragione. E' un mio diritto." —*Chandler:* "Beh, non ti faccio vedere un bel niente, chiaro?" (Back-translation [by the author of this book]: *Ross:* Alright, we're all adults. There's only one way to resolve the matter. Since you saw her tits, I believe you should show her your 'little pea' [willy]." —*Chandler:* "Y'know, I don't believe it possible." —*Ross (extra cue):* "Oh, yes!" —*Rachel:* "C'mon, he's right. It is my right." —*Chandler:* "Well, I'm going to show you nothing at all, have I made myself clear?"). This exchange was submitted to students/dubbing-translators from both Groups A and B with the task of avoiding 'idiom omission'. Group-A students first worked 'physically' together, as 'acting-translators', to find 'natural' ways of using the Italian language in rendering this exchange. They noticed in fact that, as a whole, the language employed in the dubbing translation for the Italian TV is a typical example of stilted 'Italian dubbese' as a calque from English, with the overuse of the personal pronoun 'tu' ('you'), normally omitted in Italian, and the adoption of the conditional sentence ("dovresti farle vedere" – "you should show her") in an expression where normally an Italian young adult would use the present simple with a more colloquial lexical verb ("devi mostrarle" – "you must show [display] her"), and the choice of the formal hedge "credo" ("I believe") rather than "penso" ("I think") in the turns by Ross and Chandler. Also the term "pisellino" (literally: "little pea" for "willy") used by Ross is not a natural choice that a young man would normally make. As for the actual translation of the idiom "to give tit for tat" and the related pun, Group-A students decided to attempt a translation strategy of 'analogue idiom transformation', by trying to render the original idiom into another one in Italian that is equivalent in form and meaning. Hence they opted for 'rendere pan per focaccia' (literally: "to give bread for flat bread") and so organized the whole exchange around this equivalent. Ross's prompt, therefore, was made to focus on an Italian metaphorical expression for "tits", related to the notion of 'bread', namely, "pagnottelle" ('little round loaves' for 'breasts') and on a more naughty metaphorical expression in translating "peepee" also in this case related to the notion of 'bread'—i.e., "sfilatino"

('French loaf' for 'penis'): *Ross:* "Visto che le hai guardato le pagnottelle, ora penso che devi mostrarle il tuo sfilatino" (literally: "Since you saw her little round loaves, now I think you must show her your French loaf") — *Chandler:* "Ti sbagli, penso proprio che non succederà." ("You're wrong, I really think it won't happen."). *Rachel:* "Ha ragione. Rendimi pan per focaccia." ("He's right. Gimme bread for flat bread") —*Chandler:* "Beh, non ti mostro la mia focaccia!" ("Well, I'm not going to show you my flat bread!"). Incidentally, some Group-A students went even so far as suggesting a much more vulgar alternative to the rendering of "peepee" into Italian, which was directly associated with the second term of the idiom, the "focaccia" ('flat bread')—so their choice fell on "pizza", the flat-bread food that has got the metaphorical implication of "penis" , at least in some areas of Southern Italy—yet they soon dropped this solution as too 'localized', but also too boorish for the conversational standards of the original *Friends* sitcom. Vulgarity was instead the choice made straight away by students/dubbing-translators in the control Group B, who justified their option by saying that they could not find any other possible alternative. They too worked in group before producing a translation of the above exchange based on the strategy of 'substitution', replacing the idiom "tit for tat" with the parallel Italian "occhio per occhio, dente per dente" ("an eye for an eye, a tooth for a tooth") which is equivalent in meaning to "tit for tat", and also in form, except for its lexical reduplication. Obviously, since the reference in the exchange is to Rachel's "tits", the lexical items of the Italian idiom had to be changed, though retaining the formal structure that made the idiom recognizable even with the modified words. Hence, Group-B students had Ross say his turn based on the /p/-sound alliteration "poppe" ('boobs') / "pene" ('penis'): *Ross:* "Poichè hai visto le sue poppe, credo che ora dovresti farle vedere il tuo pene" ("Since you saw her boobs, I believe that you now should show her your penis")—and Rachel claims: *Rachel:* "Dai, è giusto, poppe per poppe pene per pene" ("C'mon, it's right, boobs for boobs, a penis for a penis")—to which Chandler protests in a crude, non-metaphorical way: *Chandler:* "Non ti farò vedere il mio pene!" ("I'm not going to show you my penis!"). As evident, this solution, though clever, renders neither the naughty innuendo of the original turns, as the terms of the exchange are made even too explicit, nor its humorous effect based on metaphorical allusions. Furthermore, the language used is another variation of Italian 'dubbese' (e.g., "poiché" as a formal choice for "since", and the unusual conditional with hedging "credo che ora dovresti") that translators seem to adopt automatically every time they tackle a dubbing translation. However, to do Group-B students justice, they did work together to try to produce less vulgar alternatives, but they were not so straightforwardly clear. For instance, in an alternative translation they made Ross play with the /t/-sound alliteration "tette" ('tits') / "patta" ('[trousers] fly') by saying: *Ross:* "Dal momento che hai visto le sue tette, ora dovresti aprire la tua patta"

("Since you saw her tits, now you should open your fly"), which prompts Rachel's wordplay: *Rachel:* "Esatto. Patta per patta, tette per tette" ("Right. A fly for a fly, tits for tits")—the latter term moved to the second part of the idiomatic expression as a parallelism played on the assonance "dente" ("teeth") / "tette" ("tits") ([d][t]*e*-[n]/[t]*te*)—to which Chandler replies: *Chandler:* "Scordatelo! Non ti aprirò la mia patta" ("Forget it! I won't open my fly for you!"). Other Group-B students came up with a rendering of the exchange that they deemed less vulgar insofar as they resorted to a childish way of referring to sexual traits which, however, ended up being detrimental to the comic effect: *Ross:* "Dal momento che le hai guardato le tettine, ora dovresti mostrarle il tuo pipino" (literally: "Since you saw her little tits, now you should show her your little willie"), hence Rachel's reaction: *Rachel:* "Giusto. Tettine per tettine, pipino per pipino." ("Right. Little tits for little tits, little willie for little willie"), to which Chandler replies by neutralizing the original pun: *Chandler:* "Non ti mostro il mio pipino!" ("I'm not going to show you my little willie!"). Group-B students were aware of the humour neutralization produced by their translation and thus made another attempt at retaining the wittiness of this exchange by playing with the assonance with the original idiom—which, however, once again turned out to be too harebrained to be immediately perceived as comic. In this last attempt of theirs, Ross's prompt was: *Ross:* "Dal momento che le hai guardato le tette, ora dovresti mostrarle il tuo uccellino" (literally: "Since you saw her tits, now you should show her your little bird [willie]"), which triggers Rachel's reference to a specific type of bird, i.e., "picchio" ("woodpecker"), whose assonance with "occhio" ("eye") should justify the pun: *Rachel:* "Giusto. Picchio per picchio, tette per tette." (Literally: "Right. Woodpecker for woodpecker, tits for tits"). Chandler at this point was made to reply with another pun based on the assonance "picchio" and "picche" (literally: "spades" in the cards), metaphorically meaning "to refuse": *Chandler:* "E io ti rispondo picche!" ("And I refuse point-blank!"). (Incidentally, some students in Group B proposed another quite vulgar and unacceptable alternative based on the assonance "occhio" ["eye"] / "cacchio" ["cock"] – "dente" ["tooth"] / "tette" ["tits"] which rendered the idiom "occhio per occhio, dente per dente" into "cacchio ["cock"] per cacchio, tette ["tits"] per tette").

As evident from the discussion carried out so far, the question of idioms in dubbing translation is also closely related to the issue of rendering original metaphorical expressions and speech style into the target language by preserving their humorous implications in the sitcom conversation. Metaphor translation, in fact, implies a cognitive process of interpretation of socio-culturally marked ways of experiencing the world and categorizing it into 'embodied concepts', or 'image schemata' (Lakoff and Johnson 1980, 1999; Johnson 1987; Lakoff 1987; Kovecses 2000, 2005: 233). As cognitive structures, metaphors are also crucial in representing the image schemata underlying the incongruous scripts that determine humour in different cultures and across social groups and different historical periods (Giora 1991, 2003; Mio and Graesser 1991; Brone *et al.* 2006), but also in relation to individual experiences and mind styles (Semino 2008)—this latter aspect being crucial in the construction of sitcom fictional characters and their subsequent 'embodiment' by actors and, also, by the acting translators. Furthermore, humour may contribute to the creation of novel metaphors which deviate from the expected, conventional ones by introducing a sense of surprise at bringing together two unexpected scripts for comic effects. Indeed, in interpreting metaphors, the conceptual mechanism of 'script opposition' (Attardo 1994: 133) works by projecting an 'image schema' from a source script domain to a target one (Lakoff and Johnson 1980: 4-5). The 'logical mechanism' (Attardo 1994:144-145), to be activated, has to connect these two experientially distant and contextually diverse domains. Fauconnier and Turner (2002) define such dissimilar metaphorical script domains as 'mental spaces' (*ibidem*: 102), to be logically interconnected by a bridging inferential process, they define as 'blending', which produces a novel 'mental space' (*ibidem*: 103) representing the interpretation of the metaphor (Grady *et al.* 1999). This is a process that involves three main inferential strategies (Fauconnier and Turner 2002: 42-44), which are: 'composition', regarding the novel connections that the mind activates between the two 'blended' domains of the metaphor; 'completion', concerning the addition of elements that are not present in the metaphor, but that can however be inferred from the interpreter's background knowledge of the two domains brought together in the metaphor; and 'elaboration', entailing the addition of extra elements that are not directly connected with the two blended domains, but that could nevertheless fit them, making the metaphor a novel, unexpected, and possibly humorous one. This last inferential strategy of 'elaboration' is in line with what Mio and Graesser (1991) define as 'distance theory' of humorous metaphor, which requires the interpreter's cognitive effort to connect two very different domains, the consequent 'blend' representing the 'comic trigger'. Tsur (1992) explains such inferential effort as being induced in the interpreter's mind by the typical 'split focus' of a humorous metaphor which creates a disorienting effect by suddenly redirecting the attention from an expected experiential domain to an unexpected, very distant and incongruous one. Oring (2003) considers the 'logical mechanism' of bridging the two incongruous metaphorical domains in humorous discourse as different from the conventional, 'genuine' one occurring in everyday discourse because humour presupposes a 'spurious incongruity' as "it violates logic [...], or the sense of what traditional behaviors or expressions are supposed to do and mean" (*ibidem*: 5-6). Yet this view seems to fit only a 'nonsense humour' of the Monty Python type, but since sitcoms are typically grounded in a specific socio-cultural context—which also informs the metaphorical domains involved in their humour—the 'elaboration' strategy does not appear to be central in determining its comic effect. This seems to confirm the view expressed by Brone and Feyaert (2004) who go so far as to question the validity of the 'logical mechanism' that, in Attardo's (1994) General Theory of Verbal Humor, is central in the 'resolution' of the 'incongruity' necessary to generate the relief that triggers the comic effect (see also Perlmutter 2000) but that, in their view, does not work in trying to infer a meaning from the incongruous domains brought together in metaphor-based humour. Attardo, however, replies (in Attardo *et al.* 2002) that what ultimately triggers the comic effect is precisely the interpreter's efforts to activate the complex 'logical mechanism' necessary to resolve the incongruity in such metaphorical jokes.

The problem that students/acting-translators have to tackle in such circumstances, however, is not simply how to interpret and resolve metaphorical incongruity, but also how to render it into an equivalent dubbing translation (cf. Dobrzynska 1995) conveying equivalent comic effects. Newmark (1995) suggests a number of strategies for translating metaphors which, by ranging from foreignization to domestication ones, do not diverge too much from the taxonomies elaborated by Delabastita (1996) and Veisbergs (1997). In Newmark's (1995: 106-113) view, metaphors may be rendered into a target language by: *(a)* directly transferring the metaphorical expression from the source language to the target one; *(b)* literally translating it by transforming it into a simile, or by adding extra explanatory information; *(c)* replacing the original metaphor with another one in the target language that is equivalent in meaning, even if it does not contain the same image; *(d)* paraphrasing the meaning of the original metaphor without conveying its image; *(e)* omitting the metaphor altogether; *(f)* compensating the omission of a metaphor by adding another one. Group-A students/acting-translators, however, were required to go beyond this classical method of rendering the culture-bound metaphorical and idiomatic language of humour into the target language and culture by making mere stylistic choices as a result of their mental work carried out in isolation. In fact, they were required to apply the Acting Translator Model which aims at a team-work where each dubbing-translator 'physically embodies' the sitcom characters' language in order to understand how humorous figurative language contributes to the construction of the characters' personalities that acting translators eventually have to 'make their own' and to render into the target language.

6.3.2 *Embodying Humour constructs in* Friends *source and target scripts*

Having explored the theoretical issues underlying the dubbing translation of humour, then Group-A students worked in parallel with the control Group-B students in two distinct translation workshops on the script from *Friends* analyzed in *6.2.1*. In analyzing the exchanges in their sequence of puns and figurative language, students/dubbing-translators in both groups provided their own translation of the culture-bound metaphorical and idiomatic expressions present in the scripts. Just in turn [1], uttered by Joey, a 'deactivated, everyday metaphor' (Lakoff and Johnson 1980)—hence, not meant to be funny—can be found in the idiomatic expression "Can we drop this?", meant 'to stop talking about something'. Group-B students stuck to the conventional strategy of 'substitution' (cf. Veisbergs 1997) of a source idiom with a target one that is equivalent in meaning but not in form, and also replacing the inherent source-language metaphor with a target-language one that is, again, equivalent in meaning but different in its image (cf. Newmark 1995). Thus they rendered the idiomatic image of 'dropping' a discussion into the pragmatically equivalent expressions: "Possiamo lasciar perdere?" (Back-translation: "Can we leave it?", or, approximately, "Can we forget it?"), "Possiamo finirla/smetterla?" ("Can we stop it?"). Group-A students, instead, opted for the strategy of 'analogue idiom transformation' (Veisbergs 1997), consisting in rendering the original idiom into another one in the target language preserving its form, meaning and, in the case in point, also the original 'physical' metaphor of 'putting an end to an unpleasant discussion' as 'dropping an unpleasant object on the floor, possibly destroying it'. The students/acting-translators, therefore, investigated 'physically', in the course of an improvisation workshop, the parallel Italian metaphors that could better render the original one inherent in the idiom, first by reproducing the actual action of 'dropping something on the floor (i.e., a ball)', and then by exploring possible renderings of the metaphorical idiom into Italian. The idiomatic expression considered as formally, semantically and metaphorically equivalent to the original one was: "Possiamo lasciar cadere questa cosa?" ("Can we drop this thing?", or "Can we knock it off?"), ma anche "Possiamo piantarla?" ("Can we chuck it in?"—literally: "Can we drive it into the ground?"). Before moving to the next metaphorical expression, however, it is worth noticing a glaring misuse of 'dubbese' in Group-B students' translation of Joey's expression in turn [3]: "I've already got an apartment that I love" - with the verb "love" repeatedly rendered into the literal "un appartamento che amo" whose immediate meaning in Italian is: "an apartment I'm [romantically] in love with" or, even worse "che adoro" ("an apartment that I adore"), the latter being a choice that a young 'macho man' like Joey would never made. Instead, the more natural—and, indeed, obvious—choice was the one unanimously made by Group-A students who opted for "un appartamento che mi piace" ("an apartment I like [very much]").

The next idiomatic expression incorporating a metaphor can be found in Chandler's turn [4], as he tells Joey: "it wouldn't kill you to say it once in a while". The translator of the Italian TV version opted for the 'omission' of the source-text idiom (Veisbergs 1997)—together with its inherent metaphor (Newmark 1995)—replacing it with its implied meaning ("Perché non dici la verità una volta tanto?" - "Why don't you tell the truth, once in a while?"). Group-A students, instead, preferred, once again, to search for an 'analogue idiom transformation' to preserve the original metaphorical form and meaning of the idiom, with the addition of a small 'extension'—i.e., the word "verità" ("truth") to clarify the implied concept —as evident from their translation choices: "non ti ammazza dire la verità" ("it wouldn't kill you to tell the truth"), or "non muori se dici la verità" ("you won't die if you say the truth"), or—in a more figuratively elaborated version: "non ti strozzi se dici la verità" ("you won't choke to death if you tell the truth"). Group-B students' choices, on the other hand, were not homogenous: some students attempted a 'loan transformation' (Veisbergs 1997), providing a literal rendering of the idiom whose result, however, was not so 'natural' as it would be expected in colloquial Italian: "non ti ucciderebbe dirlo una volta ogni tanto" ("it wouldn't kill you to say it once in a while"). Other students provided an 'analogue idiom transformation' with the addition of an 'extension' which, rather than clarifying the concept, introduced a subject—"nessuno" ("no one") that was absent and unjustified by the sense of the utterance—making it much longer than the required sync-time, too: "Non ti ammazza nessuno se per una volta dici quello che pensi veramente" ("No one kills you if once in a while you say what you really think"). The other choices made by Group-B students can be classified as instances of 'substitution', equivalent in meaning, but different in form from the original one, as in "non guasterebbe se lo dicessi ogni tanto" ("it wouldn't do any harm (literally: 'it wouldn't spoil it'] if you said it now and then"), though some of them showed some semantic resemblance with the inherent 'kill' metaphor, as in: "Non ti farebbe male dire ogni tanto quello che pensi" ("It won't hurt you to say once in a while what you think"), or in the two new metaphorical expressions, as the long one: "non sarebbe la fine del mondo se lo ammettessi una volta per tutte!" ("it wouldn't be the end of the world if you admitted it once and for all!"), and the short one: "sputa il rospo una volta tanto!" ("spit it out" [literally: "spit the toad out"] once in a while!").

The next problematic metaphor students had to cope with is in Joey's turn [9] when, by addressing a highly irritated Chandler, he attacks him by asking: "What're you gettin' so bent out of shape for, huh?", thus introducing, scornfully, a typical 'deactivated metaphor' (Lakoff and Johnson 1980) representing the domain of emotional 'irritation' through the embodied domain of physical 'irritation', and the events that 'inflame' the subject's mind in terms of skin 'inflamation', producing soreness that makes the subject's body twist and 'bend out of shape' for pain. Indeed, Chandler twists his body as he speaks, as if he longed for relieving a terrible itchiness with that frantic movement, thus 'embodying' his desire to avoid listening to Joey's unexpected, irritating revelation. Joey, then, mocks him precisely on his lack of physical and emotional control, which makes Chandler even more infuriated. The translator of the Italian TV version opted again for a 'substitution' of this idiomatic-metaphorical expression, replacing it with another, more conventional one which renders 'anger' in terms of 'hot fluid boiling in the subject's body-as-a container' (*ibidem*), with the extra addition of an apology as a hedge that softens his sarcasm: "Scusa, ma vuoi dirmi perchè ti scaldi tanto?" ("Excuse me, but will you tell me why you are getting so heated?"). Group-A students tried to retain the original metaphor by looking for its occurrences also in Italian, and thus, once again, opted for the 'analogue idiom transformation' (Veisbergs 1997) which would allow them to look for equivalence in idiomatic form and meaning through the transfer of the original metaphor to the target language (cf. Newmark 1995). As acting translators, however, Group-A students had to find experiential metaphors 'within themselves', by exploring the equivalent metaphors that came up to their minds by comparing their physical 'embodied images' in Italian with the 'embodied image' triggered by the original metaphorical idiom. Hence, they suggested the following translation options: "Perché ti dimeni così?" ("Why are you wriggling [gesticulating wildly] like that?"), "Perché ti scomponi tanto?" ("What are you getting so ruffled for?"), "Perché ti contorci così?" / "Perché ti stai storcendo tanto?" ("Why are you twisting about like that?" / "Why are you warping so much?"), "Perché ti alteri così i connotati?" ("Why are you distorting your features so much?"). In all these cases, Group-A students preserved the metaphorical image of the original idiom and provided, at the same time, equivalent 'natural' renderings into the target language. Group-B students, on the other hand, opted for the 'omission' of the original idiomatic metaphor and its substitution with its implied meaning (Veisbergs 1997), and thus agreed on two possible renderings into Italian: "Perché ti agiti tanto?" ("What are you getting so upset for?"), and "Per quale motivo ti stai innervosendo tanto?" ("For what reason are you getting so nervous?"). Furthermore, the misrepresentation of Joey's words that in the TV Italian version had him express an extra meaning, absent in the original version, in the same turn: "Noi non ci siamo mica sposati, mi sembra" ("We are not married, I think") was almost ignored by both groups of students, except for a couple of cases in Group B. However, the idea of the married couple reappears in rendering into Italian the conclusive clever remark in Joey's turn [9]: "We're not Bert and Ernie". As pointed out in the previous section, the reference here is to the two puppet characters from *The Muppets Show* who are represented as living together in the same apartment, arguing all the time, sharing a bedroom but sleeping in separate beds and, crucially, never represented as a gay couple stereotype. In Italy, the two puppets were also known in the early seventies with the Italianized names of "Berto" and "Ernesto", but they were not considered among the memorable Muppets characters (such as Miss Piggy, for example). Hence the need to find an equivalent couple, well known in Italy, to substitute the "Bert and Ernie" one. Group-A students agreed on the comic duo "Stanlio e Ollio" (namely, the Italianized names of Stan Laurel and Oliver Hardy), who are also represented in the big poster Joey and Chandler have in their living room, and who are often featured as sharing the same apartment and bedroom, though sleeping in separate beds, and arguing all the time, sometimes also on matters concerning how to woo women. Another option proposed by Group-A students was the couple of comedians "Gianni e Pinotto"—namely, the Italianized names of Abbott and Costello who, in an American sitcom of the fifties, played the characters of two unemployed actors sharing the same apartment. Also the Disney cartoon characters "Cip e Ciop" (namely, Chip'n Dale, a pun for 'Chippendale'), the two squirrels who live together as friends inside a hollow trunk, were considered as an equivalent option. "Stanlio e Ollio", "Cip e Ciop" and "Gianni e Pinotto" represented also some of the options suggested by Group-B students who, however, sometimes misrepresented Joey's implicit meaning in citing Bert and Ernie and proposed other pairs that did not fit the socio-cultural implications of the original reference. For instance, equivalent translation options were considered also the cartoon characters "Olivia e Braccio di Ferro"—namely, Olive Oyl and her boyfriend Popeye—and even "Sandra e Raimondo", (i.e., Sandra Mondaini and Raimondo Vianello), a famous married couple of Italian comedians who also played the married couple in various sitcoms. The reference to a specific pair was even omitted to substitute it with the neutral "non siamo una coppia" ("we are not a pair"). In general, the rendering of this first exchange by Group-B students represented an interesting sample of 'dubbese', with all the repeated interjections "Well", "Fine", "Great" rendered into the emphatic and unnatural "Benone!" (literally: "Quite well!"), "Magnifico!" ("Magnificent!"), "Grandioso!" ("Grand!"), not to mention the customary use of a complex sentence structure with conditional forms, personal pronouns in subject position and pre-modifying adjectives that make the Italian style not at all colloquial, but rather stilted and utterly improbable.

The translation problems that students had to tackle in the second exchange of the script principally regarded, again, the rendering of culturally-marked idiomatic and metaphorical expressions. In turn [38], for instance, Monica reveals the profession of her new boyfriend to her mother: "he's a doctor". To which Mrs. Geller replies, in turn [39], with a Challenge Act: "A real doctor?", implicitly doubting the ability of her daughter to attract 'quality men'. Monica, in her turn [40], retorts with an idiom: "No, a doctor of meat". The translator of the Italian TV version preferred not to tackle the metaphorical implication of this idiom and, thus, opted for its 'omission' (Veisbergs 1997), substituting it with its assumed semantic meaning: "No, un dottore finto!" ("No, a fake doctor!"). Group-A students, instead, decided to find equivalent ways of rendering this metaphor into Italian, although this target language does not share the same metaphorical image with the source one. Naturally-sounding 'analogue idiom transformations' (*ibidem*), therefore, were deemed to be: "No, un dottore pasticciato" ("No, a butter-and-ragout doctor"), or "un dottore bollito" ("a doctor of boiled meat"), or still, to remain in the domain of cuisine: "un dottore di marzapane / di cioccolata" ("a doctor of marzipan / of chocolate"), or, more effectively, "un dottore di pastafrolla" ("a doctor of shortcrust pastry")—the term "pastafrolla" sharing with the previous adjective "bollito" the same metaphorical implication of a 'spineless, inept person'. Another solution proposed by Group-A students was: "un dottore di terracotta" ("an earthenware doctor"), an idiom which, in Italian, would stress the original reference to the fake, 'dummy' and 'fragile' (i.e., 'inadequate') quality of this specialist. Group-B students, in contrast, opted again for the 'omission' of the original idiom and its inherent metaphor, substituting it with its implied meaning. One choice, however, was in this sense more acceptable as a pun than the one made by the 'official translator': "No, un dottore per scherzo!" ("No, a doctor for fun! [in jest]"), a naturally-occurring option standing for 'a person who pretends to be a doctor for fun'. Other substitutions made by Group-B students, instead, completely lost the idiomatic, metaphorical force of the original pun: "un dottore fasullo" ("a bogus doctor"); "un finto dottore" ("a fake doctor", with the fronting of the adjective that is unusual in Italian); "No, per finta" ("No, he's just shamming"), till resorting to more explicit implications of fraud: "un dottore falso" ("a fraudulent doctor"); "No, un ciarlatano" ("No, a quack").

The next problematic idiom to tackle is in Mrs. Geller's turn [47], when she reveals to her husband that Monica, their daughter, and Richard, their friend "are something of an item" ("It seems your daughter and Richard are something of an item"). The translator of the Italian TV version opted for a 'substitution' (Veisbergs 1997), replacing the original idiom with another one in the target language equivalent in meaning but not in form: "Sembrerebbe che tra tua figlia Monica e il tuo amico Richard ci sia del tenero" ("It would seem your daughter Monica and your friend Richard are sweet on each other"). Group-A students intended once again to attempt an 'analogue idiom transformation', but this time the endeavour immediately appeared hard for the lack of direct correspondence with a similar metaphor in Italian. The solutions Group-A students came up with, therefore, ranged from newly created idioms based on the transformation of the original metaphor into an equivalent simile – "Pare che tua figlia Monica e Richard siano come tazzina e piattino" ("It seems your daughter Monica and Richard are like cup and dish"), thus producing an effect of 'cultural estrangement' in audience's reception—to more conventional equivalent choices: "siano un tutt'uno" ("[they] are one and the same", or "all one"); "siano un un insieme" ("[they] are a whole", "an ensemble"); "fanno coppia [fissa]" ("[your daughter Monica] goes steady [with Richard]"); "sono una coppietta" ("[they] are a pair of lovers"); "sono intimi" ("[they] are in intimacy"). Also the 'loan translation" was attempted, rendering verbatim the original idiom into Italian with the same 'commercial implications' of the literal domain of the metaphor: "sono come un unico articolo" ("[they] are something like a unique item") — which, again, would induce a sense of unfamiliarity in the target audience. Most of Group-B students, on the other hand, opted for the 'omission' of the source-text idiom (Veisbergs 1997), to replace it with its implied meaning. This is the case with the choice of translating Mrs. Geller's turn [47] into "Pare che tua figlia e Richard stiano insieme" ("It seems your daughter and Richard are together"). Another semi-idiomatic choice based on allusion is "Sembra che tra tua figlia e Richard ci sia qualcosa" ("It seems that between your daughter and Richard there is something"), whereas a disparaging allusion is in "Sembra che Richard e tua figlia abbiano una specie di relazione" ("It seems Richard and your daughter have a sort of affair") which is in contrast with the hint at love and tenderness implied in the choice some Group-B students shared with the 'official translator' in "ci sia del tenero" ("[they] are sweet on each other").

Mr. Geller's answer, in turn [48], introduces a metaphor, subsequently repeated across turns [49], [50] and [51], that gave students/dubbing-translators a lot of trouble in their search for 'natural' equivalence in Italian. Mr. Geller's replies, incredulous, to his wife revealing Monica's affair with Richard: "That's impossible, he's got a twinkie in the city". As already examined in *6.2.2*, the translator of the Italian TV version disregarded the cultural reference to the brand of an American sponge cake, "twinkie", used here disparagingly as the epithet for a 'young girlfriend'. In fact, s/he did not replace it with any parallel Italian brand of food equivalent in metaphorical meaning to "twinkie", not even s/he replaced it with another metaphor in the target language that could be equivalent in meaning, though not containing the same image (cf. Newmark 1995), on the contrary, what the 'official translator' did was to render "twinkie" into a sort of paraphrase of the implied meaning of the original metaphor (*ibidem*), namely, "amichetta", ("fancy girl"). Group-A students/acting-translators, instead, obstinately searched for an 'analogue transformation' of the cultural reference in the original metaphor that brought together the 'material' domain of 'food' and the 'social' domain of 'behaviour judgment' (cf. Nida and Taber 1969). Indeed, metaphors classifying 'women as food'—e.g., cookies, sweets, or tarts—are very frequent in English (cf. Goatly 1997: 155-156). What is original in this particular metaphor is that a reference is made to a specific commercial name of a food, 'Twinkies', which is forbidden in Italy where brand names cannot be mentioned outside advertisements as the consequent allegation would be that of surreptitious advertising. This, therefore, prevented students/dubbing-translators from finding equivalent food names that could work as analogue of the original metaphor. However, Group-A students, as a team, started a 'brainstorming session' during which they tried to associate the "twinkie" metaphor with parallel Italian ones which would likewise 'blend' (cf Attardo 1994) negative judgements on young women having affairs with elderly men and the figurative reference to food. One of the Italian metaphors, created anew by Group-A students, which best rendered the equivalence in both 'blended domains' of the original "twinkie" metaphor was "morosita" (*Mr. Geller:* "Impossibile, ha già una morosita in città" – "That's impossible, he's already got a morosita in the city"). Indeed, "morosita" was originally a brand name of gumdrops—'Morositas'—advertised by identifying their sweet taste with the sweetness of a black, beautiful and cheerful young woman, i.e., a kind of "sweetheart" that in Italy, in the late eighties (when this TV-ad was aired) would not have been considered as a seriously eligible fiancée. "Sweetheart", in colloquial Italian, can be translated as "morosa". After the successful advertisement of such gumdrops, the term "morosita"—namely, "young sweetheart" (precisely of Hispanic origin, as denoted by the suffix '-ita')—has today entered everyday Italian and is being used without making reference to the advertisement any longer, which justifies the adoption of this term in a domain not related to advertisement—i.e., an Italian sitcom. Other translation options for "twinkie" that the Group-A students suggested were: "ha già una *mon cherie* in città" ("he's already got a *mon cherie* in the city")—'Mon Cherie' being the famous brand of liqueur chocolates whose French name means "my darling"—to be connected again to the idea of a "sweetheart". Still applying the "woman as food" metaphor, so popular in advertising, Group-A students proposed a less effective option: "ha già una birretta in città" ("he's already got a little ale in the city"), recalling the notion of an Italian brand of beer —a 'blond ale'—represented in its advertisement as a 'blond young woman' who uttered the famous slogan: "Call me [brand name], I'll be your ale". Without making reference to other brand names, but still retaining the "woman as food" metaphor, Group-A students suggested other solutions: "ha una ciambellina /taralluccio in città" ("he's got a small doughnut / bagel in the city") – both doughnut and bagel being ring-shaped food (with a hole in the middle, easily evoking sexual associations). Also "Tarallucci", however, is the brand name of famous biscuits. Another choice made by this group of students was the common, culture-bound epithet for a young and sexually-appealing woman, namely "bocconcino" ("dish"), as in "ha già un bocconcino in città" ("he's already got a dish in the city"), but also another option was advanced, conveying the idea of a young mistress as a person who keeps his elderly lover alive, rendered by the metaphor "young woman as hot pepper", found in the version of turn [48]: "ha già una peperina in città" ("he's already got a little hot pepper [i.e., a spirited young mistress] in the city". Also Group-B students tried to tackle the metaphorical implications of "twinkle" and some of their solutions retained the "woman as food" metaphor, too, only that they missed the social implications of an epithet meant to prompt humour by disparagement. Hence, an alternative in this sense proposed by Group-B students was: "ha la sua dolce metà in città" ("he's got his 'sweet half' in the city"), whereas the solution "ha una storiella mordi e fuggi in città" ("he's got a 'nip and flee' [cursory] affair [or 'a bit on the side'] in the city"), though related in meaning to the original metaphor, is too long to fit the sync-time of Mr. Geller's utterance. The other translation choices made by Group-B students were rather of an 'omission' type, substituting the idiom with its implied meaning, as in: "ha una ragazzina / sbarbina / sciaquetta / amichetta in città" ("he's got a girl / cocky girl / flighty girl / fancy girl in the city").

The final, tough metaphor students had to cope with was in the very last turn [72] of the last exchange, when Rachel reacts angrily at Phoebe's revelation that she did not get a tattoo for fear of the needles by shouting: "Really? You don't say, because mine [my tattoo] was licked on by kittens". In the dubbing translation for the Italian television, this metaphorical expression was replaced with another one in the target language that is equivalent in meaning but that does not convey the same image. The new image, in fact, was: "Ma davvero? Non mi dire! E allora perché il mio lo hanno fatto con i gessetti?" ("Really? You don't say, so why was mine done with crayons?") – "gessetti" ("crayons"), which was believed to convey the same sense of 'delicate touch' as the 'kittens' licking' on Rachel's skin to draw the tattoo on it. Since for this task Group-A students were determined to explore ways of retaining the original idioms and metaphors also in translation—by applying the theories of rendering humour into a target language outlined in *6.3.1*—then they tried to preserve also this 'liking kittens' metaphor. A good solution was the one that rendered Rachel's final Blame Act into the rhyming lines: "perché il mio l'ha fatto la lingua del gatto!" ("because mine was done by the cat's tongue!"). An alternative and likewise rhyming and alliterating one recalled Phoebe's fear for the needle prick: "perchè il mio l'hanno fatto coi baffetti dei gatto!" ("because mine was done with the cat's whiskers"). Other choices were less effective—as, for instance: "perché il mio è fatto di bava di mici" ("because mine is done of kittens' dribble"), or another one introducing a neologism: "perchè il mio l'hanno slinguettato i mici" ("because mine was s-licked by kittens"). Group-B students did not show any wish for exploring possible translations of the original metaphor as they rather opted for its substitution with other ones that were equivalent in form, but not in meaning, as in: "perché il mio l'hanno fatto con i pennarelli / la biro / gli acquerelli / gli adesivi / le tempere" ("because mine was done with the felp-tip pens / the biro / the watercolours / the stickers / the tempera colours").

In sum, *Friends* was indeed a challenging sitcom for students/acting-translators, particularly because at this stage they were made aware of the theory that informs their professional practice, and also because they had to bring such theory/practice correlation to bear on the requirements of the Warner Bros. production that demanded a translation of *Friends* 'faithful' to the original, to the point that it appeared as a request for a 'foreignization' process aimed at (imperialistically?) convey a US-marked socio-cultural model with no regard for the possible 'estrangement effect' that the dubbed sitcom may produce on the target audience. In this same line, *Will & Grace* represents another—and even more marked—case of foreignization process that students/dubbing-translators in both Groups A and B eventually had to cope with—as reported in the next section.

6.4 'Culture-based' Humour Patterns in *Will & Grace* Sitcom and their 'Culture-biased' Rendering into Target Scripts

6.4.1 *Socio-cultural dimensions of* Will & Grace *in source and target versions*

The last sitcom to be analyzed in this book is *Will & Grace*, a successful television comedy created by David Kohan and Max Mutchnick and broadcast from 1998 to 2006 on NBC. This was a successful and influential sitcom representing another case of unconventional family unit of thirty-something people, residing on the Upper West Side in New York City at the turn of the century and composed by Will Truman (played by Eric McCormack), a gay attorney, and his flatmate and bosom friend, Grace Adler (played by Debra Messing), a straight, beautiful and self-employed interior designer. Like Rachel Green in *Friends*, also Grace drops her 'conventional family plan' by leaving her fiancé just before their wedding and choosing, instead, to live with Will, her best friend since college (who happens to have just put an end to a long-term relationship with his partner, Michael), with whom she shares the same interests and sense of humour. Their 'affective unit', based on mutual emotional support and reliance, is extended to include their flamboyant friend Jack McFarland (Sean Hayes), another gay young man and struggling stage actor who lives in the flat opposite theirs, and Karen Walker (Megan Mullally), a wealthy, apparently insensitive and alcoholic socialite who becomes Grace's assistant/receptionist at her interior design firm only to keep away from her huge house where her elderly multimillionaire husband lives with his children. Karen can also rely on another long-time friend, her Salvadorian housemaid Rosario, with whom she always has furious squabbles that always end with a hug and the admission of their mutual affection. Eventually, Rosario marries Jack just to gain the 'green card' for US residency, and then divorces from him. Indeed, during their college years, Will and Grace were dating before Will came out with her and, at that time, Grace was deeply disappointed at the revelation of his homosexuality. After a year, however, they reconciled and became best friends till starting a life together in the same apartment as 'non-romantic life partners', in their friends' words, to the point that they even planned to have a child together by resorting to artificial insemination – a plan that Grace upset when she met Leo, a surgeon working with Doctors Without Borders, and married him. Their friendship seemed to have come to an end, but Grace after some time divorced and returned to live with Will, pregnant with Leo's baby. At that stage, Will was in a relationship with Vince and, after a while, they had a child together via a biological mother. Jack, too, has a biological son, Elliot, a teenager conceived through artificial insemination with a lesbian woman. As evident from this emotionally complex plot, this 'new family unit' is quite unusual indeed, and yet it represents a modern way of building unexpected affective relationships that are as strong as conventional family ties.

As for the linguistic construction of such relationships in the sitcom, and the way they were employed to produce a comic effect, it is interesting to notice that humour, in *Will & Grace*, is based on a rapid succession of witty one-liners, as well as on language creativity, also at the morphological level, which often produces metaphorical neologisms that are themselves pun triggers. Notably, most one-liners are in-jokes about gayness that sometimes received a sharp criticism for perpetuating derogatory stereotypes of the gay community—which was also represented as confined to a privileged group of upper-middle class white gay men living in the cosmopolitan area of New York City. In fact, *Will & Grace* was actually a groundbreaking TV programme in the US at the time it was aired because it openly and humorously represented homosexual characters and their issues, which would have been inconceivable only a decade before. However, the way homosexual men were stereotypically portrayed—as classified into the humorously conflicting categories of 'metrosexual gayness', represented by the bourgeois Will, and 'flamboyant campiness', represented by the oddball Jack—is the feature of this sitcom that attracted a large amount of criticism (Gairola 2000). Jack's blatant 'queeniness' represents indeed the primary source of derogatory humour in this sitcom, and this is even more reprehensible when it is prompted by Will's frequent gay in-jokes by which he mocks the ludicrous type of 'queer man like Jack' and, in doing so, he affirms by contrast his 'straight-looking gayness' as the only socially acceptable homosexual condition. Laughing at campiness, therefore, is a disparaging way of inducing humour in this sitcom, based on the identification and derision of the related behavioural and emotional traits connected to this male-gay stereotype. For instance, in the episode to be examined in this section, *Homo for the Holidays*, in which Jack comes out to his mother, she goes over the 'clues' that she failed to notice when Jack was young—such as the fact that he was fond of the nursery rhyme "Rub-a-dub-dub, three men in a tub", which should have suggested her, since then, that Jack was gay. Also the representation of Will's gayness, however, has its drawbacks. He is often portrayed as the stereotype of the gay man as a substitute of the straight woman's best female friend and, furthermore, differently from Grace who dates various boyfriends in the course of the sitcom, Will is seldom seen involved in a romantic relationship (cf. McCauley 1998; Cooper 2003). Nevertheless, despite such shortcomings and the initial suspicion that it was a sitcom about gayness for an audience of straight people, *Will & Grace* gained also the support of GLAAD (Gay and Lesbian Alliance Against Defamation) (Finn 2006), probably because 'some' representation of gayness is always preferable to 'no' representation (Gairola 2000).

Interestingly, the dubbed version for the Italian television reveals the efforts translators made to apply a 'foreignization' approach (Venuti 1994) to the translation of this sitcom, by rendering almost literally syntactic and semantic structures into the target language, but not the socio-cultural implications of most of the jokes concerning gayness—which were, instead, often omitted in Italian, to be substituted with new ones containing totally different meanings. The peculiarity of this choice seems to be justified by a widespread ideological position—still rooted at the time of the first airing of the sitcom in Italy (in 2003) and endorsed by the initial Italian broadcasting network commissioning the dubbing translation (Tele+)—according to which the Italian society was by and large still homophobic enough not to accept the introduction of a controversial 'gay-man schema' in a popular television genre, unless, being a sitcom, such a schema was used to activate a disparagement humour which would guarantee the success of the television series. This means that retaining the general 'foreignization' approach to translation, and 'domesticating' only an otherwise morally reprehensible subject like homosexuality, would have given Italian audiences the impression that such socially and ethically unacceptable behaviour was part of a foreign culture. On the other hand, reducing the sitcom 'gay-man schema' to the assumed expectations of the target culture would have facilitated translators in their attempts to readapt it to the moral standards of the implicit Italian receivers, who were expected to appreciate a 'revised' version of this sitcom humour. To satisfy the socio-cultural needs of the target audience is in fact the objective of an influential trend in Translation Studies represented by scholars such as Lefevere and Bassnett (1990). The problematic point in this approach, however, is that there is no attempt whatsoever at questioning the authority of the people who actually ascribe to themselves the power of establishing the socio-cultural and moral 'requirements' of the implied target audience. Indeed, this approach seems to justify a complex ideological and marketing strategy which, far from accounting for the real 'requirements' of target audiences, actually imposes pre-defined socio-cultural and moral behaviours upon them. This approach has been definitely applied to the Italian dubbing translation of *Will & Grace* and, specifically, to its misrepresentation of the original 'gay-man schema', central to this sitcom, in the target language and culture. Just to remain within the context of the episode selected for the analysis in this section—namely, *Homo for the Holidays* (in Italian, *Gay per caso*)—it is possible to notice that although the whole script is constructed on a series of puns having as a target Jack and his campiness, the Italian version transforms them into a moral condemnation of homosexual behaviours. In this way, translation strengthens, through a defamatory disparagement, the implied homophobic stances of the target audiences who would thus be easily prompted to laugh at what they would deem socially and morally unacceptable. A case in point in this episode is represented by Grace's witty remarks at Jack's behaviour. For instance, Jack's overemotional negative reaction at the news that his mother was coming over is sharply described by Grace through the following one-liner: "I don't think I've seen him so upset since they hired a female urologist at the free clinic". Incredibly, this remark was mistranslated into Italian as: "Non l'ho più visto così da quando licenziarono il suo amico urologo per molestie" ("I've never seen him like this since they fired his [male] urologist friend for sexual harassment"). This derogatory mistranslation cannot be justified with any of the strategies of idiom/pun translation outlined in *6.3.1* (Delabastita 1996; Veisbergs 1997) because is it just a gratuitous homophobic attack at the 'gay-man schema' associated with a notion of a morally corrupted male-gay specialist (the "urologist") liable of harassing his male patients and justified by Jack who is disappointed for his friend's dismissal precisely because of this immoral behaviour. In the original version, instead, Grace's covert allusion was simply to Jack's taking pleasure in having a medical examination by a male urologist (who, nevertheless, may have been totally unaware of Jack's private enjoyment), which consequently justifies her overt reference to Jack's disappointment when a female urologist was instead hired at the clinic he used to go for an urological check up. Another comment by Grace in the same episode represents an instance of this type of humorous disparagement targeting gayness. When Jack claims that he cannot come out to his mother because, as he says to Will, "I don't have the same relationship with my mother as you do with yours", Grace intervenes by asking impertinently: "You never picked out her brassieres?", to which Will retorts: "We don't need that, thank you". Grace, with her cheeky remark, refers to the stereotype of the gay boy enjoying choosing clothes for his mother, underwear included. In the Italian translation, Grace's joke is mistranslated into an attack against campiness disparagingly associated with transvestism, as she is made to say: "Non ti sei mai messo I suoi vestiti?" ("Have you never worn her clothes?"), omitting the reference to mother's "brassieres" as a son associating his mother with her sexy lingerie is still considered an Oedipal taboo in Italy, however gay a son may be. One more quip said by Grace in this same episode went outrageously mistranslated into Italian. As Karen expresses her amazement at the fact that Judith, Jack's mother, does not know that her son is gay (*Karen:* How could she not know? What is she, headless?"), Grace replies: "I guess you believe what you choose to believe. One time, Judith caught him in bed with a guy, and Jack convinced her that they were doing a school check for lice". This naïve justification said by a gay schoolboy caught in the—unequivocal—act by his mother is appallingly transformed in Italian from "a school check for lice" into "a school check for AIDS", thus perpetuating the abusive stereotype of male gayness directly connected with AIDS contagion: *Grace:* "Io penso che ognuno veda ciò che vuole vedere. Un giorno Judith lo vide a letto con un ragazzo e Jack le disse che quella era una ricerca di scuola sull'AIDS." ("I guess one sees what one wants to see. One day Judith caught him in bed with a boy and Jack told her that it was a school research on AIDS"). As evident, whereas the original sentence-structure is respected according to the 'foreignization' approach overall adopted in this sitcom to render the characters' speech style, the actual pun about gayness has been completely modified to appeal to the target audience's need for strengthening their prejudices against homosexuality by disparagingly laughing at it. There are other instances of this type throughout this same episode and some of them shall be analyzed in the extract to be examined later in this section. What is interesting to point out now is instead another peculiarity of the language of this sitcom - namely, its creativity as a source of humour and the difficulty in rendering it into Italian.

Indeed, the creation of neologisms, as well as of new pragmatic ways of expressing taboo concepts, or talking about controversial issues—mostly regarding homosexuality—represents one of the innovative qualities of the language of this sitcom. A remarkable case in point is represented by the invention of the verb "to spramp" in the episode entitled *Secrets and Lays*, the title itself being a distortion of the title of a famous movie, *Secrets and Lies*, to create a pun played on the assonance "lies"/"lays" (the latter meant as a vulgar synonym of 'sexual intercourse'). In the third scene of this episode, Grace, Will and Jack are playing Scrabble at Karen's home, and Jack comes out with a invented word contending that it does instead exist:

> *Will:* Jack, that's not a word.
> *Jack:* Uh, yeah, it is.
> *Will:* Use it in a sentence.
> *Jack:* Every morning I... spramp my face with cold water. *(Makes a splash motion with his hands.)*
> *Will:* "Spramp" your face? What the hell is that?
> *Jack:* Yeah, spramp. Spramp! The bubbles from a jacuzzi spramp up. Note how the sea spramps off the jagged rocks.
> *Will:* Just 'cause you do this, *(mimicking Jack's "spramp" motion)* doesn't make it a word.
> *Karen:* I don't know, Will. Before I go to bed, I like to spramp on a little Gardenia for Stan.
> *Will:* No, you don't. You do not spramp, because no one has ever spramped

anything in the history of language.
Jack: What a carpouche.

Creativity, in the case of "spramp", is the result of a complex linguistic operation that, in natural morphology (cf. Dressler 1988), can be described as an application of specific 'economy parameters' that can justify on pragmatic grounds the natural cline of categoriality (Heine *et al.* 1991)—from a major category (noun/verb) to middle (adverb/preposition) up to minor categories (clitic/affix) in grammaticalization processes —insofar as they trigger in language-users, over time, abductive procedures of rule change (reanalysis) and meaning change (analogy) (Langacker 1977) according to strategies of minimal mental effort and simplicity of perception and production based on the cooperative principle (Grice 1975). "Spramp" is the result of an original phrasal/prepositional verb, "spray up", that went through the cliticization of the prepositional/adverbial particle to form a compact accentual unit, with the particle reduced to a suffix to which an additional inflectional suffix is also attached, as in "spramp*ed*" (parameter 1: maximization of efficiency via minimal morphonemic differentiation, cf. Zwicky 1985). The cliticization process is assumed to have developed first by keeping the semantic contribution of each part of the phrasal-verb compound clear by developing a host+suffix construction of an agglutinative type, so as to enhance ease of articulation and reception processing – namely, "spray-up" (parameter 2: maximization of effectiveness via morphosemantic and morphotactic transparency, cf. Dressler 1988). Then, a reduced speech signal have developed by means of increasing morphologization of the phrasal-verb compound and the bleaching of its particle – namely, "spray-up" → "spray-p" → "spramp" (Sweetser 1988), so as to enhance brevity in spoken discourse (parameter 3: maximization of informativeness via weakening of semantic content – i.e., from concrete to abstract meanings, cf. Talmy 1983). In this process, probably another verb has been introduced in the compound justifying the presence of an /m/ sound merged with the other labial /p/-sound—i.e., "smear"—introduced by Karen when she mimes the action of 'smearing' her face with a Gardenia cream. Once created, the novel verb "spramp" has become the basis of a new phrasal verb, namely, "spramp up" (cf. Guido 2008b) as Jack makes a splash motion with his hands from an imaginary sink 'up' to his face. As evident, linguistic creativity in this special case has followed precisely the 'economy parameters' spontaneously occurring in natural morphology. In the dubbing translation for the Italian TV, this neologism has been translated into the verb "sprempare" which does not attempt in the least to reproduce the cliticization process assumed in the original neologism. Group-A students/acting-translators, instead, produced their alternative neologism by grounding their search for metaphorical and morphological equivalence on the above outlined cognitive-experiential theories of natural morphology. Their newly created word was "susprargere", which includes the preposition "su" ("up"), the English loanword "spray", and the verb "cospargere" ("to smear"). There is also another instance of linguistic creativity in the above-reported exchange, represented by Jack's invented adjective with which he blames Will as being a nuisance: "What a carpouche"—from "to carp" meaning "to keep complaining about something in an annoying way", unaccountably translated into Italian as "guastabrizzone", where only the first part of the word has a meaning "guasta-" ("spoil") probably associated with the noun "guastafeste" ("spoilsport").

Another peculiarity of the language of this sitcom is represented by the complex structure of conversation turns, built on a series of Pre-Head and Post-Head Acts (pre-modifying and post-modifying a statement), aimed at justifying the introduction of problematic issues that arouse tension, and to facilitate a negotiation that leads to acceptance and relief in an Arousal/Safety pattern of humour. A case in point can be found precisely in the extract to be soon analyzed, focused on the central part of a Revelation plot when Jack comes out to his mother telling her that he is gay. Yet, he does not reveal his secret immediately, but after a series of conversation acts which mark an introductory pre-modification as a Negotiation move, the 'statement of offence', and the crucial 'Apology Head Act':

> *Pre-modification:*
> Mom, *[Appeal]*
> I have something to say to you *[Topic Introducer]*
> I have kept this from you for a long time, and that's wrong, because it makes it seem like I'm shamed of something I'm not shamed of. I want you to know who I am because I'm proud of who I am. *[Forewarns]*
> *Statement of the Offence:*
> Mom, *[Appeal]*
> I'm gay. *[Topic Introducer]*
> *Apology:*
> Mom, *[Appeal]*
> I'm sorry to disappoint you *[Head Act]*
> *Post-modification:*
> but this is who I am.

The Revelation plot in the episode *Homo for the Holidays*, from which the extract under analysis is taken, occurs after an introductory part where it becomes clear that Jack's mother, Judith, is not aware of her son's homosexuality. To please her, in fact, Jack has even made her believe that he had an affair with Grace, now over (but Grace, disappointed at having being dumped—even in such an imaginary situation—tells Judith that Jack has come back to her). This situation of tension is part of an overall comedy structure shared by the five sitcoms analyzed in this book, consisting in the uncompromising conflict between parents and children, two generations that are assumed to represent two different notions of family, namely, the traditional one based on family relationships hierarchically organized according to a strict set of values and roles, and the novel one based on bonds of affection and friendship that prevail over family ties even when these are also involved (as in the case with Ross and Monica in *Friends*). Such new and atypical 'family units' and that become indispensable for young people, uprooted from their original family, who have to find in themselves and in their group of friends the strength and confidence to define their own identity in order to cope with the frantic and confusing life in an American metropolis such as New York City. Such dynamic conflict between generations in these sitcoms is mediated by humour, principally of Arousal/Safety and Disparagement types. As a socio-cognitive and linguistic strategy, humour in sitcoms implies a dialogic pattern in which a character's judgement of another character represents a source of socio-cultural tension, followed by a sense of relief at the realization that the character who was assumed to be dangerous is actually innocuous (Guido 1997). The nature of such a conflict is therefore of an affective kind, reflected in the Challenge/Negotiation dynamics in all the sitcom scripts selected for the analysis in this book, which are all characterized by tense parents-children relationships in the framework of a Revelation plot. This is evident in the analyzed extracts from *The Nanny* (where Fran inadvertently reveals to her mother her indecision about marrying a rich suitor), *Roseanne* (where the teenage Darlene reveals to her parents that she is pregnant), *Friends* (where Joey reveals to Chandler that he intends to leave the apartment they share, Monica reveals to her mother she dates an elderly friend of her parents, and Phoebe reveals to Rachel that she did not have the tattoo done as they agreed), and in the extract from *Will & Grace* to be analyzed (where Jack reveal his homosexuality to his mother and she reveals her secret to Jack). The only exception among them seems to be the analyzed extract from *Dharma & Greg*, despite the fact that the whole sitcom is based on the conflicting parents/children relationships, but even there a Revelation plot is present when Judge Harper (a fatherly figure for Greg) reveals his identity to Dharma and Greg who, in their turn, refuse to reveal theirs to him.

6.4.2 *Tagged data and their comparative analysis*

In the extract from *Will & Grace* to be analyzed at this point, Jack's challenge to his mother's assumed refusal to acknowledge his gayness is mediated by his attempts at negotiating her acceptance. Then, unexpectedly, their positions are reversed as Jack's mother eventually tries to negotiate her son's acceptance of her challenging secret. In the analysis that follows, the complex interplay of conversation acts that build the Arousal/Safety/Disparagement humour of this exchange will be explored in parallel with its dubbing translation for the Italian television in order to enquire into the equivalence choices made by the translator in rendering humorous puns, idioms and cultural references into the target language so as to produce a parallel comic effect on the target audience. The enquiry will focus on the pattern of Acts (A) of *Pre-Head, Head,* or *Post-Head* types, marked for Arousal *(A)*, Safety *(S)*, or Disparagement *(D)* humour triggers to investigate the negotiation dynamics in stressful interpersonal discourse.

Will & Grace episode #2.08 *Homo for the Holidays*
(Gay per caso - Gay by chance)

Original English version:	***Italian dubbing translation:***	***Back-translation into Standard English:***
[Will's apartment]	**[Appartamento di Will]**	**[Will's apartment]**
[1] **JACK:** Mom? **[Bid A*(A)* *Head*]**	*[1]* **JACK:** Mamma? **[Bid A*(A)* *Head*]**	*[1]* **JACK:** Mom?
[2] **JUDITH: [a]** Jack ... **[b]** honey, **[c]** I'm worried. **[d]** You haven't said a thing about my bangs. **[a. Bid A*(A) Pre-Head* + b. Upgrade A*(A) Pre-Head* + c. Informative A*(A) Pre-Head* + d. Elicit A*(A) Head*]**	*[2]* **JUDITH: [a]** Jack, **[b]** tesoro, **[c]** sono preoccupata. **[d]** Non hai ancora detto una parola sui miei capelli. . **[a. Bid A*(A) Pre-Head* + b. Upgrade A*(A) Pre-Head* + c. Informative A*(A) Pre-Head* + d. Elicit A*(A) Head*]**	*[2]* **JUDITH:** Jack, darling, I'm worried. You haven't yet said a word about my hair.
[3] **JACK: [a]** They're a little short, **[b]** but they'll grow in. **[c]** Mom, **[d]** I have something I want to say to you. **[e]** I've kept this from you for a long time, **[f]** and that's wrong **[g]** because it makes seem like I'm shamed of something I'm not shamed of. **[h]** I want you to know who I am **[i]** because I'm proud of who I am. **[j]** Mom ... **[k]** are you wearing Chloe? **[a. Evaluate A*(S) Head* + b. Upgrade A*(S) Post-Head* + c. Bid A*(A) Pre-Head* + d. Starter A*(A) Pre-Head* + e. Blame A*(A) Pre-Head* + f. Evaluate A*(A) Pre-Head* + g. Comment A*(A) Pre-Head* + h. Negotiate A*(A) Pre-Head* + i. Upgrade A*(A) Pre-Head* + j. Bid A*(A) Pre-Head* + k. Check A*(A) Pre-Head*]**	*[3]* **JACK: [a]** Sono un po' corti, **[b]** ma cresceranno. **[c]** Mamma, **[d]** devo dirti una cosa, **[e]** mettiti seduta. **[f]** Io te l'ho tenuto nascosto per molto tempo **[g]** e questo è un errore **[h]** perché così sembra che mi vergogni di qualcosa, **[i]** mentre non è affatto così. **[j]** Io voglio che tu sappia chi sono **[k]** perché sono orgoglioso di essere come sono. **[l]** Mamma ... **[m]** è un profumo alla rosa? **[a. Evaluate A*(S) Head* + b. Upgrade A*(S) Post-Head* + c. Bid A*(A) Pre-Head* + d. Starter A*(A) Pre-Head* + e. Directive A*(A) Pre-Head* + f. Blame A*(A) Pre-Head* + g. Evaluate A*(A) Pre-Head* + h. Comment A*(A) Pre-Head* + i. Upgrade A*(A) Pre-Head* + j. Negotiate A*(A) Pre-Head* + k. Upgrade A*(A) Pre-Head* + l. Bid A*(A) Pre-Head* + m. Check A*(A) Pre-Head*]**	*[3]* **JACK:** It's a little short, but it'll grow in. Mom, I must tell you something, sit down. I've kept this hidden from you for a long time, and that's a mistake because it makes seem like I'm shamed of something, whereas it's not at all so. I want you to know who I am because I'm proud of being the way I am. Mom ... is it a scent of rose?
[4] **WILL:** Jack. **[Prompt A*(A)* *Head*]**	*[4]* **WILL:** Jack. **[Prompt A*(A)* *Head*]**	*[4]* **WILL:** Jack.
[5] **JACK: [a]** Mom, **[b]** I'm gay. **[a. Bid A*(A) Pre-Head* + b.**	*[5]* **JACK: [a]** Mamma, **[b]** sono gay. **[a. Bid A*(A) Pre-Head* + b.**	*[5]* **JACK:** Mom, I'm gay.

[6] **JUDITH:** Oh! **[React A*(A)* *Head*]**	*[6]* **JUDITH:** Oh! **[React A*(A)* *Head*]**	*[6]* **JUDITH:** Oh!
[7] **GRACE: [a]** Judith *(Grace puts her arm around Judith)* **[b]** It's ok. **[c]** So he's gay. **[d]** He's still the same little boy who gave you highlights for the first time. **[a. Bid A*(S)* *Pre-Head* + b. Evaluate A*(S)* *Pre-Head* + c. Acknowledge A*(S)* *Head* + d. Negotiate A*(D)* *Post-Head*]**	*[7]* **GRACE: [a]** Judith *(Grace mette un braccio attorno a Judith)* **[b]** non è cambiato niente. **[c]** È così, **[d]** lui è gay. **[e]** Resta lo stesso ragazzo buono che ti ha fatto i colpi di sole la prima volta. **[a. Bid A*(S)* *Pre-Head* + b. Evaluate A*(S)* *Pre-Head* + c. Acknowledge A*(S)* *Pre-Head* + d. Upgrade A*(S)* *Head* + Negotiate A*(D)* *Post-Head*]**	*[7]* **GRACE:** Judith *(Grace puts her arm around Judith)* nothing has changed. It's so, he's gay. He's still the same good boy who gave you highlights for the first time.
[8] **KAREN: [a]** I think you are missing the silver lining here. **[b]** When you're old and in diapers, **[c]** a gay son will know how to keep you away from chiffon and backlighting. **[a. Evaluate A*(D)* *Pre-Head* + b. Blame A*(D)* *Pre-Head* + c. Negotiate A*(D)* *Head*]**	*[8]* **KAREN: [a]** Tesoro, **[b]** hai perso di vista l'aspetto migliore. **[c]** Quando sei vecchia e depressa **[d]** un figlio gay sa come impedirti di farti fare questo color cenere e sbagliare taglio, **[e]** povera cara. **[a. Bid A*(S)* *Pre-Head* + b. Evaluate A*(D)* *Pre-Head* + c. Blame A*(D)* *Pre-Head* + d. Negotiate A*(D)* *Head* + e. Evaluate A*(D)* *Post-Head*]**	*[8]* **KAREN:** Darling, I think you've missed the best aspect. When you're old and depressed, a gay son will know how to keep you away from having this ashen hue done and getting a haircut wrong, poor thing.
[9] **JACK: [a]** Mom, **[b]** I'm sorry to disappoint you, **[c]** but ... this is who I am. **[a. Bid A*(A)* *Pre-Head* + b. Apologize A*(A)* *Head* + c. Negotiate A*(A)* *Post-Head*]**	*[9]* **JACK: [a]** Mamma, **[b]** mi dispiace di averti delusa, **[c]** io sono come sono. **[a. Bid A*(A)* *Pre-Head* + b. Apologize A*(A)* *Head* + c. Negotiate A*(A)* *Post-Head*]**	*[9]* **JACK:** Mom, I'm sorry to disappoint you, I am as I am.
[10] **JUDITH: [a]** You could never disappoint me. **[b]** I just want you to be happy. **[c]** Looking back on it... there have been clues. **[d]** When you were a child, you were overly fond of the nursery rhyme "Rub-a-dub-dub, three men in a tub". **[e]** And you do have a lot of flamboyantly gay friends. **[f]** I mean, look at Will. **[g]** No matter what, Jack... **[h]** You're what I'm most thankful in the whole world. *(Judith and Jack hug. Will, Grace, and Karen start leaving to give them privacy).* **[a. Evaluate A*(S)* *Head* + b. Directive A*(S)* *Post-Head* + c. Informative A*(D)* *Pre-Head* + d. Clue A*(D)* *Head* + e. Upgrade A*(D)* *Post-Head* + f. Evaluate A*(A)* *Head* + g. Negotiate A*(S)* *Pre-Head* + h. Evaluate A*(S)* *Head*]**	*[10]* **JUDITH: [a]** Tu non potrai mai deludermi. **[b]** Io ti vorrò sempre bene. **[c]** Ripensandoci, qualche indizio c'era. **[d]** Quando tu eri piccolo ti piaceva troppo quella filastrocca in rima "Barattò la pappa per tre uomini e una cappa". **[e]** E hai sempre avuto una quantità di favolosi gay tra i tuoi amici, **[f]** insomma, guarda quello! *(indica Will)* **[g]** A me non importa, Jack. **[h]** Tu sei la cosa per cui io mi sento grata al mondo intero. *(Judith e Jack si abbracciano. Will, Grace e Karen si accingono ad andar via per lasciarli da soli).* **[a. Evaluate A*(S)* *Head* + b. Negotiate A*(S)* *Post-Head* + c. Informative A*(D)* *Pre-Head* + d. Clue A*(D)* *Head* + e. Upgrade A*(D)* *Post-Head* + f. Evaluate A*(A)* *Head* + g. Negotiate A*(S)* *Pre-Head* + h. Evaluate A*(S)* *Head*]**	*[10]* **JUDITH:** You could never disappoint me. I will always love you. Looking back on it, there has been some clue. When you were a child, you were overly fond of the nursery rhyme "He swapped the pap for three men and a cap". And you have always had a lot of fabulous gay guys among your friends, well, look at him! *(she indicates Will).* I don't mind, Jack. You're what I'm most thankful in the whole world. *(Judith and Jack hug. Will, Grace, and Karen start leaving to give them privacy).*
[11] **JACK:** Why are you crying? **[Elicitation A*(A)* *Head*]**	*[11]* **JACK:** E perché piangi? **[Elicitation A*(A)* *Head*]**	*[11]* **JACK:** And why are you crying?
[12] **JUDITH: [a]** Because I have a secret too. *(Will, Grace, and Karen turn around).* **[b]** The man	*[12]* **JUDITH: [a]** Perché adesso mi tocca dire il mio segreto! *(Will Grace e Karen tornano*	*[12]* **JUDITH:** Because now it falls to me to reveal my secret! *(Will, Grace, and Karen turn*

you think is your father ... **[c]** is not your father. **[a. Informative A*(A) Head* + b. Negotiate A*(A) Pre-Head* + c. Revelation A*(D) Head*]**	*indietro)* **[b]** L'uomo che tu credi sia tuo padre ... **[c]** non è tuo padre! **[a. Informative A*(A) Head* + b. Negotiate A*(A) Pre-Head* + c. Revelation A*(D) Head*]**	*around).* The man you think is your father ... is not your father.
***[13]* JACK:** What? **[Loop A*(A) Head*]**	***[13]* JACK:** Cosa? **[Loop A*(A) Head*]**	***[13]* JACK:** What?
***[14]* WILL: [a]** My god, **[b]** this is like watching *Gays of Our Lives.* **[a. React A*(A) Pre-Head* + b. Blame A*(D) Head*]**	***[14]* WILL: [a]** Oh mio Dio, **[b]** è peggio che guardare *Beautiful.* **[a. React A*(A) Pre-Head* + b. Blame A*(D) Head*]**	***[14]* WILL:** Oh My god, this is worse than watching *The Bold and the Beautiful.*
***[15]* JACK:** Who's my father? **[Elicitation A*(A) Head*]**	***[15]* JACK:** E chi è mio padre? **[Elicitation A*(A) Head*]**	***[15]* JACK:** And who's my father?
***[16]* JUDITH: [a]** Well ... **[b]** it's not exactly clear. **[a. Starter A*(A) Pre-Head* + b. Negotiate A*(A) Head*]**	***[16]* JUDITH: [a]** Bé ... **[b]** non è che sia così chiaro. **[a. Starter A*(A) Pre-Head* + b. Negotiate A*(A) Head*]**	***[16]* JUDITH:** Well ... it's not exactly so clear.
***[17]* JACK: [a]** Mother, **[b]** if your explanation doesn't end with the phrase "born in a manger", **[c]** I'm gonna be violently ill. **[a. Bid A*(A) Pre-Head* + b. Challenge A*(D) Pre-Head* + c. Upgrade A*(A) Head*]**	***[17]* JACK: [a]** Madre, **[b]** se la tua spiegazione non termina con "nato in una mangiatoia" **[c]** mi verrà un attacco di bile! **[a. Bid A*(A) Pre-Head* + b. Challenge A*(D) Pre-Head* + c. Upgrade A*(A) Head*]**	***[17]* JACK:** Mother, if your explanation doesn't end with "born in a manager", I'm gonna have a rage attack.
***[18]* JUDITH: [a]** It was the sixties! **[b]** I went to this party. **[c]** Keys were thrown in a bowl, **[d]** the bowl was thrown in the pool, **[e]** off came the ponchos, **[f]** and nine months later ... **[g]** there you were. **[a. Starter A*(A) Pre-Head* + b. Informative A*(A) Head* + c. Clue A*(A) Pre-Head* + d. Upgrade A*(A) Pre-Head* + e. Upgrade A*(A) Pre-Head* + f. Upgrade A*(A) Head* + g. Revelation A*(A) Head*]**	***[18]* JUDITH: [a]** Erano gli anni Sessanta! **[b]** Andai in uno di quei party, **[c]** le chiavi delle stanze furono buttate in piscina, **[d]** fuori si spensero le luci **[e]** e nove mesi più tardi ... **[f]** arrivasti tu, **[g]** tesoro. **[a. Starter A*(A) Pre-Head* + b. Informative A*(A) Head* + c. Clue A*(A) Pre-Head* + d. Upgrade A*(A) Pre-Head* + e. Upgrade A*(A) Pre-Head* + f. Revelation A*(A) Head* + g. Negotiation A*(A) Post-Head*]**	***[18]* JUDITH:** It was the sixties! I went to one of those parties, room keys were thrown in the swimming pool, lights were turned off, and nine months later ... you arrived, darling.
***[19]* JACK: [a]** Oh. Ok. Uhh ... **[b]** I can accept that. **[c]** So ... **[d]** the guy I thought was my dad ... **[e]** wasn't. **[f]** *(Jack faints).* **[a. React A*(A) Pre-Head* + b. Acknowledge A*(A) Head* + c. Marker A*(A) Pre-Head* + d. Check A*(A) Pre-Head* + e. Blame A*(D) Head* + f. React A*(A) Post-Head*]**	***[19]* JACK: [a]** Oh. Oh. Ok. **[b]** Io posso accettare quest—a ... **[c]** L'uomo che pensavo fosse mio padre ... **[d]** non lo è. **[e]** *(Jack sviene).* **[a. React A*(A) Pre-Head* + b. Acknowledge A*(A) Head* + c. Check A*(A) Pre-Head* + d. Blame A*(D) Head* + e. React A*(A) Post-Head*]**	***19]* JACK:** Oh. Oh. Ok. I can accept thi-s ... The man I thought was my dad ... is not. *(Jack faints).*
***[20]* KAREN: [a]** So Jack's gay, huh? *(To Grace)* **[b]** Hmm. No wonder he went back to you. **[a. Acknowledge A*(A) Pre-Head* + b. Blame A*(D) Head*]**	***[20]* KAREN: [a]** Insomma, Jack è gay, eh? *(rivolgendosi a Grace)* **[b]** mmm, ecco perché era tornato da te, **[c]** cara. **[a. Acknowledge A*(A) Pre-Head* + b. Blame A*(D) Head* + c. Upgrade A*(D) Post-Head*]**	***[20]* KAREN:** So Jack's gay, huh? *(To Grace)* Hmm. That's why he went back to you, dear.

This extract represents an interesting instance of Revelation plot constructed according to an Arousal/Safety pattern of humour which focuses initially on the difficulty of a son in disclosing his secret to his mother and, soon afterwards, on an unexpected reversal of the traditional parents/children relationship with the mother finding it difficult to reveal her own secret to her son. The exchange under analysis, begins with Jack who, in turn [1], tries to attract her mother's attention with a Bid Head Act by calling her and trying to start a discourse, signalling a state of tension. Judith, his mother, however, in her turn [2], immediately interrupts him with another Bid Pre-Head Act, calling him by name and, then, adding an Upgrade Pre-Head Act which addresses him with the 'sweet' appellative "honey". Then Judith goes on with a further Pre-Head Act, still hesitating before introducing her request, and informing her son instead that she is "worried". Finally, she discloses the futile reason for her worry through an Elicit Head Act, indirectly requesting a judgement from her son under the form of a frivolous charge against him: "You haven't said a thing about my bangs". The dubbing translation for the Italian TV is faithful to the original, but for the rendering of "bangs" into the more general "capelli" ("hair"). Jack, in turn [3], patiently replies with an Evaluate Head Act offering his judgement ("They are a little short"), immediately softened by an Upgrade Post-Head Act introduced by an adversative ("but they'll grow in") meant to indulge her whims and to introduce a sense of relief. Then, with another Bid Pre-Head Act by which he addresses his mother ("Mom"), Jack reintroduces the state of tension, strengthened by a Starter Pre-Head Act by which he announces that he has something to say, but he also tries to delay the moment of revelation ("I have something I want to say to you"). This moment is postponed even further with the next Blame Pre-Head Act ("I've kept this from you for a long time"), a self-condemnation which is intensified by the negative Evaluate Pre-Head Act that follows ("and that's wrong"), by which he expresses his disapproval for his keeping this secret undisclosed, but also still delays the revelation moment and increases the sense of tension and alarm in his mother. In the Italian version, there is even the introduction of an extra Directive pre-Head Act by which Jack tells his mother to sit down by using an imperative – and Judith, in fact, at this point in the movie is actually sitting down, yet unprompted. Rather than introducing his revelation at this stage, Jack instead goes on with a series of Pre-Head Acts to avoid coming to the crucial point and, in doing so, he builds up the Arousal pattern of this exchange. He, thus, introduces a Comment Pre-Head Act to explain why he was wrong ("because it makes seem like I'm shamed of something I'm not shamed of"), which in Italian is emphasized by the addition of the adversative "mentre" ("whereas") marking a new Upgrade Pre-Head Act in a stilted Italian, inappropriate to an informal spoken discourse ("mentre non è affatto così"—whereas it's not at all so"). Then, Jack attempts some sort of mediation with a Negotiate Pre-Head Act directly appealing to his mother as a confidant ("I want you to know who I am"), to add soon afterwards another Upgrade Pre-Head Act ("because I'm proud of who I am")—this last expression mistranslated into Italian as "perché sono orgoglioso di essere come sono" ("because I'm proud of being the way I am"), as if being gay is not 'who one is', but simply 'a way of being', namely, an attitude, or a behaviour, a reversible process, not a matter of identity bound to an innate human condition. At this point, in this long and complex turn [3], Jack seems to be ready to disclose his secret and, through a Bid Pre-Head Act ("Mom") he tries once again to have his mother focus her attention on what he is going to tell her. Yet, despite the climax of tension anticipating the expected revelation, Jack unpredictably provides an anticlimax with the introduction of a Check Pre-Head Act aimed at distracting her mother, in the hope of avoiding his coming out ("are you wearing Chloe?")—translated into Italian by avoiding the reference to the perfume brand ("è un profumo alla rosa?" – "is it a scent of rose?").

It is Will's task, now, in turn [4], to redirect his friend's discourse to the topic of the exchange by means of a Prompt Head Act ("Jack"). This time Jack, in turn [5] straightforwardly comes to the point: after another Bid Pre-Head Act addressing his mother, he declares through a Revelation Head Act: "I'm gay". Tension is particularly high at this point as everybody is waiting for Judith's reaction at Jack's revelation. And, indeed, its effect on Judith seems devastating as she simply replies with the React Head Act "Oh". Grace, therefore, in turn [7], soon intervenes with a Bid Pre-Head Act addressing Judith by her name, putting her arm around her, and trying to console her by reassuring, with a positive Evaluate Pre-Head Act, that "it's ok", and with an Acknowledge Head Act that "so he's gay", aimed at relieving tension. In the Italian version, these two short clauses uttered by Grace have been enlarged to become three ones that, apart the lack of time/lip-synchronization, actually modify the implied meaning of what she was meant to say. In fact Grace in Italian is made to say: "non è cambiato niente. E' così, lui è gay" ("nothing has changed. It's so, he's gay"), superficially minimizing the emotional impact of Jack's revelation on his mother. Then Grace, in the original version, with a Negotiate Head Act goes on attempting a mediation with Judith, reminding her of moments of serenity with his son when he was a young boy, not without a touch of disparagement as the recalled event regards a young gay Jack that Grace depicts as "he's the same little boy who gave you highlights for the first time"—hence, a little boy already doing 'campy things'. The Italian translation is only apparently faithful to the original, in fact the change in an adjective referred to Jack makes a crucial difference. Grace, in the Italian version is made to say: "Resta lo stesso ragazzo buono" ("He's still the same good boy"), rather than "little boy" which, in the original version, refers to an early age. This entails that Grace, in the Italian version, is passing a derogatory view of a gay person as generally perceived as 'wicked' and 'nasty', whereas Jack—as she is made to claim—despite his being gay, is still "good".

Karen with her harsh humour strengthens even more such derogatory stances on gay men as she, in turn [8], with an Evaluate Pre-Head Act illustrates to Judith the advantages of having a gay son when a mother gets old. Hence, Karen makes her disparaging reference more specific by addressing Judith directly through a Blame Pre-Head Act: "When you're old and in diapers"—rendered into Italian by the less caustic denigration: "Quando sei vecchia e depressa" ("When you're old and depressed"). Then, she completes her comment with a Negotiate Head Act sarcastically aimed at making Judith see her luck at having a gay son: "a gay son will know how to keep you away from chiffon and backlighting". The Italian version of this Act is simply centred on the ability of a gay son to prevent an elderly mother from having her hair tastelessly dyed. However, as a whole, this turn contains the addition of two apparently sympathetic appellatives—"Tesoro" ("Darling"), at the beginning, and "povera cara" ("poor thing"), at the end—which compensate for the original perception of a pathetic Judith as Karen's object of derision. Jack at this point intervenes in turn [9] and, with his Bid Pre-Head Act, addresses directly his mother ("Mom") to introduce an Apologize Head Act ("I'm sorry to disappoint you"), followed by an attempt to make himself accepted by means of a Negotiate Post-Head Act ("but ... this is who I am"). This Act was rendered into Italian by resorting to the same prejudice introduced in turn [3] ("io sono come sono" – "I am as I am"), namely, the notion—assumed to be shared by the Italian audience—that being gay is not a matter of identity, but of attitude. Unexpectedly, in turn [10], Judith replies with a straightforward positive Evaluate Head Act referred to her son ("You could never disappoint me") introducing a sense of relief strengthened by a Directive Post-Head Act ("I just want you to be happy"), inappropriately rendered into Italian as a Negotiate Post-Head Act "Io ti vorrò sempre bene" ("I will always love you"). Differently from the corresponding original Act centred on Jack because his mother wants to see him happy with 'who he is', the translated version focused instead on Judith condescendingly disposed to love her son 'despite the way he is'. Then, however, Judith changes her tone of voice and, with an Informative Pre-Head Act, introduces her recollections of the time when Jack was young and she missed some 'clues' that now she can interpret correctly—if not disparagingly. One of them is reported in the next Clue Head Act, when Jack, as a child, was "overtly fond of the nursery rhyme 'Rub-a-dub-dub, three men in a tub'"—rendered into Italian by substituting it with another almost equivalent one, namely: "Barattò la pappa per tre uomini e una cappa" ("He swapped the pap for three men and a cap"). Such a recollection is then enhanced by an Upgrade Post-Head Act in which Judith makes a covert derogatory reference to Jack's 'campy' friends ("And you do have a lot of flamboyantly gay friends"), to focus specifically on Will with an implicitly negative Evaluate Head Act ("I mean, look at Will")—more disparagingly rendered into Italian as "insomma, guarda quello!" ("well, look at him!"), as she indicates Will by omitting his name, which makes Will become an instance of a category (the 'flamboyant gays') rather than a person with a name and identity. Finally, Judith comes to a conclusion with a Negotiate Pre-Head Act in which she dismissed any possible reservation ("No matter what, Jack...")—rendered into Italian as a first-person remark ("A me non importa, Jack" – "I don't mind, Jack")—and then, almost incongruously with what she has been saying so far, she declares emphatically with a positive Evaluate Head Act "You're what I'm most thankful in the whole world", introducing a Safety pattern of humour as she hugs her son, while Will, Grace and Karen start leaving to give them privacy.

But then Judith starts crying, which makes Jack, in turn [11], wonder about what the matter may be with her by using an Elicitation Head Act ("Why are you crying?"). In turn [12], Judith candidly declares, by means of an Informative Head Act: "because I have a secret too" thus triggering again a state of maximum tension. In the Italian translation, Judith feels, as it were, 'obliged' to reciprocate the confidence, which is absent in the original ("Perché adesso mi tocca dire il mio segreto!" – "Because now it falls to me to reveal my secret!"). This makes Will, Grace and Karen turn around as they are curious to know more about that. Judith, therefore, goes on with a Negotiate Pre-Head Act introducing the disclosure of the secret: "The man you think is your father..." to conclude with the Revelation Head Act: "is not your father". Jack's reaction through a Loop Head Act in turn [13] is quite violent ("What?"), as he implicitly asks his mother to return to the point before her revelation as he cannot believe in what she is saying. Also Will, in turn [14], is taken aback by such a revelation and, with a React Pre-Head Act ("My god"), he introduces his disparaging quip through a Blame Head Act ("this is like watching *Gays of Our Lives*") making sarcastic reference to the American TV serial *Days of Our Lives*, which is not popular in Italy and, therefore, it was substituted in translation by *Beautiful* (the Italian title of the famous American serial *The Bold and the Beautiful*) with the addition of a further disparaging comparative adverb "peggio" ("worse"): "È peggio che guardare *Beautiful*" ("this is worse than watching *The Bold and the Beautiful*"). Jack, in turn [15], tries to recover from the emotional blow and asks his mother the crucial question by means of an Elicitation Head Act that introduces a further level of Arousal anticipating some more shocking revelations: "Who's my father?". As expected, Judith's reply, in turn [16], is vague and aimed at mediating without being too abrupt, first with a Starter Pre-Head Act as a 'softener' ("Well..."), and then with a Negotiate Head Act ("it's not exactly clear"). Jack's reaction, in turn [17], is even more violent. He begins with a Bid Pre-Head Act formally addressing his mother (no longer "Mom", but "Mother", this time). Then, through a Challenge Pre-Head Act meant to disparage his mother's behaviour, he introduces a sarcastic joke: "if your explanation doesn't end with the phrase 'born in a manger'" (with an explicit reference to Jesus' birth through the agency of the Holy Spirit) ending with an Upgrade Head Act: "I'm gonna be violently ill"—more explicitly rendered into Italian as "mi verrà un attacco di bile!" ("I'm gonna have a rage attack"). Judith, in turn [18], therefore, gives her own explanation. She begins with a Starter Pre-Head Act introducing the period ("It was the sixties!"), and then, with an Informative Head Act, she gives the main contextual cue ("I went to this party"), gradually enhanced with more details about the 'orgy in darkness' through a series of Upgrade Acts (reduced in the Italian version) leading to the final consequence disclosed by means of a Revelation Head Act "there you were"—rendered into Italian with the mawkish "arrivasti tu, tesoro" ("you arrived, darling"). Jack, in turn [19], shows all his disconcert in a React Pre-Head Act ("Oh. Ok. Uhh..."). Then he seems to recover and consider the matter realistically through an Acknowledge Head Act ("I can accept that"), but when he focuses of the actual fact, first through a Marker Pre-Head Act ("So..."), and then through a Check Pre-Head Act ("the guy I thought was my dad..."), he comes to the shocking conclusion—expressed through a Blame Head Act—that "wasn't", a revelation that now makes him suddenly faint, thus marking a React Post-Head Act. At this point Karen, in turn [20], pretending to be surprised that Jack is gay through an Acknowledge Pre-Head Act ("So Jack's gay, huh?"), refers back to the imaginary situation of Jack having an affair with Grace (invented by Jack himself and supported by Grace) and, through a Blame Head Act disparagingly addressed to Grace, she claims: "No wonder he went back to you"—softened in the Italian version through an additional Upgrade Post-Head Act as "ecco perché era tornato da te, cara" ("That's why he went back to you, dear").

6.4.3 *Acting translators' embodiment of the speech-act pattern of humorous sitcom dialogues*

The conversation analysis of this extract from *Will & Grace* clearly shows the complex interplay of Acts that builds the Arousal/Safety and the Disparagement patterns of humour in this sitcom, representing one of the first serials that, at the turn of the century, dealt with the problematic issue of homosexuality within new forms of family unit. To 'embody' such conversational interplay of stressful turns, students/acting-translators in Group A were made to take part in a physical improvisation workshop as preparatory to other physical-theatre tasks meant to guide them to focus on how pragmatic theory applies to the practice of dubbing translation. One of the initial physical improvisation tasks was represented by the "shoe exercise" (cf. Guido 1992: 79), whose objective was to establish tension/relief relationships between the sitcom characters on stage, thus determining the turn-taking rhythm of the cues. In performing this task, an acting-translator is expected to utter his/her turn as soon as s/he receives the shoe thrown at him/her by another acting-translator who has just uttered his/hers, thus passing the floor to him/her. The possession of the shoe entails the control of the situation by holding the floor since an acting-translator cannot go on with his/her part until the other one who holds the shoe sooner or later decides to throw it at him/her and let him/her take the floor and speak. Obviously, this occurs in scenes where tension is very high, like the above-examined exchange from *Will & Grace*, otherwise the shoe is thrown at a regular rhythm from one acting-translator to the others taking part in the exchange and alternatively taking the floor. Before adapting this task to the exchange reported in *6.4.2*, however, Group-A students/acting-translators applied it to the improvisation of a dialogue between two characters of the *Will & Grace* sitcom. Dialogue improvisation occurred first in English, and then in Italian, so as to develop spontaneity in both languages and in relation to the personalities of the characters involved. What follows is an example of application of the "shoe exercise" to an improvised dialogue in English between Will and Jack:

> *Jack:* Where's my green jumper? *(Jack throws the shoe at Will)*
> *Will:* I don't know. I never touch your things. I don't like your clothes either. *(Will throws the shoe at Jack)*
> *Jack:* Come on! Don't be a liar! I saw it on you last Saturday! You are a liar! *(He holds the shoe for a while thus holding the floor and increasing tension as Will cannot speak and refute Jack's accusation. Then Jack throws the shoe at Will who can now take the floor).*
> *Will:* That jumper was mine! Mine! Everything you have is mine! I can take whatever I like from my home without your permission, ok? Ok? *(He holds the shoe for a longer time, preventing Jack from replying. Then he throws it at Jack)*
> *Jack:* By the way, yesterday I tore your new blue striped shirt! Well, you say nothing, so it's alright with you. *(Jack holds the shoe for a long time thus preventing Will from giving vent to his anger. Jack walks around Will holding the shoe in his hand. Then he throws it at Will).*
> *Will:* Buy it again! Immediately! That was an expensive Dolce & Gabbana shirt! I want a new one at once! *(He throws the shoe at Jack).*
> *Jack:* Ok, gimme some money. *(He throws the shoe at Will).*
> *Will:* No! Get out! I want my shirt here, by this morning, or I'll tell your secret away! *(He throws the shoe at Jack).*
> *And so on.*

At this point, Group-A students/acting-translators were introduced to more complex improvisation tasks on 'verbal planning', meant to bring pragmatic theory to bear on dubbing translation practice—which entails the development, in students/acting-translator's mind, of a Declarative Knowledge of the linguistic and pragmatic rules of usage, and of a Procedural Knowledge of how to achieve an illocutionary goal by 'verbally planning' the actualization of a specific speech act (cf. Widdowson 1978; Guido 2004). 'Verbal planning improvisation', also in this case, took place within the framework of the *Will & Grace* sitcom and involved the exploration of various speech acts 'in action', with students/acting-translators actualizing their Declarative Knowledge into a Procedural one by 'embodying' both English and Italian languages 'on stage', and within specific situation frames involving the use of specific speech acts. In this way, as 'linguists', they reflected on their theoretical, 'declarative' knowledge of the rules of usage in both languages involved in the translation process and, as 'actors', they employed improvisation techniques to explore the extent to which theory can be applied to their 'procedural' knowledge of how speech-act usage is implemented as discourse use in both languages, cultures, situations and humour patterns involved in the dubbing-translation process.

Two cases in point reported here regard the Group-A students' 'verbal-planning' improvisation tasks on two speech acts, Apology and Request, as they are deemed to enhance meaning negotiation in conversation. Students/acting-translators were thus guided to explore a number of strategies encoded in English and Italian usage, but in need of practical re-adaptation to the culture-bound context and humour of this sitcom. In tackling the Apology speech act, Group-A students/acting-translators were invited to explore the 'verbal planning' involved, for instance, in a typical situation from *Will & Grace*, marked the status gap between the character of the upper-middle class Karen Walker, wife of an elderly millionaire, and the character of her Salvadorian housemaid, Rosario, who always obeys though, suddenly, she is used to react fiercely against her mistress, as in the following example from the episode (#5.22) entitled *May Divorce Be With You*:

> *[A Fast Food Restaurant]*
> *(Rosario carries a tray of food to the table where Karen is sitting. She hands Karen a basket of onion rings.)*
> *Rosario:* Here. Now, you're gonna be disappointed. The special sauce isn't what you thought it was.
> *Karen:* Where's my J & B shake?
> *Rosario:* They said they cut you off. *(Rosario sits down.)*
> *Karen:* Hey, hey, hey, hey. Come on, take your breath burger and go eat it in the toilet with the other maids.
> *Rosario:* Oh, by the way, I poisoned one of those onion rings. Happy hunting.
> *(Rosario takes the tray and moves to a different table.)*

The series of the examples that will follow are, again, meant to be illustrative of the top-down improvisation sessions that Group-A students/acting-translators performed by embodying sitcom characters, first in English and then in Italian, thus developing a natural language style suitable for each of them—which was meant to be useful when acting translators apply it to their dubbing-translation process. Such examples, therefore, are not drawn from the actual sitcom scripts, but are top-down improvisations on the peculiar personality traits of the two characters—namely, the haughty Karen Walker who snaps orders to her maid, Rosario. This kind of improvisation task is known, in the field of the 'physical-theatre' acting method (cf. Johnstone 1981), as "Playing Status" and it is often performed as slapstick with the two stereotypical characters of Master and Servant improvising from maximum to minimum status gap, often suddenly switching from one to the other, or reversing the roles, as in the following example drawn from a workshop improvisation (Guido 1992: 65-66):

> *Master:* Where have you put my papers?
> *Servant:* I don't know ... sorry ... I can't remember
> *Master:* I think your realize they are extremely important
> *Servant:* Yes, but ... I don't know really ... maybe ... I threw them in the dustbin this morning ...
> *Master:* In the dustbin? How dare you? Are you mad?
> *Servant:* I always throw your things in the dustbin.
> *Master:* Oh, well ... that's alright, then.
> *Servant:* You are messy! I don't want to see all your papers around! Clear this table! Quick!
> *Master:* Ok, ok, please, don't be angry with me now, I'm sorry, I'll do it immediately.

This example could be well applied to the characters of Karen, the Mistress, and Rosario, the Maid, as in the following extract from the episode #5.18 entitled *Fagmalion Part Four: The Guy Who Loved Me*:

> *[The New York Palace Hotel, Karen's Suite]*
> *(Rosario is cleaning as Karen talks on the phone.)*
> *Karen: (into phone)* Hello? Maintenance? This is Mrs. Walker in 5319. Mm-hmm. I'd like to put my drink on the mantel. Could you send someone over to move the fireplace? *(Karen laughs and hangs up the phone. She holds out the phone to Rosario)* Here, Rosie, you try one.
> *Rosario: (annoyed)* You do it. I'm not in the mood.
> *Karen:* What's the matter, Ro-Ro? You've been kinda grumpy all day. Where's the usual lumber in your step? *(Karen pouts.)*
> *Rosario:* It's this new uniform you got me. It's too tight, it's itchy, I can barely breathe. *(Rosario takes off the apron.)*
> *Karen: (Karen grabs the apron)* Why, you ingrate. How dare you complain? When I found you, you were boxing donkeys for money.
> *Rosario:* You pulled me out of business school, you tipsy witch. I ain't wearing it.
> *Karen:* Oh. Why not? Seems perfectly fine to me. Look, I can do everything you do in it. *(Karen ties the apron around her waist.)* I can eat. Ang, ang, ang, ang, ang. And I can sleep. *(Loud snore.)* Cccrrrr. Oh, wait. Watch this. And I can steal. *(Karen picks up a silver teapot and 'sneaks' towards the door.)* Shh. Heh-heh-heh! Shh. *(Karen opens the door and 'sneaks' out.)*
> *Rosario:* Can you walk through doors?
> *Karen:* No.
> *(Rosario slams the door shut, leaving Karen locked outside in the hallway.)*
> *Karen:* Hey. *(Karen pounds on the door.)* Hey, let me in. Let me in. *(Karen sighs and leans against a maid's cart.)*

In sum, if, on the one hand, a drama improvisation session like the Master-&-Servant one regarding "Playing Status" requires from acting-translators 'as actors' a physical and psychological embodiment of the characters they 'play', on the other hand, a top-down physical-theatre workshop in which acting translators are involved 'as linguists' crucially entails their awareness of both the declarative and the procedural knowledge necessary to 'verbally plan' the playing of maximum and minimum status gap in improvising parallel sitcom-episode scripts. In other words, not only are acting translators required to 'become authors' of new episode scripts (cf. Blake 2005; Bull 2007; Smith 2009), but they are also asked to 'enact' their own new scripts by interacting with the other fellow acting translators in their dubbing-translation team, both in English and in Italian.

A case in point regarding a workshop on the Apology speech act is represented by a series of parallel verbally-planned situations, explored by Group-A students/acting-readers, in which Rosario, the housemaid, apologizes to her mistress, Karen Walker, for having accidentally broken a tea set. In such a context, both the social distance and the ethnic difference between the two participants in the interaction were linguistically articulated in various alternative forms (based on speech-act realization templates in Faerch and Kasper 1984) depending on the 'status' the participants played within the invented situation. What follows is an instance of verbally-planned situation parallel to the original sitcom ones and involving the Apology speech act:

> *Rosario (playing low status):*
> *Pre-modification*:
> Miss Karen *[Appeal]*
> there's something I have to tell you *[Topic Introducer]*
> I know you'll be terribly upset but *[Forewarn]*
> *Statement of the Offence:*
> the tea set has fallen down *[Impersonal Terms]*
> *Apology:*
> I'm awfully sorry *[conventionalized form, with Intensifier of Illocutionary Force]*
> *Post-modification*:
> I slipped when I carried it into the kitchen *[Explanation]*
> but I'll get you a new one. *[Promise of Compensation]*

Blum-Kulka and Olshtain (1984) identify a number of strategies adopted by the speaker who intends to apologize. In the course of the workshops on pragmatic-theory awareness, based on improvisation on Apology and Request speech acts, such Apology strategies were applied by Group-A students to the same situation of 'verbal planning' reproduced above and contextualized in the sitcom *Will & Grace*, so as to explore possible alternative 'status-gap' realizations of the Apology speech act (subsequently become the starting point of further sitcom-script improvisation sessions), which are reproduced below (cf. Guido 2004: 362-363):

> 1. *Speaker accepting responsibility by expressing traits of self-deficiency*
> *Rosario:* You know me, I'm so clumsy.

Here it is possible to notice that the speaker (the Salvadorian housemaid Rosario) is—implausibly indeed—apologizing to Karen, the lady of the house, by activating a 'maximum status gap' between herself, as she stresses a personal deficiency, and Karen, who, instead, may plausibly take a racist stance by accepting her housemaid's self-denigration as an ethnic, rather than a personal, trait—which is actually typical of the sitcom character of Karen Walker, usually employing a 'racial/social disparagement' type of humour in her quips.

> 2. *Explicit self-blame*
> *Rosario:* It's my fault/mistake.

In this example, instead, the housemaid activates a 'medium status gap': she acknowledges the accident occurred to her as 'her own fault' and, in doing so, she protects her face by accepting the social convention of 'apologizing by self-blaming'.

> 3. *Denial of fault*
> *Rosario:* It's not my fault that it fell down.

Here, the housemaid's justification is honest (she's acknowledging the accidental nature of the fact) but, in doing so, she is activating a 'minimum status gap' between herself and the lady, placing herself, as it were, on the same social 'level of reliability' as the lady, and even challenging any possible ethnic stereotype which Karen, the lady, might have activated in her mind. Apology strategies such as explanation, offer of repair, and promise of forbearance were also adopted by Group-A students/acting-translators 'verbally-planning' Rosario's Apology to signal that the offence was resulting from external factors over which she has no (or very little) control (cf. Guido 2004: 362). In the case under examination, the Salvadorian housemaid was made to adopt these strategies to reverse the status gap between herself and Karen, thus stressing her social, personal and even ethnic self-respect—which is typical of the character of Rosario in *Will & Grace*.

> 4. *Explanation or account of cause*
> *Rosario: (a)* The floor was slippery (*explicit*) / *(b)* The dog is always under my feet (*implicit*)

In these two examples, Rosario is activating a 'maximum status gap' by placing herself at a higher-status level with respect to Karen Walker, as she ascribes the responsibility of the fact not to herself, but to external causes present in the 'dangerous environment' of Karen's house.

5. *Offer of repair*
Rosario: (a) I'll pay for the damage (*specified*) / *(b)* I'll see what I can do (*unspecified*)

With these two expressions, the housemaid is establishing a 'medium status gap' though she is placing herself in a slightly advantageous position over Karen, the lady of the house, since she is displaying her social and financial capacity to cope with the problem. In doing so, she is asserting herself at an equal social – and ethnic – level as the lady.

6. *Promise of forbearance*
Rosario: This won't happen again.

With this expression the housemaid establishes again a 'medium status gap' by advancing, this time, a view of herself as a reliable person.

Another strategy that students/acting-translators adopted was 'apology intensification' (Blum-Kulka and Olshtain 1984), brought about by the following discourse strategies which, this time, are not really typical of Rosario's character:

7. *Intensification by Adverbials*
Rosario: I'm very sorry.

8. *Intensification by Repetition*
Rosario: I'm terribly, terribly sorry.

9. *Concern for the Listener*
Rosario: Are you angry/upset?

In dealing with the Request speech act, Group-A students/acting-translators once again explored its realizations by expanding the invented sitcom sequences examined above, regarding parallel improvisations on interactions between the two characters from *Will & Grace*—namely, the Salvadorian housemaid Rosario and her mistress Karen Walker, the lady of the house, with whom she is in trouble for breaking her tea-set. This time Rosario was viewed in a parallel situation in which she asks Jack for a loan of $500 to buy a new tea-set for Karen. This is one of the parallel sequences explored:

Rosario:
Jack *[Address Term]*
could you lend me 500 dollars? *[Head Act]*
I've run into problems with Miss Karen. *[Adjunct to Head Act]*

In order to examine the use of the 'Head Act' in depth, Group-A students adapted the examples from Blum-Kulka and Olshtain (*ibidem*) to the same parallel sitcom situation explored so far, introducing this time the reaction of Karen Walker, the lady of the house, requesting Rosario, her housemaid, to sweep up the broken bits of the tea-set. In performing this Request speech act, Karen was made to adopt different Request-strategy types, some receiving an 'expected' answer from Rosario, others receiving instead an 'unexpected' and 'dispreferred' one, each marking her different levels of 'status positioning' towards her housemaid. A number of these strategy types were explored by improvising parallel scripts on this invented situation. Such improvisations were assumed to be not only a 'verbal' but also–and crucially—a 'physical' playing-status task for acting-translators:

10. *Explicit, direct level*
Karen: You've left the kitchen in a mess.
Rosario: OK, I'll clean it up.

11. *Conventional, indirect level*
Karen: Would you mind cleaning up the kitchen? You've left the broken bits on the floor.
Rosario: OK, I'll clean it up.

12. *Listener-oriented, direct level*
Karen: Could you tidy up the kitchen soon?
Rosario: OK, I'll do it.

13. *Speaker-oriented, indirect level*
Karen: Do you think I could ask you to clean the kitchen now?

14. *Speaker and listener oriented, direct level*
Karen: So, could we please clean up?

15. *Impersonal, indirect (passivization)*
Karen: So it might not be a bad idea to get it cleaned up.

In all these examples it is possible to notice that the strategies adopted are marked by a 'direct level of request' that represent the speaker (Karen) positioning herself at a higher social status (and probably, in her own perception, at a higher ethnic level) with respect to her housemaid, as the ways by which she asks the housemaid for cleaning the kitchen up are more or less imperious and assertive. By using strategies marked by an 'indirect level of request', on the contrary, the speaker positions herself at a 'lower status', appearing more sympathetic and collaborative with the housemaid.

The maximum status gap, however, was achieved, in the course of the 'verbally-planning' workshop, by the use of 'Downgrading' and 'Upgrading' strategies. By the former, Karen chose to adopt the 'most indirect levels of request possible', thus positioning herself to the lowest status degrees with respect to Rosario, her listener. Downgrading strategies, however, in the case of the haughty character of Karen Walker, were adopted as humorous devices to feign a politeness which may be flouted immediately afterwards by her use of some sarcastic or rude expression which reasserts her higher status over the housemaid. By opting for the latter Upgrading strategies, instead, Karen, the speaker, was made to adopt the 'most direct and explicit levels of request', thus positioning herself, this time, to the 'highest status degrees' with respect to Rosario.

Downgrading strategies, for instance, were performed by means of 'downgraders', which are lexico-semantic and syntactic devices for achieving different effects aimed at 'softening' the act of requesting (cf. Guido 2004: 365), and realized in the following ways in the course of the workshop:

16. *Interrogative*
Karen: Could you do the cleaning up?

17. *Negation*
Karen: Look, excuse me. I wonder if you wouldn't mind cleaning it up?

18. *Past Tense*
Karen: I wanted to ask you for a cleaning up.

19. *Embedded 'if' clause*
Karen: I would appreciate if you cleaned the room up.

20. *Consultative style*
Karen: Do you think I could ask you to clean the room up?

21. *Understarters* (by which the speaker minimizes parts of the proposition)
Karen: Could you tidy up a bit before you leave?

22. *Hedges* (by which the speaker avoids specification and commitment to the illocutionary point of the utterance)
Karen: It would really help if you did something about the kitchen.

23. *Downtoner* (by which the speaker modulates the impact that her utterance may have on the listener)
Karen: Will you be able perhaps to clean the kitchen up?

Upgrading strategies were performed, instead, by means of 'upgraders' which, also in this case, are lexico-semantic and syntactic devices used to 'increase' the compelling force of the speech act of requesting (*ibidem*), and which were realized in the following ways:

24. *Intensifier* (by which the speaker offers an over-representation of reality)
Karen: Clean up this mess, it's horrible!

25. *Expletives* (by which the speaker expresses negative emotional attitudes)
Karen: You still haven't cleaned up that bloody mess!

The last part of the Request speech-act sequence regards the 'Adjuncts to Head Act'. To explore this part, the same *Will-&-Grace* parallel sitcom situation was considered in the course of the workshop, regarding the housemaid Rosario asking Jack for a loan of $500 to buy a new tea-set for Karen. Also in this case, Rosario, the speaker, embodied by students/acting-translators, was made to activate several strategies to perform her request (*ibidem*: 365-366), which were realized in the following ways:

> 26. *Checking on availability* (by which the speaker prefaces her Request speech-act with an utterance checking if the precondition necessary for compliance may be true)
> *Rosario:* Have you drawn your salary? And if so, is it possible to borrow 500 dollars from you?
>
> 27. *Getting a pre-commitment* (by which the speaker precedes the Request speech-act by trying to obtain a pre-commitment from the listener)
> *Rosario:* Will you do me a favour? Could you perhaps lend me 500 dollars?
>
> 28. *Grounder* (by which the speaker indicates the reason for her request)
> *Rosario:* Jack, I broke Miss Karen's tea-set, could I borrow some money to buy her a new one?
>
> 29. *Sweetener* (by which the speaker expresses exaggerated appreciation of the listener's ability to comply with the request)
> *Rosario:* You are my best friend, would it be possible to borrow 500 dollars from you?
>
> 30. *Disarmer* (by which the speaker indicates her awareness of a potential effrontery)
> *Rosario:* Excuse me, I hope you don't think I'm being forward, but is there any chance of a loan of 500 dollars from you?

The verbally-planning workshop on 'theory awareness' explored so far was aimed to guide Group-A students/acting-translators to focus on their declarative and procedural knowledge of speech-act usage and use in English and, subsequently, in Italian, as that was the target language of their translation activity. The instances of conversation strategies explored in the course of the workshop were precisely meant to point out the functioning of speech acts (Apology and Request in the case in point) in communicative contexts in general, and in sitcom contexts in particular. At this point, both Group-A students/acting-translators (who went through this 'embodiment' phase based on the workshop) and Group-B students/dubbing-translators were required to explore translation strategies aimed at rendering the complex conversation structure of the *Will & Grace* sitcom in general, and of the above-analyzed extract in particular, by specifically focusing on the use of cultural references as quips to convey disparaging stances. these quips are built on only one word, or on more words arranged in a fixed and recognizable order as they represent identifiable terms or expressions referred to notions that are part of the audience's shared background knowledge. Such notions could therefore belong to the domains of material, social, ecological, religious or linguistic references, according to the taxonomy outlined by Nida and Taber (1969). In the comic context of a sitcom, however, these references are grounded on a 'script opposition' (Attardo 1994: 133) according to which the generally recognized meanings of terms and fixed expressions are not simply indexical of a shared socio-cultural reference, but they are also evocative of additional socio-cultural references that are not normally associated with such meanings. And yet, the incongruous context of a sitcom allows audiences to make such unexpected associations, and the surprise effect they generate is assumed to induce their humorous response. Such double reference to different socio-cultural meaning implications represent indeed a serious problem for dubbing-translators who often resort to the domestication strategy of 'substitution' of a source term or a fixed expression with other parallel ones in the target language and culture which are different in form, but more or less similar in meaning (cf. Veisbergs 1997). The real problem, however, is to opt for solutions that are pragmatically equivalent to the original ones, in terms of appropriateness to the sitcom contexts and characters. In the above-analyzed extract from *Will & Grace* there are two instances of socio-cultural references underlying quips, based on a 'script opposition' where the former reference is the expected socio-cultural one, whereas the latter evokes an incongruous 'gay-man schema'. One of such instances can be identified soon after Jack's coming out to his mother, when she calls to her mind the 'clues' about his homosexuality that, at the time of Jack's childhood, she was unable to detect, such as the nursery rhyme Jack was fond of: "Rub-a-dub-dub, three men in a tub". Translating the multiple associations of this expression would mean accounting for the overt reference to the popular nursery rhyme about "the butcher, the backer, and the candlestick maker" together in a tub—and then also for the more learned reference to the 'rub-a-dub' dancehall reggae music. But the incongruous association that triggers the comic effect does indeed account for the covert reference to the kinky image of the "three men in a tub" made by Jack's mother to refer to her son's homosexuality – an image activating in the audience's mind the 'gay-man schema' reinforced by the allusion implicit in the verb "rub" conjuring up the action that the three men would be performing in the tub. The dubbing translator of the version for the Italian television resolves such a quandary by simply deciding not to make reference to a real Italian nursery rhyme, but rather opting for a fake one ("Barattò la pappa per tre uomini e una cappa" - "He swapped the pap for three men and a cap"), thus completely reinventing the original expression by turning it into different rhyming lines which only slightly allude to a covert homosexuality already detectable in little Jack.

Group-A students/acting-translators were instead invited to search for equivalent choices that could preserve the reference to a parallel and real Italian nursery rhyme as well as to the 'gay-man-schema' implicit in the original expression. Some students in this group came up with a convincing solution which referred to the popular nursery rhyme, "ambarabà ciccì coccò, tre scimmiette sul comò" ("ambarabà ciccì coccò, three little monkeys on the bureau")—which continues with an actual kinky innuendo in the second verse despite its being a child's counting rhyme ("che facevano l'amore con la figlia del dottore" – "who were making love with the doctor's daughter"). In their translation option, these Group-A students therefore merged the first part of the Italian nursery rhyme with an unexpected reference to the original "three men in a tub", the result of which being: "ambarabà cincìn pompòn, tre ragazzi nel sapòn" ("ambarabà chin-chin pompòn, three young men in the soap"). Also Group-B students produced interesting translation options (though they were quite vulgar and less allusive than the original) as they aimed at translating literally the original nursery rhyme without searching for equivalent references in Italian. These are some of their rhyming proposals: "Strofino strofino, tre uomini in un tino" ("I rub rub three men in a tub"); "sguazza e sguazza, tre ragazzi nella tinozza" ("splash about splash about, three young men in the tub"); "goccia su goccia, tre uomini nella doccia" ("drop by drop, three men under the shower"); "saponetta che casca, due uomini in una vasca" ("cake of soap that falls down, two men in a bathtub"). Another quip based on a socio-cultural reference to a 'script opposition' (Attardo 1994: 133) is uttered in this extract by Will who, by associating Jack's and Judith's respective revelations with the implausible 'revelation plots' typical of the popular TV serials, refers derisively to the American serial *Days of Our Lives* by distorting it into *Gays of Our Lives*. Since this serial is unfamiliar to the Italian audience (except for its fictionalized version in *Friends* as the serial in which Joey plays a role), then the translator of the Italian TV version replaced it with *Beautiful* (the Italian title of the famous American serial *The Bold and the Beautiful*) with the addition of the disparaging comparative adverb "peggio" ("worse"): "È peggio che guardare *Beautiful*" ("this is worse than watching *The Bold and the Beautiful*"), but without any reference to the 'gay schema' which was explicitly referred to by Will in his original quip. Group-A students/acting-translator produced instead a more effective and equivalent option by making reference to another worldwide famous American serial, namely *Dynasty*, turning it into *Gaynasty* and thus preserving also the original 'gay-schema' reference.

In this chapter alternatives to a 'foreignization' strategy in sitcom dubbing translation have been explored with reference to the Acting-Translator Model which, put into practice, has accounted for the application of established theories on humour translation to the acting translators' actual search for a formal and pragmatic equivalence which would avoid resorting to a 'domestication' strategy. A 'natural balance' between the two opposite strategies of domestication and foreignization was achieved by students/acting-translators who made sitcom contexts, characters and their conversational styles (both in English and in Italian) crucially 'their own', by embodying them during 'physical-improvisation' and 'verbal-planning' workshops before producing their spontaneous and 'natural' dubbing-translation options.

Conclusions

The development of the Acting Translator Model and its application to the pedagogical context of university courses that introduce the translation of audiovisual humorous texts – such as sitcoms – has involved a very complex enquiry into the principles and practice of Cognitive-Experientialist Linguistics applied to Conversation Analysis. The originality of this Model can be principally evaluated against the fact that not until recently have Applied Linguistics and Translation Theory developed an interest in audiovisual translation in general, and in the audiovisual translation of humour in particular, despite the spreading out of translation methodologies to the domains of Cognitive, Functional and Computational Linguistics, and the introduction of the notion of 'rewriting' (Lefevere 1992) encompassing techniques of 'textual redrafting'. Indeed, the processes of language/image mediation involved in audiovisual translation entail the integration of various disciplinary domains ranging from cross-cultural Semiotics to intercultural Pragmatics applied to written, spoken, and 'visual' discourse. In such wide theoretical context, the Acting Translator Model of dubbing translation is located within the domain of the Cognitive-Experientialist approach to language (Johnson 1987; Lakoff 1987; Sweetser 1990; Langacker 1991), discourse (Guido 1999, 2005) and to intercultural communication (Guido 2008). The application of the Model to the analysis of sitcoms in this book has explored the crucial concepts of the accuracy of translation with reference to the source text and culture, its pragmatic equivalence, its acceptability and appropriateness with reference to the target language and culture, and the more or less implicit conveyance of ideological, social and economic messages through the translated scripts. In particular, the analysis has investigated the processes of textual manipulation in the dubbing translation of sitcoms for the Italian television, focusing on the frequent occurrences of sociolinguistic dislocations towards the target culture, as well as of sociolinguistic conformities to the source culture, exploring their effects on the Italian audience's reception. Another distinctive dimension of this Model has been represented by the application of the concept of 'language transfer' (Selinker and Lakshmanan 1992) to the analysis of audiovisual translation. This is a concept that has never been systematically associated with the translation process but, in this book, 'language transfer' has been brought to bear on the enquiry into the translators' conveyance of specific ideological stances by means of their use of the target language, so as to comply with opposite localized/globalized realizations of the final translated product.

However, the most innovative theoretical dimension of the Model introduced in this book has been represented, first of all, by the notion of 'schemata' not simply meant as a 'cognitive construct', but rather as a background knowledge based on experiential, 'embodied' images (Johnson 1987), developing from the interaction that the human body establishes with the natural and the social environment, on the assumption that the body is the primary means through which human beings experience the world and, consequently, an essential way to semiotic conceptualization. On such grounds, therefore, this book has advanced the tenet that to achieve a thorough experience of a sitcom, dubbing translators need to engage their own schemata in their body/thought entirety. This means that they have to free themselves from their mentalist habit of 'sounding' the sitcom characters' voices within their own minds while they read and interpret the sitcom script in silence. In fact, dubbing translators are expected to 'embody' the characters and their voices, and 'inhabit' the sitcom script within a real 'physical space of representation' —i.e., a sort of actual 'stage' where they can physically 'play the script' and experience a first-person bodily and mental involvement with the humorous situations. In this way, dubbing translators become Acting Translators, as they produce 'in action' an interpretation of the source script, by initially improvising on it and its characters in order to familiarize with them and make their speech style 'their own'. Then, after this first interpretative phase, acting translators are expected to render the source script into a target language variation that is consistent with both the socio-cultural context that informs the original humorous language and the effects that the original humour produces on their own socio-cultural and experiential schemata. Indeed, humour 'in action'—as it is realized in audiovisual texts like a sitcom—implies two divergent interpretations that the acting translators need to embody, referred to, respectively, the script enacted within the visual context of the sitcom, and a completely opposite script, evoked by the peculiar use of the comic language (Attardo 1994), that disrupts the translators' conventional schematic categories (by which they make sense of reality) through the unexpected sense of surprise representing the 'humorous trigger'. Hence, acting translators, together with their embodiment of the over situation, should also physically and vocally explore the covert implications of the 'evoked' opposite script, which would give their tone of voice and bodily posture the 'ambiguous quality', required by the sitcom language structure, that prompts the comic 'real/unreal effect'. The embodiment and enactment of such 'script opposition' is also replicated in the target language, with the acting translators who first improvise on it to create new parallel scripts to the original one (so as to achieve a 'natural' variety of Italian consistent with the personality of the sitcom characters) and, then, by rendering the original script into a target one. In this sense, an acting translator encompasses all the roles usually needed in the dubbing-translation process, namely: the linguist, the script-writer (in the improvisation phase), the actor, the translator, the script adaptor, the dubbing actor, the dubbing director, and the target audience. All these roles converge in the same professional figure, despite the general disheartening situation of the dubbing translation practice—with the often unprofessional translators who have to meet limited time deadlines and marketing and political standards set by the local broadcasters of the dubbed sitcom versions, often revised by likewise unprofessional script adaptors.

The practical implications of this Acting Translator Model are therefore wholly focused on the academic and professional training of translation students who have to tackle the thorny task of providing a dubbing translation of a humorous audiovisual text like the sitcom. To this purpose, the book has shown evidence of how classroom activities informed by physical-theatre exercises, consistent with the Cognitive-Experientialist approach, can be adopted to induce in dubbing translators the activation of 'top-down', 'schema-based' strategies of 'script familiarization by embodiment'—which entails physically and verbally improvising on it in both the languages involved in the translation process. Then, a second 'bottom-up', 'text-based' phase of 'theory awareness' has been introduced with the purpose of guiding dubbing-translation students to carry out a principled analysis of the sitcom-conversation moves, acts, and characters' attitude and judgement positionings in the course of the exchanges. This phase has actually aimed at making students understand the 'script-opposition' structure of humour, based on Arousal/Safety and Disparagement patterns, that makes such conversations diverge from the expected, everyday ones. The third, 'interactive' ('top-down/bottom-up') phase concerns students/dubbing-translators becoming 'acting translators' who create their own target scripts by rehearsing them together, as a team of actors, in order to produce a 'naturalization' effect in the Italian dialogues by respecting, at the same time, the source culture producing the original sitcom. This would help them achieve a comic effect in the target version of the script that is pragmatically equivalent to the comic effect of the source version.

The ways this theoretical model was brought to bear on the pedagogical context by becoming actualized in the experience of groups of students/acting-translators majoring English Language and Translation in two Italian universities (as illustrated by the case studies in this book) was not without challenges for the researcher who devised the Model and then applied it to the translation classroom in her capacity as a university professor of Linguistics and Translation (namely, the author of this book). Indeed, creativity was not always spontaneously and easily achievable during the dubbing-translation workshops, which means that the 'researcher/professor/workshop-leader' very often had to take the responsibility of submitting to her students/acting-translators' consideration possible translation choices that they may evaluate and elaborate, or suggesting potential improvisation outcomes that they may explore, before students become capable of appropriating and autonomously using 'embodiment' techniques and interpretation/rendering strategies, thus becoming 'truly creative' acting translators. Thus, for instance, it happened that the 'workshop leader' brought to the attention of her students alternative equivalent metaphors, or idiomatic expressions, to be explored 'in action' within their 'acting-translation' team in order to ascertain that they can 'sound natural' in conversation before students could 'embody' them and, eventually, suggest further parallel translation options which, this time, were truly original and 'their own'.

This approach was adopted for the analysis of the extracts from the five American sitcoms illustrated in the last three chapters of Part Two of this book—each chapter first introducing a cross-cultural investigation of the conversation patterns in the original and the dubbed versions of these sitcoms, and then comparing them with the results of the case studies carried out with two groups of Italian undergraduate students—an experimental Group A (receiving a training according to the Acting Translator Model), and a control Group B (receiving a conventional dubbing-translation training). The comparative analysis of the original version and the dubbed one for the Italian television clearly showed how 'official' dubbing translators tended to adopt purely top-down strategies by imposing their own subjective representations of sociopragmatic contexts on the original conversation patterns, thus actually behaving as 'socio-cultural gatekeepers'—rather than 'intercultural mediators'—for the Italian audiences. For instance, in the dubbing translation of *The Nanny* (*La Tata*) the translator operated a 'sociopragmatic transfer' of Italian stereotypes into the original American cultural and linguistic patterns, with the consequent significant modifications (at the diatopic, diastratic and diaphasic levels) in the Italian scripts which, thus, represented an instance of 'product localization'. Another example of 'localization', or 'domestication' (Venuti 1995) was represented by the dubbing translation of *Roseanne* (*Pappa e Ciccia*), characterized by a 'pragmalinguistic transfer' of an Italian diatopic and diastratic variation to the rendering of a typical American working-class pragmalect, thus affecting the original socially-marked humour of this sitcom. On the contrary, the selected extract from *Dharma & Greg* represented an instance of 'product neutralization' insofar as a diatopically-marked American variation was rendered into an invented Italian variety. The Italian dubbed versions of *Friends* and *Will & Grace* represented, instead, instances of 'product globalization', or 'foreignization' (*ibidem*) characterized by a 'sociopragmatic and pragmalinguistic reverse transfer' of the American conversational styles and idiomatic expressions to the Italian version, in the attempt to render the 'foreign flair' of the original sitcom, but actually producing typical instances of artificial 'dubbese'. In sum, the dubbing translations of these sitcoms for the Italian television, far from representing examples of creativity within textual constraints, actually produced cases of either 'top-down rendering by re-authoring', or 'bottom-up rendering verbatim' the source scripts into Italian. In this respect, it was possible to notice that, on the one hand, the 'globalization-oriented' translation choices allow the expression of semiotic aspects typical of the source language and culture—thus often having an influence on the target audiences' speech styles and behaviours. On the other hand, the 'localization-oriented' choices in sitcom dubbing translation often produce, instead, a depersonalization of the reception and understanding of such audiovisual product in the target culture because of the adaptation of the source scripts to the target audience's linguistic uses and socio-cultural behaviours. Indeed, a too explicit product localization, obtained through translation and adaptation strategies oriented towards a marked 'regionalization' of accents and pragmatic uses, more than inducing a sense of familiarity, authenticity and spontaneity in the Italian audience, actually removes every sociolinguistic and cultural specificity of the original version of the sitcoms.

On such premises, then, each of the last three chapters shows evidence of how students/acting-translators actually provided more appropriate sociopragmatic and pragmalinguistic equivalent choices representing instances of 'product naturalization' as they retained the spontaneity of Italian natural conversational styles. This means that students/acting-translators in Group A activated an actual process of 'transmediation', thus becoming intercultural mediators in that they were, since the beginning, pilot-prompted to use role-play as an elicitation technique for improvising conversations (in English and in Italian) on open-ended situations parallel to the original ones selected for exploration from each sitcom. This helped them develop spontaneity and find more appropriate pragmatic equivalence in subsequent sitcom dubbing translations. Group B (the control group) did not receive this initial pilot treatment and so they could not experience, like Group A, the multidimensional diamesic level of sitcom communication, which is 'written to be spoken' and 'enacted' in a physical space of representation. Hence, students in Group B generally produced translations in artificial dialogic tones, marked by pragmatically-biased transfer and reverse-transfer patterns, and often reproducing typical written styles.

In conclusion, this book has ultimately aimed at redefining the notion of intercultural communicative competence in the domain of dubbing translation which, in the context of the Acting Translator Model, is meant as a cognitive-experiential process by which the Acting Translator develops sociopragmatic and pragmalinguistic representations of both source and target cultures, characters, and humorous situations through a process of 'embodiment' by which they engage their own schemata in their body/thought entirety. This is a competence that informs the acting translators' awareness of the sitcom conversation structures through a process of 'experiential appropriation' of the humorous scripts. This process (as demonstrated in this book) has actually facilitated the acting translators' rendering of the source scripts into a target language that has come to be perceived as natural and spontaneous by the target audience, but also faithful to the source culture—namely, the innovative turn-of-the-century American culture with the developing new 'affective communities of mutual emotional support' replacing traditional family units in their socio-cultural behaviours and novel linguistic expressions. It is said that the new century has determined the end of the sitcom genre (cf. Littlefield 2012), replaced by reality shows of the 'Big Brother' type (where real people interact before cameras that are continuously on, and where dubbing is normally replaced by the 'voice over' technique in the target language). Indeed, there are other interesting domains of audiovisual humour still to be fully explored, and the recent academic dissertations of a number of students gives proof of new developing stances on comic movies (Cuppone 2006, Maggio 2010), humorous videogames and cartoons (Iaia 2009), and novel evolutions in the sitcom genre in terms of representation of emerging social groups (Carrisi 2011). Furthermore, research on the use of 'canned laughter' as an 'amusement trigger' and a 'joke marker'—unexplored in this book—may represent another interesting area of sitcom-humour investigation. However, the crucial and ultimate purpose of this book has been to open a fresh 'experientialist' perspective on the dubbing-translation process which, it is believed, is much needed today, especially when humorous discourse is involved.

Appendix

The following scripts are untagged versions of the sitcom extracts analyzed in Chapters 4, 5 and 6.

The Nanny **(*La Tata*)** episode #304 *Dope Diamond* (*Giulio, aitante e brillante - Giulio, handsome and smart*)

Original English version:	*Italian dubbing translation:*	*Back-translation into Standard English:*
[Int. Dining Room] *(Maxwell and his children are having supper)*	**[Int. Sala da pranzo]** *(Maxwell e i suoi figli stanno cenando)*	**[Int. Dining Room]** *(Maxwell and his children are having supper)*
[1] **MAXWELL:** Please, Sylvia, why - why don't you join us?	*[1]* **MAXWELL:** Signora Assunta, non vuole sedersi a tavola con noi?	*[1]* **MAXWELL:** Signora Assunta *[approx. Mrs. Fine]*, won't you like to sit down to eat with us?
[2] **SYLVIA:** Oh, no. I just came over to see how Fran's date went. Make like I'm not even here.	*[2]* **ZIA ASSUNTA:** Oh no, io sono qui solo per sentire da Francesca com'è andata oggi. Mangi e faccia come se io non ci fossi.	*[2]* **AUNT ASSUNTA:** Oh, no. I'm here just to hear from Francesca how things were getting on today. Go on eating and make like I'm not here.
[3] **NILES:** Are you sure we can't offer you something?	*[3]* **NILES:** È sicura che non possiamo offrirle qualcosa?	*[3]* **NILES:** Are you sure we can't offer you something?
[4] **SYLVIA:** Oh, no, thank you. I had a yoplait this morning around 10:30. *(She takes a potato from Grace's dish)* Oh, such a big potato for such a little girl. Look at the time. They must be having a ball. I'm gonna go in the kitchen. I need a meat to wash this down with. *(Sylvia leaves the dining room)*	*[4]* **ZIA ASSUNTA:** No, no, no grazie, sono a dieta e sto morendo di fame, ma voi mangiate tranquilli. *(Prende una patata dal piatto di Grace)* Oh, una patata troppo grande per una bambina così piccola! Però, come tardano! Si vede che si divertiranno molto! Se non vi spiace vado in cucina, ci vuole del manzo come contorno ad una grossa patata. *(Zia Assunta esce dalla stanza)*	*[4]* **AUNT ASSUNTA:** Oh, no, thank you. I'm on diet and I'm starving, but please, go on eating easy. *(She takes a potato from Grace's dish)* Oh, a too big potato for such a little girl! Hey, how late they are! They must be having a very good time! *[idiom: they must be having a ball]* If you don't mind I'm going in the kitchen, some beef is required as a side dish for a big potato. *(Aunt Assunta leaves the dining room)*
[5] **BRIGHTON:** I don't know about you guys, but I like Jules, and he has yet to beat me in chess.	*[5]* **BRIGHTON:** Non so a voi, ma a me Giulio piace molto e non mi ha battuto neanche una volta a scacchi.	*[5]* **BRIGHTON:** I don't know if you do, but I like Giulio a lot and he has beaten me not a single time in chess.
[6] **MAXWELL:** Oh, God, Brighton, he throws every game.	*[6]* **MAXWELL:** Ma su, Brighton, è lui che vuole perdere!	*[6]* **MAXWELL:** Come on, Brighton, it's him who wants to lose!
[7] **BRIGHTON:** Do you see how easy it is to bond?	*[7]* **BRIGHTON:** È così che si diventa amici.	*[7]* **BRIGHTON:** That's how people become friends!
[8] **MAXWELL:** Well, I wouldn't get too attached to the bloke if I were you. We all know Miss Fine's relationships eventually end in disaster.	*[8]* **MAXWELL:** Guarda, se fossi in te non mi ci affezionerei troppo a Giulio. I rapporti di Francesca con gli uomini finiscono sempre in un disastro.	*[8]* **MAXWELL:** Look, if I were you I wouldn't get too attached to Giulio. Francesca's relationships with men always end up in disaster.
(Fran enters) *[9]* **FRAN:** He asked me to marry him.	*(Entra Francesca)* *[9]* **FRANCESCA:** Ragazzi, mi ha chiesto di sposarlo!	*(Francesca enters)* *[9]* **FRANCESCA:** Guys, he asked me to marry him!

[10] **NILES:** Right on the money as always, sir.	*[10]* **NILES:** Come sempre, signore, c'ha azzeccato.	*[10]* **NILES:** As always, sir, you guessed right.
[11] **BRIGHTON:** That is so cool, Fran. Congratulations.	*[11]* **BRIGHTON:** Bene, brava Francesca! Congratulazioni.	*[11]* **BRIGHTON:** Well done, bravo Francesca! Congratulations.
[12] **FRAN:** I know, I know. I can't believe it. I'm so excited. I couldn't eat a - oh, kielbasa, sweet and sour cabbage. Hit me again. *(She takes a corn from Grace's dish)* Oh, such a big corn for such a little girl.	*[12]* **FRANCESCA:** Oh che bello! Che bello! Non riesco a crederci! Sono così eccitata che neanche ceno – uh, i salsicciotti, oh e anche i cavoli in agrodolce, *(rivolta a Niles)* gli dia dentro! *(Prende una pannocchia dal piatto di Grace)* È una pannocchia troppo grande per te.	*[12]* **FRANCESCA:** Oh, how marvelous! How marvelous! I can't believe it! I'm so excited that I couldn't even dine — uh, the sausages, oh, and also the sweet and sour cabbages, *(to Niles)* let's tuck in! *(She takes a corn from Grace's dish)* This is a too big corn for you.
[13] **MAXWELL:** He asked you to marry him?	*[13]* **MAXWELL:** Ma davvero le ha chiesto di sposarlo?	*[13]* **MAXWELL:** But, did he really ask you to marry him?
[14] **FRAN:** Uh-huh.	*[14]* **FRANCESCA:** Uh-uh.	*[14]* **FRANCESCA:** Uh-huh.
[15] **MAXWELL:** You've barely known the man for two weeks.	*[15]* **MAXWELL:** Lo conosce solo da due settimane.	*[15]* **MAXWELL:** You've barely known him for two weeks.
[16] **FRAN:** What? You think it's so hard to believe a man would fall in love with me that fast?	*[16]* **FRANCESCA:** No, cosa significa? Un uomo ci deve sempre mettere anni per dire che è innamorato?	*[16]* **FRANCESCA:** No, what does it mean? A man has to wait for years before telling that he is in love?
[17] **GRACE:** Yeah. Todd and I knew each other three minutes before I got a Pudding-Pack right in the eye.	*[17]* **GRACE:** Giusto. Todd, appena conosciuto, mi ha subito buttato il primo budino in faccia.	*[17]* **GRACE:** Right. Todd, as soon as I met him, threw the first pudding at hand on my face.
[18] **FRAN:** There you go.	*[18]* **FRANCESCA:** Ecco, ha sentito?	*[18]* **FRANCESCA:** There you go, have you heard that?
[19] **MAXWELL:** You know nothing about this man. All right, so he's a doctor. Is he a specialist?	*[19]* **MAXWELL:** Oh, ragioni! Lei non sa niente di quest'uomo. D'accordo, lei saprà che fa il medico. Che medico? Specialistico?	*[19]* **MAXWELL:** Oh, be reasonable! You know nothing about this man. All right, you may know he's a doctor. What kind of doctor? A specialist?
[20] **FRAN:** You ain't just whistling "Dixie," baby.	*[20]* **FRANCESCA:** Lui è ultra specialisticissimo, è molto bravo!	*[20]* **FRANCESCA:** He is very super-highly-specialized, he's very good!
[21] **MAXWELL:** Oh, God.	*[21]* **MAXWELL:** Oh, la testa!	*[21]* **MAXWELL:** Oh, the head!
[22] **MAGGIE:** Oh, this is so exciting. So can I be a bridesmaid?	*[22]* **MAGGIE:** Sono così contenta! Mi vuoi come damigella d'onore?	*[22]* **MAGGIE:** I'm so happy! Do you want me as a bridesmaid?
(Sylvia enters behind Fran) *[23]* **FRAN:** I know the doctor asked me to marry him, but I didn't say yes. This is delicious.	*(Zia Assunta entra alle spalle di Francesca)* *[23]* **FRANCESCA:** Aspetta, Maggie, è vero che lui mi ha chiesto di sposarlo, però io non gli ho detto di sì. Oh, questo cavolo è delizioso!	*(Aunt Assunta enters behind Francesca)* *[23]* **FRANCESCA:** Hold on, Maggie, it's true that he asked me to marry him, but I didn't say yes to him. Oh, this cabbage is delicious.
(Sylvia falls to the floor behind Fran) *[24]* **SYLVIA:** Why don't you grab a knife and stick it straight through my heart.	*(Zia Assunta cade al suolo alle spalle di Francesca)* *[24]* **ZIA ASSUNTA:** Che le racconto adesso a mia sorella che poi è tua madre?	*(Aunt Assunta falls to the floor behind Francesca)* *[24]* **AUNT ASSUNTA:** What shall I say now to my sister, who is also your mother?
[25] **FRAN:** *(hinting at Grace)* That was great. She sounded just like - Ma! Ma ... Ma, let go	*[25]* **FRANCESCA:** *(riferendosi a Grace)* Ah ah ah ma che brava! Sembri proprio Zia As—ah!	*[25]* **FRANCESCA:** *(hinting at Grace)* Ah ah ah, how clever! You really sounded like Aunt As—ah!

of my ankle.	Lasciami, lasciami la caviglia! Lasciami la caviglia, Zia Assunta!	Let, let go of my ankle! Let go of my ankle, Aunt Assunta!
[26] **SYLVIA:** You better run.	*[26]* **ZIA ASSUNTA:** Ti conviene scappare!	*[26]* **AUNT ASSUNTA:** You better run!
(Fran runs around the table chased by Sylvia) *[27]* **FRAN:** Brighton, is she taking off her shoe?	*Francesca corre intorno al tavolo inseguita da Zia Assunta)* *[27]* **FRANCESCA:** Brighton, se l'è cavata una scarpa?	*(Francesca runs around the table chased by Aunt Assunta)* *[27]* **FRANCESCA:** Brighton, has she taken off her shoe?
[28] **BRIGHTON:** No. But she's gonna hurl the corn.	*[28]* **BRIGHTON:** No, però si è armata di pannocchia.	*[28]* **BRIGHTON:** No. But she's armed herself with a corn.
[Int. Kitchen]	**[Int. Cucina]**	**[Int. Kitchen]**
[29] **FRAN:** Oy, oy, oy, oy. Ma, put down the vegetable and no one gets hurt.	*[29]* **FRANCESCA:** Oh, oh, oh, oh. Bada! O metti giù quella pannocchia o apro l'acqua bollente.	*[29]* **FRANCESCA:** Oh, oh, oh, oh. Mark! Put down that corn or I'll turn the hot water on.
[30] **SYLVIA:** All right. Help me to understand which was the biggest turnoff - the fact that Jules was gorgeous, rich, or a doctor?	*[30]* **ZIA ASSUNTA:** Parliamo. Vorrei solo che mi spiegassi cos'è che ti ha spaventato così — il fatto che Giulio è stupendo, ricco e anche medico?	*[30]* **AUNT ASSUNTA:** Let's talk. I'd only want you to explain to me what has scared you so much — the fact that Giulio is gorgeous, rich and also doctor?
[31] **FRAN:** Did I mention he was Jewish?	*[31]* **FRANCESCA:** Ha un sudore che sa di pecora.	*[31]* **FRANCESCA:** He has a sweat that smells of sheep.
[32] **SYLVIA:** Oh. Darling, I only say this because I love you. You're a glorified cleaning girl. This could be your last chance.	*[32]* **ZIA ASSUNTA:** Ma che cos'hai contro le pecore? Tuo nonno ci ha fatto i milioni! E i soldi puzzano sempre di qualcosa. Questa forse è la tua ultima occasione!	*[32]* **AUNT ASSUNTA:** But why are you so against the sheep? Your grandfather made money hand over fist with it! And money always smells of something. This maybe is your last chance.
[33] **FRAN:** Oh, Ma, I didn't say no. I just said I'd think about it. Okay, I did.	*[33]* **FRANCESCA:** Ma guarda che non gli ho detto no! Gli ho detto soltanto che volevo pensarci un po' su.	*[33]* **FRANCESCA:** But, look, I didn't say no to him. I just said I'd want to think about it.
[34] **SYLVIA:** You mean I do?	*[34]* **ZIA ASSUNTA:** Oh	*[34]* **AUNT ASSUNTA:** Oh
[35] **FRAN:** Yeah.	*[35]* **FRANCESCA:** E adesso l'ho fatto.	*[35]* **FRANCESCA:** And now I did.
[36] **SYLVIA:** Oh.	*[36]* **ZIA ASSUNTA:** Cioè, dirai di sì, vero?	*[36]* **AUNT ASSUNTA:** This means that you'll say yes, won't you?
[37] **FRAN:** Ma, you may kiss the bride.	*[37]* **FRANCESCA:** Sì! Puoi baciare la sposa, Zia Assunta!	*[37]* **FRANCESCA:** Yes, you may kiss the bride, Aunt Assunta!
[38] **FRAN/SYLVIA:** Moi! Moi! Moi! Moi! Moi!	*[38]* **FRANCESCA/ZIA ASSUNTA:** Muà! Muà! Muà!	*[38]* **FRANCESCA/AUNT ASSUNTA:** Moi! Moi! Moi! Moi! Moi!
(Maxwell enters the kitchen) *[39]* **MAXWELL:** You know, Miss Fine, I think you're very wise not to rush into this. You're far too sensible a woman to marry a man - Ow!	*(Maxwell entra in cucina)* *[39]* **MAXWELL:** Guardi, Francesca, penso che sia stata molto saggia a non prendere una decisione così affrettata. Lei è una donna troppo intelligente – Ohi!	*(Maxwell enters the kitchen)* *[39]* **MAXWELL:** Look, Francesca, I think you're very wise not to take a hasty decision. You're far too intelligent a woman - Ow!
[40] **SYLVIA:** Oh, I'm sorry. Did this fork accidentally puncture your tuchas?	*[40]* **ZIA ASSUNTA:** Oh, quanto mi dispiace! Per caso non volendo le ho bucato una delle due guance posteriori?	*[40]* **AUNT ASSUNTA:** Oh, I'm so sorry! Have I by chance accidentally punctured one of your rear cheeks?

***Roseanne* (*Pappa e Ciccia*) episode #920 *Another mouth to shut up* (*Sedotti e ... sposati – Seduced and ... married*)**

Original English version:	***Italian dubbing translation:***	***Back-translation into Standard English:***
[Ext. Porch - Night]	**[Esterno, Portico - Sera]**	**[Ext. Porch - Night]**
***[1]* DAVID:** Pregnant, you mean like, pregnant?	***[1]* DAVID:** Incinta? Vuoi dire, incinta?	***[1]* DAVID:** Pregnant, you mean, pregnant?
***[2]* DARLENE:** Yes, David, you've knocked me up.	***[2]* DARLENE:** Sì, David, sono proprio rimasta incinta.	***[2]* DARLENE:** Yes, David, I've really got pregnant.
***[3]* DAVID:** How? When?	***[3]* DAVID:** Come? Quando?	***[3]* DAVID:** How? When?
***[4]* DARLENE:** When? Disney World.	***[4]* DARLENE:** Quando? A Disney World!	***[4]* DARLENE:** When? At Disney World!
***[5]* DAVID:** Oh, my god! You mean that night after the fireworks?	***[5]* DAVID:** Oh, cavolo! È successo quella notte dopo i fuochi d'artificio?	***[5]* DAVID:** Oh, gee! Did it happen that night after the fireworks?
***[6]* DARLENE:** Well, either that, or it truly is a Magic Kingdom.	***[6]* DARLENE:** O è successo allora, o è veramente un bel mistero.	***[6]* DARLENE:** Either it happened then, or it is truly quite a mystery.
***[7]* DAVID:** Wow. What are we gonna do?	***[7]* DAVID:** Wow. E adesso che facciamo?	***[7]* DAVID:** Wow. What are we gonna do now?
***[8]* DARLENE:** Oh, don't worry. You know, getting married and having a baby can't change things that much.	***[8]* DARLENE:** No, non ti preoccupare. In fondo sposarsi e avere un bambino non ti cambia drasticamente la vita.	***[8]* DARLENE:** No, don't worry. After all, getting married and having a baby don't change your life drastically.
***[9]* DAVID:** I kinda wanted a dog first.	***[9]* DAVID:** Preferivo avere prima un cane.	***[9]* DAVID:** I would have preferred to have a dog first.
***[10]* DARLENE:** Oh, it'll be okay. I'm still gonna finish school. And by getting married I can get on your health coverage, our car insurance will go down, we'll be in line for married student housing ... I mean, it just makes sense, you know.	***[10]* DARLENE:** Andrà tutto bene. Io devo ancora finire la scuola. Se ci sposiamo potrò usufruire della tua assistenza sanitaria e inoltre ci assegneranno una casa per i giovani sposi. Si sistemerà tutto, vedrai.	***[10]* DARLENE:** It'll be okay. I'm still gonna finish school. If we get married I can get on your health coverage and, furthermore, we will be assigned a house for young married couples. Everything shall right itself, you'll see.
***[11]* DAVID:** ...Wouldn't have to be a big dog.	***[11]* DAVID:** Non doveva essere un cane grande.	***[11]* DAVID:** It wouldn't have to be a big dog.
***[12]* DARLENE:** Come on. Let's go tell everybody inside and get this over with.	***[12]* DARLENE:** Vieni, andiamo a dare la bella notizia a tutta la famiglia.	***[12]* DARLENE:** Come on. Let's go tell the whole family the good news.
***[13]* DAVID:** Whoa, whoa, slow down. You mean, tell everyone in there? Look, Darlene, couldn't we wait a few months? I mean, then they would just think you were getting fat - they gotta be expecting that. So then, when we do tell them, they'll just go, "Oh, good she's not getting fat!"	***[13]* DAVID:** Ehi, ehi, aspetta. Hai intenzione di dare la notizia a tutti adesso? Oh Darlene, non potremmo, non potremmo aspettare qualche mese? All'inizio penseranno tutti che ti sei ingrassata un po' troppo, a quel punto, quando glielo diremo commenteranno 'oh che bello! Allora non è ingrassata!'	***[13]* DAVID:** Ehi, ehi, wait. Do you mean to tell everyone the news now? Oh Darlene, couldn't we wait, couldn't we wait a few months? At the beginning they all will think that you are getting a bit too fat, so then, when we do tell them, they'll comment, "Oh, how marvelous! Then she's not getting fat!"
***[14]* DARLENE:** Alright, we don't have to tell them yet. Now take a deep breath and try not to look so pasty.	***[14]* DARLENE:** D'accordo, non glielo dobbiamo dire subito. Ora fai un bel respiro e cerca di non sembrare così sconvolto.	***[14]* DARLENE:** Alright, we don't have to tell them soon. Now take a deep breath and try not to look so pasty.

[15] **DAVID:** We'll just, we'll tell them the movie we just saw affected me profoundly.	*[15]* **DAVID:** Possiamo, possiamo dire che il film che abbiamo visto mi ha colpito profondamente.	*[15]* **DAVID:** We can, we can tell them the movie we just saw affected me profoundly.
[16] **DARLENE:** Okay, let's go inside. You ready? After you ... Daddy.	*[16]* **DARLENE:** Va bene, andiamo dentro, sei pronto? Dopo di te ... paparino.	*[16]* **DARLENE:** Okay, let's go inside. You ready? After you ... Daddy.
[Int. Kitchen]	**[Interno, Cucina]**	**[Int. Kitchen]**
[17] **D.J.:** What the hell are those?	*[17]* **D.J.:** Ma che diavolo sono!	*[17]* **D.J.:** What the hell are those?
[18] **ROSEANNE:** They're cornish game hens. I, uh, bought 'em off this guy that was selling them off the back of his truck down at the, uh, gas station parking lot. It's the very same guy that I bought our stereo speakers from last week. *(Darlene and David enter from the living room)* Hey you guys just in time for dinner. Grab a plate. Sit down here, David.	*[18]* **ANNARO':** Sono galletti ruspanti di campagna. Davvero, li ho comprati da un tizio con un turbante in testa che ha un allevamento vicino a una discarica dei rifiuti naturali. Tu lo sai che senza mangiare le bottiglie di plastica questi polli pesano quasi la metà? *(Darlene e David entrano dal soggiorno)* Ehi, siete arrivati in tempo per cena. Prendetevi un piatto. Siediti qua, David.	*[18]* **ANNARO':** They're country farmyard chickens. Really, I bought them from a guy with a turban on his head who has a chicken farm near a organic-waste dump. Do you know that without eating plastic bottles these chickens are almost half heavy? *(Darlene and David enter from the living room)* Hey, You've just arrived in time for dinner. Get a plate. Sit down here, David.
[19] **DAVID:** ...Next to you?	*[19]* **DAVID:** Accanto a Lei?	*[19]* **DAVID:** ...Next to you?
[20] **ROSEANNE:** Yeah, come tell me about your, uh, new job as a graphic artist, there.	*[20]* **ANNARO':** Sì, raccontami qualche cosa del tuo nuovo lavoro di grafico, mi interessa.	*[20]* **ANNARO':** Yeah, tell me about your new job as a graphic artist, I'm interested in it.
[21] **JACKIE:** David, congratulations on the job. Is it on a computer, or do you just draw by hand?	*[21]* **GIACOMI':** Ah David, a proposito, congratulazioni per il tuo nuovo lavoro. Fai tutto con il computer, o disegni a mano?	*[21]* **GIACOMI':** Ah David, by the way, congratulations on your new job. Do you do everything on the computer, or do you draw by hand?
[22] **DAVID:** Uh, thanks, I'm fine.	*[22]* **DAVID:** Oh, grazie, sto bene.	*[22]* **DAVID:** oh, thanks, I'm fine.
[23] **DAN:** I guess you're pretty excited about moving to Chicago, huh?	*[23]* **DAN:** Scommetto che siete entusiasti di trasferirvi a Chicago, eh?	*[23]* **DAN:** I bet that you both are excited about moving to Chicago, eh?
[24] **DAVID:** Uh, uh-huh. Course it means I'll have to move to Chicago. ... Oh, I'm so confused...	*[24]* **DAVID:** Oh, oh, questo significa che mi trasferirò a Chicago. ... Oh, sono così confuso.	*[24]* **DAVID:** Oh, oh, this means I'll move to Chicago. ... Oh, I'm so confused...
[25] **D.J.:** Oh, they're some kind of tiny chickens. We didn't know what they were either.	*[25]* **D.J.:** Oh, sì, questi polli sono minuscoli, non li conoscevamo neanche noi.	*[25]* **D.J.:** Oh, yes, these chickens are tiny, we didn't know them either.
[26] **ROSEANNE:** No, I don't think that's it D.J., David's just a little excited about his new job. Isn't that right David?	*[26]* **ANNARO':** No, io dico che si tratta di qualche altra cosa e che David è assai eccitato per questo nuovo lavoro, ho ragione o mi sbaglio?	*[26]* **ANNARO':** No, I say that it is about something else and that David's very excited about this new job. Am I right of wrong?
[27] **DAVID:** The movie affected me profoundly.	*[27]* **DAVID:** Quel film mi ha colpito profondamente.	*[27]* **DAVID:** That movie affected me profoundly.
[28] **DARLENE:** Uh, David, why don't you let me sit there. You've been hogging Mom long enough.	*[28]* **DARLENE:** Eh David perché non mi fai sedere là? Hai scocciato mamma a sufficienza.	*[28]* **DARLENE:** Eh, David, why don't you let me sit there? You've been bothering mom long enough.
[29] **DAVID:** Okay, good, here.	*[29]* **DAVID:** Oh certo, siediti.	*[29]* **DAVID:** Okay, sure, sit here.
[30] **DARLENE:** Uh, but you should sit somewhere, you know.	*[30]* **DARLENE:** Ah, devi comunque sederti da qualche parte.	*[30]* **DARLENE:** Ah, you should however sit somewhere.

[31] **ROSEANNE:** What's up? I smell fear. I love that smell. But what's up?	*[31]* **ANNARO':** Che ti piglia? Sento odore di paura, è un odore che riconosco subito, ma che avete combinato?	*[31]* **ANNARO':** What's the matter with you? I smell fear. It's a smell I immediately recognize, But what are you up to?
[32] **DARLENE:** Nothing's up. God! ... Hey, D.J., that's a great shirt. Where'd you get it?	*[32]* **DARLENE:** Non abbiamo combinato niente. Ehi D.J. che bella camicia, dove l'hai presa?	*[32]* **DARLENE:** We are up to nothing. Hey, D.J., what a nice shirt. Where did you get it from?
[33] **D.J.:** My closet.	*[33]* **D.J.:** Nel mio armadio.	*[33]* **D.J.:** From my closet.
[34] **ROSEANNE:** Oh no, I think something is up. Uh, yeah, I've seen enough of that "Murder She Wrote" to figure that out. ... Let's see here, David is pale and kind of weak kneed and all nervous. So, there's no clues there. ... But Darlene wants to sit next to me, and she said something nice to her brother. Eeww, I wonder. I know, you're pregnant! *(All laugh except Darlene and David. Then everyone stops laughing)* That was my joke guess!	*[34]* **ANNARO':** Eh no, qua c'è qualcosa che non mi quadra. Eh, forse ho visto troppi episodi della "Signora in Giallo", ma non mi fregate. Esaminiamo gli indizi: David è pallido, gli tremano le ginocchia ed è molto nervoso e fin qui stiamo nella normalità. Però Darlene si vuole sedere vicino a me e tratta suo fratello quasi come un essere umano. Uuuuu, gatta ci cova! Ho capito, aspetti un bambino! *(Tutti ridono eccetto Darlene e David. Poi tutti smettono di ridere)* L'ho detto solamente per farci quattro risate!	*[34]* **ANNARO':** Eh no, there's something fishy here. Eh, maybe I've seen too many episodes of "Murder She Wrote" , but you don't cheat on me. Let's examine the clues: David is pale, his knees are shaking and he's very nervous and so far we are within the normality. Yet Darlene wants to sit next to me and she treats her brother as a human being! Eeww, there's something fishy going on here. I've got it, you're pregnant! *(All laugh except Darlene and David. Then everyone stops laughing)* I've just said that just for the laugh of it!
[35] **DAVID:** We're also getting married.	*[35]* **DAVID:** E abbiamo deciso di sposarci.	*[35]* **DAVID:** And we've decided to get married.
[36] **ROSEANNE:** Well! I'm, I'm excited for you guys. I think it's great? ... Dan, we're gonna getting grandparents! Isn't that great. I'm getting one of those sweatshirts that says "World's Greatest Grandma" on it, you know. And you can go out and get yourself, I dunno, like a cane something.	*[36]* **ANNARO':** Bene! Io sono molto, sono molto felice, una notizia stupenda, Dan! Tra un po' avremo un nipotino, non fai salti di gioia? Io mi compro subito una di quelle magliette con la scritta "Questa è la nonna più pazza del mondo" e tu invece ti potresti comprare, che so, un bel bastone per andare a passeggio.	*[36]* **ANNARO':** Well! I'm very, I'm very happy, wonderful news, Dan! We will soon have a grandchild, don't you jump for joy? I'm soon getting one of those sweatshirts that says "This is the World's Craziest Grandma" on it and you instead could you get yourself, I dunno, a nice cane to stroll around.
[37] **DAN:** Yeah. Oh boy. Good, good, good, good, good.	*[37]* **DAN:** Già. Oh mamma. Bene, bene, nonni, nonni.	*[37]* **DAN:** Yeah. Oh dear me. Good, good, grandparents, grandparents.
[38] **DAVID:** Wow, thanks, Mrs. Conner. that wasn't the reaction I was expecting.	*[38]* **DAVID:** Wow, grazie signora Conner, non era certo la reazione che mi aspettavo.	*[38]* **DAVID:** Wow, thanks, Mrs. Conner. Certainly that wasn't the reaction I was expecting.
[39] **DARLENE:** Yeah, me neither. *(to David)* I guess you peed your pants for nothing.	*[39]* **DARLENE:** già, nemmeno io. *(rivolta a David)* Te la sei fatta nei pantaloni per niente.	*[39]* **DARLENE:** Yeah, me neither. *(to David)* You did it in your pants for nothing.
[40] **ROSEANNE:** Dan! Dan!	*[40]* **ANNARO':** Dan! Dan!	*[40]* **ANNARO':** Dan! Dan!
[41] **DAN:** What? Oh, I'm just trying to figure out how to go about eating this thing.	*[41]* **DAN:** Che vuoi? Ah, stavo solo cercando di capire come si fa a mangiare questo galletto.	*[41]* **DAN:** What do you want? Ah, I was just trying to figure out how to go about eating this chicken.
[42] **JACKIE:** Well, I think it's good. That Darlene is getting pregnant, 'cause she's getting married 'cause she's has to— That's just what I did.	*[42]* **GIACOMI':** Bé, è una notizia stupenda! Che Darlene è rimasta incinta e che sta per sposarsi perché deve perché è rimasta incinta e che... proprio come è successo a me.	*[42]* **GIACOMI':** Well, that's wonderful news! That Darlene has got pregnant and that she's getting married 'cause she's has to 'cause she's got pregnant and that — That's just what happened to me.

[43] **DAVID:** D.J., stop staring at me.	*[43]* **DAVID:** D.J. smettila di fissarmi.	*[43]* **DAVID:** D.J., stop staring at me.
[44] **D.J.:** Babies having babies.	*[44]* **D.J.:** bambini che fanno bambini.	*[44]* **D.J.:** Babies making babies.

Dharma & Greg episode #2ABD14 *Dharma and Greg on a hot tin roof* (*Dharma e Greg sul tetto che scotta*)

Original English version:	***Italian dubbing translation:***	***Back-translation into Standard English:***
[Int. Golf Store - Day]	**[Int. Negozio di articoli da golf - Giorno]**	**[Int. Golf Store - Day]**
(Greg and Dharma enter) *[1]* **DHARMA:** Okay. Go ahead.	*(Entrano Greg e Dharma)* *[1]* **DHARMA:** Avanti. ***[extra cue 1a]*** **GREG:** No. ***[extra cue 1b]*** **DHARMA:** Dai, coraggio!	*(Greg and Dharma enter)* *[1]* **DHARMA:** Go ahead. ***[extra cue 1a]*** **GREG:** No. ***[extra cue 1b]*** **DHARMA:** Come on, come on!
[2] **GREG:** Dharma, I can't do this. The sales guy'll never believe I'm from the South.	*[2]* **GREG:** No, Dharma, non ci riesco, il commesso non crederà che vengo dal sud.	*[2]* **GREG:** No, Dharma, I can't do this. The salesman will never believe I'm from the South.
[3] **DHARMA:** So then he'll think you're crazy. It's more fun shopping as a crazy person anyway, and sometimes they give you free stuff just to get rid of ya. Go on. *(Dharma nudges Greg toward the salesperson.)*	*[3]* **DHARMA:** Crederà che sei svitato! E' divertente fare compere fingendosi matti, ti regalano la roba per liberarsi di te. *(Dharma spinge Greg verso il commesso)*	*[3]* **DHARMA:** He'll think you're crazy! It's funny to go shopping pretending to be a mad person, they give you free stuff just to get rid of you. *(Dharma nudges Greg toward the salesperson.)*
[4] **GREG:** *(in a Southern accent)* Excuse me, son.	*[4]* **GREG:** *(con un accento non identificato)* Salve ghiovino.	*[4]* **GREG:** *(in a non-identified accent)* Hallo, young man.
[5] **SALESPERSON:** Yes.	*[5]* **COMMESSO:** Sì?	*[5]* **SALESPERSON:** Yes?
[6] **GREG:** *(in a Southern accent)* I'm lookin' for a nan ion.	*[6]* **GREG:** *(con un accento non identificato)* farro namero nave.	*[6]* **GREG:** *(in a non-identified accent)* A number-nine iron.
[7] **SALESPERSON:** Non on?	*[7]* **COMMESSO:** Cosa ha detto?	*[7]* **SALESPERSON:** What did you say?
[8] **DHARMA:** *(in a Southern accent)* Uh, what my husband means to say is that he is in need of a nan ion.	*[8]* **DHARMA:** *(con un accento non identificato)* Mio ghiovino, quello che mio mareto voleva sapare è dove è che stanno i ferri nomero nove.	*[8]* **DHARMA:** *(in a non-identified accent)* My young man, what my husband wants to know is that where the number-nine irons are.
[9] **GREG:** *(in a Southern accent)* Yeah. I'm looking for a new, uh, nan ion.	*[9]* **GREG:** *(con un accento non identificato)* I farri namero nave, ho det-, namero nove.	*[9]* **GREG:** *(in a non-identified accent)* Number-nine irons, I say, number nine.
[10] **SALESPERSON:** I'm sorry.	*[10]* **COMMESSO:** Ah, io non capisco... eh?	*[10]* **SALESPERSON:** Ah, I don't understand... eh?
[11] **GREG:** *(in A Southern accent)* You know, a non on, six, seven, eight, nan ion.	*[11]* **GREG:** *(con un accento non identificato)* Namero nave, dai, satte, atto, nave.	*[11]* **GREG:** *(in a non-identified accent)* Number nine, come on, seven, eight, nine.
[12] **SALESPERSON:** Oh, a nine iron.	*[12]* **COMMESSO:** Oh, cerca il numero nove, ah, certo!	*[12]* **SALESPERSON:** Oh, you look for a number nine, ah, sure!

[13] **GREG:** *(in a Southern accent)* Nan ion.	[13] **GREG:** *(con un accento non identificato)* Namero nave.	*[13]* **GREG:** *(in a non-identified accent)* Number nine.
[14] **SALESPERSON:** Yes. They're right over there.	*[14]* **COMMESSO:** Ah ecco, sono là in fondo.	*[14]* **SALESPERSON:** Ah that's it, They're right over there.
[15] **GREG:** *(in a Southern accent)* Thank you. *(to Dharma)* Damn Yankees.	*[15]* **GREG:** *(con un accento non identificato)* Graz— *(rivolto a Dharma)* Maledetti Yankie!	*[15]* **GREG:** *(in a non-identified accent)* Thank— *(to Dharma)* Damn Yankees.
(Dharma and Greg walk past Judge Samuel Harper.) *[16]* **JUDGE HARPER:** I know what you're saying. It's impossible to understand these people.	*(Dharma e Greg passano accanto al Giudice Samuel Harper)* *[16]* **GIUDICE HARPER:** Ha raghione! È impotsibile capire questi comme parlano!	*(Dharma and Greg walk past Judge Samuel Harper.)* *[16]* **JUDGE HARPER:** *(from now on he will always speak in a non-identified accent)* You are right! It's impossible to understand how these people talk.
[17] **GREG:** *(laughs) (in a Southern accent)* That's true.	*[17]* **GREG:** *(ride) (con un accento non identificato)* Eh, sì è vero!	*[17]* **GREG:** *(laughs) (in a non-identified accent)* Eh, that's true.
[18] **JUDGE HARPER:** Where y'all hail from?	*[18]* **GIUDICE HARPER:** Di dove tziete voialtri?	*[18]* **JUDGE HARPER:** Where do you come from?
[19] **DHARMA:** *(in a Southern accent)* Memphis. Where the hell you from?	*[19]* **DHARMA:** *(con un accento non identificato)* Di Mamphis. Lei invece di dove?	*[19]* **DHARMA:** *(in a non-identified accent)* From Memphis. Where are you from, instead?
[20] **JUDGE HARPER:** Oh, hail from, very good. Uh, well, we're pert'near neighbors. I'm from Knoxville.	*[20]* **GIUDICE HARPER:** Oh, di Mamphis, per forza! Tziamo quazi vicini di caza, io vengo da Knoxville.	*[20]* **JUDGE HARPER:** Oh, from Memphis, of course! We're almost neighbors. I'm from Knoxville.
[21] **DHARMA:** *(in a Southern accent)* Is that right? Did you hear that, Stinkbug? This man is a Knoxidian.	*[21]* **DHARMA:** *(con un accento non identificato)* Dice davvero? Hai zentito vecchio mio. Quezto signore è un knoxvillano!	*[21]* **DHARMA:** *(in a non-identified accent)* Really? Did you hear that, old boy? This man is a Knoxvillain!
[22] **GREG:** *(in a Southern accent)* Yeah.	*[22]* **GREG:** *(con un accento non identificato)* Ah, ah.	*[22]* **GREG:** *(in a non-identified accent)* Ah, ah.
[23] **JUDGE HARPER:** Born and raised. What part of Memphis are you from?	*[23]* **GIUDICE HARPER:** Nato e cresghiuto. E di quale parte di Mamphis?	*[23]* **JUDGE HARPER:** Born and raised. What part of Memphis are you from?
[24] **GREG:** *(in a Southern accent)* Well, uh, what part of Memphis would a man such as myself be from?	*[24]* **GREG:** *(con un accento non identificato)* Bé, ecco, bé, lei vuole, vuol, vorrebbe sapere da quale parte di Mamphis vengo io, ecco, dico bane signore?	*[24]* **GREG:** *(in a non-identified accent)* Well, uh, well, you want to know what part of Memphis I come from, uh, am I right, sir?
[25] **JUDGE HARPER:** Exactly.	*[25]* **JUDGE HARPER:** Esatti!	*[25]* **JUDGE HARPER:** Exactly.
[26] **GREG/DHARMA:** *(in unison) (in a Southern accent)* Exactly!	*[26]* **GREG/DHARMA:** *(all'unisono) (con un accento non identificato)* Esatti!	*[26]* **GREG/DHARMA:** *(in unison) (in a non-identified accent)* Exactly!
[27] **JUDGE HARPER:** Allow me to introduce myself. I'm Judge Samuel Harper.	*[27]* **GIUDICE HARPER:** Permettete che mi prezanti, io sono il ghiudice Samuel Harper.	*[27]* **JUDGE HARPER:** Allow me to introduce myself. I'm Judge Samuel Harper.
[28] **GREG:** *(in a Southern accent)* Judge Samuel Harper ... the new Federal Court Judge.	*[28]* **GREG:** *(con un accento non identificato)* Il Giudice Samuel Harper ... il nuavo ghiduce della Carte Fedarale.	*[28]* **GREG:** *(in a non-identified accent)* Judge Samuel Harper ... the new Federal Court Judge.
[29] **JUDGE HARPER:** Guilty and charged. How did you know that?	*[29]* **GIUDICE HARPER:** Reo e confasso. Come fa a saparlo?	*[29]* **JUDGE HARPER:** Pleased guilty. How did you know that?

[30] **GREG:** *(in A Southern accent)* I'm — I'm with the U.S. Attorney's Office. I believe I have a motion you're hearin' in the mornin'.	*[30]* **GREG:** *(con un accento non identificato)* Bé, io lavoro con il Procuratore Distrettuale. Se non sbaglio avremo un'udienzia con Vostro Onore domani mattina.	*[30]* **GREG:** *(in a non-identified accent)* Well, I work with the District Attorney. If I'm not wrong we are having a hearing with Your Honor tomorrow morning.
[31] **JUDGE HARPER:** Is that so? And your name is?	*[31]* **GIUDICE HARPER:** Sul sario? Como si chioma lei?	*[31]* **JUDGE HARPER:** Really? What's your name?
[32] **GREG:** *(in a Southern accent)* My name?	*[32]* **GREG:** *(con un accento non identificato)* Como mi chiomo?	*[32]* **GREG:** *(in a non-identified accent)* What's my name?
[33] **DHARMA:** Tell him your name. Butterbug.	*[33]* **DHARMA:** Dì como ti chiomi bel ghiovino.	*[33]* **DHARMA:** Tell him what your name is, young man.
[34] **GREG:** *(in a Southern accent)* My name is, uh, Gregory Montgomery.	*[34]* **GREG:** *(con un accento non identificato)* Mi chiomo Gregory Montgomery.	*[34]* **GREG:** *(in a non-identified accent)* My name is Gregory Montgomery.
[35] **JUDGE HARPER:** *(laughs)* Well, it's nice to meet you, Mr. Montgomery. And this lovely flower is?	*[35]* **GIUDICE HARPER:** *(ride)* Ah ah piacere di conoscerla signor Montgomery. E questo fiore delizioso è?	*[35]* **JUDGE HARPER:** *(laughs)* Ah ah nice to meet you, Mr. Montgomery. And this lovely flower is?
[36] **GREG:** *(in a Southern accent)* Uh, Dharma.	*[36]* **GREG:** *(con un accento non identificato)* Dharma.	*[36]* **GREG:** *(in a non-identified accent)* Uh, Dharma.
[37] **DHARMA:** Dharma Jean.	*[37]* **DHARMA:** Dharma Jean.	*[37]* **DHARMA:** Dharma Jean.
[38] **JUDGE HARPER:** Dharma Jean. You're a very lucky man sir.	*[38]* **GIUDICE HARPER:** Dharma Jean. Lei è un uomo molto fortunoto.	*[38]* **JUDGE HARPER:** Dharma Jean. You're a very lucky man.
[39] **GREG:** *(in a Southern accent)* Yes sir, I am. And it is at moments like this I am made keenly aware of just how lucky I am.	*[39]* **GREG:** *(con un accento non identificato)* Sì, signore, lo so bene, ed è proprio nei momenti come questo che ho la prova concreta di quanta fortona io abbia!	*[39]* **GREG:** *(in a non-identified accent)* Yes sir, I know that well, and it is just at moments like this I have the concrete evidence of how much luck I have.
[Int. Dharma and Greg's apartment - Night.]	**[Int. Appartamento di Dharma e Greg - Notte.]**	**[Int. Dharma and Greg's apartment - Night.]**
(Dharma and Jane sit on the couch talking.) *[40]* **DHARMA:** ... so then it turns out he has to appear before this judge tomorrow morning.	*(Dharma e Jane siedono sul divano a parlare)* *[40]* **DHARMA:** Così scopriamo che domattina dovrà presentarsi proprio davanti a quel giudice.	*(Dharma and Jane sit on the couch talking.)* *[40]* **DHARMA:** So then it turns out he has to appear before this judge tomorrow morning.
[41] **JANE:** He seems to be takin' it pretty well.	*[41]* **JANE:** vedo che l'ha presa abbastanza bene!	*[41]* **JANE:** He seems to be takin' it pretty well.
(Greg sits in a chair hugging his knees, rocking.) *[42]* **DHARMA:** He's been rocking like that since we got home.	*(Greg siede su una sedia stringendosi le ginocchia e dondolandosi)* *[42]* **DHARMA:** E' da quando siamo tornati che si dondola in quel modo.	*(Greg sits in a chair hugging his knees, rocking.)* *[42]* **DHARMA:** He's been rocking like that since we got home.
[43] **JANE:** You think he'll stay that way?	*[43]* **JANE:** E continuerà a farlo?	*[43]* **JANE:** And he'll stay that way?
[44] **DHARMA:** I don't know.	*[44]* **DHARMA:** Non lo so.	*[44]* **DHARMA:** I don't know.
[45] **JANE:** I'm gonna go get my camera. *(Jane exits.)*	*[45]* **JANE:** Vado a prendere la telecamera. *(Esce Jane)*	*[45]* **JANE:** I'm gonna go get my camera. *(Jane exits.)*

[46] **DHARMA:** Honey, you wanna talk about it now?	*[46]* **DHARMA:** Tesoro, ti andrebbe di parlarne?	*[46]* **DHARMA:** Darling, you wanna talk about it?
[47] **GREG:** No. ***[INTRA]***	*[47]* **GREG:** No.	*[47]* **GREG:** No.
[48] **DHARMA:** You know, it's not that big a deal. You just have to get there like five minutes early and just explain to him that —	*[48]* **DHARMA:** Non è successo niente di grave in fondo, dovrai solo andare lì cinque minuti prima e spiegargli che—	*[48]* **DHARMA:** It's not that big a deal, you know, you just have to get there like five minutes early and just explain to him that —
[49] **GREG:** I was mocking him and his entire culture?	*[49]* **GREG:** Che ho preso in giro lui e tutta la sua cultura?	*[49]* **GREG:** I was mocking him and his entire culture?
[50] **DHARMA:** You weren't mocking. You were making believe.	*[50]* **DHARMA:** Non l'hai preso in giro, stavi solo fingendo.	*[50]* **DHARMA:** You weren't mocking him. You were making believe.
[51] **GREG:** Okay. And after he destroys me in court, I can make believe I still have a career. Hi, Greg Montgomery, attorney at law. These two gentlemen are my clients. *(Dog barks)* Okay. Were my clients.	*[51]* **GREG:** Certo, e dopo che mi avrà distrutto in tribunale potrò fingere di avere ancora un lavoro. Sono Greg Montgomery, avvocato, e i signori sono i miei clienti. *(Il cane abbaia)* E va bene. Erano i miei clienti.	*[51]* **GREG:** Sure, and after he destroys me in court, I can make believe I still have a job. I'm Greg Montgomery, attorney at law, and these two gentlemen are my clients. *(Dog barks)* Okay. Were my clients.
[Int. The Court - Day.]	**[Int. Il tribunale - Giorno.]**	**[Int. The Court - Day.]**
(Greg sits at the Attorneys' table. Dharma sits behind him in the Gallery.) *[52]* **DHARMA:** Just tell him the truth. I'm sure he'll get a kick out of it.	*(Greg siede al tavolo dei procuratori. Dharma siede dietro di lui nella sala)* *[52]* **DHARMA:** E' meglio che tu gli dica la verità, di sicuro si farà una risata.	*(Greg sits at the Attorneys' table. Dharma sits behind him in the Gallery.)* *[52]* **DHARMA:** You'd better tell him the truth, surely he'll have a good laugh.
(Pete enters) *[53]* **PETE:** What are you talking about? What truth?	*(Entra Pete)* *[53]* **PETE:** Che cosa? Che verità?	*(Pete enters)* *[53]* **PETE:** What? What truth?
[54] **GREG:** Uh, don't worry about it. As soon as I get a chance, I'll ask for a sidebar.	*[54]* **GREG:** Em, non ti preoccupare, appena sarà possibile chiederò di parlargli.	*[54]* **GREG:** Ehm, don't worry about it. As soon as I get a chance, I'll ask to talk to him.
[55] **PETE:** What's it about?	*[55]* **PETE:** Di che stai parlando?	*[55]* **PETE:** What are you talking about?
[56] **GREG:** It's not important.	*[56]* **GREG:** Niente di importante.	*[56]* **GREG:** Nothing important.
[57] **PETE:** Is it about me? Are you gonna tell the judge I went to a Caribbean law school?	*[57]* **PETE:** Si tratta di me? Vuoi dire al giudice che ho studiato legge ai Caraibi?	*[57]* **PETE:** Is it about me? Are you gonna tell the judge I studied law at the Caribbean?
[58] **GREG:** No, now just cool it.	*[58]* **GREG:** No, non ti preoccupare.	*[58]* **GREG:** No, don't worry.
[59] **PETE:** Why won't you tell me what the sidebar's about?	*[59]* **PETE:** Di che diavolo gli vuoi parlare allora?	*[59]* **PETE:** What the hell do you want to talk to him about?
[60] **GREG:** Because it has absolutely nothing to do with the case.	*[60]* **GREG:** Ti assicuro che non ha niente a che fare con il caso.	*[60]* **GREG:** I assure you that it has nothing to do with the case.
[61] **PETE:** Well, then, I might know somethin' about it.	*[61]* **PETE:** A maggior ragione vorrei saperne qualcosa.	*[61]* **PETE:** All the more reason why I'd like to know somethin' about it.
[62] **BAILIFF:** All rise.	*[62]* **UFFICIALE GIUDIZIARIO:** Tutti in piedi.	*[62]* **BAILIFF:** All rise.

(Judge Harper enters) ***[63]* JUDGE HARPER:** Sit down. I'm not the Queen. Good mornin', Counselors.	*(Entra il Giudice Harper)* ***[63]* GIUDICE HARPER:** Seduti, non sono una Reghina. Buon ghiorno, avvocati.	*(Judge Harper enters)* ***[63]* JUDGE HARPER:** Sit down. I'm not the Queen. Good morning, Counselors.
***[64]* MR. MILLER:** Howdy, Judge.	***[64]* AVVOCATO MILLER:** Ehilà, giudice!	***[64]* MR. MILLER:** Hey there, Judge.
***[65]* JUDGE HARPER:** How's that?	***[65]* GIUDICE HARPER:** Che cosa?	***[65]* JUDGE HARPER:** How's that?
***[66]* MR. MILLER:** Howdy, Your Honor?	***[66]* AVVOCATO MILLER:** Ehilà, Vostro Onore.	***[66]* MR. MILLER:** Hey there, Your Honor?
***[67]* JUDGE HARPER:** Howdy? Howdy? What are you implying, that I'm some sort of ignorant Southerner who doesn't understand proper English? If you wish to address me, say "hello".	***[67]* GIUDICE HARPER:** Ehilà? Ehilà? Acchidenti, che mi sta forse trattando come un povero ignorante del sud? Che non sa parlare se non il proprio dialatto? Se vuole salutarmi mi dica, dica "buongiorno".	***[67]* JUDGE HARPER:** Hey there? Hey there? Damn, are you perhaps treating me as a kind of poor ignorant Southerner who can speak only his own dialect? If you wish to address me, say "good morning".
***[68]* MR. MILLER:** Yes, sir, Your Honor, Hello.	***[68]* AVVOCATO MILLER:** Sì, Vostro Onore, buongiorno.	***[68]* MR. MILLER:** Yes, Your Honor, good morning.
***[69]* JUDGE HARPER:** The one thing I will not tolerate is the ridiculing of the melodic speech patterns of my people. Don't you agree, Mr. Montgomery?	***[69]* GIUDICE HARPER:** Se c'è una cosa che non tollero è chi mette in ridicolo la particolare melodica parlata della mia ghente. Condivide, Avvocato Montgomery?	***[69]* JUDGE HARPER:** If there is one thing I will not tolerate is the ridiculing of the particular melodic way of speaking of my people. Do you agree, Mr. *[Counselor]* Montgomery?
***[70]* GREG:** *(in a Southern accent)* Sho' 'nuff, Ya Honor.	***[70]* GREG:** *(con un accento non identificato)* Com' no, Vostro Onore.	***[70]* GREG:** *(in a non-identified accent)* 'v course, Your Honor.
***[71]* PETE:** *(quietly)* Sho' 'nuff? What the hell you doin'?	***[71]* PETE:** *(sottovoce)* Greg, ma come parli? Ma che sta succedendo?	***[71]* PETE:** *(quietly)* Greg, How do you speak? What's happening?
***[72]* JUDGE HARPER:** Now, the defense has, uh, made a motion here for a change of venue. Does the United States have any response to this motion?	***[72]* GIUDICE HARPER:** La difesa ha presentato rischiesta di rìnvio della causa ad altra Corte. Che cosa ha da dire lo Stato in risposta alla rischiesta suddetta?	***[72]* JUDGE HARPER:** The defense has made a motion for a change of venue. What does the State says in response to this motion?
***[73]* GREG:** *(in a Southern accent)* Yes, Your Hona, uh, I've examined counsel's motion and I find it spurious. Uh, it clearly does not meet the requirements of eighteen U.S.C. thirty-four.	***[73]* GREG:** *(con un accento non identificato)* Ecco, Vostro Onore, io ho esaminato la richiesta dell'avvocato, ma secondo me è ìmpropria. È che è schiaramente in contrasto con i requisiti rischiesti dalla diciotto trenta quattro.	***[73]* GREG:** *(in a non-identified accent)* Well, Your Honor, uh, I've examined counsel's motion but, in my view, it is spurious. It clearly does not meet the requirements of eighteen U.S.C. thirty-four.
***[74]* JUDGE HARPER:** So what you're saying, Mr. Montgomery, is that dog won't hunt?	***[74]* GIUDICE HARPER:** Sarebbe come dire, Avvocato Montgomery, che il segugio non sa cacciare?	***[74]* JUDGE HARPER:** That would mean, Mr. *(Counselor)* Montgomery, that the hound doesn't know how to hunt?
***[75]* GREG:** *(in a Southern accent)* No, sir, that dog is a ... vegetarian.	***[75]* GREG:** *(con un accento non identificato)* No, signore, quel cane è ... un vegetariano.	***[75]* GREG:** *(in a non-identified accent)* No, sir, that dog is a ... vegetarian.
***[76]* JUDGE HARPER:** Vegetarian. Very good. *(chuckles)*	***[76]* GIUDICE HARPER:** Ah ah un vegetariano, ma certo! *(ridacchia)*	***[76]* JUDGE HARPER:** Ah ah a vegetarian, but of course! *(chuckles)*
***[77]* PETE:** *(tugs on Greg's coat)* What are you doin'?	***[77]* PETE:** *(tira Greg per la giacca)* Che stai facendo?	***[77]* PETE:** *(tugs on Greg's coat)* What are you doin'?

[78] **GREG:** Well, maybe they didn't teach you this at the Bob Marley School of Law, but sometimes you have to butter up the judge.	*[78]* **GREG:** Bé, forse non te l'hanno insegnato alla Bob Marley Facoltà di Legge, ma certe volte bisogna anche compiacere il giudice.	*[78]* **GREG:** Well, maybe they didn't teach you this at the Bob Marley Faculty of Law, but sometimes you have to humour the judge.
[79] **JUDGE HARPER:** Continue, Mr. Montgomery.	*[79]* **GIUDICE HARPER:** Continui pure, avvocato.	*[79]* **JUDGE HARPER:** Please continue, Counselor.
[80] **GREG:** *(in a Southern accent)* Well, if I might, uh, beg the court's indulgence, but as it is unseasonably warm in here, I was wonderin' if there'd be any objection to my continuin' in my shirtsleeves?	*[80]* **GREG:** *(con un accento non identificato)* Ma veramante io mi appello all'indulghienzia della Corte, ma dato che fa incredibilmente caldo qui dantro chiederei di poter scontinuare il dibattimanto in maniche di camicia.	*[80]* **GREG:** *(in a non-identified accent)* Well, actually I beg the court's indulgence, but as it is incredibly warm in here, I'd like to ask if I may continue the hearing in my shirtsleeves.
[81] **JUDGE HARPER:** I don't see as how that can affect the dignity of these proceedin's.	*[81]* **GIUDICE HARPER:** Non vedo come questo possa offendere la dignità di questo procedimento.	*[81]* **JUDGE HARPER:** I don't see as how that can affect the dignity of these proceedings.
[82] **GREG:** Thank you, Your Hona.	*[82]* **GREG:** Grazie, Vostro Onore.	*[82]* **GREG:** Thank you, Your Honor.
[83] **PETE:** *(to Dharma)* Will you tell me what's goin' on?	*[83]* **PETE:** *(rivolgendosi a Dharma)* Dharma, mi spieghi che diavolo succede?	*[83]* **PETE:** *(to Dharma)* Dharma, will you tell me what's going on?
[84] **DHARMA:** What?	*[84]* **DHARMA:** Cosa?	*[84]* **DHARMA:** What?
[85] **PETE:** The accent.	*[85]* **PETE:** Come parla?	*[85]* **PETE:** How does he speak?
[86] **DHARMA:** What accent?	*[86]* **DHARMA:** Come parla?	*[86]* **DHARMA:** How does he speak?
[87] **GREG:** *(in a Southern accent)* The learned attorney for the defense has presented us with a motion that is filled with all kinds of hoo-hah — prejudicial this, fair trial that. Frankly, when I read the thing, I was more mixed up than a basketful of puppies on a Ferris wheel. *(Judge Harper laughs. Greg looks at Dharma surprised)*	*[87]* **GREG:** *(con un accento non identificato)* L'avvocato incaricato della difaisa ha presentato una mozione che potrei definire un guazzabuglio di incomprensibili termini legali — pregiudizievole qua, processo equo di là. Francamente, dopo averlo letto, mi sono sentito più sconvolto di una cesta di cuccioli sulla ruota di un battello! *(Il Giudice Harper ride. Greg guarda Dharma sorpreso).*	*[87]* **GREG:** *(in a non-identified accent)* The attorney in charge of the defense has presented us with a motion that I may define as a tangle of unintelligible legal terms — prejudicial this, fair trial that. Frankly, after having read it, I felt more mixed up than a basketful of puppies on a Ferris wheel. *(Judge Harper laughs. Greg looks at Dharma surprised)*

Friends episode #457316 *The One Where Joey Moves Out*
(I tatuaggi – The Tattoos)

Original English version:	***Italian dubbing translation:***	***Back-translation into Standard English:***
[Chandler and Joey's apartment]	**[Appartamento di Chandler e Joey]**	**[Chandler and Joey's apartment]**
(Chandler and Joey are returning from their brunch at the place of Joey's co-star who's moving and renting his apartment) *[1]* **JOEY:** Can we drop this? I am not interested in the guy's apartment.	*(Chandler e Joey sono di ritorno da una colazione a casa di un collega di Joey che sta trasferendosi ed affitta il suo appartamento)* *[1]* **JOEY:** Vuoi smetterla adesso? Ti ho già detto che non mi interessa quell'appartamento.	*(Chandler and Joey are returning from their brunch at the place of Joey's co-star who's moving and renting his apartment)* *[1]* **JOEY:** Would you come off it, now? I've already told you that I'm not interested in that apartment.

[2] **CHANDLER:** Oh please, I saw the way you were checking out his mouldings. You want it.	*[2]* **CHANDLER:** Oh, per favore, ho visto come guardavi tutte le rifiniture. Tu lo vuoi.	*[2]* **CHANDLER:** Oh please, I saw the way you were looking at all its mouldings. You want it.
[3] **JOEY:** Why would I want another apartment, huh? I've already got an apartment that I love.	*[3]* **JOEY:** E perché mai dovrei volerlo? Eh? Io ho già un appartamento che mi piace.	*[3]* **JOEY:** Why should I want it? I've already got an apartment that I like.
[4] **CHANDLER:** Well it wouldn't kill you to say it once in a while.	*[4]* **CHANDLER:** Perché non dici la verità una volta tanto?	*[4]* **CHANDLER:** Why don't you say the truth, once in a while?
[5] **JOEY:** Alright, you want the truth? I'm thinkin' about it.	*[5]* **JOEY:** D'accordo, vuoi la verità? Ci sto pensando.	*[5]* **JOEY:** Alright, you want the truth? I'm thinkin' about it.
[6] **CHANDLER:** What?	*[6]* **CHANDLER:** Cosa?	*[6]* **CHANDLER:** What?
[7] **JOEY:** I'm sorry. I'm 28 years old, I've never lived alone, and I'm finally at a place where I've got enough money that I don't need a roommate anymore.	*[7]* **JOEY:** Mi dispiace. Chandler, ho quasi ventotto anni, non ho mai abitato da solo e finalmente guadagno abbastanza da potermi permettere di prendere una casa per conto mio.	*[7]* **JOEY:** I'm sorry Chandler. I'm almost 28 years old, I've never lived alone, and I finally earn well enough to be able to afford renting a house on my own.
[8] **CHANDLER:** Whoah, whoah, whoah. I don't need a roommate either, OK? I can afford to live here by myself. Ya know, I may have to bring in somebody once a week to lick the silverware.	*[8]* **CHANDLER:** Aspetta un attimo, guarda che io ho sempre potuto permettermi un appartamento tutto mio come questo dove far venire chi voglio a leccarmi l'argenteria.	*[8]* **CHANDLER:** Wait a minute, look, I've always been able to afford an apartment on my own like this where I can make anyone I want come to lick my silverware.
[9] **JOEY:** What're you gettin' so bent out of shape for, huh? It's not like we agreed to live together forever. We're not Bert and Ernie.	*[9]* **JOEY:** Scusa, ma vuoi dirmi perché ti scaldi tanto? Noi non ci siamo mica sposati, mi sembra. E non siamo Tom e Jerry.	*[9]* **JOEY:** Excuse me, but will you tell me why you are getting so heated? We are not married, I think. And we are not Tom and Jerry.
[10] **CHANDLER:** Look, you know what? If this is the way you feel, then maybe you should take it.	*[10]* **CHANDLER:** Lo sai che ti dico? Se è così che la pensi, allora dovresti andartene.	*[10]* **CHANDLER:** You know what? If this is the way you think, then maybe you should go away.
[11] **JOEY:** Well that's how I feel.	*[11]* **JOEY:** È così che la penso.	*[11]* **JOEY:** That's how I think.
[12] **CHANDLER:** Well then maybe you should take it.	*[12]* **CHANDLER:** E allora vattene!	*[12]* **CHANDLER:** And then go away!
[13] **JOEY:** Well then maybe I will.	*[13]* **JOEY:** Me ne andrò di sicuro.	*[13]* **JOEY:** I will surely go away.
[14] **CHANDLER:** Fine with me.	*[14]* **CHANDLER:** Ne sono felice.	*[14]* **CHANDLER:** I'm happy with it.
[15] **JOEY:** Great. Then you'll be able to spend more quality time with your real friends, the spoons.	*[15]* **JOEY:** Grazie! Così finalmente potrai goderti in santa pace i tuoi veri amici, i cucchiai!	*[15]* **JOEY:** Thanks! So you'll be finally able to enjoy in peace your real friends, the spoons!
[Mr Geller's birthday party]	**[Festa di compleanno del Signor Geller]**	**[Mr Geller's birthday party]**
(Mr and Mrs. Geller enter the living room looking particularly refreshed. Monica follows looking rather pale) *[16]* **MR. GELLER:** Who's drink can I freshen?	*(Il Signore e la Signora Geller entrano nel soggiorno e appaiono particolarmente ritemprati. Poi entra Monica che appare piuttosto pallida)* *[16]* **SIG. GELLER:** Chi vuole ancora vino?	*(Mr and Mrs. Geller enter the living room looking particularly refreshed. Monica follows looking rather pale)* *[16]* **MR. GELLER:** Who wants more wine?
[17] **MRS. GELLER:** Almost time for cake.	*[17]* **SIG.RA GELLER:** È quasi ora della torta!	*[17]* **MRS. GELLER:** It's almost time for cake.

[18] **ROSS:** Mon, Mon, are you OK?	*[18]* **ROSS:** Scusa... Monica, **[c]** ma che ti succede?	*[18]* **ROSS:** Excuse me... Monica, what's wrong with you?
[19] **MONICA:** You remember that video I found of mom and dad?	*[19]* **MONICA:** Ricordi quella cassetta di mamma e papà che avevo trovato?	*[19]* **MONICA:** Do you remember that videotape I found of mom and dad?
[20] **ROSS:** Yeah.	*[20]* **ROSS:** Sì?	*[20]* **ROSS:** Yeah?
[21] **MONICA:** Well, I just caught the live show.	*[21]* **MONICA:** Bè, adesso li visti dal vivo.	*[21]* **MONICA:** Well, I just saw them in the live show.
[22] **ROSS:** Eww.	*[22]* **ROSS:** Oh.	*[22]* **ROSS:** Oh.
(Monica and Richard are alone in the kitchen). *[23]* **MONICA:** Hey there	*(Monica e Richard sono soli in cucina).* *[23]* **MONICA:** Ciao.	*(Monica and Richard are alone in the kitchen).* *[23]* **MONICA:** Hi.
[24] **RICHARD:** What?	*[24]* **RICHARD:** Che c'è?	*[24]* **RICHARD:** What's the matter?
[25] **MONICA:** Nothing, I just heard something nice about you.	*[25]* **MONICA:** Niente, ho sentito una cosa carina su di te.	*[25]* **MONICA:** Nothing, I just heard something nice about you.
[26] **RICHARD:** Humm, really?	*[26]* **RICHARD:** Umm, davvero?	*[26]* **RICHARD:** Humm, really?
(Mrs. Geller and Ross both enter) *[27]* **MRS. GELLER:** Richard. Richard. Your son isn't seeing anyone is he?	*(Entrano la Signora Geller e Ross)* *[27]* **SIG.RA GELLER:** Richard! Richard, tuo figlio non ha una ragazza fissa, vero?	*(Mrs. Geller and Ross both enter)* *[27]* **MRS. GELLER:** Richard! Richard. Your son hasn't a steady girlfriend, has he?
[28] **RICHARD:** Uhh, not that I know of.	*[28]* **RICHARD:** No, non che io sappia.	*[28]* **RICHARD:** No, not that I know of.
[29] **MRS. GELLER:** Well, I was thinking, why doesn't he give Monica a call?	*[29]* **SIG.RA GELLER:** Bè, stavo pensando, perché non gli dici di chiamare Monica.	*[29]* **MRS. GELLER:** Well, I was thinking, why don't you tell him to give Monica a call.
[30] **RICHARD:** That - that's an idea.	*[30]* **RICHARD:** Certo, certo, è un'idea.	*[30]* **RICHARD:** Sure, sure, that's an idea.
[31] **MONICA:** Well, actually, I'm already seeing someone.	*[31]* **MONICA:** Ecco, in realtà io ho già qualcuno.	*[31]* **MONICA:** Well, actually, I have already someone.
[32] **MRS. GELLER:** Oh?	*[32]* **SIG.RA GELLER:** Oh?	*[32]* **MRS. GELLER:** Oh?
[33] **RICHARD:** Oh?	*[33]* **RICHARD:** Oh	*[33]* **RICHARD:** Oh?
[34] **ROSS:** Ohh.	*[34]* **ROSS:** Ohh.	*[34]* **ROSS:** Ohh.
[35] **MRS. GELLER:** She never tells us anything. Ross, did you know Monica's seeing someone?	*[35]* **SIG.RA GELLER:** Lei non ci dice mai niente. Ross, lo sapevi che Monica aveva un ragazzo?	*[35]* **MRS. GELLER:** She never tells us anything. Ross, did you know Monica has a boyfriend?
[36] **ROSS:** Mom, there are so many people in my life. Some of them are seeing people and some of them aren't. Is that crystal?	*[36]* **ROSS:** Mamma, ci sono tanti di quei ragazzi al mondo! Ah! Alcuni di questi hanno una ragazza e altri no. Questo è vero cristallo?	*[36]* **ROSS:** Mom, there are so many boys in the world! Ah! Some of them have a girlfriend and some others haven't. Is that real crystal?
[37] **MRS. GELLER:** So, who's the mystery man?	*[37]* **SIG.RA GELLER:** Allora, chi è il fortunato?	*[37]* **MRS. GELLER:** So, who's the lucky one?
[38] **MONICA:** Well, uh, he's a doctor.	*[38]* **MONICA:** Ecco, eh, è un dottore.	*[38]* **MONICA:** Well, uh, he's a doctor.
[39] **MRS. GELLER:** A real doctor?	*[39]* **SIG.RA GELLER:** Un vero dottore?	*[39]* **MRS. GELLER:** A real doctor?
[40] **MONICA:** No, a doctor of meat. Of course he's a real doctor. And he's handsome, and	*[40]* **MONICA:** No, un dottore finto! Ma certo che è un dottore vero! Ed è affascinante, è dolcis-	*[40]* **MONICA:** No, a fake doctor! Of course he's a real doctor. And he's charming, he's very sweet,

he's sweet, and know you'd like him. *(She puts her arm around Richard).*	simo e so che ti piace da morire. *(mette un braccio attorno a Richard).*	and I know you adore him. *(She puts her arm around Richard).*
[41] **MRS. GELLER:** Well that's wonderful... I	*[41]* **SIG.RA GELLER:** Ah, mi fa piacer...	*[41]* **MRS. GELLER:** Ah, I'm pleas..
[42] **MONICA:** Mom, it's OK.	*[42]* **MONICA:** Mamma, respira adesso.	*[42]* **MONICA:** Mom, get your breath back now.
[43] **RICHARD:** It is, Judy.	*[43]* **RICHARD:** Stiamo insieme.	*[43]* **RICHARD:** We are together.
[44] **MRS. GELLER:** Jack. Could you come in for a moment? NOW!	*[44]* **SIG.RA GELLER:** Jack! Potresti venire un momento qui? Subito!	*[44]* **MRS. GELLER:** Jack. Could you come in for a moment? NOW!
[45] **MR. GELLER:** *(enters with his bat)* Found it.	*[45]* **SIG. GELLER:** *(Entra con la mazza da baseball)* L'ho trovata!	*[45]* **MR. GELLER:** *(enters with his bat)* Found it.
[46] **ROSS:** I'll take that dad *(grabs the bat).*	*[46]* **ROSS:** La prendo io questa *(gli toglie la mazza dalle mani).* ***[extra cue 1]*** **SIG. GELLER:** Ma cosa...	*[46]* **ROSS:** I'll take this (grabs the bat). ***[extra cue 1]*** **MR. GELLER:** But, what...
[47] **MRS. GELLER:** It seems your daughter and Richard are something of an item	*[47]* **SIG.RA GELLER:** Sembrerebbe che tra tua figlia Monica e il tuo amico Richard ci sia del tenero.	*[47]* **MRS. GELLER:** It would seem your daughter Monica and your friend Richard are sweet on each other.
[48] **MR. GELLER:** That's impossible, he's got a twinkie in the city.	*[48]* **SIG. GELLER:** Impossibile, lui ha già un'amichetta in città.	*[48]* **MR. GELLER:** That's impossible, he's already got a fancy girl in the city.
[49] **MONICA:** Dad, I'm the twinkie.	*[49]* **MONICA:** Sono io l'amichetta.	*[49]* **MONICA:** I'm the fancy girl.
[50] **MR. GELLER:** You're the twinkie?	*[50]* **SIG. GELLER:** Sei tu l'amichetta?	*[50]* **MR. GELLER:** You're the fancy girl?
[51] **RICHARD:** She's not a twinkie.	*[51]* **RICHARD:** Non è un'amichetta.	*[51]* **RICHARD:** She's not a fancy girl.
[52] **MONICA:** Al-alright, l-look you guys, this is the best relationship I've been in...	*[52]* **MONICA:** va bene, questa è la relazione più bella che abbia—	*[52]* **MONICA:** Alright, this is the most beautiful relationship I've had...
[53] **MRS. GELLER:** Oh please, a relationship.	*[53]* **SIG.RA GELLER:** Per favore, adesso si chiama relazione?	*[53]* **MRS. GELLER:** Please, now this is named relationship?
[54] **MONICA:** Yes, a relationship. For your information I am crazy about this man.	*[54]* **MONICA:** Certo! Una relazione! Per tua informazione io sono pazza di questo dottore.	*[54]* **MONICA:** Yes! A relationship. For your information I am crazy about this doctor.
[55] **RICHARD:** Really?	*[55]* **RICHARD:** Davvero?	*[55]* **RICHARD:** Really?
[56] **MONICA:** Yes.	*[56]* **MONICA:** Sì. ***[extra cue 2]*** **RICHARD:** Bene...	*[56]* **MONICA:** Yes. ***[extra cue 2]*** **RICHARD:** Well...
[57] **MR. GELLER:** Am I supposed to stand here and listen to this on my birthday?	*[57]* **SIG. GELLER:** E io dovrei ascoltare tutte queste idiozie nel giorno del mio compleanno?	*[57]* **MR. GELLER:** And I should listen to such foolish things on my birthday?
[58] **MONICA:** Dad, dad this is a good thing for me. Ya know, and you even said yourself, you've never seen Richard happier.	*[58]* **MONICA:** Papà, dovresti essere contento per me. L'hai detto tu stesso che non l'avevi mai visto così felice.	*[58]* **MONICA:** Dad, you should be happy for me. You said yourself that you've never seen Richard happier.
[59] **MR. GELLER:** When did I say that?	*[59]* **SIG. GELLER:** E quando l'avrei detto?	*[59]* **MR. GELLER:** And when should I've said that?

[60] **MONICA:** Upstairs in the bathroom right before you felt up mom. *(Everyone else enters and all start singing "Happy Birthday"*	*[60]* **MONICA:** Di sopra, in bagno, appena prima di buttarti sulla mamma! ***[extra cue 3]*** **ROSS:** Venite avanti. *(Entrano tutti gli altri e cominciano a cantare "Tanti Auguri")*	*[60]* **MONICA:** Upstairs in the bathroom right before you jumped at mom. ***[extra cue 3]*** **ROSS:** Come this way. *(Everyone else enters and all start singing "Happy Birthday")*
[Tattoo parlor]	**[Salone dei tatuaggi]**	**[Tattoo parlor]**
(Rachel is showing Phoebe her tattoo) *[61]* **PHOEBE:** Oh that looks so good, oh I love it.	*Rachel sta mostrando a Phoebe il suo tatuaggio)* *[61]* **PHOEBE:** Oh, è veramente carino! Mi piace da morire!	*(Rachel is showing Phoebe her tattoo)* *[61]* **PHOEBE:** Oh it's really cute! oh I'm mad about it!
[62] **RACHEL:** I know, so do I. Oh Phoebe, I'm so glad you made me do this. OK, lemme see yours.	*[62]* **RACHEL:** Anche a me, sai? Grazie per avermi convinta. Dai, fammi vedere il tuo.	*[62]* **RACHEL:** Me too, you know? Thanks for having convinced me. Come on, let me see yours.
[63] **PHOEBE:** Ahh. OK, let's see yours again.	*[63]* **PHOEBE:** Oh, va bene, rivediamo il tuo.	*[63]* **PHOEBE:** Oh, Okay, let's see yours again.
[64] **RACHEL:** Phoebe we just saw mine, let me see yours.	*[64]* **RACHEL:** L'abbiamo appena visto. Ora fammi vedere il tuo	*[64]* **RACHEL:** We just saw mine, now let me see yours.
[65] **PHOEBE:** Oh OK. *(pulls over her shirt and shows a bare shoulder)* Oh no, oh it's gone, that's so weird, I don't know how-where it went.	*[65]* **PHOEBE:** Come vuoi. *(Abbassa la camicia e scopre una spalla senza traccia di tatuaggi)* Oh no! Oh, santo cielo! È scomparso! Non ho veramente idea di dove sia finito!	*[65]* **PHOEBE:** As you like. *(pulls over her shirt and shows a bare shoulder)* Oh no! Oh, good heavens! It has disappeared! I really have no idea where it's gone!
[66] **RACHEL:** You didn't get it?	*[66]* **RACHEL:** Non te lo sei fatto?	*[66]* **RACHEL:** You didn't get it?
[67] **PHOEBE:** No.	*[67]* **PHOEBE:** No.	*[67]* **PHOEBE:** No.
[68] **RACHEL:** Why didn't you get it?	*[68]* **RACHEL:** Perché hai cambiato idea?	*[68]* **RACHEL:** Why did you change your mind?
[69] **PHOEBE:** I'm sorry, I'm sorry.	*[69]* **PHOEBE:** Scusa, ma non ne ho avuto il coraggio!	*[69]* **PHOEBE:** Sorry, but I didn't have the nerve!
[70] **RACHEL:** Phoebe, how would you do this to me? This was all your idea.	*[70]* **RACHEL:** Phoebe, ma come hai potuto farmi questo? Era stata tua l'idea!	*[70]* **RACHEL:** Phoebe, but how would you do this to me? This was all your idea!
[71] **PHOEBE:** I know, I know, and I was gonna get it but he came in with this needle and uh di-, did you know they do this with needles?	*[71]* **PHOEBE:** Sì. Lo so, lo so, avrei voluto farlo, ma quando ho visto l'ago –ma lo sapevi che i tatuaggi si fanno con gli aghi?	*[71]* **PHOEBE:** Yes, I know, I know, I would have liked to get it, but when I saw the needle — but did you know tattoos are done with needles?
[72] **RACHEL:** Really? You don't say, because mine was licked on by kittens.	*[72]* **RACHEL:** Ma davvero? Non mi dire! E allora perché il mio lo hanno fatto con i gessetti?	*[72]* **RACHEL:** Really? You don't say! So why was mine done with crayons?

Will & Grace episode #2.08 *Homo for the Holidays*
(Gay per caso - Gay by chance)

Original English version:	***Italian dubbing translation:***	***Back-translation into Standard English:***
[Will's apartment]	**[Appartamento di Will]**	**[Will's apartment]**
[1] **JACK:** Mom?	*[1]* **JACK:** Mamma?	*[1]* **JACK:** Mom?
[2] **JUDITH:** Jack ... honey, I'm worried. You haven't said a thing about my bangs.	*[2]* **JUDITH:** Jack, tesoro, sono preoccupata. Non hai ancora detto una parola sui miei capelli.	*[2]* **JUDITH:** Jack, darling, I'm worried. You haven't yet said a word about my hair.

[3] **JACK:** They're a little short, but they'll grow in. Mom, I have something I want to say to you. I've kept this from you for a long time, and that's wrong because it makes seem like I'm shamed of something I'm not shamed of. I want you to know who I am because I'm proud of who I am. Mom ... are you wearing Chloe?	*[3]* **JACK:** Sono un po' corti, ma cresceranno. Mamma, devo dirti una cosa, mettiti seduta. Io te l'ho tenuto nascosto per molto tempo e questo è un errore perché così sembra che mi vergogni di qualcosa, mentre non è affatto così. Io voglio che tu sappia chi sono perché sono orgoglioso di essere come sono. Mamma ... è un profumo alla rosa?	*[3]* **JACK:** It's a little short, but it'll grow in. Mom, I must tell you something, sit down. I've kept this hidden from you for a long time, and that's a mistake because it makes seem like I'm shamed of something, whereas it's not at all so. I want you to know who I am because I'm proud of being the way I am. Mom ... is it a scent of rose?
[4] **WILL:** Jack.	*[4]* **WILL:** Jack.	*[4]* **WILL:** Jack.
[5] **JACK:** Mom, I'm gay.	*[5]* **JACK:** Mamma, sono gay.	*[5]* **JACK:** Mom, I'm gay.
[6] **JUDITH:** Oh!	*[6]* **JUDITH:** Oh!	*[6]* **JUDITH:** Oh!
[7] **GRACE:** Judith *(Grace puts her arm around Judith)* It's ok. So he's gay. He's still the same little boy who gave you highlights for the first time.	*[7]* **GRACE:** Judith *(Grace mette un braccio attorno a Judith)* non è cambiato niente. È così, lui è gay. Resta lo stesso ragazzo buono che ti ha fatto i colpi di sole la prima volta.	*[7]* **GRACE:** Judith *(Grace puts her arm around Judith)* nothing has changed. It's so, he's gay. He's still the same good boy who gave you highlights for the first time.
[8] **KAREN:** I think you are missing the silver lining here. When you're old and in diapers, a gay son will know how to keep you away from chiffon and backlighting.	*[8]* **KAREN:** Tesoro, hai perso di vista l'aspetto migliore. Quando sei vecchia e depressa un figlio gay sa come impedirti di farti fare questo color cenere e sbagliare taglio, povera cara.	*[8]* **KAREN:** Darling, I think you've missed the best aspect. When you're old and depressed, a gay son will know how to keep you away from having this ashen hue done and getting a haircut wrong, poor thing.
[9] **JACK:** Mom, I'm sorry to disappoint you, but ... this is who I am.	*[9]* **JACK:** Mamma, mi dispiace di averti delusa, io sono come sono.	*[9]* **JACK:** Mom, I'm sorry to disappoint you, I am as I am.
[10] **JUDITH:** You could never disappoint me. I just want you to be happy. Looking back on it... there have been clues. When you were a child, you were overly fond of the nursery rhyme "Rub-a-dub-dub, three men in a tub". And you do have a lot of flamboyantly gay friends. I mean, look at Will. No matter what, Jack... You're what I'm most thankful in the whole world. *(Judith and Jack hug. Will, Grace, and Karen start leaving to give them privacy).*	*[10]* **JUDITH:** Tu non potrai mai deludermi. Io ti vorrò sempre bene. Ripensandoci, qualche indizio c'era. Quando tu eri piccolo ti piaceva troppo quella filastrocca in rima "Barattò la pappa per tre uomini e una cappa". E hai sempre avuto una quantità di favolosi gay tra i tuoi amici, insomma, guarda quello! *(indica Will)* A me non importa, Jack. Tu sei la cosa per cui io mi sento grata al mondo intero. *(Judith e Jack si abbracciano. Will, Grace e Karen si accingono ad andar via per lasciarli da soli).*	*[10]* **JUDITH:** You could never disappoint me. I will always love you. Looking back on it, there has been some clue. When you were a child, you were overly fond of the nursery rhyme "He swapped the pap for three men and a cap". And you have always had a lot of fabulous gay guys among your friends, well, look at him! *(she indicates Will).* I don't mind, Jack. You're what I'm most thankful in the whole world. *(Judith and Jack hug. Will, Grace, and Karen start leaving to give them privacy).*
[11] **JACK:** Why are you crying?	*[11]* **JACK:** E perché piangi?	*[11]* **JACK:** And why are you crying?
[12] **JUDITH:** Because I have a secret too. *(Will, Grace, and Karen turn around).* The man you think is your father ... is not your father.	*[12]* **JUDITH:** Perché adesso mi tocca dire il mio segreto! *(Will Grace e Karen tornano indietro)* L'uomo che tu credi sia tuo padre ... non è tuo padre!	*[12]* **JUDITH:** Because now it falls to me to reveal my secret! *(Will, Grace, and Karen turn around).* The man you think is your father ... is not your father.
[13] **JACK:** What?	*[13]* **JACK:** Cosa?	*[13]* **JACK:** What?
[14] **WILL:** My god, this is like watching *Gays of Our Lives.*	*[14]* **WILL:** Oh mio Dio, è peggio che guardare *Beautiful.*	*[14]* **WILL:** Oh My god, this is worse than watching *The Bold and the Beautiful.*

[15] **JACK:** Who's my father?	*[15]* **JACK:** E chi è mio padre?	*[15]* **JACK:** And who's my father?
[16] **JUDITH:** Well ... it's not exactly clear.	*[16]* **JUDITH:** Bé ... non è che sia così chiaro.	*[16]* **JUDITH:** Well ... it's not exactly so clear.
[17] **JACK:** Mother, if your explanation doesn't end with the phrase "born in a manger", I'm gonna be violently ill.	*[17]* **JACK:** Madre, se la tua spiegazione non termina con "nato in una mangiatoia" mi verrà un attacco di bile!	*[17]* **JACK:** Mother, if your explanation doesn't end with "born in a manager", I'm gonna have a rage attack.
[18] **JUDITH:** It was the sixties! I went to this party. Keys were thrown in a bowl, the bowl was thrown in the pool, off came the ponchos, and nine months later ... there you were.	*[18]* **JUDITH:** Erano gli anni Sessanta! Andai in uno di quei party, le chiavi delle stanze furono buttate in piscina, fuori si spensero le luci e nove mesi più tardi ... arrivasti tu, tesoro.	*[18]* **JUDITH:** It was the sixties! I went to one of those parties, room keys were thrown in the swimming pool, lights were turned off, and nine months later ... you arrived, darling.
[19] **JACK:** Oh. Ok. Uhh ... I can accept that. So ... the guy I thought was my dad ... wasn't. *(Jack faints).*	*[19]* **JACK:** Oh. Oh. Ok. Io posso accettare quest—a ... L'uomo che pensavo fosse mio padre ... non lo è. *(Jack sviene).*	*[19]* **JACK:** Oh. Oh. Ok. I can accept thi-s ... The man I thought was my dad ... is not. *(Jack faints).*
[20] **KAREN:** So Jack's gay, huh? *(To Grace)* Hmm. No wonder he went back to you.	*[20]* **KAREN:** Insomma, Jack è gay, eh? *(rivolgendosi a Grace)* mmm, ecco perché era tornato da te, cara.	*[20]* **KAREN:** So Jack's gay, huh? *(To Grace)* Hmm. That's why he went back to you, dear.

References

Agorni, M. 2000. "Quale teoria per la pratica della traduzione multimediale?", in R.M. Bollettieri Bosinelli, R.M. Heiss, C. Soffritti and S. Bernardini (eds) *La Traduzione Multimediale: Quale Traduzione per Quale Testo?*, Bologna: CLUEB, pp. 395-406.

Aijmer, K. 1996. *Conversational Routines in English*. London: Longman.

Aixela, J.F. 1996. "Culture-specific items in translation", in R. Alvarez and M.C.A. Vidal (eds.) *Translation, Power, Subversion*. Clevedon: Multilingual Matters, pp. 52-78.

Alden, D.L. and W.D. Hoyer. 1993. "An examination of cognitive factors related to humorousness in television advertising". *Journal of Advertising*, 23/2, pp. 29-37.

Alden, D.L., W.D. Hoyer and C. Lee. 1993. "Identifying Global and Culture-Specific Dimensions of Humor in Advertising: A Multinational Analysis". *Journal of Marketing*, 57 (April), pp. 64-75.

Alford, R. 1982. *The Evolutionary Significance of the Human Humor Response*. Atti della Terza Conferenza Internazionale sull'Umorismo. Washington, D.C., p. 238.

Anderman, G. and J. Diaz-Cintas (eds) 2009. *Audiovisual Translation: Language Transfer on Screen*. London: Palgrave MacMillan.

Anderson, J.R. 1980. *Cognitive Psychology and Its Implications*. San Francisco: Freeman.

Antonopoulou, E. 2004. "Humor theory and translation research: proper names in humorous discourse". *Humor: International Journal of Humor Research*, 18/1, pp. 41-68.

Apte, M.L. 1983. "Humor research, methodology and theory in Anthropology", in P.F. McGhee and J. Goldstein (eds.) *Handbook of Humor Research*. New York: Springer-Verlag Inc., pp. 183-212.

Apter, M.J. 1982. *The Experience of Motivation*. London: Academic Press.

Apter, M.J. and K.C.P. Smith. 1977. "Humour and the theory of psychological reversals", in A.J. Chapman and H.C. Foot (eds.) *I"s a Funny Thing, Humour*. Oxford: Pergamon Press, pp. 95-100.

Atkinson, M. 1979. "Prerequisites for Reference", in E. Ochs and B.B. Schieffelin (eds.), *Developmental Pragmatics*. New York: Academic Press, pp. 229-250.

Attardo, S. 1994. *Linguistic Theories of Humor*. Berlin: Mouton de Gruyter.

Attardo, S. 1998. "The analysis of humorous narratives". *Humor: International Journal of Humor Research*, 11/3, pp. 231-260.

Attardo, S. 2001. *Humorous Texts: A Semantic and Pragmatic Analysis*. Berlin and New York: Mouton de Gruyter.

Attardo, S. 2002. "Translation and humour: an approach based on the General Theory of Verbal Humour". *The Translator*, 8/2, pp. 173-194.

Attardo, S. and V. Raskin. 1991. "Script theory revis(it)ed: joke similarity and joke representation model". *Humor: International Journal of Humor Research*, 4/3, pp. 293-347.

Attardo, S. C. Hempelman and S. Di Maio. 2002. "Script opposition and logical mechanisms: modelling incongruities and their resolutions". *Humor: International Journal of Humor Research*, 15/1, pp. 3-46.

Austin, J.K. 1962. *How to Do Things with Words*. Oxford: The Clarendon Press.
Bach, K. 1994. "Conversational Impliciture". *Mind & Language*, 9, pp. 124-162.
Baker, M. 1992. *In Other Words: A Coursebook on Translation*. London: Routledge.
Baldry, A. and P.J. Thibault. 2006. *Multimodal Transcription and Text Analysis*. London/Oakville: Equinox.
Barbe, K. 1996. "Dubbing in the translator classroom". *Perspectives: Studies in Translatology*, 4/2, pp. 255-274.
Baron, R.A. 1978a. "Aggression-inhibiting influence of sexual humor". *Journal of Personality and Social Psychology*, 36, pp. 189-197.
Baron, R.A. 1978b. "The influence of hostile and nonhostile humor upon physical aggression". *Personality and Social Psychology Bulletin*, 4, pp. 77-80.
Basnett-McGuire, S. 1980. *Translation Studies*. London: Methuen.
Bell, R.T. 1991. *Translation and Translating: Theory and Practice*. London: Longman.
Berger, A. 1987. "Humor: an introduction". *American Behavioral Scientist*, 30/1, pp. 6-16.
Bergson, H. 1900. *Le Rire: Essai sur la signification du comique*. Alcan: Paris.
Berlyne, D.E. 1960. *Conflict, Arousal and Curiosity*. New York: McGraw-Hill.
Berlyne, D.E. 1969. "Laughter, humor, and play", in G. Lindzey and E. Aronson (eds,) *Handbook of Social Psychology*, Vol.3. New York: Addison-Wesley, pp. 795-852.
Berlyne, D.E. 1972. "Humor and its kin", in J.H. Goldstein and P.E. McGhee (eds.) *The Psychology of Humor: Theoretical Perspectives and Empirical Issues*. New York: Academic Press, pp. 43-60.
Berruto, G. 1987. *Sociolinguistica dell'Italiano Contemporaneo*. Rome: La Nuova Italia Scientifica.
Bialystok, E. 1996. "Symbolic representation and attentional control in pragmatic competence", in G. Kasper and S. Blum-Kulka (eds.), *Interlanguage Pragmatics*. New York: Oxford University Press, pp. 43-57.
Bier, J. 1988. "The problem of the Polish joke in derogatory American humor". *Humor*, 1/2, pp. 135-141.
Billig, M. 2005. *Laughter and Ridicule: Towards a Social Critique of Humour*. London: Sage Publications.
Blake, M. 2005. *How to Be a Sitcom Writer*. Chichester: Summersdale.
Bloomfield, L. 1935. *Language*. London: Allen and Unwin.
Blum-Kulka, S., and E. Olshtain. 1984. "Requests and apologies: a cross-cultural study of speech act realization pattern". *Applied Linguistics*, 3, pp. 196-213.
Bollettieri Bosinelli, R.M., 1996, "La Formazione del Traduttore: Riflessioni su un Percorso Didattico", in G. Cortese (ed.), *Tradurre i Linguaggi Settoriali*, Cortina, Torino, pp. 273-280.
Bovinelli, B. and S. Gallini. 1994. "la traduzione dei riferimenti culturali contestuali nel doppiaggio cinematografico", in R. Baccolini, R.M. Bollettieri Bosinelli and L. Gavioli (eds) *Il Doppiaggio: Trasposizioni Linguistiche e Culturali*. Bologna: CLUEB, pp. 89-98.
Braun, F. 1988. *Terms of Address: Problems of Patterns and Usage in Various Languages and Cultures*. Berlin: Mouton de Gruyter.
Brone, G. and K. Feyaerts. 2004. "Assessing the SSHT and GTVH: a view from Cognitive Linguistics". *Humor: International Journal of Humor Research*, 4/3, pp. 293-347.
Brone, G., K. Feyaerts and T. Veale. 2006. "Introduction: Cognitive linguistic

approaches to humor", in G. Brone, K. Feyaerts and T. Veale (eds), *Humor: International Journal of Humor Research (special issue)*, 19/3, pp. 203-228.

Brown, G. and G. Yule. 1983. *Discourse Analysis*. Cambridge: Cambridge University Press.

Brown, P. and S. Levinson. 1978. "Universals in language usage: politeness phenomena", in E. Goody (ed.) *Questions and Politeness: Strategies in Social Interaction*. Cambridge: Cambridge University Press, pp. 56-289.

Brown, P. and S. Levinson. 1987. *Politeness: Some Universals in Language Usage*. Cambridge: Cambridge University Press.

Brown, R. and A. Gilman. 1972. "The pronouns of power and solidarity", in P.P. Giglioli (ed.) *Language and Social Context*. Harmondsworth: Penguin, pp. 252-282.

Bryars, C. 1977. *The Real Mary Tyler Moore Show*. New York: Pinnacle.

Bucaria, C. 2007. "Humour and other catastrophes: dealing with the translation of mixed-genre TV series". *Linguistica Antverpiensia, New Series*, 6, pp. 235-254.

Bucaria, C. 2008. "Dubbing dark humour: a case study in audiovisual translation". *Lodz Papers in Pragmatism*, 4, pp. 215-240.

Bull, S. 2007. *Elephant Bucks: An Inside Guide to Writing for TV Sitcoms*. Studio City, California: Michael Wiese Productions.

Burgess, A. 1980. "Dubbing", in L. Michaels and C. Ricks (eds), *The State of the Language*. Berkeley: University of California Press, pp. 297-303.

Burton, D. 1980. *Dialogue and Discourse: A Sociolinguistic Approach to Modern Drama Dialogue and Naturally Occurring Conversation*. London: Routledge and Kegan Paul.

Camuzio, E. 1993. "Voce/Volto. Problemi della vocalità nel doppiaggio cinematografico". *Il Verri*, 1/2, pp. 192-217.

Carr, J. and L. Greeves. 2006. *Only Joking: What's So Funny About Making People Laugh?*. New York: Gotham.

Carrell, P.L. 1983. "Some issues in the role of schemata, or background knowledge, in second language comprehension". *Reading in a Foreign Language*, 1/2, pp. 81-92.

Carrisi, L. 2011. *A Cross-cultural Discourse Analysis of the Dubbing Translation of the Sitcom 'The Big Bang Theory'*. Unpublished Undergraduate Thesis (supervisor: Prof. M.G. Guido), Faculty of Foreign Languages and Literature, University of Salento (Italy).

Carter, B. 2002. "Plot twists paid off for *Friends*", in http://query.nytimes.com/gst/fullpage.html?res=9C0CE3D7113BA25751C0A9649C8B63&sec=&spon=&pagewanted=all.

Carter, R.A. 1989. "Poetry and conversation: an essay in discourse analysis", in R.A. Carter and P. Simpson (eds), *Language, Discourse and Literature: An Introductory Reader in Discourse Stylistics*. London: Unwin Hyman, pp. 59-74.

Castleman, H. and W.J. Podrazik. 1982. *Watching TV: Four Decades of American Television*. New York: McGraw-Hill.

Chapman, J. and H.C. Foot (eds). 1976. *Humour and Laughter: Theory, Research and Application*. London: John Wiley & Sons.

Chapman, J. and H.C. Foot (eds). 1977. *It's a Funny Thing, Humour*, Oxford: Pergamon Press.

Chapman, J., H.C. Foot and P. Derks (eds). 1995. *Humor and Laughter: Theory, Research, and Applications*. New Brunswick, NJ: Transaction Publishers.

Chaume, F. 2002. "Models of research in audiovisual translation". *Babel*, 48, pp. 1-13.

Chaume, F. 2004. "Discourse markers in audiovisual translation". *Meta*, XLIX, pp. 833-855.

Chaume-Varela, F. 1998. "Textual constraints and the translator's creativity in dubbing", in A. Beylard-Ozeroff, J. Kralova and B. Moser-Mercer (eds), *Translators' Strategies and Creativity*. Amsterdam: Benjamins, pp.15-22.

Chekhov, M. 1953. *To the Actor: On the Technique of Acting*. New York: Harper and Row.

Chiaro, D. 1992. *The Language of Jokes: Analyzing Verbal Play*. London: Routledge.

Chiaro, D. 2004. "Investigating the perception of translated Verbally Expressed Humour on Italian TV". *ESP Across Cultures*, 1, pp. 35-52.

Chiaro, D. 2007. "The effect of translation on humour response: the case of dubbed comedy in Italy", in Y. Gambier, M. Shlesinger and R. Stolze (eds) *Doubts and Directions in Translation Studies*. Amsterdam/Philadelphia: John Benjamins, pp. 137-152.

Chomsky, N. 1965. *Aspects of the Theory of Syntax*. Cambridge, Mass.: The MIT Press.

Chomsky, N. 1980. *Rules and Representations*. New York: Columbia University Press.

Clark, H.H. and E.F. Schaefer. 1992. "dealing with overhearers", in H.H. Clark (ed.) *Arena of Language Use*. Chicago: The University of Chicago Press, pp. 248-273.

Comuzio, E. 1993. "Voce/volto. Problemi della vocalità nel doppiaggio cinematografico". *Il Verri* 1/2, pp.192-217.

Cook, G. 1989. *Discourse*. Oxford: Oxford University Press.

Cooper, E. 2003. "Decoding *Will and Grace*: mass audience reception of a popular network situation comedy". *Sociological Perspectives*, 46/4, pp. 513-533.

Corrius, M. 2008. *Translating Multilingual Audiovisual Texts. Priorities and Restrictions. Implications and Applications*. Barcelona: Autonomous University of Barcelona.

Coulmas, F. 1981. *Conversational Routine: Explorations in Standardized Communication Situations and Prepatterned Speech*. The Hague: Mouton.

Coulthard, M. and D. Brazil. 1981. "Exchange structure", in M. Coulthard and M. Montgomery (eds), *Studies in Discourse Analysis*. London: Routledge & Kegan Paul, pp. 82-106. (Also published in M. Coulthard (ed.) 1992. *Advances in Spoken Discourse Analysis*. London: Routledge, pp. 50-78).

Coulthard, R.M. and M. Montgomery. 1981. *Studies in Discourse Analysis*. London: Routledge and Kegan Paul.

Couper-Kuhlen, E. 1986. *English Prosody*. London: Edward Arnold.

Couper-Kuhlen, E. and M. Selting (eds.) 1996. *Prosody in Conversation*. Cambridge: Cambridge University Press.

Coupland, N. and J. Coupland. 2000. "Relational frames and pronominal address/reference: the discourse of geriatric medical triads", in S. Sarangi and M. Coulthard (eds), *Discourse and Social Life*. London: Longman, pp. 207-229.

Critchley, S. 2002. *On Humour (Thinking in Action)*. London: Routledge.

Cronin, M. 2003. *Translation and Globalization*. London: Routledge.

Cruttenden, A. 1986. *Intonation*. Cambridge: Cambridge University Press.

Crystal, D. 1969. *Prosodic Systems and Intonation in English*. Cambridge: Cambridge University Press.

Culpeper, J. 2001. *Language and Characterization: People in Plays and Other Texts*. Harlow: Longman.

Cuppone, T. 2006. *A Conversational Analysis of the Intercultural Conflicts in the Film-Script 'Bend it Like Beckham'.* Unpublished Undergraduate Thesis (supervisor: Prof. M.G. Guido), Faculty of Foreign Languages and Literature, University of Lecce (Italy).

Cutler, A. and M. Pearson. 1986. "On the analysis of prosodic turn-taking cues", in C. Johns-Lewis (ed.) *Intonation in Discourse.* London: Croom Helm, pp. 139-155.

Danan, M. 1991. "Dubbing as an expression of nationalism". *Meta: Journal des Traducteurs / Translators' Journal,* 36/4, pp. 606-614.

Delabastita, D. 1989. "Translation and mass-communication: film and TV translation as evidence of cultural dynamics". *Babel,* 35, pp. 193-218.

Delabastita, D. 1994. "Focus on the pun: wordplay as a special problem in translation studies". *Target,* 6, pp.223-243.

Díaz-Cintas, J. 2004. "In search of a theoretical frame work for the study of audiovisual translation", in P. Orero (ed.) *Topics in Audiovisual Translation.* Amsterdam: Benjamins, pp. 21-34.

Díaz-Cintas, J. 2008. *The Didactics of Audiovisual Translation.* Amsterdam/Philadelphia: John Benjamins.

Dobrzynska, T. 1995. "Translating metaphor: problems of meaning. *Journal of Pragmatics,* 25, pp. 595-604.

Dore, M. 2010. "The audiovisual translation of fixed expressions and idiom-based puns", in M.C. Valero Garcés (ed.), *Dimensions of Humor: Explorations in Linguistics, Literature, Cultural Studies and Translation.* Valencia: University of Valencia Press pp. 361-385.

Dressler, W.U. 1988. "La Semiotica del Ricevente e i Parametri Universali della Fonologia/Morfologia Naturale", in T. De Mauro, S. Gensini, and M.E. Piemontese (eds) *Dalla Parte del Ricevente: Percezione, Comprensione, Interpretazione. Atti del XIX Congresso Internazionale della Società di Linguistica Italiana,* 26. Rome: Bulzoni, pp. 5-21.

Dries, J. 1995. *Dubbing and Subtitling: Guidelines for Production and Distribution.* Dusseldorf: The European Institute for the Media.

Dworkin, E.S. and J.S. Efran. 1967. "The angered: their susceptibility to varieties of humor". *Journal of Personality and Social Psychology,* 6, pp. 233-236.

Edmonson, W. 1981. *Spoken Discourse: A Model for Analysis.* London: Longman.

Eisner, J. and D. Krinsky. 1984. *Television Comedy Series.* Winston-Salem: McFarland.

Empson, W. 1961. *Seven Types of Ambiguity.* Harmondsworth: Penguin.

Erickson, F. 1975. "Gatekeeping and the melting pot: interaction in counselling interviews". *Harvard Education Review,* 45, pp. 44-70.

Ericsson, A.K. and H.A. Simon. 1984. *Protocol Analysis: Verbal Reports as Data.* Cambridge, Mass.: The MIT Press.

Faerch, C., and G. Kasper. 1984. "Pragmatic knowledge: rules and procedures". *Applied Linguistics,* 3, pp. 214-225.

Faerch, C. and G. Kasper (eds.) 1987. *Introspection in Second Language Research.* Clevedon: Multilingual Matters.

Fairclough, N. 1995. *Critical Discourse Analysis.* London: Longman.

Fauconner, G. and M. Turner. 2002. *The Way We Think: Conceptual Blending and the Mind's Hidden Complexities.* New York: Basic Books.

Fawcett, R.P., A. van der Mije, and C. van Wissen. 1988. "Towards a Systemic

Flowchart Model for Discourse Structure", in R.P. Fawcett and D. Young (eds), *New Developments in Systemic Linguistics*. London: Pinter, pp. 116-143.
Ferrari, C.F. 2011. *Since When Is Fran Drescher Jewish?: Dubbing Stereotypes in The Nanny, The Simpsons, and The Sopranos*. Austin: University of Texas Press.
Fine, G.A. 1983. "Sociological approaches to the study of humor", in P.F. McGhee and J. Goldstein (eds) *Handbook of Humor Research*. New York: Springer-Verlag Inc., pp. 159-181.
Fink, G. 1984. "Pride and prejudice: Italian dubbing and Hollywood stereotypes". *Rivista di Studi Anglo-Americani*, 3, pp.213-225.
Finn, N. 2006. "Racy 'Grace' made mark by creating laughter". *Television Week*, 31 July, p. 34.
Firth, J.R. 1957. "The techniques of semantics", in *Papers in Linguistics: 1934-1951*. London: Oxford University Press, pp. 7-33.
Fish, S.E. 1980. *Is There a Text in this Class? The Authority of Interpretative Communities*. Cambridge, Mass.: Harvard University Press.
Fleet, F.R. 2010. *An Analysis of Wit and Humour*. Memphis: General Books LLC.
Fodor, I. 1976. *Film Dubbing: Phonetic, Semiotic, Aesthetic and Psychological Aspects*. Hamburg: Buske.
Forster, E.M. 1966. *Aspects of the Novel*. London: Penguin.
Fowler, R. 1977. *Linguistics and the Novel*. London: Methuen.
Francis, G. and S. Hunston. 1992. "Analysing everyday conversation", in M. Coulthard (ed.), *Advances in Spoken Discourse Analysis*. London: Routledge, pp. 1-34.
Franklyn, B. 2008. *Towards a Theory of Postmodern Humour: South Park, Seriousness, and Social Control*. VDM: Verlag Dr. Mueller Aktiengesellschaft & Co. KG.
Frascerra, M. 2006. *A Discourse Analysis of the Intercultural and Conversational Dynamics in Three American Sitcoms*. Unpublished Undergraduate Thesis (supervisor: Prof. M.G. Guido), Faculty of Foreign Languages and Literature, University of Lecce (Italy).
French, P. and J. Local. 1986. "Prosodic features and the management of interruptions", in C. Johns-Lewis (ed.) *Intonation in Discourse*. London: Croom Helm.
Freud, S. 1963. *Jokes and their Relations to the Unconscious*. New York: W.W. Norton & Company. (1st Ed. 1905).
Fries, C.C. 1952. *The Structure of English: An Introduction to the Construction of English Sentences*. New York: Harcourt, Brace & Co.
Fry, W.F.Jr. 1987. "Humor and paradox". *American Behavioral Scientist*, 30/1, pp. 42-71.
Frye, N. 1957. *Anatomy of Criticism: Four Essays*. Princeton: Princeton University Press.
Frye, N. 1959. *Fables of Identity: Studies in Poetic Mythology*. New York: Harcourt Brace Jovanovich.
Fuentes-Luque, A. 2003. "An empirical approach to the reception of AV translated humour: a case study of the Marx Brothers' *Duck Soup*". *The Translator*, 9, pp. 293-306.
Gaiba, F. 1994. "La traduzione di alcuni aspetti umoristici nel doppiaggio cinematografico", in R. Baccolini, R.M. Bollettieri Bosinelli and L. Gavioli (eds) *Il doppiaggio. Trasposizioni linguistiche e culturali*. Bologna: CLUEB, pp. 105-112.
Gairola, R. 2000. "Will & Grace: watching with ambivalence". *Pop Matters Television*, October 3 (http://www.popmatters.com/tv/reviews/w/will-and-grace.html).

Galassi, G. 1994. "La norma traviata", in R. Baccolini, R.M. Bollettieri Bosinelli, R.M. and L. Gavioli (eds) *Il Doppiaggio: Trasposizioni Linguistiche e Culturali*. Bologna: CLUEB, pp.61-70.

Gambier, Y. 2003. "Introduction. Screen transadaptation: perception and reception". *The Translator*, 9/2, pp. 171-189.

Garfinkel, H. 1967. *Studies in Ethnomethodology*. Englewood Cliffs, NJ: Prentice-Hall.

Giles, H. and P. Powesland. 1975. *Speech Style and Social Evaluation*. New York: Academic Press.

Giora, R. 1991. "On the cognitive aspects of jokes". *Journal of Pragmatics*, 16, pp. 465-485.

Giora, R. 2003. *On Our Mind: Salience, Context and Figurative Language*. New York: New York University Press.

Goatly, A. 1997. *The Language of Metaphors*. London and New York: Routledge.

Godkewitsch, M. 1972. "The relationship between arousal potential and funniness in jokes", in J.H. Goldstein and P.E. McGhee (eds) *The Psychology of Humor: Theoretical Perspectives and Empirical Issues*. New York, Academic Press, pp. 143-158.

Godkewitsch, M. 1976. "Physiological and verbal indices of arousal in rated humour", in A.J. Chapman and H.C. Foot (eds) *Humour and Laughter: Theory, Research and Application*. London: John Wiley & Sons, pp. 117-138.

Goffman, E. 1967. *Interaction Ritual: Essays on Face-To-Face Behaviour*. New York: Doubleday Anchor.

Goffman, E. 1978. "Response cries". *Language*, 54, pp. 787-815.

Goffman, E. 1981. *Forms of Talk*. Philadelphia: University of Pennsylvania Press.

Goldstein, J.H. 1970. "Repetition, motive arousal, and humor appreciation". *Journal of Experimental Research in Personality*, 4, pp. 90-94.

Goldstein, J.H. and P.E. McGhee (eds). 1972. *The Psychology of Humor: Theoretical Perspectives and Empirical Issues*. New York: Academic Press.

Goldstein, J.H., J.M. Suls and S. Anthony. 1972. "Enjoyment of specific types of humor content: motivation or salience?", in J.H. Goldstein and P.E. McGhee (eds.) *The Psychology of Humor*. New York: Academic Press.

Goody, E. 1978. "Towards a theory of questions", in E. Goody (ed.) *Questions and Politeness: Strategies in Social Interaction*. Cambridge: Cambridge University Press, pp. 17-43.

Gotti, M. 1996. "Il Linguaggio della Divulgazione: Problematiche di Traduzione Intralinguistica", in G. Cortese (ed.), *Tradurre i Linguaggi Settoriali*. Turin: Cortina, pp. 217-235.

Gottlieb, H. 1994. "Subtitling: diagonal translation". *Perspectives: Studies in Translatology*, 1, pp. 101-123.

Grady, J.E., T. Oakley and S. Coulson. 1999. "Blending and metaphor", in R.W. Gibb Jr. and G.J. Steen (eds) *Metaphor in Cognitive Linguistics*. Amsterdam: John Benjamins, pp. 101-124.

Greenberg, J.H. 1963. *Universals of Language*. Cambridge, Mass.: The MIT Press.

Greimas, A.J. 1983 [1966]. *Structural Semantics*. Lincoln: University of Nebraska Press.

Grice, H.P. 1975. "Logic and conversation", in P. Cole and J. Morgan (eds) *Syntax and Semantics 3. Speech Acts*. New York: Academic Press, pp. 41-58.

Gruner, C. and C.R. Gruner. 1999. *The Game of Humor: A Comprehensive Theory of Why We Laugh*. New Brunswick, NJ: Transaction Publishers.

Guido, G. 2001. *The Salience of Marketing Stimuli: An Incongruity-Salience Hypothesis on Consumer Awareness.* Boston, Mass.: Kluwer Academic Publishers.

Guido, G. 2005. *L'Ontoso Anonimato.* Nardò: Besa Editrice.

Guido, M.G. 1992. *King Lear Workshop.* Galatina: Congedo.

Guido, M.G. 1996. *The Representation Model of Second Language Learning: A Computer-Hypertext Approach to Sociolinguistic Cognition and L2 Personalization.* Rome: Bulzoni.

Guido, M.G. 1997. *Aspetti Sociolinguistici, Cognitivi e Pedagogici del Discorso Umoristico: Il Caso dell'Umorismo Australiano.* Galatina: Congedo.

Guido, M.G. 1999. *The Acting Reader: Schema/Text Interaction in the Dramatic Discourse of Poetry.* New York, Toronto, Ottawa: Legas.

Guido, M.G. 2004. *Mediating Cultures: A Cognitive Approach to English Discourse for the Social Sciences.* Milan: LED.

Guido, M.G. 2005. *The Imaging Reader: Visualization and Embodiment of Metaphysical Discourse.* New York, Toronto, Ottawa: Legas.

Guido, M.G. 2008a. *English as a Lingua Franca in Cross-cultural Immigration Domains.* Bern: Peter Lang.

Guido, M.G. 2008b. "The Case of Phrasal Verbs in the Interlanguage of Italian Immigrants in England", in S. Kermas and M. Gotti (eds) *Socially-conditioned Language Change: Diachronic and Synchronic Insights.* Lecce: Edizioni del Grifo, pp. 271-291.

Guido, M.G. 2009. "Cross-cultural Pragmatic Markedness: Migration of Discoursal Forms in Professional Encounters on Immigration Issues", in D. Torretta, M. Dossena, A. Sportelli (eds) *Forms of Migration – Migration of Forms.* Bari: Progedit, pp. 127-141.

Gumperz, J.J. 1982. *Discourse Strategies.* Cambridge: Cambridge University Press.

Gumperz, J.J. and D. Hymes. 1964. *The Ethnography of Communication.* Washington: American Anthropological Association.

Hall, E.T. and M. R. Hall. 1990. *Understanding Cultural Differences: German, French and Americans.* Boston: Nicholas Brealey Publishing.

Halliday, M.A.K. 1973. *Explorations in the Functions of Language.* London: Edward Arnold.

Halliday, M.A.K. 1978. *Language as Social Semiotic: The Social Interpretation of Language and Meaning.* London: Edward Arnold.

Halliday, M.A.K. 1994. *An Introduction to Functional Grammar* (1st ed. 1985) London: Edward Arnold.

Hatim, B. 2004. *Translation: An Advanced Resource Book.* London: Routledge.

Hatim, B. and I. Mason. 1997. *The Translator as Communicator.* London and New York: Routledge.

Heine, B., U. Claudi and F. Hunnemeyer. 1991. *Grammaticalization: A Conceptual Framework.* Chicago: University of Chicago Press.

Hempelmann, C.F. 2004. "Script opposition and logical mechanism in punning". *Humor: International Journal of Humor Research,* 17/4, pp. 381-392.

Herbst, T. 1996. "Why dubbing is impossible", in C. Heiss and R.M. Bollettieri Bosinelli (eds) *Traduzione Multimediale per il Cinema, la Televisione e la Scena.* Bologna: CLUEB, pp. 97-115.

Herbst, T. 1997. "Dubbing and the Dubbed Text – Style and Cohesion: Textual Characteristics of a Special Form of Translation", in A. Trosborg (ed.) *Text*

Typology and Translation. Amsterdam and Philadelphia: John Benjamin, pp. 291-308.

Hervey, S. and I Higgins. 2001. *Thinking Translation*. London and New York: Routledge.

Herzog, T.R. and D.A. Larwin. 1988. "The appreciation of humor in captioned cartoons". *Journal of Psychology*, 122/6, pp. 597-607.

Hickey, L. 1998. "Perlocutionary equivalence: marking, exegesis and recontextualization", in L. Hickey (ed.) *The Pragmatics of Translation*. Clevedon: Multilingual Matters, pp. 217-232.

Himmelstein, H. 1985. *Television Myth and the American Mind*. New York: Praeger.

Hofstede, G. 1983. "National cultures in four dimensions". *International Studies of Management and Organization*, 13/2, p. 52.

Hofstede, G. 1991. *Cultures and Organizations: Software of the Mind*. New York, NYM McGraw-Hill.

Hockett, C.F. 1967. "Where the tongue slips there slip I", in V.A. Fromkin (ed.) *Speech Errors as Linguistic Evidence*. The Haugue: Mouton, pp. 93-119.

Hockett, C.F. 1977. "Jokes", in C.F. Hockett (ed.) *The View from Language: Selected Essays 1948-1964*. Athens, GA: University of Georgia Press, pp. 257-289.

Hymes, D. 1972. "On communicative competence", in J.B. Pride and J. Holmes (eds) *Sociolinguistics: Selected Readings*. Harmondsworth: Penguin, pp. 269-293.

Iaia, P.L. 2009. *Lexico-semantic, Structural and Pragmatic Aspects of Humour in TV Cartoons: From 'Family Guys' to 'I Griffin'*. Unpublished Undergraduate Thesis (supervisor: Prof. M.G. Guido), Faculty of Foreign Languages and Literature, University of Salento (Italy).

Jacquier, S. 1995. "Prima era il silenzio: traduzione e adattamento del doppiaggio cinematografico e televisivo". *Libri e Riviste d'Italia. La traduzione: saggi e documenti II*. Rome: Ministero per I Beni Culturali e Ambientali, Divisione Editoria, pp. 255-266.

Jakobson, R. 1960. "Closing statement: linguistics and poetics", in T.A. Sebeok (ed.) *Style and Language*. Cambridge, Mass.: The MIT Press, pp. 350-377.

Johnson, M. 1987. *The Body in the Mind: The Bodily Basis of Meaning, Imagination, and Reason*. Chicago: The University of Chicago Press.

Johnstone, K. 1981. *Impro: Improvisation and the Theatre*. London: Methuen.

Jones, J.M. 1970. *Cognitive Factors in the Appreciation of Humor: A Theoretical and Experimental Analysis*, Doctoral dissertation, Yale University, New Haven, Connecticut.

Jung, C.G. 1953. *The Collected Works of C.G. Jung*. Vol. V. London: Routhledge.

Kant, I. 1790. *Kritik der Urteilskraft*. Berlin: Lagarde.

Kaplan, A. 1964. *The Conduct of Inquiry*. Scranton, Pennsylvania: Chandler Publishing.

Keith-Spiegel, P. 1972. "Early conceptions of humor: varieties and issues", in J.H. Goldstein and P.E. McGhee (eds.) *The Psychology of Humor*. New York: Academic Press, pp. 3-39.

Kilborn, R. 1989. "'They don't speak proper English': a new look at the dubbing and subtitling debate". *Journal of Multilingual and Multicultural Development*, 10/5, pp. 421-434.

Koestler, A. 1964. *The Act of Creation*. New York: Dell.

Koestler, A. 1974. "Humour and wit". *Encyclopaedia Britannica*, Vol. 9. Chicago: Benton, pp. 5-11.

Kovecses, Z. 2000. *Metaphor and Emotion: Language, Culture and Body in Human Feeling.* Cambridge: Cambridge University Press.

Kovecses, Z. 2005. *Metaphor in Culture: Universality and Variation.* New York: Cambridge University Press.

Kuhlman, T.J. 1985. "A study of salience and motivational theories of humor". *Journal of Personality and Social Psychology*, 49/1, pp. 281-286.

Labov, W. 1970. "The study of language in its social context". *Studium Generale*, 23, pp. 30-87.

Labov, W. 1972. *Sociolingistic Patterns.* Philadelphia: University of Pennsylvania Press.

Ladd, D.R. 1996. *Intonational Phonology.* Cambridge: Cambridge University Press.

Ladegaard, H.J. 1995. "Audience design revisited: persons, roles, and power relations in speech interactions". *Language and Communication*, 15, pp. 89-101.

Lado, R. 1957. *Linguistics Across Cultures.* Ann Arbor: University of Michigan Press.

La Fave, L., J. Haddad and W.A. Maesen. 1976. "Superiority, enhanced self-esteem, and perceived incongruity humour theory", in A.J. Chapman and H.C. Foot (eds) *Humour and Laughter: Theory, Research and Application.* London: John Wiley & Sons, pp. 63-92.

Lakoff, G. 1987. *Women, Fire, and Dangerous Things: What Categories Reveal About the Mind.* Chicago: The University of Chicago Press.

Lakoff, G. and M. Johnson. 1980. *Metaphors We Live By.* Chicago: The University of Chicago Press.

Lakoff, G. and M. Johnson. 1999. *Philosophy in the Flesh: The Embodied Mind and its Challenge to Western Thought.* New York: Basic Books.

Lakoff, R. 1973. "The logic of politeness: minding your p's and q's". *Papers from the 9th Regional Meeting, Chicago Linguistics Society*, pp. 292-305.

Lamb, C.W. 1968. "Personality correlates of humor enjoyment following motivational arousal". *Journal of Personality and Social Psychology*, 12, pp. 66-71.

Landy, E. and S. Matee. 1969. "Evaluation of an aggressor as a function of exposure to cartoon humor". *Journal of Personality and Social Psychology*, 12, pp. 66-71.

Langacker, R.W. 1977. "Syntactic Reanalysis", in Li (ed.) *Mechanisms of Syntactic Change.* Austin: University of Texas Press, pp. 57-139.

Langacker, R.W. 1991. *Foundations of Cognitive Grammar.* Two Vols. Stanford: Stanford University Press.

La Polla, F. 1994. "Quel che si fa dopo mangiato: doppiaggio e contesto culturale", in R. Baccolini, R.M. Bollettieri Bosinelli, R.M. and L. Gavioli (eds) *Il Doppiaggio: Trasposizioni Linguistiche e Culturali.* Bologna: CLUEB, pp. 51-60.

Lauer, M. 2005. "*Friends* creators share show's beginnings", in http://www.msnbc.msn.com/id/4899445/. MSNBC.

Lefevere, A. 1992. *Translation, Rewriting and the Manipulation of Literary Fame.* London and New York: Routledge.

Lefevere, A. and S. Bassnett. 1990. *Translation, History and Culture.* London: Pinter Publishers.

Leibold, A. 1989. "The translation of humour: who says it can't be done". *Meta*, 34, pp. 109-111.

Lendvai, E. 1996. "Types of untranslatable jokes", in K. Klaudy, J. Lambert and A. Sohar (eds) *Translation Studies in Hungary.* Budapest: Scholastica, pp. 89-98.

Leppihalme, R. 1996. "Caught in the frame: a target-culture viewpoint on allusive wordplay". *The Translator*, 2/2, pp. 199-218.

Leppihalme, R. 1997. *Culture Bumps: An Empirical Approach to the Translation of Allusions*. Clevedon: Multilingual Matters.

Levinson, S.C. 1983. *Pragmatics*. Cambridge: Cambridge University Press.

Lionello, O. 1994. "Il falso in doppiaggio", in R. Baccolini, R.M. Bollettieri Bosinelli, R.M. and L. Gavioli (eds) *Il Doppiaggio: Trasposizioni Linguistiche e Culturali*. Bologna: CLUEB, pp. 41-50.

Littlefield, W. 2012. *Top of the Rock: Inside the Rise and Fall of the Must See TV*. New York: Doubleday.

Luyken, G.M., T. Herbst, J. Langham-Brown, H. Reid and H. Spinhof. 1991. *Overcoming Language Barriers in Television: Dubbing and Subtitling for the European Audience.* Manchester: European Institute for the Media.

Maggio, M. 2010. *A Cross-cultural Analysis of Humour in the Dubbing Translation of the Movie 'Monty Python and the Holy Grail'*. Unpublished Undergraduate Thesis (supervisor: Prof. M.G. Guido), Faculty of Foreign Languages and Literature, University of Salento (Italy).

Malinowski, B. 1935. *Coral Gardens and their Magic*. London: Allen and Unwin.

Mangiron, C. and M. O'Hagan. 2006. "Game localisation: unleashing imagination with 'restricted' translation". *The Journal of Specialized Translation*, 6, pp. 10-21.

Maraschio, N. 1982. "L'italiano del doppiaggio", in *La Lingua Italiana in Movimento*, Firenze: Accademia della Crusca Publications, pp. 135-158.

Marc, D. 1998. *Comic Visions: Television Comedy and American Culture*. Oxford: Blackwell.

Martin, J.R. 2000. "Beyond exchange: appraisal systems in English", in S. Hunston and G. Thompson (eds), *Evaluation in Text: Authorial Stance in the Construction of Discourse*. Oxford: Oxford University Press, pp. 143-175.

Martin, J.R. and P.R.R. White 2005. *The Language of Evaluation: Appraisal in English*. New York: Palgrave Macmillan.

Martínez-Sierra, J.J. 2005a. "Translating Audiovisual Humour. A Case Study". *Perspectives: Studies in Translatology*, 13, pp. 289-296.

Martìnez-Sierra, J.J. 2005b. "The manipulation of the text: on the foregnizing/domestication duality in the translation of humor in audiovisual texts". *Translation Studies in the New Millennium: An International Journal for Translation and Interpreting*, 3, pp. 89-99.

Massara, G. 2007. *La Lingua Invisibile: Aspetti Teorici e Tecnici del Doppiaggio in Italia*. Rome: NEU.

Matuella, M.G. 2000. *Dimensioni Interculturali nella Traduzione*. Unpublished Undergraduate Thesis (supervisor: Prof. M.G. Guido), Faculty of Foreign Languages and Literature, University of Rome "San Pio V" (Italy).

Mazzoleni, M. 1995. "Il vocativo", in L. Renzi, G. Salvi and A. Cardinaletti (eds), *Grande Grammatica di Consultazione, Vol.3. Tipi di Frase, Deissi, Formazione delle Parole*. Bologna: Il Mulino, pp. 377-402.

McCarroll, C. 2004. "A *family* sitcom for Gen X – *Friends* cast a new TV mold". *The Christian Science Monitor*, http://www.csmonitor.com/2004/0506/p01s01-ussc.html.

McCauley, S. 1998. "He's gay, she's straight, they're a trend". *The New York Times*, 20 September, p. 31.

McGhee, P.E. 1972. "On the cognitive origins of incongruity humor: fantasy assimilation versus reality assimilation", in J.H. Goldstein and P.E. McGhee (eds) *The Psychology of Humor: Theoretical Perspectives and Empirical Issues*. New York:

Academic Press, pp. 61-79.
McGhee, P.E. 1983. "The role of arousal and hemispheric lateralization in humor", in P.E. McGhee and J.H. Goldstein (eds.) *Handbook of Humor Research*, Vol.1. New York: Springer-Verlag, pp. 13-37.
McGhee, P.E. and J.H. Goldstein (eds). 1983. *Handbook of Humor Research*. New York: Springer-Verlag Inc.
Merritt, M. 1976. "On questions following questions (in service encounters)". *Language in Society*, 5, pp. 315-357.
Mio, J.S. and A. Graesser. 1991. "Humour, Language and Metaphor". *Metaphor and Symbolic Activity*, 6/2, pp. 87-102.
Moerman, M. 1988. *Talking Culture: Ethnography and Conversation Analysis*. Philadelphia: University of Pennsylvania Press.
Moon, R. 1998. *Fixed Expressions and Idioms in English: A Corpus-based Approach*. Oxford and New York: Clarendon Press.
Morreall, J. 1983. *Taking Laughter Seriously*. Albany, New York: State University of New York Press.
Morris, C. 1964. *Signification and Significance: A Study of the Relations of Signs and Values*. Cambridge: Mass.: The MIT Press.
Mueller, C.W. and E. Donnerstein. 1983. "Film-induced arousal and aggressive behaviour". *Journal of Social Psychology*, 119, pp. 61-67.
Munro, D.H. 1951. *Argument of Laughter*. Melbourne: University of Melbourne Press.
Myers Scotton, C. 1983. "The negotiation of identities in conversation: a theory of markedness and code choice". *International Journal of the Sociology of Language*, 44, pp. 115-136.
Nash, W. 1985. *The Language of Humour: Style and Technique in Comic Discourse*. London and New York: Longman.
Neisser, U. 1967. *Cognitive Psychology*. New York: Appleton-Century-Crofts.
Nerhardt, G. 1970. "Humor and inclinations of humor: emotional reactions to stimuli of different divergence from a range of expectancy". *Scandinavian Journal of Psychology*, 11, pp. 185-195.
Newcomb, H. 1974. *TV: The Most Popular Art*. New York: Anchor/Doubleday.
Newmark, P. 1995. *A Textbook of Translation*. London: Phoenix.
Nida, E. 1964. *Towards a Science of Translating*. Leiden: Brill.
Nida, E. and C.R. Taber. 1969. *The Theory and Practice of Translation*. Leiden: Brill.
Niemeier, S. 1991. "Intercultural dimensions of pragmatics in film synchronization", in J. Blommaert and J. Verschueren (eds), *The Pragmatics of Intercultural and International Communication*. Amsterdam: Benjamins, pp. 145-162.
Nisbett, R.E. and T.D. Wilson. 1977. "Telling more than we can know: verbal reports on mental processes". *Psychological Review*, 84, pp. 231-259.
Norrick, N.R. 1993. *Conversational Joking: Humor in Everyday Talk*. Bloomington: Indiana University Press.
Olohan, M. 2004. *Introducing Corpora in Translation Studies*. London: Routledge.
Oppliger, P.A. and J. Sherblom. 1988. "Late night with David Letterman: a humorous balance". *Communication Research Reports*, 5/2, pp. 193-196.
Oring, E. 2003. *Engaging Humour*. Urbana and Chicago: University of Illinois Press.
Paivio, A. 1969. "Mental imagery in associative learning and memory". *Psychological Review*, 76, pp. 241-263.
Palmer, J. 1994. *Taking Humour Seriously*. London and New York: Routledge.

Paolinelli, M. 2004. "Nodes and boundaries of global communications: notes on the translation and dubbing of audiovisuals". *Meta*, 49, pp. 172-181.

Paolinelli, M. and E. Di Fortunato (eds) 2005. *Tradurre per il Doppiaggio. La Trasposizione Linguistica dell'Audiovisivo: Teoria e Pratica di un'Arte Imperfetta*. Milan: Hoepli.

Pavesi, M. 1994. "Osservazioni sulla (socio)linguistica del doppiaggio", in in R. Baccolini, R.M. Bollettieri Bosinelli, R.M. and L. Gavioli (eds) *Il Doppiaggio: Trasposizioni Linguistiche e Culturali*. Bologna: CLUEB, pp. 129-142.

Pavesi, M. 1996. "L'allocuzione nel doppiaggio dall'inglese all'italiano", in C. Heiss and R.M. Bollettieri Bosinelli (eds) *Traduzione Multimediale per il Cinema, la Televisione e la Scena*. Bologna: CLUEB, pp. 117-130.

Pavesi, M. 2005. *La Traduzione Filmica: Aspetti del Parlato Doppiato dall'Inglese all'Italiano*. Rome: Carocci.

Pavesi, M. and E. Perego. 2006. "Profiling film translators in Italy: a preliminary analysis". *The Journal of Specialized Translation*, 6, pp. 99-114.

Peirce, C.S. 1992. *The Essential Peirce*, 2 Vols. N. Houser and C. Kloesel (eds.). Bloomington: Indiana University Press.

Perego, E. 2005. *La Traduzione Audiovisiva*. Rome: Carocci.

Perlmutter, D.D. 2000. "On incongruities and logical inconsistencies in humour: the delicate balance". *Humor: International Journal of Humor Research*, 15/2, pp. 155-168.

Petillo, M. 2008. *Doppiaggio e Sottotitolazione. Problemi Linguistici e Traduttivi nel Mondo della Screen Translation*. Bari: Digilabs.

Pick, A.D. 1980. "Cognition: psychological perspectives", in H.C. Triandis and W. Lonner (eds.) *Handbook of Cross-Cultural Psychology*, Vol. 3. Boston, MA: Allyn and Bacon, pp. 117-153.

Pisek, G. 1997. "Wordplay and the dubber/subtitler". *Aaa-Arbeiten Aus Anglistik Und Amerikanistik*, 22, pp. 37-51.

Pomerantz, A. and J. Fehr. 1997. "Conversation analysis: an approach to the study of social action and sense-making practices", in T. Van Dijk (ed.), *Discourse as Social Interaction*. Thousand Oaks: Sage, pp. 1-37.

Propp, V. 1968. *Morphology of Folktale*. Austin: University of Texas Press.

Purpel, D.E. 1981. "Humour in the great scheme of things – a response to Elizabeth Vallance". *Curriculum Inquiry*, 11, pp. 231-237.

Raffaelli, S. 1994. "Il parlato cinematografico e televisivo", in L. Serianni, P. Trifone and P. Ramière (eds) *Storia della Lingua Italiana: Scritto e Parlato*. Turin: Einaudi, pp. 271-290.

Ramière, N. 2006. "Reaching a foreign audience: cultural transfers in audiovisual translation". *The Journal of Specialized Translation*, 6, pp. 152-166.

Rannow, J. 2000. *Writing Television Comedy*. New York: Allworth Press.

Raskin, V. 1985. *Semantic Mechanisms of Humor*. Dordrecht: D. Reidel.

Roberts, C., E. Davies, and T. Jupp. 1992. *Language and Discrimination: A Study of Communication in Multi-ethnic Workplaces*. London: Longman.

Robinson, D. 2003. *Becoming a Translator: An Introduction to the Theory and Practice of Translation*. London: Routledge.

Ronen, S. 1986. *Comparative and Multinational Management*. New York: John Wiley & Sons, Inc.

Rosch, E. 1977. "Human categorization", in N. Warren (ed.) *Studies in Cross-Cultural Psychology*. New York: Academic Press, Inc., pp. 1-49.

Rosch, E. and C.B. Mervis. 1975. "Family resemblances: studies in the internal structure of categories". *Cognitive Psychology*, 7, pp. 573-605.

Ross, A. 1998. *The Language of Humour*. London: Routledge.

Ross, N. 1995. "Dubbing American in Italy". *English Today. International Review of the English Language*, 11/1, pp.45-50.

Rothbart, M.K. 1973. "Laughter in young children". *Psychological Bulletin*, 80/3, pp. 247-256.

Rothbart, M.K. 1976. "Incongruity, problem solving and laughter", in A.J. Chapman and H.C. Foot (eds) *Humour and Laughter: Theory, Research and Application*. Oxford: Pergamon Press, pp. 37-40.

Rothbart, M.K. 1977. "Psychological approaches to the study of humour", in A.J. Chapman and H.C. Foot (eds) *It's a Fanny Thing, Humour*. Oxford: Pergamon Press, pp. 87-94.

Rowe, T. 1960. "The English dubbing text". *Babel*, 6, pp.116-120.

Ruch, W., S. Attardo, and V. Raskin. 1993. "Toward an empirical verification of the general theory of verbal humour". *Humor: International Journal of Humor Research*, 6/2, pp. 123-136.

Rumelhart, D.E. 1980. "Schemata: the building blocks of cognition", in R.J. Spiro, B. Bruce, and W. Brewer (eds) *Theoretical Issues in Reading Comprehension: Perspectives from Cognitive Psychology, Linguistics, Artificial Intelligence and Education*. Hillsdale, N.J.: Erlbaum, pp. 33-58.

Ryan, P. 2007. *The Art of Comedy: Getting Serious About Being Funny*. Back Stage Books.

Sacks, H. 1974. "An analysis of the course of a joke's telling in conversation", in R. Baumann and J.F. Scherzer (eds) *Explorations in the Ethnography of Speaking*. Cambridge: Cambridge University Press, pp. 337-353.

Sacks, H., E.A. Schegloff and G. Jefferson. 1974. "A simplest systematics for the organization of turn-taking in conversation". *Language*, 4, pp. 696-735.

Salmon Kovarski, L. 2000. "Tradurre l'etnoletto: come doppiare in italiano l''accento hebraico'", in R.M. Bollettieri Bosinelli, C. Heiss, M. Soffritti and S. Bernardini (eds) *La Traduzione Multimediale. Quale traduzione per quale testo?* Bologna: CLUEB, pp. 67-84.

Sandler, E. 2007. *The TV Writer's Workbook: A Creative Approach To Television Scripts*. New York: Delta.

Sanford, A.J. and S.C. Garrod. 1981. *Understanding Written Language*. Chichester: Wiley.

Schachter, S. and J.E. Singer. 1962. "Cognitive, social, and physiological determinants of emotional states". *Psychological Review*, 69, pp. 379-399.

Schank, R. and R. Abelson. 1977. *Plans, Scripts, Goals and Understanding*. Hillsdale, N.J.: Erlbaum.

Schank, R., Goldman, C. Rieger, and C. Riesbeck. 1975. *Conceptual Information Processing*. Amsterdam: North Holland.

Schegloff, E.A. 1972. "Sequencing in conversational openings", in J. Gumperz and D. Hymes (eds), *Directions in Sociolinguistics*. New York: Holt, Rinehart and Winston, pp. 346-380.

Schiffrin, D. 1987. *Discourse Markers*. Cambridge: Cambridge University Press.

Schumann, J.H. 1986. "Research on the acculturation model for second language acquisition". *Journal of Multilingual and Multicultural Development*, 7, pp. 379-392.

Shuttleworth and Cowie 1997

Searle, J.R. 1969. *Speech Acts: An Essay in the Philosophy of Language*. Cambridge: Cambridge University Press.

Searle, J.R. 1975. "Indirect speech acts", in P. Cole and J.L. Morgan (eds), *Speech Acts, Vol.3, Syntax and Semantics*. New York: Academic Press, pp. 59-82.

Searle, J.R. 1983. *Intentionality*. Cambridge: Cambridge University Press.

Sedita S. 2005. *The Eight Characters of Comedy: Guide to Sitcom Acting And Writing*. New York: Atides Publishing.

Selinker, L. and U. Lakshmanan. 1992. "Language transfer and fossilization: the 'Multiple Effect Principle'", in S. Gass and L. Selinker (eds) *Language Transfer in Language Learning*. Amsterdam: John Benjamins, pp. 197-216.

Semino, E. 2008. *Metaphor in Discourse*. Cambridge: Cambridge University Press.

Shales, T. 2004. "A big hug goodbye to Friends and maybe to the sitcom". *The Washington Post*, May 7, 2004. http://www.washingtonpost.com/wp-dyn/articles/A7176-2004May7.html.

Sherzer, J. 1978. "Oh! That's a pun and I didn't mean it". *Semiotica*, 22, pp. 335-350.

Short, M.H. 1989. "Discourse analysis and the analysis of drama", in R. Carter and P. Simpson (eds), *Language, Discourse and Literature: An Introductory Reader in Discourse Stylistics*. London: Unwin Hyman, pp. 139-168.

Schröter, T. 2004. "Of holy goats and the NYPD: a study of language-based screen humour in translation", in G. Hansen *et al.* (eds) *Claims, Changes and Challenges in Translation Studies: Selected Contributions from the EST Congress, Copenhagen 2001*. Amsterdam/Philadelphia: John Benjamins, pp. 157-168.

Shultz, T.R. 1972. "The role of incongruity and resolution in children's appreciation of cartoon humor". *Journal of Experimental Child Psychology*, 13, p.77.

Shultz, T.R. 1974a. "Development of the appreciation of riddles". *Child Development*, 45, pp. 100-105.

Shultz, T.R. 1974b. "Order of cognitive processing in humour appreciation". *Canadian Journal of Psychology*, 28, pp. 409-420.

Shultz, T.R. 1976. "A cognitive-developmental analysis of humour", in J. Chapman and H.C. Foot (eds) *Humour and Laughter: Theory, Research and Application*. London: John Wiley & Sons, pp. 11-36.

Shultz, T.R. 1977. "A cross-cultural study of the structure of humour", in A.J. Chapman and H.C. Foot (eds) *It's a Funny Thing, Humour*. Oxford: Pergamon Press, pp. 175-180.

Shuttleworth, M. and M. Cowie. 1997. *Dictionary of Translation Studies*. Manchester: St. Jerome Publishing.

Silverstein, M. 1998. "Contemporary Transformations of Local Linguistic Communities". *Annual Review of Anthropology*. 27, 401-426.

Sinclair, J. McH. and R.M. Coulthard. 1975. *Towards an Analysis of Discourse: The English Used by Teachers and Pupils*. London: Oxford University Press.

Singer, D.L. 1968. "Aggression, arousal, hostile humor, and catharsis". *Journal of Personality and Social Psychology Monograph Supplements*, 8, pp. 1-14.

Smith, E.S. 2009. *Writing Television Sitcoms*. New York: Perigee Trade.

Snell, J. 2006. "Schema theory and the humour of *Little Britain*". *English Today*, 85, pp. 59-64.

Speck, P.S. 1991. "The humorous message taxonomy: A framework for the study of humorous ads". *Current Issues and Research in Advertising*, 5, pp. 1-44.

Spencer, H. 1860. "The physiology of laughter". *Macmillan's Magazine*, 1, pp. 395-402.

Stanislavski, K. 1981a. *An Actor Prepares*. London: Methuen.

Stanislavski, K. 1981b. *Building a Character*. London: Methuen.

Stanislavski, K. 1981c. *Creating a Role*. London: Methuen.

Stenstrom, A.B. 1994. *An Introduction to Spoken Interaction*. London: Longman.

Strawson, P.F. 1964. "Intention and convention in speech acts". *Philosophical Review*, 73, pp. 439-460.

Strawson, P.F. (ed.) 1971. *Philosophical Logic*. Oxford: Oxford University Press.

Stubbs, M. 1983. *Discourse Analysis*. Oxford: Blackwell.

Suls, J.M. 1972. "A two-stage model of the appreciation of jokes and cartoons: an information-processing analysis", in J.H. Goldstein e P.E. McGhee (eds) *The Psychology of Humour: Theoretical Perspectives and Empirical Issues*. New York: Academic Press, pp. 81-100.

Suls, J.M. 1977. "Cognitive and disparagement theories of humour: a theoretical and empirical synthesis", in A.J. Chapman and H.C. Foot (eds) *It's a Funny Thing, Humour*. Oxford: Pergamon Press, pp. 41-45.

Suls, J.M. 1983. "Cognitive processes in humor appreciation", in P.E. McGhee and J.H. Goldstein (eds.) *Handbook of Humor Research*. New York: Springer-Verlag Inc., pp. 39-58.

Sweetser, E.E. 1988. "Grammaticalization and Semantic Bleaching", in Axmaker, S., A. Jaisser and H. Singmaster (eds) *Berkeley Linguistics Society: General Session and Parasession on Grammaticalization. Berkeley Linguistic Society* 14. Berkeley: University of California Press, pp. 389-405.

Sweetser, E.E. 1990. *From Etymology to Pragmatics: Metaphorical and Cultural Aspects of Semantic Structure*. Cambridge: Cambridge University Press.

Tagliamonte, S. and C. Roberts. 2005. "So weird; so cool; so innovative: the use of intensifiers in the television series Friends". *American Speech*, 80/3, pp. 280-300.

Talmy, L. 1983. "How Language Structures Space", in H. Pick and L. Acredolo (eds) *Spatial Orientation: Theory, Research and Application*. New York: Plenum Press, pp. 225-282.

Tannen, D. 1981. "New York Jewish conversational style". *International Journal of the Sociology of Language*, 30, pp.133-149.

Tannen, D. 1984. *Conversational Style: Analyzing Talk Among Friends*. Norwood, NJ: Ablex.

Tannen, D. 1993. "The relativity of linguistic strategies: rethinking power and solidarity in gender and dominance", in D. Tannen (ed.) *Gender and Conversational Interaction*. New York: Oxford University Press, pp. 165-188.

Tannen, D. 1994. *Gender and Discourse*. Oxford and New York: Oxford University Press.

Thibault, P.J. 2000. "The multimodal transcription of a television advertisement: theory and practice", in A. Baldry (ed.), *Multimodality and Multimediality in the Distance Learning Age*. Campobasso: Palladino, pp. 311-385.

Thomas, J. 1983. "Cross-cultural pragmatic failure". *Applied Linguistics*, 4/2, pp. 91-112.

Thomas, J. 1984. "Cross-cultural discourse as 'unequal encounter': towards a pragmatic analysis". *Applied Linguistics*, 5/3, pp. 226-135.

Titone, R. (ed.) 1995. *Come Parlano gli Adolescenti: Storia di una Ricerca*, Rome: Armando.

Togerson, W.S. 1958. *Theory and Methods of Scaling*. New York: John Wiley and Sons, Inc.

Triandis, H.C., R. Bontempo, M.J. Villareal, M. Asai and N. Lucca. 1988.

"Individualism and collectivism: cross-cultural perspectives on self-ingroup relationships". *Journal of Personality and Social Psychology*, 54/2, pp-. 323-338.

Trice, A.D. 1982. "Ratings of humor following experience with unsolvable tasks". *Psychological Reports*, 51, p. 1148.

Trudgill, P. 1983. *Sociolinguistics: An Introduction to Language and Society.* Harmondsworth: Penguin.

Tsakona, V. 2003. "Jab lines in narrative jokes". *Humor: International Journal of Humor Research*, 16/3, pp. 315-329.

Tsohatzidis, S.L. (ed.), 1994. *Foundations of Speech Act Theory: Philosophical and Linguistic Perspectives.* London: Routledge.

Tsui, A.B. 1989a. "Systemic choices as discourse processes" *Word*, 40, pp. 163-187.

Tsui, A.B., 1989b. "Beyond the adjacency pair". *Language in Society*, 18, pp. 545-564.

Tsur, R. 1992. *Toward a Theory of Cognitive Poetics.* Amsterdam: Elsevier Science Publishers.

Ulrych, M. 1994. "Film dubbing and the translatability of modes of address: power relations and social distance in The French Lieutenant's Woman", in R. Baccolini, R.M. Bollettieri Bosinelli, and L. Gavioli (eds) *Il Doppiaggio: Trasposizioni Linguistiche e Culturali.* Bologna: CLUEB, pp. 139-160.

Van Antwerp, C. and M. Maxwell (1982). Speaker Sex, Regional Dialect and Employability: A Study in Language Attitudes, in Di Pietro, R.J. (ed.) *Linguistics and the Professions. Proceedings of the Second Annual Delaware Symposium on Language Studies.* Norwood, NJ: Ablex.

Van Dijk, T.A. and W. Kintsch. 1983. *Strategies of Discourse Comprehension.* New York: Academic Press.

Vandaele, J. 1999. "'Each Time We Laugh'. Translated humour in screen comedy", in J. Vandaele (ed.) *Translation and the (Re)location of Meaning, Selected Papers of the CETRA Research Seminars in Translation Studies 1994-1996.* Lovain: Catholic University of Lovain, pp. 237-272.

Vandeale, J. 2002. "Humor mechanisms in film comedy: incongruity and superiority". *Poetics Today*, 23/2, pp. 221-249.

Veisbergs, A. 1997. "The contextual use of idioms, wordplays, and translation", in D. Delabastita (ed.), *Traductio: Essays on Punning and Translation.* Manchester: St. Jerome Publishing, pp. 155-176.

Venuti, L. 1995. *The Translator's Invisibility: A History of Translation.* London and New York: Routledge.

Venuti, L. 1998. *The Scandals of Translation: Towards an Ethics of Difference.* London and New York: Routledge.

Vermeer, H. 1994. "Translation today: old and new problems", in M. Snell-Hornby, F. Pochhacker and K. Kaindl (eds), *Translation Studies – An Interdiscipline.* Amsterdam: Benjamins, pp. 3-16.

Voge, H. 1977. "The translation of film: sub-titling versus dubbing". *Babel*, 2, pp. 120-125.

Walte, I. 2007. *The American Way of Comedy: A Comprehensive Analysis of Humour on the Basis of the US Sitcom* Friends. Munich: GRIN Verlag.

Wannan, B. (ed.) 1981. *Treasury of Australian Humour. 1796-1950.* Victoria: Currey O'Neil Ross Pty Ltd.

Warren, N. (ed.) 1977. *Studies in Cross-Cultural Psychology.* New York: Academic

Press, Inc.

Webb, L.S. 2002. *Multicultural Cookbook of Life-cycle Celebrations*. Westport: Greenwood Publishing.

Whitman-Linsen, C. 1992. *Through the Dubbing Glass: The Synchronization of American Motion Pictures into German, French and Spanish*. Frankfurt: Peter Lang.

Wichmann A. 2000. *Intonation in Text and Discourse: Beginnings, Middles and Ends*. London: Longman Pearson Education.

Wicker, F.W., I.M. Thorelli, W.L. Barron III and M.R. Ponder. 1981. "Relationships among affective and cognitive factors in humor". *Journal of Research in Personality*, 15, pp. 359-370.

Widdowson, H.G. 1975. *Stylistics and the Teaching of Literature*. London: Longman.

Widdowson, H.G. 1978. *Teaching Language as Communication*. London: Oxford University Press.

Widdowson, H.G. 1979. *Explorations in Applied Linguistics*. Oxford: Oxford University Press.

Widdowson, H.G. 1984. *Explorations in Applied Linguistics 2*. Oxford: Oxford University Press.

Widdowson, H.G. 1991. "Types of equivalence in translation". *Triangle 10, The Role of Translation in Foreign Language Teaching*. Paris: Didier Erudition, pp. 153-165.

Widdowson, H.G. 1992. *Practical Stylistics: An Approach to Poetry*. Oxford: Oxford University Press.

Wild, D. 2004. *Friends Till the End: The Official Celebration of All Ten Years*. New York: Time Inc. Home Entertainment.

Wimsatt, W.K. 1946. "The intentional fallacy". *Sewanee Review*, 54, pp. 468-488.

Yampolsky, M. and L.P. Joseph (eds & tr.). 1993. "Voice devoured: Artaud and Borges on dubbing", *October*, 64, pp. 57-77.

Zabalbeascoa, P. 1994. "Factors in dubbing television comedy". *Perspectives: Studies in Translatology*, 2/1, pp. 89-99.

Zabalbeascoa, P. 1996a. "Translating jokes for dubbed television situation comedies". *The Translator*, 2/2, pp. 235-257.

Zabalbeascoa, P. 1996b. "In search of a model that will work for the dubbing of television comedy", in M. Edo-Juliá (ed.) *Actes del I Congrés Internacional sobre Traducció 1992*. Barcelona: Autonomous University of Barcelona, pp. 351-366.

Zabalbeascoa, P. 1997. "Dubbing and the nonverbal dimension of translation", in F. Poyatos (ed.) *Nonverbal Communication and Translation: New Perspectives and Challenges in Literature, Interpretation and the Media*. Amsterdam/Philadelphia: John Benjamins, pp. 327-342.

Zabalbeascoa, P. 2003. "Translating audiovisual screen irony", in A. Sánchez-Macarro and L. Pérez-González (eds), *Speaking in Tongues: Languages Across Contexts and Users, English in the World Series*. Valencia: University of Valencia, pp. 305-322.

Zabalbeascoa, P. 2005. "Humour and translation – an interdiscipline". *Humor: International Journal of Humor Research*, 18/2, pp. 185-207.

Zillmann, D. 1983. "Disparagement Humor", in P.E. McGhee and J.H. Goldstein (eds), *Handbook of Humor Research*, Vol.1. New York: Springer Verlag: pp. 85-108.

Zillmann, D. and J.R. Cantor. 1976. "A disposition theory of humour and myrth", in A.J. Chapman and H.C. Foot (eds) *Humour and Laughter: Theory, Research and Application*. London: John Wiley & Sons, pp. 93-116.

Zwicky, A. 1985. "Clitics and Particles". *Language* 61, pp. 283-305.

MIX
Paper from
responsible sources
FSC
www.fsc.org
FSC® C100212